THE ULTIMATE REFERENCE BOOK

~ BOOK ~
THE WIT'S THESAURUS

THE ULTIMATE REFERENCE BOOK

BOOK

THE WIT'S THESAURUS

LANCE DAVIDSON

AVON BOOKS ◆ NEW YORK

THE ULTIMATE REFERENCE BOOK: THE WIT'S THESAURUS is an original publication of Avon Books. This work has never before appeared in book form.

AVON BOOKS
A division of
The Hearst Corporation
1350 Avenue of the Americas
New York, New York 10019

Copyright © 1994 by Lance Davidson
Published by arrangement with the author
Cover art by Culver, Inc.
Library of Congress Catalog Card Number: 93-50926
ISBN: 0-380-76957-3

Library of Congress Cataloging in Publication Data:

Davidson, Lance.
    The ultimate reference book : the wit's thesaurus / Lance Davidson.
    p. cm.
    1. Wit and humor—Dictionaries. I. Title. II. Title: Wit's thesaurus.
PN6151.D37 1994   93-50926
808.87'003—dc20   CIP

First Avon Books Trade Printing: August 1994

AVON TRADEMARK REG. U.S. PAT. OFF. AND IN OTHER COUNTRIES, MARCA REGISTRADA, HECHO EN U.S.A.

Printed in the U.S.A.

ARC 10 9 8 7 6 5 4 3 2 1

◆ ABSENCE

Foreign Words and Phrases

en conge (Fra)
(on kon-JAY) on leave

Quotations

"Absence makes the heart grow fonder."

> *Anonymous,* Poetical Rhapsody *(1602)*

Classical Phrases and Myths

lacuna (Lat)
(la-KOO-na) gap, blank space, hiatus, missing part of text, etc. (plu: lacunae)

in absentia (Lat)
(in ab-SEN-tee-ah) in the absence of the one concerned

Jokes, Stories and Anecdotes

"There are 100 jails in this state and I'm proud to say that nobody in my family has ever been in one of them," boasted the political candidate. Shouted a heckler, "And which one is that?"

◆ ACCIDENT

Quotations

"What is better than presence of mind in a railway accident? Absence of body."

> Punch, *(1849), vol. XVI, p. 231*

Jokes, Stories and Anecdotes

Attorney: "Just what did you do to prevent the accident?" Defendant: "I closed my eyes and screamed as loud as I could."

A waitress tripped and spilled a tray of food on a woman waiting to be served. The woman turned to her group and remarked, "Breakfast is on me."

◆ ACCOMPANIMENT

Foreign Words and Phrases

basso continuo (Ita)
(BAHS-so kon-TIN-u-oh) figured bass line composed at the keyboard; adroit extemporization

en masse (Fra)
(on MAHS) as a group, in force

Quotations

"Come with me to the Casbah."

> *Charles Boyer (1898–1978), French actor (misattributed to Boyer in the film* Algiers*)*

◆ ACCOMPLISHMENT

Foreign Words and Phrases

fait accompli (Fra)
(feh ta-KOM-plee) *lit:* an accomplished fact; something already done

Quotations

"Knowledge may give weight, but accomplishments give lustre, and many more people see than weigh."

> *Philip Dormer Stanhope,*
> *4th Earl of Chesterfield (1694–1773),*
> *British statesman and writer,*
> *letter to his son, May 8, 1750*

"The reward of a thing well done is to have done it."

> *Ralph Waldo Emerson (1803–1882),*
> *U.S. writer, poet and philosopher,*
> Essays: Second Series *(1844),*
> *"Nominalist and Realist"*

"Saying is one thing and doing is another."

> Michel Eyquem de Montaigne
> (1533–1592), French writer,
> Essays (1580), bk. II

"Let the end try the man."

> William Shakespeare (1564–1616),
> British playwright and poet, Henry IV,
> Part II (1598), Act II, sc. ii

"Is there anything in life so disenchanting as attainment?"

> Robert Louis [Balfour] Stevenson
> (1850–1894), British writer and poet,
> New Arabian Nights (1882),
> "The Adventure of the Hansom Cab"

Classical Phrases and Myths

quod erat faciendum (Lat)
(kwod e-rai FAK-ee-END-um) that which was to be carried out (abbr: QEF)

According to Greek myth, Herakles (HER-a-kleez) (Lat: Hercules) performed ten labors for Eurystheus, the favored king of Mycenae born two months ahead of Herakles, in order to become immortal. But because Eurystheus refused to count two of them, Herakles performed 12 great labors. His fifth and cleverest labor was to clean the stables of Augeas, king in Elis. The Augean stables, which housed an enormous and magnificent herd, had not been cleaned in years. Augeas thought the task impossible to perform before nightfall as Herakles had promised, so Augeas promised in exchange a tenth of the herd. Herakles cleaned the stables by diverting the course of the rivers Alpheus and Peneus through them. Hence, to clean the Augean stables is to accomplish a seemingly unperformable task.

Jokes, Stories and Anecdotes

A scene in a Robert Benchley movie short required that the humorist be strung up in a mess of telephone wires above a street. While waiting for the shoot, he remarked to his wife, "You know how good I was in school at Latin?" "Yes." "Well, look where it got me."

> Robert Charles Benchley (1889–1945),
> U.S. humorist

"How do you do it, Arthur?" asked President Kennedy while congratulating Goldberg, then secretary of labor, for averting a labor strike. Goldberg winked and answered, "The trick is, be there when it's settled."

> Arthur J[oseph] Goldberg
> (1908–1990), U.S. politician and lawyer

◆ ACCURACY & FOCUS

Foreign Words and Phrases

stimmt (Ger)
(shtimmt) correct; precisely

Quotations

"This hitteth the nail on the head."

> John Heywood (c. 1497–c. 1580),
> British poet, Proverbs (1546)

Classical Phrases and Myths

omphalus (Grk)
(OM-fal-us) boss on shield; conical stone at Delphi considered to be the earth's central point

ad unguem (Lat)
(ad UNG-wem) lit: to the fingernail; precisely, to a nicety

◆ ACCUSATION

Quotations

"The Right Honourable Gentleman is indebted to his memory for his jests, and to his imagination for his facts."

> Richard Brinsley Sheridan (1751–1816), Irish-born British playwright and politician, replying to a mocking accusation by the Earl of Dundas

"J'accuse." (I accuse.)

> Emile Zola (1840–1902), French writer, title of an open letter to the president of the French Republic in connection with the Dreyfus case, L'Aurore (January 13, 1898)

Classical Phrases and Myths

tu quoque (Lat)
(too KWO-kwe) lit: and you also; statement suggesting that accusation may be turned against the accuser

Jokes, Stories and Anecdotes

The ensign returned from leave so drunk that he could not assume his duties until the third day out to sea. He was horrified when he saw in the ship's log the damning statement: "Unfortunately, Ensign Jones too drunk for duty." He rushed below and begged the captain to erase the entry. But the captain scowled mercilessly. "You know the log can't be changed. It's true, it stays, and you should have thought about your future before you got drunk." So the ensign resumed his duties and entered in the log: "Fortunately, Captain Harrison sober all day."

◆ ACQUISITION & DISPOSITION

Classical Phrases and Myths

caveat emptor (Lat)
(KA-way-at EMP-tor) lit: let him beware; let the buyer beware (buyer alone is responsible for making a bad purchase)

Jokes, Stories and Anecdotes

The great banker J. P. Morgan, as president of the Metropolitan Museum of Art in New York City, recruited Sir Caspar Purdon Clarke, director of the Victoria and Albert Museum in London, to be the Metropolitan's new director. When the secretary of the Victoria and Albert Museum returned from a vacation, he inquired about some artwork that he had hoped to purchase for the museum, which had come up for auction in his absence. "I'm afraid J. P. Morgan bought them, sir," replied the clerk. "Good God," said the secretary, "I must tell Sir Purdon." "Sorry, sir," replied the clerk uneasily. "Mr. Morgan bought him also."

> John Pierpont Morgan, Sr. (1837–1913), U.S. financier

◆ ACTION & ACTIVITY

Foreign Words and Phrases

faire sans dire (Fra)
(FEHR son DEER) lit: to do without speaking; fig: to act rather than talk

Quotations

"What you do speaks so loud that I cannot hear what you say."

> Ralph Waldo Emerson (1803–1882), U.S. writer, poet and philosopher

3

Classical Phrases and Myths

facta non verba (Lat)
(FAK-ta nohn WER-ba) *lit:* deeds not words; (what is required is) action not speeches

---

◆ ACTORS & ACTING

Quotations

"Tallulah Bankhead barged down the Nile last night as Cleopatra—and sank."

> *John Mason Brown (1900–1969),*
> *U.S. critic,* New York Post
> *(November 11, 1937)*

"To see him [Kane] act, is like reading Shakespeare by flashes of lightning."

> *Samuel Taylor Coleridge (1772–1834),*
> *British poet and writer,* Table Talk
> *(April 27, 1823)*

"All through the five acts of that Shakespearean tragedy he played the king as though under a momentary apprehension that someone else was about to play the ace."

> *Eugene Field (1850–1895), U.S. humorist*
> *and writer, reviewing Creston Clarke's*
> *performance as King Lear*

"The most important thing in acting is honesty; once you've learned to fake it, you're in."

> *Samuel Goldwyn [Samuel Goldfish]*
> *(1882–1974), Russian-born U.S. film*
> *producer [authenticity unverified]*

"Katharine Hepburn runs the gamut from A to B."

> *Dorothy Parker (1893–1967), U.S. wit*
> *and writer, quipping during intermission*
> *of the 1933 premiere of* The Lake

Classical Phrases and Myths

Thespis (THES-pis) was an Attic poet who reputedly founded tragic drama. It is said that to rest his actors and vary the entertainment, he introduced monologues and perhaps dialogues; until then choruses performed as a unit to the leader. Accordingly, a *thespian* is an actor or something pertaining to drama.

> *Thespis (c. 550 B.C.), Greek poet*

Jokes, Stories and Anecdotes

Although his drinking became a serious problem near the end of his career, Junius Booth, the great Shakespearean actor and the father of John Wilkes Booth, could rely on his talent and experience to win the day. The aged actor reportedly once staggered from his dressing room at curtain time and asked, "What's the play, and where's the stage?"

> *Junius Brutus Booth (1796–1852),*
> *U.S. actor*

After watching an actor give a wretched performance in one of his Gilbert and Sullivan light operas, W. S. Gilbert entered the man's dressing room after the show and exclaimed, "My dear chap! Good isn't the word!"

> *Sir W[illiam] S[chwenck] Gilbert*
> *(1836–1911), British writer*

"I don't think I can do that naturally," the then young actress Ingrid Bergman informed Alfred Hitchcock about a particular scene. She gave a lengthy explanation for her discomfort and believed that she had converted Hitchcock to her position. In what Bergman would later admit was the best acting advice she ever received, Hitchcock suggested, "If you can't do it naturally, then fake it."

> *Sir Alfred Hitchcock (1889–1980),*
> *British film director*

During the filming of *Marathon Man*, Dustin Hoffman returned to the dressing room of Laurence Olivier. Said Olivier, "Gawd, what happened to you? You're dripping wet." Hoffman replied, "I was running around Central Park. My part requires me to be a marathon runner, and I'm a method actor preparing for my role." Responded Olivier: "That's just it, though. An actor is supposed to *act*."

Sir Laurence Olivier (1907–1989), British actor

◆ ADULTERY

Jokes, Stories and Anecdotes

Q: "What's the difference between a wife and a mistress?" A: "30 pounds." Q: "And the difference between a husband and a lover?" A: "30 minutes."

"I've been unfaithful to Cheryl for years," said Fred to his friend Bill. "I'm going to come clean with my wife and beg for her forgiveness." "Don't reveal the names of your mistresses," cautioned Bill, "since it would get them in trouble." That night Fred confessed his infidelity, and to Fred's surprise his wife's curiosity outweighed her anger. "So who did you go to bed with?" demanded Cheryl. "That slut Mrs. Jones?" "I can't tell you," replied Fred. "I'll bet it was that hussy Ginny. She's slept with everyone!" "Discretion forbids," he begged off. "Shirley," she said confidently. "You slept with that whore!" Again Fred was silent, so his wife gave up. The next day Bill asked Fred how things went. "Great," said Fred. "Not only did my wife forgive me, but she gave me three new leads!"

Two men were walking down the street together in the twilight when one squinted and ducked his head, saying, "Well, I'll be damned. See those two women approaching us? One's my wife and the other's my mistress!" The other man then ducked his head, too. "What's wrong?" asked the first man. The second answered, "Small world, isn't it?"

Mrs. Jones awoke in her lover's arms and was distressed to realize that it was after midnight. "My husband will kill me!" she groaned. Calling home, she had a sudden inspiration. When her husband answered the telephone, she panted, "Honey, don't pay the ransom. I've escaped!"

Disentangling herself, the woman answered the phone. After she hung up, her companion asked who the caller was. "My husband," she replied, nuzzling his neck. "He was calling to say he'd be out late playing poker with you."

◆ ADULTHOOD

Foreign Words and Phrases

bar mitzvah (Heb)
(bar MITS-vah) *lit:* son of the commandment; Jewish ceremony for boys reaching adulthood at age 13

Quotations

"If you can keep your head when all about you
Are losing theirs and blaming it on you,
If you can trust yourself when all men doubt you,
But make allowance for their doubting too; ...
If you can dream—and not make dreams your master;
If you can think—and not make thoughts your aim;

5

If you can meet with Triumph and
Disaster
And treat those two impostors just
the same . . .
If you can make one heap of all
your winnings
And risk it on one turn of pitch-
and-toss,
And lose, and start again at your
beginnings
And never breathe a word about
your loss . . .
If you can talk with crowds and
keep your virtue,
Or walk with Kings nor lose the
common touch
If neither foes nor loving friends
can hurt you,
If all men count with you, but none
too much;
If you can fill the unforgiving min-
ute
With sixty seconds' worth of dis-
tance run,
Yours is the Earth and everything
that's in it,
And—which is more—you'll be a
Man, my son!"

> *Rudyard Kipling (1865–1936),*
> *British writer and poet, Rewards*
> *and Fairies (1919), "If—"*

"Behold me now.
A man not old, but mellow, like
good wine. Not over-jealous, yet an
eager husband."

> *Stephen Phillips (1864–1915), British*
> *playwright, Ulysses (1902), Act III, sc. ii*

"A child becomes an adult when he
realizes that he has a right not only
to be right but also to be wrong."

> *Thomas Szasz (1920–   ),*
> *U.S. psychiatrist*

Jokes, Stories and Anecdotes

The actress Ethel Barrymore was in
her Hollywood dressing room one
day when a studio usher knocked
on the door and announced, "A
couple of ladies in the reception

room, Miss Barrymore, claim they
went to school with you. What
should I do?" "Wheel them in."

> *Ethel Barrymore (1879–1959),*
> *U.S. actress*

When the English poet Dame Edith
Sitwell informed her parents that
she was leaving the family estate,
she explained, "I can write so much
better when I'm alone." Sir George
Sitwell, her father, challenged her.
"And you prefer poetry to human
love?" "As a profession," replied
Dame Edith, "yes."

> *Dame Edith Sitwell (1887–1964),*
> *British poet*

◆ ADVANTAGE

Quotations

"It is a great advantage to have produced nothing, but you must not
abuse it."

> *Antoine de Rivarol (1753–1801), French*
> *writer and wit, replying to a merciless*
> *critic, considered unproductive*

Classical Phrases and Myths

cum privilegio (Lat)
(kum pri-vil-LEG-io) with privilege

Jokes, Stories and Anecdotes

The evangelist Billy Graham, upon
being introduced to the Shakespearean actress Dame Edith Evans,
said to her, "We in the ministry
could learn a good deal from you
about how to put our message
across." "You in the ministry have
an advantage over us," replied

Dame Edith. "You have long-term contracts."

Dame Edith Evans (1888–1976),
British actress

◆ ADVERSITY

Foreign Words and Phrases

contretemps (Fra)
(KON-truh-tom) *lit:* against time; mishap, inconvenience

Quotations

"Some people are so fond of ill-luck that they run half-way to meet it."

Douglas William Jerrold (1803–1857),
British playwright and humorist, Wit and Opinions of Douglas Jerrold *(1859)*

Murphy's Law: "If anything can go wrong, it will." *Murphy's Corollary:* "If nothing can go wrong, it still will." *Nichol's Observation:* "Murphy is an optimist."

[Named after Ed Murphy, a development engineer at Edwards Airforce Base, who remarked about a lab technician: "If there's any way to do it wrong, he will!"]

"I had never had a piece of toast
Particularly long and wide,
But fell upon the sanded floor,
And always on the buttered side."

James Payn (1830–1898), British humorist

"When you are down and out something always turns up—and it is usually the noses of your friends."

[George] Orson Welles (1915–1985),
U.S. actor and filmmaker

"A reasonable amount o' fleas is good fer a dog—keeps him from broodin' over bein' a dog, mebbe."

Edward Noyes Westcott (1847–1898),
U.S. writer, David Harum *(1898), ch. 32*

Classical Phrases and Myths

per ardua ad astra (Lat)
(per ARD-u-a ad AS-tra) through adversity to reach the stars (the motto of the Royal Air Force)

hamartia (Grk)
(ham-ART-ia) in classic drama, the tragic flaw, defect or failure in character that brings disaster upon its bearer

"It is difficulties that show what stuff men are made of."

Epictetus (c. 55–c. 135), Greek
philosopher, Discourses, *bk. I, ch. 24*

"*Aequam memento rebus in arduis Servare mentem.*" (Remember when life's path is steep to keep your mind even.)

Horace (65 B.C.–8 B.C.), Roman poet,
Odes, *III, I*

According to Greek mythology, Pandora was the first woman on earth. She had been sent by Zeus to be the lovely wife for Epimetheus, the brother of Prometheus, who loved mankind and had given the gift of fire. Zeus wanted revenge, so he arranged that Pandora be given the box into which Prometheus had shut all the evils that might plague the world. She yielded to her curiosity and ignored the order not to open the box she had been given as a dowry, thus releasing all the adversities and evil that beset mankind. Only hope remained. Hence, a *Pandora's box* is a source of great and unexpected troubles.

In Greek mythology and in Homer's *Odyssey* Scylla (SIL-a) and Charybdis (ka-RIB-dis) were monsters. Scylla was a six-headed monster who lived in a cave, and if a ship came within her reach, she would seize and devour the sailors six at a time; Charybdis was a whirlpool adjacent to Scylla in the Straits of Messina. Avoiding one put the sailors in danger of being killed by the other. Thus, to be *between Scylla and Charybdis* is to be in a serious predicament, a dual danger, in which the avoidance of one requires facing the other.

Jokes, Stories and Anecdotes

"Well, you win some and you lose some," said the friend consolingly. Replied the hapless loser, "If only that were true!"

Benjamin Disraeli had meticulously corrected himself during a parliamentary debate by substituting the word "misfortune" for "calamity." Questioned afterward about his reason for drawing a distinction between the two words, Disraeli, using the name of his great political rival William Gladstone, explained, "If, for example, Mr. Gladstone were to fall accidentally into the Thames, that would be a misfortune; but if anyone were then to pull him out, that would be a calamity."

Benjamin Disraeli, 1st Earl of Beaconsfield (1804–1881), British prime minister

One of the earliest Goldwynisms from the malaprop-prone Samuel Goldwyn occurred when, as a young producer facing severe financial problems, he complained that he was "on the brink of an abscess."

Samuel Goldwyn [Samuel Goldfish] (1882–1974), Russian-born U.S. film producer [authenticity unverified]

◆ ADVICE

Foreign Words and Phrases

éminence grise (Fra)
(AY-mee-nonce greez) *lit:* gray cardinal; behind the scenes; power or force behind the throne; phrase originally applied to Richelieu's confessor

kibitzer (Yid)
(KIB-it-zer) onlooker offering unsolicited advice, meddler, backseat driver

Quotations

"Anyone who has ever struggled with poverty knows how extremely expensive it is to be poor."

James Baldwin (1924–1987), U.S. writer, Nobody Knows My Name (1961), "Fifth Avenue, Uptown: A Letter from Harlem"

"When a man comes to me for advice, I find out the kind of advice he wants, and I give it to him."

Josh Billings [Henry Wheeler Shaw] (1818–1885), U.S. humorist

"Advice is seldom welcome; and those who want it the most always like it the least."

Philip Dormer Stanhope, 4th Earl of Chesterfield (1694–1773), British statesman and writer, letter to his son, January 29, 1748

"You're only here for a short visit, so don't hurry, don't worry, and be sure to smell the flowers along the way."

Walter Hagen (1892–1969), U.S. golfer, providing the secret of his success

"A good scare is worth more to a man than good advice."

Edgar Watson Howe (1853–1937), U.S. writer, Country Town Sayings (1911)

"Don't look back. Something may be gaining on you."

Leroy Robert ["Satchel"] Paige (1904–1982), U.S. baseball player, printed on the back of his business card as one of his "Six Rules for a Happy Life"

Jokes, Stories and Anecdotes

Dante did not enjoy the best relationship with his patron, Can Grande della Scala, but a jester at Can Grande's court was lavishly rewarded with money and gifts for his fooleries. Once the arrogant fool asked Dante, "Why is it that I, who am so ignorant and foolish, should be so rich and favored, while you, who are so learned and wise, should be a beggar?" Dante replied, "Because you have found a lord who resembles you, and when I find one who resembles me, undoubtedly I shall be as rich as you are."

Dante Alighieri (1265–1321), Italian poet

Upon completing his examination of the then-ill poet Otto Hartleben, a doctor prescribed abstaining from both smoking and drinking. Hartleben picked up his hat and coat and moved to leave. "That will be three marks, Herr Hartleben, for my advice." Hartleben growled, "But I'm not taking it," and left.

Otto Erich Hartleben (1864–1905), German poet

A young man approached the renowned composer Wolfgang Amadeus Mozart, seeking his advice on composing symphonies. Mozart advised him to wait until he was older and had acquired more experience. The young man looked astonished. "But, Herr Mozart, you yourself wrote symphonies when you were only ten years old." "Ah," said Mozart, "but I did so without asking advice."

Wolfgang Amadeus Mozart (1756–1791), Austrian composer

In the Wei River of the province of the philosopher and administrator Teng Shih, the corpse of a wealthy man who had drowned was retrieved by a man who demanded a large payment from the mourning family to return the body. The deceased's relatives were advised by Teng, "Wait, for no one else will pay for the body." They took his counsel and waited. But then the finder of the corpse became concerned, and he, too, consulted Teng. "Wait," counseled Teng, "for nowhere else can they obtain the body."

Teng Shih (500s B.C.), Chinese philosopher and administrator [Teng's equivocations eventually led the state ruler to have him put to death]

◆ AFFECTEDNESS

Foreign Words and Phrases

contraposto (Ita) (kon-trah-POHS-toh) *lit:* juxtaposed; (sculpture or painting of a figure) in difficult or unlikely pose

mie (Jap) (may) stylized poses at moments of high Kabuki drama

Quotations

"So Harry says, 'You don't like me any more. Why not?' And he says, 'Because you've got so terribly pretentious.' And Harry says, 'Pretentious? *Moi?*' "

John Cleese (1939–   ), and Connie Booth (c. 1940–   ), British comedians, Fawlty Towers, "The Psychiatrist," BBC television program, 1979

"A highbrow is a person educated beyond his intelligence."

> *J. Brander Matthews (1852–1929),*
> *U.S. writer*

"[He] believes in the fine arts with all the earnestness of a man who does not understand them."

> *George Bernard Shaw (1856–1950),*
> *Irish playwright*

"It's a naive domestic Burgundy without any breeding, but I think you'll be amused by its presumption."

> *James Thurber (1894–1961),*
> *U.S. cartoonist and humorist,* New Yorker *cartoon caption, March 27, 1937*

Classical Phrases and Myths

infra dig(nitatem) (Lat)
(EEN-fra dig-nee-TAH-tem) beneath one's dignity

Jokes, Stories and Anecdotes

It was a hot afternoon during the couple's first summer in their new home. The windows were closed, so the husband asked, "Please open the windows." "Are you crazy!" the wife exclaimed. "And let our neighbors know our house isn't air-conditioned?"

Q: "Why didn't the socialite get a colostomy?" A: "She couldn't find shoes to match the bag."

A flustered society matron approached Dean Acheson in a Washington hotel. "I am so embarrassed," she said. "Could you please help me with my zipper that has stuck? I am due at a meeting." Acheson cordially helped her, averting his eyes as best he could, and pulled the zipper back up to the top. The lady thanked him profusely. "I should tell you," she remarked, "that I am vice president of the Daughters of the American Revolution." "My dear lady," said Acheson, "what a moment ago was a rare privilege now appears to have been a really great honor."

> *Dean [Gooderham] Acheson (1893–1971),*
> *U.S. diplomat*

Watching Abraham Lincoln cleaning the mud off his boots, a foreign diplomat expressed his surprise. Inquired Lincoln, "Do not European gentlemen black their own boots?" "Certainly not." "Then whose boots do they black?"

> *Abraham Lincoln (1809–1865),*
> *U.S. president [authenticity unverified]*

◆ AFFLICTION

Foreign Words and Phrases

l'oer naque (Fra)
(luhr na-Kuh) the sting

écrasez l'infime (Fra)
(ay-KRAZ-ay lahn-FAHM) crush the filthy object, Voltaire's reference to the Catholic Church

Quotations

"To have a grievance is to have a purpose in life."

> *Eric Hoffer (1902–1983),*
> *U.S. labor leader and philosopher*

"Something is rotten in the state of Denmark."

> *William Shakespeare (1564–1616), British*
> *playwright and poet,* Hamlet *(1601),*
> *Act I, sc. iv*

Jokes, Stories and Anecdotes

After a fierce hurricane struck Washington, D.C., local officials estimated that the storm did $100 million worth of improvements.

◆ AFTERLIFE

Quotations

"One world at a time."

Henry David Thoreau (1817–1862), U.S. writer, naturalist and poet, answering what he thought of the world to come

"Heaven for climate; Hell for society."

Mark Twain [Samuel Langhorne Clemens] (1835–1910), U.S. humorist, writer and speaker

Jokes, Stories and Anecdotes

Father Andrew, the BBC's adviser on Roman Catholic affairs, was asked how he could confirm the truth of the Roman Catholic view of heaven and hell. Andrew's answer contained just one word: "Die."

Father Agnellus Andrew (1908–), British clergyman

At a dinner party, the subject of heaven and hell was discussed at length. Mark Twain took no part, so the woman seated next to him asked: "Why haven't you said anything? Surely you must have some opinion about this." "Madam, you must excuse me," Twain replied. "I am silent because of necessity. I have friends in both places."

Mark Twain [Samuel Langhorne Clemens] (1835–1910), U.S. humorist, writer and speaker [attributed also to Jean Cocteau]

◆ AGE

Quotations

"Alonso of Aragon was wont to say in commendation of age, that age appears to be best in four things— old wood best to burn, old wine to drink, old friends to trust, and old authors to read."

Francis Bacon (1561–1626), British lawyer and writer, Apothegms (1624), 97 [attributed also to Sir Francis Drake]

"The arrogance of age must submit to be taught by youth."

Edmund Burke (1729–1797), British statesman, philosopher and writer, letter to Fanny Burney, July 29, 1782

"If youth only knew; if age only could."

Henri Estienne (c. 1531–1598), French writer, Les Prémices (1594)

"At twenty years of age, the will reigns; at thirty, the wit; and at forty, the judgment."

Benjamin Franklin (1706–1790), U.S. statesman and scientist, Poor Richard's Almanac (1732–1757)

"To be 70 years young is sometimes far more cheerful and hopeful than to be 40 years old."

Oliver Wendell Holmes, Sr. (1809–1894), U.S. writer and physician, commenting on the 70th birthday of Julia Ward Howe, 1889

"The four stages of man are infancy, childhood, adolescence and obsolescence."

Art Linkletter (1912–), U.S. musician and writer, A Child's Garden of Misinformation (1965), ch. 8

"Growing old is like being increasingly penalized for a crime you haven't committed."

Anthony Powell (1905–), British writer, Temporary Kings (1973), ch. 1

"When I was a boy of 14, my father was so ignorant I could hardly stand to have the old man around. But when I got to be 21, I was astonished at how much he had learned in seven years."

Mark Twain [Samuel Langhorne Clemens] (1835–1910), U.S. humorist, writer and speaker

"The old believe everything; the middle aged suspect everything; the young know everything."

Oscar [Fingal O'Flahertie Wills] Wilde (1854–1900), British playwright, writer and wit

Classical Phrases and Myths

"Singula de nobis anni praedantur euntes." (The years as they pass plunder us of one thing after another.)

Horace (65 B.C.–8 B.C.), Roman poet, Epistles, II, ii, l.55

Cicero (SIS-e-roh), the Roman orator and statesman, was conversing with a well-preserved matron who asserted vainly, "Why, I am only 30 years old." "It must be true," replied Cicero, "for I have heard it these twenty years."

Marcus Tullius Cicero (106 B.C.–43 B.C.), Roman statesman and man of letters

Jokes, Stories and Anecdotes

Descending the grand stairway at the Paris Opera, a friend of Daniel Auber's engaged him in conversation. "My friend, we're all getting older, aren't we?" he observed. "Well, there's no helping it," sighed Auber. "Aging seems to be the only available way to live a long time."

Daniel Francois Esprit Auber (1782–1871), French composer

A friend greeting German statesman Prince von Bismarck on his 80th birthday wished him many more happy years. Bismarck thanked him, adding, "But, you are aware, the first 80 years of a man's life are always the happiest."

Otto Eduard Leopold, Prince von Bismarck (1815–1898), German statesman

When he was an elderly man, an admirer gushed to novelist Alexandre Dumas, "How do you grow old so gracefully?" "Madame, I give all my time to it."

Alexandre [pere] Dumas (1802–1870), French writer and playwright

Somerset Maugham spoke at a dinner given in honor of his 80th birthday at London's Garrick Club. "There are many virtues in growing old," he began, then paused. As he fumbled through his notes, the delay grew agonizingly long. At last, the exasperated novelist cleared his throat and murmured, "I'm just trying to think what they are."

W[illiam] Somerset Maugham (1874–1965), British writer and playwright

Despite concern over Ronald Reagan's age of 69 when he ran for President in 1980, he nevertheless won the election. During a televised debate with Walter Mondale in the 1984 presidential campaign, Reagan was asked whether he was too old to serve another term. "I'm not going to inject the issue of age into this campaign," replied Reagan. "I am not going to exploit for political gain my opponent's youth and inexperience."

Ronald Reagan (1911–   ), U.S. actor and president

An interviewer once asked British conductor Sir Malcolm Sargent, when he was 70 years old, "To what do you attribute your advanced age?" "Well," he responded, "I suppose I must attribute it to the fact that I have not yet died."

Sir Malcolm Sargent (1895–1967), British conductor and organist

◆ AGGRAVATION

Foreign Words and Phrases

inquiter (Fra)
(an-KEET-er) to disturb

agent provocateur (Fra)
(AH-jon pro-vok-ah-TUHR) *lit:* agent of provocation; one who is commissioned or planted to incite others to riot or criminal acts

fisselig (Ger)
(FIS-sel-ish) being flustered due to another's harassment

picador (Spa)
(pee-kah-DOR) horseman who starts bullfight by provoking bull

Quotations

"The authorities were at their wit's end, nor had it taken them long to get there."

Desmond MacCarthy (1877–1952), British writer

◆ AGREEMENT

Quotations

"A verbal contract isn't worth the paper it's written on."

Samuel Goldwyn [Samuel Goldfish] (1882–1974), Russian-born U.S. film producer [authenticity unverified]

Driftwood (Groucho Marx): "It's all right. That's—that's in every contract. That's—that's what they call a sanity clause." Fiorello (Chico Marx): "You can't fool me. There ain't no Sanity Claus."

George S. Kaufman (1889–1961)), U.S. playwright, writer and wit, and Morrie Ryskind (1895–1985), U.S. playwright, A Night at the Opera (1935 film)

"The big print giveth and the fine print taketh away."

Fulton J[ohn] Sheen (1895–1979), U.S. clergyman, educator and writer, reviewing his television contract

Classical Phrases and Myths

non est factum (Lat)
(nohn est FAK-tum) *lit:* it is not done; in law, principle that a party to a contract is not bound by its terms because he or she did not understand its provisions

◆ AID (SUPPORT)

Quotations

"It was as helpful as throwing a drowning man both ends of a rope."

Arthur ["Bugs"] Baer (1897–1975), U.S. writer

"When a dog is drowning, everyone offers him a drink."

George Herbert (1593–1633), British clergyman and poet, Jacula Prudentum (1651), no. 77

"An arch never sleeps."

Indian saying

Classical Phrases and Myths

auxilium ab alto (Lat)
(owx-IL-i-umab AL-toh) help from on high

In Greek mythology, the aegis (EE-gis) was the wondrous and terrifying breastplate worn by Zeus and

Athena, and sometimes by Apollo. A Gorgon's head occupied its center. Hence, to be under the *aegis* of a person or thing is to enjoy protection or patronage.

Jokes, Stories and Anecdotes

A customer asked the clerk at a New Age bookstore where the self-help section was. Said the clerk, "If I told you, that would defeat the whole purpose."

An acquaintance of Lord Berners would constantly say to him: "I have been sticking up for you." This was repeated once too often, and Berners snapped, "Yes, and I have been sticking up for you. Someone said you aren't fit to live with pigs, and I said that you are."

Gerald Tyrwhitt-Wilson,
14th Baron Berners (1883–1950),
British musician and artist

A sawyer cutting up some wood was being watched by Ralph Waldo Emerson when he was a child. Though incapable of splitting wood himself, the little Emerson helpfully inquired, "May I do the grunting for you?"

Ralph Waldo Emerson (1803–1882),
U.S. writer, poet and philosopher

The wit Dorothy Parker awoke on the morning of June 13, 1963, to find her husband, Alan Campbell, dead beside her. Among those standing with Parker and others as Campbell's body was carried from the house was a certain officious Mrs. Jones, who solicitously asked if she could do anything for Parker. "Get me a new husband." Silence. Before anyone who would have laughed could laugh, Mrs. Jones said, "I think that is the most callous and disgusting remark I ever heard in my whole life." "So sorry," sighed Parker. "Then run down to the corner and get me a ham and cheese on rye and tell them to hold the mayo."

Dorothy Parker (1893–1967),
U.S. wit and writer

◆ ALLURE (CHARM & FLIRT)

Foreign Words and Phrases

coquette (Fra)
(ko-KET) a flirt

piquant (Fra)
(pee-KAHN) sharp, stinging, or pointed

Quotations

"Merely innocent flirtation,
Not quite adultery, but adulteration."

George Gordon, Lord Byron (1788–1824),
British poet, Don Juan *(1823),*
Canto XII, st. lxiii

"All charming people have something to conceal, usually their total dependence on the appreciation of others."

Cyril Connolly (1903–1974),
British writer, Enemies of Promise
(1938), ch. 16

"She who trifles with all
Is less likely to fall
Than she who trifles with one."

John Gay (1685–1732), British poet and
playwright, The Coquet Mother and the
Coquet Daughter

"I never resist temptation, because I have found that things that are bad for me do not tempt me."

George Bernard Shaw (1856–1950),
Irish playwright, The Apple Cart
(1930), interlude

"What, when drunk, one sees in other women, one sees in Garbo sober."

Kenneth [Peacock] Tynan (1927–1980), British writer, Curtains *(1961), pt. 2, p. 347*

"I couldn't help it. I can resist everything except temptation."

Oscar [Fingal O'Flahertie Wills] Wilde (1854–1900), British playwright, writer and wit, Lady Windermere's Fan *(1891), Act I*

"Vous savez ce qu'est le charme: une manie re de s'entendre repondre oui sans avoir pose aucune question claire." (You know what charm is: a way of getting the answer yes without having asked any clear question.)

Albert Camus (1913–1960), French philosopher and writer, La Chute (The Fall), *(1956)*

"Quand elle le ve ses paupie res, on dirait qu'elle se de shabille." (When she raises her eyelids, it is as if she is undressing.)

Colette [Sidonie-Gabrielle Colette] (1873–1954), French writer, Claudine s'en va (Claudine Goes Away) *(1931), p. 59*

Classical Phrases and Myths

In Greek mythology, Tantalus (TAN-ta-lus) committed crimes including the stealing of nectar of ambrosia (food reserved for the gods) and providing it to his mortal friends, killing his son Pelops and serving him as a stew to the gods at a dinner to test their omniscience, and deceitfully denying under oath to Zeus that he knew the whereabouts of the golden dog that had protected Zeus in his infancy. Zeus condemned Tantalus to Tartarus, the bottom of the underworld, where he would eternally try to fill his cup or snatch fruit from trees, but they remained always just beyond his reach. Thus, something

which is available but unobtainable is *tantalizing*.

Jokes, Stories and Anecdotes

In her later years, actress Sarah Bernhardt lived in an upper-story Paris apartment. One day, after the long climb, a visitor arrived at her door and breathlessly inquired, "Madame, why do you live so high up?" Answered the actress, "It is the only way I can still make the hearts of men beat faster."

Sarah Bernhardt (1844–1923), French actress

After being squired to dinner, first by British Labour politician William Gladstone and then, the following evening, by Conservative Benjamin Disraeli, a young lady was asked what impressions the two political rivals had left on her. "When I left the dining room after sitting next to Mr. Gladstone I thought he was the cleverest man in England," she said. "But after sitting next to Mr. Disraeli, I thought I was the cleverest woman in England."

Benjamin Disraeli, 1st Earl of Beaconsfield (1804–1881), British prime minister

The journalist and critic H. L. Mencken once posed the rhetorical question: "If you find so much that is unworthy of reverence in the United States, why do you live here?" He then supplied the answer: "Why do men go to zoos?"

H[enry] L[ouis] Mencken (1880–1956), U.S. critic and writer

◆ ALOOFNESS

Quotations

"I never forget a face, but in your case I'll be glad to make an exception."

Groucho [Julius] Marx (1895–1977), U.S. comedian, replying to a drunk who had slapped him on the back and said, "You probably don't remember me."

"The Englishman has all the qualities of a poker except its occasional warmth."

> *Daniel O'Connell (1775–1847),*
> *Irish politician*

Irish playwright George Bernard Shaw received the following invitation from a woman infamous for courting celebrities: "I will be at home on Tuesday between four and six o'clock." On the returned card she read Shaw's message: "Mr. Bernard Shaw likewise."

> *George Bernard Shaw (1856–1950),*
> *Irish playwright*

Notable snob Oscar Browning once approached poet laureate Lord Tennyson on the Isle of Wight and proudly announced, "I am Browning." Tennyson, who knew only of Robert Browning, eyed him coldly, said, "No, you're not," and left.

> *Alfred Tennyson, 1st Baron Tennyson*
> *(1809–1892), British poet*

◆ ALTERABILITY

Classical Phrases and Myths

"Panta rhei." (PAN-ta ray) (All is flux, nothing is stationary.)

> *Heraclitus (c. 535 B.C.–475 B.C.),*
> *Greek philosopher*

"Nothing endures but change."

> *Heraclitus (c. 535 B.C.–475 B.C.),*
> *Greek philosopher*

In Roman mythology, Mercury (MER-kyoo-ree) (Grk: Hermes) was the swift-footed god of commerce, messenger of the gods and patron of travelers and athletes. He wore winged sandals. Thus, to travel quickly is *to wear the winged sandals of Mercury.* Because Mercury was also the tutelary deity for thieves and deceivers, to be *mercurial* is to be changeable, volatile and quick-witted.

In classical mythology, Proteus (PRO-tee-us) was an oracular sea god who had the ability to assume different shapes. If caught and held until he reassumed his own shape, however, he was compelled to answer questions. On his way home from Troy, Menelaus successfully disguised himself in a seal skin to catch Proteus napping and to obtain answers. Hence, a person or thing which is *protean* readily assumes different shapes.

◆ ALTRUISM

Classical Phrases and Myths

amor proximi (Lat)
(AM-or PROX-ee-mee) love of one's neighbor

"Nam tua res agitur, paries cum proximus ardet." (It is your own interest that is at stake when your next neighbor's wall is ablaze.)

> *Horace (65 B.C.–8 B.C.), Roman poet,*
> *Epistles, I, xviii, l. 80*

Jokes, Stories and Anecdotes

Returning from the South Pole, Robert Falcon Scott and his expedition team were beset by horrendous blizzards. The feet of a young member of the team, Lawrence Oates, were frostbitten and turning gangrenous. Oates courageously offered to be left behind to avoid slowing up the rest of the party.

The others dissuaded him, and all doggedly progressed another day. The snowstorm was still raging the next morning. Oates simply said, "I am just going outside and may be some time." He then walked out of the tent and vanished forever into the blizzard. Sadly, Oates's heroism was in vain, because the entire party died before reaching safety. Months later, a search party found Scott's diaries, which revealed the story of Oates's sacrifice. Near the spot where Oates walked into the blizzard, a cross commemorates him as "a very gallant gentleman."

Lawrence Edward Grace Oates (1880–1912), British explorer

◆ AMBIGUITY

Foreign Words and Phrases

double entendre (Fra)
(DOUB-luh-on-TON-druh) ambiguous expression, phrase with two meanings; often a deliberate and risque ambiguity

Classical Phrases and Myths

Prior to attacking the Persian king Cyrus in 546 B.C., Croesus (KROW-sooz), the rich king of Lydia who controlled much of Asia Minor, consulted the oracle at Delphi to learn the fate of his undertaking. Encouraged by the oracle's response that if he went to war he would destroy a great empire, Croesus marched against the Persians. He was decisively beaten and the Persians then invaded Lydia and captured its capital, Sardis. Croesus became Cyrus's prisoner. Cyrus later freed Croesus in return for his wisdom in pointing out that when Cyrus's troops were carrying off riches from Sardis, they were actually plundering Cyrus's own bounty. Croesus again sent messengers to Delphi, reproaching it for the deceptive oracle. The priestess of the oracle replied that he had not been deceived; Croesus had indeed destroyed a great empire—his own.

Croesus (c. 550 B.C.), Lydian king

Darius I became king of Persia in troubled times, and so in 512 B.C. he sought to secure the northern boundaries of his empire by conquering the Scythians. But instead of meeting for battle, the Scythians stayed a day's march ahead of Darius's troops, practicing a scorched-earth policy that exasperated Darius. He sent messengers to the Scythians, inquiring whether they would fight or surrender. The Scythians sent back a mouse, a frog, a bird, and five arrows. "Victory is ours," Darius said to his captains. "The mouse means the land of Scythia will be surrendered to us; the frog means that their rivers and lakes will also be ours; like a bird, the Scythian army will fly from our army; and these arrows signify that the Scythians will lay down their arms." An adviser to Darius, however, interpreted the message differently: "The Scythians mean that unless you turn into mice and burrow in the ground for safety, or turn into frogs and hide in the waters, or turn into birds and fly away, you will all be slain by the Scythian archers." After deliberations, Darius accepted the second interpretation and retreated from Scythia.

Darius I (550 B.C.–486 B.C.), Persian king

Jokes, Stories and Anecdotes

Two Irish youngsters passed a Methodist minister. Seeing the reversed collar, one little boy said automatically, "Hello, Father." The

17

other child sharply elbowed the first. "He's no father," she said. "He's married and got two kids."

◆ AMBITION

Foreign Words and Phrases

abondance déclaré e (Fra) (ah-bonn-DAHNSE day-klah-RAY) (in whist) the attempt to win all the tricks; also used generally to indicate ambition

Quotations

"Well is it known that ambition can creep as well as soar."

> Edmund Burke (1729–1797),
> British statesman, philosopher and writer,
> Letters on a Regicide Peace, *letter I*

Guildenstern: "The very substance of the ambitious is merely the shadow of a dream."
Hamlet: "A dream itself is but a shadow."
Rosencrantz: "Truly, and I hold ambition of so airy and light a quality that it is but a shadow's shadow."

> William Shakespeare (1564–1616),
> British playwright and poet,
> Hamlet (1601), Act II, sc. ii

Jokes, Stories and Anecdotes

Alan Brooke, chief of the imperial general staff, commented to King George VI in 1944 that the imperious field marshal Bernard Law "Monty" Montgomery, who had won the famous Battle of El Alamein against Rommel, was "a very good soldier, but I think he is after my job." George quipped, "I thought he was after mine."

> George VI (1895–1952), British king

The novelist Sinclair Lewis began a lecture at Columbia University on the writer's craft by asking, "How many here are really serious about being writers?" A forest of hands eagerly rose. "So why the hell aren't you all home writing?" asked Lewis, and sat down.

> [Harry] Sinclair Lewis (1885–1951),
> U.S. writer

◆ AMERICANS

Quotations

"America is the only nation in history which miraculously has gone directly from barbarism to degeneration without the usual interval of civilization."

> Georges Clemenceau (1841–1929),
> French prime minister

"The thing that impresses me most about America is the way parents obey their children."

> Edward VIII (1894–1972), British king,
> subsequently Duke of Windsor

"I am willing to love all mankind, except an American."

> Samuel Johnson (1709–1784), British man
> of letters, letter to James Boswell,
> April 15, 1778

"Boobus Americanus."

> H[enry] L[ouis] Mencken (1880–1956),
> U.S. critic and writer

"Our national flower is the concrete cloverleaf."

> Lewis Mumford (1895–1990),
> U.S. writer, philosopher and scholar

"America is a large, friendly dog in a very small room. Every time it wags its tail it knocks over a chair."

> Arnold J[oseph] Toynbee (1889–1975),
> British scholar, News Summaries
> (July 14, 1954)

"It was wonderful to find America, but it would have been more wonderful to miss it."

Mark Twain [Samuel Langhorne Clemens] (1835–1910), U.S. humorist, writer and speaker

"It is absurd to say that there are neither ruins nor curiosities in America when they have their mothers and their manners."

Oscar [Fingal O'Flahertie Wills] Wilde (1854–1900), British playwright, writer and wit

"The youth of America is their oldest tradition. It has been going on now for three hundred years."

Oscar [Fingal O'Flahertie Wills] Wilde (1854–1900), British playwright, writer and wit, A Woman of No Importance (1893), Act I

◆ AMUSEMENT

Foreign Words and Phrases

tchotchke (Yid)
(TCHOTCH-keh) knickknack; toy; attractive woman

pour le sport de (Fra)
(por le spoor duh) for the sport of [it]

divertissement (Fra)
(dee-vair-TEES-mon)   small-scale work (often a foil for a major presentation)

Quotations

"The only difference between men and boys is the cost and number of their toys."

Dorothy Parker (1893–1967), U.S. wit and writer [authenticity unverified]

"To play billiards well was a sign of an ill-spent youth."

Herbert Spencer (1820–1903), British philosopher and economist, repeating a remark from a Mr. Charles Roupell [attributed also to Robert Louis Stevenson]

"This is the biggest electric train set any boy ever had!"

[George] Orson Welles (1915–1985), U.S. actor and filmmaker describing the RKO studio to his associate, Richard Wilson

Jokes, Stories and Anecdotes

Answering the society matron's question at a formal dinner party, the Latin American consul said, "Our most popular sport is bullfighting." The matron shook her head, muttering, "I've always thought that was revolting." Without hesitation, the consul replied, "No, that's our second most popular pastime."

Although he appeared as a gross buffoon, Lord Castlerosse, an *intime* of Lord Beaverbrook, had a nimble wit. On one occasion on the golf course, Nancy Cunard asked him, "What is your handicap?" "Drink and debauchery."

Valentine Browne, Lord Castlerosse (1891–1943), Irish aristocrat

---

◆ ANCESTRY

Quotations

"I can trace my ancestry back to a protoplasmal primordial atomic globule. Consequently, my family pride is something inconceivable. I can't help it. I was born sneering."

Sir W[illiam] S[chwenck] Gilbert (1836–1911), British writer, The Mikado (1885), Act I

"I can't claim my folks were *Mayflower* descendants; but I recall they were here to meet the boat."

> Will[iam Penn Adair] Rogers (1879–
> 1935), U.S. comedian, speaking to the
> Daughters of the American Revolution
> [Rogers was part Cherokee]

"I would rather make my name than inherit it."

> William Makepeace Thackeray
> (1811–1863), British writer

Classical Phrases and Myths

omne vivum ex vivo (Lat)
(OM-ne WEE-wum ex WEE-woh)
lit: every living thing from a living thing; assertion that nothing can be spontaneously created, i.e., that all living things are descended from other living things

A descendant of Harmodius, who with Aristogiton had attacked the tyrant Hippias in 514 B.C., enjoyed a life of privilege due to the reverence of Athenians for his ancestor. He arrogantly ridiculed Iphicrates, a general who had developed superior battle tactics for Athenian troops against Sparta during the Corinthian war, for being the son of a sandalmaker. Iphicrates retorted, "The difference between you and me is that my family begins with me, whereas yours ends with you."

> Iphicrates (d. 353 B.C.), Athenian general

Jokes, Stories and Anecdotes

Though earlier unconcerned about her ancestry, on marrying into the Gardner family of Boston, Isabella Stewart Gardner had her lineage traced all the way to King Fergus I of Scotland, a contemporary of Alexander the Great. When the much-discussed topic of lineage came up, Mrs. Gardner had to endure a Boston dowager's monologue about her American Revolutionary ancestry. "Ah yes," said Mrs. Gardner.

"They were much less careful about immigration in those days, I believe."

> Isabella Stewart ["Mrs. Jack"] Gardner
> (1840–1924), U.S. social leader and
> art collector

"Caroline's very bright, smarter than you were, Jack, at that age," commented patriarch Joseph Kennedy about his granddaughter to John. "Yes, she is," agreed John. "But look who she has for a father."

> John Fitzgerald Kennedy (1917–1963),
> U.S. president

The lyric poet and novelist Detlev von Liliencron listened quietly during dinner while one of a group of noblemen boasted about his aristocratic ancestors who had fought in the Crusades, sailed with Columbus, and so on. "You remind me of a potato," Liliencron said finally. "How is that?" "The best part is underground."

> Detlev von Liliencron (1844–1909),
> German poet and writer

"I'm a Democrat!" shouted a heckler while Theodore Roosevelt was giving a campaign speech. Roosevelt quieted the crowd and inquired, "May I ask the gentleman why he is a Democrat?" "My grandfather was a Democrat, my father was a Democrat and I am a Democrat." Thinking he had the situation in hand, Roosevelt then asked, "My friend, suppose your grandfather had been a jackass and your father was a jackass, what would you then be? "A Republican?"

> Theodore Roosevelt (1858–1919),
> U.S. president

◆ ANGER & RESENTMENT

Foreign Words and Phrases

ressentiment (Fra)
(re-SOHNT-ee-mohn) obtuse outrage

Quotations

"Heav'n has no rage, like love to hatred turn'd,
Nor Hell a fury, like a woman scorned."

> *William Congreve (1670–1729),*
> *British playwright,* The Mourning
> Bride *(1697), Act III, sc. viii*

"We boil at different degrees."

> *Ralph Waldo Emerson (1803–1882),*
> *U.S. writer, poet and philosopher,*
> Society and Solitude *(1870), "Eloquence"*

Jokes, Stories and Anecdotes

When a major general accused Lincoln's secretary of war Edwin Stanton of favoritism, Stanton complained to Lincoln, who suggested that he write the officer a strongly worded letter. Stanton did and showed it to Lincoln, who asked what Stanton would do with it. The surprised Stanton replied, "Send it." "You don't want to send that letter," Lincoln said. "Put it in the stove. That's what I do when I have written a letter while angry. It's a good letter and you had a good time writing it and feel better. Now, burn it, and write another."

> *Abraham Lincoln (1809–1865),*
> *U.S. president*

◆ ANIMAL HUSBANDRY & ZOOLOGY

Classical Phrases and Myths

A Thessalian brought an exceptionally beautiful horse, named Bucephalus, to the Macedonian court, offering to sell it to King Philip. When the royal grooms tried to test its paces, however, Bucephalus proved too unmanageable. When young Alexander (later the Great) asked his father for permission to try his skill, Philip reluctantly agreed on condition that if Alexander failed to ride Bucephalus he would pay his father a forfeit equal to its price. Alexander walked to the horse's head and turned it to face into the sun, for he had noticed that the horse was upset by its own shadow. He calmed it, then mounted it, and Bucephalus obediently showed off his paces. The court, which had feared for Alexander's safety, applauded loudly. The proud father Philip kissed his son, saying, "Seek another kingdom that may be worthy of your abilities, for Macedonia is too small for you."

> *Alexander III [Alexander the Great]*
> *(356 B.C.-323 B.C.), Macedonian king*

Jokes, Stories and Anecdotes

Baron Cuvier at Paris's Museum of Natural History helped develop the science of paleontology by reconstructing whole skeletons by induction from the apparent function of fragmentary fossils. As a practical joke, his students one night broke into Cuvier's rooms, and one, dressed in a threatening outfit of horns, tail, and hoofed feet, growled, "Cuvier, I have come to eat you!" Cuvier cocked one eye and said sleepily, "All animals with horns and hooves are herbivorous. You won't eat me." And he went back to sleep.

> *Georges Léopold, Baron Cuvier*
> *(1769–1832), French zoologist*

◆ ANIMALS & INSECTS

Quotations

"Animals are such agreeable friends—they ask no questions, they pass no criticisms."

> *George Eliot [Mary Ann Evans Cross]*
> *(1819–1880), British writer,*
> *Mr. Gilfil's Love-Story*

"Oh, a wondrous bird is the pelican!
His beak holds more than his belican.
He takes in his beak
Food enough for a week.
But I'll be darned if I know how the helican."

> *Dixon Lanier Merritt (1879–1972),*
> *U.S. lawyer, Nashville Banner*
> *(April 12, 1913)*

"The turtle lives 'twixt plated decks
Which practically conceal its sex.
I think it clever of the turtle
In such a fix to be so fertile."

> *Ogden Nash (1902–1971), U.S. humorist,*
> *Hard Lines (1931), "Autres Bates,*
> *Autres Moeurs"*

"I know two things about the horse
And one of them is rather coarse."

> *Naomi Royde-Smith (1875–1964), British*
> *poet, Weekend Book (1928), p. 231*

Jokes, Stories and Anecdotes

"Q: What's the last thing that goes through a bug's mind when it hits the windshield?" A: "Its ass."

As Beatrice Lillie and her Pekingese puppy were emerging from a taxi in front of a fancy London hotel, she and the driver saw a small puddle on the seat. The taxidriver started to complain. Slipping him a large tip, Lillie said flatly, "I did it," and swept away.

> *Beatrice Lillie (1898–1989),*
> *Canadian-born British actress*

The Scottish historical novelist and poet Sir Walter Scott and his wife, while walking on the Abbotsford estate in spring, passed a field full of gamboling lambs. "No wonder that poets from the earliest times have made lambs the symbols of peace and innocence," Scott murmured. "Delightful creatures indeed," agreed Lady Scott. "Especially with mint sauce."

> *Sir Walter Scott (1771–1832),*
> *British writer and poet*

One day Lord Brougham's one-horse coach (the carriage that he invented was named after him) passed clergyman Sydney Smith while he was walking in London. Smith eyed the splendid *B* surrounded by a coronet on the panel of the carriage. Remarked Smith to a friend, "There goes a carriage with a *B* outside and a wasp within."

> *Sydney Smith (1771–1845),*
> *British clergyman and writer*

◆ ANSWER

Quotations

"How many roads must a man walk down
Before you can call him a man?...
The answer, my friend, is blowin' in the wind,
The answer is blowin' in the wind."

> *Bob Dylan [Robert Zimmerman]*
> *(1941–   ), U.S. songwriter,*
> *Blowin' in the Wind (1962 song)*

Classical Phrases and Myths

quaesitum (Lat)
(KWAI-see-tum) *lit:* (something) that is sought after; that which is to be determined, the answer or solution

Jokes, Stories and Anecdotes

Once, when George Bernard Shaw scathingly critiqued G. K. Chesterton's economic views, Chesterton failed to reply. Historian Hilaire Belloc reproached him for this strange behavior. "My dear Belloc, I have answered him," said Chesterton. "To a man of Shaw's wit, silence is the one unbearable repartee."

> G[ilbert] K[eith] Chesterton (1874–1936),
> British man of letters

The short story writer O. Henry made a written request for a $50 advance from his publisher, Frank Munsey. Noting that O. Henry was already several stories in arrears, Munsey responded there would be "no advance unless I know its purpose." By return mail Munsey received an envelope containing a single long hair. O. Henry received the advance.

> O. Henry [William Sydney Porter]
> (1862–1910), U.S. writer

◆ ANXIETY

Foreign Words and Phrases

malaise (Fra)
(mah-LEHZ) discomfort, uneasiness

Torschlusspanik (Ger)
(TOHR-shloos-PAWN-ik) anxiety of being "locked out" or alone (especially as an unmarried)

Sturm und Drang (Ger)
(SHTURHM unt DRAHNG) storm and struggle; emotional turmoil (also a period in German literature derived from eponymous 1776 play by Frederick von Klinger)

Quotations

"Worry is interest paid on trouble before it falls due."

> William Ralph Inge (1860–1954),
> British clergyman

"Though this may be play to you, 'tis death to us."

> Sir Roger L'Estrange (1616–1704),
> British fabulist [paraphrasing Bion:
> "Though boys throw stones at frogs
> in sport, the frogs die in earnest"]

Jokes, Stories and Anecdotes

Lamented the anxious but lazy man: "Yesterday I was a man. Today I'm a man. Tomorrow I'll probably still be a man. (Sigh.) There's so little hope for advancement!"

The patient complained to his psychiatrist that he was having horrible alternating nightmares—first he would dream he was a tepee, and then a wigwam. "Doc, what should I do?" "Relax, you're two tents."

After succumbing to a knockout, a boxer finally came to as his manager and trainer crowded around him. Still groggy, he announced, "Boy, did I have him worried back then! He thought he'd killed me."

◆ APOCALYPSE

Quotations

"This is the way the world ends
Not with a bang but a whimper."

> T[homas] S[tearns] Eliot (1888–1965),
> U.S. poet, Poems 1909–1925 (1925),
> "The Hollow Men"

"Je vais vous dire un grand secret, mon cher. N'attendez pas le jugement dernier. Il a lieu tous les jours." (I'll tell you a great secret, my friend. Don't wait for the last judgment. It happens every day.)

Albert Camus (1913–1960),
French philosopher and writer,
La Chute (The Fall), (1956)

◆ APOLOGY

Quotations

"A stiff apology is a second insult."

G[ilbert] K[eith] Chesterton (1874–1936),
British man of letters

Jokes, Stories and Anecdotes

The frontiersman Davy Crockett, viewing a menagerie exhibition in Washington, D.C., with friends, was amusingly pointing out the similarity between the features of a monkey on display and those of a congressman. Crockett turned around to find the congressman standing just behind him. "I guess I should apologize," Crockett began, "but I don't know whether to apologize to you or to the monkey."

Davy Crockett (1786–1836),
U.S. frontiersman and congressman

Baron Beaverbrook ran into young British MP Edward Heath in his London club's washroom soon after printing an insulting editorial in his newspaper. "I've been thinking it over, and I was wrong," said Beaverbrook contritely. "Here and now, I apologize." "Very well," said Heath. "But next time, please insult me in the washroom and apologize in your newspaper."

Edward Heath (1916–   ),
British prime minister

"The hotel room where I'm staying is so small that the rats are round-shouldered," cracked Bob Hope once in a show, borrowing an oft-repeated joke. The irked hotel proprietor threatened to sue for damages, so Hope agreed to retract the insult. At his next show Hope told his audience, "I apologize for saying that the rats in my hotel were round-shouldered. They're not."

Bob Hope [Leslie Townes]
(1903–   ),
British-born U.S. comedian

George C. Scott, when he had to get into bed with an actress for a love scene, was rumored to have told her, "I apologize if I get an erection and I apologize if I don't."

George C[ampbell] Scott
(1927–   ), U.S. actor

◆ APPROVAL

Quotations

"Do not trust to the cheering, for those very persons would shout as much if you and I were going to be hanged."

Oliver Cromwell (1599–1658),
British lord protector

"Some people pay a compliment as if they expected a receipt."

Frank McKinney ["Kin"] Hubbard
(1868–1930), U.S. humorist and writer

"He who praises everybody praises nobody."

Samuel Johnson (1709–1784),
British man of letters

"Fondly we think we honour merit then,
When we but praise ourselves in other men."

Alexander Pope (1688–1744),
British poet and writer

"Usually we praise only to be praised."

François, Duc de La Rochefoucauld
(1613–1680), French writer,
Maximes (1678), 146

"If you applaud me at the start, that is faith; midway through, that is hope. But, ah, dear friends, if you applaud me at the end, that would be charity!"

Fulton J[ohn] Sheen (1895–1979),
U.S. clergyman, educator and writer,
responding to applause before
addressing a rally

"I can live for two months on a good compliment."

Mark Twain [Samuel Langhorne Clemens]
(1835–1910), U.S. humorist,
writer and speaker

Classical Phrases and Myths

imprimatur (Lat)
(im-preem-AH-tur) official, especially papal, sanction (to publish a text)

O si sic omnes (Lat)
(OH see seek OM-nes) if only everyone were like that

Jokes, Stories and Anecdotes

The politician droned on in his speech to the crowd from the caboose platform when suddenly the train began pulling away. Immediately the crowd broke into applause, accompanied by cheering and shouting. With the shouts fading in the distance, the politician settled into his seat and remarked to an aide: "I don't know whether they were applauding me or the engineer."

Supreme Court Chief Justice Salmon P. Chase was introduced soon after the Civil War to a beautiful Alabama belle, who declared, "I must warn you that I'm an unreconstructed rebel." "In your case, madam," replied Chase, "reconstruction—even in the slightest—would be nothing short of sacrilege."

Salmon Portland Chase (1808–1873),
U.S. statesman and jurist

"Mr. Foote, I swallow all the good things you say," said the Duke of Cumberland to the farce dramatist. "Indeed, sir," replied Foote, "then Your Royal Highness has an excellent digestion, for you never bring any of it up again."

Samuel Foote (1720–1777),
British actor and playwright

French philosopher and wit Voltaire was visited in his home in Switzerland by Casanova, who was on a two-year sojourn throughout Europe. Having been reading works by the Swiss physiologist and polymath Albrecht von Haller, Voltaire praised them to Casanova. "That praise is ill-returned," replied Casanova, "since he has said that your work is nonsense." "Perhaps," said Voltaire, "we are both mistaken."

Voltaire [François-Marie Arouet] (1694–1778), French philosopher, writer and wit

◆ ARCHITECTURE

Foreign Words and Phrases

Bauhaus (Ger)
(BOW-hows) modern style of architecture and design, named after school of early 20th century

Quotations

"A large number of us have developed a feeling that architects tend to design houses for the approval of fellow architects and critics—not for the tenants."

Charles, Prince of Wales
(1948–   ), British prince

"Under this stone, Reader, survey Dead Sir John Vanbrugh's house of clay.
Lie heavy on him, Earth! for he
Laid many heavy loads on thee!"

Abel Evans (1679–1737), British poet,
Epitaph on Sir John Vanbrugh,
Architect of Blenheim Palace

"Architecture in general is frozen music."

Friedrich von Schelling (1775–1854),
German writer, Philosophie der Kunst

Jokes, Stories and Anecdotes

One rainy evening in 1937, industrialist Hibbard Johnson was proudly entertaining guests for dinner in his newly built Frank Lloyd Wright house in Wisconsin. Suddenly, water that had seeped through a roof leak started to drip steadily on the bald pate of Johnson directly below. He indignantly telephoned Wright in Phoenix, Arizona. "Frank, you built this beautiful house for me and we enjoy it very much," he began. "But I have told you the roof leaks, and right now I am with some friends and distinguished guests and it is leaking right on top of my head." "Well, Hib," replied Wright, overheard by the guests, "why don't you move your chair?"

Frank Lloyd Wright (1869–1956),
U.S. architect

◆ AREA (DESOLATION)

Quotations

"The purity of the air of Newfoundland is without doubt due to the fact that the people of the outposts never open their windows."

J. G. Millais (1907–   ),
Canadian politician

"If I owned two plantations and one was located in Texas and the other one was in hell, I'd rent out the one in Texas and live on the other one."

Philip Henry Sheridan (1831–1888),
U.S. general

Jokes, Stories and Anecdotes

First college roommate to second: "Let's spend the summer working in Buffalo." Second: "Why, all they have in Buffalo is prostitutes and hockey players!" First: "My sister lives up there!" Second: "What team does she play for?"

◆ ARMS

Quotations

"Our ships have been salvaged and are retreating at full speed toward the Japanese fleet."

William Frederick Halsey, Jr.
(1882–1959), U.S. admiral, wiring
after Japanese claims that most of the
American Third Fleet had been sunk
or were retreating, October 1944

"Ohne Butter werden wir fertig, aber nicht biespielsweise ohne Kanonen." (We can do without butter but not, for example, without guns.)

Joseph Goebbels (1897–1945),
German statesman, speech in Berlin,
January 17, 1936

◆ ARROGANCE

Foreign Words and Phrases

de haut en bas (Fra)
(de oat on bah) *lit:* from above to

26

below; contemptuously, superciliously

hauteur (Fra)
(oat-UHR) haughty manner

Quotations

"Snobs talk as if they had begotten their own ancestors."

> Herbert Agar (1897–1980), U.S. writer

"If he ever went to school without any boots it was because he was too big for them."

> Ivor Bulmer-Thomas (1905–),
> British politician, after being informed
> that Labour rival Harold Wilson had been
> obliged as a child to go to school without
> boots, speech at Conservative Party
> Conference, 1949 [misattributed to
> Harold MacMillan]

"Are there any writers on the literary scene whom I consider truly great? Yes. Truman Capote. But there are others who, while not quite in this exalted orbit, are still commendable."

> Truman Capote (1924–1984), U.S. writer

"There but for the grace of God goes God."

> Sir Winston Spencer Churchill (1874–
> 1965), British prime minister and writer

"Jean Lesage is the only person I know who can strut sitting down."

> John G. Diefenbaker (1895–1979),
> Canadian prime minister, mocking Jean
> Lesage, the former premier of Quebec

"He was like a cock who thought the sun had risen to hear him crow."

> George Eliot [Mary Ann Evans Cross]
> (1819–1880), British writer, Adam Bede
> (1859), ch. 33

"The difficulty lies not so much in buying Monsieur Chateaubriand, but in paying him the price he thinks he's worth."

> Napoleon I [Napoleon Bonaparte]
> (1769–1821), French general
> and emperor, commenting on the
> vain Vicomte de Chateaubriand's
> disaffection with his diplomatic post

"They remind me of a very tired rich man who said to his chauffeur, 'Drive off that cliff, James, I want to commit suicide.' "

> Adlai E[wing] Stevenson (1900–1965),
> U.S. politician

"How haughtily he cocks his nose, To tell what every schoolboy knows."

> Jonathan Swift (1667–1745),
> Anglo-Irish clergyman and writer,
> The Country Life, 1, 81

Classical Phrases and Myths

"He may forget that he is Caesar, but I always remember that I am Caesar's daughter."

> Julia (39 B.C.–A.D. 14), Roman aristocrat,
> declining to live simply, as wished by her
> father, Augustus Caesar,
> Rome's first emperor

Jokes, Stories and Anecdotes

The streets were wet and the martinis were dry, and when humorist Robert Benchley emerged from an elegant New York nightclub, he tapped the resplendently uniformed man at the door, saying, "Get me a cab." "Sir, I happen to be a rear admiral of the Fleet in the United States Navy," snorted the affronted gent, drawing himself up proudly. "OK," said Benchley, "call me a battleship."

> Robert Charles Benchley (1889–1945),
> U.S. humorist

A pompous woman complained once to Lord Berners that the head waiter of a restaurant had not immediately shown her and her husband to a table. She recounted, "We had to tell him who we were." Inquired Berners, "And who were you?"

Gerald Tyrwhitt-Wilson Berners,
14th Baron (1883–1950),
British musician and artist

The Harvard economist and ambassador to India John Kenneth Galbraith was having breakfast with President Kennedy on the morning that the *New York Times* published a profile of Galbraith, and Kennedy asked him his opinion of the article. Galbraith said it was all right but he did not understand why they called him arrogant. "I don't see why not," Kennedy replied, "everybody else does."

John Fitzgerald Kennedy (1917–1963),
U.S. president

George Kittredge, a Harvard English professor, was once asked why, although he was such a great scholar, he had never gotten a Ph.D. "My dear sir," Kittredge replied, "who could examine me?"

George Lyman Kittredge (1860–1941),
U.S. scholar [attributed also to others]

A young man loftily looking around at a party remarked in a bored tone, "I'm afraid I simply cannot bear fools." "Odd," replied Dorothy Parker. "Apparently your mother could."

Dorothy Parker (1893–1967),
U.S. wit and writer

Irritated by painter James Whistler's egregious conceit, someone once pointedly remarked to him, "It's a good thing we can't see ourselves as others see us." Quipped Whistler, "Isn't it? I know in my case I would grow intolerably conceited."

James Abbott McNeill Whistler
(1834–1903), U.S.-born British painter

◆ ARTIST

Foreign Words and Phrases

poite maudit (Fra)
(po-ET moe-DEE) *lit:* accursed poet; poet unappreciated by contemporaries

Quotations

"Art is a jealous mistress, and if a man have a genius for painting, poetry, music, architecture or philosophy, he makes a bad husband and an ill provider."

Ralph Waldo Emerson (1803–1882),
U.S. writer, poet and philosopher,
The Conduct of Life *(1860), "Wealth"*

"The writer's only responsibility is to his art. He will be completely ruthless if he is a good one.... Everything goes by the board: honor, pride, decency, security, happiness, all, to get the book written. If a writer has to rob his mother, he will not hesitate; the *Ode on a Grecian Urn* is worth any number of old ladies."

William Faulkner (1897–1962),
U.S. writer, Paris Review *(Spring 1956)*

"*Engravit* is the inscription on the tombstone where he lies;
Dead he is not, but departed,—for the artist never dies."

Henry Wadsworth Longfellow
(1807–1882), U.S. poet, Nuremberg, *xiii*

"An artist must know how to convince others of the truth of his lies."

Pablo [Ruiz y] Picasso (1881–1973),
Spanish-born French artist

"The notion of making money by popular work, and then retiring to do good work on the proceeds, is the most familiar of all the devil's traps for artists."

Logan Pearsall Smith (1865–1940),
U.S. writer, After-Thoughts (1931),
"Arts and Letters"

Classical Phrases and Myths

The acclaimed painter Apelles called upon the talented but unrecognized painter Protogenes at his home in Rhodes, but Protogenes was away. When a servant asked the name of the unknown visitor, Apelles took a brush and traced upon a panel, with a single continuous line, a shape of extreme delicacy. Later, Protogenes returned and saw the panel, commenting, "Only Apelles could have drawn that line." He then drew an even finer line inside that of Apelles, telling his servant to show it to his visitor if he returned. Apelles did return, and drew a third line of even greater fineness between the first two. When Protogenes saw it, he acknowledged that he had been bested and hurried to catch Apelles to celebrate together. The panel with the triple outline was preserved as a masterpiece, but was destroyed by a fire in Rome.

Apelles (c. 450 B.C.), Greek painter

Jokes, Stories and Anecdotes

The artist Salvador Dali was asked if it was hard to paint a picture. "No," he replied. "It's either easy or impossible."

Salvador Dali (1904–1990), Spanish artist

When asked with what he mixed his colors to obtain the vibrant hues, the British painter John Opie replied sincerely, "I mix them with my brains, sir."

John Opie (1768–1807), British painter

Once when film producer Samuel Goldwyn was in London, he sat for tea with George Bernard Shaw to enlist the playwright as a writer for his movie studio. Goldwyn had the gist of the conversation cabled to his publicity chief, Howard Dietz, who in turn cabled back a distillation of Shaw's reply for release in London: "The trouble, Mr. Goldwyn, is that you are only interested in art and I am only interested in money."

George Bernard Shaw (1856–1950),
Irish playwright

"I only know of two painters in the world," gushed a female admirer to the painter James Whistler, "yourself and Velasquez." "Why," answered Whistler sweetly, "why drag in Velasquez?"

James Abbott McNeill Whistler
(1834–1903), U.S.-born British artist

◆ ASCETICISM

Quotations

"Remember that there is always a limit to self-indulgence, but none to self-restraint."

Mohandas Karamchand [Mahatma]
Gandhi (1869–1948), Indian statesman
and spiritual leader

"The Puritan through Life's sweet garden goes
To pluck the thorn and cast away the rose."

Kenneth Hare (1888–1962),
British poet and writer

"Abstinence is as easy to me as temperance would be difficult."

Samuel Johnson (1709–1784),
British man of letters

Classical Phrases and Myths

ascesis (Grk)
(as-KA Y-sis) the practice of self-discipline

Diogenes once observed a child drinking from his cupped hands. The Cynic philosopher, who preached that true happiness consisted of satisfying one's essential needs, immediately reached into his satchel, withdrew his goblet and threw it away. He said, "In the practice of moderation, a child has become my teacher."

Diogenes (c. 412 B.C.–323 B.C.),
Greek philosopher

Diogenes was living stoically in a large tub on the outskirts of Corinth. He was sunning himself when the powerful king Alexander the Great came to visit. Alexander politely asked if Diogenes wanted anything. Diogenes replied, "Yea, that I do—that you stand out of my sun a little."

Diogenes (c. 412 B.C.–323 B.C.),
Greek philosopher

Jokes, Stories and Anecdotes

"My grandfather doesn't drink, smoke, eat fried meat, philander with women, gamble, or even swear," said Mrs. Grundy. "And tomorrow he's going to celebrate his 90th birthday." Fred looked at her and asked, "How?"

Mahatma Ghandi, despite becoming an internationally recognized statesman, persisted in leading the ascetic lifestyle of the impoverished. He wore simple clothes, stayed in slums and traveled by foot or by railroad economy class. Lord Mountbatten, the British viceroy, conveyed his surprise about Gandhi's apparent exposure to danger to a member of Gandhi's party at a railroad station. He was told that all the Untouchables in the carriage had been carefully selected and checked by the security services: "If only Bapu [Ghandi] knew

the cost of setting him up in poverty!"

Mohandas Karamchand [Mahatma]
Gandhi (1869–1948), Indian statesman
and spiritual leader

◆ ASSENT (AFFIRMATION)

Foreign Words and Phrases

jawohl (Ger)
(ya-VOL) yes!

Quotations

"When you say that you agree to a thing in principle you mean that you have not the slightest intention of carrying it out in practice."

Otto Eduard Leopold, Prince von
Bismarck (1815–1898), German statesman

" 'My idea of an agreeable person,' said Hugo Bohun, 'is a person who agrees with me.' "

Benjamin Disraeli, 1st Earl of Beaconsfield
(1804–1881), British prime minister,
Lothair (1870), ch. 35

Classical Phrases and Myths

placet (Lat)
(PLAK-et) statement of an assenting vote

After Alexander the Great had conquered Egypt, the Persian king Darius sent a letter offering generous terms for peace and future friendship with the Macedonian king: cession of all the countries west of the Euphrates, 10,000 talents in ransom for Persian prisoners, and Darius's daughter as a bride. Alexander consulted his lieutenants about how to respond. "If I were Alexander," said his general Parmenion, "I would accept this generous offer." "So would I," responded Alexander, "if I were Parmenion."

*Alexander III [Alexander the Great]
(356 B.C.–323 B.C.), Macedonian king*

◆ ASSOCIATE

Foreign Words and Phrases

gregario (Ita)
(greh-GAR-yoh) follower, private retainer

compere (Fra)
(KOM-pare) entertainment announcer, partner in crime, prank, etc.

Quotations

"He that lies with the dogs, riseth with fleas."

*George Herbert (1593–1633),
British clergyman and poet,
Jacula Prudentum (1651), no. 343*

"As with the Christian religion, the worst advertisement for Socialism is its adherents."

*George Orwell [Eric Blair] (1903–1950),
British writer, The Road to Wigan Pier
(1937), ch. 11*

Jokes, Stories and Anecdotes

"Father, what is meant by business ethics?" "I am pleased, my son, that you ask," replied the proud father. "Let me explain this subtle concept to you by an example. Assume an elderly widow places a $20 bill on the counter for a garment. You make the change, and leave. When you later return, you notice that she has mistakenly left the change. Understand, my son?" "Yes, Father." "So now the question of business ethics. Do I, or do I not, tell my partner?"

◆ ASSOCIATION

Foreign Words and Phrases

coterie (Fra)
(koh-ter-EE) clique, closed group

Gemeinschaft (Ger)
(ge-MYN-shaft) association based on love or kinship (*cf. Geselischaft*)

Geselischaft (Ger)
(ge-ZELL-shaft) company, society, association, organization based on self-interest and contractual agreement (*cf. Gemeinschaft*)

Gruppe (Ger)
(GROO-pe) group, association (especially of artists, writers, etc.)

zoku (Jap)
(ZOH-koo) informal political coalitions using bribes

Quotations

"I don't want to belong to any club that will accept me as a member."

*Groucho [Julius] Marx (1895–1977),
U.S. comedian, resigning from the
Friar's Club in Hollywood by telegram*

"Most clubs have the atmosphere of a Duke's house with the Duke lying dead upstairs."

*Douglas Sutherland (1919–   ),
British writer*

Jokes, Stories and Anecdotes

"I pay dues to too many organizations," lamented the society matron. "My epitaph is going to read: 'Elsie Jones—Clubbed to death.'"

One partner did not try to conceal his jubilation. "Guess," he said to his partner, "how much I cleared in that deal I closed?" "Half!" responded his partner.

On his way to the House of Lords, British barrister and Conservative

MP F. E. Smith often used the bathrooms of London's prestigious Athenaeum Club. When a porter courteously explained to Smith that the club was for members only, Smith replied, "Is it a club as well?"

F[rederick] E[dwin] Smith,
1st Earl of Birkenhead (1872–1930),
British lawyer and politician

◆ ATHEISM & AGNOSTICISM

Foreign Words and Phrases

kaffir (Arab)
(KAH-feer) infidel, lower-order person

Quotations

"An atheist is a man who has no invisible means of support."

John Buchan, Baron Tweedsmuir (1875–1940), British writer and statesman

"There are no atheists in the foxholes."

William Thomas Cummings (1903–1945),
U.S. soldier

Jokes, Stories and Anecdotes

The film director Luis Buñuel was educated as a Catholic by the Jesuits. Asked as an older man if he had been deeply affected by his Jesuit education, Buñuel responded, *"Grâce à Dieu, je suis toujours athée."* (Thanks to God, I am still an atheist.)

Luis Buñuel (1900–1983),
French filmmaker

◆ ATONEMENT

Quotations

"Repentance is but want of power to sin."

John Dryden (1631–1700), British poet, playwright and writer, Palamon and Arcite, bk. III, l. 813

Jokes, Stories and Anecdotes

Though the practice was disclaimed by Boston's Episcopal Church of the Advent, Boston tradition held that Isabella Stewart Gardner was taken to church by her chauffeur-driven limousine every Ash Wednesday and, armed with a bucket and mop, would wash the steps of the church as a penance for her sins of the preceding year.

Isabella Stewart ["Mrs. Jack"] Gardner (1840–1924), U.S. social leader and art collector

◆ ATTACK

Foreign Words and Phrases

Blitzkrieg (Ger)
(BLITZ-kreeg) *lit:* lightning warfare; a sudden and devastating strike (associated historically with German attack in WWII)

jihad (Arab)
(jee-HAHD) holy war or crusade by Muslims against infidels

Quotations

"Mon centre cède, ma droite recule, situation excellente, j'attaque." (My center is giving way, my right is retreating, situation excellent, I am attacking.)

Marshal Ferdinand Foch (1851–1929), French general, message sent during the first Battle of the Marne, September 1914

Jokes, Stories and Anecdotes

The charge of the Light Brigade, in which the British cavalry attacked the Russian guns at Balaclava, exemplified military discipline and parade-ground steadiness of pace. The foolish heroism, however, resulted in near total annihilation. Watching the doomed advance of his allies, General Pierre Bosquet made the memorable comment, *"C'est magnifique, mais ce n'est pas la guerre."* (It's magnificent, but it's not war.)

> Pierre François Joseph Bosquet
> (1810–1861), French general

◆ ATTENTIVENESS

Foreign Words and Phrases

Achtung (Ger)
(ahk-TUHNG) attention! (military command)

Quotations

"The wheel that squeaks the loudest Is the one that gets the grease."

> Josh Billings [Henry Wheeler Shaw]
> (1818–1885), U.S. humorist, The Kicker

"Depend upon it, Sir, when a man knows he is to be hanged in a fortnight, it concentrates his mind wonderfully."

> Samuel Johnson (1709–1784),
> British man of letters

"Men are generally more careful of the breed of their horses and dogs than of their children."

> William Penn (1644–1718),
> British-born U.S. religious leader,
> Some Fruits of Solitude (1693)

"I am as vigilant as a cat to steal cream."

> William Shakespeare (1564–1616),
> British playwright and poet, King
> Henry IV, Part I (1598), Act IV, sc. ii

"Put all your eggs in the one basket, and—WATCH THAT BASKET."

> Mark Twain [Samuel Langhorne Clemens]
> (1835–1910), U.S. humorist, writer and
> speaker, Pudd'nhead Wilson
> (1894), ch. 15

Classical Phrases and Myths

nota bene (Lat)
(NOH-ta BE-ne) *lit:* note well; take note of what follows (usually a qualification to something that has gone before)

ecce homo (Lat)
(EK-ke HO-moh) *lit:* behold the man; picture of Christ wearing a crown of thorns

Jokes, Stories and Anecdotes

A professor was reminiscing about his 30 years of teaching. "In nearly every class, there's one student eager to argue. Although my first impulse was to silence him or her, I soon learned better," he said. "That student is probably the only one listening."

Dr. Bell, the model for Sir Arthur Conan Doyle's *Sherlock Holmes*, would test the powers of perception of each new class of medical students with an experiment. He would display a tumbler of an unknown liquid (often described as urine), and say, "We could analyze this chemically, but I want you to test it by smell and taste as I do," and then he would dip a finger into the liquid and suck his finger. Grimacing, he then would pass the tumbler around the class and each student would dip a finger into the unknown substance, suck it, and shudder at the bitter taste. When the experiment was over, Bell announced: "Gentlemen, not one of you has developed his power of perception for, if you had watched me closely, you would have noticed that, although I placed my forefinger in the bitter medicine, it was the middle finger which went into my mouth!"

> Joseph Bell (1837–1911), British surgeon

◆ ATTRACTION

Jokes, Stories and Anecdotes

During rush hour, trying to catch a train, a plump, middle-aged woman sprinted to the gate, lost her footing on the smooth floor and slid on her back into a young man. Regaining her composure, she said, "Do you always have beautiful women falling at your feet?"

◆ ATTRIBUTION

Quotations

"You've got to be careful quoting Ronald Reagan, because when you quote him accurately it's called mud-slinging."

> *Walter F. Mondale (1928–),*
> *U.S. vice president*

Jokes, Stories and Anecdotes

Picasso, who lived in Paris, was harassed by the Nazis who occupied the city during WWII. A gestapo officer, while inspecting his apartment, noticed a photograph of *Guernica*, Picasso's masterpiece depicting the destruction of the Basque capital by German aircraft during the Spanish Civil War. "Did you do that?" demanded the officer. Picasso retorted, "No, you did."

> *Pablo [Ruiz y] Picasso (1881–1973),*
> *Spanish-born French artist*

◆ AUDIENCE

Quotations

"Theatre habitués and sons of habitués."

> *Marc Klaw (1858–1936), U.S. theater*
> *producer, describing the two classes of*
> *first-night audiences*

"There are only three things that hiss—a goose, a snake, and a fool. Stand forth, and let us identify you."

> *Charles Lamb (1775–1834), British writer,*
> *responding to a hiss from*
> *the lecture audience*

Classical Phrases and Myths

mobile vulgus (Lat)
(MOH-bil-e WUL-gus) (the) fickle crowd

Jokes, Stories and Anecdotes

Q: "What has 200 legs and four teeth?" A: "The front row at a Johnny Cash concert."

The writer Charles Lamb's farce *Mr. H* was a miserable failure at its debut. He joined in the hissing at the Drury Lane Theatre, because, as he later explained, he was "so damnably afraid of being taken for the author."

> *Charles Lamb (1775–1834), British writer*

The actress Laurette Taylor enjoyed a pleasant conversation with a stranger at a party given following a poorly attended performance. The stranger then left her to talk to others at the party. Taylor turned to her host and exclaimed, "That man walked out on me tonight at the theater!" "Are you sure?" "Of course I'm sure," replied the actress. "I may forget a face, but I never forget a back!"

> *Laurette Taylor (1884–1946), U.S. actress*

Chief Justice Earl Warren, then governor of California, addressed a crowd by beginning, "I'm pleased to see such a dense crowd here tonight." A heckler in the audience shouted back, "Don't be too pleased, Governor, we ain't all dense."

Earl Warren (1891–1974),
U.S. jurist and politician

◆ AUTHORITY

Foreign Words and Phrases

carte blanche (Fra)
(kart BLAHNSH) *lit:* white card; complete freedom, authority to act at will

de par le roi (Fra)
(de par le RWA) in the name of the king

coup d'autorite (Fra)
(koo doh-tor-ee-tay) *lit:* blow of authority; act of authority

Quotations

"He did not seem to care which way he travelled providing he was in the driver's seat."

William Maxwell Aitken, 1st Baron
Beaverbrook (1879–1964),
British publisher and politician,
describing David Lloyd George, Decline
and Fall of Lloyd George (1963), ch. 7

"If a rhinoceros were to enter this restaurant now, there is no denying he would have great power here. But I should be the first to rise and assure him that he had no authority whatever."

G[ilbert] K[eith] Chesterton (1874–1936),
British man of letters, distinguishing the
meanings of "power" and "authority" to
Alexander Woollcott

Classical Phrases and Myths

ex cathedra (Grk/Lat)
(ex kath-HED-ra) *lit:* from seat; from a position of authority, official

ex officio (Lat)
(ex of-FIK-ee-oh) by virtue of an office held

ad litem (Lat)
(ad LEE-tem) in law, guardian appointed to represent an infant

Jokes, Stories and Anecdotes

A frosty colonel was testing new lieutenants. Turning to the class goof-off, the colonel asked, "So, to pitch a tent, what would be your first order?" "Sir, my first, my only, order would be 'Sergeant, pitch a tent.'"

◆ AVOIDANCE

Quotations

"That, sir, is a matter of too great importance to discuss in a five-minute interview—now rapidly drawing to its close."

[Stephen] Grover Cleveland (1837–1908),
U.S. president, declining a reporter's
request for a foreign policy statement

Jokes, Stories and Anecdotes

"Can I make an appointment with the dentist?" "Sorry, he's out now." "When will he be out again?"

◆ AWARD

Foreign Words and Phrases

grand prix (Fra)
(grohn PREE) *lit:* great prize; Formula One motor racing event forming part of the world championship

Quotations

"He got the peace prize; we got the problem. If I'm following a general, and the enemy gives him rewards, I tend to get suspicious. Especially if he gets a peace award before the war is over."

Malcolm X [Malcolm Little] (1925–1965), U.S. social reformer, describing Martin Luther King, Jr.

Jokes, Stories and Anecdotes

"I really don't deserve this," said Jack Benny, accepting an award. "But I have arthritis and I don't deserve that either."

Jack Benny (1894–1974), U.S. comedian

eagerly sought her husband, who had died several years before. "Excuse me," she said to St. Peter, "have you seen my husband?" "What was his name?" St. Peter inquired. "Paul Simpson." St. Peter shook his head. "That's a common name here. Anything else to identify him?" She blurted out the first thing that came to mind: "The last thing he said before he died was that if I were ever unfaithful to him, he would turn in his grave." "Aha!" said St. Peter, "you're looking for Pinwheel Paulie."

◆ BACHELORHOOD (WIDOWHOOD)

Foreign Words and Phrases

Fraulein (Ger)
(FROY-lyn) unmarried young lady

en gare on (Fra)
(on gahr-SOHN) as a bachelor

Quotations

"Being an old maid is like death by drowning, a really delightful sensation after you cease to struggle."

Edna Ferber (1887–1968), U.S. writer

"Bachelors know more about women than married men; if they didn't they'd be married too."

H[enry] L[ouis] Mencken (1880–1956), U.S. critic and writer

"Somehow a bachelor never quite gets over the idea that he is a thing of beauty and a boy forever."

Helen Rowland (1875–1950), U.S. writer, A Guide to Men (1922), p. 25

Jokes, Stories and Anecdotes

No sooner had Mrs. Simpson arrived at the Pearly Gates than she

◆ BANKS

Quotations

"I don't trust a bank that would lend money to such a poor risk."

Robert Charles Benchley (1889–1945), U.S. humorist, after closing his account at a bank that had quickly approved his loan request

"A bank is a place that will lend you money if you can prove that you don't need it."

Bob Hope [Leslie Townes] (1903–   ), British-born U.S. comedian

"Banker: a person who lends you his umbrella when the sun is shining and wants it back the minute it rains."

Mark Twain [Samuel Langhorne Clemens] (1835–1910), U.S. humorist, writer and speaker

Jokes, Stories and Anecdotes

The rich tycoon was astonished when he received back from his bank a personal check stamped "Insufficient Funds." Below the stamped words was the handwritten notation: "Not you . . . us."

Finding his savings and loan branch office closed, the man angrily pounded on the door. Finally, the manager appeared and shouted through the glass, "We're closed!" "But your sign says you're open nine to five," the customer replied. "Those aren't our hours. They're the odds we'll open tomorrow."

If you buy a toaster in Texas, you receive a free savings and loan.

◆ BEAUTY

Foreign Words and Phrases

grand amateur (Fra)
(grond AM-ah-tuhr) great collector, lover of beautiful things

beaux yeux (Fra)
(boh ZYER) *lit:* beautiful eyes; pretty

Quotations

"There is no excellent beauty that hath not some strangeness in the proportion."

> *Francis Bacon (1561–1626),*
> *British lawyer and writer,*
> Essays *(1625), "Of Gardens"*

"It was a blonde. A blonde to make a bishop kick a hole in a stained glass window."

> *Raymond Chandler (1888–1959),*
> *U.S. writer,* Farewell, My Lovely
> *(1940), ch. 13*

"Beauty is in the eye of the beholder."

> *Margaret Wolfe Hungerford (1855–1897),*
> *British writer,* Molly Bawn *(1878)*
> *[phrase quoted]*

"What ills from beauty spring."

> *Samuel Johnson (1709–1784), British man*
> *of letters,* Vanity of Human Wishes
> *(1749), l. 321*

"I'm tired of all this nonsense about beauty being only skin deep. That's deep enough. What do you want—an adorable pancreas?"

> *Jean Kerr (1923–   ), U.S. writer*
> *and playwright,* The Snake Has All the
> Lines *(1958), p. 142*

"She got her good looks from her father—he's a plastic surgeon."

> *Groucho [Julius] Marx (1895–1977),*
> *U.S. comedian*

"I always say beauty is only sin deep."

> *Saki [Hector Hugh Munro] (1870–1916),*
> *British writer,* Reginald *(1904),*
> *"Reginald's Choir Treat"*

"To me, fair friend, you never can be old
For as you were when first your eye I eyed,
Such seems your beauty still."

> *William Shakespeare (1564–1616), British*
> *playwright and poet,* Sonnets *(1609), 104*

"Beauty is all very well at first sight; but who ever looks at it when it has been in the house three days?"

> *George Bernard Shaw (1856–1950),*
> *Irish playwright,* Man and Superman
> *(1903), Act IV*

"She stood, a sight to make an old man young."

> *Alfred Tennyson, 1st Baron Tennyson*
> *(1809–1892), British poet,*
> The Gardener's Daughter *(1842)*

Classical Phrases and Myths

In Greek mythology, Adonis (a-DON-is) was a young man of unsurpassed beauty who was the lover of Aphrodite and Persephone. Adonis was killed by a wild boar while on the hunt; the bloodred flower, the anemone, which blooms briefly, sprang from his drops of blood that fell to earth. An *adonis* is a handsome young man.

In Greek mythology, Apollo (A-POL-oh), the god of the sun, music, poetry, prophecy and medicine, had many love affairs and was exceedingly handsome. Hence an *Apollonian* man is an extremely handsome man.

◆ BELIEF

Foreign Words and Phrases

bonne foi (Fra)
(bonn FWA) good faith

Quotations

" 'I can't believe that!' said Alice. 'Can't you?' the Queen said in a pitying tone. 'Try again: draw a long breath, and shut your eyes.' Alice laughed. 'There's no use trying,' she said: 'one can't believe impossible things.' 'I daresay you haven't had much practice,' said the Queen. 'When I was your age, I always did it for half-an-hour a day. Why, sometimes I've believed as many as six impossible things before breakfast.' "

> *Lewis Carroll [Charles Lutwidge Dodgson] (1832–1898), British writer and mathematician*, Through the Looking-Glass *(1872), ch. 5*

"Fanaticism consists in redoubling your effort when you have forgotten your aim."

> *George Santayana (1863–1952), Spanish-born U.S. philosopher, poet and writer,* Life of Reason *(1905), vol. 1, introduction*

"We are paid for our suspicions by finding what we suspected."

> *Henry David Thoreau (1817–1862), U.S. writer, naturalist and poet*

Classical Phrases and Myths

"Fere libenter homines id quod volunt credunt." (Men willingly believe what they wish.)

> *Gaius Julius Caesar (100 B.C.–44 B.C.), Roman general and statesman,* De Bello Gallico, *III, xviii*

Jokes, Stories and Anecdotes

The statesman Comte de Mirabeau, perhaps because he was sincere in his own beliefs, was quick to perceive the true convictions of others in the violent days of the French Revolution. On first hearing the great orator Robespierre speak, Mirabeau remarked to a colleague, "That man will go far. He believes all he says."

> *Honoré Gabriel Riqueti, Comte de Mirabeau (1749–1791), French revolutionary statesman*

When asked once if he would be prepared to die for his beliefs, mathematician, logician and Nobel laureate Bertrand Russell responded, "Of course not. After all, I could be wrong."

> *Bertrand Arthur William Russell, 3rd Earl (1872–1970), British mathematician and philosopher*

◆ BELIEVABILITY

Quotations

"All argument is against it; but all belief is for it."

> *Samuel Johnson (1709–1784), British man of letters, commenting on the appearance of the spirit of a person after death*

"The best lack all conviction, while the worst
Are full of passionate intensity."

> *William Butler Yeats (1865–1939), Irish poet and playwright,* Michael Robartes and the Dancer *(1920), "The Second Coming"*

Classical Phrases and Myths

cum grano salis (Lat)
(kum GRAH-noh SAL-ees) with a grain of salt; thus, do not be so gullible

"Prorsus credibile est, quia ineptum est." (PROR-sus kred-IB-il-eest, KWEE-a in-EPT-um est) (It is believable because it is absurd.)

> Tertullian [Quintus Septimius Florens Tertullianus] (c. 160–c. 225)
> Roman writer, De Carne Christi, 5

Jokes, Stories and Anecdotes

A rationalist, after waxing to French diplomat Talleyrand about the difficulty of converting the French peasants, then asked, "What could one do to impress these people?" Talleyrand remarked, *"Mais,* you could try being crucified and rising again on the third day."

> Charles Maurice de Talleyrand-Périgord (1754–1838), French diplomat [attributed also to Voltaire]

◆ BETRAYAL

Foreign Words and Phrases

lése majesté (Fra)
(LEHS MAH-jest-ay) *lit:* injured sovereignty; high treason, affront to the sovereign

quisling (Nor)
(KWIZ-ling) collaborator with enemy, traitor; named after Norwegian officer who supported Nazis in Norway in WWII

Quotations

"Cosmus, Duke of Florence, was wont to say of perfidious friends, that 'We read that we ought to forgive our enemies; but we do not read that we ought to forgive our friends.' "

> Francis Bacon (1561–1626), British lawyer and writer, Apothegms (1624), 206

"To betray you must first belong. I never belonged."

> Harold Adrian Russell [Kim] Philby (1912–1988), British-born Russian spy

Antony: This was the most unkindest cut of all.

> William Shakespeare (1564–1616), British playwright and poet, Julius Caesar (1600), Act III, sc. ii

La quinta columna. (The fifth column.)

> Emilio Mola (1887–1937), Spanish general, Radio Address given during the Spanish Civil War (1936–1939)

Jokes, Stories and Anecdotes

The Lone Ranger and his inseparable friend Tonto, who had rescued the Lone Ranger from certain death, are surrounded by hostile Indians. "Well, Tonto," says the Lone Ranger, turning to his trusted companion, "I think we are in the gravest danger." Tonto's immortal words were: "What do you mean 'we,' paleface?"

◆ BETWEEN

Foreign Words and Phrases

intermezzo (Ita)
(een-tayr-MEH-tsoh) *lit:* in between; in music, short movement as interlude between major movements in a piece

entr'acte (Fra)
(ON-trakt) *lit:* between acts; brief interlude, performance between two larger works

Jokes, Stories and Anecdotes

Roger Fry, the tireless promoter of post-Impressionist art, was guiding Lady Violet Bonham-Carter through the post-Impressionist exhibition in London, and finally led her to Matisse's *La Ronde*, which was hanging in the place of honor on the end wall of the Grafton Gallery. "What do you think of that?" he solicitously inquired. Lady Bonham-Carter tiredly looked at the painting and remarked at last, "I don't think I quite like the shape of their legs." "Ah!" said Roger, triumphantly, "but don't you like the shape of the spaces between their legs?"

Roger Fry (1866–1934),
British painter and art critic

"I say, Sherry," said one of two aristocrats who happened upon Anglo-Irish playwright Richard Sheridan in London's Piccadilly, "we were just discussing whether you are more of a rogue or a fool." "Why," replied Sheridan, taking each duke by the arm, "I believe I am between both."

Richard Brinsley Sheridan (1751–1816),
Irish-born British playwright
and politician

◆ BIG SHOT

Foreign Words and Phrases

shtarker (Yid)
(SHTARK-er) an important person, a big shot

pasha (Turk)
(PAH-shah) high official in former Turkish empire

magnifico (Ita)
(mah-NYEE-fee-koh) great man (often used pejoratively)

incontournable (Fra argot)
(an-kon-tor-NAB-le) one so important in a field of human endeavor that he literally "cannot be gotten around"

sangron (Spa)
(SAN-gron) big shot

macher (Yid)
(MAHK-er) important person, big shot

caballero (Spa)
(kah-bah-LYARE-oh) cavalier, gentleman, knight, nobleman

Quotations

"You can always tell a Harvard man, but you can't tell him much."

James Barnes (1866–1936), U.S. writer
[authenticity unverified]

Mendoza: "I am a brigand: I live by robbing the rich." *Tanner:* "I am a gentleman: I live by robbing the poor."

George Bernard Shaw (1856–1950),
Irish playwright, Man and Superman
(1903), Act III

Jokes, Stories and Anecdotes

During the three months in which the influential founder of the *New York Tribune*, Horace Greeley, served in Congress, another congressman boasted to him that he was a self-made man. "That, sir," replied Greeley, "does relieve the Almighty of a great responsibility."

Horace Greeley (1811–1872),
U.S. publisher and politician

◆ BIGNESS

Quotations

"The dinosaur's eloquent lesson is that if some bigness is good, an overabundance of bigness is not necessarily better."

Eric A[llen] Johnston (1896–1963),
U.S. businessman

Classical Phrases and Myths

a maximis ad minima (Lat)
(ah MAX-ee-mees ad MIN-ee-ma)
from the largest to the smallest

In ancient Greece, a colossus (KOL-os-sus) was a gigantic human statue, and the most famous, the Colossus of Rhodes, was one of the Seven Wonders of the Ancient World. It was reputedly more than 100 feet high and was made of bronze, supposedly from the weapons abandoned by Demetrius after his failed siege of the island Rhodes. Hence, anything *colossal* is gigantic, huge or splendid.

In Greek mythology, the Titans (TEE-tanz) were the 12 children of the goddess of the earth, Gaea, and the god of the skies, Uranus. Incited by Gaea, the Titans warred on Uranus, dethroned him and replaced him with Cronus. Then Zeus overthrew Cronus. The Titans had a fierce struggle against Zeus, but he, the other Olympians and the Cyclops defeated the Titans. All except Atlas and Prometheus were banished to Tartarus, an abyss below Hades. Hence, a *titan* is one of superhuman size and strength.

Jokes, Stories and Anecdotes

The longtime headmaster of Westminster School in London, the diminutive Dr. Richard Busby, was in a crowded London coffeehouse. A very large Irish nobleman said to him, "May I pass to my seat, O giant?" "Certainly, O pygmy!" replied Busby, making way. Apologetic, the nobleman tried to recant. "My expression alluded to the size of your intellect." Busby replied, "And my expression to the size of yours."

Richard Busby (1606–1695),
British teacher and headmaster

◆ BIGOTRY

Quotations

"Bigotry may be roughly defined as the anger of men who have no opinions."

G[ilbert] K[eith] Chesterton (1874–1936),
British man of letters, Heretics
(1905), ch. 20

"Much may be made of a Scotchman, if he be caught young."

Samuel Johnson (1709–1784), British man
of letters, describing Lord Mansfield, who
was educated in England

"The Irish are a fair people; they never speak well of one another."

Samuel Johnson (1709–1784), British man
of letters, commenting to Dr. Barnard,
Bishop of Killaloe

Jokes, Stories and Anecdotes

The English literary lion Samuel Johnson once mocked Scotland by declaring, "Sir, it is a very vile country." A Scotsman countered, "Well, sir, God made it." Rejoined Dr. Johnson, "Certainly he did, but we must remember that He made it for Scotchmen; and comparisons are odious, Mr. S—, but God made Hell."

Samuel Johnson (1709–1784),
British man of letters

◆ BIOGRAPHY (AUTOBIOGRAPHY)

Quotations

"One of the new terrors of death."

John Arbuthnot (1667–1735),
British writer and physician, describing
Edmund Curll's biographies

"George the Third
Ought never to have occurred.
One can only wonder
At so grotesque a blunder."

> *Edmund Clerihew Bentley (1875–1956),*
> *British poet, More Biography (1929),*
> *"George the Third"*

"Every artist writes his own autobiography."

> *[Henry] Havelock Ellis (1859–1939),*
> *British psychologist and writer,*
> *New Spirit (1890), "Tolstoi"*

"Autobiography is now as common as adultery, and hardly less reprehensible."

> *John Grigg [Edward Poynder]*
> *(1924–   ), British writer*

"Biography is a region bounded on the north by history, on the south by fiction, on the east by obituary, and on the west by tedium."

> *Philip Guedalla (1889–1944),*
> *British writer*

"I don't care what is written about me so long as it isn't true."

> *Dorothy Parker (1893–1967), U.S. wit*
> *and writer [authenticity unverified]*

"The affair between Margot Asquith and Margot Asquith will live as one of the prettiest love stories in all literature."

> *Dorothy Parker (1893–1967), U.S. wit*
> *and writer, reviewing Margot Asquith's*
> *fourth-volume autobiography, The New*
> *Yorker (October 22, 1927),*
> *"Lay Sermons"*

"This book doesn't seem to be about me, but it's pretty interesting about somebody."

> *John Steinbeck (1902–1968), U.S. writer,*
> *after reading his biography by*
> *Frank William Watt*

"My problem is that I am not frightfully interested in anything, except myself. And of all forms of fiction autobiography is the most gratuitous."

> *Tom Stoppard (1937–   ),*
> *British playwright and writer, Lord*
> *Malquist and Mr Moon (1966), pt. 2*

"I should not talk so much about myself if there were anybody else whom I knew as well."

> *Henry David Thoreau (1817–1862),*
> *U.S. writer, naturalist and poet,*
> *Walden (1854), "Economy"*

"Every great man now has his disciples, and it is always Judas who writes the biography."

> *Oscar [Fingal O'Flahertie Wills] Wilde*
> *(1854–1900), British playwright,*
> *writer and wit*

◆ BIRTH

Quotations

"If newborns could remember and speak, they would emerge from the womb carrying tales as wondrous as Homer's."

> *Anonymous, Newsweek (1982)*

Jokes, Stories and Anecdotes

Joseph Addison once began a parliamentary address, "Mr. Speaker, I conceive—I conceive, sir—sir, I conceive—"At which point he was interrupted by a colleague: "The right honorable secretary of state has conceived thrice and brought forth nothing."

> *Joseph Addison (1672–1719),*
> *British writer and politician*

The German mathematician Dirichlet intensely disliked corresponding, but he did make one exception. When his first child was born, he wired his father-in-law: "2 + 1 = 3."

Peter Gustav-Lejeune Dirichlet (1805–1859), German mathematician

Telegraphing congratulations to Mrs. Robert Sherwood upon the birth of her baby, Dorothy Parker wired collect: "Good work, Mary. We all knew you had it in you."

Dorothy Parker (1893–1967), U.S. wit and writer

Although the wit Alexander Woollcott was childless, he was often godparent to the children of friends. At the baptism of Mary MacArthur, daughter of Charles MacArthur and Helen Hayes, he was overheard saying, "Always a godfather—never a god!"

Alexander Woollcott (1887–1943), U.S. writer, broadcaster and wit

◆ BIRTH CONTROL

Quotations

"I must say . . . a fast word about oral contraception. I asked a girl to go to bed with me and she said 'no.' "

Woody Allen [Allen Stewart Konigsberg] (1935–   ), U.S. comedian and filmmaker, at a Washington nightclub, April 1965

"Contraceptives should he used on all conceivable occasions."

Terence Alan ["Spike"] Milligan (1918–   ), British comedian and writer

"Impotence and sodomy are socially OK but birth control is flagrantly middle-class."

Evelyn Waugh [Arthur St. John] (1903–1966), British writer

"Those right-to-lifers. They're with you up to the moment of birth, and then it's 'I gotta go.' "

Robin Williams (1951–   ), U.S. comedian and actor

Classical Phrases and Myths

Julia, the licentious daughter of Rome's first emperor, Augustus Caesar, had five children by her second husband, Marcus Vipsanius Agrippa. With her infidelities common knowledge, someone remarked about the uncanny resemblance of the children to Agrippa. Replied Julia, "It is because passengers are never allowed on board until the hold is full."

Julia (39 B.C.–A.D. 14), Roman aristocrat

Jokes, Stories and Anecdotes

Q: "What do [lawyers] use for birth control?" A: "Their personalities."

Heard about the new male birth-control pill? A man takes it the day after and it changes his blood type.

◆ BITTERSWEETNESS

Foreign Words and Phrases

chantpleure (Fra)
(shan-PLUR) to sing and to weep simultaneously, torch-singing

comedie noire (Fra)
(kom-AY-dee NWAR) *lit:* black comedy; comedy based on tragic or desperate circumstances

Quotations

"Let us eat and drink; for tomorrow we shall die."

Isaiah 22:13

Classical Phrases and Myths

rictus sardonicus (Lat)
(RIK-tus sar-DOHN-ee-kus) *lit:* sardonic laughter; when one's heart may be breaking but one never stops smiling

"Smiling through her tears."

> *Homer (c. 900 B.C.), Greek poet,*
> *Iliad, bk. VI, l. 484*

"*Felix . . . opportunitatemortis.*" (FAY-lix opp-or-TYOON-ee-TATE mor-TIS) (Fortune favored him . . . in the opportune moment of his death.)

> *Cornelius Tacitus (c. 55–117),*
> *Roman historian, Agricola (c. 98), 45*

Jokes, Stories and Anecdotes

The artist asked the gallery owner if there had been any interest in his paintings currently on display. "I've got good news and bad news," the owner replied. "The good news is that a man, asked if your work would appreciate in value after your death. I told him 'yes,' so he bought all 12 of your paintings." "That's great!" the artist exclaimed. "What's the bad news?" "He was your doctor."

"Oh, I assure you, Mr. Longfellow," said the queen, "you are very well known. All my servants read you." "Sometimes," said Longfellow to Oscar Wilde, "I will wake up in the middle of the night and wonder if it was a deliberate slight."

> *Henry Wadsworth Longfellow*
> *(1807–1882), U.S. poet*

◆ BLAME (LIABILITY)

Classical Phrases and Myths

"The gods
Visit the sins of the fathers upon the children."

> *Euripides (480 B.C.–406 B.C.),*
> *Greek playwright, Phrixus*

"*Delicta maiorum immeritus lues.*" (For the sins of your sires, albeit you had no hand in them, you must suffer.)

> *Horace (65 B.C.–8 B.C.), Roman poet,*
> *Odes, III, vi, I*

◆ BOASTING

Quotations

"It is nice to make heroic decisions and to be prevented by 'circumstances beyond your control' from ever trying to execute them."

> *William James (1842–1910),*
> *U.S. philosopher and psychologist*

"Look at him, a rhinestone in the rough."

> *Dorothy Parker (1893–1967),*
> *U.S. wit and writer, appraising a drunk*
> *who had assured her that he was a good*
> *person and a man of real talent*
> *[authenticity unverified]*

Classical Phrases and Myths

"*Qualis artifex pereo!*" (KWAL-is ART-i-fex PER-eo) (What an artist dies with me!)

> *Nero [Lucius Domitius Ahenobarbus]*
> *(37–68), Roman emperor*

Jokes, Stories and Anecdotes

Writer Franklin Pierce Adams once asked Beatrice Kaufman, "Whose birthday is it today?" "Yours?" she guessed. "No, but you're getting warm," replied Adams. "It's Shakespeare's."

Franklin Pierce Adams (1881–1960),
U.S. writer

One of the best ripostes to pretensions of grandeur was made by the first actor to receive a knighthood, Sir Henry Irving. A new member to London's Garrick Club, frequented by actors, wanted to impress the great Shakespearean actor and Lyceum Theatre manager. He approached Irving and casually began a story concerning his being stopped in the street by a total stranger who had gasped, "My God, is that you?" Inquired Irving: "And, ah, was it?"

Sir Henry Irving (1838–1905),
British actor and theater manager

Virtuoso violinists Mischa Elman and Jascha Heifetz were eating together when a waiter handed them a note labeled: "To the greatest violinist in the world." Heifetz gracefully handed it to Elman. "For you, Mischa." Elman returned it. "No, Jascha, for you." The note was traded until they agreed to open it together. The note began, "Dear Fritz."

Fritz Kreisler (1875–1962), U.S. violinist

When the young heavyweight James ("Quick") Tillis arrived in Chicago by bus from Tulsa, he eagerly made his way to the great Sears Tower. He put down his cardboard suitcases, looked up at the Tower and thought to himself, "I'm going to conquer Chicago." When he looked down at his feet, his suitcases had disappeared.

James ["Quick"] Tillis
(1957–   ), U.S. boxer

Returning to New York after a three-week vacation fishing in the Maine woods in the off-season, Mark Twain boasted of his successful fishing exploits to a stranger in the lounge car of the train. The stranger, at first unresponsive, turned grim. At length, Twain airily asked for the stranger's identity. "I'm the state game warden. Who are you?" Twain almost swallowed his cigar. "A-ah, to be perfectly candid, warden," he responded hastily, "I'm the biggest damn liar in the entire United States."

Mark Twain [Samuel Langhorne Clemens]
(1835–1910), U.S. humorist,
writer and speaker

Sir Redvers Henry Buller, British commander during the Boer War, was forced to retreat by the Boers numerous times. On one occasion, he put the best face possible on the setback by noting that he had retreated without losing a man, a flag or a cannon. "Or," added the painter James Whistler, when he heard the report, "a minute."

James Abbott McNeill Whistler
(1834–1903), U.S.-born British painter

◆ BOOK (PERIODICAL)

Quotations

"Don't place books by married male authors next to those by female authors and vice versa."

Anonymous, entry in Victorian-era
Lady Gough's Book of Etiquette

"Some books are undeservedly forgotten; none are undeservedly remembered."

W[ystan] H[ugh] Auden (1907–1973),
British-born poet, Dyer's Hand
(1963), "Reading"

"Some books are to be tasted, others to be swallowed, and some few to be chewed and digested."

> Francis Bacon (1561–1626),
> British lawyer and writer,
> (1625), "Essays Of Studies"

"A man's library is a sort of harem."

> Ralph Waldo Emerson (1803–1882),
> U.S. writer, poet and philosopher,
> The Conduct of Life (1860),
> "In Praise of Books"

"As a work of art it has the same status as a long conversation between two not very bright drunks."

> Clive James (1939–   ),
> Australian writer, critiquing
> Princess Daisy by Judith Krantz

"From the moment I picked up your book until I laid it down, I was convulsed with laughter. Some day I intend reading it."

> Groucho [Julius] Marx (1895–1977),
> U.S. comedian, writing a blurb for
> S. J. Perelman's book, Dawn Ginsberg's
> Revenge (1928)

"An anthology is like all the plums and orange peel picked out of a cake."

> Sir Walter Raleigh (1861–1922),
> British aristocrat, letter to
> Mrs. Robert Bridges, January 15, 1915

"All books are divisible into two classes: the books of the hour, and the books of all time."

> John Ruskin (1819–1900), British writer
> and social reformer, Sesame and Lilies
> (1865), "Of Kings' Treasuries"

"A library is thought in cold storage."

> Herbert Louis, 1st Viscount Samuel
> (1870–1963), British statesman and
> writer, A Book of Quotations
> (1947), p. 10

" 'Classic.' A book which people praise and don't read."

> Mark Twain [Samuel Langhorne Clemens]
> (1835–1910), U.S. humorist, writer, and
> speaker, Following the Equator (1897),
> ch. 25 [attributed by Twain also to
> Professor Caleb Winchester]

Classical Phrases and Myths

locus classicus (Lat)
(LO-kus KLAS-sik-us) standard source of an idea or reference, most authoritative reference on a subject

opere citato (Lat)
(OP-er-ekit-AH-toh) (occurring) in the work cited (*abbr:* op cit)

locus communis (Lat)
(LO-kus kom-MUNE-is) a commonly quoted passage (cliché)

Jokes, Stories and Anecdotes

After making his fortune, "Lord" Timothy Dexter of Newburyport, Massachusetts, wrote in his autobiography, *A Pickle for the Knowing Ones,* names of the men he wanted to serve as his pallbearers. When the 24-page pamphlet became notorious for its complete absence of punctuation, the indignant Dexter repented by including an extra page in the second edition filled with punctuation marks.

> "Lord" Timothy Dexter [Timothy
> Dwight] (1747–1806), U.S. businessman

A proof copy of Thomas Wolfe's first and inordinately long novel, *Look Homeward, Angel,* a fictionalized autobiography, which was dedicated to his editor Maxwell Perkins, was sent to novelist and short-story writer F. Scott Fitzgerald for his review. Fitzgerald replied, "Dear Max, I liked the dedication, but after that I thought it fell off a bit."

> F[rancis] Scott [Key] Fitzgerald
> (1896–1940), U.S. writer

◆ BORE

Foreign Words and Phrases

nudnik (Yid)
(NOOD-nik) a bore or pest

Quotations

"He is not only dull in himself, but the cause of dullness in others."

Samuel Foote (1720–1777), British actor and playwright [parodying Shakespeare's Henry IV, Part II, *Act I, sc. ii]*

"Sir, you have but two topics, yourself and me. I am sick of both."

Samuel Johnson (1709–1784), British man of letters

"A bore is a man who spends so much time talking about himself that you can't talk about yourself."

Melville D. Landon (1839–1910), U.S. lecturer and wit

"A bore is a man who, when you ask him how he is, tells you."

Bert Leston Taylor (1866–1901), U.S. humorist and writer, The So Called Human Race *(1922), p. 163*

"He is an old bore. Even the grave yawns for him."

Sir Herbert Beerbohm Tree (1853–1917), British actor and theater manager, describing Israel Zangwill

"One out of three hundred and twelve Americans is a bore . . . a healthy male adult bore consumes each year one and a half times his own weight in other people's patience."

John Updike (1932–   ), U.S. writer, Assorted Prose *(1965), "Confessions of a Wild Bore"*

Jokes, Stories and Anecdotes

A friend of Tristan Bernard once found the playwright staring despondently at a shop window in the pouring rain. "But you can't just stand out here in the rain!" exclaimed his friend. "Why don't you go home?" "I cannot," replied Bernard. "My wife's lover is there." The friend was going to offer appropriate sympathy when Bernard added, "And he's a goddamn bore!"

Tristan Bernard (1866–1947), French playwright and writer

An orator was giving yet another long, dull speech on the floor of the House of Commons when he spied Winston Churchill dozing off. "*Must* you fall asleep while I'm speaking?" demanded the speaker. "No," Churchill replied, eyes remaining shut, "it's purely voluntary."

Sir Winston Spencer Churchill (1874–1965), British prime minister and writer

"Ah, I simply talk the way I think," chattered a woman known for her vacuity. Commented the bored Lucien Guitry, "Yes, but more often."

Lucien Guitry (1860–1925), French actor

While relaxing with fellow club members, the humorist Oliver Herford was approached by the club's notorious bore. "I just heard that someone said that he'd offer me $50 to resign my membership," harumphed the insulted man. "What do you suggest that I do, Oliver?" "Hold out for a hundred."

Oliver Herford (1863–1935), British-born U.S. humorist and illustrator

Informed that Calvin ("Silent Cal") Coolidge had just died, the American wit Wilson Mizner asked, "How do they know?"

Wilson Mizner (1876–1933), U.S. wit and writer [attributed to others]

Welsh poet and writer Dylan Thomas suddenly stopped after drinking and talking at length. "Somebody's boring me," he said, "I think it's me."

Dylan [Marlais] Thomas (1914–1953), British poet and writer

"Do you think oysters have brains?" a loquacious bore once asked lawyer William Travers at a dinner. "I d-d-do," replied Travers, a stutterer. "J-j-just enough b-b-brains to k-k-keep their mouths s-s-shut."

William R. Travers (1819–1887),
U.S. lawyer and wit

◆ BOREDOM & TEDIUM

Foreign Words and Phrases

megillah (Yid)
(meh-GIL-ah) long boring speech, recital, etc.

ennui (Fra)
(ON-nwee) boredom, weariness from inactivity

tirare la carretta (Ita)
(tee-RAH-ray lah kuh-REH-tuh) *lit:* to pull the little cart; to perform uninteresting and burdensome work

Quotations

"Bore, n. A person who talks when you wish him to listen."

Ambrose [Gwinnet] Bierce
(1842–c. 1914), U.S. writer and poet,
Cynic's Word Book (1906)

"A yawn is a silent shout."

G[ilbert] K[eith] Chesterton (1874–1936),
British man of letters

"We were nearly as bored as enthusiasm would permit."

Sir Edmund Gosse (1849–1928),
British writer, commenting on a play
by Algernon Charles Swinburne

"We frequently forgive those who bore us, but cannot forgive those whom we bore."

François, Duc de La Rochefoucauld
(1613–1680), French writer,
Maximes (1678), 304

"Boredom is . . . a vital consideration for the moralist, since at least half the sins of mankind are caused by the fear of it."

Bertrand Arthur William Russell, 3rd Earl
(1872–1970), British mathematician and
philosopher, Sceptical Essays (1928),
"Eastern and Western Ideals
of Happiness"

Classical Phrases and Myths

taedium vitae (Lat)
(TEE-di-um WEE-fee) weariness with life

Jokes, Stories and Anecdotes

Robert Browning had to listen to a volley of questions concerning his poetry when cornered by a bore at an affair. Eventually he escaped. "But my dear fellow, this is too bad," he exclaimed. "I am monopolizing you." And he exited.

Robert Browning (1812–1889),
British poet

David Hartley, a soporific speaker, was addressing his peers in the House of Commons in 1783. Only 80 members, mostly asleep, remained of an audience originally numbering about 300. Just when he appeared to conclude his speech, he ordered the clerk of the House to read the 1715 Riot Act to illustrate a point he had made. Unable to contain himself, Edmund Burke rose, shouting, "The Riot Act? The Riot Act? To what purpose? Don't you see that the mob is already quietly dispersed?"

Edmund Burke (1729–1797),
British statesman, philosopher and writer

A biologist was rhapsodizing about the intricate social organization of ant colonies to the British actress Mrs. Patrick Campbell. "Do you know," he added enthusiastically, "they have their army and their own police force?" Arching an eyebrow, Mrs. Campbell asked, "What, no navy?"

Mrs. Patrick [Beatrice] Campbell (1865–1940), British actress

Much of the Amherst home of the poet Emily Dickinson, in particular the holograph manuscripts of some of her most famous poems, is off-limits to the general public. "Silent Cal" Coolidge, however, was given a special guided tour. After scrutinizing her handwritten poems, Coolidge made his one comment of the visit, saying, "Wrote with a pen, eh? I dictate."

[John] Calvin Coolidge (1872–1933), U.S. president

While at the premiere of a play of his at the *Theatre Français*, the novelist and dramatist Alexandre Dumas remarked to his friend that he had seen Fournet's *Gladiator* there just the previous night. "How was it?" asked the friend. "Dull," answered Dumas. "People fell asleep." Then the friend, spying a snoring member of the audience, said sneeringly, "Apparently your own play isn't too interesting either." "*Mon ami*, you are mistaken. He's left over from last night."

Alexandre [pere] Dumas (1802–1870), French writer and playwright

King Frederick William was exiting the royal box after attending the performance of a tedious and thankfully forgotten play. Nodding toward the snoring loge attendant, the king remarked to an aide, "An eavesdropper."

Frederick William IV (1795–1861), Prussian king

Jean de La Fontaine, attending a lackluster social gathering, excused his departure by explaining that he was due to speak before the French Academy. "But the Academy isn't scheduled to meet for a whole hour," the hostess protested. "It will take only 20 minutes to get there by the quickest route." La Fontaine bowed and said, "But, Madame, I prefer the longest way."

La Jean de La Fontaine (1621–1695), French fabulist

"Where do you think all these people go when they leave Alec's?" someone asked Dorothy Parker, referring to the mind-numbing weekend guests at Alexander Woollcott's country home. "Back into the woodwork."

Dorothy Parker (1893–1967), U.S. wit and writer [authenticity unverified]

At a tedious social function, the hostess anxiously inquired of the Irish playwright George Bernard Shaw, "Are you enjoying yourself, Mr. Shaw?" "Indeed," responded Shaw. "There is no one else here to enjoy."

George Bernard Shaw (1856–1950), Irish playwright [attributed also to Oscar Wilde]

◆ BRITISH

Quotations

"The maxim of the British people is 'Business as usual.' "

Sir Winston Spencer Churchill (1874–1965), British prime minister and writer, speech at Guild Hall, November 9, 1914

"Paralytic sycophants, effete betrayers of humanity, carrion-eating servile imitators, arch-cowards and collaborators, gang of women-murderers, degenerate rabble, parasitic traditionalists, play-boy soldiers, conceited dandies."

Officially sanctioned German Socialist Republic terms of abuse to describe Great Britain, 1953

"The devil take these people and their language! They take a dozen monosyllabic words in their jaws, chew them, crunch them and spit them out again, and call that speaking. Fortunately they are by nature fairly silent, and although they gaze at us open-mouthed, they spare us long conversations."

> *Henrich Heine (1797–1856),*
> *German poet and writer*

"An Englishman, even if he is alone, forms an orderly queue of one."

> *George Mikes (1912–   ),*
> *Czech humorist,* How To Be an Alien
> *(1946), p. 44*

"Continental people have sex lives; the English have hot-water bottles."

> *George Mikes (1912–   ),*
> *Czech humorist*

"Gorgonised me from head to foot, with a stony British stare."

> *Alfred Tennyson, 1st Baron Tennyson*
> *(1809–1892), British poet,* Maud *(1855)*

"How hard it is to make an Englishman acknowledge that he is happy."

> *William Makepeace Thackeray*
> *(1811–1863), British writer*

"Unmitigated noodles."

> *William II [Kaiser Wilhelm II]*
> *(1859–1941), German emperor,*
> *describing England*

Jokes, Stories and Anecdotes

Eager to flatter the fiercely nationalistic Lord Palmerston, once Britain's prime minister, a honey-tongued Frenchman commented, "If I were not a Frenchman, I should wish to be an Englishman." "If I were not an Englishman," retorted the unimpressed Palmerston, "I should wish to be an Englishman."

> *Henry John Temple, 3d Viscount*
> *Palmerston (1784–1865),*
> *British prime minister*

While Voltaire was in exile in London between 1726 and 1729, anti-French sentiment was so great that at one point the French philosopher and satirist was surrounded by an unruly mob yelling, "Hang him! Hang the Frenchman!" "Men of England! You desire to hang me merely because I am a Frenchman!" Voltaire shouted back. "Is it not punishment enough not to be born an Englishman?" The crowd was so pleased that they cheered and he was escorted safely away.

> *Voltaire [François-Marie Arouet]*
> *(1694–1778), French philosopher,*
> *writer and wit*

◆ BROAD-MINDEDNESS

Foreign Words and Phrases

sunao (Jap)
(soo-NAY-oh) seeing the world as it is, not as we would have it

au fond (Fra)
(oh fon) at root, fundamentally

Quotations

"It's dull (as well as draughty) to keep an open mind."

> *Philip Guedalla (1889–1944),*
> *British writer*

"You see things; and you say 'Why?' But I dream things that never were; and I say 'Why not?' "

> *George Bernard Shaw (1856–1950),*
> *Irish playwright,* Back to Methuselah
> *(1921), pt. 1, Act I*

◆ BUREAUCRACY

Foreign Words and Phrases

apparatchik (Rus)
(ap-PAR-aht-chik) (Communist party) functionary

echelon (Fra)
(AY-shel-lon) ladder rung, level within a hierarchy

Quotations

"Guidelines for bureaucrats: (1) When in charge, ponder. (2) When in trouble, delegate. (3) When in doubt, mumble."

> *James H. Boren (1925–   ),*
> *U.S. citizen*

"This place needs a laxative."

> *Bob Geldof (1954–   ),*
> *British music promoter, describing the*
> *bureaucracy of the European*
> *Economic Community*

"The longer the title, the less important the job."

> *George McGovern (1922–   ),*
> *U.S. politician*

Jokes, Stories and Anecdotes

Q: "How does a civil servant wink?" A: "He opens one eyelid."

Three youngsters were bragging about their fathers. First: "My dad's so fast he can shoot an arrow from his bow and beat the arrow to the target." Second: "So what. My dad's so fast he can shoot a bear from 400 yards and get to the bear before it falls." Third: "That's nothing. My dad works for the government. He gets off work at five but he's so fast he gets home by three-thirty."

The government official reviewed the new employees with displeasure and then shouted, "I have a nice easy job for the laziest employee here. Will the laziest person come forward?" Instantly, everyone came forward—all but one. "Why don't you come forward with the others?" demanded the official. "Too much trouble."

◆ BUSINESSMAN

Foreign Words and Phrases

affaire d'intérêt (Fra)
(ah-FAIR dan-te-REH) matter involving self-interest; matter of money

Quotations

"Every crowd has a silver lining."

> *P[hineas] T[aylor] Barnum (1810–1891),*
> *U.S. showman*

"For the merchant, even honesty is a financial speculation."

> *Charles [Pierre] Baudelaire (1821–1867),*
> *French poet,* Intimate
> Journals *(1887), 97*

"Here's the rule for bargains: 'Do unto other men, for they would do you.' That's the true business precept."

> *Charles Dickens (1812–1870),*
> *British writer,* Martin Chuzzlewit
> *(1843–1844), ch. 11*

"There are very honest people who do not think that they have had a bargain unless they have cheated a merchant."

> *Anatole France [Jacques-Anatole-François*
> *Thibault] (1844–1924),*
> *French writer and poet*

"Who is worse shod than the shoemaker's wife?"

> *John Heywood (c. 1497-c. 1580),*
> *British poet,* Proverbs *(1546)*

"Nothing is as irritating as the fellow that chats pleasantly while he's overcharging you."

> *Frank McKinney ["Kin"] Hubbard*
> *(1868–1930), U.S. humorist and writer*

"When you are skinning your customers you should leave some skin on to grow again so that you can skin them again."

> *Nikita Sergeyevich Khrushchev (1894–1971), Russian leader, advising British businessmen*

"The secret of business is to know something that nobody else knows."

> *Aristotle [Socrates] Onassis (1906–1975), Greek businessman*

"If Max [Beaverbrook] gets to heaven he won't last long. He will be chucked out for trying to pull off a merger between heaven and hell . . . after having secured a controlling interest in key subsidiary companies in both places, of course."

> *H[erbert] G[eorge] Wells (1866–1946), British writer*

"*Le client n'a jamais tort.*" (The customer is never wrong.)

> *Cesar Ritz (1850–1918), French businessman*

Jokes, Stories and Anecdotes

"Business is so bad," said the tailor, "that yesterday I only sold one suit. And today it was even worse." "How could it be worse?" asked his wife. Wailed the tailor, "Today the customer returned the suit he bought yesterday."

"I don't understand," asked the new accountant. "If you're selling these copiers way under cost, how come you're showing a profit?" "Simple," was the reply. "We make our money fixing them."

"I'm going into business," bragged the modern entrepreneur. "It'll be a partnership." "How much capital are you contributing?" asked his friend. "None. We go into business for four years. My partner puts in the capital, and I put in the experience. After four years, I'll have the

capital, and he'll have the experience."

Before Joseph Duveen became one of the world's foremost art dealers, he learned a lesson when dealing with the savvy banker and financier J. P. Morgan, Sr., who was also a major benefactor of the arts. Young Joseph once showed Morgan a collection of 30 miniatures. Only six pieces of the otherwise unremarkable collection were extremely rare. Morgan quickly looked over the collection and asked the total price, which Duveen happily supplied. Morgan pocketed the six rare pieces, and gave Duveen 20 percent of the total price. "You are just a boy, Joe," Uncle Henry later said to the downcast Joseph. "It takes a man to deal with Morgan."

> *Joseph Duveen, Baron Duveen of Millbank (1869–1939), British art dealer*

◆ CALIFORNIA

Quotations

"California is a fine place to live— if you happen to be an orange."

> *Fred Allen [John Sullivan] (1894–1957), U.S. comedian*

"His great aim was to escape from civilization, and, as soon as he had money, he went to Southern California."

> *Anonymous*

"If you live there [in California] long enough, you turn into a Mercedes."

> *Dustin Hoffman (1937–   ), U.S. actor*

"What was the use of my having come from Oakland . . . there is no there there."

> *Gertrude Stein (1874–1946), U.S. writer, Everybody's Autobiography (1937), ch. 4*

◆ CANNIBALISM

Quotations

"I have been assured by a very knowing American of my acquaintance in London, that a young healthy child well nursed is at a year old a most delicious, nourishing, and wholesome food, whether stewed, roasted, baked, or boiled, and I make no doubt that it will equally serve in a fricassee, or a ragout."

Jonathan Swift (1667–1745), Anglo-Irish clergyman and writer, A Modest Proposal for Preventing the Children of Ireland from Being a Burden to Their Parents or Country (1729)

Jokes, Stories and Anecdotes

Victor Biaka-Boda, who represented the Ivory Coast in the French Senate and was once a witch doctor, went on a tour of the hinterlands in January 1950 to broadcast his stand on the issues to his people and to understand their concerns—one of which was apparently the food supply. His constituents ate him.

Victor Biaka-Boda (c. 1895–1950), Ivory Coast politician

Herman Melville used numerous sources to write the great American novel Moby Dick, including an account of the sinking in 1620 of the whaleship Essex by a whale. Captain Pollard and other sailors aboard the Essex survived the long ordeal at sea by resorting to cannibalism. A relative of one of the Essex crew members aproached Captain Pollard years later and timidly asked if the old salt remembered the sailor. "Remember him!" Pollard bellowed. "Hell, son, I et him!"

Herman Melville (1819–1891), U.S. writer

In 1874 Alferd Packer, guiding five homesteaders along the Mormon Trail into Colorado during a heavy winter, emerged alone from the San Juan Mountains. When sentencing Packer to hang for cannibalism, Judge Melville B. Gerry reportedly shouted, "Stand up, yah voracious man-eatin' sonofabitch and receive your sintince! Thar were only sivin Dimocrats in all of Hinsdale County 'n ya et five of thim!" The cafeteria at the University of Colorado at Boulder is known as the Alfred G. Packer Grill.

Alferd G. Packer (d. 1907), U.S. frontiersman [authenticity of Gerry's remarks controverted]

◆ CAPRICE

Foreign Words and Phrases

capriccio (Ita)
(kah-PREE-cho) lit: caprice; in music or art, lively and whimsical

Quotations

"Vogue la galè re!" (voag la ga-LEHR) (Let the galley sail; let's chance it.)

François Rabelais (c. 1494–1553), French scholar, physician and writer, Works, bk. I, ch. 40

◆ CAREFULNESS

Foreign Words and Phrases

doveryai no proveryai (Rus)
(doh-VEHR-yay noh proh-VEHR-yay) trust but verify

una bocca chiusa non prende mosche (Ita)
(oo-na bo-CHO CHEE-oo-sa non PREN-day Mos-chay) a closed mouth catches no flies; proverb

Quotations

"You never test the depth of a river with both feet."

African proverb

"You will find in politics that you are much exposed to the attribution of false motive. Never complain and never explain."

Stanley Baldwin, Earl Baldwin of Bewdley (1867–1947), British prime minister

"Look ere you leap."

John Heywood (c.1497–c.1580), British poet, Proverbs (1546)

Jokes, Stories and Anecdotes

While visiting sculptor Jacob Epstein's studio, George Bernard Shaw spied a huge block of stone in a corner and asked its purpose. "I'm not sure yet," answered the sculptor. "I'm still planning." "You mean you plan your work?" asked the surprised Shaw. "I change my mind several times a day!" "That's all very well with a four-ounce manuscript," said Epstein, "but not with a four-ton block."

Sir Jacob Epstein (1880–1959), British sculptor

◆ CAUSE

Foreign Words and Phrases

raison d'etre (Fra)
(ray-ZON DET-ruh) *lit:* reason for being; justification, purpose

Quotations

"Nothing is worth doing unless the consequences may be serious."

George Bernard Shaw (1856–1950), Irish playwright, Misalliance *(1914)*

Classical Phrases and Myths

casus belli (Lat)
(KAH-sus BEL-ee) *lit:* cause of war; grounds for a quarrel or war

◆ CAUSE & EFFECT

Quotations

"Thou canst not stir a flower
Without troubling of a star."

Francis Thompson (1859–1907), British poet, Poems *(1913)*

Classical Phrases and Myths

a posteriori (Lat)
(ah pos-TER-ree-o-ree) in logic, the reasoning from effects to causes, reasoning based on past experience (*opp: a priori*)

ergo (Lat)
(ERR-go) therefore, thus

a priori (Lat)
(ah pree-OHR-ree) in logic, deductive reasoning, reasoning from causes to effects, *i.e.,* without reference to experience (*opp: a posteriori*)

post hoc ergo propter hoc (Lat)
(post hok ERG-oh PROP-ter hok) *lit:* after this, therefore because of this; the fallacy that because an effect follows a cause in time, it may therefore be attributed to that cause

Jokes, Stories and Anecdotes

Two politicians were lamenting the recent death of another. "Apparently our friend," observed one, "left very few effects." "It wouldn't be otherwise," replied the other. "He had very few causes."

◆ CAUTION

Quotations

"As the ancients
Say wisely, Have a care o' th' main chance,
And look before you ere you leap;
For, as you sow, you are like to reap."

> Samuel Butler (1612–1680), British poet and writer, Hudibras, Part II (1664), c. II, l. 501

"The better part of valour is discretion."

> William Shakespeare (1564–1616), British playwright and poet, Henry IV, Part I (1598), Act V, sc. iv

Classical Phrases and Myths

"Fallentis semita vitae." (The untrodden paths of life.)

> Horace (65 B.C.–8 B.C.), Roman poet, Epistles, I. xviii. l. 103

◆ CENSORSHIP

Quotations

"Those expressions are omitted which cannot with propriety be read aloud in the family."

> Thomas Bowdler (1754–1825), British editor and expurgator

"[The film] is so cryptic as to be almost meaningless. If there is a meaning, it is doubtless objectionable."

> British Board of Film Censors, banning Jean Cocteau's 1929 film The Seashell and the Clergyman, 1956

"It's red hot, mate. I hate to think of this sort of book getting into the wrong hands. As soon I've finished this, I shall recommend they ban it."

> Ray Galton (1930–   ), and Alan Simpson (1929–   ), British writers, "Hancock's Half Hour," television program for British comedian Tony Hancock, 1974

"They can't censor the gleam in my eye."

> Charles Laughton (1899–1962), British actor

"And art made tongue-tied by authority."

> William Shakespeare (1564–1616), British playwright and poet, Sonnets (1609), 66

"Assassination is the extreme form of censorship."

> George Bernard Shaw (1856–1950), Irish playwright, Shewing Up of Blanco Posnet (1911), "Limits to Toleration"

"It is now virtually impossible for the media in Britain to expose official wrongdoing without technically breaking the law."

> Donald Trelford (1937–   ), British editor, 1986

"I believe in censorship. After all, I made a fortune out of it."

> Mae West (1892–1980), U.S. film actress

Classical Phrases and Myths

nihil obstat (Lat)
(ni-hil OB-stat) lit: nothing hinders; statement from a censor that a text contains nothing that hinders its printing or production

Jokes, Stories and Anecdotes

According to journalist and writer John Gunther, immediately before WW II an American journalist wrote home to a friend: "Don't know if this will ever arrive because the Japanese censor may open it." Some time later, he received a note from the Japanese post office reading: "The statement in your letter is not correct. We do not open letters."

John Gunther (1901–1970), U.S. writer

◆ CERTAINTY

Foreign Words and Phrases

alla prima (Ita)
(al-a PREE-mah) painting quickly without subsequent retouching

Quotations

"Our constitution is in actual operation; everything appears to promise that it will last; but in this world nothing is certain but death and taxes."

Benjamin Franklin (1706–1790), U.S. statesman and scientist, letter to Jean Baptiste Le Roy, November 13, 1789

"I wish I was as cocksure of anything as Tom Macaulay is of everything."

William Lamb, 2nd Viscount of Melbourne (1779–1848), British prime minister

"It is the dull man who is always sure, and the sure man who is always dull."

H[enry] L[ouis] Mencken (1880–1956), U.S. critic and writer

"Rose is a rose is a rose is a rose, is a rose."

Gertrude Stein (1874–1946), U.S. writer, Sacred Emity (1913), p. 187 [misquoted often as "a rose is a rose is a rose"]

Classical Phrases and Myths

"Certum est quia impossible est." (KER-tum est KWEE-a im-poss-IB-il-e) (It is certain because it is impossible.)

Tertullian [Quintus Septimius Florens Tertullianus] (c. 160–c. 225), Roman writer, De Carne Christi, 5 [sometimes rendered as: "Credo quia absurdum" (KRAY-doh KWEE-A ab-SURD-um) (I believe because it is absurd); thus, faith must sometimes supplant reason]

Jokes, Stories and Anecdotes

"How old are these dinosaur bones?" the tourist asked the native. "One hundred million and six years old." Inquired the tourist, "How can you be so definite?" "A geologist told me they were 100 million years old," replied the native, "and that was exactly six years ago."

◆ CHANCE (LUCK)

Foreign Words and Phrases

par hasard (Fra)
(par AZ-ar) by chance

Quotations

"How else do you explain the success of those you don't like?"

Jean Cocteau (1889–1963), French writer, artist, and filmmaker, answering whether he believed in luck

"If at first you do succeed, don't take any more chances."

Frank McKinney ["Kin"] Hubbard (1868–1930), U.S. humorist and writer

"Chance is a word that does not make sense. Nothing happens without a cause."

Voltaire [François Marie Arouet] (1694–1778), French philosopher, writer and wit

"Le hasard est un sobriquet de la Providence." (Chance is a nickname for Providence.)

Sébastien Roch Nicolás Chamfort (1741–1794), French writer and wit, Maxims and Thoughts, 62

Jokes, Stories and Anecdotes

A fellow asked for condoms from a drugstore clerk, who looked him up and down and said, "Wouldn't you rather have a lottery ticket?" "Why?" "The odds are better."

◆ CHANGE

Foreign Words and Phrases

Verkla rung (Ger)
(fehr-KLAI-rung)   transfiguration, transformation

Quotations

"Well, I find that a change of nuisance is as good as a vacation."

> *David Lloyd George, 1st Earl (1863–1945), British prime minister, answering how he retained his good spirits in spite of the crises during his ministry*

"There is nothing in this world constant, but inconstancy."

> *Jonathan Swift (1667–1745), Anglo-Irish clergyman and writer,* A Critical Essay upon the Faculties of the Mind *(1707)*

Classical Phrases and Myths

mutatis mutandis (Lat)
(moo-TAH-tees moo-TAND-ees) *lit:* things having been changed which should be changed; allowing for the appropriate changes

---

◆ CHANGE OF MIND

Quotations

"Treason doth never prosper: what's the reason?
For if it prosper, none dare call it treason."

> *Sir John Harington (1561–1612), British writer,* Of Treason, *bk. iv, no. 5*

"Whenever a Republican leaves one side of the aisle and goes to the other, it raises the intelligence quotient of both parties."

> *Clare Boothe [Brokaw] Luce (1903–1987), U.S. writer, playwright and diplomat, commenting on a Republican senator's affiliation with the Democratic party*

"Some praise at morning what they blame at night;
But always think the last opinion right."

> *Alexander Pope (1688–1744), British poet and writer,* An Essay on Criticism

Classical Phrases and Myths

Among the conspirators who attacked Caesar on the fatal Ides of March in 44 B.C. at the Roman Senate house was Marcus Junius Brutus, whom Caesar had trusted and favored as a son. According to Roman historians, Caesar first resisted the assassins, but when he saw Brutus among them with his dagger ready to strike, he ceased to struggle. Pulling the top part of his toga over his face, Caesar cried, *"Kai su, teknon?"* (You too, my son?)

> *Gaius Julius Caesar (100 B.C.–44 B.C.), Roman general and statesman [Caesar spoke in Greek but the Latin form as depicted in Shakespeare's* Julius Caesar, *Act III, sc. i, is best known:* "Et tu, Brute?"]

Jokes, Stories and Anecdotes

Benjamin Butler, Union general and later Massachusetts govenor, was about to administer the oath of allegiance at the end of the Civil War when a Confederate soldier shouted, "We gave you hell at Chickamauga, General!" Butler, furious, threatened to have the man shot unless he took the oath.

The rebel reluctantly complied. "General, I suppose I am a good Yankee and citizen of the United States now?" "I hope so," Butler replied cautiously. "Well, General, the rebels did give us hell at Chickamauga, didn't they?"

Benjamin Franklin Butler (1818–93), U.S. general and politician

◆ CHARITY & BEGGING

Quotations

"Beggars should be abolished. It annoys one to give to them, and it annoys one not to give to them."

Friedrich [Wilhelm] Nietzsche (1844–1900), German philosopher

"Charity is injurious unless it helps the recipient to become independent of it."

John D[avison] Rockefeller, Sr. (1839–1937), U.S. industrialist and philanthropist

"No one would remember the Good Samaritan if he'd only had good intentions. He had money as well."

Margaret Thatcher (1925–   ), British prime minister, television interview, January 6, 1986

Classical Phrases and Myths

"*Proxumus sum egomet mihi.*" (PROX-um-us sum EG-oh-met MEE-hee) (Charity begins at home.)

Terence [Publius Terentius Afer] (c.190 B.C.–159 B.C.), Roman playwright, The Woman of Andros (166 B.C.)

Jokes, Stories and Anecdotes

Begging off the Hare Krishna cultists, the hurried man said, "I gave in a previous lifetime."

Passing by a Salvation Army player, Tallulah Bankhead dropped a $50 bill into his extended tambourine. "Don't bother to thank me," said Bankhead, waving aside the man's gratitude. "I know what a perfectly ghastly season it's been for you Spanish dancers."

Tallulah Bankhead (1903–1968), U.S. actress

The collector for charitable organization solicited a donation from Horace Greeley, founder of the *New York Tribune*, by saying, "Your money will save millions of your fellow men from going to hell." "I won't give a damned cent, then," Greeley snorted. "Not half enough of them go there now."

Horace Greeley (1811–1872), U.S. publisher and politician

One of humorist Douglas Jerrold's circle was infamous for his requests for financial assistance from his acquaintances. Once again short of money, he sent an intermediary to request Jerrold's contribution. "How much does he want this time?" Jerrold asked irritably. "Just a four and two noughts will put him straight," said the man uneasily. Responded Jerrold, "Put me down for one of the noughts."

Douglas Jerrold (1803–1857), British playwright and humorist

◆ CHASTITY

Quotations

"A woman's chastity consists, like an onion, of a series of coats."

Nathaniel Hawthorne (1804–1864), U.S. writer, Journals (March 16, 1854)

"An unattempted woman cannot boast of her chastity."

Michel Eyquem de Montaigne (1533–1592), French writer, Essays *(1580)*

Classical Phrases and Myths

"*Da mihi castitatem et continentiam, sed noli modo.*" (Give me chastity and continence, but not yet).

St. Augustine of Hippo (354–430) North African Catholic theologian, Confessions, *bk. viii, ch. 7*

nisi caste, saltem caute (Lat)
(NEE-si KAS-te SAL-tem KOW-te) if you are not chaste, at least be careful (first canon of religious prudence)

Jokes, Stories and Anecdotes

Mother Superior called in all the nuns and declared, "I found a condom in the dormitory!" There was an audible gasp from all the nuns, save one who said, "Tee-hee." "And that condom had a hole in it," continued the Mother Superior. "Tee-hee," chuckled the nuns in unison, save for one audible gasp.

"I have learned that immorality is rampant in our small town," declared the preacher. "It is said that no virgins are left. This vile lie must and shall be refuted. I ask every virgin in the congregation to rise." Nobody stirred. "Modesty is of no concern here," begged the preacher. "All virgins, rise!" Again, no woman moved. "Will you avoid a small shame to incur a great one? The Almighty commands: Let all virgins stand!" thundered the preacher. A young woman, with a baby in her arms, rose bashfully. The preacher stared at the baby, then said, "Young woman, I'm asking virgins to stand." Replied the woman, "Do you expect this six-month-old girl to stand by herself?"

Lord Lyndhurst was asked by a social matron if he believed in platonic friendship between men and women. "After, not before."

John Singleton Copley, Lord Lyndhurst (1772–1863), British lord chancellor

◆ CHEERFULNESS

Foreign Words and Phrases

entrain (Fra)
(on-tren) warmth, zest, vivacity, spirit

bon diable (Fra)
(bon dee-AHBL) good-humored man

Quotations

"Happy the man, and happy he alone,
He, who can call to-day his own:
He who, secure within, can say,
Tomorrow do thy worst, for I have lived to-day."

John Dryden (1631–1700), British poet, playwright and writer, Imitation of Horace, *bk. III, ode 29 (1685), l. 65*

"By happy alchemy of mind
They turn to pleasure all they find."

Matthew Green (1696–1737), British poet, The Spleen

"Keep a stiff upper lip, Bertha dear. What, knocked a tooth out? Never mind, dear, laugh it off, laugh it off; it's all part of life's rich pageant."

Arthur Marshall (1910–1989), British comedian, The Games Mistress, *recorded monologue, 1937*

"He was born with a gift of laughter and a sense that the world was mad. And that was all his patrimony."

Rafael Sabatini (1875–1950), Italian writer, Scaramouche (1921), bk. 1, ch. 1

"He laughs best who laughs last."

Sir John Vanbrugh (1664–1726), British playwright, The Country House (1706), Act II, sc. 5

"Je me presse de rire de tout, de peur d'être oblige d'en pleurer." (I hasten to laugh at everything for fear of being obliged to weep at it.)

Pierre-Augustin Caron de Beaumarchais (1732–1799), French playwright, Le Barbier de Seville (1775), Act I, sc. ii

Classical Phrases and Myths

"Nihil est ab omni Parte beatum." (No lot is happy on all sides.)

Horace (65 B.C.–8 B.C.), Roman poet, Odes, II, xvi, l. 27

◆ CHEST

Foreign Words and Phrases

Heldenbrust (Ger)
(HELD-en-broost) maiden's heroic-sized bosom

decolletage (Fra)
(DAY-kol-let-TAJ) low cut of a dress, revealed neck, shoulders and often upper chest

Quotations

"It was not a bosom to repose upon, but it was a capital bosom to hang jewels upon."

Charles Dickens (1812–1870), British writer

"There are two good reasons why men go to see her. Those are enough."

Howard Hughes (1905–1976), U.S. industrialist, describing film actress Jane Russell

"I am the only topless octogenarian here."

Alice Roosevelt Longworth (1884–1980), U.S. socialite, following surgical removal of her second breast due to cancer at age 86

"I have one criticism. You can't expect the public to get excited about a film where the leading man's chest is bigger than the leading lady's."

Groucho [Julius] Marx (1895–1977), U.S. comedian, commenting at a private screening to the buoyant producer of the film Samson and Delilah starring Victor Mature

---

◆ CHILDREN

Quotations

"We want better reasons for having children than not knowing how to prevent them."

Countess Dora Russell (1894–1986), British writer, Hypatia (1925), ch. 4

"How sharper than a serpent's tooth it is
To have a thankless child."

William Shakespeare (1564–1616), British playwright and poet, King Lear (1606), Act I, sc. iv

Mother: "It's broccoli, dear." Child: "I say it's spinach, and I say the hell with it."

E[lwyn] B[rooks] White (1899–1985), U.S. humorist and writer, New Yorker cartoon caption (December 8, 1928)

"Children begin by loving their parents; after a time they judge them; rarely, if ever, do they forgive them."

> Oscar [Fingal O'Flahertie Wills] Wilde (1854–1900), British playwright, writer and wit, A Woman of No Importance (1893), Act I

Jokes, Stories and Anecdotes

Q: "What term is similar to umbilical cord describing the sometimes hard-to-break tie between an older child and a parent?" A: "Purse string."

◆ CHINESE

Jokes, Stories and Anecdotes

When Wellington Koo was representing his country at the 1921 Washington Conference, many Americans were still unaccustomed to meeting sophisticated foreigners. At a social function he found himself next to a young lady who, after some minutes of embarrassed silence, attempted to begin a conversation with "Likee soupee?" Koo just nodded and continued with his soup. At the end of the meal Koo rose to give a speech, which he did for ten minutes in impeccable English. When he returned to his seat, he blandly asked the woman, "Likee speechee?"

> Wellington Koo [Ku Wei-chain] (1887–1985), Chinese politician and diplomat

◆ CHOICE

Foreign Words and Phrases

embarras du choix (Fra)
(om-BA-ra doo-SHWA) *lit:* embarrassment of choice; the more alternatives, the more difficult the choice

Quotations

"Look here, Steward, if this is coffee, I want tea; but if this is tea, then I wish for coffee."

> G. D. Armour (1864–1949), British cartoonist, Punch cartoon caption (July 23, 1902)

"When you come to a fork in the road, take it."

> Lawrence ["Yogi"] Berra (1925–), U.S. baseball player and manager [authenticity unverified]

"Of all the 36 alternatives, running away is best."

> Chinese proverb

Classical Phrases and Myths

tertium quid (Lat)
(TER-tee-um kwid) last choice

ex gratis (Lat)
(ex GRAH-tee-ah) *lit:* out of grace, (an action) performed by choice not necessity

◆ CHOICE, ABSENCE OF

Foreign Words and Phrases

cul de sac (Fra)
(kool de sack) *lit:* bottom of a sack; street closed at one end

Quotations

"People can have the Model T in any color—so long as it's black."

> Henry Ford (1863–1947), U.S. industrialist

"There was only one catch and that was Catch-22, which specified that a concern for one's own safety in the face of dangers that were real and immediate was the process of a rational mind. Orr was crazy and could be grounded. All he had to do was ask; and as soon as he did, he would no longer be crazy and would have to fly more missions. Orr would be crazy to fly more missions and sane if he didn't, but if he was sane he had to fly them. If he flew them he was crazy and didn't have to; but if he didn't want to then he was sane and had to. Yossarian was moved very deeply by the absolute simplicity of this clause of Catch-22 and let out a respectful whistle. 'That's some catch, that Catch-22,' he observed."

> *Joseph Heller (1923–   ),*
> *U.S. writer*, Catch-22 *(1961), ch. 5*

"Beggars should be no choosers."

> *John Heywood (c.1497–c.1580),*
> *British poet,* Proverbs *(1546)*

"There's small choice in rotten apples."

> *William Shakespeare (1564–1616), British playwright and poet,* The Taming of the Shrew *(1594), Act I, sc. i*

Jokes, Stories and Anecdotes

"Hobson's choice," an expression that means either taking what is offered or taking nothing, is derived from the practice of the Cambridge, England stabler Thomas Hobson. His patrons were given the "choice" of only the horse nearest the stable door, thereby ensuring that Hobson's customers and his horses were given equally fair treatment.

> *Thomas Hobson (c. 1544–1631),*
> *British stabler*

◆ CIRCUITOUSNESS (ROTATION)

Classical Phrases and Myths

"Per caputque pedesque." (per CAP-ut-kay PED-es-kay) (Over head and heels.)

> *Gaius Valerius Catullus*
> *(87 B.C.–c. 54 B.C.), Roman poet*

Jokes, Stories and Anecdotes

Fred was at the local bar one evening when the fellow next to him put down his empty glass, walked over to the wall and, without hesitation, walked up its surface and onto the ceiling. He crossed the ceiling upside down, walked down the wall to the top of the front door and somersaulted out the door. Fred, astonished, remarked to the bartender, "That's an odd way of leaving." The bartender shrugged. "You get used to it. He always leaves without saying goodbye."

◆ CIRCUMSTANCES

Foreign Words and Phrases

en passant (Fra)
(on PASS-sohn) incidentally, in passing, by the way; a move in chess by which a pawn captures another

Quotations

"Circumstances! I make circumstances!"

> *Napoleon I [Napoleon Bonaparte]*
> *(1769–1821), French general and emperor*

Classical Phrases and Myths

status quo (ante) (Lat)
(STA-tus kwoh AN-tay) state of affairs (beforehand)

Jokes, Stories and Anecdotes

Robert Ingersoll, a well-known 19th-century agnostic, was visiting Reverend Henry Ward Beecher and admired Beecher's beautiful globe depicting the various constellations and stars of the heavens. He asked who had made it. "Who made it?" said Beecher, seizing the opportunity to challenge his guest. "Why, nobody made it. It just happened."

> *Henry Ward Beecher (1813–1887),*
> *U.S. clergyman and writer*

◆ CIVILIZATION

Foreign Words and Phrases

Geisteswissen (Ger)
(GYST-es-VISS-en-shaf-ten) theory that each facet of cultural and intellectual life shares certain characteristics

Quotations

"That would be a good idea."

> *Mohandas Karamchand [Mahatma]*
> *Gandhi (1869–1948), Indian statesman*
> *and spiritual leader answering what he*
> *thought of modern civilization*

"One of the surest signs of the Philistine is his reverence for the superior tastes of those who put him down."

> *Pauline Kael (1919–   ),*
> *U.S. writer*

"All the greatest things we know have come to us from neurotics. It is they and they only who have founded religions and created great works of art. Never will the world be conscious of how much it owed to them, nor above all of what they have suffered in order to bestow their gifts on it."

> *Marcel Proust (1871–1922),*
> *French writer, Le côté de Guermantes*
> (Guermantes Way) *(1921), vol. 1, p. 418*

"The reasonable man adapts himself to the world: the unreasonable one persists in trying to adapt the world to himself. Therefore all progress depends on the unreasonable man."

> *George Bernard Shaw (1856–1950),*
> *Irish playwright,* Man and Superman
> *(1903), "Maxims for Revolutionists:*
> Reason"

"The plain working truth is that it is not only good for people to be shocked occasionally, but absolutely necessary to the progress of society that they should be shocked pretty often."

> *George Bernard Shaw (1856–1950),*
> *Irish playwright*

Andrea: "Unglu cklich des Land, das keine Helden hat! . . . " Galilei: "Nein. Unglu cklich des Land, das Helden no-tig hat." (Andrea: Pity the country that has no heroes! . . . Galileo: No, pity the country that needs heroes.)

> *Bertolt Brecht (1898–1956),*
> *German playwright,* Leben des Galilei
> (Life of Galileo) *(1939), sc. 13*

Jokes, Stories and Anecdotes

"You're a lost civilization!" exulted the anthropologist to the chief in the deep jungle. "We don't mind being lost," remarked the chief. "It's being discovered that worries us."

The young men of the Bloomsbury Group, an intellectual clique comprised of writers, philosophers and artists, were notorious for their pedantry and narcissism. The avant-garde writer Gertrude Stein reportedly once referred pointedly to them as "the Young Men's Christian Association—with Christ left out, of course." They tended to be conscientious objectors, not a particularly popular view during the early days of World War I. It was then the practice to hand white feathers to able-bodied men not in uniform, and a woman, about to do so, witheringly challenged a member of the group on why he wasn't in uniform to fight for civilization. The young man replied, "Madam, I *am* the civilization they are fighting for."

◆ CLASS-CLIMBING

Foreign Words and Phrases

parvenu (Fra)
(par-VEN-oo) social climber, upstart, newly rich

arriviste (Fra)
(ah-ree-VEEST) social climber, person with money who lacks class

dé classement (Fra)
(day-KLASS-mon) loss of social position, to fall from one class to a lower class

Quotations

"Mrs. Montagu has dropt me. Now, Sir, there are people whom one should like very well to drop, but would not wish to be dropped by."

Samuel Johnson (1709–1784),
British man of letters

"To establish oneself in the world, one does all one can to seem established there already."

François, Duc de La Rochefoucauld
(1613–1680), French writer,
Maximes *(1678), 56*

" 'My boy,' he says, 'always try to rub up against money, for if you rub up against money long enough, some of it may rub off on you.' "

Damon Runyon (1884–1946), U.S. writer,
Cosmopolitan *(August 1929), "A Very*
Honourable Guy"

"'Tis a common proof,
That lowliness is young ambition's ladder,
Whereto the climber-upward turns his face;
But when he once attains the upmost round,
He then unto the ladder turns his back,
Looks in the clouds, scanning the base degrees
By which he did ascend."

William Shakespeare (1564–1616), British
playwright and poet, Julius Caesar
(1600), Act II, sc. i

Classical Phrases and Myths

"*Magnas inter opes inops.*" (A pauper in the midst of wealth.)

Horace (65 B.C.–8 B.C.), Roman poet,
Odes, *III, xvi, l. 28*

Jokes, Stories and Anecdotes

"The only reason you married me is because my Aunt Muffie willed me $1 million," sniffled the young wife. "Don't be silly!" shot back her husband. "I don't care who left it to you."

Romance novelist Barbara Cartland became remotely connected to royal circles when her step-granddaughter became the Princess of Wales in 1981. Interviewed on BBC radio, she was asked whether she thought that class barriers had broken down in Britain. "Of course they have," replied Cartland, "or I wouldn't be sitting here talking to someone like you."

> *Barbara Cartland (1902–   ),*
> *British writer*

◆ CLOTHING (SEWING & WEAVING)

Foreign Words and Phrases

endimanche (Fra)
(on-DEE-mon-shay)   dressed   in one's Sunday best

en grande tenue (toilette) (Fra)
(on GROND ten-EW (twa-LET)) dressed up (tenue is general; but toilette refers to women)

schmatte (Yid)
(SHMAT-ta) (dressed in) rags; lower-order person

Quotations

"She just wore
Enough for modesty—no more."

> *Robert Williams Buchanan (1841–1901),*
> *U.S. poet,* White Rose and Red, *iv*

"I dress for women. I undress for men."

> *Angie Dickinson [Angeline Brown]*
> *(1931–   ), U.S. film actress*

"One morning I shot an elephant in my pajamas. How, he got into my pajamas I'll never know."

> *George S. Kaufman (1889–1961)),*
> *U.S. playwright, writer and wit, and*
> *Morrie Ryskind (1895–1985), U.S.*
> *playwright,* Animal Crackers (*1930 film*)

"He has 75 winter overcoats, 25 spring coats, 600 suits, a thousand neckties, and 11 jock straps for both fast or feast days."

> *H[enry] L[ouis] Mencken (1882–1958),*
> *U.S. critic and writer, describing the*
> *sartorial critic George Jean Nathan*

"There was a young belle of old Natchez
Whose garments were always in patchez.
When comment arose
On the state of her clothes,
She drawled, When Ah itchez, Ah scratchez."

> *Ogden Nash (1902–1971), U.S. humorist,*
> *I'm a Stranger Here Myself*
> *(1938), "Requiem"*

"Brevity is the soul of lingerie."

> *Dorothy Parker (1893–1967), U.S. wit*
> *and writer [authenticity unverified]*

Jokes, Stories and Anecdotes

The naive vixen came home from the store and showed her husband the new dress she'd bought. "But honey," the young man gasped, "it's made of plastic and transparent. People will see right through it!" "No they won't, dummy." She giggled. "I'll be inside of it."

"To congratulate certain employees at his firm, Armour and Co., for their increased efficiency, Philip Armour offered to buy each of them a new suit of clothes. Each man would order a suit of his choice and send the bill to Armour. One young man greedily selected an expensive evening suit. Armour nonetheless agreed to pay the bill, commenting to his clerk, "I've packed a great many hogs in my time, but I never dressed one before."

> *Philip Danforth Armour (1832–1901),*
> *U.S. industrialist*

A flamboyant dresser was once boasting that he was so well-dressed that his tailor gave him a discount because he was such an excellent advertisement for the firm. "My tailor also allows me a discount," said French playwright Tristan Bernard, a careless dresser. "It's on condition that I never tell anyone where I buy my suits."

Tristan Bernard (1866–1947),
French playwright and writer

Thomas Du Pont once checked into his room at a Chicago hotel, only to find a sheer nightgown apparently left behind by a woman who had previously occupied his room. He summoned the manager and, handing him the garment, said, "Fill it, and bring it back."

Thomas Coleman Du Pont (1863–1930),
U.S. entrepreneur and politician

While Frederick William the Just lay on his deathbed, the attending minister read to him from the Book of Job: "Naked came I out of my mother's womb and naked shall I return thither." The king muttered his last words, "No, not quite naked. I shall have my uniform on."

Frederick William I (1688–1740),
Saxon king

When Mrs. Horace Greeley happened to run into Margaret Fuller on the street one day, she noticed that Fuller was wearing kid gloves. Shuddering with distaste, Greely exclaimed, "Skin of a beast!" "Why, what do you wear?" asked Fuller. "Silk." Retorted Fuller with equal distaste, "Entrails of a worm!"

Margaret Fuller, Marchioness d'Ossoli
(1810–1850), U.S. writer and philosopher

At a banquet while the papal nuncio to France, the future Pope John XXIII was seated next to a lady wearing a very low-cut dress, which he affected not to notice during most of the meal. During dessert the popular prelate selected an apple and offered it to the woman. She politely declined. "Please take it, madam," he pressed. "Only after Eve ate the apple did she become aware of how little she had on."

John XXIII [Angelo Roncalli]
(1881–1963), Roman Catholic pope

When the English comic actor Edward Shuter was chided for having holes in his stocking, he replied that he would rather have 20 holes than one darn: "A hole is the accident of a day, whilst a darn is premeditated poverty."

Edward Shuter (1728–1776), British actor
[attributed also to others]

◆ COERCION

Quotations

"There is a homely old adage which runs: 'Speak softly and carry a big stick; you will go far.' If the American nation will speak softly, and yet build and keep at a pitch of the highest training a thoroughly efficient navy, the Monroe Doctrine will go far."

Theodore Roosevelt (1858–1919),
U.S. president, speech in Chicago,
April 3, 1903

Classical Phrases and Myths

vi et armis (Lat)
(WEE et AR-mes) by force of arms

ultima ratio regum (Lat)
(UL-tee-ma RA-tee-oh REG-um) the final argument (of kings) is force

---

◆ COINCIDENCE

Foreign Words and Phrases

stretto (Ita)
(STREH-toh) *lit:* arrow; in music,

passage in a fugue where the subject overlaps its answer, quicker time

Quotations

"[W]herever the long arm of coincidence intrudes, the author seizes it and shakes hands."

Heywood Broun (1888–1939),
U.S. writer, reviewing the play
Just Outside the Door *(1915)*

The long arm of coincidence.

Charles Haddon Chambers (1860–1921),
British playwright, Captain Swift, *Act II*

"It is only in literature that coincidences seem unnatural."

Robert Lynd (1879–1949),
Anglo-Irish writer

Classical Phrases and Myths

catastasis (Grk)
(ka-ta-STA-sis) in drama, climax of the action

Jokes, Stories and Anecdotes

Distraught upon learning that her husband had cheated on her, Vera Czermak decided to kill herself by jumping out of her third-story window. She later awoke in the hospital to discover that she was still alive, having landed on her husband. Her fall, however, killed him.

Jazz clarinetist Benny Goodman shared a flat with saxophonist Jimmy Dorsey early in their careers and, since both could play either instrument, there was fierce competition for any opportunity to play a gig. To mete out jobs, they decided that whoever answered the telephone first got the job. Once there was a tie. "Jimmy got the mouthpiece of the phone and accepted the date," recalled Goodman. "But I had the receiver and knew where the job was."

Benny Goodman [Benjamin David]
(1909–1986), U.S. clarinetist

Posters announced that novelist Joseph Hergesheimer and critic H. L. Mencken would speak "together" in New York. Taking the pronouncement literally, they walked onstage together, stood side by side, and gave their own separate lectures simultaneously.

Joseph Hergesheimer (1880–1954),
U.S. writer

◆ COLLECTION

Foreign Words and Phrases

cadre (Fra)
(kahd-re) *lit:* frame, outline; a tight-knit unit

falange (Spa)
(fah-LAHN-heh) *lit:* phalanx; Spanish Fascists supporting Franco

ensemble (Fra)
(on-sehm-bleh) group of people (usually gathered for a specific purpose, e.g., a musical ensemble)

galimafre e (Fra)
(ga-ee-MAH-fray) jumble (English: gallimaufry)

◆ COMBINATION

Foreign Words and Phrases

Gesamtkunstwerk (Ger)
(ge-ZAMT-koonst-VERK) work of art as a combination of distinct parts (*e.g.,* opera's music and libretto)

Jokes, Stories and Anecdotes

Two movers struggled with a baby grand piano in a doorway. It wouldn't budge, despite their pushing and pulling. Finally, one said, "I give up, we'll never get this in." The other said, "What do you mean, 'in'? I thought you were trying to get it out."

◆ COMEDY

Quotations

"Jack Benny couldn't ad-lib a belch at a Hungarian dinner."

> Fred Allen [John Sullivan] (1894–1956),
> U.S. comedian

Jokes, Stories and Anecdotes

While rehearsing a scene being performed poorly, Sir Herbert Beerbohm Tree, the actor and theater manager, instructed a young actor to step back. The man complied, and when Tree later stopped the rehearsal again with the same request, the actor again obeyed. But when Tree made the request a third time, the actor finally protested, "But should I step back further, I'll be right off the stage." Tree raised an eyebrow. "That is correct."

> Sir Herbert Beerbohm Tree (1853–1917),
> British actor and theater manager

◆ COMEUPPANCE

Quotations

"To give the devil his due."

> Miguel de Cervantes (1547–1616),
> Spanish writer, Don Quixote de la
> Mancha, Part I (1605), bk. III, ch. 3

"Beaten with his own rod."

> John Heywood (c. 1497–c. 1580),
> British poet, Proverbs (1546)

"He is, as we all know, a man of most unusual intellectual brilliance ... But ... he has adopted ... a most unhappy and an entirely wrong approach. He has been too clever by half."

> Robert Arthur James Gascoyrie-Cecil,
> 5th Marquess of Salisbury (1893–1972),
> British politician, describing Iain Macleod,
> colonial secretary

"My pride fell with my fortunes."

> William Shakespeare (1564–1616),
> British playwright and poet,
> As You Like It (1600), Act I, sc. ii

"For 'tis the sport to have the engineer
Hoist with his own petard."

> William Shakespeare (1564–1616),
> British playwright and poet,
> Hamlet (1601), Act III, sc. iv

Classical Phrases and Myths

"Major privato visus dum privatus fuit, et omnium consensu capax imperil nisi imperasset." (MAY-or PREE-vat-ohvee-SUS dum PREE-vat-us FOO-it, et OM-nee-um kon-SEN-su ka-PAX imPER-il NEE-si im-per-ASS-et) (When he was a commoner he seemed too big for his station, and had he never been emperor, no one would have doubted his ability to reign.)

> Cornelius Tacitus (c. 55–117),
> Roman historian, describing
> Emperor Servius Galba, Histories I, xlix

◆ COMFORT

Foreign Words and Phrases

a l'aise (Fra)
(ah LEHS) to be at ease

douceur de vivre (Fra)
(DOUC-yuhr de VEE-vruh) countrylike ease of living

gemutlich (Ger)
(ge-MEWT-lik) cozy (place), genial (person)

Weltlust (Ger)
(VELT-loost) worldly pleasure, hedonism

Quotations

"One day I sat thinking, almost in despair; a hand fell on my shoulder and a voice said reassuringly: 'Cheer up, things could get worse.' So I cheered up and, sure enough, things got worse."

> *James Hagerly (1909–1981),*
> *U.S. statesman*

Classical Phrases and Myths

bene esse (Lat)
(BE-ne ES-se) well-being

Jokes, Stories and Anecdotes

"Get me out of this wet suit and into a dry martini."

> *Charles Butterworth (1896–1946),*
> *U.S. film actor [misattributed to Robert*
> *Benchley, who spoke a similar line in the*
> *1942 film* The Major and the Minor; *similar line spoken by Mae West in the*
> *1937 film* Every Day's a Holiday]

◆ COMMAND (ORDER)

Foreign Words and Phrases

le roi le veut (Fra)
(le rwah le vuh) the king wishes it; it is the will of the king

Sieg Heil (Ger)
(zeeg HYL) *lit:* hail victory; Nazi salute and cheer

Quotations

"You press the button, and we'll do the rest."

> *Advertisement for first Kodak*
> *cameras, c. 1888*

Jokes, Stories and Anecdotes

On his first command, the green lieutenant marched his men into a fence. "Company-y-y halt!" They stopped. "At ease, men." "Now what, Lieutenant?" snickered a sergeant. The lieutenant thought a bit. "Company-y-y, fall out! Company-y-y, fall in—on the other side of the fence."

◆ COMMERCE & ECONOMICS

Foreign Words and Phrases

cartel (Fra)
(kar-tel) group of companies with common interests

Quotations

"Respectable Professors of the Dismal Science [Political Economy]."

> *Thomas Carlyle (1795–1881),*
> *British historian,* Latter Day
> Pamphlets *(1850), no. I*

"There Ain't No Such Thing as a Free Lunch." [Title of book (1975).]

> *Milton Friedman (1912–   ),*
> *U.S. economist [origin of phrase*
> *believed to predate Mayor La Guardia's*
> *"E finita la cuccagna!" (No more*
> *free lunch!), meaning "no more graft,*
> *the party is over" (1934).]*

"Capitalists are no more capable of self sacrifice than a man is capable of lifting himself up by his boot-straps."

Nikolai Lenin [Vladimir Ilich Ulyanov]
(1870–1924), Russian statesman

"Monopolies are like babies: nobody likes them until they have got one of their own."

Lord Mancroft (1914–   ),
British aristocrat

"Every one lives by selling something."

Robert Louis [Balfour] Stevenson
(1850–1894), British writer and poet,
Across the Plains (1892), "Beggars"

"Business first; pleasure afterwards."

William Makepeace Thackeray
(1811–1863), British writer, The Rose
and the Ring (1855), ch. I

"It's a recession when your neighbor loses his job. It's a depression when you lose yours."

Harry S Truman (1884–1972),
U.S. president

Jokes, Stories and Anecdotes

A businessman expressed concern about the national economy in 1961 soon after President Kennedy blocked an increase in steel prices. "Things look great," Kennedy remarked consolingly. "Why, if I weren't president, I'd buy stock myself." "If you weren't president," replied the businessman, "so would I."

John Fitzgerald Kennedy (1917–1963),
U.S. president

◆ COMMITTEE & FORUM

Foreign Words and Phrases

junta (Spa)
(HOON-tah) *lit:* council; group of military men or group with military support serving as an interim government

Quotations

"Committee—a group of men who individually can do nothing, but as a group decide that nothing can be done."

Fred Allen [John Sullivan] (1894–1957),
U.S. comedian

"A camel is a horse designed by a committee."

Anonymous, Financial Times
(January 31, 1976)

"No grand idea was ever born in a conference, but a lot of foolish ideas have died there."

F[rancis] Scott [Key] Fitzgerald
(1896–1940), U.S. writer

"Two heads are better than one."

John Heywood (c. 1497–c. 1580),
British poet, Proverbs (1546)

"The length of a meeting rises with the square of the number of people present."

Eileen Shanahan (c.1900s), U.S. citizen
[authenticity unverified]

"In the first place God made idiots. This was for practice. Then he made school boards."

Mark Twain [Samuel Langhorne Clemens]
(1835–1910), U.S. humorist, writer, and
speaker, Following the Equator
(1897), p. 225

◆ COMMUNICATION

Quotations

"You were about to tell me something, child—but you left off before you began."

William Congreve (1670–1729),
British playwright, The Old Bachelor
(1693), Act IV, sc. vii

"But words, once spoke, can never be recall'd."

> Wentworth Dillon, Earl of Roscammon (c. 1633–1685), British poet, Art of Poetry, l. 438

"Every man has a right to utter what he thinks truth, and every man has a right to knock him down for it."

> Samuel Johnson (1709–1784), British man of letters

"The Medium is the Message."

> Marshall [Herbert] McLuhan (1911–1980), Canadian scholar, Understanding Media (1964), title of ch. 1

"Grant me the power of saying things
Too simple and too sweet for words!"

> Coventry Patmore (1823–1896), British poet, The Angel in the House (ed. 1904), bk. I, canto I, prelude I, "The Impossibility"

"I disapprove of what you say, but I will defend to the death your right to say it."

> Voltaire [François Marie Arouet] (1694–1778), French philosopher, writer and wit [authenticity unverified; claimed by S. G. Tallentyre to be a paraphrase of words in Voltaire's Essay on Tolerance]

"I am not arguing with you—I am telling you."

> James Abbott McNeill Whistler (1834–1903), U.S.-born British artist, The Gentle Art of Making Enemies (1890)

Jokes, Stories and Anecdotes

The cub reporter was excited about her first assignment to cover the upcoming elections but, due to inexperience, she asked a veteran newsman how to determine whether a politician was lying. "No problem, kid," the vet said. "Just watch the body language. If he touches his ear or scratches his nose, he's telling the truth. But if he opens his mouth and moves his lips . . . "

Laurence Olivier, his young son and the playwright Noel Coward were walking along together when they came upon two dogs copulating. When the boy innocently asked what they were doing, Coward explained, "It's like this, dear boy. The one in front is blind and the kind one behind is pushing him."

> Sir Noel Coward (1899–1973), British playwright and actor

◆ COMPARISON

Quotations

"There is no settling the point of precedency between a louse and a flea."

> Samuel Johnson (1709–1784), British man of letters, responding to Maurice Morgann, as to whether Derrick or Smart was the better poet

Classical Phrases and Myths

"Si parva licet componere magnis." (If it be met to measure small by great.)

> Virgil [Publius Vergilius Maro] (70 B.C.–19 B.C.), Roman poet, Georgics, bk. IV, l. clxxvi

◆ COMPENSATION

Quotations

"Alfred and I would have worked for less, but nobody asked us."

> Alfred Lunt (1893–1977) and Lynn Fontanne (1887–1983), U.S. husband-wife acting team answering, in front of speechless MGM executives, a reporter who had inquired whether they were receiving $60,000 for their part in the film The Guardsman

Jokes, Stories and Anecdotes

A farmer, needing extra hands for the harvest, finally asked the lazy son of the town's richest family if he'd like work. "What'll you pay?" inquired the youth. "I'll pay what you're worth," answered the farmer. The lad hesitated, then said, "I won't work for that!"

"Whenever I have a headache," the patient explained to her doctor, "I take aspirin. When I have stomach trouble, I take bicarbonate of soda. If I have a cold, I go to bed and drink liquids. Am I doing the right things?" "Yes, you are," replied the doctor. "That will be $140, please."

In a career trough, screenwriter Michael Arlen was in New York and went to the upscale "21." In the lobby, he ran into Sam Goldwyn, who strangely suggested that he should buy racehorses. At the bar Arlen met Louis B. Mayer, an old acquaintance, who asked him what were his future plans. "I was just talking to Sam Goldwyn—" began Arlen. "How much did he offer you?" interrupted Mayer. Arlen hesitated. Evasively, he replied, "Not enough." "Would you take $15,000 for 30 weeks?" asked Mayer. Without hesitating, Arlen said, "Yes."

Michael Arlen [Dikran Kouyoumdjian] (1895–1956), Armenian-born British writer

After refusing to accept payment for a charity performance, comedian Jack Benny asked, "But in case I was accepting money, just how much was I refusing?"

Jack Benny (1894–1974), U.S. comedian

"How can I ever show my appreciation?" a client gleefully asked Clarence Darrow after he had solved her legal problems. "Ever since the Phoenicians invented money," replied Darrow, "there has been only one answer to that question."

Clarence Seward Darrow (1857–1938), U.S. lawyer

After a poor year pitching for the New York Yankees in the 1930s, Lefty Gomez was asked to accept a salary cut from $20,000 to $7,500 per year. "How about," countered Gomez, reeling, "you keep the salary and pay me the cut."

Vernon ["Lefty"] Gomez (1910–), U.S. baseball player

Screenwriter George S. Kaufman was so incensed at Paramount Pictures' offer of $30,000 for the film rights to one of his plays that he countered by offering $40,000 for Paramount.

George S[imon] Kaufman (1889–1961), U.S. playwright, writer and wit

Home run king Babe Ruth held out for his $80,000 contract rather than accept a cut in salary during the Depression. A club official protested, "But that's more money than Hoover got for being president last year." "I know," said the Sultan of Swat, "but I had a better year."

George Herman ["Babe"] Ruth (1895–1948), U.S. baseball player

The impressario Flo Ziegfeld once offered Gracie Allen $750 a week to appear in one of his London shows. When she asked his fee if George Burns, her husband and straight man, was included, Ziegfeld responded, "$500."

Florenz Ziegfeld (1867–1932), U.S. theatrical producer

◆ COMPETENCE

Foreign Words and Phrases

schtick (Yid)
(shtik) one's forte or (contrived) act, what one does

di bravura (Ita)
(dee brah-VOO-rah) *lit:* with bravado; in music, with virtuosity

soigne (Fra)
(SWAH-nyeh) well-performed (undertaking), well-kept (person)

bricoleur (Fra)
(BRIK-oh-leuhr) skillful and clever handyman, jack-of-all-trades

forte (Ita)
(FOR-tay) in music, strong, loud; one's skill, strong point

Quotations

"There is great skill in knowing how to conceal one's skill."

François, Duc de La Rochefoucauld (1613–1680), French writer, Maximes *(1678), 245*

"Consistency is the last refuge of the unimaginative."

Oscar [Fingal O'Flahertie Wills] Wilde (1854–1900), British playwright, writer and wit

Jokes, Stories and Anecdotes

"Dammit," screamed the tailor's customer, "I bought this coat last week, and the seams already burst!" Responded the tailor, "Yes, but see how well the buttons were sewn on!"

To select the most able man as his bodyguard, the Arab sheik informed the three swordsmen that they would compete in a contest. To each he gave a box containing a wasp. When the first opened his box, no sooner had the wasp appeared than his scimitar sliced the insect in two. Aware that he had to do even better, the second swordsman released his wasp and swiftly cut off its wings. Watching it fall, the impressed sheik turned to the third, who released his wasp, made a swift movement with his scimitar, then casually watched the wasp fly away. "Your wasp still lives," observed the sheik. "True," replied the swordsman, "but it will have no children."

After completing the filming of *A Bill of Divorcement*, Katharine Hepburn turned to co-star John Barrymore, saying, "Thank God I don't have to act with you anymore!" He replied, "I didn't know you ever had, darling."

John Barrymore (1882–1942), U.S. actor

A slightly nervous soprano was performing during an operatic recital for the First Family and guests at the White House. A guest turned to President Calvin Coolidge and whispered, "What do you think of the singer's execution?" Coolidge whispered back, "I'm all for it."

[John] Calvin Coolidge (1872–1933), U.S. president

Within earshot of writer Charles Lamb, English Romantic poet William Wordsworth boasted, "I could write like Shakespeare if I had a mind to." Mumbled Lamb, "So only the mind which is lacking."

Charles Lamb (1775–1834), British writer

◆ COMPETITION (CONTENTION)

Foreign Words and Phrases

mêlée (Fra)
(MEL-lay) confused fight, scuffle, muddle

Quotations

"I called off his players' names as they came marching up the steps behind him, 'Walker, Cooper, Mize, Marshall, Kerr, Gordon, Thomson. Take a look at them. All nice guys. They'll finish last. Nice guys. Finish last."

Leo Durocher (1906–1991), U.S. baseball manager [generally contracted to "Nice guys finish last"]

"The reason academic battles are so fierce is the stakes are so low."

Henry Kissinger (1923–   ), U.S. diplomat

"I strove with none; for none was worth my strife;
Nature I loved, and, next to Nature, Art;
I warmed both hands before the fire of life;
It sinks, and I am ready to depart."

Walter Savage Landor (1775–1864), British poet and writer, I Strove with None (1853)

"We're eyeball to eyeball, and I think the other fellow just blinked."

[David] Dean Rusk (1909–   ), U.S. statesman, commenting on the Cuban missile crisis, October 24, 1962

"We throw all our attention on the utterly idle question of whether A has done as well as B, when the only question is whether A has done as well as he could."

William Graham Sumner (1840–1910), U.S. sociologist

Classical Phrases and Myths

agon (Grk)
(AG-ohn) conflict, struggle, contest

Jokes, Stories and Anecdotes

Two hunters wheeled around to face a bear. One hunter calmly sat down, took off his boots, and began to lace up his running shoes. "What good are those shoes going to do you?" asked the other hunter, smirking. "You can't outrun a bear!" "I don't have to outrun the bear," replied the first hunter. "I just need to outrun you."

Mischa Elman, the violinist, and Leopold Godowsky were in the audience for the American debut of child prodigy Jascha Heifetz at Carnegie Hall in 1917. As the 16-year-old Heifetz played, Elman grew restless, sticking a finger in his collar and wiping his brow. He leaned over to Godowsky and whispered, "It's much too hot here." Said Godowsky, "Not for pianists."

Leopold Godowsky (1870–1938), Russian-born U.S. pianist and composer [variations also attributed to others]

An organ grinder who had stationed himself outside popular composer Jacques François Halévy's window was busy grinding out melodies from rival composer Rossini's *Barber of Seville*. Driven to distraction, Halévy approached the organ grinder and said, "I will give you a louis d'or if you go to Rossini's place and play my tunes outside his window." "But, monsieur," replied the man, "M. Rossini has paid me *two* louis d'or to play his music outside your window."

Gioacchino Antonio Rossini (1792–1868), Italian composer

◆ COMPLEXITY

Foreign Words and Phrases

grottesca (Ita)
(gro-TESS-kah) decoration with humans and animals intertwined in foliage; elaborate tangle

indebrouillable (Fra)
(aan-day-broo-yabl) cannot be un-raveled, inexplicable

Quotations

"It is quite a three-pipe problem, and I beg that you won't speak to me for fifty minutes."

> *Sir Arthur Conan Doyle (1859–1930), British writer,* Adventures of Sherlock Holmes *(1892),* "Red-Headed League"

♦ COMPREHENSIBILITY

Quotations

"I have suffered from being mis-understood, but I would have suf-fered a hell of a lot more if I had been understood."

> *Clarence Seward Darrow (1857–1938), U.S. lawyer*

"Nowadays to be intelligible is to be found out."

> *Oscar [Fingal O'Flahertie Wills] Wilde (1854–1900), British playwright, writer and wit*

♦ COMPREHENSION

Quotations

"The reason you don't understand me is because I'm talkin' to you in English and you're listenin' in Dingbat."

> *"All in the Family," 1970s television program, Archie Bunker (Carroll O'Connor) to his wife Edith (Jean Stapleton)*

"Anyone who isn't confused doesn't really understand the situation."

> *Edward R. Murrow (1908–1965), U.S. broadcaster, commenting on Vietnam*

"To have great poets, there must be great audiences, too."

> *Walt[er] Whitman (1819–1892), U.S. poet and writer,* Notes Left Over, *"Ventures on an Old Theme"*

Classical Phrases and Myths

felix qui potuit rerum cognoscere causas (Lat)
(FAY-lix kwee POT-u-it REHR-um kog-NOS-ker-e KOW-sas) fortunate is the man who understands the causes of things

♦ COMPUTER

Quotations

"To err is human but to really foul things up requires a computer."

> *Anonymous,* Farmers' Almanac for 1978 *(1977),* "Capsules of Wisdom"

Jokes, Stories and Anecdotes

During WWII, noted mathematician John von Neumann, an incurable practical joker, constructed and delivered to the federal government an electronic "brain" that he labeled a Mathematical Analyzer, Numerical Integrater, and Computer. It took several days before scientists realized that the first letters of the computer's name spelled MANIAC.

> *John von Neumann (1903–1957), U.S. mathematician*

♦ CONCEALMENT

Quotations

"Keep up appearances; there lies the test;

The world will give thee credit for the rest.
Outward, be fair, however foul within;
Sin if thou wilt, but then in secret sin."

Charles Churchill (1731–1764),
British poet, Night, l. 311

Classical Phrases and Myths

apocrypha (Grk)
(ap-Ō-kri-fah) *lit:* things which have been hidden; secrets, hidden things (especially expunged Scripture)

◆ CONDEMNATION

Quotations

"When I came back to Dublin, I was courtmartialled in my absence and sentenced to death in my absence, so I said they could shoot me in my absence."

Brendan Behan (1923–1964),
Irish playwright and wit,
The Hostage *(1958), Act I*

"You pronounce sentence upon me with greater fear than I receive it."

Giordano Bruno (1548–1600), Italian
philosopher, speaking to the Inquisitors
who had condemned him to death

"Are you going to hang him *anyhow*—and try him afterward?"

Mark Twain [Samuel Langhorne Clemens]
(1835–1910), U.S. humorist, writer and
speaker, The Innocents at Home
(1875), ch. 5

Classical Phrases and Myths

Socrates was condemned to drink poisonous hemlock after his *Apology* failed to overturn the charge of corrupting the young of Athens. When his wife, Xantippe, visited him in prison and bemoaned the jury's condemnation, Socrates said to her consolingly, "They are by their nature also condemned." Xantippe, unmoved, cried, "But the condemnation is unjust!" Replied Socrates, "Would you prefer it to be just?"

Socrates (469 B.C.–399 B.C.),
Greek philosopher

Jokes, Stories and Anecdotes

Because of his notorious indiscretions while Prince of Wales, Edward VII was excluded by his mother, Queen Victoria, from active participation in affairs of state. The leading article in *the Times* upon the accession of Edward VII to the throne euphemistically summed up the prevailing jaundiced view (unwarranted during his reign) of proper British citizenry: "We shall not pretend that there is nothing in his long career which those who respect and admire him would wish otherwise."

Edward VII (1841–1910), British king

◆ CONDITION, LIMITING

Foreign Words and Phrases

c'est selon (Fra)
(seh se-Ion) that depends (on circumstances, etc.)

Quotations

O horrid provisos!

William Congreve (1670–1729),
British playwright, The Way
of the World *(1700), Act IV, sc. v*

"Reasons are not like garments, the worse for wearing."

Robert Devereux, Earl of Essex
(1566–1601), British aristocrat

"Sir, your favor is received and your name is on my list, but I am compelled to warn you that the list is long, and I grant no preferences."

Honoré Gabriel Riqueti, Comte de Mirabeau (1749–1791), French revolutionary statesman, replying to challenges to duel

Classical Phrases and Myths

sine qua non (Lat)
(sine kwah non) essential precondition

lemma (Grk)
(LAY-ma) assumed or demonstrated proposition used in argument or proof

quo jure (Lat)
(kwoh yoo-re) by what right, on what authority (do you act)?

ceteris paribus (Lat)
(KET-er-ees PAR-ri-bus) other things being equal, if other conditions remain unchanged (in order to measure the impact of a single variable)

Jokes, Stories and Anecdotes

Befitting a secretary of state, Cordell Hull was an extremely cautious man, loath to assume past the evidence. Once, on a train trip, Hull and a companion watched while the locomotive dragged its load of cars slowly past a large flock of sheep. Making conversation, Hull's companion said, "Those sheep have recently been sheared." Hull stared thoughtfully, then said, "Appears so. At least on the side facing us."

Cordell Hull (1875–1955), U.S. statesman [attributed also to others]

◆ CONDUCT

Foreign Words and Phrases

se comporter (Fra)
(zuh kom-PORT-er) to behave

Quotations

"We are the President's men, and we must behave accordingly."

Henry Kissinger (1923–   ), U.S. diplomat

Classical Phrases and Myths

ad vitam aut culpam (Lat)
(ad WEE-tam owl KUL-pam) in law, allowing for good behavior

Jokes, Stories and Anecdotes

In 1900 social reformer Jane Addams was elected to honorary membership by the Daughters of the American Revolution. The association later expelled her, however, because of her antiwar stance during World War I and her insistence that even subversives had a right to trial by due process of law. Addams remarked that she had thought her election was for life, but now knew it was for good behavior.

Jane Addams (1860–1935), U.S. social reformer

One day Columbia Studio mogul Harry Cohn, as usual, was quarreling furiously with his brother Jack over some creative differences. Suddenly, the tinkling bell of an ice-cream wagon was heard from the street below. Cohn stopped in his tracks, took orders, ran over to the window, yelled down, "One chocolate! Two strawberry!" and then went back to throttling his brother while they waited for the ice cream.

Harry Cohn (1891–1958), U.S. film producer

◆ CONFIDENCE

Foreign Words and Phrases

savoir faire (Fra)
(sat-wahr fehr) knowhow, sophistication, self-confidence

77

Classical Phrases and Myths

In August of 216 B.C. Hannibal won one of the great tactical battles in history, the Battle of Cannae, whereby the Romans were allowed to charge Hannibal's infantry center, only to be routed by his cavalry on the enveloping flanks. Rome lost over 60,000 men compared to Hannibal's losses of some 6,000, and, since many leaders of the Roman republic perished, over 170 new senators had to be elected to restore that assembly's count to 300. Maharbal, commander of the cavalry under Hannibal, insisted on a day's rest after the devastating battle, declaring, *"Vincere scis, Hannibal, victoria uti nescis"* (You know how to win a battle, Hannibal, but not how to use it). The enemy was allowed to recoup, and eventually Hannibal was defeated by a newly strengthened, but wilier, Rome.

Maharbal (d. c. 210 B.C.),
Carthaginian soldier

Jokes, Stories and Anecdotes

Georges Clemenceau, the French statesman and prime minister during World War I, was in numerous duels. On the way to one he surprised his second by asking for a one-way ticket at the Paris railroad station. His second asked, "Isn't that a little pessimistic?" *"Pas de tout,"* replied Clemenceau. "I always use my opponent's return ticket for the trip back."

Georges Clemenceau (1841–1929),
French prime mininster

During the 1863 battle of the Wilderness in the Civil War, Union general John Sedgwick was inspecting his troops. An *aide de camp* advised the general to lower his head because he was a target for the Confederate sharpshooters. "Nonsense," snapped the general. "Why,

they couldn't hit an elephant at this dist—"

John Sedgwick (1813–1864), U.S. general

"No one is going to beat us one-handed," confidently claimed Clair Bee about his undefeated (for three seasons) championship Long Island University basketball team, set to meet underdog Stanford with Hank Luisetti at Madison Square Garden. Luisetti, with 15 points and remarkable defensive play, led Stanford to a stunning 45–31 upset. Bee remarked later, "I hate to think how badly they'd have beaten us if he'd used both hands."

Hank Luisetti (1916–   ),
U.S. basketball player

Prior to exhibitions at the prestigious Academy for British Artists, artists enjoyed a brief period in which to touch up and revarnish their works. Famed landscape painter Joseph Turner would use this period to complete his huge canvases. A masterpiece of his, celebrated for its evocation of an immensely complex scene caught at a moment of high drama, was his painting of the fire that destroyed the old Houses of Parliament in 1834. When Turner finished his *alla prima*, he simply snapped shut his paintbox and left without a final look at his work.

Joseph Mallord William Turner
(1775–1851), British painter

◆ CONFINEMENT & RESTRAINT

Foreign Words and Phrases

cordon sanitaire (Fra)
(KOR-don san-ee-TEHR) quarantining an infected or a politically sensitive area or subject

en prise (Fra)
(on PREEZ) in chess, piece open to immediate capture; seized

Quotations

"She's a bird in a gilded cage. [Title of song (1900).]
> Arthur J. Lamb (1870–1928),
> U.S. songwriter

The most anxious man in a prison is the governor.
> George Bernard Shaw (1856–1950),
> Irish playwright

"We're all of us sentenced to solitary confinement inside our own skins, for life!"
> Tennessee Williams [Thomas Lanier Williams] (1911–1983), U.S. playwright,
> Orpheus Descending (1958),
> Act II, sc. 1

Classical Phrases and Myths

habeas corpus (Lat)
(HAB-ay-as KOR-pus) writ requiring the appearance of a prisoner in court to determine the legality of his detention; the Habeas Corpus Act of 1679 introduced this crucial tenet of British justice, which prohibits the police from holding a person for more than a short period without a court deciding whether detention is justified

durance vile (Lat)
(DOOH-an-cevee-le) vile prison

Jokes, Stories and Anecdotes

"Answer two questions," said the warden to the instigators of a failed prison riot, "and I'll go easier on you. "Why did you revolt?" Answered one convict, "Warden, we rebelled because the food here is horrible." "OK. And to escape from your cell, what did you use to break the bars?" "Toast."

◆ CONFLICT (QUARREL)

Foreign Words and Phrases

brouhaha (Fra)
(BREW-ha-ha) hubbub, commotion

Quotations

"I will make a bargain with the Democrats. If they will stop telling lies about Republicans, we will stop telling the truth about them."
> Chauncey Mitchell Depew (1834–1928),
> U.S. lawyer and politician

"Agreed to differ."
> Robert Southey (1774–1843), British poet and man of letters, Life of Wesley (1820)

"The honorable member disagrees. I can hear him shaking his head."
> Pierre Elliott Trudeau (1919–   ),
> Canadian prime minister

Classical Phrases and Myths

advocatus diaboli (Lat)
(ad-wok-AH-ius dee-A-bol-ee) the devil's advocate

"*Concordia discors.*" (Harmony in discord.)
> Horace (65 B.C.–8 B.C.), Roman poet,
> Epistles, I, xii, l. 19

Jokes, Stories and Anecdotes

Breaking the long silence after a quarrel, the husband said meekly to his wife, "Honey, I've decided after all to agree with you." "Too late," she snapped. "I've changed my mind."

The French salonnière Mme. Geoffrin was once engaged in a heated argument with a French writer. After listening in silence for some time, the materialist philosopher Baron d'Holbach approached them and asked with a smile, "Perchance, are you two secretly married?"

Paul Henri Dietrich, Baron d'Holbach (1723–1789), French philosopher

Joe Louis served in the Army during his reign as world heavyweight boxing champion. Once, while driving with a fellow GI, he was involved in a minor collision with a large truck. The truck driver screamed, got out and sweared at the nonchalant Louis, who just sat in the driver's seat. After the other man had left, Louis' buddy inquired, "Why didn't ja get out and flatten the SOB?" "Why should I?" responded Louis. "If somebody insulted Caruso, did he sing an aria for him?"

Joe Louis (1914–1981), U.S. boxer

During an argument between *avant-garde* writer Gertrude Stein and Mortimer Adler, the philosopher and educator, her confidante Alice B. Toklas commented, "Oh my! Gertrude is saying some things tonight that she herself won't understand for six months."

Gertrude Stein (1874–1946), U.S. writer

Composer Giacomo Puccini would customarily send colleagues and friends a cake each Christmas. One year, however, after a cake was sent too hastily to maestro Toscanini following a quarrel, Puccini dispatched the following telegram: "Cake sent by mistake." The conductor replied by return: "Cake eaten by mistake."

Arturo Toscanini (1867–1957), Italian conductor

◆ CONFORMITY (NORMALITY)

Foreign Words and Phrases

j'adoube (Fra)
(ja-DOOB) *lit:* I adjust; in chess, statement indicating that a player does not intend to move a touched piece but is merely placing it in its correct square

Classical Phrases and Myths

"Si fueris Romae, Romano vivito more; si fueris alibi, vivito aicut ibi." (*lit:* If you are at Rome live in the Roman style; if you are elsewhere live as they live elsewhere. When in Rome, do as the Romans do.)

St. Ambrose [Aurelius Ambrosius] (c. 340–397), Italian clergyman

Jokes, Stories and Anecdotes

Mary Wollstonecraft Shelley, author of *Frankenstein* and widow of the Romantic poet Percy Bysshe Shelley, sought the advice of a lady for choosing a school for her son. The woman flippantly remarked, "Oh, send him somewhere where they will teach him to think for himself." "Teach him to think for himself?" Mrs. Shelley replied, considering her deceased husband. "Oh, my God, teach him rather to think like other people!"

Mary Wollstonecraft Shelley (1797–1851), British writer

◆ CONFUSION (DISTRACTION)

Foreign Words and Phrases

divertimento (Ita)
(dee-ver-ti-MEN-toh) in music, light instrumental work; a pleasing diversion

affole (Fra)
(ah-fol-LAY) driven to madness, distracted (*e.g.*, love, anger)

Quotations

" 'Are you lost, Daddy?' I asked tenderly. 'Shut up,' he explained."

Ring [Ringgold Wilmer] Lardner (1885–1933), U.S. writer, The Young Immigrants (recreated, from the child's viewpoint, from an actual situation when Lardner moved his family from Chicago and became lost in the Bronx)

Jokes, Stories and Anecdotes

"I have brought a frog fresh from a pond," said the elderly, bespectacled professor to his zoology class, "for purposes of dissection." He carefully unwrapped the package, and inside was a finely prepared turkey sandwich. He looked at it quizzically. "Odd," he said. "I distinctly remember having eaten my lunch."

Upon receiving from William Bowles a Bible, Bessie Moore, wife of the poet Tom Moore, asked Bowles to inscribe it. She was astonished to see that the absent-minded clergyman had written: "From the Author."

William Lisle Bowles (1762–1850), British clergyman

The great mathematician Karl Gauss was deeply engrossed in a problem when someone attending to his wife on her deathbed said that she was about to die. Murmured Gauss absently, "Tell her to wait until I've finished."

Karl Friedrich Gauss (1777–1855), German mathematician

◆ CONSENT (PERMISSION)

Foreign Words and Phrases

conge (Fra)
(kon-JAY) leave, permission to depart

Classical Phrases and Myths

quod licet Jovi non licet bovi (Lat) (kwod LEE-ket YO-vee nohn LEE-ket BO-vi) *lit:* what is permitted to Jove is not permitted to an ox; ordinary mortal may not do what a god may, such as park in an assigned space

communi consensu (Lat) (kom-MOON-ee con-SEN-soo) by common consent

The Greek philosopher Aristippus once requested a favor for a friend from Dionysius, tyrant of Syracuse. When Dionysius refused, Aristippus threw himself at the tyrant's feet, pleading until the favor was granted. Criticized for this conduct as being unworthy of a philosopher, Aristippus replied, "But that is where the tyrant's ears are."

Aristippus (c. 435 B.C.–c. 356 B.C.), Greek philosopher

◆ CONSPICUOUSNESS

Quotations

"He looked as inconspicuous as a tarantula on a slice of angel food."

Raymond Chandler (1888–1959), U.S. writer

"Among the defects of the Bill, which were numerous, one provision was conspicuous by its presence and another by its absence."

John Russell, 1st Earl (1792–1878), British prime minister, speech to the electors of the City of London, April, 1859

"Is that a gun in your pocket, or are you just glad to see me?"

Mae West (1892–1980), U.S. film actress

◆ CONTAINER & CONTENTS

Jokes, Stories and Anecdotes

Humorist Mark Twain, still a fledgling reporter, was once walking along the street in Virginia City, Nevada, carrying a cigar box under his arm. "You promised me that you would give up smoking," scolded an older woman of his acquaintance. "Madam, this box does not contain cigars," responded Twain. "I'm just moving."

Mark Twain [Samuel Langhorne Clemens] (1835–1910), U.S. humorist, writer and speaker

◆ CONTEMPT

Quotations

"This party of two is like the Scotch terrier that was so covered with hair that you could not tell which was the head and which was the tail."

John Bright (1811–1889), British politician, speech to House of Commons, March 13, 1866

"This man, I thought, had been a lord among wits; but I find he is only a wit among lords."

Samuel Johnson (1709–1784), British man of letters, describing Lord Chesterfield [cf. "Those who wish to appear wise among fools, among the wise seem foolish." Quintilian, Institutio Oratoria, bk. X, 7, 21]

Jokes, Stories and Anecdotes

The politician and famed orator Henry Clay was addressing a crowd, but hissing from a group of slaveowners was drowning out his voice. "Gentlemen," he shouted, "that is the sound you hear when the waters of truth drop upon the fires of hell."

Henry Clay (1777–1852), U.S. politician and orator

After American wit Wilson Mizner's intemperate remark during a heated argument with the magistrate, the magistrate exclaimed: "You've been showing contempt for this court!" Mizner snapped: "No, your honor, I've been trying to conceal it."

Wilson Mizner (1876–1933), U.S. wit and writer

Illinois congressman William M. Springer quoted Henry Clay's line "I had rather be right than be president" during a debate while Thomas Reed was speaker of the House of Representatives. Reed, in an aside, murmured, "The gentleman need not worry, for he will never be either."

Thomas Brackett Reed (1839–1902), U.S. politician

When English Romantic poet William Wordsworth declared that he had "the greatest contempt for Aristotle," Scottish historical novelist and poet Sir Walter Scott remarked, "But not, I take it, that contempt which familiarity breeds."

Sir Walter Scott (1771–1832), British writer and poet

Following a formal dinner with the sheriffs and judges at London's Old Bailey law courts, the biographer James Boswell complained that he had his pocket picked and his handkerchief stolen. "Pooh," scoffed the English politician and journalist John Wilkes, a tireless fighter for individual and press freedom, "this is nothing but the ostentation of a Scotsman to let the world know that

he had possessed a pocket handkerchief."

John Wilkes (1725–1797),
British politician and writer

◆ CONTINUITY

Foreign Words and Phrases

legato (Ita)
(lay-GAH-toh) in music, without
breaks between notes

Quotations

"The opera ain't over 'til the fat
lady sings."

Daniel Cook (1926–   ),
U.S. sportscaster, April 1978, commenting
on basketball playoffs between San Antonio
Spurs and Washington Bullets

Classical Phrases and Myths

ad infinitum (Lat)
(ad in-fee-NEE-tum) endlessly, to
infinity

"dicebamus hesterna die." (di-KAY-
bam-us hes-TERN-a die) (We were
saying yesterday.)

Luis de Leon (c. 1528–1591), Spanish
educator, resuming a lecture at Salamanca
University after five years in prison

◆ CONVERSATION & SOLILOQUY

Foreign Words and Phrases

schmoos (Yid)
(shmooz) gossip, small talk

Quotations

"In the room the women come and
go

Talking of Michelangelo."

T[homas] S[tearns] Eliot (1888–1965),
U.S. poet, Prufrock (1917), "The Love
Song of J. Alfred Prufrock"

"He [William Ewart Gladstone]
speaks to me as if I was a public
meeting."

Victoria (1819–1901), British queen

"He knew the precise, psychologi-
cal moment when to say nothing."

Oscar [Fingal O'Flahertie Wills] Wilde
(1854–1900), British playwright, writer
and wit, The Picture of Dorian Gray
(1891), ch. 2

Classical Phrases and Myths

"I wept as I remembered how often
you and I
Had tired the sun with talking and
sent him down the sky."

Callimachus (c. 300 B.C.–250 B.C.),
Greek poet, Heraclitus

Jokes, Stories and Anecdotes

While conversing with his son Randolph, Winston Churchill interrupted him to express his own
opinion. Randolph listened and
then attempted again to speak.
"Don't interrupt me when I am interrupting!" snapped Winston.

Sir Winston Spencer Churchill (1874–
1965), British prime minister and writer

A reporter had the temerity to ask
legendary lawyer and author Clarence Darrow for a prepared copy of
a speech he was to give later that
evening. Irritated, Darrow handed
him a blank piece of paper and
turned his heel. "But Mr. Darrow,"
the reporter called out, "this is the

same speech you gave last week."

Clarence Seward Darrow (1857–1938),
U.S. lawyer [authenticity unverified]

◆ CONVERSION

Foreign Words and Phrases

volte face (Fra)
(VOL-te fass) reversal of opinion, about-face, repudiation of a previous situation

perestroika (Rus)
(PEHR-es-TROY-kau) restructuring of system

Classical Phrases and Myths

peripateia (Grk).
(per-i-pat-AY-a) *lit:* turning point; sudden change of fortune (especially in drama)

◆ COOKING

Foreign Words and Phrases

maitre de cuisine (Fra)
(MET-ruh de KWEE-ZEEN) chief cook, head chef

à la broche (Fra)
(ah lah BROSH) *lit:* in the spit; cooked on a skewer, barbecued

al dente (Ita)
(al DEN-tay) *lit:* to the tooth; not overcooked (especially pasta)

Quotations

"The cook was a good cook, as cooks go; and as cooks go she went."

Saki [Hector Hugh Munro] (1870–1916),
British writer, Reginald (1904),
"Reginald on Besetting Sins"

" 'But why should you want to shield him?' cried Egbert; 'the man is a common murderer.' 'A common murderer, possibly, but a very uncommon cook.' "

Saki [Hector Hugh Munro] (1870–1916),
British writer, Beasts and Super-Beasts
(1914), "The Blind Spot"

Jokes, Stories and Anecdotes

"The two best things I cook are hamburger and apple pie," noted the groom. Asked the bride, "Which is this?"

"You think your wife's a lousy cook," said one husband to the other. "Mine uses the smoke detector as a timer."

Mother to her 12-year-old daughter helping her bake: "Check if that cake in the oven is ready. Just stick a knife inside and see if it comes out clean." Daughter, a few minutes later: "The knife came out so clean I stuck in all the other dirty knives."

"Fred, wake up! There's a burglar in the kitchen." "Quick! What's he doing?" "He's eating up the pie we started at dinner." "Go back to sleep. I'll bury him in the morning."

After his cook served a mediocre meal, the hot-headed poet, essayist, and critic Walter Landor promptly threw him out an open window. As the cook landed in the flower bed below, breaking a limb, Landor exclaimed, "Good God, I forgot the violets!"

Walter Savage Landor (1775–1864),
British poet and writer

◆ COOPERATION

Foreign Words and Phrases

wa (Jap)
(wah) Confucian notion of social harmony, team spirit

esprit de corps (Fra)
(es-SPREE de kohr) *lit:* spirit of the group; common bond or loyalty between members of a group

entente cordiale (Fra)
(on-TONT-kor-DYAL) friendly relationship, informal alliance between states

Quotations

"Alliance, n. In international politics, the union of two thieves who have their hands so deeply inserted in each other's pocket that they cannot separately plunder a third."

> Ambrose [Gwinnet] Bierce (1842–
> c. 1914), U.S. writer and poet,
> Cynic's Word Book (1906)

Tous pour un, un pour tous. (All for one, one for all.)

> Alexandre [pere] Dumas (1802–1870),
> French writer and playwright, Les Trois
> Mousquetiers (1844) ch. 9

"Those who know the least obey the best."

> George Farquhar (1678–1707),
> Irish playwright

"What a night, buddy! Seventy-three points between us!

> Rodney Hundley (1934–   ),
> U.S. basketball player, commenting
> triumphantly to Elgin Baylor after Baylor
> had scored 71 points in one game

Jokes, Stories and Anecdotes

Another classicist hopefully suggested to Oxford don Richard Porson that they should collaborate on a project. The renowned scholar replied, "Put in all I know and all you don't know, and it will make a great work."

> Richard Porson (1759–1808),
> British scholar

◆ COPY & IMITATION

Foreign Words and Phrases

ersatz (Ger)
(EHR-zatz) *lit:* replacement; (usually inferior) substitute, imitation

rechauffe (Fra)
(RAY-sho-EAY) reheated, rehash, unoriginal creation

à la (Fra)
(ah lah) in the manner or style of

pastiche (Fra)
(pass-TEESH) something done as imitation (or ridicule) of another's style

Quotations

"A lotta cats copy the Mona Lisa, but people still line up to see the original."

> Louis ["Satchmo"] Armstrong
> (1900–1971), U.S. musician
> and singer, answering a question
> about whether he objected to the
> impressions of him frequently given
> by other singers and comedians

"Tout est dit et l'on vient trop tard depuis plus de sept mille ans qu'il y a des hommes et qui pensent." (Everything has been said, and we are more than seven thousand years of human thought too late.)

> Jean de la Bruyère (1645–1696),
> French writer, Les Caractères (1688),
> "Des Ouvrages de l'Esprit"

"Imitation is the sincerest of flattery."

> C[harles] C[aleb] Colton (c. 1780–1832),
> British clergyman and writer, Lacon
> (1820–1822), vol. I, no. 217

"If you steal from one author, it's plagiarism; if you steal from many, it's research."

Wilson Mizner (1876–1933), U.S. writer and wit [variations also attributed to others]

"The only good copies are those which make us see the absurdity of bad originals."

François, Duc de La Rochefoucauld (1613–1680), French writer Maximes (1678)

"I often quote myself. It adds spice to my conversation."

George Bernard Shaw (1856–1950), Irish playwright

Classical Phrases and Myths

verbatim (et literatim) (Lat) (wer-BAY-tim et lit-er-AH-tim) word for word (and letter for letter) as it was written, quoted exactly

"El mimesis eine psysiologhikon enstikton." (El MEE-mee-sees AY-neh phiz-ee-oh-loh-gee-KON EN-stik-ton) Imitation is an instinct of nature.

Aristotle (384 B.C.-322 B.C.), Greek philosopher, Poetics

"O imitatores, servum pecus." (O imitators, you slavish herd.)

Horace (65 B.C.-8 B.C.), Roman poet, Epistles, I, xix, l. 19

Jokes, Stories and Anecdotes

The musician Baron von Bulow was once asked by a young composer to listen to his latest composition. Its most notable feature was the extent of its borrowings from other composers. "How do you like it?" asked the composer once he had finished playing the piece. Said von Bulow, "I have always liked it."

Hans Guido, Baron von Bulow (1830–1894), German conductor and pianist

After first entertaining guests at a Hollywood dinner party with impressions of famous people, silent screen star Charlie Chaplin sang an operatic aria. Exclaimed a guest, "Why, I never knew you could sing so beautifully!" "I can't sing," said Chaplin. "I was only imitating Caruso."

Charles Spencer ["Charlie"] Chaplin (1889–1977), British-born actor

Asked whether she objected to being imitated by other performers, Marlene Dietrich replied, "Only if they do it badly."

Marlene Dietrich [Maria Magdalene von Losch] (1904–1992), German actress and singer

Without acknowledgment, a writer incorporated many of mathematician, logician and Nobel laureate Bertrand Russell's thoughts in a book he had written. When the plagiarist solicited Russell to write the book's introduction, Russell politely declined, saying, "Modesty forbids."

Bertrand Arthur William Russell, 3rd Earl (1872–1970), British mathematician and philosopher

◆ CORRELATION

Jokes, Stories and Anecdotes

An impoverished Chinese laundry operator, whose establishment was located next to a prosperous Chinese restaurant, would daily plant his chair close to the restaurant during dining hours and eat his simple bowl of rice while sniffing the appealing aromas. One day, his neighbor sent him a bill "for smell of food." He disappeared into his laundry and returned with his tiny money box. He rattled it loudly for his creditor, saying, "Here's payment for the smell of your food with the sound of my money."

later they received a reply: "He did."

Mark Twain [Samuel Langhorne Clemens] (1835–1910), U.S. humorist, writer and speaker

◆ CORRESPONDENCE

Foreign Words and Phrases

billet doux (Fra)
(bi-vav doo) lit: sweet note; love letter

Jokes, Stories and Anecdotes

The avant-garde writer Gertrude Stein once received from her editor, A. J. Fifield, the following parody-cum-rejection slip: "I am only one, only one, only one. Only one being, one at the same time. Not two, not three, only one. Only one life to live, only sixty minutes in one hour. Only one pair of eyes. Only one brain. Only one being. Being only one, having only one pair of eyes, having only one time, having only one life, I cannot read your MS three or four times. Not even one time. Only one look, only one look is enough. Hardly one copy would sell here. Hardly one. Hardly one."

Gertrude Stein (1874–1946), U.S. writer

During Christmas 1955, President Harry Truman found his wife, Bess, burning in the fireplace letters that he had written to her over the years. "But think of history," he protested. Responded his wife, "I have."

Harry S. Truman (1884–1972), U.S. president

Because a group of Mark Twain's friends and admirers in New York did not know the address of the peripatetic humorist on a lecture tour, they mailed him birthday greetings addressed: "Mark Twain, God Knows Where." Several weeks

◆ CORRUPTION

Foreign Words and Phrases

guandào (Chi)
(GWAN-day-oh) official profiteering, money politics

kinken-seiji (Jap)
(KEEN-kehn SAY-gee) money politics (dubious, but long-tolerated)

Quotations

"They wouldn't be sufficiently degraded in their own estimation unless they were insulted by a very considerable bribe."

Sir W[illiam] S[chwenck] Gilbert (1836–1911), British writer, The Mikado (1885), Act I

Jokes, Stories and Anecdotes

Unsuccessful in inducing a shopkeeper to carry his product, a salesman finally offered a bottle of cognac as a bribe. "Oh, my conscience wouldn't let me take a gift!" protested the shopkeeper. "How about I sell it to you for a nickel?" asked the salesman. "In that case," responded the shopkeeper, "I'll take two."

◆ COSTLESSNESS

Classical Phrases and Myths

gratis (Lat)
(GRAH-tees) lit: for nothing; gratuitous, free

Jokes, Stories and Anecdotes

Two lovers were walking hand in hand when the woman noticed a beautiful diamond ring in a jewelry store window. "What I'd give to own that," she said, sighing. "No problem," the man said, throwing a rock through the glass and grabbing the ring. A block later, the woman admired a full-length mink coat. "Boy, I'd love to have that!" she gushed. "No problem," he said, throwing a rock through the window and grabbing the coat. Down the street, they passed a car dealership. "Boy, I'd do anything for that Rolls!" she exclaimed. "Jeez, baby," he moaned, "You think I'm made of rocks?"

French statesman Talleyrand, reviewing a draft budget prepared for Louis XVIII, noted that salaries for deputies had not been included. Explained the monarch, "I believe they should perform their duties without remuneration. It should be an honorary position." "Without any payment?" Talleyrand exclaimed. "Your Majesty, it would cost too much!"

Charles Maurice de Talleyrand-Périgord (1754–1838), French diplomat

---

◆ COSTLINESS

Classical Phrases and Myths

Asked by a rich Athenian to teach his son philosophy, the Greek philosopher Aristippus demanded 500 drachmas. "What!" the Athenian protested. "I could buy a slave for that much." "Do so," replied Aris-tippus. "Then you will have two slaves."

Aristippus (c. 435 B.C.–c. 356 B.C.), Greek philosopher

Jokes, Stories and Anecdotes

When Valentine Dale was informed of his new diplomatic post in Flanders, Queen Elizabeth said that he would receive 20 shillings a day expenses. Dale said, "Then, madam, I shall spend 19 shillings a day." "What will you do with the odd shilling?" asked Elizabeth. "I will reserve that for my wife and children." Taking the hint, Elizabeth increased the allowance.

Valentine Dale (d. 1589), British diplomat

While traveling, King George II stopped at a village inn for a brief meal. The innkeeper served an egg and charged a guinea. "Eggs must be very scarce around here," remarked the king. "Oh, no, Your Majesty," said the innkeeper, "it is kings that are scarce."

George II (1683–1760), British king [attributed also to others]

After examining the menu at a posh New York restaurant, film comedian Chico Marx turned to playwright and wit George S. Kaufman and commented rhetorically, "Jeez, what the hell can you get here for 50 cents?" Kaufman answered, "A quarter."

George S[imon] Kaufman (1889–1961), U.S. playwright, writer and wit

Picasso was entertaining several lunch guests at his villa in the south of France when someone noticed that the immensely successful artist displayed none of his own works. "Why?" one inquired. "Don't you like them?" "No, I like them very much," answered Picasso. "It is only that I cannot afford them."

Pablo [Ruiz y] Picasso (1881–1973), Spanish-born French, artist

◆ COUNTERACTION

Quotations

"*Ils ne passeront pas.*" (eel ne PASS-er-ohn pas) (They shall not pass.)

[Henri] Philippe Pétain (1856–1951), French general and statesman, prophesying correctly, but at the cost of 1 million lives, that the Germans would not penetrate Allied defenses at Verdun, 1916 [attributed also to General Robert Nivelleat]

Jokes, Stories and Anecdotes

When a weaver set up an eight-loom workshop next door to Botticelli's home, the noise drove the painter to distraction. After his protests went unheeded, Botticelli finally hoisted a boulder onto the roof of his own house. He had balanced it such that it overhung the neighbor's roof and threatened to come crashing down upon it at the slightest disturbance. The weaver gave in to Botticelli's version of a sword of Damocles.

Sandro [Alessandro di Mariano Filipepi] Botticelli (c. 1445–1510), Italian painter

◆ COUNTRY

Quotations

"One thing I will say for the Germans—they're always perfectly willing to give somebody else's land to somebody else."

Will[iam Penn Adair] Rogers (1879–1935), U.S. comedian

"I should like my country well enough if it were not for my countrymen."

Horace Walpole, Fourth Earl of Oxford (1717–1797), British writer

Mrs. Allonby: "They say, Lady Hunstanton, that when good Americans die they go to Paris." *Hunstanton:* "Indeed? And when bad Americans die, where do they go to?" *Lord Illingworth:* "Oh, they go to America."

Oscar [Fingal O'Flahertie Wills] Wilde (1854–1900), British playwright, writer and wit, A Woman of No Importance (1893), Act I

Classical Phrases and Myths

"*Crimine ab uno,*
Disce omnes." (From a single crime know the nation.)

Virgil [Publius Vergilius Maro] (70 B.C.–19 B.C.), Roman poet, Aeneid, bk. II, l. lxv

◆ COURAGE

Foreign Words and Phrases

escudo (Spa)
(es-KOO-doh) shield; courage

matador (Spa)
(ma-tah-DOR) *lit:* one who kills; bullfighter

Quotations

"I'm not the heroic type, really. I was beaten up by Quakers."

Woody Allen [Allen Stewart Konigsberg] (1935–   ), U.S. comedian and filmmaker, and Marshall Brickman (1941–   ), U.S. humorist, Sleeper (1973 film)

"Come closer, boys. It will be easier for you."

> Erskine Childers (1870–1922),
> British writer, shouting to his firing squad

"If hopes were dupes, fears may be liars;
It may be in yon smoke concealed."

> A[rthur] H[ugh] Clough (1819–1861),
> British poet, Qua Cursum Ventus

"The object, in war, is not to die for your country. The object, in war, is to make the other poor bastard die for his country!"

> Francis Ford Coppola (1939–   ),
> U.S. screenwriter and film director,
> Patton (1969 film)

"A hero is no braver than an ordinary man, but he is brave five minutes longer."

> Ralph Waldo Emerson (1803–1892),
> U.S. writer and philosopher, Essays:
> First Series (1841), "Heroism"

"Damn the torpedoes, go ahead!"

> David Glasgow Farragut (1801–1870),
> U.S. admiral attacking the Confederates in
> August 1864 at the heavily guarded
> Mobile Bay during the Civil War

"You know the old saying, 'The bigger they are, the further they have to fall.'"

> Robert Fitzsimmons (1862–1917),
> British boxer answering whether he was
> concerned about fighting the considerably
> larger James J. Jeffries in San Francisco in
> July 1902 [authenticity unverified]

"Grace under pressure."

> Ernest [Miller] Hemingway (1899–1961),
> U.S. writer, responding to Dorothy
> Parker's inquiry during an interview of
> what he meant by "guts"

"He was a bold man who first swallowed an oyster."

> James I (1566–1625), British king

"He can run, but he can't hide."

> Joe Louis (1914–1981), U.S. boxer
> expressing confident unconcern about

opponent Billy Conn's agility before a
heavyweight title match, 1946

"Cowards die many times before their deaths;
The valiant never taste of death but once."

> William Shakespeare (1564–1616),
> British playwright and poet,
> Julius Caesar, (1600), Act II, sc. ii

Le courage de l'improviste. (le kor-AHG de lim-PROH-veest) (Unprepared courage.)

> Napoleon I [Napoleon Bonaparte]
> (1769–1821), French general and emperor
> explaining "Two o'clock in the
> morning courage" remark at St. Helena
> (December 4–5, 1815)

Classical Phrases and Myths

"*Fortis fortuna adiuvat.*" (FOR-tis for-TOON-a ad-YOO-vat) (Fortune favors the brave.)

> Terence [Publius Terentius Afer]
> (c. 190 B.C.–159 B.C.), Roman playwright,
> Phormio (161 B.C.) [Adapted to
> "Audentes Fortuna iuvat"
> in Virgil's Aeneid.]

Jokes, Stories and Anecdotes

"You may eat anything for your last meal," explained the warden to the condemned man. "Filet mignon? Lobster? Caviar?" "No, I'll just have mushrooms," said the convict. "Why mushrooms?" asked the curious warden. "Always been afraid to eat 'em."

For failure of duty, Admiral Byng came up before the firing squad. It was suggested that his face be concealed with a handkerchief. Referring to his executioners, Byng said, "If it will frighten them, let it be done. They do not frighten me."

> John Byng (1704–1757), British admiral

Evariste Galois, the founder of group theory in mathematics, was rushed to a hospital fatally wounded in a duel. To his younger brother who was sobbing at his bedside, Galois said, "Don't cry, I need all my courage to die at 20."

Evariste Galois (1811–1832), French mathematician

◆ COURTESY (CIVILITY)

Foreign Words and Phrases

saper vivere (Ita)
(suh-PARE vee-VARE-ay) to know how to deal with others smoothly, to act like a smooth operator

Quotations

"The propriety of some persons seems to consist in having improper thoughts about their neighbours."

F. H. Bradley (1846–1924), British philosopher, Aphorisms (1930), no. 9

"He was so generally civil, that nobody thanked him for it."

Samuel Johnson (1709–1784), British man of letters

"Good breeding consists in concealing how much we think of ourselves and how little we think of the other person."

Mark Twain [Samuel Langhorne Clemens] (1835–1910), U.S. humorist, writer and speaker, Notebooks (1935), p. 345

"A gentleman is one who never hurts anyone's feelings unintentionally."

Oscar [Fingal O'Flahertie Wills] Wilde (1854–1900), British playwright, writer and wit

Noblesse oblige (no-BLESS oh-BLEEGE) (Nobility obliges)

Gaston Pierre Marc, Duc de Lévis (1764–1830), French writer [Those of high rank must be noble, gallant and responsible.]

Jokes, Stories and Anecdotes

A noted French statesman was in the habit of bluntly speaking his mind, much to the dismay of his political advisers. "You must be more tactful," they urged him. "Your strong language only makes you enemies." The politician couldn't see it that way. "It also makes me friends," he argued. "I have as my supporters all the enemies of my enemies."

An old pensioner entered the grocery store and asked the clerk for half a head of lettuce. Startled, the clerk pulled aside the manager to ask for permission, saying, "There's a jerk who wants half a head of lettuce and . . . " He looked over his shoulder and saw the pensioner had followed him. Thinking quickly, he continued, "And this kind gent the other half."

Although ultimately beheaded on royal instructions for having an affair with one of Queen Elizabeth's ladies in waiting, the courtly Sir Walter Raleigh traditionally enjoyed great favor with the monarch for a singular incident. In 1581 she was treading along a slightly muddy way and, when she hesitated in front of a large puddle, Raleigh sprang forward, took off his new plush cloak with a flourish, and gallantly spread it on the ground for the queen to step upon.

Sir Walter Raleigh (c. 1552–1618), British soldier, explorer and privateer [authenticity unverified]

◆ COWARDICE

Quotations

"When I give the order abandon ship, it doesn't matter what time I leave. If some people want to stay, they can stay."

Yiannis Avranas (c. 1900s), Greek ship captain, explaining why he was among the first to abandon ship on the cruise liner Oceanos, *which went down off the coast of South Africa, 1991*

"I remember, when I was a child, being taken to the celebrated Barnum's circus, which contained an exhibition of freaks and monstrosities, but the exhibit on the programme which I most desired to see was the one described as 'The Boneless Wonder'. My parents judged that that spectacle would be too revolting and demoralizing for my youthful eyes, and I have waited 50 years to see the boneless wonder sitting on the Treasury Bench."

Sir Winston Spencer Churchill (1874– 1965), British prime minister and writer, describing Sir Ramsay MacDonald

"I'm a hero with coward's legs."

Terence Alan ["Spike"] Milligan (1918–   ), British comedian and writer

"[William] McKinley has no more backbone than a chocolate eclair!"

Theodore Roosevelt (1858–1919), U.S. president

"If you can't stand the heat, get out of the kitchen."

Harry Vaughan (c. 1900s), U.S. citizen [misattributed to Harry S. Truman]

Jokes, Stories and Anecdotes

Early in his career as a courtier at the court of Queen Elizabeth I of England, Sir Walter Raleigh scratched on a window of the royal palace: "Faith would I climb, yet fear I to fall." Queen Elizabeth completed the couplet: "If thy heart fails thee, climb not at all."

Elizabeth I (1533–1603), British queen

Khrushchev was censuring Stalin for the 20 million deaths he author-

ized during his rule in front of a throng of people when a member of the audience shouted, "You were an associate of Stalin. Why didn't you do anything to stop him?" Khrushchev bellowed, "Who said that?" Silence. Nodding, Khrushchev said, "Now you know why."

Nikita Sergeyevich Khrushchev (1894–1971), Soviet statesman

◆ CRIME

Quotations

"Crimes, like virtues, are their own rewards."

George Farquhar (1678–1707), Irish playwright, The Inconstant, *Act IV, sc. ii*

Classical Phrases and Myths

in flagrante delicto (Lat)
(in flag-RAN-tay day-LEEK-toh) *lit:* in the heat of the crime; in the act, in compromising circumstances

maleficium (Lat)
(mal-eh-FIK-ium) evil deed, crime

The Greek legislator and statesman Solon, who overhauled Draco's legal code, was asked what measures could be taken to eliminate legal violations and crime. "Wrongdoing can only be avoided, responded Solon, "if those who are not wronged feel the same indignation at it as those who are."

Solon (c. 639 B.C.-c. 559 B.C.), Greek legislator and statesman

◆ CRITIC

Quotations

"Critics are like eunuchs in a harem. They're there every night, they see it done every night, they see how it should be done every night, but they can't do it themselves."

Brendan Behan (1923–1964),
Irish playwright and wit

"A critic is a man who knows the way but can't drive the car."

Kenneth [Peacock] Tynan (1927–1980),
British writer, New York Times
Magazine (January 9, 1966), p. 27

Jokes, Stories and Anecdotes

Alexander Woollcott took Tallulah Bankhead to see an inferior revival of a Maeterlinck tragedy. As they rose to leave, Bankhead remarked, "There's less here than meets the eye."

Tallulah Bankhead (1903–1968),
U.S. actress

◆ CRITICISM OF ARTS

Quotations

"One cannot review a bad book without showing off."

W[ystan] H[ugh] Auden (1907–1973),
British-born poet, Dyer's Hand
(1963), "Reading"

"Darling, they've absolutely ruined your perfectly dreadful play."

Tallulah Bankhead (1903–68),
U.S. actress, commenting on the screen
adaptation of Tennessee Williams's play
Orpheus Descending

"It was one of those plays in which all the actors unfortunately enunciated very clearly."

Robert Charles Benchley (1889–1945),
U.S. humorist

"Ouch!"

Wolcott Gibbs (1902–1958), U.S. writer
reviewing the Broadway farce Wham!

"Asking a working writer what he thinks about critics is like asking a lamp-post what it feels about dogs."

Christopher Hampton (1946–   ),
British playwright

"Her only flair is in her nostrils."

Pauline Kael (1919–   ),
U.S. writer, reviewing the actress
Candice Bergen in the 1971 film
Carnal Knowledge

"Hook and Ladder is the sort of play that gives failures a bad name."

Walter Kerr (1913–   ),
U.S. writer

"He [Samuel Johnson] gets at the substance of a book directly; he tears out the heart of it."

Mary Knowles (1733–1807),
British writer

"That's a person who surprises the playwright by informing him of what he meant."

Wilson Mizner (1876–1933), U.S. writer
and wit, describing a drama critic

"It is a terrible, harrowing experience for a playwright to be forced by his conscience to praise critics for anything. There is something morbid and abnormal about it, something destructive to the noble traditions of what is correct conduct for dramatists."

Eugene [Gladstone] O'Neill (1888–1953),
U.S. playwright, reply to request for New
York Drama Critics Circle for
welcoming statement, 1939

"This is not a novel to be tossed aside lightly. It should be thrown with great force."

Dorothy Parker (1893–1967), U.S. wit
and writer, reviewing A. A. Milne's The
House at Pooh Corner in her column
"Constant Reader"

"He's a writer for the ages—for the ages of four to eight."

> Dorothy Parker (1893–1967),
> U.S. wit and writer

"I never read a book before reviewing it; it prejudices one so."

> Sydney Smith (1771–1845),
> British clergyman and writer

"The play was a great success, but the audience was a disaster."

> Oscar [Fingal O'Flahertie Wills] Wilde
> (1854–1900), British playwright,
> writer and wit

"The work of a queasy undergraduate scratching his pimples."

> [Adeline] Virginia Woolf (1882–1941),
> British writer, referring to
> James Joyce's writings

"The scenery was beautiful but the actors got in front of it . . . The play left a taste of lukewarm parsnip juice."

> Alexander Woollcott (1887–1943),
> U.S. writer, broadcaster and wit

"My leg is the only sensible part of my body. It has gone to sleep."

> Israel Zangwill (1864–1926), British
> writer and playwright, watching a tedious
> Sardou melodrama

"Ich sitze in dem kleinsten Zimmer in meinem Hause. Ich habe Ihre Kritik vor mir. Im nächsten Augenblick wird sie hinter mir sein." (I am sitting in the smallest room of my house. I have your review before me. In a moment it will be behind me.)

> Max Reger (1873–1916),
> German composer and organist,
> letter to Munich critic Rudolph Louis
> in response to his review in Munchener
> Neueste Nachrichten
> (February 7, 1906)

Classical Phrases and Myths

"Great book, great bore."

> Callimachus (c. 300 B.C.–250 B.C.),
> Greek poet, describing traditional epics,
> Fragments

Jokes, Stories and Anecdotes

A theater critic was leaving the Broadway theater after an opening and met the producer in the lobby. Haughtily eyeing the critic's suit, which was rumpled, as usual, the producer smirked. "Apparently you cannot afford to dress properly for premieres. Your suit looks as if it had been slept in." "Since you mention it," the critic replied, "I just woke up."

While humorist Robert Benchley was attending the Broadway premiere of a play, a telephone rang on the otherwise deserted stage. "I believe that's for me," remarked Benchley, and he rose and left the theater.

> Robert Charles Benchley (1889–1945),
> U.S. humorist

"I'm amazed the audience didn't hiss it," commented critic Ludwig Sternaux to his friend, critic Oskar Blumenthal, about a recently opened play. Replied Blumenthal, "Well, you can't yawn and hiss at the same time."

> Oskar Blumenthal (1852–1917),
> German playwright, journalist and critic

John Singer Sargent, the popular portraitist of the European elite, bristled when criticized. Once, when a lady sitting for a portrait complained about his rendering of her mouth, he said, "Perhaps, madam, we should leave it out altogether." When another woman sitting for her $5,000 portrait objected to his treatment of her nose, he said, "Oh, you can easily right a little thing like that when you get it home," and handed her the canvas.

John Singer Sargent (1856–1925), U.S. painter

Composer Igor Stravinsky was inveighing against critics who had written harshly about his work. "No one can please everyone," said a friend consolingly. "Even God does not please everyone." Stravinsky jumped up and exclaimed, "Especially God!"

Igor Feodorovitch Stravinsky (1882–1971), Russian-born composer

Poet laureate Tennyson's poem, *Maud,* which dealt with murder, suicide, love and madness, met with a hostile reception among the critics. *Maud* had one vowel too many in the title, suggested one reviewer, and would make sense no matter which was deleted.

Alfred Tennyson, 1st Baron Tennyson (1809–1892), British poet

◆ CULTURE

Foreign Words and Phrases

évolué (Fra)
(eh-vol-OO-eh) *lit:* evolved; non-European who has adjusted to and been absorbed by European culture

Zeitgeist (Ger)
(TSYT-guyst) *lit:* spirit of the time (especially its literature, philosophy, etc.)

Kultur (Ger)
(kul-TOOR) culture or civilization (suggesting racial superiority)

Quotations

"And the wind shall say: 'Here were decent godless people:

Their only monument the asphalt road
And a thousand lost golf balls.' "

T[homas] S[tearns] Eliot (1888–1965), U.S. poet, The Rock (1934), pt. I

"I wish you would read a little poetry sometimes. Your ignorance cramps my conversation."

Sir Anthony Hope [Hawkins] (1863–1933), British writer, Dolly Dialogues (1894), no. 22

"I respect Millar [a bookseller], sir; he has raised the price of literature."

Samuel Johnson (1709–1784), British man of letters

"*Wenn ich Kultur hore . . . entsichere ich meinen Browning.*" (When I hear the word Culture, I release the safety catch of my revolver.)

Hanns Johst (1890–1978), German playwright, Schlageter (1934), Act I, sc. 1 [paraphrased by Hermann Goering]

Jokes, Stories and Anecdotes

A scandal erupted in June 1906 when the architect Stanford White was shot by Harry Thaw in a quarrel over Evelyn Nesbit. Years later, in a gaudy Palm Beach hotel designed by Joseph Urban, the wit Wilson Mizner quipped, "Harry Thaw shot the wrong architect."

Wilson Mizner (1876–1933), U.S. writer and wit [attributed also to others]

◆ CURE & TREATMENT

Quotations

"Cure the disease and kill the patient."

Francis Bacon (1561–1626), British lawyer and writer, Essays (1625), "Of Friendship"

"I enjoy convalescence. It is the part that makes illness worth while."

George Bernard Shaw (1856–1950), Irish playwright, Back to Methuselah *(1921), pt. 2*

Classical Phrases and Myths

placebo (Lat)
(PLAK-e-bo) *lit:* I shall please; in medicine, a harmless substance that might make one well because the person believes it will

nostrum (Lat)
(NOS-trum) *lit:* our own; patent medicine (or scheme)

Jokes, Stories and Anecdotes

"Help me, I'm not feeling well, Doc," said the patient. "Do you drink?" asked the doctor. "Nope." "Smoke?" "No." "Go to bed late?" "No." Shaking his head, the doctor said, "How can I cure you if you have nothing to give up?"

The doctor was conferring with the intern in the hospital corridor when suddenly his patient Fred ran by, his hands cupping his genitals. Hot on his heels was the patient's nurse, carrying a still-steaming pot. Grabbing the nurse's arm, the doctor roared, "Dammit, nurse, you misunderstood! I said 'prick his boil'!"

"Your impotency is only temporary," the physician informed the young man. "Just put a little more wheat in your diet and you'll soon have erections." The young man raced out the doctor's office, down the street and into a bakery. Breathless, he asked for five loaves of whole wheat bread. "Having a party?" chuckled the baker. When informed that the young man intended all the bread for himself, the baker warned him, "But it'll get hard in a day or two." "Then lemme have 20 loaves."

The emperor Menelik took literally Francis Bacon's maxim that "some books are to be tasted, others to be swallowed, and some few to be chewed and digested." Recovering from a stroke in December 1913, the emperor, who felt eating the Bible would help him recover from feeling ill, commanded that the complete Book of Kings be fed to him, page by page. He died anyway.

Menelik II (1844–1913), Ethiopian emperor

◆ CURIOSITY

Foreign Words and Phrases

yenta (Yid)
(YEN-ta) female busybody, shrew, a gossip

Quotations

" 'Is there any point to which you would wish to draw my attention?' 'To the curious incident of the dog in the night time.' 'The dog did nothing in the night time.' 'That was the curious incident,' remarked Sherlock Holmes."

Sir Arthur Conan Doyle (1859–1930), British writer, The Memoirs of Sherlock Holmes *(1894), "Silver Blaze"*

◆ CURSE & BLASPHEMY

Foreign Words and Phrases

en cuiller (Fra argot)
(on KWE-yer) up yours

gâchis (Fra)
(gah-SHE) curse for a bungled opportunity, opportunity missed because of ineptness

yeb vas (Rus)
(yeb vuhs) fuck you

Quotations

"May the fleas of a thousand camels infest your armpits."

Arab curse

"But th' best thing about a little judicyous swearin' is that it keeps th' temper. 'Twas intinded as a compromise between runnin' away an' fightin'. Befure it was invinted they was on'y two ways out iv an argymint."

Finley Peter Dunne (1867–1936), U.S. writer and humorist, Observations by Mr. Dooley (1902), "Swearing"

"[W]hen I call him an s.o.b. I am not using profanity but am referring to the circumstances of his birth."

Huey [Pierce] Long (1893–1967), U.S. politician commenting on the Imperial Wizard of the Ku Klux Klan

"Who can refute a sneer?"

William Paley (1743–1805), British philosopher, Moral Philosophy (1785), vol. II, bk. V, ch. 9

"Let me be cruel, not unnatural; I will speak daggers to her, but use none."

William Shakespeare (1564–1616), British playwright and poet, Hamlet (1601), Act III, sc. ii

"A footman may swear but he cannot swear like a lord. He can swear as often, but can he swear with equal delicacy, propriety and judgement?"

Jonathan Swift (1667–1745), Anglo-Irish clergyman and writer

"Profanity furnishes a relief denied even to prayer."

Mark Twain [Samuel Langhorne Clemens] (1835–1910), U.S. humorist, writer and speaker

"May you inherit a shipload of gold; may it not be enough to pay your doctor's bills."

Yiddish curse

Classical Phrases and Myths

anathema sit (Gk/Lat)
(an-A-them-a sit) may he be accursed; pronouncement of excommunication (now used as a general exclamation)

"'Twas but my tongue, not my soul that swore."

Euripides (480 B.C.–406 B.C.), Greek playwright, Hippolytus (428 B.C.), l. 612

Jokes, Stories and Anecdotes

A passionate golfer dies and is greeted by St. Peter. "Your life has been exemplary," says St. Peter, "but according to our records, once you took the Lord's name in vain during a game of golf." "Let me explain," says the man. "I was playing a few years ago, a hole away from claiming the club trophy. When I came to the 18th hole, my tee shot was long but landed in the rough." "Is that when you took the Lord's name in vain?" asked St. Peter. "No, then I hit the ball long again but it ended in a sand trap." "Awful," said St. Peter. "Then is that when you took the Lord's name in vain?" "No, but I was frustrated. I used my pitching iron but the ball stopped rolling inches from the cup." "Oh, no," said St. Peter, "don't tell me you missed the goddamn putt!"

Two priests were out playing golf, but Father Riley, who was flubbing his drives and putts, would hiss after each missed shot, "Damn, I missed!" Good Father O'Rourke finally said, "Don't swear! You risk divine anger, and a lightning bolt might hit you the next time." But

Father Riley, on the next shot, said, "Damn, I—" Suddenly, a fierce lightning bolt ripped through the atmosphere. When the smoke cleared, Father Riley saw that although he was fine, there was but a charred pit where good Father O'Rourke had stood. From the clouds, a voice boomed, "Damn, I missed!"

◆ CUSTOM

Foreign Words and Phrases

epater le bourgeois (Fra)
(ay-PAT-ayle BOOR-jwa) *lit:* amaze bourgeois; to shock (deliberately) people with conventional values, to challenge conventionality for effect

de rigueur (Fra)
(de ree-GUHR) necessary, compulsory; required by the rules of etiquette

autre temps, autre moeurs (Fra)
(OH-tre tohm OH-tre muhr) *lit:* other times, other ways; values change with the times

gaiatsu (Jap)
(gay-ee-AHT-soo) external pressure

comme il faut (Fra)
(kom eel foh) *lit:* as is necessary; proper (behavior), socially acceptable (usually used ironically or sarcastically in English)

Quotations

"A gentleman never strikes a lady with his hat on."

Fred Allen [John Sullivan] (1894–1956),
U.S. comedian

"Custom reconciles us to everything."

Edmund Burke (1729–1797),
British statesman, philosopher and writer,
Tracts on the Popery Laws, *ch. 3, pt. i*

"Custom, that unwritten law,
By which the people keep even kings in awe."

Sir William Davenant (1606–1668),
British poet, Circe, *bk. II, iii*

"They teach the morals of a whore, and the manners of a dancing master."

Samuel Johnson (1709–1784), British man
of letters, commenting on Lord
Chesterfield's letters to his son

"Nobody can live in society without conventions. The reason why sensible people are as conventional as they can bear to be, is that conventionality saves so much time and thought and trouble and social friction of one sort or another that it leaves them much more leisure for freedom than unconventionality does."

George Bernard Shaw (1856–1950),
Irish playwright

"The total want of all the usual courtesies of the table, the voracious rapidity with which the viands were seized and devoured; the strange uncouth phrases and pronunciation; the loathsome spitting, from the contamination of which it was absolutely impossible to protect our dresses; the frightful manner of feeding with their knives, till the whole blade seemed to enter into the mouth; and the still more frightful manner of cleaning the teeth afterwards with a pocket-knife, soon forced us to feel that we were not surrounded by the generals, colonels and majors of the old world."

Frances Trollope (1780–1863),
British writer, describing Americans

Classical Phrases and Myths

mores (Lat)
(MOR-es) conduct, morals, customs (generally of country, society, etc.)

mos maiorum (Lat)
(mohs mai-OR-um) the custom of one's ancestors; tradition

Jokes, Stories and Anecdotes

During a Grover Cleveland White House dinner, a young European attache was served a salad that included a worm. The attache was about to draw a servant's attention to the unsavory serving before him but caught Mrs. Cleveland's eye, fixed on him in a challenging stare. The attache obligingly ate the salad, worm and all. Mrs. Cleveland smiled approvingly, remarking, "You will go far, young man." Fifteen years later he returned as a full ambassador.

> *Frances Folsom Cleveland (1864–1947),*
> *U.S. presidential wife*

At a dinner party, attended by several Hollywood stars, thrown by film producer and epicure Arthur Hornblow, Jr., the journalist and scriptwriter Herman Mankiewicz threw up at the table after drinking too much. The guests were in stunned silence. "It's all right, Arthur," gulped Mankiewicz. "The white wine came up with the fish."

> *Herman J. Mankiewicz (1897–1953),*
> *U.S. writer*

Dorothy Parker, rising from her seat at the Algonquin Hotel's Round Table, announced, "Excuse me, everybody, I have to go to the bathroom." She paused, then confided sheepishly, "I really have to use the telephone, but I'm too embarrassed to say so."

> *Dorothy Parker (1893–1967),*
> *U.S. wit and writer*

◆ DANCE

Foreign Words and Phrases

pirouette (Fra)
(pee-ro-WET) *lit:* spinning top; ballet dancer's spin

fandango (Spa)
(fan-DAN-goh) very lively dance for two, music for it; nonsense, foolishness

entrechat (Fra)
(ON-tray-sha) leap in ballet in which dancer crosses his legs more than once (i.e., *entrechat-douze*, where legs criss-crossed 12 times)

baile flamenco (Spa)
(BY-lay flah-MEN-koh) *lit:* flamingo dance; flamenco dance, a traditional Spanish gypsy dance

corps de ballet (Fra)
(kor de bah-lay) members of ballet troupe who do not dance solo parts

danse macabre (Fra)
(dahnse mah-CAH-br) dance of death

Quotations

"O body swayed to music, O brightening glance
How can we know the dancer from the dance?"

> *William Butler Yeats (1865–1939),*
> *Irish poet and playwright*, October Blast
> (1927), "Among School Children"

Classical Phrases and Myths

In Greek mythology, Terpsichore (terp-SIK-oh-ree) was the muse of dancing and the patroness of lyric poetry. She was depicted holding a lyre, and by some accounts was a mother of the Sirens. Thus, something *terpsichorean* pertains to dancing.

Jokes, Stories and Anecdotes

Although Lord Sandwich is now known for the snack which he invented to sustain him while gambling, his contemporaries recognized him by his ungainliness. One wag remarked that Sandwich could be recognized from a distance because "he walked down both sides of the street at once." Sandwich once took dancing lessons in Paris, and when he bid farewell to his dancing master, he offered to recommend him to London socialites visiting Paris. "I would take it as a particular favor," replied the bowing instructor, "if your lordship would never disclose to anyone from whom you learned to dance."

John Montagu, 4th Earl of Sandwich (1718–1792), British politician

der, in the Greek colony of Syracuse in Italy, who was an ardent sycophant. To challenge Damocles, the tyrant invited Damocles to a splendid banquet and had him feast with a sword suspended above his head by a single horsehair. Thus, a *sword of Damocles* or something *damoclean* connotes an imminent threat or danger.

Damocles (c. 375 B.C.), Greek courtier

◆ DANGER

Quotations

"In skating over thin ice, our safety is in our speed."

Ralph Waldo Emerson (1803–1892), U.S. writer, poet and philosopher, Essays: First Series (1841), "Prudence"

"Nothing is more dangerous than a friend without discretion; even a prudent enemy is preferable."

Jean de La Fontaine (1621–1695), French fabulist, Fables (1668)

Classical Phrases and Myths

"*Incedis per ignis* Suppositos cineri doloso." (You tread over fires hidden under a treacherous crust of ashes.)

Horace (65 B.C.–8 B.C.), Roman poet, Odes, II. i.

"*De calcaria in carbonarium.*" (de kal-KARE-ee-a in kar-BON-air-ee-um) (Out of the frying pan into the fire.)

Tertullian [Quintus Septimius Florens Tertullianus] (c. 160–c. 225) Roman writer, De Carne Christi, 6

Damocles (dam-ok-leez) was a member of the court of Dionysus the El-

◆ DEATH

Foreign Words and Phrases

belle mort (Fra) (BEL more) natural death

karoshi (Jap) (ka-ROH-shi) *lit:* death from overwork

Quotations

"On the plus side, death is one of the few things that can be done as easily lying down."

Woody Allen [Allen Stewart Konigsberg] (1935–), U.S. comedian and filmmaker, Without Feathers (1976), "Early Essays"

"It's not that I'm afraid to die. I just don't want to be there when it happens."

Woody Allen [Allen Stewart Konigsberg] (1935–), U.S. comedian and filmmaker, Death (1975), p. 63

"One of the fathers saith . . . that old men go to death, and death comes to young men."

Francis Bacon (1561–1626), British lawyer and writer, Apothegms (1624), 270

"I do not believe that any man fears to be dead, but only the stroke of death."

*Francis Bacon (1561–1626),
British lawyer and writer,* Essays *(1625)*

"I am prepared to meet my Maker. Whether my Maker is prepared for the great ordeal of meeting me is another matter."

*Sir Winston Spencer Churchill
(1874–1965), British prime minister
and writer, Washington, D.C., news
conference on eve of 80th birthday, 1954*

"Death, in itself, is nothing; but we fear,
To be we know not what, we know not
where."

*John Dryden (1631–1700), British poet,
playwright and writer,* Aureng-Zebe
(1676), Act IV, sc. i

"It matters not how a man dies, but how he lives."

*Samuel Johnson (1709–1784),
British man of letters*

"I [Death] was astonished to see him in Baghdad, for I had an appointment with him tonight in Samarra."

*Amy [Lawrence] Lowell (1874–1925),
U.S. poet and writer,* Sheppy
(1933), Act III

"There is no cure for birth and death save to enjoy the interval."

*George Santayana (1863–1952),
Spanish-born U.S. philosopher, poet
and writer,* Soliloquies in England *(1922),
"War Shrines"*

"Life is a gamble at terrible odds—if it was a bet, you wouldn't take it."

*Tom Stoppard (1937–   ), British
playwright and writer,* Rosencrantz and
Guildenstern Are Dead *(1967), Act III*

"Better be killed than frightened to death."

*Robert Smith Surtees (1803–1864),
British writer,* Mr. Facey Romford's
Hounds *(1864), ch. 32*

"My wallpaper and I are fighting a duel to the death. One or the other of us has to go."

*Oscar [Fingal O'Flahertie Wills] Wilde
(1854–1900), British playwright, writer
and wit, dying words*

Classical Phrases and Myths

de mortuis (nil nisi bonum) (Lat)
(day MOR-too-eesnil nee-see BOH-num) (say) nothing but good of the dead

in extremis (Lat)
(in ex-TRAY-mees) at the point of death, at the extreme, of dire circumstances

post mortem (Lat)
(post MOR-tem) *lit:* after death; usually applied to examination of a corpse to discover the cause of death

"Those whom the gods love die young."

*Menander (c. 342 B.C.–292 B.C.),
Greek playwright,* The Double Deceiver

"*Abiit ad plures.*" (AB-ee-itad PLU-res) (He has gone over to the majority.)

*Petronius, Gaius [Petronius Arbiter]
(d. c. 66), Roman writer,*
Cena Trimalchionis, *xlii, 5*

One of the queerest deaths ever recorded happened to the Greek poet Aeschylus. Ancient biographies record that an eagle, seeking to smash the shell of the tortoise held in its talons mistook the poet's bald head for a stone and dropped the tortoise on him.

*Aeschylus (525 B.C.–456 B.C.),
Greek playwright*

Jokes, Stories and Anecdotes

Li Bo, considered one of China's greatest poets, reveled in beauty both in life and death. In a boat one evening, according to popular tradition, he tried to embrace the reflection of the full moon shining in the still water, fell in and drowned.

Li Bo (701–762), Chinese poet

To induce Louis B. Mayer to donate to a charity, another contributor reasoned with him, "You can't take it with you when you go." "If I can't take it with me," snorted Mayer, "I won't go."

Louis B. Mayer (1885–1957),
U.S. film producer

Alistair Cooke paid a visit in 1955 to critic and fellow journalist H. L. Mencken, who had suffered a stroke in 1948, which had crippled his mental faculties. Conversation turned to Edgar Lee Masters, who Cooke suggested had died in 1948. Mencken agreed. "That's right, I believe he died the year I did."

H[enry] L[ouis] Mencken (1880–1956),
U.S. critic and writer

Wilson Mizner was close to his extremely successful architect brother Addison, and the two often exchanged ideas. When Addison had retired to Palm Beach close to his death, Wilson sent him a telegram from Hollywood, "Stop dying. Am trying to write a comedy."

Wilson Mizner (1876–1933),
U.S. writer and wit

"So sorry to be late," exclaimed Arthur Rubinstein, the virtuoso pianist, to Clifton Fadiman as he sat down for lunch. "For two hours I have been at my lawyer's, making a testament. What a nuisance, this business of a testament. One figures, one schemes, one arranges, and in the end—what? It is practically impossible to leave anything for yourself!"

Arthur Rubinstein (1886–1982),
Polish-born U.S. pianist

The English politician and journalist John Wilkes dined with the Earl of Sandwich one night at the famous Beef Steak Club in London's Covent Garden. At one point Lord Sandwich said to Wilkes, "Egad, sir, I have often mused how you would meet your end. I should say that you would either die of the halter [gallows] or of the pox." "That will depend, my lord," retorted Wilkes, "on whether I embrace your principles or your mistress."

John Wilkes (1725–1797),
British politician and writer
[attributed also to Samuel Foote
and Benjamin Disraeli]

◆ DEBACLE

Foreign Words and Phrases

débâcle (Fra)
(day-BAH-cl) collapse, complete breakdown, fiasco

Quotations

"Calamities are of two kinds: misfortune to ourselves, and good fortune to others.

Ambrose [Gwinnet] Bierce
(1842–c. 1914), U.S. writer and poet,
The Devil's Dictionary (1911)

"There cannot be a crisis next week. My schedule is already full."

Henry Kissinger (1923–   ),
U.S. diplomat

"If the temperature of the bath water rises one degree every ten minutes, how will the bather know when to scream?"

Marshall [Herbert] McLuhan
(1911–1980), Canadian scholar,
commenting rhetorically on people's
tendency to adjust to, rather than
confront or escape, an impending disaster

"Fortunately for themselves and the world, nearly all men are cowards and dare not act on what they believe. Nearly all our disasters come of a few fools having the 'courage of their convictions.'"

Coventry Patmore (1823–1896),
British poet

Classical Phrases and Myths

hinc illae lacrimae (Lat)
(HEENK EEL-lai LAK-rim-ai) *lit:* hence these tears; this was the cause of the disaster

---

◆ DEBT

Quotations

"Bankruptcy is a legal proceeding in which you put your money in your pants pocket and give your coat to the creditors.

Joey Adams (1911–),
U.S. comedian

"Some people use one half their ingenuity to get into debt, and the other half to avoid paying it."

George D[ennison] Prentice (1802–1870),
U.S. editor and poet

"He that dies pays all debts."

William Shakespeare (1564–1616),
British playwright and poet,
The Tempest (1612), Act III, sc. ii

"The day of judgment. But, no—stay—that will be a busy day. Make it the day after."

Richard Brinsley Sheridan (1751–1816),
Irish-born British playwright and
politician, answering a creditor when
asked to name a payment date

Jokes, Stories and Anecdotes

"Don't you think you're being a bit extravagant?" said the husband to his new bride. "You've got five electric fans running." "Don't worry,

dear," she replied. "They're not ours. I borrowed them from the neighbors."

Frustrated by an overdue account, the sales rep forwarded the following collection note: "Although we appreciate your business, your account is now 10 months overdue. We've carried you longer than your mother did. Immediate delivery is expected."

Daughter to father: "Lend me $20, but just give me $10. That way you'll owe me $10 and I'll owe you $10 and we'll be even."

Austrian poet Peter Altenberg, though of solid means, had a mania for begging. The poet and critic Karl Kraus was repeatedly beseeched by Altenberg for a hundred kronen, and consistently refused. Finally, losing his patience, Kraus exclaimed, "Peter, I'd gladly give it to you, but I really, really, do not have the money." Replied Altenberg, "Then, I'll lend it to you."

Peter Altenberg (c. 1862–1919),
Austrian poet

The hard-driving and independent statesman Charles Fox was once reprimanded for his immense debts by his father, who remarked that he wondered how Fox could sleep or enjoy life with such obligations hanging over him. "Your lordship need not be surprised," was Fox's cool reply. "You should rather be astonished that my creditors can sleep."

Charles James Fox (1749–1806),
British statesman

Early in his career, Oliver Herford was somewhat impoverished. The sympathetic manager of the hotel where he was living merely allowed Herford's bill to grow larger rather than insisting on immediate payment each week. After permitting this arrangement for some time, the manager stopped Hereford and asked whether he had received his latest bill. "Yes," Herford replied. "Is that all you can say?" "At present," said the humorist. "But if the bill gets any larger, I'll need to ask you for a larger room."

Oliver Herford (1863–1935), British-born U.S. humorist and illustrator

The lyric poet and novelist Detlev von Liliencron, typically impoverished, was stopped by a creditor who demanded immediate payment. "So sorry, but I have no money," replied Liliencron. "Please be patient." "But you told me that four weeks ago." "So," remarked Liliencron triumphantly, "did I not keep my word?"

Detlev von Liliencron (1844–1909), German poet and writer

Anglo-Irish dramatist Richard Sheridan's tailor, owed money, finally pleaded, "At least you could pay me the interest on it." Sheridan retorted, "It is not my interest to pay the principal, nor my principle to pay the interest."

Richard Brinsley Sheridan (1751–1816), Irish-born British playwright and politician

◆ DECEIVER

Quotations

"[Three sets of budget figures were maintained by the War Office:] one to mislead the public, another to mislead the Cabinet, and the third to mislead itself."

Herbert Henry Asquith, Earl of Oxford and Asquith (1852–1928), British prime minister

"It is the wisdom of crocodiles, that shed tears when they would devour."

Francis Bacon (1561–1626), British lawyer and writer, Essays (1625), "Of Wisdom for a Man's Self"

"An open foe may prove a curse, But a pretended friend is worse."

John Gay (1685–1732), British poet and playwright, Fables, Part I (1727), "The Shepherd's Dog and the Wolf"

"*C'est double plaisir de tromper le trompeur.*" (It is doubly pleasing to trick the trickster.)

Jean de La Fontaine (1621–1695), French fabulist, Fables (1668), "Le Coq et Le Renard"

Classical Phrases and Myths

splendide mendax (Lat) (SPLEN-did-e MEN-dax) splendidly false; Horace describing Cleopatra, the enemy of Rome

A wolf became desperate after lurking near a flock of sheep because the shepherd had been so diligent in guarding them from him. The wolf found a sheepskin, and, slipping it over its own hide, mingled with the sheep. Even the shepherd was deceived, and the disguised wolf was shut up the sheep in the fold. But at night, the shepherd went to the fold to kill the first animal he found. The wolf's deceptive appearance was so clever, the shepherd mistakenly killed the wolf in sheep's clothing.

Aesop (c. 600 B.C.), Greek fabulist

Jokes, Stories and Anecdotes

A new lawyer was sitting at her desk at her newly opened office. As she saw her door opening, she thought "A client already. I must impress him." She picked up the telephone and said loudly, "No,

I'm just too busy to take your case, even for $10,000." Putting down the phone, she looked up at her prospective client and asked, "So how can I help you?" "Oh," was the reply. "I just came to connect your telephone."

NASA was interviewing professionals to be sent to Venus. Only one could go—and couldn't return to Earth. The first applicant, an engineer, was asked how much he wanted to be paid for going. "A million dollars," he answered "because I want to donate it to Cal-Tech." Asked the same question, the next applicant, a doctor, asked for $2 million. "I want to give $1 million to my family," he explained, "and leave the other million for the advancement of medical research." When asked how much money he wanted, the third applicant, a lawyer, whispered in the interviewer's ear, "$3 million dollars." "Why so much more than the others?" asked the interviewer. The lawyer replied, "If you give me $3 million, I'll give you $1 million, I'll keep $1 million, and we'll send the engineer to Venus."

◆ DECEPTION

Foreign Words and Phrases

yentz (Yid)
(yehntz) to defraud

Quotations

"If a man deceives me once, shame on him; if he deceives me twice, shame on me."

Italian proverb

"You can fool all of the people some of the time, and some of the people all of the time, but you cannot fool all of the people all of the time."

Abraham Lincoln (1809–1865),
U.S. president [attributed also to
P. T. Barnum]

"In baiting a mouse-trap with cheese, always leave room for the mouse."

Saki [Hector Hugo Munro] (1870–1916),
British writer, The Square Egg
(1924), "The Infernal Parliament"

"O what a tangled web we weave, When first we practise to deceive!"

Sir Walter Scott (1771–1832),
British writer and poet,
Marmion (1808), canto VI, st. 17

Classical Phrases and Myths

According to Greek legend and recounted in Homer's *Iliad*, after ten years beseiging the city of Troy, the Greeks feigned retreat and left behind a wooden horse, the Trojan horse, as a "gift." The Trojans, not suspecting that the horse in fact contained Greek soldiers, brought it into the city. The Greeks hidden within launched a surprise attack, opened the gates of Troy, and thereby conquered the city. Hence, a *Trojan horse* is a trap to defeat an enemy, and ever since, it has been considered wise to *beware of Greeks bearing gifts.*

◆ DECISION

Quotations

"When the decision is up before you—and on my desk I have a motto which says 'The buck stops

---

here'—the decision has to be made."

Harry S Truman (1884–1972),
U.S. president, speech at National
War College, December 19, 1952

Jokes, Stories and Anecdotes

Poor Morris had never made the right decision—all his life he had taken the slowest traffic lane, bet on the wrong horse, and had his picnics rained out. Forced to travel in a hurry to Gnome, he began to weep happily, for he had no choice that could result in harm to him. As fate would have it, however, the plane developed engine trouble. Morris began to pray fervently to his patron saint, St. Francis. Suddenly, a giant hand swooped down out of the clouds and snatched him from the doomed plane. There he was, miraculously suspended five miles in the air, when a heavenly voice boomed, "I can save you, my son, if you in fact called me. Is it St. Francis Xavier or St. Francis of Assissi?"

◆ DEFAMATION

Foreign Words and Phrases

far secco qualcuno (Ita)
(far SEK-koh kwal-KOO-noh) to leave someone speechless with a biting remark

Quotations

"No one can have a higher opinion of him than I have—and I think he is a dirty little beast."

Sir W[illiam] S[chwenck] Gilbert
(1836–1911), British writer

"[A] pig, an ass, a dunghill, the spawn of an adder, a basilisk, a ly-ing buffoon, a mad fool with a frothy mouth. . . "

Martin Luther (1483–1546),
German Protestant theologian,
describing Henry VIII

"Aside from the fact that he is a squinteyed, consumptive liar, with a breath like a buzzard and a record like a convict, I don't have anything against him. He means well enough, and if he can evade the penitentiary and the vigilance committee for a few more years, there is a chance he'll end his life in a natural way. If he doesn't tell the truth a little more plentifully, however, the Green River people will rise as one man and churn him up till there won't be anything left of him but a pair of suspenders and a wart."

Edgar Wilson ["Bill"] Nye (1850–1896),
U.S. writer and humorist feuding with the
editor of Wyoming's Sweetwater Gazette
Laramie Boomerang (c. 1893)

"Satire is a sort of glass, wherein beholders do generally discover everybody's face but their own."

Jonathan Swift (1667–1745),
Anglo-Irish clergyman and writer,
The Battle of the Books (1704), preface

Classical Phrases and Myths

argumentum ad hominem (Lat)
(ar-gu-MEN-tum ad HOM-in-em) argument based on personal slander or praise that obscures the real points at issue

"To add insult to injury."

Phaedrus (c. 20), Roman fabulist,
Fables, bk. V, l. 3

Jokes, Stories and Anecdotes

While Reverend Henry Ward Beecher was speaking, a heckler in the crowd imitated a cock crow. The audience roared with laughter. Beecher merely withdrew his watch and studied it until the noise had died down. Then he said, "Odd. My watch says it's ten o'clock, but there can't be any mistake. It must be morning, for the instincts of the lower animals are absolutely infallible."

Henry Ward Beecher (1813–1887),
U.S. clergyman and writer

William Jennings Bryan was once asked while campaigning to make a speech to a crowd of people assembled in a field. Climbing up onto the manure spreader that served as an impromptu dais, he commented, "This is the first time I have ever spoken from a Republican platform."

William Jennings Bryan (1860–1925),
U.S. politician [attributed also to others]

While Buddha, the Indian prince whose teachings formed the basis of Buddhism, was once preaching, he was interrupted by a man hurling abuses. Buddha waited until he had finished and then asked, "If a man offered a gift to another but the gift was declined, to whom would the gift belong?" "To the one who offered it," answered the heckler. "Then," said Buddha, "I decline to accept your abuse and request that you keep it for yourself."

Gautama Buddha (563 B.C.–483 B.C.),
Indian prince and religious pedagogue

Playwright and wit George S. Kaufman was buttonholed at a Hollywood dinner party by an author who began loudly hurling invectives against the reputation of a film actress. "And," concluded the man, "she's her own worst enemy." Kaufman replied wryly, "Not while you're alive."

George S[imon] Kaufman (1889–1961),
U.S. playwright, writer and wit

A mutual friend of Dorothy Parker and Clare Boothe Luce extolled the latter's virtues to Parker, "Actually, she's very kind to her inferiors." "Oh? Where does she find them?"

Dorothy Parker (1893–1967), U.S. wit
and writer [authenticity unverified]

Long-time New York governor and journalist Alfred Smith paused while speaking during a political rally because of a heckler's incessant interruptions. "Go ahead, Al, don't let me bother you," shouted the heckler. "Tell 'em all you know. It won't take you long." "If I tell 'em all we both know," Smith shouted back. "That won't take any longer."

Alfred Emanuel Smith (1873–1944),
U.S. politician and writer

A member of the landed gentry was arguing about the Church of England with British clergyman and wit Sydney Smith. The squire concluded by remarking that if he had a son who was a fool he would make him a parson. "Most probably," replied Smith, "but I see your father was of a different mind."

Sydney Smith (1771–1845),
British clergyman and writer

The British painter and sculptor Frederic Leighton happened to run into James Whistler in Piccadilly. "My dear Whistler, you leave your pictures in such a crude, sketchy state," commented Leighton, who prided himself on the detail of his draftsmanship. "Why do you not ever finish them?" "My dear Leighton," retorted Whistler, who tended toward Impressionism, "why do you ever begin yours?"

James Abbott McNeill Whistler
(1834–1903), U.S.-born British painter
[authenticity unverified]

◆ DEFEAT

Quotations

"[Sir John R.] Jellicoe was the only man on either side who could lose the war in an afternoon."

> Sir Winston Spencer Churchill (1874–1965), British prime minister and writer, World Crisis (1927), pt. 1, ch. 5

"How could God do this to me after all I have done for him?"

> Louis XIV (1638–1715), French king, learning news of the French army's crushing defeat at Blenheim, 1709 [authenticity unverified]

"By trying we can easily learn to endure adversity. Another man's, I mean."

> Mark Twain [Samuel Langhorne Clemens] (1835–1910), U.S. humorist, writer and speaker, Following the Equator (1897), ch. 39

"De toutes choses ne m'est demeuré que l'honneur et la vie est sauvé." (All is lost save honor.)

> François I (1494–1547), French king, letter to his mother after his defeat at Pavia, 1525 [modern French translation: Tout est perdu fors l'honneur]

Classical Phrases and Myths

"Vae victis." (vay VIK-tus) (Woe to the vanquished.)

> Livy [Titus Livius] (59 B.C.–A.D. 17), Roman historian, History, bk. V, xlviii

◆ DEFIANCE

Foreign Words and Phrases

émeute (Fra)
(ay-moat) popular rising, insurrection, riot

Quotations

"I cannot and will not cut my conscience to fit this year's fashions."

> Lillian Hellman (1905–1984), U.S. playwright, letter to John S. Wood, chairman of the House Committee on Un-American Activities, May 19, 1952

"Nuts!"

> Anthony McAuliffe (1898–1975), U.S. general, responding to the German demand to surrender at Bastogne, Belgium, December 22, 1944

"Il nous faut de l'audace, encore l'audace, toujours de l'audace." (Audacity, more audacity, always audacity.)

> Georges Jacques Danton (1759–1794), French revolutionary leader, speech to the legislative assembly, September 2, 1792

Classical Phrases and Myths

When Alexander the Great conquered the known world, he adopted the Eastern custom of having his subjects worship him as a god. Rather than risk Alexander's wrath, the Greek cities obeyed his command and even erected temples to him. Only Sparta resisted. Alexander sent envoys to Sparta to obtain its submission. Sparta's dismissive reply was: "If Alexander wishes to be a god, let him be one."

> Alexander the Great (356 B.C.–323 B.C.), Macedonian king

Jokes, Stories and Anecdotes

Reminiscing about their wayward youth, a former hippie asked another, "Hey, were you ever picked up by the fuzz?" "No," she replied, "but I bet it would hurt."

Benjamin Disraeli's maiden speech to the House of Commons on December 7, 1837, was an eloquent response to an old adversary, Daniel O'Connell. Jeered loudly by O'Connell's supporters, Disraeli, before being forced to sit down, roared at his tormentors, "Though I sit down now, the time will come when you will hear me."

Benjamin Disraeli, 1st Earl of Beaconsfield (1804–1881), British prime minister

Although Galileo's support of Copernicus' theory that the earth revolved around the sun was declared by the Church to be heresy in 1616, Galileo published his *Dialogue on Two Chief World Systems* in 1632. Galileo was summoned to Rome. Threatened with torture, he recanted and had imposed on him a life sentence of house arrest. Rising, following his solemn renunciation of the Copernican doctrine, Galileo muttered, "*E pur si muove* (But yet it moves). The phrase has since gained currency as a statement of defiance against conservative or unwarranted beliefs.

Galileo (1564–1642), Italian astronomer and physicist [Authenticity unverified].

◆ **DEMAND**

Quotations

"I am the emperor, and I want dumplings."

Ferdinand I (1793–1875), Austrian emperor

Jokes, Stories and Anecdotes

"My grandfather fought at Lexington, my father fought at New Orleans and my husband was killed at Monterey," began a woman demanding from President Lincoln a colonel's commission for her son. "I ask for the commission not as a favor, but as a right." "I guess, madam," replied Lincoln, "your family has done enough for the country. It's time to give somebody else a chance."

Abraham Lincoln (1809–1865), U.S. president

◆ **DEMOCRACY & CAPITALISM**

Quotations

"Democracy is the power of equal votes for unequal minds."

Charles I (1600–1649), British king

"Democracy is the theory that the common people know what they want, and deserve to get it good and hard."

H[enry] L[ouis] Mencken (1880–1956), U.S. critic and writer, Little Book in C Major (1916), p. 42

"Democracy is a form of religion. It is the worship of jackals by jackasses."

H[enry] L[ouis] Mencken (1880–1956), U.S. critic and writer

"Man's capacity for justice makes democracy possible, but man's inclination to injustice makes democracy necessary."

Reinhold Niebuhr (1892–1971), U.S. theologian, Christian Realism and Political Problems (1953)

"Democracy substitutes election by the incompetent many for appointment by the corrupt few."

George Bernard Shaw (1856–1950), Irish playwright, Man and Superman (1903), "Maxims for Revolutionists: Democracy"

"Democracy is the recurrent suspicion that more than half of the people are right more than half of the time."

E[lwyn] B[rooks] White (1899–1985), U.S. humorist and writer, New Yorker (July 3, 1944)

Classical Phrases and Myths

"*Salus populi suprema est lex.*" (Sal-us POH-pu-liSUP-reem-a est lex) (The good of the people is the supreme law.)

Marcus Tullius Cicero (106 B.C.–43 B.C.), Roman statesman and man of letters, De Legibus, III, iii

◆ DEPARTURE

Foreign Words and Phrases

adieu (Fra)
(ad-YUH) goodbye (firmly)

au revoir (Fra)
(oh re-VWAR) goodbye (until we meet again)

vamoose (Spa)
(vah-MOOS) go away!

roppo (Jap)
(ROH-poh) a leaping exit in Kabuki drama

Quotations

"The government declared a state of emergency, so I obediently emerged."

Sir Thomas Beecham (1879–1961), British conductor, answering why he had left England while his country was at war

"Well, God bless you, McNulty, goddamn it."

Harold Ross (1892–1951), U.S. publisher bidding John McNulty farewell as he, like many of Ross's New Yorker writers, was lured to Hollywood

"Away, you scullion! you rampallion! you fustilarian!

I'll tickle your catastrophe."

William Shakespeare (1564–1616), British playwright and poet, Henry IV, Part II (1598), Act II, sc. i

Classical Phrases and Myths

bene decessit (Lat)
(be-ne day-KESS-it) *lit:* he has left well; conclusion that one's leaving of a situation is not due to misconduct or ill will

Jokes, Stories and Anecdotes

Georges Clemenceau, the French statesman and prime minister during World War I, was in numerous duels. In one duel with longtime political rival Paul Deschanel, each time Clemenceau lunged, Deschanel retreated further. Finally Clemenceau shrugged, tucked his sword under his arm, and commented, "Monsieur is leaving us."

Georges Clemenceau (1841–1929), French prime minister

S. N. Behrman postponed his departure and then screenwriter George S. Kaufman ran into him on the studio lot. Quipped Kaufman, "Ah, forgotten, but not gone."

George S[imon] Kaufman (1889–1961), U.S. playwright, writer and wit

◆ DESCENT

Foreign Words and Phrases

glissando (Ita)
(glee-SAHN-doh) in music, sliding between notes

Jokes, Stories and Anecdotes

There was no love lost between the actress Henrietta Hodson and librettist W. S. Gilbert, who prepared for the production of his light operas like a drill sergeant. Rehearsing for a Gilbert and Sullivan comedy, she missed her chair when sitting down, and fell heavily on the stage. An applauding Gilbert called out, "I always thought you would make an impression on the stage someday."

Sir W[illiam] S[chwenck] Gilbert (1836–1911), British writer

◆ DESIRE

Foreign Words and Phrases

grande passion (Fra)
(grohnde PASS-y-on) all-consuming love affair, overwhelming passion

coup de foudre (Fra)
(koo de FOO-dra) *lit:* flash of lightning; sudden passion or shock

Quotations

"The trouble with life is that there are so many beautiful women and so little time."

John Barrymore (1882–1942), U.S. actor

"It is with our passions as it is with fire and water, they are good servants, but bad masters."

Sir Roger L'Estrange (1616–1704), British fabulist, Fables (1692), "Reflection"

"Adam was but human—this explains it all. He did not want the apple for the apple's sake; he wanted it only because it was forbidden."

Mark Twain [Samuel Langhorne Clemens] (1835–1910), U.S. humorist, writer and speaker, Pudd'nhead Wilson (1894), ch. 2

Classical Phrases and Myths

agnosco veteris vestigia flammae (Lat)
(AG-noh-kohveh-TER-isVES-tee-

gia FLAM-mie) I feel again a spark of that ancient flame

libido (Lat)
(lib-EE-doh) *lit:* lust; sexual drive; in psychology, generally sexual impulse, but may be applied to all motivations

desideratum (Lat)
(day-SEED-er-AH-tum) something much desired or needed (plu: *desiderata*)

"We desire nothing so much as what we ought not to have."

Publilius Syrus (c. 100 B.C.), Roman writer, Sententiae, 559

Jokes, Stories and Anecdotes

The San Jose tourist visiting San Francisco was approached by a lady of the night. "I'll do anything you want—satisfy your wildest fantasies—for $75," she purred. The tourist thought for a moment and replied, "OK. Paint my house."

The Earl of Albemarle took with him on a diplomatic mission to Paris in 1748 his mistress Lolotte Gaucher, an actress known for her avarice and guile. One evening, seeing her gazing pensively at a star, he said, "It's no good, my dear, I can't buy it for you."

William Anne Keppel, 2d Earl of Albemarle (1702–1754), British soldier and diplomat

◆ DESPERATION

Foreign Words and Phrases

âme perdue (Fra)
(AHM per-DOO) *lit:* lost soul; desperate individual

Quotations

"A horse! a horse! my kingdom for a horse!"

William Shakespeare (1564–1616),
British playwright and poet,
King Richard III *(1593), Act V, sc. iv*

Tempt not a desperate man.

William Shakespeare (1564–1616),
British playwright and poet,
Romeo and Juliet *(1595), Act V, sc. iii*

The mass of men lead lives of quiet desperation.

Henry David Thoreau (1817–1862),
U.S. writer, naturalist and poet,
Walden *(1854), "Economy"*

Classical Phrases and Myths

A fox accidentally fell into a well and could not escape. To a goat who later came along, the fox cried, "To avoid the drought now coming it is best to share this water with me. It is the best water I have tasted. I have drunk so much that I can scarcely move." Hearing this, the goat jumped in the well. The fox quickly scrambled up its back and scrambled to safety. *"Look before you leap,"* the fox advised the unfortunate goat. "And *beware of the entreaties of the desperate."*

Aesop (c. 600 B.C.), Greek fabulist

◆ DEVIATION

Foreign Words and Phrases

démarche (Fra)
(DAY-marsh) step, maneuver, generally to indicate change in policy or direction

Quotations

"If you would hit the mark, you must aim a little above it;

Every arrow that flies feels the attraction of earth."

Henry Wadsworth Longfellow
(1807–1882), U.S. poet, Elegiac Verse

◆ DIFFICULTY

Quotations

"Put you in this pickle."

Miguel de Cervantes (1547–1616),
Spanish writer, Don Quixote de la Mancha, *Part I (1605), bk. I, ch. 5*

"Negotiating with [Irish politician Eamon] de Valera . . . is like trying to pick up mercury with a fork."

David Lloyd George, 1st Earl
(1863–1945), British prime minister

◆ DIPLOMACY

Foreign Words and Phrases

Machtpolitik (Ger)
(macht-POH-li-TEEK) *lit:* politics of might; theory that power dictates foreign policy and international relations

Quotations

"He looked at foreign affairs through the wrong end of a municipal drainpipe."

Sir Winston Spencer Churchill
(1874–1965), British prime minister and
writer, describing Sir Neville Chamberlain

"Diplomacy is to do and say
The nastiest thing in the nicest way."

Isaac Goldberg (1887–1938), U.S. writer

"Diplomacy: lying in state."

Oliver Herford (1863–1935), British-born U.S. humorist and illustrator

"We hear the Secretary of State boasting of his brinkmanship—the art of bringing us to the edge of the abyss."

Adlai E[wing] Stevenson (1900–1965), U.S. politician commenting on John Foster Dulles speech in Hartford, Connecticut, February 25, 1956

"A diplomat ... is a person who can tell you to go to hell in such a way that you actually look forward to the trip."

Caskie Stinnett (1911–   ), U.S. writer, Out of the Red (1960), ch. 4

"A diplomat these days is nothing but a head-waiter who's allowed to sit down occasionally."

Sir Peter [Alexander] Ustinov (1921–   ), British actor and writer, Romanoff and Juliet (1956), Act I

"I've always had a weakness for foreign affairs."

Mae West (1892–1980), U.S. film actress

◆ DIRECTION

Quotations

"Go west, young man."

John Babsone Lane Soule (1815–1902), U.S. writer, article in the Terre Haute (Indiana) Express (1851) [expression popularized by Horace Greeley in his New York Tribune]

Classical Phrases and Myths

quo vadis (Lat)
(kwo WAH-dis) where are you going? where are you heading?

Jokes, Stories and Anecdotes

Among the Germans, Berlin is considered the epitome of Prussian brusqueness and efficiency, while Vienna is the epitome of Austrian charm and laxness. There is the story that a Berliner, visiting Vienna, became lost, so he grabbed the lapel of the first passing Viennese, and barked out, "Where is the train depot?" The startled Viennese removed the other's fist, smoothed his lapel, and said gently, "Sir, it would have been more delicate if you had politely asked me, 'Sir, could you please direct me to the depot?'" The Berliner, taken aback, growled, "I'd rather be lost!" and stomped away. The Viennese later visited Berlin, and he became lost. He stopped a Berliner, and said politely, "Sir, could you please direct me to the train depot?" The Berliner barked, "About face, two blocks forward, sharp left under arch and into depot." Replied the Viennese, "Thank you, kind sir." The Berliner snatched the other's lapel and shouted, "Forget the thanks. Repeat *the instructions!*"

The actress Tallulah Bankhead bought herself a Bentley when she first became successful in London. Although she greatly enjoyed driving the automobile, she often became lost in the bewildering streets of London. She then took to hiring a taxi to lead the way, while she drove behind in the Bentley.

Tallulah Bankhead (1903–1968), U.S. actress

Field Marshal Montgomery hopped into a taxi in London and instructed the driver that his destination was Waterloo. The driver inquired, "Station?" "Of course," replied Montgomery, glancing at his watch. "We're a bit late for the battle."

> *Bernard Law Montgomery,*
> *Viscount Montgomery of Alamein*
> *(1887–1976), British general*

month, she sighed, "Promises, promises."

> *Dorothy Parker (1893–1967),*
> *U.S. wit and writer*

◆ DISAPPOINTMENT

Quotations

"Like the boy who stubbed his toe—I am too big to cry and too badly hurt to laugh."

> *Abraham Lincoln (1809–1865),*
> *U.S. president, answering how he felt*
> *after the 1858 Illinois legislature elected*
> *Stephen A. Douglas senator instead of him*

"Blessed is the man who expects nothing, for he shall never be disappointed."

> *Alexander Pope (1688–1744), British poet*
> *and writer, letter to Fortescue*
> *September 23, 1725*

Jokes, Stories and Anecdotes

The skydiving instructor reassured his student, as the student climbed out on the airplane wing at 10,000 feet, "You jump, count to 100 and pull your ripcord. If that doesn't work, pull your reserve. Once you land, a van will pick you up." The student took a breath and plunged. After free-falling, he pulled his ripcord. Nothing. He pulled his reserve. Cobwebs drifted out. "Damn," he said, shaking his head. "With my luck the van's not down there, either."

The wit Dorothy Parker was admitted to a sanatorium late in life because she would turn to the bottle when despondent. When her physician urged her to stop drinking, or she would be dead within a

◆ DISAPPROVAL

Foreign Words and Phrases

mal vu (Fra)
(mal VEW) viewed with disapproval, resented

à bas (Fra)
(ah BAH) down with!

Quotations

"[H. L.] Mencken, with his filthy verbal hemorrhages, is so low down in the moral scale, so damnably dirty, so vile and degenerate, that when his time comes to die it will take a special dispensation from Heaven to get him into the bottommost pit of Hell."

> *Anonymous editorial in* Jackson News

"There is so much good in the worst of us,
And so much bad in the best of us,
That it hardly becomes any of us
To talk about the rest of us."

> *Edward Wallis Hoch (1849–1925),*
> *U.S. politician, Good and Bad*
> *[attributed also to others]*

"People who like this sort of thing will find this the sort of thing they like."

> *Abraham Lincoln (1809–1865),*
> *U.S. president, judging a book*

" . . . nattering nabobs of negativism."

> *William Safire (1929–   ),*
> *U.S. writer*

"The critic's symbol should be the tumble-bug; he deposits his egg in somebody else's dung, otherwise he could not hatch it."

Mark Twain [Samuel Langhorne Clemens] (1835–1910), U.S. humorist, writer and speaker

"We are not amused!"

Victoria (1819–1901), British queen, seeing herself parodied by Alexander Grantham Yorke, her groom-in-waiting [other variations attributed]

Jokes, Stories and Anecdotes

A young man joined a monastery where each monk took a vow of silence, limiting conversation to two words with his superior. At the end of the first year, the young man said to his superior, "Food plain." The following year, he said, "Room cold." Another year passed and he exclaimed to his superior, "I quit!" "I'm not surprised," said the superior. "All you've done since you arrived is complain, complain, complain."

MP Bessie Braddock approached Winston Churchill after a late convivium. "Winston," she exclaimed accusingly. "You're drunk!" Drawled Churchill, "Bessie, you're ugly. And tomorrow morning I shall be sober."

Sir Winston Spencer Churchill (1874–1965), British prime minister and writer [authenticity unverified]

In the heyday of his career as an art critic, John Ruskin always maintained that it should in no way affect his friendship with an artist if he panned the artist's work. The artists, of course, saw matters in a rather different light. "Next time I meet you, I shall knock you down," one of his victims retorted, "but I trust it will make no difference to our friendship."

John Ruskin (1819–1900), British writer and social reformer

The poet and Lincoln biographer Carl Sandburg was once asked by a young playwright to attend the dress rehearsal of his new play. Sandburg slept through the performance. Afterward, the disappointed dramatist, who had badly wanted to hear the poet's opinion, scolded Sandburg. Sandburg replied, "Sleep *is* an opinion."

Carl Sandburg (1878–1967), U.S. poet and writer

Seeing a fabulous diamond ring on the actress's hand, Princess Margaret remarked to Elizabeth Taylor, "That's a bit vulgar." After persuading the princess to try on the ring, Taylor inquired, "There, it's not too vulgar now, is it?"

Elizabeth Taylor (1932–   ), U.S. film actress

After criticizing a young actor for his overbearing attitude, British actor and theater manager Sir Herbert Beerbohm Tree was informed by the conceited actor, "I assure you, sir, that I am not suffering from a swelled head." "It is not the swelling that causes suffering," Tree snapped. "It is the subsequent shrinkage which hurts."

Sir Herbert Beerbohm Tree (1853–1917), British actor and theater manager

After hearing a witty remark from painter James Whistler, the aesthete Oscar Wilde exclaimed, "I wish I had said that!" Replied Whistler, "You will, Oscar, you will."

James Abbott McNeill Whistler (1834–1903), U.S.-born British painter

◆ DISBELIEF

Foreign Words and Phrases

louche (Fra)
(loosh) cross-eyed, oblique, suspicious

Quotations

"George [Gershwin] died on July 11, 1937, but I don't have to believe that if I don't want to."

> John O'Hara (1905–1970), U.S. writer

Jokes, Stories and Anecdotes

A visitor to the eminent physicist Niels Bohr noted a horseshoe nailed to his wall. "Surely, Dr. Bohr, you don't believe in such superstition," teased the visitor. "Of course not," replied Bohr, "but I'm told it brings you luck whether you believe in it or not."

> Niels Henrik David Bohr (1885–1962), Danish physicist

◆ DISCLOSURE

Quotations

"Oh fie, Miss, you must not kiss and tell."

> William Congreve (1670–1729), British playwright, Love for Love (1695), Act I, sc. x

Classical Phrases and Myths

apocalypsis (Grk)
(ap-o-kal-IP-sis) uncovering, revelation, disclosure

Jokes, Stories and Anecdotes

Wife to husband: "I have some good news and some bad news." Husband: "What's the good news?" Wife: "The airbags work."

Having less money to support herself in the manner to which she had grown accustomed, the paramour Harriette Wilson decided around 1820 to write her memoirs and went public that she was going to name names. Several former lovers made substantial cash contributions to her to buy themselves out of the narrative, but the war hero Duke of Wellington supposedly declined the extortion by responding, "Publish and be damned!" Wilson did publish and the book was a smashing success.

> Harriette Wilson (1786–1846), British courtesan

◆ DISCOURTESY

Jokes, Stories and Anecdotes

Returning to her concert seat, the stocky society matron asked the man at the end of the row, "Pardon, did I step on your foot before?" Expecting an apology, the pain-wracked man replied, "Yes, you did." The woman smiled. "Aha, then this is my row."

The actress Ethel Barrymore had exquisite manners and expected the same from others. Once, a young actress whom she had invited to dinner not only failed to appear but did not even bother to apologize for her absence. Some time later, the two women unexpectedly ran into each other. The young woman lamely began, "I think I was invited to your house for dinner the other evening." "Oh, yes," replied Barrymore. "Did you come?"

> Ethel Barrymore (1879–1959), U.S. actress [attributed also to Beatrice Lillie]

◆ DISCOVERY

Foreign Words and Phrases

objet trouvé (Fra)
(OB-jay TROO-vay) lit: found object; beautiful or artistically valid

object that is found, not created; Surrealist theory

Quotations

"Discovery consists of seeing what everybody has seen and thinking what nobody has thought."

Albert von Nagyrapolt Szent-Gyorgyi (1893–1986), Hungarian-born U.S. scientist

Classical Phrases and Myths

The tyrant Hiero of Syracuse believed that an artisan to whom he had given a quantity of gold to shape into a crown had debased the gold with an inferior metal. Hiero therefore asked Archimedes (ark-i-MEED-eez) to prove or disprove his suspicions. The traditional story is that Archimedes, while taking a bath, noticed that the water overflowed the deeper his body was submerged, and that his body seemed to weigh less; leaping from the bath, Archimedes ran naked through the streets of Syracuse crying, "Eureka!" (I have found it!) He had conceived of Archimedes' Principle—that the apparent loss of weight of a floating body is equal to the weight of water it displaces, and that the density, or weight per volume, of a body determines its displacement. Archimedes applied his principle by submerging first the crown and then the same weights of gold and a less dense metal, and thus was able to demonstrate that the crown was indeed adulterated.

Archimedes (287 B.C.-212 B.C.), Greek mathematician and scientist

Jokes, Stories and Anecdotes

A fellow bought some "smart" pills (medication to increase intelligence) from his doctor and told him, after a week, "They're not working, and the more I take, the more I think they taste like rabbit droppings." Replied the doctor: "See? You are getting smarter."

◆ DISEASE

Quotations

"I was born eight drinks below par."

O. Henry [William Sydney Porter] (1862–1910), U.S. writer, appraising his lifelong hypoglycemic condition

Jokes, Stories and Anecdotes

"I have bad news and I have *terrible* news!" shouted the doctor into the phone. Max moaned, "Bad news and terrible news? Good Lord, give me the bad news first." "The bad news is that you've got 24 hours to live," said the physician. "Omigod! What could the *terrible* news possibly be?" Answered the doctor, "I've been calling you since yesterday!"

President Eisenhower was to attend a performance in Washington of *La Boheme* and the Secret Service men were worried about security. "We understand the girl dies," one agent asked the noted opera manager Sir Rudolph Bing. "How is she killed?" "She dies of consumption," he replied. "But it isn't contagious at a distance."

Sir Rudolf Bing (1902–   ), opera administrator

Reelected in 1946 as mayor of Boston, James Curley, known as the Purple Shamrock, and the model for Edwin O'Connor's hero-villain in *The Last Hurrah*, was convicted on fraud charges and obliged to fulfill his duties from a prison cell. He petitioned the court for his release, citing as grounds that he was suffering from 12 potentially fatal illnesses. Asked to name one, he responded, "An imminent cerebral hemorrhage."

James Michael Curley (1874–1958), U.S. politician

◆ DISHONESTY

Jokes, Stories and Anecdotes

Two lawyers were walking along negotiating a case. "Look," said one to the other, "let's be honest with each other." "OK, you first," replied the other. That was the end of the discussion.

The senior partner of a prestigious law firm was concluding the interview of the associate who was to join the ranks of the firm's partners. "So, are you an honest attorney?" he asked. "Of course," the lawyer replied. "In fact, I repaid in full my education loan from the government after my very first case." "Indeed, and which case was that?" The attorney squirmed slightly. "The government sued me for the money."

After a long talk on the politics of the day, the disgraced ex-senator was asked by the network television interviewer whether the politician would ever consider running again for his seat. "Yes." "Honestly?" the stunned broadcaster asked. "No," the pol answered. "Same as last time."

Secretary of War Simon Cameron was implicated in a scandal over the awarding of army contracts in the early 1860s, and Pennsylvania congressman Thaddeus Stevens had publicly declared that Cameron would steal anything except a red-hot stove. President Lincoln, urged by Cameron, requested that Stevens say that he had been misquoted. "Certainly, I would say that I have been misquoted," Stevens growled. "What I said actually was that Cameron would steal anything—even a red-hot stove."

Thaddeus Stevens (1792–1868), U.S. politician and lawyer

◆ DISLIKE

Foreign Words and Phrases

slizistyi (Rus) (SLEEZ-eet-yee) slimy

Quotations

"I regard you with an indifference closely bordering on aversion."

Robert Louis [Balfour] Stevenson (1850–1894), British writer and poet, New Arabian Nights (1882), "The Rajah's Diamond–Story of the Bandbox"

Classical Phrases and Myths

The Roman emperor Augustus had ordered the dismissal from his service of a young man of bad character. The man came to him and pleaded for pardon, saying, "How can I go home? What would I tell my father?" Answered Augustus, "Tell your father that you didn't find me to your liking."

Augustus [Gaius Julius Caesar Octavianus] (63 B.C.–A.D. 14), Roman emperor

Jokes, Stories and Anecdotes

Q: "What's the difference between a lawyer and an onion?" A: "You cry when you cut up an onion."

At a formal dinner, the young Winston Churchill, then sporting a mustache, and an elderly lady were arguing politics. Finally the lady said haughtily, "Young man, I care neither for your politics nor your mustache." "Madam," replied Churchill, "you are unlikely to come into contact with either."

Sir Winston Spencer Churchill (1874–1965), British prime minister and writer

Lady Nancy Astor was renowned for her acute repartee; she was reportedly bettered only once. Following a heated debate with Winston Churchill on some trivial matter, Lady Astor scornfully shouted, "If I were your wife I would put poison in your coffee." "And if I were your husband," Churchill answered, "I would drink it."

Sir Winston Spencer Churchill (1874–1965), British prime minister and writer [attributed also to others]

After Samuel Goldwyn and his rival Louis Mayer got into a shoving match in the locker room at the Hillcrest Country Club in Los Angeles, Goldwyn was chided by a friend for it. "What? We're like friends, we're like brothers. We love each other. We'd do anything for each other," replied Goldwyn, apparently sincere. "We'd even cut each other's throats for each other!"

Samuel Goldwyn [Samuel Goldfish] (1882–1974), Russian-born U.S. film producer

déraciné (Fra)
(DAY-ras-see-NAY) *lit:* uprooted; removed from (one's) natural environment

mal du pays (Fra)
(MALL doo pez) homesickness

Jokes, Stories and Anecdotes

Lost, the tycoon stopped his large and expensive car on the country road next to a farmer. "Hey, you, how far to Glenville?" Answered the farmer, "Don't know." "OK, so what's the best way to get there?" Again the farmer thought and said, "Don't know." The tycoon snapped, "You don't know much, do you?" Replied the farmer, "I'm not lost."

The old woman had lived her entire life in a little house on the North Dakota side of the North Dakota–South Dakota border. One day, the surveyors informed her that in fact she lived in South Dakota. "Whew!" she said. "I couldn't suffer another one of those damn North Dakota winters."

While painting Daniel Boone's portrait, American artist Chester Harding asked the frontiersman, then in his 80s, if he had ever been lost. "No, I can't say I was ever lost," mused Boone, "but I was bewildered once for three days."

Daniel Boone (1734–1820), U.S. frontiersman

◆ DISLOCATION

Foreign Words and Phrases

émigré (Fra)
(ay-mee-gray) exile, emigrant; (originally applied to aristocrats fleeing the French Revolution)

dépaysé (Fra)
(day-PAY-zay) beyond one's country or natural environment

◆ DISORDER (CHAOS)

Foreign Words and Phrases

fracas (Fra)
(frah-kah) a disturbance

dérangé (Fra)
(DAY-ron-JAY) disordered things, deranged person

Quotations

"There is nothing stable in the world; uproar's your only music."

> *John Keats (1795–1821), British poet, letter to G. and T. Keats, January 13, 1818*

"Confusion is a word we have invented for an order which is not understood."

> *Henry Miller (1891–1980), U.S. writer, The Tropic of Capricorn (1938), "Interlude"*

"The whole worl's in a state o' chassis!"

> *Sean O'Casey (1884–1964), Irish playwright, Juno and the Paycock (1925), Act I*

"The lunatics have taken charge of the asylum."

> *Richard Rowland (1881–1947), U.S. writer, commenting on the takeover of United Artists film studios by Charles Chaplin, Mary Pickford, Douglas Fairbanks, and D. W. Griffith*

Classical Phrases and Myths

disjecta membra (Lat)
(dis-YEK-ta MEM-bra) *lit*: scattered limbs; disordered fragments of a work or task

"*Rudis indigestaque moles.*" (An unformed and confused mass.)

> *Ovid [Publius Ovidius Naso] (43 B.C.–c. A.D. 18) Roman poet, Metamorphoses, I, 7*

◆ DISREPUTE

Foreign Words and Phrases

demi monde (Fra)
(DEM-ee MOHND) *lit*: half-world; class peripheral to society, those of questionable reputation

Quotations

"I hate the man who builds his name
On ruins of another's fame."

> *John Gay (1685–1732), British poet and playwright, Fables, Part I (1727), "The Poet and the Rose"*

"Damn with faint praise, assent with civil leer,
And, without sneering, teach the rest to sneer."

> *Alexander Pope (1688–1744), British poet and writer, Epistles and Satires of Horace Imitated (1734), Prologue, Epistle to Dr. Arbuthnot, l. 193*

"His passion still, to covet general praise,
His life, to forfeit it a thousand ways."

> *Alexander Pope (1688–1744), British poet and writer, describing the Duke of Wharton*

◆ DISRESPECT

Foreign Words and Phrases

demi mondaine (Fra)
(DEM-ee MOHND-en) woman (person) who lives on the fringe of society or is of doubtful repute

Quotations

"Posterity will ne'er survey
A nobler grave than this:
Here lie the bones of Castlereagh
Stop, traveller, and piss."

> *George Gordon, Lord Byron (1788–1824), British poet*

"Don't look at me, Sir, with that tone of voice."

> *Punch, (1884), vol. LXXXVII, p. 38*

Jokes, Stories and Anecdotes

Once an unidentified man approached writer Hilaire Belloc, saying, "You don't know me." Belloc, a master of insult, replied, "Yes, I do," turned on his heel, and walked off.

[Joseph] Hilaire [Pierre] Belloc (1870–1953), British writer

Although the German composer Johannes Brahms could be agreeable, he could also launch into unprovoked attacks of sarcasm and rudeness, even at his friends. Once he upset a gathering with his difficult behavior, rose and left the room, stopping at the door merely to say, "If there is anyone here whom I have not insulted, I beg his pardon."

Johannes Brahms (1833–1897), German composer

"Here I am between wit and beauty," exclaimed a foppish young bore at a dinner party, seated between French writer Mme. de Stae I and a beautiful woman. "Quite so," Mme. de Stae I sneered, "and without possessing either."

Anne Louise Germaine, Baronne de Stae I (1766–1817), French writer

---

◆ DISSENT

Quotations

"Raise a hue and cry."

Miguel de Cervantes (1547–1616), Spanish writer, Don Quixote de la Mancha, Part I (1605), bk. III, ch. 8

"Sometimes a scream is better than a thesis."

Ralph Waldo Emerson (1803–1892), U.S. writer, poet and philosopher, Journals (1836)

"In a democracy dissent is an act of faith. Like medicine, the test of its value is not in its taste, but its effects."

J[ames] William Fulbright (1905–   ), U.S. politician

"I disagree with you entirely. What was it you said?"

Anthony Trollope (1815–1882), British writer, challenging the prior speaker at a surveyors' meeting

"It were not best that we should all think alike; it is difference of opinion that makes horse races."

Mark Twain [Samuel Langhorne Clemens] (1835–1910), U.S. humorist, writer and speaker, Pudd'nhead Wilson (1894), ch. 19

"The rule is perfect: in all matters of opinion our adversaries are insane."

Mark Twain [Samuel Langhorne Clemens] (1835–1910), U.S. humorist, writer and speaker

"It is dangerous to be right in matters on which the established authorities are wrong."

Voltaire [François Marie Arouet] (1694–1778), French philosopher, writer and wit

Classical Phrases and Myths

non placet (Lat)
(nohn PLAK-et) *lit:* it does not please (me); statement of a negative vote

---

◆ DISSUASION

Jokes, Stories and Anecdotes

There was the woman who became so disturbed with everything she read about the connection between smoking and cancer that she finally gave up reading.

In violent disagreement with an opinion expressed by poet and critic Lascelles Abercrombie, Ezra Pound wrote to him, "Stupidity carried beyond a certain point becomes a public menace. I hereby challenge you to a duel, to be fought at the earliest moment that is suited to your convenience . . . " Abercrombie was naturally disturbed by the challenge, and aware of Pound's skill at fencing, but with relief he remembered that the choice of weapons lay with the party challenged. "May I suggest," he replied, "that we bombard each other with unsold copies of our own books?" Since Pound had far more "weapons" than his opponent, he withdrew his challenge.

Lascelles Abercrombie (1881–1938), British poet and critic

Political reformer and heralded pathologist Rudolf Virchow so antagonized German Chancellor Otto von Bismarck that Bismarck challenged him to a duel. "As the challenged party, I choose the weapons," replied Virchow to Bismarck's messenger, "and I choose these." He displayed two seemingly identical sausages. He added, "One of these is infected with deadly germs. The other is perfectly fine. Let His Excellency choose which one he shall eat, and I shall eat the other." The chancellor called off the duel.

Rudolf Virchow (1821–1902), German pathologist and politician

---

◆ DIVORCE & SEPARATION

Quotations

"It was partially my fault that we got divorced. . . . I tended to place my wife under a pedestal."

Woody Allen [Allen Stewart Konigsberg] (1935–   ), U.S. comedian and filmmaker, Chicago nightclub, March 1964

"You never realize how short a month is until you pay alimony."

John Barrymore (1882–1942), U.S. actor

"Judges, as a class, display, in the matter of arranging alimony, that reckless generosity which is found only in men who are giving away someone else's cash."

P[elham] G[renville] Wodehouse (1881–1975), British writer and humorist

Jokes, Stories and Anecdotes

The actress and novelist Ilka Chase happened to find a packet of visiting cards engraved with the name "Mrs. Louis Calhern" while going through her things. This occurred soon after her just-divorced husband Louis Calhern had married Julia Hoyt. Disinclined to waste the cards, Chase mailed them to her successor with a note: "Dear Julia, I hope these reach you in time."

Ilka Chase (1903–1978), U.S. actress, writer and playwright

Pioneering sexologists William Masters and Virginia Johnson agreed to divorce after 21 years of marriage and 35 years of research on orgasm, impotence and sexual dysfunction, and co-writing *Human Sexual Response*. Asked for comment, William Young, director of the Masters and Johnson Institute, said, "I'm sure people will say, 'If these two people can't get along, who can?'"

William Howell Masters (1915–   ) and Virginia Johnson (1925–   ), U.S. physicians

◆ DOMINATION & SUBMISSION

Quotations

"There is an old political adage which says 'If you can't lick 'em, jine 'em.'"

> Quentin Reynolds (1902–1965),
> British writer, Wounded Don't Cry
> (1941), ch. 1

Classical Phrases and Myths

testibus prehende, cortis sequentur et mentis (Lat)
(TES-tee-bus preh-HEND-e KOR-tis SEK-wi-tur et MEN-tis) when you grab them by the balls, their hearts and minds will follow

Aristippus, the Greek philosopher who advocated hedonism, had insinuated himself into the court of Dionysius, tyrant of Syracuse, with assiduous flattery. Aristippus once came upon Diogenes the Cynic while Diogenes was washing lentils before making the soup that was the main article of his diet. Aristippus said, "Oh, Diogenes, if you could but learn to flatter Dionysius, you would not have to live on lentils." And Diogenes answered, "Oh Aristippus, if you could but learn to live on lentils, you would not have to flatter Dionysius."

> Diogenes (c. 412 B.C.–323 B.C.),
> Greek philosopher

Jokes, Stories and Anecdotes

Future president Lyndon Johnson was a driving taskmaster as Senate majority leader. Working hard and late, one senator wearily complained to another, "What's the hurry? Rome wasn't built in a day." The reply: "No, but Lyndon wasn't foreman on that job."

> Lyndon Baines Johnson (1908–1973),
> U.S. president

Soviet Foreign Minister Vyacheslav Molotov was overhead talking to Stalin by telephone. Molotov kept repeating, "Yes, Comrade Stalin. Yes, comrade." Then his tone changed. "No, comrade. No." Astonished at hearing Molotov dare disobedience, someone asked, after Molotov hung up, "What did Stalin say that caused you to reply 'no'?" "He asked me if there was anything he said which I disagreed with."

> Vyascheslav Molotov (1890–1986),
> Soviet diplomat [authenticity unverified]

◆ DRAMA

Foreign Words and Phrases

Lehrstiick (Ger)
(LAYR-shtook) lit: oral tale; form of theater, championed by Bertolt Brecht in the 1930s, the intention of which was primarily to instruct the performer rather than entertain or instruct the audience

coup de théâtre (Fra)
(koo de tay-AHT-ra) dramatically sudden act, sensational occurrence, or stage trick performed for effect

Quotations

"Don't look now, but your show's slipping."

> Heywood Broun (1888–1939),
> U.S. writer, remarking to Tallulah
> Bankhead [authenticity unverified]

"An actor is something less than a man, while an actress is something more than a woman."

Richard Burton (1925–1984), British actor

"I understand that your play is full of single entendres."

George S[imon] Kaufman (1889–1961), U.S. playwright, writer and wit, commenting to the author of a panned Broadway play

"The bad end unhappily, the good unluckily. That is what tragedy means."

Tom Stoppard (1937–   ), British playwright and writer, Rosencrantz and Guildenstern Are Dead *(1967), Act II*

Jokes, Stories and Anecdotes

When too many members of the audience began coughing during his performance, an irate John Barrymore sent out for a fish during intermission. "Busy yourself with that, you damned walruses," he cried, throwing the fish from the stage at his tormentors, "and let the rest of us proceed with the play."

John Barrymore (1882–1942), U.S. actor [authenticity unverified]

Rachel rose from being an itinerant Jewish peddler's daughter to become the leading tragedienne at the Comédie-Française. "Goodness!" she once boasted after a successful new debut. "When I came out onstage, the audience sat there simply openmouthed." "Nonsense!" sneered another actress. "They never all yawn at once."

Rachel [Élisa Fèlix], (1820–1858), French actress

Ada Rehan was once in a romantic comedy playing opposite a young, inexperienced actor. In one scene his character was to ask hers an important question, and before the delayed answer, his next line was to be: "You don't reply." But the young actor forgot his line. "You don't reply . . . you don't reply," instructed a loud whisper from offstage. Responded the exasperated young actor, "How the hell can I when I don't know what to say?"

Ada Rehan (1860–1916), Irish-born U.S. actress

◆ DREAM

Quotations

"I do not know whether I was then a man dreaming I was a butterfly, or whether I am a butterfly dreaming I was a man."

Chuang-Tzu (369 B.C.–286 B.C.), Chinese philosopher, On Leveling All Things

Jokes, Stories and Anecdotes

It was an unwritten rule that Jack Warner, co-founder of Warner Brothers, was not to be disturbed during his habitual afternoon nap at his office. Bette Davis once raged into his office, however, complaining about a certain script. Warner, eyes shut fast, reached for the phone and called his secretary: "Come quickly and wake me up. I'm having a nightmare." The laughing Bette Davis and Warner Brothers resolved the crisis.

Jack Warner (1892–1978), U.S. film producer

◆ DRINKING

Foreign Words and Phrases

Brau (Ger)
(brow) brew

c'est la même chose de coleur (Fra)
(seh la mehm chose de koh-LUHR)
drinks on the house

pineau (Fra)
(PEEN-o) cheap wine

ube hoch (Ger)
(OOH-be HOACH) to your health!
cheers!

Quotations

"If all be true that I do think,
There are five reasons we should
drink;
Good wine—a friend—or being
dry—
Or lest we should be by and by—
Or any other reason why."

Henry Aldrich (1648–1710), British poet

"One evening in October, when I
was one-third sober,
An' taking home a 'load' with
manly pride;
My poor feet began to stutter, so I
lay down in the gutter,
And a pig came up an' lay down
by my side;
Then we sang 'It's all fair weather
when good fellows get together,'
Till a lady passing by was heard to
say:
'You can tell a man who "boozes"
by the company he chooses'
And the pig got up and slowly
walked away."

Benjamin Hapgood Burt (1880–1950),
U.S. songwriter, The Pig Got Up and
Slowly Walked Away (1933 song)

"Alcohol is like love: the first kiss
is magic, the second is intimate, the
third is routine. After that you just
take the girl's clothes off."

Raymond Chandler (1888–1959),
U.S. writer

"Always remember, Clemmie, that
I have taken more out of alcohol
than alcohol has taken out of
me."

Sir Winston Spencer Churchill (1874–
1965), British prime minister and writer

"I always keep a supply of stimulant handy in case I see a snake—
which I also keep handy."

W. C. Fields [William Claude Dukenfield]
(1879–1946), U.S. film actor
and comedian

"One of the disadvantages of wine
is that it makes a man mistake
words for thoughts."

Samuel Johnson (1709–1784),
British man of letters

"You're not drunk if you can lie on
the floor without holding on."

Dean Martin (1917–   ),
U.S. singer and actor

"A torchlight procession marching
down your throat."

John Louis O'Sullivan (1813–1895),
U.S. politician, describing whiskey

"One more drink and I'd have been
under the host."

Dorothy Parker (1893–1967),
U.S. wit and writer

"'Tis not the drinking that is to be
blamed, but the excess."

John Selden (1584–1654), British jurist
and scholar, Table Talk (1892), "Law"

"He'll probably never write a good
play again."

George Bernard Shaw (1856–1950),
Irish playwright, learning that playwright
Eugene O'Neill had given up drinking
[authenticity unverified]

"But I'm not so think as you drunk
I am."

Sir John Collings Squire (1884–1958),
British poet and writer

Classical Phrases and Myths

delirium tremens (Lat)
(day-LEE-ree-um TRE-inens) alco-

holic distress, with delusions and trembling

"What soberness conceals, drunkeness reveals." Latin proverb

"In vino veritas." (in WEE-no WER-ee-tas) (In wine is truth.)

> Pliny the Elder [Gaius Plinius Secundus] (23–79), Roman writer and scientist, Historia Naturalis, bk. XIV, cxli [Pliny wrote: "Vulgoque veritas iam attributa vino est." (Now truth is commonly said to be in wine)]

According to classical mythology, Bacchus (Bak-us) was the god of wine, and Bacchanalia was the festival devoted to him. Hence *bacchic* or *bacchanalian* refers to riotous behavior, or a tendency to indulge in drunken revelry.

The Roman orator and statesman Cicero (SIS-e-roh) was dining with a friend when his host proudly offered a bottle of wine, saying, "Try this Falernian. It's 40 years old." Cicero tasted the mediocre wine, remarking, "Young for its age."

> Marcus Tullius Cicero (106 B.C.–43 B.C.), Roman statesman and man of letters

Jokes, Stories and Anecdotes

[An alcoholic is] a man you don't like who drinks as much as you do.

> Dylan [Marlais] Thomas (1914–1953), British poet and writer

Asked about his attitude toward whiskey, a congressman reportedly replied, "If you mean the demon drink that poisons the mind, pollutes the body, desecrates family life, and inflames sinners, then I'm against it. But if you mean the elixir of Christmas cheer, the shield against winter chill, the taxable potion that puts needed funds into public coffers to comfort little crippled children, then I'm for it. This is my position, and I will not compromise."

After banging on it all night, the unsteady drunk fumbled at the door, trying to open it. The commotion awakened his wife, who opened the upstairs window and shouted, "Don't you have your key?" "Yeah, I have the damn key," he yelled. "Send down the damn keyhole!"

"Don't you know alcohol is slow poison?" a friend once scolded humorist Robert Benchley. Benchley replied, "So who's in a hurry?"

> Robert Charles Benchley (1889–1945), U.S. humorist

Drenched in a sudden thundershower, journalist and novelist Heywood Broun ran into the nearest bar for refuge. He ordered a glass of wine to warm himself and, drinking it despite his distate for it, he remarked, "Oh well, any port in a storm."

> Heywood Broun (1888–1939), U.S. writer [authenticity unverified]

One-time Secretary of State William Evarts, a bon vivant, was once asked whether drinking many different wines had caused him to feel ill the following day. "Not at all, madam," he replied, "it's the indifferent wines that produce that result."

> William Maxwell Evarts (1818–1901), U.S. lawyer and statesman

Eager to help film comedian W. C. Fields recover from a hangover, a waiter solicituously inquired, "Can I fix you a Bromo-Seltzer, sir?" "Ye gods, no," moaned Fields, "I can't stand the noise."

> W. C. Fields [William Claude Dukenfield] (1879–1946), U.S. film actor and comedian

The sardonic Ring Lardner and Arthur Jacks once shared a hotel room which they had stocked with liquor, including good Canadian whiskey and some rotgut Kentucky corn. The following morning, after an evening of heavy drinking, Jacks awoke with a hangover. Using the spurious remedy of another drink, he poured himself a glass of the Canadian whiskey. He became sick, poured another and again became sick. After another unsuccessful attempt to keep the liquor down, Lardner cocked an eye and asked, "If you're just practicing, Arthur, would you use the corn?"

> *Ring [Ringgold Wilmer] Lardner*
> *(1885–1933), U.S. writer*

Comic Marty Brill, striking up a conversation with legendary imbiber Dean Martin, asked the singer why he drank so much. "I drink to forget." "That's sad." "It could be a lot sadder," replied Martin. "What could be sadder than drinking to forget?" asked Brill. "Forgetting to drink."

> *Dean Martin (1917–),*
> *U.S. singer and actor*

◆ DRUGS

Quotations

"I'll die young, but it's like kissing God."

> *Lenny Bruce [Leonard Alfred Schneider]*
> *(1925–1966), U.S. comedian commenting*
> *on taking drugs (heroin)*

"The only reason that cocaine is such a rage today is that people are too dumb and lazy to get themselves together to roll a joint."

> *Jack Nicholson (1937–),*
> *U.S. film actor*

◆ DUPE

Foreign Words and Phrases

schnook (Yid)
(shnook) one who is (has been) easily deceived, a pitiful person

Quotations

"Never give a sucker an even break."

> *Edward Francis Albee (1857–1930),*
> *U.S. writer [attributed also*
> *to W. C. Fields]*

"There's a sucker born every minute."

> *P[hineas] T[aylor] Barnum (1810–1891),*
> *U.S. showman*

"There are more fools than knaves in the world, else the knaves would not have enough to live upon."

> *Samuel Butler (1835–1902), British writer*

"It is in the ability to deceive oneself that one shows the greatest talent."

> *Anatole France [Jacques-Anatole-François*
> *Thibault] (1844–1924),*
> *French writer and poet*

"The true way to be deceived is to believe oneself more clever than others."

> *François, Duc de La Rochefoucauld*
> *(1613–1680), French writer,*
> *Maximes (1678), 127*

Jokes, Stories and Anecdotes

"Oh, you go ahead, John," said Mary to her husband. "The cleaners are late getting my costume." So John went on alone to the masquerade party. Tired of waiting, she instead got out a duchess costume. She gaily realized that her husband would not recognize her, because he was expecting to see her as a bunny. She would be able to observe how he behaved when he thought she was absent. At the masquerade, she had no trouble locating him. A half dozen woman were around him in his gorilla outfit. Furious, Mary sidled up to him and nibbled on his ear. It merely enraged her further when he quickly responded. She led him into the garden, determined to see how far he would go with an unknown, but willing, woman. After sex, she came home furious, waiting for her husband to appear. Eventually, John returned home, with his gorilla costume slung over his shoulder. "Where were you?" he asked. "Never mind me," she hissed. "What about you?" "Me?' said John. "Oh, I got sick so I lent my costume to Bob. He kept bragging about his evening of sex."

◆ DURABILITY & SURVIVAL

Quotations

"One can survive anything these days except death."

> Oscar [Fingal O'Flahertie Wills] Wilde
> (1854–1900), British playwright,
> writer and wit

"J'ai vécu." (jay VAY-ku) (I survived.)

> Emmanuel Joseph, Comte Sieyè s
> (1748–1836), French revolutionary,
> answering what he had done during the
> bloody Reign of Terror

Classical Phrases and Myths

A tortoise, at whom a hare had continually poked fun for its slowness, was finally goaded into challenging the hare to a foot race. When the fox barked the start of the race, the hare bounded rapidly out

of sight while the tortoise plodded along at its usual unhurried pace. The hare, waiting further along the course to jeer at the tortoise, decided to take a quick nap, confident that it could win the race later. Meanwhile, the tortoise plodded on, passed the sleeping hare and approached the finish line. The hare awoke with a start but could not catch up—*slow and steady wins the race.*

> Aesop (c. 600 B.C.), Greek fabulist

◆ DUTY

Quotations

"It is my duty, and I will . . . It was their duty, and they did."

> Sir W[illiam] S[chwenck] Gilbert
> (1836–1911), British writer, The "Bab"
> Ballads (1866–1871), "Captain Reece"

"I ought, therefore I can."

> Immanuel Kant (1724–1804),
> German philosopher [authenticity
> unverified; a play on Descartes's
> "I think, therefore I am"]

"When a stupid man is doing something he is ashamed of, he always declares that it is his duty."

> George Bernard Shaw (1856–1950),
> Irish playwright, Caesar and Cleopatra
> (1901), Act III

Classical Phrases and Myths

The model leader Hadrian was once approached by a woman with a petition. Informing her that he was too occupied, he brushed her aside. She angrily exclaimed, "Then cease to be emperor." He heard her petition.

> Hadrian (76–138), Roman emperor

Jokes, Stories and Anecdotes

The German musician Baron von Bulow, who championed both Wagner and Brahms, was once invited to play for Napoleon III. When the emperor soon became inattentive to the music and instead began talking animatedly to a guest, von Bulow stopped playing. "When his majesty speaks," he said, hiding his annoyance as best he could, "all must be silent."

> *Hans Guido, Baron von Bulow (1830–1894), German conductor and pianist*

◆ DYING

Quotations

"Why fear death? It is the most beautiful adventure in life."

> *Charles Frohman (1860–1915), U.S. actor, dying words before going down on the Lusitania*

"Gentlemen, I am so sorry for keeping you waiting like this. I am unable to concentrate."

> *George V (1865–1936), British king, speaking on his deathbed*

"I never thought I'd live to see the day."

> *Samuel Goldwyn [Samuel Goldfish] (1882–1974), Russian-born U.S. film producer, dying words (coined by Clifton Fadiman)*

"If Mr. Selwyn calls again, show him up. If I am alive, I shall be delighted to see him, and if I am dead, he would like to see me."

> *Henry Fox Holland, 1st Baron (1705–1774), British statesman, dying words for British politician and wit George Selwyn*

"My exit is the result of too many entrees."

> *Richard Monckton Milnes, 1st Baron Houghton (1809–1885), British writer politician and epicure, dying words*

"Why should I talk to you? I've just been talking to your boss."

> *Wilson Mizner (1876–1933), U.S. writer and wit, waving away a priest on his deathbed, after awakening briefly from a coma*

"Everybody has got to die, but I have always believed an exception would be made in my case. Now what?"

> *William Saroyan (1908–1981), U.S. writer, phoning the Associated Press preceding his death*

"I am dying beyond my means."

> *Oscar [Fingal O'Flahertie Wills] Wilde (1854–1900), British playwright, writer and wit, dying words as he drank champagne, though impoverished [authenticity unverified; in another version, this remark is made when a fee for an operation is mentioned]*

"Dieu me pardonnera. C'est son métier." (God will pardon me. It is His trade.)

> *Henrich Heine (1797–1856), German poet and writer, dying words*

Classical Phrases and Myths

"The hour of departure has arrived, and we go our ways—I to die, and you to live. Which is the better, God only knows."

> *Socrates (469 B.C.–399 B.C.), Greek philosopher [in Plato's Apologia these are Socrates' last words; Socrates' last words in Plato's Phaedo are: "Crito, we owe a cock to Aesculapius; pay it, therefore, and do not neglect it"]*

Jokes, Stories and Anecdotes

The Marchese d'Azeglio's second marriage to Luisa Blondel ended in separation. But in 1866, upon learning that Azeglio was dying, Blondel rushed to his deathbed. "Ah, Luisa," sighed Azeglio, "You always arrive just as I'm leaving."

> Massimo Taparelli, Marchese d'Azeglio (1798–1866), Italian statesman and writer

"Cheer up, Your Majesty, you will soon be at Bognor again," assured a doctor attending to George V on his deathbed, referring to the king's preferred seaside resort of Bognor Regis on the south coast of England. The king said, "Bugger Bognor," and died.

> George V (1865–1936), British king [statement may also have been made in 1929]

A lamp was accidentally overturned adjacent to Henry Labouchere's deathbed on the day before he died. Labouchere opened his eyes and laughed, "Flames? Not yet, I think."

> Henry Labouchere (1831–1912), British politician and writer

The mistress of Louis XV lay dying. Gathering her strength, Mme de Pompadour shouted to God, "Wait a moment," as she dabbed her cheeks with rouge.

> Jeanne-Antoinette Poisson Pompadour, Marquise d'Étoiles (1721–1764), French courtier

◆ EAGERNESS

Foreign Words and Phrases

recherché (Fra)
(re-sher-SHAY) in great demand, affected, refined

aficionado (Spa)
(ah-fee-SEE-oh-NAH-doh) *lit*: amateur; enthusiast, devotee

gung ho (Chi)
(gung hoh) *lit*: work together; (excessively) enthusiastic, loyal

dilettante (Ita)
(deel-eh-TAN-tay) *lit*: amateur; lover of the arts; one who approaches subjects in a trifling manner

Quotations

"There are few more impressive sights in the world than a Scotsman on the make."

> Sir J[ames] M[atthew] Barrie (1860–1937), British writer and playwright, What Every Woman Knows (1918), Act 1

"Worth seeing? yes; but not worth going to see."

> Samuel Johnson (1709–1784), British man of letters, replying to Boswell's question, "Is not the Giant's Causeway worth seeing?"

"Why, then the world's mine oyster,
Which I with sword will open."

> William Shakespeare (1564–1616), British playwright and poet, The Merry Wives of Windsor (1601), Act II, sc. ii

Classical Phrases and Myths

perfervidum ingenium (Lat)
(per-fer-WID-um in-GEN-ium) extreme ardour or enthusiasm

"*Audax ornnia perpeti Gens humana ruit per vetitum nefas.*" (In its boldness to bear and to dare all things, the race of man rushes headlong into sin, despite law.)

> Horace (65 B.C.–B.C.), Roman poet, Odes, I. iii, l. 25

◆ EATING

Foreign Words and Phrases

gourmet (Fra)
(GOOR-may) *lit*: winetaster; connoisseur of wines, food, etc.

nosh (Yid)
(nosh) (to) snack

bon appétit (Fra)
(bon AP-eh-tee) have a good appetite; *fig:* enjoy your meal

Quotations

"He hath eaten me out of house and home."

> William Shakespeare (1564–1616),
> British playwright and poet, Henry IV,
> Part II (1598), Act II, sc. i

"*Le mejor salsa del mundo es el hambre.*" (la me-HOR SAL-sa del MOON-doh es el am-BRAY) (The best sauce in the world is hunger.)

> Miguel de Cervantes (1547–1616),
> Spanish writer, Don Quixote de la
> Mancha, Part II (1615), ch. 5

"*Il faut manger pour vivre et non pas vivre pour manger.*" (One should eat to live, not live to eat.)

> Molière [Jean Baptiste Poquelin]
> (1622–1673), French playwright,
> L'Avare (1668), Act III, sc. v

"*L'appetit vient en mangeant.*" (The appetite grows by eating.)

> François Rabelais (c. 1494–1553),
> French scholar, physician and writer,
> Gargantua and Pantagruel (1532), ch. 5

Classical Phrases and Myths

"It is a difficult matter, my fellow citizens, to argue with the belly, since it has no ears."

> Marcus Porcius Cato [the Elder]
> (234 B.C.–149 B.C.), Roman statesman

Jokes, Stories and Anecdotes

Said one cannibal to the other, "You know, I really can't stand my wife." "To hell with her, then," said the other, "eat the noodles."

Sylvia Llewelyn-Davies scolded her young son, "You'll be sick tomorrow, Jack, if you eat any more chocolates." Dismissing the warning, Jack said, "I shall be sick tonight," and grabbed a handful. Overhearing the two, Sir James Barrie was so pleased with the quip that he incorporated it in *Peter Pan* and paid the young Llewelyn-Davies a copyright fee of a halfpenny a performance.

> Sir J[ames] M[atthew] Barrie
> (1860–1937), British writer
> and playwright

At a dinner party, the vegetarian playwright George Bernard Shaw had been served a special plate of salad greens with dressing. Sir James Barrie, who was seated next to Shaw, eyed the unpleasant-looking dish and whispered to Shaw, "Tell me, have you already eaten that or are you just starting?"

> Sir J[ames] M[atthew] Barrie
> (1860–1937), British writer
> and playwright

The Wagnerian contralto Ernestine Schumann-Heink loved food, and had the ample girth to prove it. She was dining at a restaurant when tenor Enrico Caruso entered. Seeing her ready to begin on a huge steak, he asked, "Surely you are not going to eat that alone?" "Oh, no, not alone," she responded, "mit potatoes."

> Ernestine Schumann-Heink (1861–1936),
> German opera singer

◆ ECCENTRICITY

Jokes, Stories and Anecdotes

The eccentric poet and writer Gérard de Nerval, who suffered bouts of insanity before finally hanging himself, once walked in the gardens of the Palais-Royal in Paris trailing a blue ribbon. At the end of this leash was a lobster, which, he explained, was less extravagant than a dog, cat or tame lion, none of which could match the lobster's quiet, gravity and knowledge of the secrets of the sea. On another occasion, the journalist Paul Meurice was startled one night when he saw Nerval, by lighted candle, picking snails in his garden and carefully placing them on his prized rose bushes.

Gérard de Nerval (1808–1855),
French poet and playwright

◆ ECONOMIST

Quotations

"If all economists were laid end to end, they would not reach a conclusion."

George Bernard Shaw (1856–1950),
Irish playwright

"All my economists say, 'on the one hand . . . on the other.' Give me a one-handed economist!"

Harry S. Truman (1884–1972),
U.S. president

Jokes, Stories and Anecdotes

"Why did you negotiate so fiercely about the price?" asked the young wheeler-dealer. "You don't intend to pay his bill anyway." "But I'm a nice guy," replied his mentor. "I don't want him to lose more than is necessary."

◆ EFFORT

Foreign Words and Phrases

coup d'essai (Fra)
(koo des-SAY) first attempt

nintendo (Jap)
(niyn-TEN-doh) work hard, but in the end it is in heaven's hands

Classical Phrases and Myths

"Nil mortalibus ardui est." (No height is too arduous for mortal men.)

Horace (65 B.C.–8 B.C.), Roman poet,
Odes, I, i, l. 37

Jokes, Stories and Anecdotes

While traveling on a tour of America, the British writer Oscar Wilde observed a notice posted above a saloon piano in the rowdy mining town of Leadville, Colorado. It read: "Please don't shoot the pianist. He is doing his best."

◆ ELDERLY

Quotations

"To me old age is always fifteen years older than I am."

Bernard Mannes Baruch (1870–1965),
U.S. financier and statesman

"[James O'Hara] Tyrawley and I have been dead these two years; but we do not choose to have it known."

Philip Dormer Stanhope, 4th Earl of
Chesterfield (1694–1773),
British statesman and writer, referring
to the despair of both in their last years

"When one has reached 81 . . . one likes to sit back and let the world turn by itself, without trying to push it."

Sean O'Casey (1884–1964),
Irish playwright

"An old man gives good advice to console himself for no longer being able to set a bad example."

François, Duc de La Rochefoucauld (1613–1680), French writer, Maximes (1678), 93

Classical Phrases and Myths

In Greek legend and in Homer's *Iliad*, Nestor was a friend of Herakles and performed feats in his youth that he later used in counseling Agamemnon and the Greeks in the Trojan War. As the oldest and wisest of the Greeks in the Trojan War, he was noted for "words flowing from his smooth tongue sweeter than honey." Hence, a *Nestor* is any wise old man or elder statesman.

Jokes, Stories and Anecdotes

Said the sage, "You know you're old when it takes you all night to do what you used to do all night long."

Maurice Chevalier, the famous French singer, was asked how he felt about advancing years on his 72nd birthday. "Considering the alternative," he said, "it's not too bad at all."

Maurice Chevalier (1888–1972), French singer and actor

An admirer gushed to the elderly novelist Alexandre Dumas, "How do you grow old so gracefully?" "Madame, I give all my time to it."

Alexandre [pere] Dumas (1802–1870), French writer and playwright

Oliver Wendell Holmes, Jr., an eminent Supreme Court Justice, in his late 80s, was out walking with another elderly friend. A pretty girl passed by. The judge turned to watch her and then sighed, "Oh, to be 75 again!"

Oliver Wendell Holmes, Jr. (1841–1935), U.S. jurist

Asked at the age of 88 how he felt upon getting up in the morning, Ludwig von Mises replied, "Amazed."

Ludwig von Mises (1881–1973), Austrian economist

◆ EMBARRASSMENT (HUMILIATION)

Foreign Words and Phrases

désagrément (Fra) (DAY-zag-ray-MON)   embarrassment, unpleasantness

Quotations

"Man is the Only Animal that Blushes. Or needs to."

Mark Twain [Samuel Langhorne Clemens] (1835–1910), U.S. humorist, writer and speaker, Following the Equator (1897), ch. 27

Jokes, Stories and Anecdotes

Comedian George Burns once reproached Ed Sullivan after he disclosed the embarrassing fact that Burns wore a toupee. "But George," protested Sullivan, "I didn't think you would mind." "If I didn't mind," pointed out Burns, "why would I wear a toupee?"

George Burns [Nathan Birnbaum] (1896–   ), U.S. comedian and actor

The French diplomat Talleyrand disapproved of Napoleon's invasion of Spain and Portugal. On January 28, 1809, an enraged Napoleon gave Talleyrand one of history's most infamous dressings down in the crudest language in front of his other ministers, ending by shouting, *"Tenez, vous êtes de la merde dans un bas de soie."* (You're shit in a silk stocking) Talleyrand, silent during the verbal attack, only remarked as he left the council chamber, "What a pity such a great man should be so ill-bred!"

> *Charles Maurice de Talleyrand-Périgord (1754–1838), French diplomat*

◆ EMPIRE

Foreign Words and Phrases

Reich (Ger)
(rike) empire, nation (Hitler's regime titled the Third Reich)

Quotations

"He who rides a tiger is afraid to dismount."

> *Chinese proverb*

"A man may build himself a throne of bayonets, but he cannot sit on it."

> *William Ralph Inge (1860–1954), British clergyman*

"All empires die of indigestion."

> *Napoleon I [Napoleon Bonaparte] (1769–1821), French general and emperor*

"We [the English] seem, as it were, to have conquered and peopled half the world in a fit of absence of mind."

> *Sir John Robert Seeley (1831–1896), British scholar and historian, The Expansion of England, lecture I*

◆ EMPLOYEE (SUBORDINATE)

Jokes, Stories and Anecdotes

"So, can you handle a variety of work?" asked the interviewer. "I should be able to," responded the young lady. "I've had six different jobs in four months."

An arriviste in Berlin was guiding his guest, the German renaissance man Ernst Hoffman through his lavish home. The wealthy man airily mentioned that he required for his personal needs three servants. Hoffmann countered that, just to handle his bath, he required four attendants: one to lay out the towels, another to test the water's temperature and yet another to ensure that the faucets were functioning properly. "And the fourth?" "Ah, he's most important—he takes my bath for me."

> *Ernst Theodor Wilhelm Hoffmann (1776–1822), German writer, composer and impressario*

A servant of J. P. Morgan, known for his enterprise, decided to retire, and notified his employer. Morgan asked him to locate a suitable replacement before leaving. The next day, the servant presented Morgan with two candidates, of whom Morgan selected one. Said the servant, "And I'll take the other, Mr. Morgan."

> *John Pierpont Morgan, Jr. (1867–1943), U.S. banker*

◆ END

Foreign Words and Phrases

finale (Fra)
(fee-NAL) concluding part of a piece

Quotations

"This is not the end. It is not even the beginning of the end. But it is, perhaps, the end of the beginning."

Sir Winston Spencer Churchill (1874–1965), British prime minister and writer, describing the Battle of Egypt, speech at the Mansion House, November 10, 1942

"*Voilà le commencement de la fin.*" (vwah-LAH le koh-MONS-monde la fah) (This is the beginning of the end.)

Charles Maurice de Talleyrand-Périgord (1754–1838), French diplomat, learning the news of Napoleon's defeat at the Battle of Borodino

Classical Phrases and Myths

omega (Grk)
(OH-me-ga) last letter of the Greek alphabet; last of series

ad finem (Lat)
(ad FEE-nem) at the end of a page or text (abbr: *ad fin*)

◆ ENERGY AND POWER

Foreign Words and Phrases

con brio (Ita)
(kon BREE-oh) in music, with spirit, with great life and vivacity

joie de vivre (Fra)
(JWA de VEE-vru) enthusiasm for life, high spirits

élan (Fra)
(ay-LON) flair, dashing quality

Quotations

"President Nixon says presidents can do almost anything, and President Nixon has done many things that nobody would have thought of doing."

Golda Meir (1898–1978), U.S.-born Israeli prime minister

"One, on God's side, is a majority."

Wendell Phillips (1811–1884), U.S. social reformer, speech November 1, 1859

"Daniel Webster struck me much like a steam-engine in trousers."

Sydney Smith (1771–1845), British clergyman and writer

Classical Phrases and Myths

"*Non onmia possumus onmes.*" (All of us do not have the power of everything.)

Virgil [Publius Vergilius Maro] (70 B.C.–19 B.C.), Roman poet, Eclogues, VIII, l. lxiii

Jokes, Stories and Anecdotes

At a cocktail party, Isaac Asimov said to an attending novelist, "And when will you be publishing your next book, Miss Coolidge?" She at once replied, "And when will you *not* be publishing your next book, Mr. Asimov?"

Isaac Asimov (1920–1992), U.S. writer

◆ ENTERTAINER

Quotations

"For an actress to be a success, she must have the face of a Venus, the brains of a Minerva, the grace of Terpsichore, the memory of a Macaulay, the figure of Juno, and the hide of a rhinoceros."

Ethel Barrymore (1879–1959), U.S. actress

"On the stage he was natural, simple, affecting;
'Twas only that when he was off he was acting."

> Oliver Goldsmith (1728–1774),
> Irish-born British poet, playwright
> and writer, Retaliation (1774),
> l. 101, describing David Garrick

"God makes stars. I just produce them."

> Samuel Goldwyn [Samuel Goldfish]
> (1882–1974), Russian-born U.S. film
> producer [authenticity unverified]

"Acting is merely the art of keeping a large group of people from coughing."

> Sir Ralph Richardson (1902–1983),
> British actor

Jokes, Stories and Anecdotes

The movie musical producer had convinced his director to listen to the producer's young girlfriend sing when they were casting the lead role. When her audition was over, the producer leaned over to the director and said, "Her voice ain't much, I know, but it can be dubbed. But what you think of her execution?" Mustering uncharacteristic candor, the director replied, "I'm in favor."

Singer reminiscing about her cabaret career: "I didn't mind the audience walking out on me, but when they started coming toward me—that's when I began to worry!"

A notoriously vain actor boasted to the humorist, poet and cartoonist Oliver Herford, "I'm a smash hit! Only yesterday, during the last act, I had the audience glued in their seats!" "Wonderful! Wonderful!"

congratulated Herford. "Clever of you to think of it."

> Oliver Herford (1863–1935),
> British-born U.S. humorist
> and illustrator [authenticity unverified]

As a guest of Noel Coward in Jamaica, Sir Laurence Olivier accompanied Coward to a mountaintop to see the playwright's favorite view. Looking out over the terraced landscape below, Olivier said, "It looks like rows and rows of empty seats."

> Sir Laurence Olivier (1907–1989),
> British actor

◆ ENTITLEMENT

Quotations

"To whom nothing is given, of him can nothing be required."

> Henry Fielding (1707–1754),
> British writer, playwright and lawyer,
> Joseph Andrews (1742), bk. II, ch. 8

"If you can't handle the weight, don't carry the freight."

> U.S. prison wisdom

"Toute nation a le gouvernement qu'elle mérite." (Every country has the government it deserves.)

> Joseph de Maistre (1753–1821),
> French politician, Lettres et
> Opuscules Inédits, (August 15, 1811)

Classical Phrases and Myths

volenti non fit injuria (Lat)
(wo-LEN-tee non fit in-YOO-ria)
there can be no injury to the who consents

According to Greek mythology, Nemesis (NEM-e-sis) was the goddess of divine retribution, particularly for human presumption. Personifying divine wrath and vengeance, she was, by extension, the goddess of the inevitable. Thus, one's *nemesis* is the coming of one's due. According to some accounts, Helen of Troy was born from an egg produced by the union of Zeus and Nemesis, who had been disguised as a swan.

Jokes, Stories and Anecdotes

The cocky yuppie couldn't find a seat on the crowded commuter train, so he yelled into the last car: "All change here. This car isn't going." The disgruntled passengers cleared the car, and the young man sat down, grinning to himself, and waited, and waited. Finally the station agent appeared. "You the clever fella who said this car wasn't going?" "Yep." "Well, it isn't," said the agent, "You sounded so much like a director, they just uncoupled the car."

The shipping tycoon Aristotle Onassis lived aboard his yacht the *Christina.* Adjoining his office, he installed a luxurious private bathroom whose door was a one-way mirror to enable Onassis from within to observe secretly unsuspecting visitors. During a business meeting Onassis went to the bathroom. Once enthroned, he voyeurishly looked up at the door. To his embarrassment, he was staring at his own reflection, for a workman repairing the door had inverted the mirror.

Aristotle [Socrates] Onassis (1906–1975),
Greek industrialist

Following a sensational trial in which he was sentenced to two years' hard labor for his affair with Lord Alfred Douglas, Oscar Wilde stood handcuffed in a pounding rain waiting for his transport to prison. Even in the depths of despair, his wit did not take leave: "If this is the way Queen Victoria treats her prisoners, she doesn't deserve to have any."

Oscar [Fingal O'Flahertie Wills] Wilde
(1854–1900), British playwright,
writer and wit

◆ ENVY

Foreign Words and Phrases

Schadenfreude (Ger) (SHAH-den-FROYD-uh) selfish enjoyment, malicious delight in the misery of others, mixed the pleasure and guilt one feels for another's misfortune

Quotations

"Some folks rail against other folks, because other folks have what some folks would be glad of."

Henry Fielding (1707–1754),
British writer, playwright and lawyer,
Joseph Andrews (1742), bk. IV, ch. 6

"Whenever a friend succeeds, a little something in me dies."

Gore Vidal (1925–   ), U.S. writer

Classical Phrases and Myths

"Treat your friend as if he will one day be your enemy, and your enemy as if he will one day be your friend."

Laberius (105 B.C.–43 B.C.),
Roman writer, Fragment

A dog seeking a comfortable place to sleep jumped into the manger of the ox and lay on its hay. The ox returned, exhausted from work, but the dog barked and snapped whenever the ox approached. Its patience spent, the ox protested: "Dog, eat my dinner or lie elsewhere. But it is churlish when *others begrudge one for what they cannot enjoy themselves.*"

Aesop (c. 600 B.C.), Greek fabulist

Some of the less fortunate tend to be awestruck in their admiration for the gilded lifestyle, some visiting subjects of Emperor Heliogabulus occasioned an embarrassment of riches when one airily commented, to the others' applause, how divine it would be to be smothered in the scent of roses that adorned the imperial table. Inviting the same guests again, the emperor took them at their word and had several tons of petals dumped over the dinner table. The reaction of the guests is unrecorded—they all suffocated.

Heliogabulus (204–222), Roman emperor

Jokes, Stories and Anecdotes

A Mercedes pulled up beside a Rolls-Royce just parking at a country club. "Not only do I have a phone in my car," the Mercedes driver shouted, "but a fax machine as well." "Harumph," the Rolls owner replied, "I've got a water bed in the back." Stung with fury, the Mercedes driver sped off to an auto-specialty shop and had a fancy water bed installed in the rear of his car. He was delighted to see the Rolls several days later, and honked. Finally, the Rolls window rolled down. "You have nothing on me," the Mercedes driver boasted. "I have a $10,000 water bed in back." The Rolls owner stuck his head out of the window and shouted, "You got me out of the shower to tell me that?"

◆ EPITAPH

Quotations

"I'll be right back."

> *Johnny Carson (1925–   ), U.S. television entertainer suggesting own epitaph (pun on traditional television segue into commercial breaks)*

"Epitaph: A belated advertisement for a line of goods that has been discontinued."

> *Irvin S[hrewsbury] Cobb (1876–1944), U.S. humorist and writer, Vanity Fair (1925)*

"Here lies W. C. Fields. I would rather be living in Philadelphia."

> *W. C. Fields [William Claude Dukenfield] (1879–1946), U.S. film actor and comedian, suggesting his own epitaph, Vanity Fair (June 1925)*

"Over my dead body!"

> *George S[imon] Kaufman (1889–1961), U.S. playwright, writer and wit, suggesting his own epitaph, Vanity Fair (1925)*

"Excuse my dust."

> *Dorothy Parker (1893–1967), U.S. wit and writer suggesting her own epitaph (1925)*

"Good friend, for Jesus sake forbear
To dig the dust enclosed here.
Best be the man that spares these stones,
And curst be he that moves my bones."

> *William Shakespeare (1564–1616), British playwright and poet, epitaph*

Jokes, Stories and Anecdotes

As a little child, Charles Lamb was walking with his sister in a graveyard, where he read the epitaphs praising the deceased as "beloved," "virtuous" and so forth. He turned to his sister and asked, "Mary, where are all the naughty people buried?"

Charles Lamb (1775–1834), British writer

◆ EQUALITY

Foreign Words and Phrases

d'égal à égal (Fra)
(deg-al ah eg-AL) *lit:* equal to equal; equally, on equal terms

Quotations

"The defect of equality is that we only desire it with our superiors."

Henri [François] Becque (1837–1899), French playwright

"All animals are equal but some animals are more equal than others."

George Orwell [Eric Blair] (1903–1950), British writer, Animal Farm (1945), ch. 10

Classical Phrases and Myths

premus inter pares (Lat)
(PREE-mus in-ter PAH-rays) first among equals; spokesman of a group that is not differentiated by rank

pari passu (Lat)
(PAR-ee PAH-soo) *lit:* with equal pace; side by side, equitably

◆ EQUIPMENT & SUPPLIES

Foreign Words and Phrases

entrepét (Fra)
(ON-tray-POH) storehouse, warehouse from which goods are distributed; port serving a large hinterland.

schlock (Yid)
(shlok) junk, cheap quality items

Jokes, Stories and Anecdotes

The multimillionaire decided to take up scuba diving in his early retirement. With the same determination that had earned his fortune, he spent thousands of dollars on lessons and equipment before sailing for Hawaii. Diving deep along the coral reefs, he was taking notes with his waterproof pen and pad when he saw another man diving nearby without a lick of equipment. The outraged retiree swam over to the free diver and wrote out on his pad, "I spent a fortune to scuba dive, yet you're doing it free form. How come?" Wrote back the stranger, "I'm drowning!"

A Muscovite asked a butcher for chicken and was told there was none. She asked for pork. None. Lamb? None. Beef? None. Veal? None. After the dejected shopper had left, the butcher murmured admiringly, "What a memory!"

◆ ERROR (MISTAKE)

Foreign Words and Phrases

faux pas (Fra)
(foh pah) *lit:* false step; social misstep, error in taste, manners, etc.

Quotations

"Don't make the wrong mistakes."

Lawrence ["Yogi"] Berra (1925–), U.S. baseball player and manager

"A fool must now and then be right, by chance."

William Cowper (1731–1800), British poet, Conversation (1782), l. 96

"When I make a mistake, it's a beaut!"

> *Fiorello La Guardia (1882–1947),*
> *U.S. politician, regretting his appointment*
> *of Herbert O'Brien as a judge, 1936*

"The man who makes no mistakes does not usually make anything."

> *Edward John Phelps (1822–1900),*
> *British politician, speech at*
> *Mansion House, January 24, 1899*

Classical Phrases and Myths

errare est humanum (Lat)
(err-AH-ray est hoo-MAH-num) to err is human

corrigendum (Lat)
(KOR-rig-END-um) correction, or something to be corrected (plu: *corrigenda*)

Jokes, Stories and Anecdotes

Perhaps the most embarassing typographical error in modern times occurred in the *Washington Post* in 1915. In a news story about President Woodrow Wilson having taken his fiancée Edith Galt to the theater the previous night, the article noted that, rather than watching the play, Wilson "spent most of his time entering [cf. entertaining] Mrs. Galt."

> *Anonymous*

Several North American ice-hockey players went to Moscow to play the Soviet team in the early 1970s, and were suspicious that their hotel room was bugged. Phil Esposito recalled, "We searched the room for microphones. In the center of the room, we found a funny-looking, round piece of metal embedded in the floor, under the rug. We figured we had found the bug. We dug it out of the floor . . . and we heard a crash beneath us. We had released

the anchor to the chandelier in the ceiling below."

> *Phil Esposito (1942–   ),*
> *Canadian-born ice-hockey player*

Napoleon, then emperor of France, having received intelligence apparently linking Duc d'Enghien with royalist conspiracies trying to overthow him, stubbornly had the duke executed before a firing squad in 1804. The incident strengthened antagonism against Napoleon, eventually leading to his downfall. The Comte Antoine Boulay de Meurthe wryly observed, "C'est pire qu'un crime, c'est une faute." (It's worse than a crime, it's a blunder.)

> *Comte Antoine Boulay de la Meurthe*
> *(1761–1840), French aristocrat*

◆ ESCAPE

Foreign Words and Phrases

sauve qui peut (Fra)
(soav kee puh) run for your life; every man for himself

Jokes, Stories and Anecdotes

The director Michael Curtiz was bent on having realism in his films. In one swashbuckling scene in which he had extras throw authentic spears at Errol Flynn, Flynn dodged the hail of lethal points and began to go after Curtiz. "Lunch!" yelled Curtiz.

> *Michael Curtiz (1888–1962),*
> *Hungarian-born U.S. film director*

As a pallbearer carrying out the coffin of the renowned escape artist Houdini, Broadway producer Charles Dillingham whispered to fellow impresario Florenz Ziegfeld, "Ziggie, I bet you he isn't in here."

Harry [Ehrich Weiss] Houdini (1874–1926), U.S. magician

◆ ESSENCE & NATURE (CHARACTER)

Foreign Words and Phrases

Geist (Ger)
(gyst) spirit or soul (of individual, nation, era, etc.)

Ding an sich (Ger)
(DING an ZICH) *lit:* the thing in itself, what really exists behind the surface appearance

Gestalt (Ger)
(ge-SHTALT) structure, form; a school of psychoanalysis focusing on the shape of the whole personality

Quotations

"The greatest of faults, I should say, is to be conscious of none."

Thomas Carlyle (1795–1881), British historian, Heroes and Hero Worship *(1841), "The Hero as Prophet"*

"To see ourselves as others see us is a most salutary gift. Hardly less important is the capacity to see others as they see themselves."

Aldous Huxley (1894–1963), British writer

"Every man likes the smell of his own farts."

Icelandic proverb

"Every man has three characters: that which he shows, that which he has, and that which he thinks he has."

Alphonse Karr (1808–1890), French writer

"The first time you meet Winston [Churchill] you see all his faults and the rest of your life you spend in discovering his virtues."

Pamela Frances Audrey, Countess of Lytton (1874–1971), British writer, letter to Sir Edward Marsh, December 1905

"The measure of a man's real character is what he would do if he knew he would never be found out."

Thomas Babington Macaulay, 1st Baron (1800–1859), British statesman and writer

"We only confess our little faults to persuade people that we have no big ones."

François, Duc de La Rochefoucauld (1613–1680), French writer, Maximes *(1678), 327*

Classical Phrases and Myths

id (Lat)
(id) *lit:* that; in psychology, the group of unconscious impulses and energies which motivate one

ego (Lat)
(EE-go) *lit:* I, myself; in psychology, an individual's consciousness of himself

anima (Lat)
(AN-ee-ma) *lit:* mind, soul; inner self, true part of the personality. Jung contrasted the anima (true self) with the persona (assumed or externalized self)

per se (Lat)
(per say) by itself, inherently

ethos (Grk)
(ee-THOS) the distinctive character of a people or an institution; in aesthetics, an ideal or universal quality

◆ ETHICS & CONSCIENCE

Quotations

"It is easier to fight for one's principles than to live up to them."

Alfred J. Adler (1870–1937),
Austrian psychiatrist

"Morality comes with the sad wisdom of age, when the sense of curiosity has withered."

Graham Greene (1904–1992),
British writer and playwright

"I'm not saying it's right, I'm saying it is."

William Randolph Hearst (1863–1951),
U.S. publisher, commenting on his long
affair with actress Marion Davies despite
public mores

"I know only that what is moral is what you feel good after and what is immoral is what you feel bad after."

Ernest [Miller] Hemingway (1899–1961),
U.S. writer, Death in the Afternoon
(1932), ch. 1

"Men are never so good or so bad as their opinions."

Sir James Mackintosh (1765–1832),
British philosopher, Dissertation on
Ethical Philosophy (1830), "Remarks
on Jeremy Bentham"

"Do not do unto others as you would that they should do unto you. Their tastes may not be the same."

George Bernard Shaw (1856–1950), Irish
playwright, Man and Superman (1903),
"Maxims for Revolutionists:
The Golden Rule"

"The golden rule is that there are no golden rules."

George Bernard Shaw (1856–1950), Irish
playwright, Man and Superman (1903),
"Maxims for Revolutionists:
The Golden Rule"

"Conscience is, in most men, an anticipation of the opinion of others."

Sir Henry Taylor (1800–1886),
British writer

"Erst kommt das Fressen, dann kommt die Moral." (Grub first, then morality.)

Bertolt Brecht (1898–1956),
German playwright, Dreigroschenoper
(Threepenny Opera) (1928), Act II, sc. 3

Classical Phrases and Myths

casus conscientiae (Lat)
(KAH-sus KON-ski-ENT-ia) case of conscience

◆ EVENT

Foreign Words and Phrases

pièce d'occasion (Fra)
(pyes do-KAY-zhon) piece (of art, music, etc.) composed for special occasion

Jokes, Stories and Anecdotes

Writer Franklin Pierce Adams escorted Beatrice Kaufman, wife of playwright George S. Kaufman, to a party. She happened to sit down on a cane-seated chair. The seat suddenly broke, ensnaring Beatrice in the frame with her legs in the air. As the shocked partygoers stood in silence, Adams said sternly, "I've told you a hundred times, Beatrice, that's not funny."

Franklin Pierce Adams (1881–1960),
U.S. writer

◆ EVIL

Quotations

"Two wrongs don't make a right, but they make a good excuse."

> Thomas Szasz (1920–   ), U.S. psychiatrist, The Second Sin (1973), "Social Relations"

"When I'm good, I'm very very good, but when I'm bad, I'm better."

> Mae West (1892–1980), U.S. film actress, I'm No Angel (1933 film)

"Wickedness is a myth invented by good people to account for the curious attractiveness of others."

> Oscar [Fingal O'Flahertie Wills] Wilde (1854–1900), British playwright, writer and wit

Classical Phrases and Myths

contra bonos mores (Lat) (KON-tru BON-ohs MOHR-es) contrary to good morality

Jokes, Stories and Anecdotes

Asked whether he had ever been wrong, John Foster Dulles, President Eisenhower's secretary of state, considered the question thoughtfully. "Yes," he finally admitted, "once—many, many years ago. I thought I had made a wrong decision. Of course, it turned out that I had been right all along. But I was wrong to have thought that I was wrong."

> John Foster Dulles (1888–1959), U.S. statesman

◆ EXAGGERATION

Quotations

"A practitioner in panegyric, or, so to speak more plainly, a professor of the art of puffing."

> Richard Brinsley Sheridan (1751–1816), Irish-born British playwright and politician, The Critic (1779), Act I, sc. ii

Jokes, Stories and Anecdotes

The French actress Sarah Bernhardt was so renowned for her wild exaggeration both on- and off-stage that, in reference to her almost skeletal thinness, Alexandre Dumas fils commented, "She's such a liar, she may even be fat!"

> Alexandre [fils] Dumas (1824–1895), French writer and playwright

"Why do you reject my drawings," a cartoonist complained to The New Yorker magazine founder and editor Harold Ross, "and print stuff by that fifth-rate artist, Thurber?" Ross corrected him. "Third-rate."

> Harold Ross (1892–1951), U.S. publisher

The editor of the New York Journal, who had heard a rumor of Mark Twain's or imminent death, cabled the London correspondent: "If Mark Twain dying in poverty in London send 500 words" and "If Mark Twain has died in poverty send 1000 words." Learning of the cables, Twain proffered that a cousin, James Ross Clemens, although seriously ill in London, had recovered. The cabled reply concluded: "The report of my death was an exaggeration."

> Mark Twain [Samuel Langhorne Clemens] (1835–1910), U.S. humorist, writer, and speaker

◆ EXAMINATION

Quotations

"I was thrown out of college for cheating on the metaphysics exam: I looked into the soul of another boy."

Woody Allen [Allen Stewart Konigsberg]
(1935–), U.S. comedian
and filmmaker

Jokes, Stories and Anecdotes

"Just how far are you from the correct answer?" demanded the pupil's teacher. "Three seats, ma'am."

A newspaper held a competition for the best answer to the question: "If a fire broke out in the Louvre and you could save only one painting, which one would it be?" French playwright Tristan Bernard won with the reply: "The one nearest the exit."

Tristan Bernard (1866–1947),
French playwright and writer

The 23-year-old physicist J. Robert Oppenheimer underwent his doctoral examination by Professor James Franck, a physicist at Gottingen University. "I got out of there just in time," quipped Franck following the oral examination. "He was beginning to ask *me* questions."

J[ulius] Robert Oppenheimer (1904–1967),
U.S. physicist

William Phelps, a professor of English literature at Yale, was grading examinations before the Christmas school break when he read in the margin of one paper a message: "God only knows the answer to this question. Merry Christmas."

Phelps returned the paper to the student with an annotation: "God gets an A. You get an F. Happy New Year."

William Lyon Phelps (1865–1943),
U.S. scholar and critic

◆ EXCESS

Foreign Words and Phrases

embarras de richesses (Fra)
(om-BA-ra de ree-SHESS) embarrassment of riches, choices

troppo (Ita)
(TROH-poh) too much

de trop (Fra)
(de troh) something or someone superfluous (often vulgar)

Quotations

"Can we ever have too much of a good thing?"

Miguel de Cervantes (1547–1616),
Spanish writer, Don Quixote de la
Mancha, Part I *(1605), bk. I, ch. 6*

"I have climbed to the top of the greasy pole."

Benjamin Disraeli, 1st Earl of Beaconsfield
(1804–1881), British prime minister
speaking to friends on being made
prime minister (1868)

"Moderation is a fatal thing. Nothing succeeds like excess."

Oscar [Fingal O'Flahertie Wills] Wilde
(1854–1900), British playwright,
writer and wit

Classical Phrases and Myths

nihil nimis (Lat)
(NI-hil NI-mis) nothing in excess

ad nauseam (Lat)
(ad NAW-see-am) to the point of sickness or disgust

Jokes, Stories and Anecdotes

As British minister of health, Nye Bevan often worked late into the night on cabinet matters in a small bedroom at the top of his house. After several hours' work one night, he asked his wife to bring up a second set of papers. "No. One you can have," she said, adding, "but taking two to bed is positively immoral."

Aneurin ["Nye"] Bevan (1897–1960),
British politician

◆ EXCHANGE

Quotations

"A government which robs Peter to pay Paul can always depend on the support of Paul."

George Bernard Shaw (1856–1950),
Irish playwright, Everybody's Political
What's What? (1944), ch. 30

Classical Phrases and Myths

quid pro quo (Lat)
(kwid proh kwoh) *lit:* something for something; compensation for a concession, etc.; (something given) in return for a service rendered

Jokes, Stories and Anecdotes

Once Tallulah Bankhead was in a stall in a ladies' room, and since the toilet paper dispenser was empty, she asked the lady in the next stall, "Da-a-h-ling, is there any toilet paper in there?" "Sorry, no more left." "Then have you any facial tissue?" "Afraid not." Then Bankhead said, "My dear, have you two fives for a ten?"

Tallulah Bankhead (1903–1968),
U.S. actress [authenticity unverified]

Sigmund Freud related a story that a marquis at the court of Louis XIV returned to his wife only to find her in the arms of a bishop. The cuckold calmly walked to the window and started blessing everyone in the street below. Puzzled, his wife asked what he was doing. The marquis replied: "Monseigneur is performing my function, so I am performing his."

"Excuse me," a man said to the clerk at the auto-parts store. "I'd like to get a new gas cap for my Yugo." "OK," the clerk replied. "Sounds like a fair exchange."

While governor of New Jersey, Woodrow Wilson was informed of the sudden death of a personal friend, a New Jersey senator. Still recovering from the shock, Wilson was called to the telephone to talk to another prominent New Jersey politician. "Governor," said the caller, "I should like to take the senator's place." Wilson replied, "It is agreeable to me as long as it is agreeable to the undertaker."

[Thomas] Woodrow Wilson (1856–1924),
U.S. president and scholar

◆ EXERCISE & FITNESS

Quotations

"That's not exercise, it's flagellation."

Sir Noel Coward (1899–1973),
British playwright and actor,
commenting on the game of squash

"I get my exercise acting as a pallbearer to my friends who exercise."

Chauncey Mitchell Depew (1834–1928),
U.S. lawyer and politician

"Whenever I feel like exercise I lie down until the feeling passes."

Robert Maynard Hutchins (1899–1977),
U.S. educator

Classical Phrases and Myths

mens sana in corpore sano (Lat) (MENS SAH-na in KOR-por-e SAH-noh) a healthy mind (will exist) in a healthy body

Jokes, Stories and Anecdotes

A coach was putting his team through a tough exercise of sprints, sit-ups and the "bicycle." This exercise requires a player to lie on his back and move his raised legs as if riding a bicycle. "Gotta problem?" the coach asked one motionless player. "No problem," he replied. "I'm coasting."

There are some people who think exercise means running up bills, jumping to conclusions, bending over backward, stretching the truth, sidestepping responsibility, lying down on the job and pushing their luck.

◆ EXERTION

Quotations

"When the going gets tough, the tough get going."

Knute Rockne (1888–1931),
U.S. football coach [attributed also to
Joseph P. Kennedy]

Classical Phrases and Myths

"Leave no stone unturned."

Euripides (480 B.C.–406 B.C.), Greek
playwright, Heraclidae (c. 428 B.C.)

The battle of Marathon (MARE-a-thon) in 490 B.C. was one of history's

greatest battles, ending efforts to conquer Greece by Darius, the Persian king. Prior to the battle, the renowned Greek messenger Phidippides is reputed to have run 150 miles in two days to secure aid from Sparta for the Athenians, and then run a little over 26 miles to carry news of the victory to Athens, collapsing dead at the end of his ordeal. Hence, a *marathon* is a 26-mile race or an endeavor requiring extreme endurance.

Jokes, Stories and Anecdotes

Standing next to his drums, the slavemaster on a galley ship told the sweating rowers: "Men, I have some good news and some bad news. The good news is that you all get an extra ration of stale bread." Cheers. "The bad news is that the captain wants to go waterskiing."

In his old age Johannes Brahms informed his friends that he would stop composing music and enjoy the time left to him. After several months without writing a note, Brahms issued a new composition. "But you weren't going to write any more," a friend reminded him. "I wasn't," said the composer, "but after a short absence from it, I was so elated at not having to write that the music came to me without effort."

Johannes Brahms (1833–1897),
German composer

◆ EXONERATION

Classical Phrases and Myths

"Pardon one offense, and you encourage the commission of many."

Publilius Syrus (c. 100 B.C.),
Roman writer, Sententiae, 750

"Iudex damnatur ubi nocens absolvitur. (EE-u-dex dam-NAT-ur oo-bee no-KENS ab-SOL-wee-tur) (The judge is condemned when the criminal is acquitted.)

> *Publilius Syrus (c. 100 B.C.),*
> *Roman writer, Sententiae, 247*

Jokes, Stories and Anecdotes

A day before a case came to trial against a certain film producer in Hollywood's early years, the producer sent a dwarf and two nondescript performers to each deliver outlandish messages to a woman preparing to give damaging court testimony against him. The next day the producer's attorney opened his defense by stating that the woman was mentally unbalanced. And when she was on the stand, sure enough, she was led to describe the story of her strange visitors and the messages. According to F. Scott Fitzgerald's unused notes for *The Last Tycoon,* "the jury shook their heads, winked at each other and acquitted" the defendant producer.

> *F[rancis] Scott [Key] Fitzgerald*
> *(1896–1940), U.S. writer*

◆ EXPECTATION

Quotations

"I almost had to wait."

> *Louis XIV (1638–1715), French king,*
> *commenting about a coach that he had*
> *ordered which had arrived just in time*
> *[authenticity unverified]*

"I have noticed that the people who are late are often so much jollier than the people who have to wait for them."

> *E[dward] V[errall] Lucas (1868–1938),*
> *British writer and poet, 365 Days and*
> *One More (1926), p. 277*

Jokes, Stories and Anecdotes

When Louis XIII, the father of Le Roi Soleil (the Sun King), was dying, he playfully teased the precocious four-year-old dauphin by asking, "Now, what is your name?" "Louis the Fourteenth," declared the boy. "Not quite yet, my son."

> *Louis XIV (1638–1715), French king*

◆ EXPEDIENCE

Foreign Words and Phrases

à contrecoeur (Fra)
(ah KON-tre-KUHR) *lit:* against the wishes of the heart; reluctantly, making a logical or expedient choice despite contrary emotions or feelings

Lebensraum (Ger)
(LAY-bens-ROWM) *lit:* living space; Hitler Germany's justification for territorial aggrandizement

pis aller (Fra)
(pees al-LAY) the worst, last resort

Quotations

"The graveyards are full of indispensable men."

> *Charles Andre Joseph Marie de Gaulle*
> *(1890–1970), French president and general*

"The most important tool of the theoretical physicist is the wastebasket."

> *Albert Einstein (1879–1955),*
> *German-born physicist*

"We do what we must, and call it by the best names."

> *Ralph Waldo Emerson (1803–1882),*
> *U.S. writer, poet and philosopher,*
> *The Conduct of Life (1860),*
> *"Considerations by the Way"*

"Well, I'd rather have him inside the tent pissing out, than outside pissing in."

Lyndon Baines Johnson (1908–1973), U.S. president, concluding that J. Edgar Hoover would remain FBI chief

"You can't learn too soon that the most useful thing about a principle is that it can always be sacrificed to expediency."

W[illiam] Somerset Maugham (1874–1965), British writer and playwright, The Circle, (1921), Act III

"Never interrupt an enemy while he's making a mistake."

Napoleon I [Napoleon Bonaparte] (1769–1821), French general and emperor

"The race is not always to the swift. The battle is not always to the strong. But that's the way to bet."

Damon Runyon (1884–1946), U.S. writer

Classical Phrases and Myths

ad hoc (Lat)
(ad HOK) impromptu, improvised; for a particular occasion

"Cui bono." (kwee-BOH-noh) (To whose benefit?)

Marcus Tullius Cicero (106 B.C.–43 B.C.), Roman statesman and man of letters, Pro Milone, XII, xxxii

"Honesta turpitudo est pro causa bona." (hon-EST-aTUR-pee-TU-dohest pro KAUS-a BOH-na) (For a good cause, wrongdoing is virtuous.)

Publilius Syrus (c. 100 B.C.), Roman writer, Sententiae, 244

According to Greek legend, Procrustes (proh-KRUS-teez) was an outlaw who offered hospitality to travelers coming to Athens but insisted that they use a certain bed. Those too short he stretched on a rack to fit it, and those too tall had their legs cut off to the proper length. He was killed by Theseus. A *Procrustean bed*, therefore, represents a tendency to find conforming solutions that are arbitrary and often imposed.

Jokes, Stories and Anecdotes

A king riding through a forest saw a target painted on many trees and in the middle of each target, an arrow. Amazed, he sent his attendants to find the talented archer. They returned with a young boy. The king asked the boy to explain his remarkable feat. "Simple," said the boy. "First shoot the arrow and then paint the target."

Jesse James and his gang were given much needed hospitality by a lonely and impoverished widow who was expecting a visit by the debt collector. Out of the take from a recent bank robbery, James gave her the required $1,400 to pay off the debt, and reminded the shocked woman to obtain a receipt in exchange for payment. James and his men hid along the road leading to the farmhouse, and shortly the grim-looking debt collector came. He soon emerged from the farmhouse, looking very content. James and his gang stopped the collector, reclaimed the $1,400, and rode off.

Jesse James (1847–1882), U.S. outlaw

◆ EXPERIMENT

Foreign Words and Phrases

ballon d'essai (Fra)
(bal-LON des-SAY) *lit:* trial balloon; tentative approach, prototype or model

Quotations

"We're all of us guinea pigs in the laboratory of God. Humanity is just a work in progress."

Tennessee [Thomas Lanier] Williams (1911–1983), U.S. playwright, Camino Real (1953), block 12

Jokes, Stories and Anecdotes

With his Ballets Russes Company triumphing in Paris during the 1920s, Sergei Diaghilev was always looking to surprise his sophisticated public. The impresario was once asked for some direction by Jean Cocteau, who was to provide a scenario for a new ballet. In a statement that encapsulated an era, Diaghilev simply replied, "*Étonne-moi!*" (Astonish me!)

Sergei [Pavlovich] Diaghilev (1872–1929), Russian impresario

Q: "A lawyer and an IRS agent jump off a skyscraper at the same time—who hits the ground first?"
A: "Who cares?"

◆ EXPERTISE

Foreign Words and Phrases

mavin (Yid)
(MAY-vin) expert

idiot savant (Fra)
(id-EE-oh sah-VAHN) *lit:* knowing idiot; an idiot or mentally retarded person expert in one craft

virtuoso (Ita)
(vur-too-OH-soh) *lit:* skillful, learned; (one) with great ability and skill (especially art)

tour de force (Fra)
(tour de force) powerful display of virtuosity

Quotations

"The definition of a specialist as one who 'knows more and more about less and less' is good and true."

Charles H. Mayo (1865–1939), U.S. physician, Modern Hospital (September 1938), p. 69

Jokes, Stories and Anecdotes

The social matron asked her dress designer for a unique design. The man smiled, took a roll of satin, and within several minutes had fashioned a beautiful dress. "I love it, Pascal," she said. "How much, dear?" "Three thousand dollars, Madame." "But, Pascal, that's so expensive for just a roll of satin." The man unwound the satin and presented it to the lady with a slight bow. "The satin, madame, is free."

General Electric recalled retired inventor and electrical engineer Charles Steinmetz to try to locate a malfunction in a system of complex machinery that had baffled all of GE's experts. After walking around and testing aspects of the machinery, he marked an "X" in chalk at a certain location on one machine. Lo and behold, when the GE engineers disassembled the machine, the defect was located where Steinmetz had left his chalk mark. When GE received a $10,000 bill from Steinmetz, company auditors protested the amount and asked for an itemization. The itemized bill he returned disclosed: Making one chalk mark . . . $1; Knowing where to place it . . . $9,999.

Charles Proteus Steinmetz (1865–1923), German-born U.S. engineer

◆ FACE

Quotations

"My face looks like a wedding-cake left out in the rain."

> *W[ystan] H[ugh] Auden (1907–1973),*
> *British-born poet*

"His ears made him look like a taxi-cab with both doors open."

> *Howard Hughes (1905–1976),*
> *U.S. industrialist, describing film actor*
> *Clark Gable*

"At 50, everyone has the face he deserves."

> *George Orwell [Eric Blair] (1903–1950),*
> *British writer, notebook, April 17, 1949*

"Barring that natural expression of villainy which we all have, the man looked honest enough."

> *Mark Twain [Samuel Langhorne Clemens]*
> *(1835–1910), U.S. humorist, writer and*
> *speaker, A Mysterious Visit (1875)*

"One of those characteristic British faces that, once seen, are never remembered."

> *Oscar [Fingal O'Flahertie Wills] Wilde*
> *(1854–1900), British playwright,*
> *writer and wit*

Jokes, Stories and Anecdotes

For a role, the actor John Drew shaved off his identifiable mustache. Later, running into the British wit Max Beerbohm, Drew was unable to recall who Beerbohm was. Beerbohm did recognize Drew, however, saying, "Mr. Drew, I'm afraid you don't recognize me without your mustache."

> *Sir Max Beerbohm (1872–1956),*
> *British writer, caricaturist and wit*

On one occasion the classical scholar and professor C. Maurice Bowra and a group of other dons were bathing *au naturel* at Parsons' Pleasure, a stretch of river at Oxford exclusively for men's bathing. A boatload of women, disregarding the "men only" signs, rowed into their midst. Hurriedly, the dons on the bank grabbed towels to fashion impromptu loincloths—except for Bowra, who threw his towel over his face. "I believe, gentlemen," Bowra later explained, "that I am recognized by my face."

> *Sir C. Maurice Bowra (1898–1971),*
> *British scholar [attributed also to others]*

◆ FAILURE

Foreign Words and Phrases

manqué (Fra)
(mon-KAY) *lit:* missed, lost, a lost opportunity (e.g., a professor manque can teach well but is unsuccessful—double-edged) (cf. [ ] *se manque* (Fra) to miss)

Quotations

"There are two kinds of men who never amount to much: those who cannot do what they are told, and those who can do nothing else."

> *Cyrus H. Curtis (1850–1933),*
> *U.S. publisher*

"Show me a good loser and I will show you a loser."

> *Paul Newman (1925–   ),*
> *U.S. film actor*

"[Herbert Bayard Swope] enunciated no rules for success, but offered a sure formula for failure: just try to please everyone."

> *Herbert Bayard Swope (1882–1958),*
> *U.S. writer and editor*

Classical Phrases and Myths

damnum sine injuria (Lat)
(DAM-num SEE-ne in-YOO-ree-ah)
in law, loss not subject to remedy,
loss for which there can be no rep-
aration

dis aliter visum (Lat)
(DEES AL-ee-ter WEE-sum) *lit*: the
gods thought otherwise; used in explanation of same apparently inexplicable human failure

---

◆ FALSENESS

Quotations

"She tells enough white lies to ice a
wedding cake."

> Margot Asquith, Countess of Oxford and
> Asquith (1864–1945), British writer and
> socialite, describing Lady Desborough

"I do not mind lying, but I hate inaccuracy."

> Samuel Butler (1835–1902),
> British writer, Notebooks (1912),
> "Truth and Inconvenience: Falsehood"

"The word liberty in the mouth of
Mr. [Daniel] Webster sounds like
the word love in the mouth of a
courtesan."

> Ralph Waldo Emerson (1803–1882),
> U.S. writer, poet, and philosopher

"Without lies humanity would perish of despair and boredom."

> Anatole France [Jacques Anatole François
> Thibault] (1844–1924), French writer and
> poet, Bloom of Life, afterword

"Strip away the phony tinsel of
Hollywood and you find the real
tinsel underneath."

> Oscar Levant (1906–1972),
> U.S. pianist and wit

"A lie is like a snowball; the longer
it is rolled the larger it is."

> Martin Luther (1483–1546),
> German Protestant theologian

"Good lies need a leavening of
truth to make them palatable."

> William McIlvanney (1936–   ),
> British writer

"A little inaccuracy sometimes
saves tons of explanation."

> Saki [Hector Hugh Munro] (1870–1916),
> British writer, The Square Egg (1924),
> "Clovis on the Alleged
> Romance of Business"

"The liar's punishment is not in the
least that he is not believed, but that
he cannot believe anyone else."

> George Bernard Shaw (1856–1950),
> Irish playwright

"Liars ought to have good memories."

> Algernon Sidney (1622–1683),
> British writer and poet, Discourses on
> Government (1698)

"He will lie even when it is inconvenient, the sign of the true artist."

> Gore Vidal (1925–   ), U.S. writer

Classical Phrases and Myths

suggestio falsi (Lat)
(sug-GEST-ioh FAL-see) misrepre-
sentation to conceal truth; suppres-
sion of the truth that is not quite a
lie (*cf* suppressio veri)

suppressio veri (Lat)
(sup-PRESS-ee-oh WER-ee) *lit*: sup-
pression of truth; wilful misrepre-
sentation

A little shepherd boy grew tired of
watching his father's flock alone, so

one day, to stir up excitement, he cried, "Wolf! Wolf!" The villagers dashed to his spot to answer the alarm, but of course found no wolf. The foolish boy repeated this, and each time the villagers came to the rescue, only to be laughed at by the little boy. But finally a wolf really did appear. The boy cried for help, but the villagers, who would not believe the liar even when he was telling the truth, ignored him. The wolf devoured the sheep as the boy who cried "Wolf!" watched helplessly.

Aesop (c. 600 B.C.), Greek fabulist

According to Roman and Etruscan mythology, Janus (JAY-nus) was the god of doorways and the patron of the beginning of all undertakings. The month of January is named after him. As the god of the sun's rising, Janus was depicted with two faces. Hence, to be Janusfaced is to be two-faced, i.e., false.

According to Greek legend and recounted in Homer's *Iliad*, Sinon (SEE-non) was a cousin of Odysseus who accompanied the Greeks to Troy. He induced King Priam of the Trojans to accept the Trojan horse as a gift from the Greeks, who had apparently abandoned their siege of Troy after ten years of fighting. The Trojans believed Sinon's lie and allowed the massive wooden horse to be wheeled within the "impregnable" walls surrounding the city. In the stealth of the night, Sinon signaled the Greek warriors hidden within the horse to come out; the Greeks entered the gates of the city. Troy fell, and ever since it has been considered wise to *beware of Greeks bearing gifts* and of a *liar like Sinon*.

Jokes, Stories and Anecdotes

Asked whether Frank Harris, a British writer and critic, had ever been known to speak the truth, the wit Max Beerbohm replied, "Sometimes, when his invention flagged."

Sir Max Beerbohm (1872–1956),
British writer, caricaturist and wit

American writer Mary McCarthy crusaded against inaccuracy, cant, evasion, dishonesty and bad writing. Thus, on television's *Dick Cavett Show,* she said of Lillian Hellman that "every word she says is a lie, including 'and' and 'the.' " Hellman sued her.

Mary McCarthy (1912–1992), U.S. writer

While the pianist and composer Anton Rubenstein was practicing, his servant François answered an untimely telephone call. A woman tenderly asked to speak with the maestro. Although the piano was clearly audible, François assured the caller that Rubenstein was not in. "But I hear him playing," she protested. "You are mistaken, madame," replied François. "I am dusting the piano keys."

Anton Rubenstein (1829–1924),
Russian pianist and composer

Shigeru Yoshida was Japan's ambassador to England during the 1930s when he advised his staff that he wished to avoid a visiting Japanese cabinet minister. The minister tried in vain to reach the ambassador, and finally called at the embassy in person. Passing Yoshida in the foyer, he asked to speak to the ambassador. "The ambassador is out," replied Yoshida. With sudden recognition the minister asked, "But aren't you the ambassador?" "I am," said Yoshida. "And, sir, when you hear from Yoshida himself that Yoshida is out, you can believe it!"

Shigeru Yoshida (1878–1967),
Japanese politician

◆ FAMILY

Foreign Words and Phrases

bol (Maya)
(bowl) idiotic in-laws
chez la famille (Fra)

(shav la fain-EEYE) at the family home, with the family

Quotations

"There's nothing wrong with incest just as long as you keep it in the family."

Milton Mayer (1908–   ),
writer and educator

"God gives us our relatives; thank God we can choose our friends."

Ethel Watts Mumford (1878–1940),
U.S. writer

"All happy families are alike, but an unhappy family is unhappy in its own way."

Leo Nikolaevich Tolstoy (1828–1910),
Russian writer, Anna Karenina
(1875–1877) Pt. I, ch. i

Jokes, Stories and Anecdotes

"So you want to become my son-in-law, do you?" asked the father. Replied the fiancé, "No sir. But I want to marry your daughter, so I don't see how to avoid it."

Winston Churchill was not particularly fond of his actress daughter Sarah's husband, Vic Oliver. Once Oliver asked his father-in-law whom he had admired in the war. "Mussolini," growled Churchill, surprisingly. "He had the courage to have his son-in-law shot."

Sir Winston Spencer Churchill (1874–
1965), British prime minister and writer
[Count Galeazzo Ciano, husband of Edda
Mussolini, had been convicted on a charge
of high treason and executed in 1944]

A man burst into the dressing room of Mischa Elman immediately before he was to perform on the violin and greeted him: "We're related, Mr. Elman! Your wife's aunt is married to the uncle of my ex-wife's first husband's present wife." Elman, at first taken aback, said with relief, "Well, you're not so close that I need to give you a free ticket to the concert this evening."

Mischa Elman (1891–1967),
Russian-born U.S. violinist

◆ FASTIDIOUSNESS & PRIGGISHNESS

Quotations

"He was so neat that he put hospital corners on the newspaper he lined the hamster cage with."

Nora Ephron (1945–   ),
U.S. writer, Heartburn *(1983)*

Jokes, Stories and Anecdotes

In one course, Oxford professor Christopher Atkinson realized that his class was entirely composed of young female students. One morning he began his lecture by saying that his subject would be the sexual prowess of the natives of the Polynesian islands. Shocked, the women made a concerted rush for the door. Atkinson shouted after them. "You needn't hurry, ladies. There's not another boat for a month."

Christopher Thomas Atkinson
(1874–1964), British professor

Samuel Johnson's *Dictionary* had recently been published. Two Victorian matrons were praising Dr. Johnson, particularly for his tome's omission of all off-color words. "What! My dears!" Johnson declared. "Then you have been looking for them?" The deeply embarrassed ladies abruptly changed the subject.

Samuel Johnson (1709–1784),
British man of letters

John O'Hara was unusually sensitive to criticism of his writings. "John," said a friend, commenting on the film version of one of his novels, "I've just seen *Pal Joey* again, and I like it even better than I did the first time." "So," retorted O'Hara, "what was the matter with it the first time?"

John O'Hara (1905–1970), U.S. writer

The popular interpreter of Chopin, Vladimir Pachmann, would often begin a recital by adjusting the piano stool to the appropriate height for him to sit at the keyboard. If unsatisfied after numerous failed attempts, he would dash into the wings and return with a thick telephone book, which he would then place on the seat and sit on. But if still unhappy, he would indicate to the audience that he had a brilliant idea. He would open the book, tear out a single page and sit down again. Only, then was he ready to play.

Vladimir de Pachmann (1848–1933),
Russian pianist

Chances are that sparks will fly when two great egos clash. So when the author Mark Twain first met the artist James Whistler, a fellow American living in London, there was a noticeable chill in the air as the two men sized each other up. Then Twain walked over to one of Whistler's canvases in progress and nearly touched it with a gloved hand. "For the love of God!" cried Whistler. "Be careful, Clemens. Apparently you don't realize that the

paint's still fresh." "No need to be concerned," remarked Twain. "I have my gloves on."

Mark Twain [Samuel Langhorne Clemens]
(1835–1910), U.S. humorist,
writer and speaker

◆ FATE (DESTINY)

Foreign Words and Phrases

karma (Skt)
(KAR-mah) fate, destiny, retribution (upon death); essence of one's life

kismet (Arab)
(KIS-met) fate, the will of Allah

Quotations

"God works in mysterious ways."

James Anderton (1932–   ), British
policeman [attributed also to others]

"He that is born to be hanged shall never be drowned."

English proverb

"Live and let die." [Title of novel (1954).]

Ian Fleming (1908–1964), British writer

Classical Phrases and Myths

amor fati (Lat)
(AM-or FAT-ee) love of one's fate

"*Permitte divis cetera.*" (All else I leave to the gods.)

Horace (65 B.C.-8 B.C.), Roman poet,
Odes, I, ix, l. 9

"*Nam homo proponit, sed Deus disponit.*" (Man proposes but God disposes.)

Thomas à Kempis [Thomas Hamerken von
Kempen] (c. 1380–1471), German monk
and writer, Imitatio Christi (c. 1420),
bk. I, ch. 19

The Stoic philosopher Zeno once caught his slave stealing and beat him. "But it was fated that I should steal," protested the slave, philosophically. Replied Zeno, "And that I should beat you."

*Zeno (335 B.C.-263 B.C.),
Greek philosopher*

◆ FEELINGS

Foreign Words and Phrases

honne, tatemae (Jap)
(HOHN-nay ta-TEE-may) separation of private feelings and public diplomacy that permits Japanese society to function so well

schmaltz (Yid)
(shmaltz) excessive sentimentality; cooking fat

Quotations

"Sentimentality is the emotional promiscuity of those who have no sentiment."

*Norman Mailer (1923–   ),
U.S. writer*, Cannibals and Christians (1966), p. 51

"Sentimentality is only sentiment that rubs you up the wrong way."

W[illiam] Somerset Maugham (1874–1965), British writer and playwright, A Writer's Notebook (1941)

"The young man who has not wept is a savage, and the old man who will not laugh is a fool."

George Santayana (1863–1952), Spanish-born U.S. philosopher, poet and writer, Dialogues in Limbo (1925), ch. 3

"The advantage of the emotions is that they lead us astray."

Oscar [Fingal O'Flahertie Wills] Wilde (1854–1900), British playwright, writer and wit

Classical Phrases and Myths

aesthesis (Grk)
(ees-THAY-sis) feeling, perception, sensitivity

pathos (Grk)
(pa-THOS) with great emotion

Jokes, Stories and Anecdotes

Asked to describe her relationship with her famous father, President Johnson's daughter replied: "Blood."

*Lyndon Baines Johnson (1908–1973),
U.S. president*

◆ FEMALE

Foreign Words and Phrases

femme du monde (Fra)
(fam doo MOHND) *lit:* woman of the world; sophisticated woman

femme fatale (Fra)
(fam feh-TAHL) *lit:* deadly woman; fatally fascinating woman; woman who drives her lovers to disaster

Ewigweibliche (Ger)
(Ay-vig vyb-lich-uh) women's power to spiritualize mankind

Hausfrau (Ger)
(HOWS-frow) housewife

Quotations

"A woman, especially, if she have the misfortune of knowing anything, should conceal it as well as she can."

Jane Austen (1775–1817), British writer

"Brigands demand your money *or* your life; women demand both."

*Samuel Butler (1835–1902),
British writer*, Further Extracts from Notebooks (1934), p. 315

"A lady of a certain age, which means certainly aged."

*George Gordon, Lord Byron (1788–1824),
British poet*, Don Juan (1823),
Canto VI, lxix

"A lady is one who never shows her underwear unintentionally."

Lillian Day (1893–1991), U.S. writer

"Not if it means I have to carry the male dancers instead of them carrying me!"

Dame Margot Fonteyn [nee Margaret Hookham] (1919–1991), British ballerina, answering whether she was in favor of the women's liberation movement

"But if God had wanted us to think with our wombs, why did He give us a brain?"

Clare Boothe [Brokaw] Luce (1903–1987), U.S. writer, playwright and diplomat

"A woman is like a teabag—only in hot water do you realize how strong she is."

Nancy [Davis] Reagan (1921–   ), former U.S. first lady

"A woman without a man is like a fish without a bicycle."

Gloria Steinem (1934–   ), U.S. social reformer [authenticity unverified]

"Now, we are becoming the men we wanted to marry."

Gloria Steinem (1934–   ), U.S. social reformer, Ms. Magazine (July/Aug. 1982)

"Once a woman is made man's equal, she becomes his superior."

Margaret Thatcher (1925–   ), British prime minister

"Whatever women do they must do twice as well as men to be thought half as good. Luckily, this is not difficult."

Charlotte Whitton (1896–1975), Canadian politician, Canada Month (June 1963)

"Woman begins by resisting a man's advances and ends by blocking his retreat."

Oscar [Fingal O'Flahertie Wills] Wilde (1854–1900), British playwright, writer and wit

Classical Phrases and Myths

"The poet was right: can't live with them, or without them!"

Aristophanes (c. 450 B.C.–380 B.C.), Greek playwright, Lysistrata (411 B.C.) l. 1038

According to Greek mythology, the Sirens (*SIE-renz*) were sea nymphs, half-birds and half-maidens, whose singing lured passing sailors onto rocks, where the sailors perished. The sirens lost their feathered wings when they were defeated in a singing contest with the Muses. To protect his crew from the charms of the Sirens, Odysseus sealed his sailors' ears with wax and lashed himself to the mast, and Orpheus saved the Argonauts by singing even more enchantingly than the Sirens. A siren is thus an alluring or seductive woman.

Jokes, Stories and Anecdotes

A reporter was interviewing Sir Winston Churchill. "What do you say, sir," he asked, "to the prediction that in the year 2000, women will be ruling the world?" Churchill smiled his wise old cherub smile. "They still will, eh?"

Sir Winston Spencer Churchill (1874–1965), British prime minister and writer

The replies of famous women to the question "What is the first thing you notice about a woman?" were printed in a women's magazine. Said mystery novelist Agatha Christie, "Her way of speaking." Opera singer Maria Callas responded, "Her hands." Zsa Zsa Gabor replied, "Her husband."

Zsa Zsa [Sari] Gabor (1919–   ), Hungarian-born U.S. actress

◆ FIGURE OF SPEECH

Quotations

"Fuddle-duddle!"

Pierre Elliott Trudeau (1919–),
Canadian prime minister correcting a
quote [amused Canadian took up the new
expression with enthusiasm]

"He is every other inch a gentleman."

Dame Rebecca West [Cicily Isabel
Fairfield] (1892–1983), British writer,
describing Michael Arlen

"I've been things and seen places."

Mae West (1892–1980), U.S. film actress,
I'm No Angel (1933 film)

Jokes, Stories and Anecdotes

A talkative bore ran into humorist Douglas Jerrold as he was walking on the street and inquired, "What's going on, Jerrold?" "I am," Jerrold replied firmly, and did.

Douglas Jerrold (1803–1857),
English writer and humorist

Business correspondence is replete with empty clichés, and even celebrities are not immune, but on occasion they strike back. After Groucho Marx had received a letter from his bank manager closing with, "If I can be of any service to you, do not hesitate to call on me," Marx replied, "The best thing you can do to be of service to me is to steal some money from the account of one of your richer clients and credit it to mine."

Groucho [Julius] Marx (1895–1977),
U.S. comedian

◆ FILM

Foreign Words and Phrases

ciné aste-(Fra)
(seen-ay-ast) devotee of the cinema

Quotations

"An associate producer is the only guy in Hollywood who will associate with a producer."

Fred Allen [John Sullivan] (1894–1957),
U.S. comedian

"Dramatic art in her opinion is knowing how to fill a sweater."

Bette [Ruth Elizabeth] Davis (1908–1992),
U.S. actress describing Jayne Mansfield

"Nobody can change night into day, or vice versa, without asking me first!"

Samuel Goldwyn [Samuel Goldfish]
(1882–1974), Russian-born U.S. film
producer, reprimanding a director for
changing a daylight scene into a
nighttime shot [authenticity unverified]

"Pictures are for entertainment, messages should be delivered by Western Union."

Samuel Goldwyn [Samuel Goldfish]
(1882–1974), Russian-born U.S. film
producer, answering what the "message"
was of a particular film

"Movies are so rarely great art that if we cannot appreciate the great trash we have very little reason to be interested in them."

Pauline Kael (1919–),
U.S. writer

"It's a trip through a sewer in a glass-bottomed boat."

Wilson Mizner (1876–1933), U.S. writer
and wit, describing Hollywood

"A director must be a policeman, a midwife, a psychoanalyst, a sycophant and a bastard."

Billy [Samuel] Wilder (1906–),
U.S. film director and writer

"They get excited about the sort of stuff I could get shooting through a piece of Kleenex."

Billy [Samuel] Wilder (1906–),
U.S. film director and writer, remarking
about European cinema

Jokes, Stories and Anecdotes

Contemptuous of the film medium, John Barrymore refused to learn his lines for his movie roles. During filming Barrymore would read his lines from boards held up by stagehands. If a director or actor castigated him for this inconvenient habit, he would refrain: "My memory is full of beauty—Hamlet's soliloquies, the Queen Mab speech, King Magnus's monologue from *The Apple Cart*, most of the Sonnets. Do you expect me to clutter up all that with this horseshit?"

> *John Barrymore (1882–1942), U.S. actor*

◆ FINANCIAL CREDIT

Quotations

"Creditors have better memories than debtors."

> *Benjamin Franklin (1706–1790),*
> *U.S. statesman and scientist,*
> *Poor Richard's Almanac (1732–1757)*

Jokes, Stories and Anecdotes

The red-faced seamstress explained, "I'm sorry, madam, but I can't give you further credit. Your bill is already more than it should be." "I know that," snapped the society matron. "If you'll make it out for what it should be, I'll pay it."

A ne'er-do-well named Schweiger nagged Ferenc Molnár for a loan, and was given a measly 20 pengos. "What?" sneered the affronted Schweiger. "From a Molnár, 20 pengos?" "No, to a Schweiger, 20 pengos."

> *Ferenc Molnár (1878–1952),*
> *Hungarian playwright and writer*

◆ FLATTERY

Foreign Words and Phrases

kowtow (Chi)
(KOW-tow) fawning, obsequious behavior; bowing low

Quotations

"Nothing is so silly as the expression of a man who is being complimented."

> *André Gide (1869–1951), French writer*

"Self-love is the greatest of all flatterers."

> *François, Duc de La Rochefoucauld*
> *(1613–1680), French writer,*
> *Maximes (1678) 2*

"Madame, I have cried only twice in my life—once when I dropped a wing of truffled chicken into Lake Como, and once when for the first time I heard you sing."

> *Gioacchino Antonio Rossini (1792–1868),*
> *Italian composer, congratulating diva*
> *Adelina Patti on her singing*

"But when I tell him he hates flatterers,
He says he does, being then most flattered."

> *William Shakespeare (1564–1616),*
> *British playwright and poet,*
> *Julius Caesar (1600), Act II, sc. i*

Classical Phrases and Myths

Consistent with his claim to be on an equal footing with the gods, the evil Roman emperor Caligula would invite the moon goddess to his bed at the full moon. "Did you not see her?" he demanded of Aulus Vitellius. "No," said Vitellius, a future emperor, tactfully, "only you gods can see one another."

> *Aulus Vitellius (15–69), Roman emperor*

Jokes, Stories and Anecdotes

Lawyer and diplomat Joseph Choate, once asked who he would like to be if he were not himself, quickly thought through a list of famous people. Then, catching his wife's eye, he said, "If I could not be myself, I would like to be Mrs. Choate's second husband."

Joseph Hodges Choate (1832–1917),
U.S. lawyer and diplomat

◆ FOLLOWING

Classical Phrases and Myths

et sequentes (Lat)
(et se-KWEN-tes) and following (abbr: *et seq.*)

seriatum (Lat)
(SER-ee-at-um) serially, in sequence

secundum ordinem (Lat)
(sek-UND-um OR-di-nem) *lit:* according to sequence; in order, arranged sequentially

Jokes, Stories and Anecdotes

For a forthcoming recital, a singer once asked Johannes Brahms to give her some of his least-known songs. "Take some of my posthumous ones," offered the composer. "No one will know them."

Johannes Brahms (1833–1897),
German composer

Addison Mizner, brother of the wit Wilson Mizner, became an architect to the rich and famous during a great land boom in Florida. The cachet of a Mizner-designed residence may have helped to make up for the man's lack of qualifications; once, he forgot to install a stairway between the first and second stories. On another occasion a client, William Gray Warden, asked for a copy of the blueprints of his Palm Beach house to show these to his friends. "Why, the house isn't built yet!" protested Mizner. "Construction first, blueprints afterward."

Addison Mizner (d. 1933),
U.S. architect and entrepreneur

◆ FOOD

Foreign Words and Phrases

haute cuisine (Fra)
(oat kwee-ZEEN) *lit:* high cooking; (the art of) fine cooking

Quotations

"Boiled cabbage à l'Anglaise is something compared with which steamed coarse newsprint bought from bankrupt Finnish salvage dealers and heated over smoky oil stoves is an exquisite delicacy."

William Connor ["Cassandra"]
(1909–1967), U.S. writer

"Most vigitaryans I iver see looked enough like their food to be classed as cannybals."

Finley Peter Dunne (1867–1936),
U.S. writer and humorist,
Mr. Dooley's Opinions (1900),
"Casual Observations"

"This was a good enough dinner, to be sure; but it was not a dinner to ask a man to."

Samuel Johnson (1709–1784),
British man of letters

"You know, this piece of cod passeth all understanding."

Sir Edwin Landseer Lutyens (1869–1944),
British architect, struggling through the
fish course in a famous London restaurant

"Dinner at the Huntercombes' possessed only two dramatic features—the wine was a farce and the food a tragedy."

Anthony Powell (1905–   ), British
writer, Acceptance World (1955), ch. 4

"I don't worry about my arteries. I worry about the arteries of the chicken."

Isaac Bashevis Singer (1904–1991), U.S. writer, answering whether he abstained from meat for his health

Classical Phrases and Myths

a fabis abstinete (Lat)
(ah FAB-is ab-STIN-et-e) eat no beans, Latin translation of Greek, attributed to Pythagoras

In Greek mythology, ambrosia (am-BROH-zia) was the food of the Greek gods and conferred everlasting youth and beauty. The gods also drank nectar, a sweet concoction. Hence, *ambrosia* is used to indicate a food or substance that is sweet or pleasing.

Jokes, Stories and Anecdotes

The newlywed man came home to find his wife weeping. "I made a pie from mother's recipe," she sobbed, "and I put it out to cool but the dog ate it." "Don't worry, honey," he comforted her. "I'll buy a puppy tomorrow."

"This food isn't fit for a pig," bellowed the angry diner. "So sorry," replied the waiter, "I'll get you some that is."

◆ FOOD SERVICE

Quotations

"God finally caught his eye."

George S[imon] Kaufman (1889–1961), U.S. playwright, writer and wit suggesting an epitaph for a dead waiter

Jokes, Stories and Anecdotes

"We have practically everything on the menu," boasted the waiter. Replied the restaurant patron, "So I

see. Would you bring me a clean one?"

Taken to a famous restaurant of which he had never heard, Yogi Berra scanned the packed place. "No wonder nobody comes here," observed the baseball player. "It's too crowded."

Lawrence ["Yogi"] Berra (1925–), US baseball player and manager

At a restaurant, the farce dramatist Feydeau was once served a lobster with only one claw. When he protested, the waiter apologetically explained that lobsters can lose a claw because they fight in their tank. "So take this one away," instructed Feydeau, "and bring me the victor."

Georges Feydeau (1862–1921), French playwright

The novelist Irwin Shaw waited an interminably long time for a waiter at a French restaurant when finally the maître d' came over and genteely informed Shaw that snails were the specialty of the house. "I know," responded Shaw, nodding his head, "and you have them dressed as waiters."

Irwin Shaw (1913–1984), U.S. writer

◆ FOOL

Quotations

"Ordinarily he was insane, but he had lucid moments when he was merely stupid."

Henrich Heine (1797–1856), German poet and writer, describing Savoye when appointed ambassador to Frankfurt, 1848

"It has been said that there is no fool like an old fool, except a young fool. But the young fool has first to grow up to be an old fool to realise what a damn fool he was when he was a young fool."

[Maurice] Harold Macmillan,
1st Earl of Stockton (1894–1986),
British prime minister

"However big the fool, there is always a bigger fool to admire him."

Nicolas Boileau-Despré aux (1636–1711),
French poet and writer

"They never open their mouths without subtracting from the sum of human knowledge."

Thomas Brackett Reed (1839–1902),
U.S. politician, commenting on
fellow congressmen

"A fool and his words are soon parted; a man of genius and his money."

William Shenstone (1714–1763), British
poet, Essays on Men and Manners
(1764), "On Reserve"

"Let us be thankful for the fools. But for them the rest of us could not succeed."

Mark Twain [Samuel Langhorne Clemens]
(1835–1910), U.S. humorist, writer and
speaker, Following the Equator
(1897), ch. 28

Classical Phrases and Myths

"Wise men benefit more from fools than fools from wise men; for the wise avoid the fools' mistakes, but fools do not follow the wise's successes."

Marcus Porcius Cato [the Elder]
(234 B.C.-149 B.C.), Roman statesman

"Talk sense to a fool and he calls you foolish."

Euripides (480 B.C.–406 B.C.),
Greek playwright, The Bacchae
(c. 407 B.C.), l. 480

"*Tantia stultitia mortalium est.*" (What fools these mortals be.)

Seneca [Lucius Annaeus Seneca]
(c. 5 B.C.–A.D. 65), Roman writer,
philosopher and statesman, Epistles, I, iii

◆ FOOLISHNESS

Foreign Words and Phrases

finita la commedia (Ita)
(fin-EE-tah la kom-MED-yah) the farce is over, the game is up

Schlaraffenland (Ger)
(shlar-AHF-en-lant) fool's paradise

outré (Fra)
(OO-tray) improper, outrageous, unconventional

Quotations

" 'You are old, Father William,' the young man said,
'And your hair has become very white;
And yet you incessantly stand on your head—
Do you think, at your age, it is right?'
'In my youth,' Father William replied to his son.
'I feared it might injure the brain;
But now that I'm perfectly sure I have none,
Why, I do it again and again.' "

Lewis Carroll [Charles Lutwidge
Dodgson] (1832–1898),
British writer and mathematician,
Alice's Adventures in
Wonderland (1865), ch. 5

"Boys, I may not know much, but I know the difference between chicken shit and chicken salad."

Lyndon Baines Johnson (1908–1973),
U.S. president, commenting on
contents of Vice President
Richard Nixon's speech

"The follies which a man regrets most, in his life, are those which he didn't commit when he had the opportunity."

Helen Rowland (1875–1950), U.S. writer,
A Guide to Men (1922), p. 87

Classical Phrases and Myths

"On occasion discretion should be discarded, and with the foolish we should play the fool."

*Menander (c. 342 B.C.-292 B.C.),
Greek playwright*, Those Offered for Sale

◆ FOREIGNER

Foreign Words and Phrases

gringo (Spa)
(GREEN-goh) *lit:* foreign; stranger in Mexico; (used pejoratively) foreigner, especially from U.S.

Auslinder (Ger)
(OWS-len-der) foreigner, alien (often pejorative, suggesting boorishness)

Quotations

"They spell it Vinci and pronounce it Vinchy; foreigners always spell better than they pronounce."

*Mark Twain [Samuel Langhorne Clemens]
(1835–1910), U.S. humorist, writer and
speaker*, The Innocents Abroad
(1869), ch. 19

Jokes, Stories and Anecdotes

As the Englishman registered in the Hawaiian hotel, the concierge, hearing his accent, said warmly, "Ah, a foreigner." The Englishman turned crimson and said, "Certainly not! English!"

◆ FORESIGHT

Quotations

"What all the wise men promised has not happened, and what all the

damned fools said would happen has come to pass."

*William Lamb, 2nd Viscount of
Melbourne (1779–1848), British prime
minister, commenting on Catholic
emancipation*

Jokes, Stories and Anecdotes

Married to the Duke of York, later George VI, Elizabeth visited Marshal Lyautey's Colonial Exhibition at Vincennes. At one point, Elizabeth said to the marshal, "Monsieur le Marechal, you are so powerful. You created the beautiful country of Morocco and this fine exhibition. Would you do something for me?" The marshal courteously asked what he could do. "The sun is in my eyes," said the duchess. "Would you make it disappear?" Just then a cloud passed in front of the sun. Other guests within earshot looked with wonder at Lyautey. Explained the smiling Elizabeth to a friend, "I saw the cloud coming."

*Elizabeth the Queen Mother
(1900–   ), British queen*

Puzzled by the play *Rosencrantz and Guildenstem Are Dead*, which became an international success, a friend of British dramatist Tom Stoppard asked, "What's it about?" Responded Stoppard, "It's about to make me a rich man."

*Tom Stoppard (1937–   ),
British playwright*

◆ FORGETFULNESS

Quotations

" 'The horror of that moment,' the King went on, 'I shall never, never forget!' 'You will, though,' the

Queen said, 'if you don't make a memorandum of it.' "

Lewis Carroll [Charles Lutwidge Dodgson] (1832–1898), British writer and mathematician, Through the Looking-Glass (1872), ch. I

"May I please see your program, madam? I forget what comes first."

Josef Casimir Hofmann (1876–1957), Polish-born pianist, to a spectator in the front row of a concert at which he was performing

Classical Phrases and Myths

lapsus memoriae (Lat)
(LAP-sus mem-OR-ee-ay) lapse or fault of memory

In Greek mythology, the Lethe (LEE-theh) was one of the rivers in Hades, the underworld; drinking its waters caused one to forget the past. Hence, to be *lethean* is to be forgetful and unable to recollect past events.

Jokes, Stories and Anecdotes

To remind herself that there was something she wanted to be sure to do, an absentminded woman put a rubber band around her wrist. She later noticed the rubber band but couldn't remember why it was there. She fretted until 3 A.M., and only then remembered why—she had wanted to go to bed early that night.

In the foyer of a hotel, British conductor Sir Thomas Beecham vaguely recognized a distinguished-looking woman whose name he could not remember. Pausing to talk to her, he remembered that she had a brother, so, hoping for a clue, he asked how her brother was and if he was still working at the same job. "Oh, he's very

well," she answered, "and still king."

Sir Thomas Beecham (1879–1961), British conductor

The absentminded Bishop of Exeter, William Cecil, was traveling by rail but had mislaid his ticket and was unable to produce it for the ticket collector. "No problem, my lord," said the collector, "we know who you are." "That's all very well," replied the bishop, "but without the ticket, how am I to know where I'm going?"

William Cecil (1863–1936), British clergyman [attributed also to Ambassador Dwight Morrow]

When the British writer G. K. Chesterton became engaged to be married, he went straight home and devotedly wrote his mother a long letter informing her of the happy event. The delighted Mrs. Chesterton was not at all surprised to receive his letter; she was in the room with him when he wrote it.

G[ilbert] K[eith] Chesterton (1874–1936), British man of letters

The actor Leslie Howard once froze onstage, having forgotten his lines. He whispered desperately to the stage prompter, "What's my line?" Whispered back the prompter, "What's the play?"

Leslie Howard (1890–1943), British actor

Even after Transcendentalist philosopher Immanuel Kant discharged his faithful servant Lampe, Kant could not dismiss Lampe from his mind. He thus wrote in his journal, "Remember, in the future the name of Lampe must be completely forgotten."

Immanuel Kant (1724–1804), German philosopher

During a murder trial, defense barrister Sir John Maynard challenged

Lord Jeffreys, the presiding judge, on a point of law. "Sir," the judge said reprovingly, "you have grown so old you have forgotten the law." Maynard countered, "I have forgotten more law than you ever knew, but allow me to say, I have not forgotten much."

*Sir John Maynard (1602–1690),
British lawyer*

◆ FORGIVENESS

Foreign Words and Phrases

tout comprendre c'est tout pardonner (Fra)
(too KOM-pren seh too par-DON-eh) to understand everything is to pardon everything

Quotations

"Why don't you sin a little? Doesn't God deserve to have something to forgive you for!"

*Martin Luther (1483–1546),
German Protestant theologian, encouraging
his virtuous and reserved friend
Philips Melanchthon*

"I never forgive but I always forget."

*Arthur James Balfour, 1st Earl of Balfour
(1848–1930), British prime minister*

"There is, however, a limit at which forbearance ceases to be a virtue."

*Edmund Burke (1729–1797),
British statesman, philosopher and writer,
Observations on a Publication,
"The Present State of the Nation" (1769)*

"One should forgive one's enemies, but not before they are hanged."

*Henrich Heine (1797–1856),
German poet and writer*

"The stupid neither forgive nor forget; the naive forgive and forget;

the wise forgive but do not forget."

*Thomas Szasz (1920–   ),
U.S. psychiatrist, The Second Sin
(1973), "Personal Conduct"*

Jokes, Stories and Anecdotes

Alexander Korda first offered a film part to English actress Ann Todd, but then made the film with another actress. Upset by his treachery, Todd stormed at Korda. "I wouldn't have done it to anyone else," said Korda. Taken aback, Todd inquired, "What do you mean?" "You and I are such good friends," Korda replied sweetly, "I knew that you would forgive me."

*Sir Alexander Korda (1893–1956),
British film producer and director*

◆ FREEDOM & LIBERATION

Quotations

"We sure liberated the hell out of this place."

*Anonymous U.S. soldier in ruined
French village*

"The condition upon which God hath given liberty to man is eternal vigilance; which condition if he break, servitude is at once the consequence of his crime, and the punishment of his guilt."

*John Philpot Curran (1750–1817),
Irish lawyer and judge, speech on the
right of election of lord mayor of Dublin,
July 10, 1790 [attributed also to
Thomas Jefferson; commonly quoted as
"The price of liberty is eternal vigilance"]*

"O Freedom, what liberties are taken in thy name!"

*Daniel George [Bunting] (c. 1900s),
U.S. poet, Perpetual Pessimist
(1963), p. 58*

"I know not what course others may take; but as for me, give me liberty, or give me death!"

> Patrick Henry (1736–1799),
> U.S. politician, speech in
> Virginia Convention March 23, 1775

"*Il vaut mieux mourir debout que de vivre à genoux!*" (It is better to die standing than to live on your knees!)

> Dolores Ibárruri ["La Pasionaria"]
> (1895–1989), Spanish politician,
> speech in Paris, September 3, 1936
> [attributed also to Emiliano Zapata]

"Freedom is never voluntarily given by the oppressor; it must be demanded by the oppressed."

> Martin Luther King, Jr. (1929–1968),
> U.S. social reformer

"Freedom's just another word for nothin' left to lose,
Nothin' ain't worth nothin', but it's free."

> Kris Kristofferson (1936–   ),
> U.S. songwriter, singer and actor and
> Fred Foster (c. 1900s), U.S. songwriter,
> Me and Bobby McGee (1969 song)

"It is true that liberty is precious— so precious that it must be rationed."

> Nikolai Lenin [Vladimir Ilich Ulyanov]
> (1870–1924), Russian statesman

"Many politicians lay it down as a self-evident proposition that no people ought to be free until they are fit to use their freedom. The maxim is worthy of the fool in the old story who resolved not to go into the water until he had learned to swim."

> Thomas Babington Macaulay, 1st Baron
> (1800–1859), British statesman and writer

"Liberty consists in doing what one desires."

> John Stuart Mill (1806–1873), British
> philosopher, On Liberty (1859), ch. 5

"He that would make his own liberty secure must guard even his enemy from oppression."

> Thomas Paine (1737–1809), British writer
> and revolutionary, Dissertation on First
> Principles of Government (1795)

"No human being, however great, or powerful, was ever so free as a fish."

> John Ruskin (1819–1900), British writer
> and social reformer, The Two Paths,
> Lecture V

"Liberty means responsibility. That is why most men dread it."

> George Bernard Shaw (1856–1950),
> Irish playwright, Man and Superman
> (1903), "Maxims for Revolutionists:
> Democracy"

"My definition of a free society is a society where it is safe to be unpopular."

> Adlai E[wing] Stevenson (1900–1965),
> U.S. politician, speech in Detroit,
> October 7, 1952

"We have . . . fought for our place in the sun and have won it."

> William II [Kaiser Wilhelm II]
> (1859–1941), German emperor

"*O liberté! O liberté! Que de crimes on commet en ton nom!*" (O liberty! O liberty! What crimes are committed in thy name!)

> Jeanne Manon Roland (1754–1793),
> French aristocrat, exclaiming, while
> mounting the steps to the guillotine, at
> the statue of Liberty set up in the Place de
> la Revolution

Classical Phrases and Myths

"*Nullius addictus iurare in verba magistri,
Quo me cumque rapit tempestas, deferor hospes.*" (I am not bound over to swear allegiance to any master; where the wind carries me, I put into port and make myself at home.)

> Horace (65 B.C.-8 B.C.), Roman poet,
> Epistles, I, i, l, 14

◆ FRIENDSHIP

Foreign Words and Phrases

bon compagnon (Fra)
(bon com-pan-NJON) good companion

camaraderie (Fra)
(kahm-ah-RAHD-er-EE) friendship, clique

intime (Fra)
(an-TEEM) an intimate friend

l'amour est aveugle, l'amitié ferme les yeux (Fra)
(la-MOUR ay a-VYOO-gle la-MEE-tee-ay fehrm lay-ZUH) love is blind, friendship closes its eyes

faux bonhomme-(Fra)
(foh bon-OM) *lit:* falsely good-natured man; hypocrite who feigns good intentions or fellowship

Quotations

"Acquaintance, n. A person whom we know well enough to borrow from, but not well enough to lend to. A degree of friendship called slight when its object is poor or obscure, and intimate when he is rich or famous."

Ambrose [Gwinnet] Bierce (1842-c. 1914),
U.S. writer and poet,
Cynic's Word Book (1906)

"In prosperity our friends know us; in adversity we know our friends."

John Churton Collins (1848–1908),
British writer and scholar

"A friend in need is a friend indeed." *English proverb* [*cf.* "No one is more friendly to a man than a friend in need."]

Titus Maccius Plautus, Epidicius,
Act III, sc. iii

"A man, sir, should keep his friendship in a constant repair."

Samuel Johnson (1709–1784),
British man of letters

"God gives us our relatives—thank God we can choose our friends."

Ethel Watts Mumford (1878–1940),
U.S. writer; Oliver Herford (1863–1935),
U.S. humorist and illustrator; Addison
Mizner (1872–1933), U.S. architect and
entrepreneur, Cynic's Calendar *(1903)*

"I do not believe that friends are necessarily the people you like best, they are merely the people who got there first."

Sir Peter [Alexander] Ustinov
(1921–   ), British actor and writer

"We cherish our friends not for their ability to amuse us, but for ours to amuse them."

Evelyn Waugh [Arthur St. John]
(1903–1966), British writer

"He hasn't an enemy in the world, and none of his friends like him."

Oscar [Fingal O'Flahertie Wills] Wilde
(1854–1900), British playwright, writer
and wit, describing George Bernard Shaw

Classical Phrases and Myths

alter ego (Lat)
(AL-ter EH-go) *lit:* one's second self; very close friend (often used inaccurately to refer to another aspect of one's personality)

koinonia (Grk)
(KOH-in-ohn-ia) a spirit of fellowship; collegiality, e.g., the Academy

"What is a friend? A single soul dwelling in two bodies."

Aristotle (384 B.C.-322 B.C.),
Greek philosopher

"Every man is known by the company he keeps."

> Euripides (480 B.C.-406 B.C.),
> Greek playwright, Phoenix

Jokes, Stories and Anecdotes

Alexander I's accession to the Russian throne was achieved through the murder of his father, Czar Paul I. Similarly, a generation earlier, Alexander's grandmother, Catherine the Great, had arranged for the murder of her husband, Peter III, to seize power herself. Although Alexander had preferred to believe that the conspirators would only imprison—not murder—his father, the conspirators nonetheless continued in his favor, and some became his closest counselors. The Countess de Bonneuil, a French spy, reported: "The young emperor goes about preceded by the murderers of his grandfather, followed by the murderers of his father, quite surrounded by his friends."

> Alexander I (1777–1825), Russian czar
> [attributed also to Talleyrand]

◆ FRIGHT & FRIGHTFULNESS

Foreign Words and Phrases

bête noire-(Fra)
(bet nwah) lit: black beast; pet aversion, something provoking fear and trepidation

Quotations

"The time of fear is over. Now comes the time of hope."

> Tristan Bernard (1866–1947),
> French playwright and writer, remarking
> to his wife as they were arrested by
> the Gestapo during WW II

"There is no terror in a bang, only in the anticipation of it."

> Sir Alfred Hitchcock (1899–1980),
> British film director

"Even a paranoid has real enemies."

> Henry Kissinger (1923–   ),
> U.S. diplomat

Classical Phrases and Myths

"My heart was in my mouth."

> Petronius, Gaius [Petronius Arbiter]
> (d.c. 66), Roman writer, Satyricon, sec. 62

"Quid si nunc caelum ruat?" (kwid see nunc KAY-lum ROO-at) (It is asked what if the sky were to fall?)

> Terence [Publius Terentius Afer]
> (c. 190 B.C.-159 B.C.), Roman playwright,
> Heauton Timoroumenos

Jokes, Stories and Anecdotes

"Give me all the money. I don't want to hurt you," ordered the tall burly man, pointing a revolver, who tried to rob a Tenderloin liquor store in San Francisco on March 8, 1991. The 35-year-old clerk responded with an adamant "no," and the gunman immediately burst into tears, but had sufficient composure to flee.

Two priests died and arrived at the Pearly Gates, and were quickly followed by two debt collectors. St. Peter motioned the clergy aside and first admitted the collectors. "Why them ahead of us?" asked the priests. "Didn't we do everything to spread the good word?" "Yes," said St. Peter, "but the collectors scared the hell out of more people than you did."

Asked about his thoughts just before taking off into space, John Glenn, the first U.S. astronaut in space, replied: "I looked around me and suddenly realized that everything had been built by the lowest bidder."

John Glenn (1927–   ),
U.S. astronaut and politician

◆ FUNERAL

Quotations

"The only reason I might go to the funeral is to make absolutely sure that he's dead."

Anonymous "eminent editor"
commenting on Lord Beaverbrook, 1965

"The reason so many people showed up at his funeral was because they wanted to make sure he was dead."

Samuel [Samuel Goldfish] Goldwyn
(1882–1974), Russian-born U.S. film
producer, explaining the large attendance
at film producer Louis Mayer's funeral

Jokes, Stories and Anecdotes

When the great actor Maurice Barrymore was being laid to rest, the straps supporting the coffin became twisted. In order to make an adjustment, the coffin, already lowered into the grave, had to be raised again. When it reappeared, Lionel Barrymore leaned over to his brother John and whispered, "How like Father—a curtain call!"

Lionel Barrymore (1878–1954), U.S. actor

At Dorothy Parker's funeral service, the actor Zero Mostel, noting that she had requested there be no formal ceremony, quipped, "In fact, if she had her way, I suspect she would not be here at all."

Zero Mostel (1915–1977), U.S. actor

◆ FUTURE

Quotations

"Cheer up! The worst is yet to come!"

Philander Chase Johnson (1866–1939),
U.S. writer, Everybody's Magazine
(May 1920)

"The best way to predict the future is to invent it."

Allen Kay (1945–   ),
U.S. inventor

"In the long run we are all dead."

Baron John Maynard Keynes
(1883–1946), British economist,
Tract on Monetary Reform *(1923), ch. 3*

"I have heard tell of a Professor of Economics who has a sign on the wall of his study, reading 'the future is not what it was.' The sentiment was admirable; unfortunately, the past is not getting any better either."

Bernard Levin (1928–   ), British
writer, Sunday Times *(May 22, 1977)*

◆ GAMBLE

Foreign Words and Phrases

a cheval (Fra)
(ah she-VAHL) *lit:* on horseback; used in roulette to indicate a bet placed across two adjacent numbers

pari mutuel (Fra)
(PAR-ee MOOT-oo-ell) *lit:* mutual betting; horse racing lottery in which the total of losers' stakes on any race is divided, after the deduction of a legally fixed amount from the pool, among the winners in proportion to the amount each has staked

faites vos jeux (Fra)
(FEHT vo-ZJUH) *lit:* make your
sport; place your bets

Quotations

*"Il y a deux grand plaisirs dans le jeu,
celui de gagner et celui de perdre."*
(There are two great pleasures in
gambling: that of winning and that
of losing.)

French proverb

"Death and dice level all distinc-
tions."

*Samuel Foote (1720–1777),
British actor and playwright*

Classical Phrases and Myths

meo periculo (Lat)
(me-oh per-IK-ul-oh) at my risk

Jokes, Stories and Anecdotes

"Now I need $50 more," said the
prospective borrower to the banker.
"I bet my partner $50 that you'd
turn me down."

Sign in the window of a clothier in
Atlantic City: "While You're Here,
Why Don't You Have Your Clothes
Cleaned, Too?"

Then there was the banker who
drove his $90,000 Mercedes to Las
Vegas and returned on a $1,400,000
Greyhound.

Franklin Pierce Adams belonged to
a poker club that included among
its members Herbert Ransom, an
actor. Because Ransom's lack of a
poker face always revealed when
he held a good hand, Adams suggested a new rule for the club:
"Anyone who looks at Ransom's
face is cheating."

*Franklin Pierce Adams (1881–1960),
U.S. writer*

French playwright Tristan Bernard
was wearing a jaunty new yachting
cap, and a friend commented on it.
Bernard stated that he had just
bought it with his winnings from the
previous night's play at the casino.
The friend was congratulating him
when Bernard said, "Ah, but with
what I lost I could have bought the
yacht."

*Tristan Bernard (1866–1947),
French playwright and writer*

President "Silent Cal" Coolidge
was sitting at dinner next to a
woman who tried to coax him into
talking to her. "Oh, Mr. President,
I bet a friend of mine that I could
persuade you to say more than two
words to me. Would you?" He answered: "You lose."

*[John] Calvin Coolidge (1872–1933),
U.S. president [authenticity unverified]*

The husband was silently sneaking
into bed at 2 A.M., after a long evening playing poker, when his wife
said, "Ha! 2 o'clock! I suppose
you're going to tell me you were
out somewhere holding a sick
friend's hand." "If I'd been holding
his hand," replied the man sadly,
"we'd be far richer tonight!"

◆ GAMES

Foreign Words and Phrases

cercle privé (Fra)
(SER-klapree-VAY) *lit:* private
group; private gaming party
Kriegspiel (Ger)
(KREEG-shpeel) *lit:* war game;
chess-playing in which opponent's
position is unseen but gleaned from
information given by an umpire, *ie,*
legality of move, taking of pieces, etc.

Quotations

"Life's too short for chess."

*Henry James Byron (1834–1884),
British playwright, Our Boys, Act I*

Jokes, Stories and Anecdotes

A man surprised his wife in the arms of his best friend. To calm the shocked husband, the friend suggested they play dominoes. "If I win," he said, "you divorce her so I can marry her. If you win, I'll leave you two alone, OK?" "OK," agreed the husband. "But what about a penny a point to make it interesting?"

Facing Algonquin wit George S. Kaufman's icy stare of disapproval, a fellow bridge player inquired, "All right, George, how would you have played it?" "Under an assumed name."

George S[imon] Kaufman (1889–1961), U.S. playwright, writer and wit

◆ GENERATION

Quotations

"Every new generation is a fresh invasion of savages."

Hervey Allen (1889–1949), U.S. educator, poet and writer

"Every generation laughs at the old fashions, but follows religiously the new."

Henry David Thoreau (1817–1862), U.S. writer, naturalist and poet, Walden (1854), "Economy"

"*Une génération perdue.*" (A lost generation.)

Gertrude Stein (1874–1946), U.S. writer, referring to Hemingway's literary generation; the remark is originally from a certain Monsieur Pernollet, commenting on the undereducated generation that spent its youth in WWI trenches

◆ GENEROSITY

Jokes, Stories and Anecdotes

"When I drink, everybody drinks!" the man shouted throughout the tavern. A loud cheer went up. After downing his Scotch, he hopped onto a bar stool, shouting, "When I have another drink, everybody has another drink." Another cheer and round of drinks. After finishing his second drink, the man hopped onto the bar. "And when I pay," he bellowed, slapping $5 into the bartender's hand, "everybody pays!"

U.S. automobile manufacturer Henry Ford answered a plea for a donation to a new orphanage while vacationing in Dublin, Ireland, by contributing 2,000 pounds. His generosity made headlines, but the sum was wrongly quoted as 20,000 pounds. "I'll phone the editor and tell him to correct the mistake," said the orphanage director, who had called on Ford at his hotel to apologize. Ford instead took out his checkbook and pen. "I'll give you a check for the remaining 18,000 pounds, but on one condition," said Ford. "I want the new building to bear this inscription on it: 'I Was a Stranger, and You Took Me In.'"

Henry Ford (1863–1947), U.S. industrialist

As he was boarding a moving train, Mahatma Gandhi, who lived an extremely spartan existence despite his international renown, lost one of his shoes. Unable to retrieve it, he blithely discarded his other shoe. Asked to explain his behavior, Gandhi replied, "The poor man who finds the shoe lying on the track will now have a pair he can use."

Mohandas Karamchand [Mahatma] Gandhi (1869–1948), Indian statesman and spiritual leader [authenticity unverified]

◆ GENIUS

Quotations

"Conversation enriches the understanding, but solitude is the school of Genius."

> Edward Gibbon (1737–1794),
> British historian, Memoirs (1796)

"There sit the sainted sage, the bard divine,
The few, whom genius gave to shine
Thro' every unborn age, and undiscover'd clime."

> Thomas Gray (1716–1771), British poet,
> Ode for Music (1769)

"Genius does what it must, and talent does what it can.

> Owen Meredith [Edward Robert Bulwer-Lytton, Earl of Lytton] (1831–1891),
> British poet, Poems. Last Words of a Sensitive Second-Rate Poet

"Anybody can make the simple complicated. Creativity is making the complicated simple."

> Charles Mingus (1922–1979),
> U.S. musician

"It takes chaos in the soul to give birth to a dancing star."

> Friedrich [Wilhelm] Nietzsche (1844–1900), German philosopher,
> Thus Spake Zarathustra (1883–1891)

"Everybody denies I am a genius—but nobody ever called me one!"

> [George] Orson Welles (1915–1985),
> U.S. actor and filmmaker

"Genius is one per cent inspiration, ninety-nine per cent perspiration."

> Thomas Alva Edison (1847–1931),
> U.S. inventor, c. 1903

"You may have genius. The contrary is, of course, probable."

> Oliver Wendell Holmes, Jr. (1841–1935),
> U.S. jurist

Classical Phrases and Myths

cathexis (Grk)
(kath-EX-is) burst of thought from an idea or object

"There is no great genius without tincture of madness."

> Seneca [Lucius Annaeus Seneca] (c.5 B.C.-65), Roman writer, philosopher and statesman, Moral Essays, "On Tranquility of the Mind," paraphrasing Aristotle's Problemata, XXX and Plato's Phaedrus, CCILV

◆ GIFT

Foreign Words and Phrases

lagniappe (Fra)
(lan-YAP) unexpected gift to stranger or customer; a bribe

Quotations

"We do not quite forgive a giver. The hand that feeds us is in some danger of being bitten."

> Ralph Waldo Emerson (1803–1882),
> U.S. writer, poet and philosopher,
> Essays: Second Series (1844), "Gifts"

"It's better to give than to lend, and it costs about the same."

> Sir Philip Gibbs (1877–1962),
> British writer

Jokes, Stories and Anecdotes

The Romantic poet Lord Byron once gave a beautifully bound Bible to his publisher, John Murray, who would proudly display it on a table where guests might see it. A visitor admiring the book noticed that at John 18:40, in the sentence "Now Barabbas was a robber," Byron had deleted the word "robber" and substituted "publisher." The book was thereafter removed from display.

George Gordon, Lord Byron (1788–1824), British poet

Burlesque and comedy writer Paul Scarron was about to marry his beautiful but impoverished young bride, who would later become Louis XIV's second wife. When the notary drawing up the marriage contract asked Scarron what dowry he intended to bestow upon her, he replied, "Immortality."

Paul Scarron (1610–1660), French poet, playwright and writer

◆ GLORY & HERO

Foreign Words and Phrases

preux chevalier (Fra)
(preoh shev-A-lee-ay) *lit:* peerless knight; knight in shining armor

Quotations

"No man is a hero to his valet."

Mme Cornuel (1605–1694), French aristocrat, Lettress de Mlle Aissé (August 13, 1728)

"Show me a hero and I will write you a tragedy."

F[rancis] Scott [Key] Fitzgerald (1896–1940), U.S. writer, Note-Books E

Classical Phrases and Myths

"*Sic transit gloria mundi:* " (seek TRAN-sit GLOR-ee-a MUND-ee) (Thus passes away the glory of the world.)

Thomas à Kempis [Thomas Hamerken von Kempen] (c. 1380–1471), German monk and writer, Imitatio Christi (c. 1420), bk. I, ch. 3

Alexander the Great wept at his father's military conquests not for the misery and casualties endured by the soldiers and civilians, but for

fear that no fame or glory would remain for him.

Alexander III [Alexander the Great] (356 B.C.–323 B.C.), Macedonian king

In Greek mythology, Prometheus (pro-ME-thee-us) was a Titan who fought his brothers with Zeus. Some say it was he who split the skull of Zeus so that Athena could emerge. Athena taught Prometheus many arts—how to walk erect and lift his head to the sun and stars, how to use numbers and letters, how to sail the seas in ships, how to cultivate the fields and to tame wild beasts, and the creative arts—which he passed on to mankind. In pity of man, Prometheus stole fire from the gods and gave it to man. As punishment, Prometheus was bound to a rock in the Caucasus to have his liver forever gnawed by an eagle, which was eventually killed by Herakles. Chiron exchanged places with Prometheus, who assumed his role in Olympus as adviser to the gods. Hence, a promethean accomplishment is a glorious, wonderful achievement.

◆ GLUTTONY & FASTING

Foreign Words and Phrases

gourmand (Fra)
(GOOR-man) glutton and self-indulgent hedonist

Quotations

"They have digged their grave with their teeth."

Thomas Adams (1612–1653), British writer

◆ GOD & GODS

Foreign Words and Phrases

Gotterdammerung (Ger)
(GUH-ter-DEHM-er-ung) twilight of the gods; title of a Wagner opera

Quotations

"If it turns out that there is a God, I don't think that he's evil. But the worst that you can say about him is that basically he's an underachiever."

Woody Allen [Allen Stewart Konigsberg] (1935–   ), U.S. comedian and filmmaker, Love and Death (1975 film)

"I believe in the incomprehensibility of God."

Honoré de Balzac (1799–1850), French writer, letter to Madame Hanska, 1837

"Why don't You come on down and fight like a man!"

Tommy Bolt (1919–   ), U.S. golfer, shaking his fist at the heavens and making a challenge after a series of muffed putts

"God moves in a mysterious way His wonders to perform."

William Cowper (1731–1800), British poet, Olney Hyms (1779), no. 35

"It is the final proof of God's omnipotence that he need not exist in order to save us."

Peter De Vries (1910–1993), U.S. writer, Mackerel Plaza (1958), ch. 1

"Of course there's no such thing as a totally objective person, except Almighty God, if she exists."

Antonia Fraser (1932–   ), British historian

"Good God, how much reverence can you have for a Supreme Being who finds it necessary to include such phenomena as phlegm and tooth-decay in His divine system of creation?"

Joseph Heller (1923–   ), U.S. writer, Catch-22 (1961), ch. 18

"Operationally, God is beginning to resemble not a ruler but the last fading smile of a cosmic Cheshire cat."

Julian Huxley (1887–1975), British writer, Religion Without Revelation (1957 ed.), ch. 3

"If God made us in His image we have certainly returned the compliment."

Voltaire [François Marie Arouet] (1694–1778), French philosopher, writer and wit

"God will provide—ah, if only He would till He does!"

Yiddish proverb

"*Si Dieu n'existait pas, il faudrait l'inventer.*" (see deuh nex-EEST-ay pah, eel foh-DRAY luhn-VEHNT-ay) (If God did not exist, it would be necessary to invent him.)

Voltaire [François Marie Arouet] (1694–1778), French philosopher, writer and wit, Épître à l'Auteur du Livre des Trois Imposteurs (November 10, 1770)

◆ GOOD PERSON (GENTLEMAN)

Foreign Words and Phrases

mensch (Yid) (mensh) a good man

Quotations

"I joked about every prominent man in my lifetime, but I never met a man I didn't like."

Will[iam Penn Adair] Rogers (1879–1935), U.S. comedian, epitaph

"Any man who hates dogs and babies can't be all bad."

Leo [Calvin] Rosten (1908–   ), U.S. humorist, ad-libbing at a Friar's Club banquet to honor W. C. Fields's 40th year in show business, February 16, 1939 [misattributed to Fields as "Any man who hates children and dogs can't be all bad"]

"This above all: to thine own self be true,
And it must follow, as the night the day,
Thou canst not then be false to any man."

William Shakespeare (1564–1616), British playwright and poet, Hamlet (1601), Act I, sc. iii

"It is better to be beautiful than to be good. But . . . it is better to be good than to be ugly."

Oscar [Fingal O'Flahertie Wills] Wilde (1854–1900), British playwright, writer and wit, The Picture of Dorian Gray (1891), ch. 17

Jokes, Stories and Anecdotes

A newspaper ran a competition to recognize the most moral, respectable citizen. One entry received read: "I don't smoke, touch intoxicants or gamble. I am faithful to my wife and never look at another woman. I am hard-working, quiet and obedient. I go to bed early every night and rise with the dawn. I attend chapel regularly every Sunday. I've been like this for the past three years. But just wait until next spring, when they let me out of here!"

◆ GOSSIP

Quotations

"Alas! they had been friends in youth;
But whispering tongues can poison truth."

Samuel Taylor Coleridge (1772–1834), British poet and writer, Christabel (1797), pt. II

"There are many who dare not kill themselves for fear of what the neighbours will say."

Cyril Connolly (1903–1974), British writer

"Love and scandal are the best sweeteners of tea."

Henry Fielding (1707–1754), British writer, playwright and lawyer, Love in Several Masques (1743)

"If you haven't got anything good to say about anyone come and sit by me."

Alice Roosevelt Longworth (1884–1980), U.S. socialite, maxim embroidered on a cushion

"She poured a little social sewage into his ears."

George Meredith (1828–1909), British writer

"Walls have tongues, and hedges ears."

Jonathan Swift (1667–1745), Anglo-Irish clergyman and writer, Pastoral Dialogue, l. 8

"It is perfectly monstrous the way people go about nowadays saying things against one, behind one's back, that are absolutely and entirely true."

Oscar [Fingal O'Flahertie Wills] Wilde (1854–1900), British playwright, writer and wit

"There is only one thing in the world worse than being talked about, and that is not being talked about."

Oscar [Fingal O'Flahertie Wills] Wilde (1854–1900), British playwright, writer and wit, The Picture of Dorian Gray (1891), ch. 1

"Gossip is the art of saying nothing in a way that leaves practically nothing unsaid."

Walter Winchell (1897–1972), U.S. writer

"When a thing ceases to be a subject of controversy, it ceases to be a subject of interest."

William Hazlitt (1778–1830), British writer

◆ GOVERNMENT

Quotations

"How can one govern a country that has three hundred and fifty kinds of cheese?"

Charles André Joseph Marie de Gaulle (1890–1970), French president and general

"Now and then an innocent man is sent to the legislature."

Frank McKinney ["Kin"] Hubbard (1868–1930), U.S. humorist and writer

"Our greatest growth industry is the Civil Service."

Lord Lucas (1896–1967), British aristocrat

"Laws are like sausages; you should never watch them being made."

Honore Gabriel Riqueti, Comte de Mirabeau (1749–1791), French revolutionary statesman

"I don't make jokes. I just watch the government and report the facts."

Will[iam Penn Adair] Rogers (1879–1935), U.S. comedian

"If 'pro' is the opposite of 'con,' then 'progress' is the opposite of 'congress.' "

William Howard Taft (1857–1930), U.S. president and jurist

"In general, the art of government consists in taking as much money as possible from one part of the citizens to give to the other."

Voltaire [François Marie Arouet] (1694–1778), French philosopher, writer and wit

Classical Phrases and Myths

Themistocles, the Athenian leader who led the Greeks to the great naval victory over the Persians at Salamis (480 B.C.), once said that his infant son ruled all of Greece. When asked how this could be, he explained: "Athens dominates all Greece; I dominate Athens; my wife dominates me; and my infant son dominates her."

Themistocles (c. 527 B.C.–c. 460 B.C.), Greek statesman

Jokes, Stories and Anecdotes

A farmer said to his companion, "You know, that weather forecaster on the government radio station is always wrong." "Don't complain," remarked the second farmer. "Think how bad it would be if the government started regulating the weather instead of just predicting it!"

Ben Franklin was asked following the Constitutional Convention, "Well, doctor, do we have a republic or a monarchy?" Responded Franklin, "A republic, if we can keep it."

Benjamin Franklin (1706–1790), U.S. statesman and scientist

A customer in a major Delhi bookstore asked a store clerk for a copy of India's constitution soon after Indira Gandhi had declared a state of emergency in 1975. "I am sorry, sir," the bookseller said, "but we don't stock periodicals."

Indira Gandhi (1917–1984),
Indian prime minister

◆ GRANDILOQUENCE

Quotations

"He could not blow his nose without moralising on the state of the handkerchief industry."

Cyril Connolly (1903–1974),
British writer describing George Orwell

"I could deny myself the pleasure of talking, but not to others the pleasure of listening."

Oscar [Fingal O'Flahertie Wills] Wilde
(1854–1900), British playwright,
writer and wit

Classical Phrases and Myths

olet lucernam (Lat)
(OL-et loo-KER-nam) *lit:* it smells of the lamp; labored piece of writing which betrays the effort and pedantry put into it

dithyramb (Grk)
(DEE-thir-am) Greek hymn of wild character; Bacchanalian song; any passionate or inflated writing or speech

Alcibiades was telling Pericles, 40 years his senior, how best to govern Athens. "Alcibiades," said Pericles reproachfully, "when I was your age, I talked just as you do now." "How I should like to have known you then," replied Alcibiades, "when you were at your best."

Alcibiades (c. 450 B.C.–404 B.C.),
Greek general and politician

◆ GRATITUDE

Foreign Words and Phrases

Danke schon (Ger)
(DAN-ke SHUHN) many thanks

Quotations

"Isn't God good to me?"

Louis B. Mayer (1885–1957), U.S. film
producer driving away from the funeral of
Irving Thalberg, originally his protégé and
then his rival

"*La reconnaissance de la plupart des hommes n'est qu'un secrète envie de recevoir de plus grands bienfaits.*" (The gratitude of most men is only a secret desire to receive greater favors.)

François, Duc de La Rochefoucauld
(1613–1680), French writer,
Maximes (1678), 298

Jokes, Stories and Anecdotes

After a ten-year-old girl was rescued by a boy, she asked how she could reward him. "The best way," he replied, "is to say nothing about it. If my friends knew I'd pulled you out, they'd throw me in."

◆ GREATNESS & SUPERIORITY

Foreign Words and Phrases

non pareil (Fra)
(non PAR-ehv) without equal, incomparable

par excellence (Fra)
(par ex-SEL-ehnse) above all others of a similar type, preeminent(ly)

Quotations

"I'm the greatest."

> Muhammad Ali [Cassius Clay]
> (1942–   ), U.S. boxer,
> catch-phrase used c. 1962

"Anything you can do, I can do better,
I can do anything better than you."

> Irving Berlin [Israel Baline] (1888–1989),
> U.S. songwriter, Anything You Can Do
> (1946 song)

"The world's great men have not commonly been great scholars, nor its great scholars great men."

> Oliver Wendell Holmes, Sr. (1809–1894),
> U.S. writer and physician, The Autocrat
> of the Breakfast Table (1858), ch. 6

"What men prize most is a privilege, even if it be that of a chief mourner at a funeral."

> James Russell Lowell (1819–1891),
> U.S. poet

"We are both great men, but I have succeeded better in keeping it a profound secret than he has."

> Edgar Wilson ["Bill"] Nye (1850–1896),
> U.S. writer and humorist, referring to
> Mark Twain

"Some men are born great, some achieve greatness, and some have greatness thrust upon them."

> William Shakespeare (1564–1616),
> British playwright and poet,
> Twelfth Night (1600), Act II, sc. v

Classical Phrases and Myths

sui generis (Lat)
(SWU-ee GEN-er-is) in a class by itself, unique

"Unless degree is preserved, the first place is safe for no one."

> Publilius Syrus (c. 100 B.C.),
> Roman writer, Sententiae, 1042

According to Greek mythology, Olympus (oh-LIM-pus) was the mountain on the borders of Thessaly and Macedonia on which the 12 high gods dwelt. Hence, something olympian is something giant, magnificent or superior—and removed.

◆ GREED

Quotations

"If all the rich people in the world divided up their money among themselves, there wouldn't be enough to go round."

> Christina Stead (1902–1983),
> British writer, House of All Nations
> (1938), "Credo"

Classical Phrases and Myths

auri socra fames (Lat)
(OW-ree SAK-ra FAM-es) (the) accursed lust for gold

A farmer who went to check on his goose was pleasantly surprised one day to find in its nest an egg of solid gold. His joy increased daily, for the goose would lay another golden egg each morning. But as the farmer grew rich, he grew greedy. Thinking he could have all his treasure at once, he killed the golden goose only to find nothing inside; the greedy who want more lose all.

> Aesop (c. 600 B.C.), Greek fabulist

Jokes, Stories and Anecdotes

Last winter it was so cold that lawyers walked around with their hands in their own pockets.

◆ GUILT

Foreign Words and Phrases

qui s'excuse s'accuse (Fra)
(kee sex-KOOZ sah-KOOZ) he who
excuses himself, accuses himself

vergangenheitsverabeitung (Ger)
(FEHR-gahng-en-hite-sver-a-BIE-
tuhng) overcoming or conquering
the past, especially the Nazi chapter
in German history

Quotations

"Conscience: the inner voice which
warns us that someone may be
looking."

> H[enry] L[ouis] Mencken (1880–1956),
> U.S. critic and writer, Little Book in C
> Major (1916) p. 42

"The Eleventh Commandment:
Thou shalt not be found out."

> George John Whyte-Melville (1821–1878),
> British writer

Classical Phrases and Myths

mea culpa (Lat)
(ME-a KUL-pa) *lit:* I am guilty; admission of guilt

◆ HABIT

Foreign Words and Phrases

moeurs de province (Fra)
(MUHR de pro-VONS) provincial
habits, parochial manners

Quotations

"I've done it a hundred times!"

> Mark Twain [Samuel Langhorne Clemens]
> (1835–1910), U.S. humorist, writer and
> speaker, on quitting smoking

Jokes, Stories and Anecdotes

Dashiell Hammett, referring to Tallulah Bankhead's cocaine addiction,
told her at the opening-night party
for Lillian Hellman's *The Little
Foxes*, in which she starred, that he
did not care for people who took
drugs. Bankhead retorted, "Cocaine
habit-forming? Of course not. I
ought to know. I've been using it
for years."

> Tallulah Bankhead (1903–1968),
> U.S. actress

◆ HAIR

Quotations

"There was an Old Man with a
beard,
Who said, 'It is just as I feared!
Two Owls and a Hen,
Four Larks and a Wren,
Have all built their nests in my
beard!' "

> Edward Lear (1812–1888), British poet,
> Book of Nonsense (1846)

Classical Phrases and Myths

Before one battle, Alexander the
Great commanded his soldiers to
shave off their beards, explaining,
"There is nothing like a beard to get
hold of in a fight."

> Alexander III [Alexander the Great]
> (356 B.C.–323 B.C.), Macedonian king

Jokes, Stories and Anecdotes

"Split hair is a problem," the bald-
ing man agreed. "Mine split about
eight years ago."

Having had his hair cut at a new
barbershop, the French comedian
Fernandel was handed a mirror by
the proud barber anxious to please
his illustrious client. After the chair

was rotated so that Fernandel could see the back of his head, Fernandel studied the barber's handiwork and asked with a smile, "Just a little longer at the back, please."

Fernandel [Fernand Joseph Desiré Contandin] (1903–1971), French comedian

As Christopher Morley and William Rose Benet gazed through a shopwindow in which two identical small wigs were displayed on their stands, Morley quipped, "They're alike as toupees in a pod."

Christopher Morley (1890–1957), US writer

◆ HANDS

Quotations

"Give a man a free hand and he'll try to put it all over you."

Mae West (1892–1980), U.S. film actress, Klondike Annie (1936 film)

Jokes, Stories and Anecdotes

One cold day, Le Roi Soleil (the Sun King), who never wore gloves while hunting, rode past two peasants. To one, who expressed his alarm that Louis XIV took no precautions against the cold, the other peasant remarked, "Why should he? His hands are always in our pockets."

Louis XIV (1638–1715), French king

On the back of a picture postcard of the Venus de Milo that comedian Will Rogers sent to his niece from Paris, he wrote: "See what will happen to you if you don't stop biting your fingernails."

Will[iam Penn Adair] Rogers (1879–1935), U.S. comedian [attributed to others]

◆ HANDWRITING

Quotations

"There, I guess King George will be able to read that."

John Hancock (1737–1793), U.S. politician, remarking on signing in large, bold lettering the Declaration of Independence, July 4, 1776

"My handwriting looks as if a swarm of ants, escaping from an ink bottle, had walked over a sheet of paper without wiping their legs."

Sydney Smith (1771–1845), British clergyman and writer

Jokes, Stories and Anecdotes

Prince Charles awoke one morning to see that a beautiful snowfall had blanketed the grounds of Buckingham Palace. To his horror, however, pissed into the snow outside his window was the message: "Charles sucks." Indignant, he immediately called MI5, Scotland Yard, and the palace guards to find the villain responsible. Later, his aide informed him that he had bad news and terrible news regarding the insult. The bad news was that Prince William was the culprit. "What's the terrible news, then?" asked Charles. "It was Princess Diana's handwriting."

The great tragic actor William Macready handwrote a complimentary letter of admission to a theater as a favor to someone while on an American tour. Unable to decipher Macready's notoriously bad handwriting, the donee went to an apothecary, reasoning that a pharmacist, familiar with illegible doctor's prescriptions, could read the letter's contents. After quickly examining the paper, the young apothecary began mixing ingedients from assorted vials and jars to make a compound. But after puzzling over one ingredient, he summoned his boss who, after studying the paper, confidently finished the mixture. "A cough mixture, and a very good one," said the apothecary, handing the compound over the counter. "Fifty cents, please."

William Charles Macready (1793–1873), British actor

◆ HAPPINESS

Foreign Words and Phrases

bien être (Fra)
(byen etr) well-being

sans souci (Fra)
(song SOO-see) without care, concern, worry, etc.

khushi (Hin)
(KOO-shee) contentment, bliss

bon vivant (Fra)
(bon vee-VANT) *lit:* good living; one who enjoys the good things in life

Quotations

"A man hath no better thing under the sun than to eat and to drink and to be merry."

Ecclesiastes 8:15

"His best companions, innocence and health;
And his best riches, ignorance of wealth."

Oliver Goldsmith (1728–1774), Irish-born British poet, playwright and writer, The Deserted Village (1770), l. 51

"Only do always in health what you have often promised to do when you are sick."

Sigismund (1368–1437), Holy Roman Emperor, giving his recipe for lasting happiness in this world

"Happiness is no laughing matter."

Richard Whately (1787–1863), Irish clergyman, Apophthegms, p. 218

"On n'est jamais si heureux ni si malheureux qu'on s'imagine." (One is never so happy or so unhappy as one thinks.)

François, Duc de La Rochefoucauld (1613–1680), French writer, Maximes (1678), 49

Classical Phrases and Myths

horus non numero nisi serenas (Lat)
(HOR-us non NUM-er-oh SER-enas) I count only the serene hours

compos voti (Lat)
(KOM-pos WOH-tee) to have obtained one's wish(es)

vive ut vivas (Lat)
(WEE-we ut WEE-was) live that you may live (hereafter)

ataraxia (Grk)
(ah-tar-AX-ia) calmness, inner contentment, passiveness; the serenity and indifference aimed at by the Stoics

◆ HASTE

Quotations

"What is the use of running when you are on the wrong road?"

Proverb

"Half our life is spent trying to find something to do with the time we have rushed through life trying to save."

Will[iam Penn Adair] Rogers (1879–1935), U.S. comedian, letter to New York Times, September 29, 1930

"The haste of a fool is the slowest thing in the world."

Thomas Shadwell (c. 1642–1692), British playwright, A True Widow (1679), Act III, sc. i

"Hurry? I never hurry. I have no time to hurry."

Igor Feodorovitch Stravinsky (1882–1971), Russian-born composer, replying to his impatient publisher

Classical Phrases and Myths

festina lente (Lat)
(FES-tee-na LEN-te) more haste, less speed; Greek proverb

sine mora (Lat)
(sine MOHR-ah) without delay

"Sat celeriter fieri quidquid fiat satis bene." (Well done is quickly done.)

Augustus
[Gaius Julius Caesar Octavianus] (63 B.C.–14), Roman emperor; Latin proverb

Jokes, Stories and Anecdotes

Two privates, carrying a steaming caldron between them from the kitchens, were stopped by an officious lieutenant. "Put it down and get me a ladle," ordered the officer. "B-b-but, sir—" "That's an order!" snapped the officer. The privates produced a ladle, the officer dipped it into the caldron, brought it out, blew and swallowed a mouthful. "Yuk! Call that soup?" "N-no, sir," stammered a private, "it's dishwater."

Cop scribbling speeding ticket: "I'll make it quick; I see you're in a hurry."

Back on his estate after WWI, French general Louis Lyautey requested his gardener to plant a certain tree. The tree the marshal had chosen was particularly slow growing, the gardener protested, and would not reach maturity for at least a century. "Then there is no time to lose," the marshal replied. "Plant it this afternoon."

Louis Hubert Gonzalve Lyautey (1854–1934), French general

◆ HATE

Quotations

"Now hatred is by far the longest pleasure;
Men love in haste, but they detest at leisure."

George Gordon, Lord Byron (1788–1824), British poet, Don Juan (1818), Canto XIII, vi

"At Harvard, it took me ten years to achieve an environment of total hostility. Here [in Washington, D.C.] I've done it in 20 months."

Henry Kissinger (1923–   ), U.S. diplomat, responding to Attorney General John Mitchell's characterization of him as an "egocentric maniac"

"Any kiddie in school can love like a fool,
But hating, my boy, is an art."

Ogden Nash (1902–1971), U.S. humorist, Happy Days (1933), "Plea for Less Malice Toward None"

"To have a good enemy, choose a friend: he knows where to strike."

Diane de Poitiers (1499–1566), French aristocrat

"What dire offense from amorous causes springs,

What mighty contests rise from trivial things!''

Alexander Pope (1688–1744), British poet and writer, The Rape of the Lock (1712), Canto I, l. I

"Put an Irishman on the spit, and you can always get another Irishman to turn him."

George Bernard Shaw (1856–1950), Irish playwright

"I have only ever made one prayer to God, a very short one: 'O Lord, make my enemies ridiculous'. And God granted it."

Voltaire [François Marie Arouet] (1694–1778), French philosopher, writer and wit

"I'm lonesome. They are all dying. I have hardly a warm personal enemy left."

James Abbott McNeill Whistler (1834–1903), U.S.-born British artist

Classical Phrases and Myths

"I love treason but hate a traitor."

Gaius Julius Caesar (100 B.C.–44 B.C.), Roman general and statesman

"Io Proprium humani ingenii est odisse quem laeseris." (EE-oh PROH-pree-umhyoo-MAN-ee in-GEN-ee est oh-DEES kyem lay-SEHR-is) (It is human nature to hate the man whom you have hurt.)

Cornelius Tacitus (c. 55–117), Roman historian, Agricola (c. 98) 42, paraphrasing Seneca

Jokes, Stories and Anecdotes

"I suppose that when I die, soldier, you'll make a special trip to my grave just to spit on it," said the cruel drill instructor. "Not I, sir," replied the recruit. "Once I get outta here I'll never stand in line again."

The dying Frederick William the Just was admonished by the attending minister that he would have to forgive all of his enemies in order to reach heaven. With his hated brother-in-law, George II of England, foremost in his thoughts, the reluctant king instructed his wife, "Well, then, write to your brother and inform him that I forgive him, but be sure not to do so until after my death."

Frederick William I (1688–1740), Saxon king

A fiercely patriotic woman rebuked President Lincoln when he spoke mercifully about the erring Southerners at a reception during the Civil War, imploring the president to speak instead about destroying his enemies. "Why, madam," said Lincoln, "do I not destroy my enemies when I make them my friends?"

Abraham Lincoln (1809–1865), U.S. president

◆ HEALTH

Foreign Words and Phrases

Gesundheit (Ger) (ge-ZUHND-hyl) good health to you (often used after a sneeze)

Quotations

"If I'd known I was gonna live this long, I'd have taken better care of myself."

Eubie Blake [James Hubert Blake] (1883–1983), U.S. songwriter and composer, commenting on his 100th birthday (1983)

"I know a man who gave up smoking, drinking, sex and rich food. He was healthy right up to the time he killed himself."

Johnny Carson (1925–), U.S. television entertainer

"Be careful about reading health books. You may die of a misprint."

Mark Twain [Samuel Langhorne Clemens] (1835–1910), U.S. humorist, writer and speaker

Jokes, Stories and Anecdotes

A woman died and went to heaven, finding it even more beautiful than she'd expected. Months later when her grouchy husband arrived, she said, "Really heavenly, isn't it?" "Yeah," he grumbled, "and if it weren't for your damn oat bran we'd have gotten here six years ago."

◆ HEALTH CARE

Foreign Words and Phrases

maison de santi (Fra)
(meh-ZON de SON-lay) hospital or asylum (usually private)

Jokes, Stories and Anecdotes

Patient to psychiatrist: "Doctor, I'm beside myself. My husband thinks he's a piano." Psychiatrist: "Bring him in." Patient: "Are you crazy? Do you know what it costs to move a piano?"

A man had the flu last week. He was so full of penicillin that whenever he sneezed he cured somebody.

A doctor sent his patient to Miami for asthma. He finally got it.

After suffering a stroke in 1900, the playwright Henrik Ibsen had to abandon his writing and live the remaining six years of his life as a helpless invalid. One day he heard his nurse suggest that he was feeling a little better. He snapped, "On

the contrary!" and promptly died.

Henrik Ibsen (1828–1906), Norwegian playwright and poet

Soon after the appendectomy became a widely performed operation, German political reformer and heralded pathologist Rudolf Virchow was asked if humans could survive without the appendix. "Human beings, yes," the scientist remarked, "but not surgeons."

Rudolf Virchow (1821–1902), German pathologist and politician

---

◆ HEAVEN

Foreign Words and Phrases

nirvana (Skt)
(neer-VAH-nah) in Hinduism, the perfect state, in which needs and desires are nonexistent as one's identity is extinguished and absorbed into Brahman

Jokes, Stories and Anecdotes

Phillips Brooks refused to receive any visitors, even his dearest friends, while recovering from a serious illness. The Episcopal bishop did, however, make an exception for the agnostic Robert Ingersoll. Ingersoll, realizing the privilege, was curious to know the reason behind it. "I feel confident of seeing my friends in the next world," Brooks explained, "but this may be my last chance of seeing you."

Phillips Brooks (1835–1893), U.S. bishop

Bishop Fulton J. Sheen was scheduled to speak one evening at the town hall in Philadelphia but became lost *en route*. He approached a gang of toughs to ask directions. Asked by a gang member on what subject he was going to lecture, Sheen answered, "On how to get to heaven." Then he added, "Do you want to come along?" "Are you kidding?" replied the tough. "You don't even know how to get to the town hall!"

Bishop Fulton J[ohn] Sheen (1895–1979), U.S. clergyman, educator and writer

---

◆ HEAVINESS

Foreign Words and Phrases

bombé (Fra)
(bom-BAY) *lit:* bomb-shaped; bulging; swollen, especially a furniture style

Quotations

"Of course he was a wonderful all-round man, but the act of walking round him has always tired me."

Sir Max Beerbohm (1872–1956), British writer, caricaturist and wit, describing William Morris, letter to S. N. Behrman, c. 1953

"Just the other day in the Underground I enjoyed the pleasure of offering my seat to three ladies."

G[ilbert] K[eith] Chesterton (1874–1936), British man of letters, noting that his great girth afforded him moments of gallantry

"Imprisoned in every fat man a thin one is wildly signalling to be let out."

Cyril Connolly (1903–1974), British writer, Unquiet Grave (1944), pt. 2

"He must have had a magnificent build before his stomach went in for a career of its own."

Margaret Halsey (1910–   ), U.S. writer

"The Right Hon. was a tubby little chap who looked as though he had been poured into his clothes and had forgotten to say 'When!' "

P[elham] G[renville] Wodehouse (1881–1975), British writer and humorist, Very Good, Jeeves (1930), "Jeeves and the Impending Doom"

Jokes, Stories and Anecdotes

The French ambassador to London, the Duke of Guines, was a dandy despite his enormous girth. In his closet he kept two pairs of breeches for each outfit—one for occasions on which he would be standing, and the other, much bigger, for those on which he would sit. For those days when he was to remain standing, Guines would put on his breeches by climbing onto two chairs and lowering himself into the breeches as they were held up by two servants.

Adrien-Louis de Bonnières, Duke of Guines (1735–1806), French diplomat

A vain, corpulent actress confessed to Abbé Mugnier that she occasionally looked at her naked body in the mirror. "Is it a sin?" she demurely inquired. "No, madame," responded the abbé, eyeing her portly figure. "It's an error."

Abbé Arthur Mugnier (1853–1944), French clergyman

G. K. Chesterton, the author best known for his Father Brown detective stories, swung his ample girth up the steps of his club and met George Bernard Shaw, emerging. Chesterton, looking at Shaw's reed-thin figure, commented, "Shaw, to look at you, anyone would think that famine had struck England." "And to look at you, Chesterton," replied Shaw, "anyone would think that you had caused it."

George Bernard Shaw (1856–1950), Irish playwright [attributed also to others]

British barrister and Conservative MP F. E. Smith once teased Lord

Chief Justice Gordon Hewart about his enormous girth, asking him if he was expecting a boy or a girl. Hewart snorted. "If it's a boy, I shall call him John, and if it's a girl I shall call her Mary. Yet if, as I suspect, it's only wind, I shall call it F. E. Smith."

> F[rederick] E[dwin] Smith, 1st Earl of Birkenhead (1872–1930), British lawyer and politician [attributed also to William Howard Taft]

◆ HELL

Quotations

"He will not, whither he is now gone, find much difference, I believe, either in the climate or the company."

> Samuel Johnson (1709–1784), British man of letters, commenting on a Jamaican gentleman's recent death

"The infliction of cruelty with a good conscience is a delight to moralists. That is why they invented Hell."

> Bertrand Arthur William Russell, 3rd Earl (1872–1970) British mathematician and philosopher, Sceptical Essays (1928), "On the Value of Scepticism"

"Hell is paved with good intentions, not bad ones. All men mean well."

> George Bernard Shaw (1856–1950), Irish playwright, Man and Superman (1903), "Maxims for Revolutionists: Stray Sayings"

"Alors, c'est ça l'Enfer . . . l'Enfer, c'est les Autres." (So that's what Hell is . . . Hell is other people.)

> Jean-Paul Sartre (1905–1980), French philosopher, playwright and writer, Huis Clos (Closed Doors) (1944), sc. 5

Jokes, Stories and Anecdotes

According to British writer and playwright Sir James Barrie, a certain author was once executed for murdering his publisher. Reportedly, when the author was on the scaffold, he said goodbye to the minister and to the reporters. To some publishers sitting in the front row below, however, he said, "I'll see you later."

As is true for all lawyers, Sam went to hell when he died. While being led to his eternal damnation by the devil, he passed his ex-partner Merv making love to the most beautiful woman Sam had ever seen. "Is this hell thing some kinda joke?" he complained to the devil. "I've been condemned to spend eternity up to my neck in molten excrement, but Sam gets to screw himself silly!" The devil prodded Sam with his pitchfork, roaring, "Who are you to criticize that poor woman's punishment?"

◆ HISTORY

Foreign Words and Phrases

Geistesgeschichte (Ger) (GYST-es-ge-SHIK-te) lit: history of the spirit; cultural history

Quotations

"It's the good girls who keep the diaries; the bad girls never have the time."

> Tallulah Bankhead (1903–1968), U.S. actress

"History is a distillation of rumour."

> Thomas Carlyle (1795–1881), British historian, History of the French Revolution (1837), Pt. I, bk. VII, ch. 5

"History repeats itself. Historians repeat each other."

Philip Guedalla (1889–1944),
British writer

"Historians are like deaf people who go on answering questions that no one has asked them."

Leo Nikolaevich Tolstoy (1828–1910),
Russian writer

"History will say that the right honorable gentleman was wrong in this matter. I know it will, because I shall write the history."

Sir Winston Spencer Churchill
(1874–1965), British prime minister
and writer, arguing against a governmental
policy of Prime Minister Stanley
Baldwin in the House of Commons

"History is more or less bunk. It's tradition. We don't want tradition. We want to live in the present and the only history that is worth a tinker's damn is the history we make today."

Henry Ford (1863–1947),
U.S. industrialist [often contracted to
"History is bunk"]

"History repeats itself, first as tragedy, second as farce."

Karl Marx (1818–1883),
German philosopher

"History is littered with the wars which everybody knew would never happen."

Enoch Powell (1912–   ),
British politician speech to Conservative
Party Conference, October 19, 1967

"The people of Crete unfortunately make more history than they can consume locally."

Saki [Hector Hugh Munro] (1870–1916),
British writer, Chronicles of Clavis
(1914), "The Jesting of Arlington
Stringham"

"I always say, keep a diary and someday it'll keep you."

Mae West (1892–1980), U.S. film actress,
Every Day's a Holiday (1937 film)

"*Le nez de Cléopâtre: s'il eût été plus court, toute la face de la terre aurait changé.*" (Had Cleopatra's nose been shorter, the whole history of the world would have been different.)

Blaise Pascal (1623–1662),
French mathematician and writer,
Pensées (1670), no. 2, 162

Classical Phrases and Myths

"*At ingenium ingens*
Inculto latet hoc sub corpore." (But genius lies subsumed under that uncouth exterior.)

Horace (65 B.C.–8 B.C.), Roman poet,
Satires, I, iii, l. 33

◆ HOME

Foreign Words and Phrases

pied-à-terre (Fra)
(pee-AY ah TAIR) second home, temporary residence

chez moi (Fra)
(shaé, MWA) at my home

Quotations

"For a man's house is his castle, *et domus sua cuique est tutissimum refugium.*"

Sir Edward Coke (1552–1634),
British lawyer, Third Institute (1644)

"Old houses mended,
Cost little less than new before they're ended."

Colley Cibber (1671–1757),
British playwright, The Double Gallant
(1707), prologue

"Ah, my good friend, I wish God would let me stay at Whitton."

Sir Godfrey Kneller (1646–1723), German-born British painter, on his deathbed, preferring to remain at his country house rather than to pass on to a better place

"A man's home may seem to be his castle on the outside; inside, it is more often his nursery."

Clare Boothe [Brokaw] Luce (1903–1987), U.S. writer, playwright and diplomat

"I hate housework! You make the beds, you do the dishes—and six months later you have to start all over again."

Joan Rivers (1935–   ), U.S. comedian

Classical Phrases and Myths

"*Quae est domestica sede iucundior?*" (kay est DOHM-est-i-ka seed ee-uk-UND-ior) (What is better than one's home?)

Marcus Tullius Cicero (106 B.C.–43 B.C.), Roman statesman and man of letters, De Familiares, IV, viii

Jokes, Stories and Anecdotes

An English nobleman was proudly guiding Ben Franklin, then living in London, on a tour of the former's newly constructed home. Owing to the narrow, irregular shape of the lot on which the house had been built, however, the house had an impracticable floor plan behind its handsome colonnaded facade. "All you need to do to enjoy your house, my lord," observed Franklin, "is to rent a spacious apartment directly across the street."

Benjamin Franklin (1706–1790), U.S. statesman and scientist

In 1930 in Danbury, Connecticut, novelist Rex Stout hand-built a 14-room house on a hilltop. Sometime later, the architect Frank Lloyd Wright was invited by Stout to give an opinion. "A superb spot," Wright remarked after thoughtful consideration, "Someone should build a house here."

Frank Lloyd Wright (1869–1956), U.S. architect

◆ HOMOSEXUALITY

Quotations

"On bisexuality: It immediately doubles your chances of getting a date on Saturday night."

Woody Allen [Allen Stewart Konigsberg] (1935–   ), U.S. comedian and filmmaker

Classical Phrases and Myths

Sappho (SAF-oh) was a lyric poet from Lesbos who was believed to have been the center of attention among a literary coterie of women tied together by affection and intimacy. The poetry of Sappho was notable for its rich personal quality and melodious grace of language, and she was admired all over ancient Greece after her death. Hence, female lovers are described as *lesbian* and involved in *sapphism*.

Sappho (c. 600 B.C.), Greek poetess

◆ HONESTY

Quotations

"There's one way to find out if a man is honest—ask him. If he says 'yes,' you know he is crooked."

Groucho [Julius] Marx (1895–1977), U.S. comedian

"Though I am not naturally honest, I am so sometimes by chance."

William Shakespeare (1564–1616), British playwright and poet, The Winter's Tale *(1611), Act IV, sc. iii*

"It should seem that indolence itself would incline a person to be honest; as it requires infinitely greater pains and contrivance to be a knave."

William Shenstone (1714–1763), British poet

Classical Phrases and Myths

While marching through Asia Minor, Alexander the Great became dangerously ill. His physicians were afraid to treat him on the chance that he would die, but one physician, Philip the Acarnanian, was willing to take the risk, confident both of his abilities and of his friendship with Alexander. While the medicine was being prepared, an enemy of Philip's had delivered to Alexander a letter that accused the physician of having been bribed by the Persian king to poison his master. Alexander read the letter and hid it under his pillow without informing anyone of its contents. Later, when Philip handed Alexander the cup of medicine, Alexander handed Philip the letter. While the physician was reading it, Alexander calmly drank the contents of the cup. Horrified at the deceit, Philip threw himself at the king's feet, but Alexander assured him that he had complete confidence in Philip's honor. After three days the king recovered to lead his army again.

Alexander III [Alexander the Great] (356 B.C.—323 B.C.), Macedonian king

◆ HONOR

Foreign Words and Phrases

croix de guerre (Fra)
(krwa de GERR) *lit:* cross of war; medal

affaire d'honneur (Fra)
(ah-FAIR don-UHR) matter of principle, duel (often used ironically in English)

Quotations

"The louder he talked of his honor, the faster we counted our spoons."

Ralph Waldo Emerson (1803–1882), U.S. writer, poet and philosopher, The Conduct of Life *(1860), "Worship"*

"Remember, you're fighting for this woman's honor . . . which is probably more than she ever did."

Bert Kalmar (1884–1947); Harry Ruby (1895–1974); Arthur Sheekman (1891–1978); and Nat Perrin (c. 1900s), U.S. writers, Duck Soup *(1933 film)*

Classical Phrases and Myths

magna cum laude (Lat)
(MAG-na koom LOW-day) with much distinction, with high honors

honoris causa (Lat)
(hon-OR-is KOW-sa) *lit:* for the sake of honor; generally, an honor conferred without examination in recognition of some particular achievement

"*Ave Caesar, morituri te salutant.*"
(AY-vay KAY-sar, MOR-ee-toor-ee te SAL-oo-tant) (Hail Caesar, those who are about to die salute you.)

Suetonius (c. 70–140), Roman historian, salutation of Roman gladiators upon entering the arena

Jokes, Stories and Anecdotes

If everyone were from the South, it wouldn't be such an honor.

The great Cunard linear R.M.S. *Queen Mary* was originally to have been christened *Queen Victoria*. But when a Cunard executive informed King George V that the company wanted to name it after "the greatest of all English queens," the king happily exclaimed, "Oh, my wife will be pleased!"

George V (1865–1936), British king

As their taxi drove past the Arc de Triomphe in Paris with its "eternal fire," Valery Larbaud asked the novelist James Joyce, "How long do you think that will burn?" Joyce, revealing his contempt for monuments, replied, "Until the Unknown Soldier gets up in disgust and blows it out."

James Joyce (1882–1941), Irish writer

◆ HOPE & OPTIMISM

Quotations

"Hope is a good breakfast, but it is a bad supper."

Francis Bacon (1561–1626), British lawyer and writer, Apothegms (1624), 36

"Optimism: the world is the best of all possible worlds, and everything in it is a necessary evil."

F. H. Bradley (1846–1924), British philosopher, Aphorisms (1930)

"The optimist proclaims that we live in the best of all possible worlds; and the pessimist fears this is true."

James Branch Cabell (1879–1958), U.S. writer, The Silver Stallion (1926), ch. 26

"He that lives upon hope will die fasting."

Benjamin Franklin (1706–1790), U.S. statesman and scientist, Poor Richard's Almanac (1732–1757)

"Idealism increases in direct proportion to one's distance from the problem."

John Galsworthy (1867–1933), British writer and playwright

"An optimist is a guy who has never had much experience."

Don[ald Robert Perry] Marquis (1878–1937), U.S. writer and poet, archy and mehitabel (1933), "archy says"

Classical Phrases and Myths

dum spiro, spero (Lat)
(dum SPEE-roh SPEE-roh) while I breathe, I hope

Deo volente (Lat)
(DE-oh vol-EN-tay) God willing (it will be achieved)

"*Modo liceat vivere, est sepes.*"
(MOH-doh LIK-ee-at VEE-ve-ray est SEP-es) (While there is life, there is hope.)

Terence [Publius Terentius Afer] (c.190 B.C.-159 B.C.), Roman playwright, Heauton Timoroumenos

---

◆ HOPELESSNESS & PESSIMISM

Foreign Words and Phrases

mal du siécle (Fra)
(mal doo see-EKL) world-weariness (usually applied to the 19th century)

Weltschmerz (Ger)
(VELT-shmairtz) *lit:* grief of the world; anguish about the world situation

189

Quotations

"I do not see any way of realizing our hopes about world organization in five or six days. Even the Almighty took seven."

> Sir Winston Spencer Churchill
> (1874–1965), British prime minister
> and writer, replying to President Franklin
> D. Roosevelt's expressed hope that the
> Yalta conference would not last more than
> five or six days

" 'Twixt the optimist and pessimist
The difference is droll;
The optimist sees the doughnut
But the pessimist sees the hole."

> McLandburgh Wilson (fl. 1915),
> U.S. poet, Optimist and Pessimist

Classical Phrases and Myths

nil desperandum (Lat)
(nil DAY-spay-RAND-um) do not despair; no reason to despair

"Cantabit vacuos coram latrone viator." (The traveler with empty pockets will sing even in the robber's face.)

> Juvenal [Decimus Junius Juvenalis]
> (c. 50-c. 130), Roman writer,
> Satires X, l. 22

According to Greek mythology, the river Styx (stix) was one of the five rivers surrounding Hades, over which the ghosts of the properly buried dead must pass. Thus, something stygian is dark, gloomy or infernal.

◆ HOSPITALITY

Foreign Words and Phrases

à bras ouverts (Fra)
(ah BRAHS oo-ver) lit: with open arms, cordially (receiving guests, etc.)

accueil (Fra)
(ah-KWEE) greeting, welcome

Quotations

"It was a delightful visit—perfect, in being much too short."

> Jane Austen (1775–1817), British writer,
> Emma (1815), ch. 13

"Fish and visitors smell in three days."

> Benjamin Franklin (1706–1790), U.S.
> statesman and scientist, Poor Richard's
> Almanac (1732–1757) [cf. "No guest is
> so welcome in a friend's house without
> becoming a nuisance in three days." Titus
> Maccius Plautus, Miles Gloriosus,
> Act III, sc. i]

"His handshake ought not to be used except as a tourniquet."

> Margaret Halsey (1910–   ),
> U.S. writer, With Malice Toward Some
> (1938)

Classical Phrases and Myths

"A host is like a general—calamities often reveal his genius."

> Horace (65 B.C.–8 B.C.), Roman poet

Jokes, Stories and Anecdotes

As an ambassador and President Coolidge were winding up an important private conference, Mrs. Coolidge came in and suggested to her husband, "Why don't you offer the ambassador a drink?" Replied "Silent Cal" testily, "He's already had one." When asked later by reporters if he had any comment about the conference, Coolidge said, "No. I have nothing to say about anything else either." He added, "And don't quote me!"

> [John] Calvin Coolidge (1872–1933),
> U.S. president

◆ HUMAN BODY

Jokes, Stories and Anecdotes

Three surgeons were discussing different kinds of patients. The first said, "I like artists because when you cut them open, they are awash with color inside." The second doctor said, "I prefer engineers. When you cut them open, everything is orderly and numbered." "The easiest are attorneys," said the third doctor. "They have only two parts, their rears and their mouths, both interchangeable."

Duc d'Aumale, son of King Louis Philippe, was renowned in his youth for his love affairs, but he acknowledged his failing powers in his old age. "As a young man I used to have four supple members and one stiff one," he observed. "Now I have four stiff and one supple."

> Henri, Duc d'Aumale (1822–1897),
> French aristocrat

◆ HUMANS

Quotations

"The significance of man is that he is insignificant and is aware of it."

> Carl Lotus Becker (1873–1945),
> U.S. writer, Progress and Power
> (1936), ch. 3

"No man is an Island entire of itself; every man is a part of the continent, a part of the main . . . [A]ny man's death diminishes me, because I am involved in Mankind; And therefore never send to know for whom the bell tolls; It tolls for thee."

> John Donne (1571–1631), British poet,
> Devotions upon Emergent
> Occasions (1624)

"I believe man will not merely endure, he will prevail. He is immortal, not because he, alone among creatures, has an inexhaustible voice but because he has a soul, a spirit capable of compassion and sacrifice and endurance."

> William Faulkner (1897–1962),
> U.S. writer, Nobel Prize speech, 1950

"This world may be divided into those who take it or leave it and those who split the difference."

> Monsignor Ronald Knox (1888–1957),
> British clergyman and writer

"When someone behaves like a beast, he says: 'After all, one is only human.' But when he is treated like a beast, he says: 'After all, one is human.' "

> Karl Kraus (1874–1936), Austrian poet
> and writer, Spruche und Widerspruche
> (Dicta and Contradictions) (1909)

"Ah! what is man? Wherefore does he why? Whence did he whence? Whither is he withering?"

> Dan Leno [George Galvin] (1860–1904),
> U.S. writer, Hys Booke (1901), ch. 1

"Know then thyself, presume not God to scan,
The proper study of mankind is man."

> Alexander Pope (1688–1744), British poet
> and writer, An Essay on Man
> (1733–1734), Epistle II, l. I

"What a piece of work is a man! How noble in reason! how infinite in faculty! in form, in moving, how express and admirable! in action how like an angel! in apprehension how like a god! the beauty of the world! the paragon of animals! And yet, to me, what is this quintessence of dust? man delights not me; no, nor woman neither, though, by your smiling, you seem to say so. And yet; to me, what is this quintessence of dust?"

William Shakespeare (1564–1616),
British playwright and poet,
Hamlet *(1601), Act II, sc. ii*

"All the world's a stage;
And all the men and women
merely players:
They have their exits and their entrances;
And one man in his time plays
many parts,
His acts being seven ages."

William Shakespeare (1564–1616),
British playwright and poet,
As You Like It *(1600), Act II, sc. vii*

Classical Phrases and Myths

"Man is a little soul carrying around a corpse."

Epictetus (c. 55–c. 135),
Greek philosopher, Discourses

"*Panton anthropon metron einai.*"
(PAN-tohn AN-throh-pon MET-ron AY-nay) (Man is the measure of all things.)

Protagoras (c. 485 B.C.–c. 410 B.C.),
Greek philosopher, quoted by Plato

◆ HUMILITY

Quotations

"The English instinctively admire any man who has no talent, and is modest about it."

James Agate (1877–1947), British writer

"Modesty is the only sure bait when you angle for praise."

Philip Dormer Stanhope, 4th Earl of Chesterfield (1694–1773), British statesman and writer, letter to his son

"Don't be humble, you're not that great."

Golda Meir (1898–1978),
U.S.-born Israeli prime minister

Jokes, Stories and Anecdotes

An American writer of some repute, upon being introduced to the novelist Thomas Mann, self-deprecatingly declared that he scarcely considered himself a writer in comparison with Mann. Later the Nobel laureate commented, "He has no right to make himself so modest. He's not that great."

Thomas Mann (1875–1955),
German writer

◆ HUMOR & WIT

Foreign Words and Phrases

bon mot (Fra)
(bon moh) witty comment, aphorism, memorable remark

bel esprit (Fra)
(BELL es-PREE) real wit; plu: *beaux esprits*

jeu de mots (Fra)
(jeu de moe) *lit:* game of words; play on words, pun

blagueur (Fra)
(blahg-UHR) one who tells jokes

buffo (Ita)
(BOO-foh) comic, burlesque (*una buffonata*—a joke)

légèreté (Fra)
(lay-JEHR-ay-tay) frivolity, levity, agility

Quotations

"Ready to split his sides with laughing."

Miguel de Cervantes (1547–1616),
Spanish writer, Don Quixote de la Mancha, *Part I (1605), bk. III, ch. 13*

"Wit is a sword; it is meant to make people feel the point as well as see it."

G[ilbert] K[eith] Chesterton (1874–1936), British man of letters

The Wit's Thesaurus. [Book Subtitle (1994).]

Lance S. Davidson (1953-), U.S. writer, The Wit's Thesaurus (1994)

"A man who could make so vile a pun would not scruple to pick a pocket."

John Dennis (1657–1734), British playwright

"I told him my funniest story, and he laughed so hard you could have heard a pin drop."

Ring [Ringgold Wilmer] Lardner (1885–1933), U.S. writer, describing a visit with "Silent Cal" Coolidge at the White House

"Everything is funny as long as it is happening to Somebody Else."

Will[iam Penn Adair] Rogers (1879–1935), U.S. comedian, Illiterate Digest (1924), "Warning to Jokers: Lay Off the Prince"

"Brevity is the soul of wit."

William Shakespeare (1564–1616), British playwright and poet, Hamlet (1601), Act II, sc. ii

"Look, he's winding up the watch of his wit, by and by it will strike."

William Shakespeare (1564–1616), British playwright and poet, The Tempest (1612), Act II, sc. i

"His fine wit
Makes such a wound, the knife is lost in it."

Percy Bysshe Shelley (1792–1822), British poet, letter to Maria Gisborne, l. 240

"May you live all the days of your life."

Jonathan Swift (1667–1745), Anglo-Irish clergyman and writer

Classical Phrases and Myths

"*Pereant qui ante nos nostra dixerunt.*" (Damn those who said our good things before us.)

Aelius Donatus (c. 300s), Roman grammarian

Jokes, Stories and Anecdotes

The playwright Charles MacArthur, brought to Hollywood to write a screenplay, was describing the difficulty of writing visual jokes to Charlie Chaplin, the little tramp. "How, for example, could I make a fat lady, walking down Fifth Avenue, slip on a banana peel and still get a laugh? It's been done a million times," said MacArthur. "What's the best way to get the laugh? Do I show first the banana peel, then the fat lady approaching: then she slips? Or do I show the fat lady first, then the banana peel, and then she slips?" "Neither," replied Chaplin. "You show the fat lady approaching. Then you show the banana peel. Then you show the fat lady and the banana peel together. Then she steps over the banana peel and disappears down a manhole."

Charles Spencer ["Charlie"] Chaplin (1889–1977), British-born actor

When told that puns were the lowest form of wit, British lord chancellor Thomas Erskine remarked, "That's very true, and therefore [the pun is] the foundation of all wit."

Thomas Erskine, 1st Baron (1750–1823), British lawyer and politician

Comedian Carol Channing once invited actor John Gielgud to an event. Gielgud, taken ill, gave her the following note: "Sorry, love, cannot attend. Gielgud doesn't fielgud."

Sir John Gielgud (1904–   ), British actor

"What are you going to do when you run out of continents?" Clifton Fadiman teased world affairs chronicler John Gunther after publication of his seventh "Inside" book. Gunther replied, "Try incontinence."

John Gunther (1901–1970), U.S. writer

"Mr. President," comedian Will Rogers said to President Harding during an audience at the White House, "I'd like to tell you all of the latest jokes." "You don't have to," quipped Harding. "I already appointed them to office."

Warren G[amaliel] Harding (1865–1923), U.S. president [authenticity unverified]

◆ HUNTING & FISHING

Quotations

"She watches him, as a cat would watch a mouse."

Jonathan Swift (1667–1745), Anglo-Irish clergyman and writer, Polite Conversation (c. 1738), "Dialogue III"

"The English country gentleman galloping after a fox—the unspeakable in full pursuit of the uneatable."

Oscar [Fingal O'Flahertie Wills] Wilde (1854–1900), British playwright, writer and wit, A Woman of No Importance (1893), Act I

Jokes, Stories and Anecdotes

"You can't possibly believe your husband's story that he spent the day fishing," sniffed the local gossip. "Why, he didn't come home with a single fish." Responded the wife, "That's why I believe him."

◆ HYGIENE

Quotations

"I feel as I always have, except for an occasional heart attack."

Robert Charles Benchley (1889–1945), U.S. humorist, addressing underclassman at his 25th reunion at Harvard University, 1937

"There was no need to do any housework at all. After the first four years the dirt doesn't get any worse."

Quentin Crisp (1908–), British writer, Naked Civil Servant (1968), ch. 15

"I test my bath before I sit,
And I'm always moved to wonderment
That what chills the finger not a bit
Is so frigid upon the fundament."

Ogden Nash (1902–1971), U.S. humorist, Good Intentions (1942), "Samson Agonistes"

Classical Phrases and Myths

catharsis (Grk)
(kath-AR-sis) cleansing from guilt or defilement; purification; in drama, the period of suffering to expiate a sin

Jokes, Stories and Anecdotes

When a speck of dust happened to land on an uncovered culture plate, Sir Alexander Fleming fortunately noticed that the mold Penicillium notatum destroyed surrounding bacteria, and so discovered penicillin. Years later he was being led on a tour through a modern research laboratory. "Too bad you did not have a place like this to work in," said his guide, proudly waving his arm around the sterile, dust-free, air-conditioned environment. "Who knows what you could have discovered in such surroundings!" Murmured Fleming, "Not penicillin."

Sir Alexander Fleming (1881–1955),
British microbiologist

Dr. William Spooner, the Oxford scholar celebrated for the verbal trick of (usually unintentionally transposing the first syllables of words, accidentally spilled a salt shaker at a meal. Whereas a home remedy calls for sprinkling salt over spilled wine to prevent a stain, Dr. Spooner reached for his wineglass and poured his red wine over the spilled salt.

William Archibald Spooner (1844–1930),
British scholar [authenticity unverified]

At a party, a guest happened to comment that Cecil Chesterton, brother of writer G. K. Chesterton, was extremely hygenic despite having a "dingy" complexion. In fact, the guest added, when Cecil bathed at Le Touquet, "he came out of the water just as gray-blue as when he went in." Rebecca West, the novelist and political journalist, interjected, "But did you look at the Channel?"

Dame Rebecca West [Cicily Isabel
Fairfield] (1892–1983), British writer

◆ HYPOCRISY

Jokes, Stories and Anecdotes

The French novelist Alexandre Dumas employed a factory of ghost writers to help him produce his prodigious output of literature. On one occasion, Dumas asked his son and namesake whether he had read Dumas's latest novel. Replied Alexandre *fils,* "No. Have you?"

Alexandre [fils] Dumas (1824–1895),
French writer and playwright

◆ IDEA

Foreign Words and Phrases

Schwerpunkt (Ger)
(SHVEHR-poonkt) the main point (e.g., of a discussion)

idée force (Fra)
(EE-day FORS) *lit:* powerful idea; notion that "an idea can move men"

Quotations

"There is one thing stronger than all the armies in the world; and that is an idea whose time has come."

Anonymous, Nation *(April 15, 1943)*

"As usual the Liberals offer a mixture of sound and original ideas. Unfortunately none of the sound ideas is original and none of the original ideas is sound."

[Maurice] Harold Macmillan, 1st Earl of
Stockton (1894–1992), British prime
minister speech to London conservatives,
March 7, 1961

"A man with a new idea is a crank until the idea succeeds."

Mark Twain [Samuel Langhorne Clemens]
(1835–1910), U.S. humorist,
writer, and speaker

Classical Phrases and Myths

Plato was an Athenian philosopher who was a pupil of Socrates and who, as author of the *Dialogues,* profoundly shaped the development of philosophy. In the series of *Dialogues* culminating in the *Republic,* Plato applies uncompromising idealism to construct a perfect human community. Hence, something *platonic* relates to ideas generally, rather than action, and *platonic love* is a spiritual, nonsexual relationship.

Plato [Aristocles] (c. 428 B.C.–c. 347 B.C.),
Greek philosopher

◆ IDEAL

Jokes, Stories and Anecdotes

A man had fruitlessly spent a decade searching for the meaning of life. Then he learned of a guru on a remote mountaintop in India who could give him the answer. Inspired, the man hired a Sherpa guide, climbed for a week to the top of the mountain, and finally obtained an audience with the guru. "O, guru, I have traveled from far away to find the answer to this question: What is the meaning of life?" The guru stroked his beard and pondered the sky. After a long silence he said, "Life is a fountain." "That's it? That's the meaning? Life is a fountain?" the man asked. The guru was surprised. "You mean it's *not* a fountain?"

◆ IDENTITY

Quotations

"Monkeys are superior to men in this: when a monkey looks into a mirror, he sees a monkey."

Malcolm de Chazal (1902–   ),
French writer

"*Quand j'ai écrit que Victor Hugo était un fou qui se croyait Victor Hugo, je ne plaisantais pas.*" (When I wrote that Victor Hugo was a madman who thought he was Victor Hugo, I was not joking.)

Jean Cocteau (1889–1963), French writer,
artist and filmmaker,
Opium (1930), p. 77

Classical Phrases and Myths

ad hominem (Lat)
(ad HOM-in-em) personal, relating to an individual

"*Cogito, ergo sum.*"
(KOG-ee-toh ER-go SUM) (I think, therefore I am.)

René Descartes (1596–1650),
French philosopher

Jokes, Stories and Anecdotes

Closing his folder, the psychiatrist smiled at his patient and said, "I'm pleased to pronounce you cured." Sighed the patient gloomily, "Gee, I'm thrilled." "But you should be pleased" "Why?" snapped the patient. "A year ago I was Charlemagne. Now I'm nobody!"

King Charles II was visiting Oxford in 1675 with his mistress, the English actress Nell Gwyn. The crowd angrily shook her coach in the mistaken belief that the king was accompanied by Louise de Kérouaille, his unpopular Roman Catholic mistress. The unruffled Nell leaned out of the window, calling, "Pray, good people, be civil. It is I, the Protestant whore."

Nell [Eleanor] Gwyn (1650–1687),
British actress

At London's Garrick Club a stranger once approached the comedy playwright Freddy Lonsdale and inquired, "Aren't you Freddy Lonsdale?" Freddy eyed him, then replied, "No, not tonight."

Frederick Lonsdale (1881–1954),
British playwright [attributed also to
Peter Sellers]

During a squad meeting coach Bear Bryant informed his football players at the University of Alabama: "This is a class operation. I want your shoes to be shined. I want you to have a tie on, get your hair cut and keep a crease in your pants. I also want you to go to class. I don't want no dumbbells on this team. If there is a dumbbell in the room, I wish he would stand up." Joe Namath, his quarterback, rose to his feet. "Joe," said Bryant. "How come you're standing up? You ain't dumb." "Coach, I just hate like the devil for you to be standing up there by yourself."

> *Joe Namath (1943–   ),*
> *U.S. football player*

◆ IDOLATRY

Quotations

Claire: "How do you know you're ...God?" *Earl of Curney:* "Simple. When I pray to Him I find I'm talking to myself."

> *Peter Barnes (1931–   ),*
> *British playwright,* The Ruling
> Class *(1969), Act I, sc. 4*

Jokes, Stories and Anecdotes

While touring his own Scotland, James Boswell took his idol Samuel Johnson to his home in Edinburgh. Mrs. Boswell, though civil, was scornful of her husband's devotion to the ungainly, ill-complexioned and ill-mannered Johnson, saying, "I have seen many a bear led by a man, but I never before saw a man led by a bear."

> *James Boswell (1740–1795),*
> *British lawyer*

In Zurich a young man approached the novelist James Joyce and inquired, "May I kiss the hand that wrote *Ulysses?*" "No," Joyce replied, à la King Lear, "it did lots of other things, too."

> *James Joyce (1882–1941), Irish writer*

◆ IGNORANCE

Foreign Words and Phrases

bétise (Fra)
(bet-EEZ) ignorance, stupidity

Quotations

"What you don't know would make a great book."

> *Sydney Smith (1771–1845),*
> *British clergyman and writer*

"His ignorance was an Empire State Building of ignorance. You had to admire it for its size."

> *Dorothy Parker (1893–1967), U.S. wit*
> *and writer, describing* New Yorker *editor*
> *Harold Ross*

Classical Phrases and Myths

terra incognita (Lat)
(TER-ra in-KOG-nit-a) unknown land or area (e.g., in geography or a field of study)

argumentum ad ignorantiam (Lat)
(ar-gu-MEN-tum ad ig-nor-ANT-ee-am) argument based on an adversary's ignorance

Jokes, Stories and Anecdotes

Two little girls were walking to first grade when one confided, "Guess what. I found a contraceptive in the attic." Asked the other, "What's an attic?"

◆ ILLEGALITY

Foreign Words and Phrases

agiotage (Fra)
(ah-jyo-TAJ) illicit speculation, stock manipulation

na levo (Rus)
(nuh LEHV-oh) on the left, or corrupt markets

entourloupette (Fra)
(on-TOUR-lew-PET) underhand commercial dealing

plunderbund (Dut)
(PLOON-duhr-boond) political or financial cabal to exploit the public

Quotations

"A burglar who respects his art always takes his time before taking anything else."

O. Henry [William Sydney Porter] (1862–1910), U.S. writer

"It was beautiful and simple as all truly great swindles are."

O. Henry [William Sydney Porter] (1862–1910), U.S. writer, Gentle Grafter (1908), "Octopus Marooned"

"The study of crime begins with the knowledge of oneself."

Henry Miller (1891–1980), U.S. writer, The Air-Conditioned Nightmare (1945), "The Soul of Anaesthesia"

"When the President does it, that means that it is not illegal."

Richard Milhous Nixon (1913–   ), U.S. president

"Laws were made to be broken."

Christopher North [John Wilson] (1785–1854), British writer, Noctes Ambrosianae, No. 24 (May 1830)

Classical Phrases and Myths

abusus non tollit usum (Lat)
(ab-USE-us non TOL-lit USE-um) in law, the dictum that the abuse of a right or privilege does not invalidate its use

ignorantio legis ne hominem excusat (Lat)
(ig-nor-AHN-tee-oh LAY-gis ne HOH-mee-nem ex-KOO-sat) ignorance of the law excuses no man

animus furandi (Lat)
(AN-ee-mus fu-RAND-ee) in law, the intention of stealing

Jokes, Stories and Anecdotes

As both a military commander and an administrator in India, Baron Clive enjoyed numerous opportunities for corruption. Indeed, he was impeached by Parliament, though later cleared. While being cross-examined during the parliamentary proceedings against him, he exclaimed defensively, "My God, Mr. Chairman, at this moment I stand astonished at my own moderation!"

Robert Clive, Baron Clive of Plassey (1725–1774), British administrator

To avoid a conflict with Prince Feliks Yusupov, Metro-Goldwyn-Mayer in the film *Rasputin and the Empress* changed the name of his character, a conspirator in the murder of Rasputin, to Prince Chegodieff. Angered that he did not receive due credit, the prince sued the studio in a London court and won a large sum from MGM. But then a real Prince Chegodieff emerged and sued for libel. MGM had to pay off again.

◆ ILLUSION

Foreign Words and Phrases

trompe l'oeil (Fra)
(tromp loy) *lit:* trick the eye; optical illusion in art

Quotations

"Journalists say a thing that they know isn't true, in the hope that if they keep on saying it long enough it *will* be true."

[Enoch] Arnold Bennett (1867–1931), British writer and playwright, The Title (1918), Act II

"I wish he would explain his explanation."

George Gordon, Lord Byron (1788–1824), British poet, Don Juan (1818), Canto I, dedication ii

"Things sweet to taste prove in digestion sour."

William Shakespeare (1564–1616),
British playwright and poet,
King Richard II (1596), Act I, sc. iii

"Se non è vero, è molto ben trovato." (If it is not true, it is a happy invention.)

Anonymous (c. 1500s) [misattributed to
Giordano Bruno (1585)]

Jokes, Stories and Anecdotes

Early in his career P. T. Barnum originated an exhibit called "The Happy Family" in which a lion, tiger, panther, and baby lamb were featured, all dwelling harmoniously in the same cage. The unusual display made newspaper headlines and generated strong attendance. Asked several weeks after its opening about the display's future promise, Barnum replied, "The display will become a permanent feature if the supply of lambs holds out!"

P[hineas] T[aylor] Barnum (1810–1891),
U.S. showman

◆ IMAGINATION

Foreign Words and Phrases

chateaux en Espagne (Fra)
(shoh-TOH on esp-ANG-nh) lit: castles in Spain; castles in the air

Quotations

" 'Have some wine,' the March Hare said in an encouraging tone. Alice looked all round the table, but there was nothing on it but tea. 'I don't see any wine,' she remarked.

'There isn't any,' said the March Hare."

Lewis Carroll [Charles Lutwidge
Dodgson] (1832–1898), British writer and
mathematician, Alice's Adventures in
Wonderland (1865), ch. 7

"His imagination resembled the wings of an ostrich. It enabled him to run, though not to soar."

Thomas Babington Macaulay, 1st Baron
Macaulay (1800–1859), British statesman
and writer, describing John Dryden,
Edinburgh Review (January 1828)

Classical Phrases and Myths

ex umbris et imaginibus in veritatem (Lat)
(ex OOM-bris et im-AG-in-ee-bus) from shadows and imagination to the reality

According to Greek mythology, the Chimaera (KIM-ee-ra) was a fire-breathing monster with a lion's head, goat's body and serpent's tail. It dwelt in Lycia and was slain by Bellerophon while he was riding the flying horse Pegasus. Hence, to be chimerical is to be wildly fanciful.

In Greek mythology, there were originally three Muses (MYOO-zez) as goddesses of memory, meditation and song. Zeus slept for nine nights with the Muse of memory, from which the nine Muses were born. They presided over the arts: history, music, comedy, tragedy, dance, lyric poetry, religious hymn and dance, astronomy and epic poetry. Hence, a muse is a (goddess) inspiration for a creative artist.

Jokes, Stories and Anecdotes

Honoré de Balzac lived in an unheated, bare garret during his years of poverty. On one bare wall the writer inscribed: "Rosewood paneling with commode"; on another: "Gobelin tapestry with Venetian mirror"; and over the empty fireplace: "Picture by Raphael."

Honoré de Balzac (1799–1850),
French writer

Film director Alfred Hitchcock never sat among the audience to watch his films. Asked if he missed hearing them scream, he replied, "No, I can hear them when I'm making the picture."

Sir Alfred Hitchcock (1889–1980),
British film director

Actress Ruth Gordon was describing her latest play to playwright and wit George Kaufman: "In the first scene I'm on the left side of the stage, and the audience has to imagine I'm eating dinner in a crowded restaurant. Then in scene two I run over to the right side of the stage and the audience imagines I'm in my own drawing room." "And the second night," Kaufman added, unimpressed, "you have to imagine there's an audience out front."

George S[imon] Kaufman (1889–1961),
U.S. playwright, writer and wit

The children's book author and illustrator once received the following letter from an eight-year-old: "Dear Dr. Seuss, you sure thunk up a lot of funny books. You sure thunk up a million funny animals . . . who thunk you up, Dr. Seuss?"

Dr. Seuss [Theodore Seuss Geisel]
(1904–1992), U.S. humorist

◆ IMMORTALITY

Quotations

"I don't want to achieve immortality through my work . . . , I want to achieve it through not dying.

Woody Allen [Allen Stewart Konigsberg]
(1935–   ), U.S. comedian
and filmmaker

"I can't die. I'm booked."

George Burns [Nathan Birnbaum]
(1896–   ), U.S. comedian
and actor

"He had decided to live for ever or die in the attempt."

Joseph Heller (1923–   ),
U.S. writer, Catch-22 (1961), ch. 1

"Martyrdom . . . is the only way in which a man can become famous without ability."

George Bernard Shaw (1856–1950),
Irish playwright, The Devil's
Disciple (1901), Act III

Classical Phrases and Myths

"Life is short, but art is long."

Hippocrates (c. 440 B.C.–c. 377 B.C.),
Greek physician, Aphorisms, I, i.

"Non onmis moriar." (I shall not all die.)

Horace (65 B.C.–8 B.C.), Roman poet,
Odes, III, xxx, l. 6

Jokes, Stories and Anecdotes

It was reputed that Alessandro Cagliostro, an adventurer, alchemist and charlatan, was 300 years old. Asked to verify this, one of his servants said, "I cannot. I have only been in his service a hundred years myself."

Alessandro Cagliostro (1743–1895),
Italian adventurer

It was said of James Fenimore Cooper, a founder of American fiction, that he "came to the gates of immortality with a vast amount of excess baggage."

James Fenimore Cooper (1789–1851),
U.S. writer

A successful playwright, Nathaniel Lee was confined to the London asylum Bedlam after he became insane in his early 30s. A friend went to see him there. The friend's hopes that Lee had recovered were bolstered by Lee's rational discourse during the course of the visit and as Lee conducted a guided tour of the asylum. When they walked onto the roof of the building, Lee suddenly grabbed his friend's arm. "Let us immortalize ourselves!" he exclaimed. "Let us leap down this moment!" "Er, any man could leap down, so we should not immortalize ourselves that way," replied the friend coolly. "Instead, let us go down and, if we can, leap up." Lee, delighted, raced downstairs to be the first thus to achieve immortality.

Nathaniel Lee (c. 1653–1692),
British playwright

The mathematician, logician and Nobel laureate Bertrand Russell once had a nightmare taking place approximately 200 years in the future. In his dream he saw a librarian moving along the shelves, pulling out book after book, and either returning it to the shelf or disposing of it in a large bucket. He then came to three large volumes that Russell recognized as the last surviving copy of his early masterpiece co-authored with Alfred North Whitehead, *Principia Mathematica:* The librarian removed a volume, puzzled over the writing, closed the book, balanced it in his hand and hesitated.

Bertrand Arthur William Russell, 3rd
Earl (1872–1970), British mathematician
and philosopher

◆ IMPASSIVITY

Foreign Words and Phrases

blasé (Fra)
(blah-ZAY) world-weary, tired of pleasure

au-dessus de la mêlée (Fra)
(oh-de-SOO de la MEH-lay) *lit:* above the struggle; expression of detachment from and indifference to World War I

Quotations

"Those who would make us feel— must feel themselves."

Charles Churchill (1731–1764), British
poet, The Rosciad (1761), l. 962

"Qu'ils mangent de la brioche." (Let them cat cake.)

Marie Antoinette (1755–1793),
French queen, replying when informed that
the French people had no bread to eat
[authenticity unverified]

"Aujourd'hui, maman est morte. Ou peut-être hier, je ne sais pas." (Mother died today. Or perhaps it was yesterday, I don't know.)

Albert Camus (1913–1960), French
philosopher and writer, L'Etranger
(The Outsider) (1944)

Jokes, Stories and Anecdotes

A lawyer was sitting in high-priced seats ready to watch the stage performance when a man in front of her, noticing the empty seat next to her, asked why such a valuable commodity was unused. The lawyer replied, "My husband can't attend." "Don't you have relatives or friends who could use the seat." "Oh, they're all at the funeral."

◆ IMPERFECTION

Quotations

"I may have my faults, but being wrong ain't one of them."

Jimmy Hoffa (1913–c. 1983),
U.S. labor leader

Classical Phrases and Myths

"We must as second best . . . take the lesser of two evils."

Aristotle (384 B.C.–322 B.C.),
Greek philosopher, Nichomachean Ethics,
bk. II, ch. 9 [said differently by Homer]

According to Greek legend, the mother of Achilles (a-KIL-eez), holding him by the heel, when he was a baby, dipped him into the river Styx to render him invulnerable. He became a great hero, the strongest, bravest and swiftest at the siege of Troy, described in Homer's *Iliad*. He was killed, however, by an arrow shot by Paris, son of Troy's King Priam, at Achilles' heel. Hence, the *Achilles' heel* implies a weak spot, a point vulnerable to attack.

Jokes, Stories and Anecdotes

Greatly irritated by a street organ-grinder who played his well-known one-act opera *Cavalleria Rusticana* at about half-speed below his apartment, the composer Pietro Mascagni marched into the street. "I am Mascagni," he announced to the organ-grinder. "I will show you how to play this music correctly." And he played several bars. The next day Mascagni again saw in the street the organ-grinder, bearing a sign over his instrument: "Pupil of Mascagni."

Pietro Mascagni (1863–1945),
Italian composer

◆ IMPOSITION

Jokes, Stories and Anecdotes

The nobleman checked into a European hotel that prided itself on offering everything a client might desire. The traveler at once called room service. "Bring to me a beautiful virgin under 20, a cat-o'-nine-tails made of Moroccan leather, the finest port from Portugal and a burly Tibetan monk. Hurry, I'm tired." An hour later, room service called back, apologetic. "Sir, we have the cat-o'-nine-tails. We ultimately found the virgin, and went across the border to locate the port. But all we could find was an Indian monk. Will that do?" "No," answered the nobleman. "Just send up a Danish pastry and tea."

After returning from an exploration, Sir Richard Burton, the Renaissance man and translator of *The Arabian Nights*, was attracted by a young woman in Boulogne. Unseemly rumors had spread among the fashionable English colony there concerning Burton's travels, so the young woman's mother summoned Burton because, she said, "I think it is my duty to ask what are your intentions with regard to my daughter." Burton, who regarded his relationship with the daughter as little more than a pleasant flirtation, was amused and a bit nonplussed by the formal interview. "Your duty, madam?" "Yes." "Alas," Burton sighed, "strictly dishonorable."

Sir Richard Burton (1821–1890),
British scholar and explorer

◆ IMPOSSIBILITY

Foreign Words and Phrases

pas possible (Fra)
(pah poss-EE-ble) it cannot be done!
it is impossible!

Quotations

"There ain't no way to find out
why a snorer can't hear himself
snore."
Mark Twain [Samuel Langhorne Clemens]
(1835–1910), U.S. humorist, writer and
speaker, Tom Sawyer Abroad
(1894), ch. 10

Jokes, Stories and Anecdotes

A plump woman visited her podi-
atrist, complaining of swollen feet.
After he pried her foot from the
shoe, he glanced first at her foot,
then the shoe. "It could be," he suggested, "pride in accomplishing the
impossible."

Seeking approval from her peers, a
society matron proudly displayed a
new antique on her mantle and
boasted; "This is the knife that
killed Julius Caesar." "Are you sure
it's authentic?" gasped the paceset-
ter. "Authentic? Why it even has 44
B.C. inscribed on it!"

◆ IMPULSIVENESS (SPONTANEITY)

Foreign Words and Phrases

acte gratuit (Lat)
(AKT grat-WEE) impulsive act; act
without ostensible cause

à l'improviste (Fra)
(ah lahm-pro-VEEST) suddenly, un-
awares

Quotations

"It usually takes more than three
weeks to prepare a good impromptu speech."
Mark Twain [Samuel Langhorne Clemens]
(1835–1910), U.S. humorist,
writer and speaker

Classical Phrases and Myths

ate (Grk)
(AH-tay) infatuation, blindness of
judgment sent by the gods (often
used in a literary context)

ad libitum (Lat)
(ad LIB-ee-tum) *lit:* at pleasure; ex-
temporaneously (abbr: *ad lib*)

ex tempore (Lat)
(ex TEM-por-AY) *lit:* out of the
time; spontaneously

"*Horatii curiosa felicitas.*" (HOR-a-
tee-ee kur-ee-OH-safay-LEE-kee-
tas) (The studied spontaneity of
Horace.)
Petronius, Gaius [Petronius Arbiter]
(d. c.66), Roman writer, Satyricon, sec.
118 [originally a kudo for adapting the
rhythms and language of everyday speech
to poetry]

Jokes, Stories and Anecdotes

George Bernard Shaw, at the time a
music critic, was eating at a restaurant that featured a minor musical
ensemble. Its leader, who recognized Shaw, asked him *in a note*
what he would like to hear played.
Shaw responded, "Dominoes."
George Bernard Shaw (1856–1950),
Irish playwright

◆ INACTION & INACTIVITY

Foreign Words and Phrases

dolce far niente (Ita)
(DOL-che far NYEN-tay) *lit:* gentle
inactivity; blissful idleness

wei-wu-wei (Chi)
(WAY-woo-WAY) conscious inaction, from knowing when to do nothing

das war nicht schwimmen, das war baden (Ger)
(dahs wahr neecht SHWIM-men dahs war BAH-den) that was not swimming, that was bathing; feeble effort

fainéant (Fra)
(fay-NAY-on) idler, do-nothing

infingardo (Ita)
(een-feen-GAHR-doh) lazy, slothful

Quotations

"It is related of an Englishman that he hanged himself to avoid the daily task of dressing and undressing."

Johann Wolfgang Von Goethe (1749–1832), German poet, playwright and writer

"It is impossible to enjoy idling thoroughly unless one has plenty of work to do."

Jerome K[lapka] Jerome (1859–1927), British writer, Idle Thoughts of an Idle Fellow *(1886), "On Being Idle"*

"Mr. [Calvin] Coolidge's genius for inactivity is developed to a very high point. It is far from being an indolent activity. It is a grim, determined, alert inactivity which keeps Mr Coolidge occupied constantly. Nobody has ever worked harder at inactivity, with such force of character, with such unremitting attention to detail, with such conscientious devotion to the task."

Walter Lippmann (1889–1974), U.S. writer, Men of Destiny *(1927), p. 12*

Classical Phrases and Myths

In Greek legend and recounted in Homer's *Odyssey*, the lotus (LOH-tus) was a plant whose fruit, when eaten, caused a dreamy and contented forgetfulness, removing all desire to return home. Thus, a *lotus-eater* is one given to indulgence and indolence.

Jokes, Stories and Anecdotes

German jurist and historian Felix Dahn was invited to be the guest of honor at a dinner after a lecture in Hamburg. He declined, citing as a reason that he had already wasted enough time during six weeks which he had spent in Hamburg doing nothing but sleeping and drinking. His concerned host asked Dahn when this had happened. "During the first six weeks of my life."

Felix Dahn (1834–1912), German jurist and historian

An efficiency expert asked by U.S. automobile manufacturer Henry Ford to review the Ford Motor Company submitted his report but drew attention to one employee. "That man down the corridor. Every time I go by his office he's just sitting there with his feet on his desk," he noted. "He's wasting your money." "That man," Ford said, "once had an idea that saved us millions of dollars. And I believe his feet at the time were planted exactly where they are now."

Henry Ford (1863–1947), U.S. industrialist

As a young boy, Daniel Webster was left at home with his brother Ezekiel by their father, who had assigned them tasks to be performed for the day. When Captain Webster returned, however, the work was left untouched. "What have you been doing, Ezekiel?" demanded Captain Webster. "Nothing, sir."

"And Daniel, what have you been doing?" "Helping, Ezekiel, sir."

Daniel Webster (1782–1852), U.S. lawyer, politician and orator

Asked what he was working at, Oscar Wilde would reply, "At intervals."

Oscar [Fingal O'Flahertie Wills] Wilde (1854–1900), British playwright, writer and wit

◆ INATTENTIVENESS

Foreign Words and Phrases

ta (Chi)
(tah) to understand things and thereby take them lightly

Quotations

"What is Matter?—Never mind. What is Mind?—No matter."

Punch (1855), vol. XXIX, p. 19

Classical Phrases and Myths

Although Demosthenes is generally recognized as the greatest orator of classical Greece, his political views did not always please those assembled to hear his speeches. On one occasion, booed by the gathered throngs, he announced that he would set aside his speech to relate a story. The crowd quieted. "A youth hired an ass during the summer to travel from his home to Megara," began Demosthenes. "At the hottest point of the day, both he who had hired the ass, and the owner of the beast, desired to sit in the shade of the ass, and fell into shoving each other. The youth insisted that he had hired the ass, so he should enjoy its shade; the animal's owner insisted that the youth had hired only the beast of burden, not its shadow." At this point, Demosthenes stopped, but the crowd beckoned him to continue. "How can you insist upon hearing a story about the shadow of an ass," cried Demosthenes, "and not give an ear to the matters of great moment?" The abashed Athenians listened to Demosthenes' intended address.

Demosthenes (c.384 B.C.–322 B.C.), Greek orator

Jokes, Stories and Anecdotes

The humorist Robert Benchley was watching a tennis tournament at a women's nudist camp in California with the actor Charles Butterworth and other friends. There was a sustained silence as the men's eyes remained glued on the action before them until Butterworth, breaking up the party, deadpanned, "Who's winning."

Charles Butterworth (1896–1946), U.S. film actor

The writer Charles Lamb once recalled an encounter in London with the poet, critic and philosopher Samuel Taylor Coleridge in London: "Brimful of some new idea, and in spite of my assuring him that time was precious, he drew me within the door of an unoccupied garden by the road-side, and there, sheltered from observation by a hedge of evergreens, he took me by the button of my coat, and closing his eyes commenced an eloquent discourse, waving his right hand gently, as the musical words flowed in an unbroken stream from his lips. I listened entranced; but the striking of a church clock recalled me to a sense of duty. I saw it was no use to attempt to break away, so taking advantage of his absorption in his subject, 1, with my penknife, quietly severed the button from my coat, and decamped. Five hours afterwards, in passing the same garden on my way home, I heard

Coleridge's voice, and on looking in, there he was, with closed eyes—the button in his fingers—and his right hand gracefully waving, just as when I left him. He had never missed me!"

Samuel Taylor Coleridge (1772–1834),
British poet and writer

To one question put to him by the cross-examining attorney, British aesthete Oscar Wilde made some irrelevant remark concerning his physician. "Never mind your physician," said the lawyer angrily. Wilde answered loftily, "I never do."

Oscar [Fingal O'Flahertie Wills] Wilde
(1854–1900), British playwright,
writer and wit

◆ INCLUSION & EXCLUSION

Foreign Words and Phrases

Berufsverbot (Ger)
(be-ROOFS-ver-BOHT) law prohibiting people considered politically unsuitable from entering public service

clique (Fra)
(kleek) coterie, exclusive group

Quotations

"Gentlemen, include me out."

Samuel Goldwyn [Samuel Goldfish]
(1882–1974), Russian-born U.S. film
producer, resigning from the Motion
Pictures Producers and Distributors of
America, October 1933

Classical Phrases and Myths

inter alia (Lat)
(IN-ter AL-ee-a) among other things

exceptis excipiendis (Lat)
(ex-KEP-tees ex-kip-ee-END-ees) *lit:*

things excluded that should be excluded; accounting for the necessary exceptions

Jokes, Stories and Anecdotes

After missing four swings and finally driving the ball 30 feet, the poor golfer looked up and, to his embarrassment, saw that he was being watched by a passing equestrian. "Look here!" he shouted at the stranger. "Only golfers are allowed on this course!" "I know," the equestrian replied. "But I won't say anything if you won't, either!"

◆ INCOMPETENCE

Foreign Words and Phrases

gauche (Fra)
(gohsh) awkward, tactless, vulgar

Quotations

"Why do we have to have all these third-rate foreign conductors around when we have so many second-rate ones of our own?

Sir Thomas Beecham (1879–1961),
British conductor

"He has delusions of adequacy."

Walter Kerr (1913–   ),
U.S. writer, reviewing an
anonymous actor

"Sending Dan Quayle to a disaster is a redundancy."

Los Angeles Times (October 1992)
"Letters to the Editor"

"The Peter Principle: In a Hierarchy Every Employee Tends to Rise to His Level of Incompetence."

Lawrence Peter (1919–   ) and
Raymond Hull (c. 1900s), U.S. writers,
The Peter Principle (1969), ch. 1

Classical Phrases and Myths

"Not worth his salt."

> *Petronius, Gaius [Petronius Arbiter]*
> *(d. c. 66), Roman writer, Satyricon,*
> *sec. 57 [salt was a form of*
> *currency for soldiers]*

According to Greek legend as recounted in Homer's epic poems, the *Iliad* and the *Odyssey*, Odysseus (oh-DIS-ee-us) (Roman: Ulysses), after an absence of 20 years due to the Trojan War and travels, returned to his home in Ithaca. His faithful wife, Penelope, who did not recognize him, had spurned many wooers by challenging them to bend the great bow he had left behind. Since all wooers were *unable to bend Ulysses' bow*—not equal to the task—Penelope remained free. When Odysseus, in disguise, bent the bow, she instantly knew her husband had returned home. He then turned the bow on the suitors and slew all.

Jokes, Stories and Anecdotes

The scene required 15 takes, but it finally was finished. The novice actress sprinted to the nearest phone, dialing her agent. "Isn't it wonderful?" she gushed. "The director just told me he's making two films with me!" "Two?" asked the agent, mystified. "Yes, my first and my last."

When comedian Jack Benny was a boy, he faithfully practiced his violin every day. One Saturday, a neighboring dog passed by and started howling dolefully under the window of the room in which Benny was sawing away. Finally Benny's father shouted downstairs, "For pity's sake, Jack, can't you play some piece the dog doesn't know!"

> *Jack Benny (1894–1974), U.S. comedian*

A conspirator in the Decembrist uprising against Nicholas I, czar of Russia, was condemned to be hanged, but the rope broke. The fortunate condemned man, Kondraty Ryleyev, smirked, "In Russia they do not know how to make anything properly, not even a rope." A pardon normally results from such provident interference, so a messenger was sent to Nicholas to learn the czar's pleasure. Informed of Ryleyev's comment, the czar blithely said, "Well, let the contrary be proved."

> *Nicholas I (1796–1855), Russian czar*

Upon the death of Alfred Tennyson, the British poet laureateship became vacant, and several candidates were anxious to secure the prestigious post. Sir Lewis Morris, a poet of limited ability, complained to the British wit Oscar Wilde that critics were ignoring him. "I'm a victim of a conspiracy of silence, Oscar," he said. "What shall I do?" Wilde suggested, "Join it!"

> *Oscar [Fingal O'Flahertie Wills] Wilde*
> *(1854–1900), British playwright,*
> *writer and wit*

◆ INCOMPREHENSIBILITY

Foreign Words and Phrases

indechiffrable (Fra)
(aan-day-she-frah-bl) undecipherable, incomprehensible

Quotations

"It is a riddle wrapped in a mystery inside an enigma."

> *Sir Winston Spencer Churchill*
> *(1874–1965), British prime minister*
> *and writer, describing Russia,*
> *radio broadcast, October 1, 1939*

"[President Nixon's latest statement] is the operative White House position ... and all previous statements are inoperative."

Ronald L. Ziegler (1939–   ),
U.S. statesman, commenting after being
reminded of the president's prior
statements that the White House was not
involved in the Watergate affair

Classical Phrases and Myths

obscurum per obscurius (Lat)
(ob-SKOO-rum per ob-SKOO-rius)
explanation of something obscure by means of something even more obscure

"*Brevis essel aboro,*
Obscurus fio." (When I struggle to be brief, I become obscure.)

Horace (65 B.C.–8 B.C.), Roman poet,
Ars Poetica, l. 25

In Greek legend, Orpheus (OR-fee-us) was the most famous poet and musician. Apollo, the god of music, poetry and dance, gave Orpheus a lyre, and the Muses taught him to play it so beautifully that trees and stones danced to his music and wild beasts were tamed by it. His music outcharmed that of the Sirens when Jason and the Argonauts passed, and he invented and taught the Mysteries of Dionysus to Thrace and King Midas. With his singing, Orpheus charmed the judges and Hades of the underworld into restoring his dead wife Eurydice to life on earth, on the condition that he would not look at her until she reached the upper world. Unsure that she was indeed following him, he looked back, and she was forever lost to him. Orpheus returned to Thrace and pursued young lads instead of women, but was later torn to pieces by Ciconian women. Hence, something *Orphean* or *Orphic* is mysterious, oracular or mystical, as well as pertaining to the mysterious legends of Orpheus.

Jokes, Stories and Anecdotes

Finally working up enough courage, an employee went into his boss's office, closed the door and demanded a raise. The high-ranking government official sat back in her seat and said, "Due to the fluctuational predisposition of your position's productive capacity, juxtaposed to government standards, it would be monetarily injudicious to advocate an increment." Dumbfounded, the employee said, "I-I don't get it." The supervisor responded, "Correct you are."

"Only one man ever understood me," said the German philosopher Hegel, famous for his obscure writings on idealism, on his deathbed. Silence. He then added, "And he didn't understand me."

Georg Wilhelm Hegel (1770–1831),
German philosopher

Lyndon Johnson's press secretary, Bill Moyers, was once saying grace at lunch. "Speak up, Bill," ordered Johnson. "I can't hear a damn thing." Moyers calmly replied, "I wasn't addressing you, Mr. President."

Lyndon Baines Johnson (1908–1973),
U.S. president

◆ INCREDULITY

Quotations

"Why, that's the most unheard-of thing I've ever heard of."

Joseph R[aymond] McCarthy
(1908–1957), U.S. politician

"Believe It or Not." [Title of syndicated newspaper feature (1918–present).]

Robert L[eroy] Ripley (1893–1949),
U.S. writer

Classical Phrases and Myths

*"Olim quod vulpes aegroto cauta leoni
Respondit referam: 'quia me vestigia
terrent,
Omnia te adversum spectantia, nulla
retrorsum.' "*
(The wary fox in the fable declined
the invitation of the sick lion to join
him in his den: "Because I am
frightened at seeing that all the
footprints point towards your den
and none the other way.")

> Horace (65 B.C.–8 B.C.), Roman poet,
> Epistles, I, epistle i., l. 73

Jokes, Stories and Anecdotes

The story of how St. Denis was de-
capitated at Montmartre and then,
carrying his head in his hands,
walked a whole league to the village named after him, was pains-
takingly explained by Cardinal de
Polignac to the Marquise du Def-
fand. Perturbed that she failed to
make any response, the cardinal
queried, "Do you deny that he carried his head in his hands for a
whole league?" Quipped the marquise, *"Il n'y a que le premier pas qui
coûte."* (It's only the first step that
counts.)

> Marquise Marie Anne du Deffand
> (1697–1780), French aristocrat

◆ INDECENCY

Quotations

"Naughty But Nice." [Title of film
(1939).]

> Jerry Wald (1911–1962) and Richard
> Macaulay (c. 1900s), U.S. writers

"There was a young lady of Exeter,
So pretty that men craned their
necks at her,

And one daring young knave
Even ventured to wave
The distinguishing mark of his sex
at her."

> Anonymous

◆ INDESCRIBABILITY

Foreign Words and Phrases

je ne sais quoi (Fra)
(je ne say kwa) *lit:* I do not know
what; an indescribable something

ça se sent, ça ne s'explique pas (Fra)
(sah suh sahn, sah nuh sex-PLEEK
pah) one can feel it, one cannot explain it

Quotations

"Englishwomen's shoes look as if
they had been made by someone
who had often heard shoes described, but had never seen any."

> Margaret Halsey (1910–   ),
> U.S. writer, With Malice Toward Some
> (1938), pt. 2, p. 107

"You say you are incapable of ex-
pressing your thought. How then
do you explain the lucidity and
brilliance with which you are ex-
pressing the thought that you are
incapable of thought?"

> Jacques Rivière (c. 1900s), French painter,
> letter to Antonin Artoud, c. 1923

Jokes, Stories and Anecdotes

One hot summer evening the English writer Elizabeth Bowen threw
a dinner party. Not only was she
extremely myopic, but she had to
shop at the last minute. The buffet
dinner was decidedly unappealing
for the guests. The salad, which appeared to have been briefly sham-
pooed, was tasted first by Bowen.
She turned to Howard Moss and

said, "You know, this just doesn't have that *je ne sais quoi*."

> Elizabeth Dorothea Cole Bowen
> (1899–1973), British writer

◆ INEQUALITY

Foreign Words and Phrases

apartheid (Afr)
(uh-PAR-tayt) South African state-sanctioned racial segregation

Quotations

"His lordship may compel us to be equal upstairs, but there will never be equality in the servant's hall."

> Sir J[ames] M[atthew] Barrie
> (1860–1937), British writer
> and playwright,
> The Admirable Crichton (1903), Act 1

Classical Phrases and Myths

im pari marte (Lat)
(im-PAR-ee MAR-tay) in unequal combat

◆ INEXCITABILITY (COMPOSURE)

Foreign Words and Phrases

zanshin (Jap)
(ZAHN-sheen) the state of relaxed mental alertness in the face of danger

jishuku (Jap)
(jeesh-OO-koo) self-restraint

Quotations

"If you can keep your head when all about you are losing theirs, it's just possible you haven't grasped the situation."

> Jean Kerr (1923–   ), U.S. writer
> and playwright, Please Don't Eat the
> Daisies (1957), introduction

Classical Phrases and Myths

nil admirari (Lat)
(nil ad-meer-AHR-i) *lit*: nothing surprises; (state of) equanimity, perfect composure

Jokes, Stories and Anecdotes

An American being entertained by his French hosts asked, "What does it mean when you say 'savoir faire'?" "Ah. Savoir faire!" the first Frenchman answers. "Imagine, monsieur, that you return home unexpectedly, and oh, *mon dieu*, your wife is in bed with another man. You say, 'Pardon. Continue.' That is savoir faire." "No, no!" the second Frenchman says. "Imagine instead, monsieur, that you discover your wife in bed with another woman. You say, 'Pardon, Continue.' That is savoir faire." The third Frenchman interjects, "No, no! Imagine instead, monsieur, that it is your wife, not you, who returns home unexpectedly and discovers you in bed with another woman. She says, 'Pardon, continue.' If you can continue, that, monsieur, is savoir faire."

Before being an MP for many years, Henry Labouchere was an attaché with the British consul in St. Petersburg. One day a pompous nobleman came and demanded to see the ambassador. "Please take a chair. The ambassador will be here soon," said Labouchere. The insulted nobleman asked, "Do you know who I am?" and recited his pedigree. Labouchere replied, "Please take two chairs."

> Henry Labouchere (1831–1912), British
> politician and writer [variations also
> attributed to others]

◆ INFANT

Jokes, Stories and Anecdotes

"My three-year-old's been walking since she was two," said the mother to her aunt. Replied the aunt, "Doesn't she ever get tired?"

◆ INFLUENCE & PERSUASION

Foreign Words and Phrases

blat (Rus)
(bluht) influence (legal tender in some markets)

Quotations

"It was said that Mr. Gladstone could persuade most people of most things, and himself of anything."

William Ralph Inge (1860–1954),
British clergyman

Classical Phrases and Myths

argumentum ad populum (Lat)
(ar-gu-MEN-lum ad POP-u-lum) argument appealing to the crowd

The Athenian statesman Themistocles had alienated allies of Athens by extorting money from them. With his naval fleet nearby, he sent a message to the Andrians to compel them to pay him money: "I have with me two gods, Persuasion and Compulsion." The islanders sent back their reply that they already had two great deities on their side who hindered them from giving him his funds: Penury and Despair.

Themistocles (c. 527 B.C.–c. 460 B.C.),
Greek statesman

◆ INFLUENCE & PERSUASION, LACK OF

Quotations

"Let every man mind his own business."

Miguel de Cervantes (1547–1616),
Spanish writer, Don Quixote de la
Mancha, Part I *(1605), bk. III, ch. 8*

"My people and I have come to an agreement which satisfies us both. They are to say what they please, and I am to do what I please."

Frederick II [Frederick the Great]
(1712–1786), Prussian king
[authenticity unverified]

Classical Phrases and Myths

"However many you put to death, you will never kill your successor."

Seneca [Lucius Annaeus Seneca]
(c. 5 B.C.–A.D. 65), Roman writer,
philosopher and statesman, trying
unsuccessfully to curb Nero's cruelty

Jokes, Stories and Anecdotes

The wife of a mediocre writer approached the accomplished writer François Coppe to vote for her husband, who was seeking a prestigious membership in the French Academy. She pleaded, "He'll die if he's not elected." Coppe assented but his vote was insufficient. Another seat became available sometime later, so the wife reiterated her plea to Coppe. "No, I consider myself free of any obligation," he said. "I kept my promise but he did not keep his."

François Edouard Joachim Coppe
(1842–1908), French writer

◆ INFORMALITY

Foreign Words and Phrases

en famille (Fra)
(on fah-MEE) as one of the family, informally

en pantoufles (Fra)
(on PAN-foo-ful) *lit:* in slippers; in a relaxed manner

◆ INFORMATION

Foreign Words and Phrases

tout court (Fra)
(too COOR) without further explanation or description

Jokes, Stories and Anecdotes

Bored waiting for the press conference to begin, the reporter sidled up to a man standing alone in a corner. "Have you heard the latest joke about Senator Bloomley?" asked the reporter. The man eyed her narrowly. "Before you say it, I must inform you that I work for him." "Thanks for warning me," replied the reporter. "I'll tell it slowly."

Russell Baker, while the *New York Times* correspondent on Capitol Hill in early 1961, was emerging from the Senate when he was collared by Vice-President Lyndon Johnson. Johnson exclaimed, "You, I've been looking for you," pulled him into his office and embarked on a monologue concerning his insider position and importance within the Kennedy administration. While talking, he scribbled on a piece of paper and buzzed for his secretary. She took the paper, left the room, soon reappeared and returned the paper to Johnson. Johnson, still talking, glanced at the paper, crumpled it, and threw it away. Later Baker learned what Johnson had written: "Who is this I'm talking to?"

> *Lyndon Baines Johnson (1908–1973), U.S. president*

◆ INHERITANCE

Quotations

"The weeping of an heir is laughter in disguise."

> *Michel Eyquem de Montaigne (1533– 1592), French writer,* Essays *(1580)*

Classical Phrases and Myths

damnosa haereditas (Lat)
(dam-NOH-sa hee-RED-ee-tas) *lit:* inheritance of damnation; ruinous legacy

"*In necessariis, unitas; in dubiis, libertas; in omniis, caritas.*" (in NEK-essar-ee-is UN-ee-tas in DUB-ee-is LIB-er-tas in OM-nee-is KARE-eetas) (In necessary things, unity; in doubtful things, liberty; in all things, charity.)

> *Richard Baxter (1615–1691), British divine, Motto*

Jokes, Stories and Anecdotes

All relatives, particularly the greedy niece, Gertrude, listened expectantly to the reading of the dead millionaire's will. Then the lawyer said, "And to my niece, Gertrude, whom I promised to remember— 'Hi, there, Gertie!' "

After comedian Jack Benny's death, his widow, Mary, received a single long-stemmed rose, sent without a card from the local florist. The following day, a second rose was delivered. Mystified, Mary called the florist. It turned out that Benny had provided in his will for the florist to supply "one perfect red rose daily for the rest of Mary's life."

> *Jack Benny (1894–1974), U.S. comedian*

Perhaps the most unusual legacy left in a will was by the poet and radical writer Heinrich Heine. Married for 15 years to a vain and boorish wife, he bequeathed to her his whole estate on condition that she marry again, "because then there will be at least one man who will regret my death."

Heinrich Heine (1797–1856), German poet and writer

Scottish novelist Robert Louis Stevenson had a young friend who once confided that she felt cheated because, being born on Christmas Day, she received presents only once a year. Drawing up his will, Stevenson remembered the girl and bequeathed his own birthday to her. Later, he modified his legacy: "If, however, she fails to use this bequest properly, all rights shall pass to the President of the United States."

Robert Louis [Balfour] Stevenson (1850–1894), British writer and poet

---

◆ INHOSPITALITY

Foreign Words and Phrases

pariah (Hin)
(puh-RIE-uh) outcast

Quotations

"And do come back, when you've a little less time to spare."

Walter Richard Sickert (1860–1942), British painter, bidding farewell to guests who overstayed their welcome

"He said it in a moment of excitement, when chasing Americans out of his backyard with brickbats... At bottom he was probably fond of them, but he was always able to conceal it."

Mark Twain [Samuel Langhorne Clemens] (1835–1910), U.S. humorist, writer and

speaker, describing Thomas Carlyle, New York World (December 10, 1899), "Mark Twain's Christmas Book"

"Frank Harris is invited to all the great houses of England—once."

Oscar [Fingal O'Flahertie Wills] Wilde (1854–1900), British playwright, writer and wit

Classical Phrases and Myths

persona non grata (Lat)
(per-SOH-na nohn GRAH-ta) *lit:* person not welcome; an unacceptable person (opp: *persona grata*)

Roman consul Scipio Nasica once visited the house of his friend, the poet Quintus Ennius. Although Nasica saw Ennius disappearing into a back room, his slave told Nasica that his master was not at home. Nasica left. Later, Ennius called on Nasica. "Not home!" Nasica said through the door. Ennius replied, "You cannot have me think this—I recognize your voice." Retorted Nasica, "Well, I believed your slave, and you won't believe me."

Scipio Nasica Serapio, Publius Cornelius (c. 138 B.C.), Roman politician [attributed also to Jonathan Swift]

Jokes, Stories and Anecdotes

The stocky union boss, though uninvited, showed up at a political function. "Why, you're here!" said a friend. "I thought you weren't invited." "I wasn't," said the crasher, grabbing a plateful of hors d'oeuvres, "but I thought I'd show up anyway to prove I wasn't mad at not being asked."

A reporter once called on Peter Pan's creator, Sir James Barrie, at his home. When Barrie came to the door, the reporter said, "Sir James Barrie, I presume?" Barrie, who resented any intrusion into the privacy of his home, answered "You do," and slammed the door.

Sir J[ames] M[atthew] Barrie (1860–1937), British writer and playwright

"How do you deal with insistent visitors who overextend their welcome?" asked the British ambassador, after a long meeting with German chancellor Prince von Bismarck. "My method is excellent," replied Bismarck. "I merely have my servant appear to inform me that my wife has an urgent matter requiring my attention." At that instant, there was a knock at the door and a servant entered with a message from his wife.

Otto Eduard Leopold, Prince von Bismarck (1815–1898), German statesman

Returning home after a long day, Winston Churchill was determined to avoid his last appointment. He instructed his valet to "tell him I'm out." Then, after reflecting, he added, "And to convince him, smoke one of my cigars when you open the door."

Sir Winston Spencer Churchill (1874–1965), British prime minister and writer

An English duchess, who had invited noted pianist Ignace Paderewski to play for her dinner guests, was displeased by his high fee, and wrote him: "Dear Maestro, accept my regrets for not inviting you to dinner. As a professional artist you will be more at ease in a nice room where you can rest before the concert." "Dear Duchess, thank you for your letter," Paderewski responded. "As you so kindly inform me that I am not obliged to be present at your dinner, I shall be satisfied with half of my fee."

Ignace Jan Paderewski (1860–1941), Polish pianist, composer and statesman

A stranger once approached the colonial Virginia politician John Randolph and began, "I have had the pleasure of passing your house recently." Randolph simply replied, "I am glad of it. I hope you will always do, sir."

John Randolph (1773–1833), U.S. politician

◆ INJUSTICE

Foreign Words and Phrases

misfeasance (Fra)
(MIS-feez-ahnse) injustice or wrong judgment given by legally constituted authority

Quotations

Ninotchka (Greta Garbo): "Why should you carry other people's bags?" Porter: "Well, that's my business, madame." Ninotchka: "That's no business. That's social injustice." Porter: "That depends on the tip."

Charles Brackett (1892–1969), U.S. writer, Billy [Samuel] Wilder (1906–1993), U.S. director and writer, and Walter Reisch (1903–1983), U.S. writer, Ninotchka (1939 film)

"Justice is my being allowed to do whatever I like. Injustice is whatever prevents my doing so."

Samuel Butler (1835–1902), British writer

"*Ils commencent ici [Paris] par faire pendre un homme et puis ils lui font son proces.*" (Here, in Paris, they hang a man first, and try him afterwards.)

Molière [Jean Baptiste Poquelin] (1622–1673), French playwright, Monsieur de Pourceaugnac, Act III, sc. ii

Classical Phrases and Myths

"*Raro aritecedentem scelestum Deseruit pede Poena claudo.*" (Rarely has Punishment, though halt of foot, left the track of the criminal in the way before her.)

Horace (65 B.C.–8 B.C.), Roman poet, Odes, III, ii, l. 31

"Ius summum saepe summa est mala-tia." (ee-US SUM-mum sayp SUM-ma est MAL-ay-tia) (Extreme law is often extreme injustice.)

> Terence [Publius Terentius Afer]
> (c. 190 B.C.–159 B.C.), Roman playwright,
> Heauton Timoroumenos

◆ INNOCENCE

Foreign Words and Phrases

jusqu'au boutiste (Fra)
(JOOSK-oh boh-TEEST) passionate, virgin innocence

débutante (Fra)
(day-BOO-TAHNT) person making a first appearance, performance, etc.

ingénue (Fra)
(an-JAY-new) simple and pure young (woman) or one assuming such role

Quotations

"He was a simple soul who had not been introduced to his own subconscious."

> Warwick Deeping (1877–1950),
> British writer

"Men do not suspect faults which they do not commit."

> Samuel Johnson (1709–1784),
> British man of letters

"I used to be Snow White . . . but I drifted."

> Mae West (1892–1980), U.S. film actress

◆ INQUIRY

Foreign Words and Phrases

investigaciones (Spa)
(een-VEST-ee-ga-SEE-ohnz) police investigators

Classical Phrases and Myths

"Tu ne quaesieris, scire nefas." (Pray, ask not, such knowledge is not for us.)

> Horace (65 B.C.–8 B.C.), Roman poet,
> Odes, I, xi, l. 1

The fifth-century theologian St. Augustine was once asked, "What was God doing through all the eternity of time before He created heaven and earth?" Responded St. Augustine, "Creating hell for those who ask questions like you."

> St. Augustine of Hippo (354–430),
> North African Catholic theologian
> [authenticity unverified]

Jokes, Stories and Anecdotes

A man told the lawyer referred to him, "I need advice fast. I just found $700. If I pay it to you, will you answer two questions?" "Sure. What's your second question?"

The mountain-climbing party was traversing a steep wall when there was a sudden shudder and the ice broke away, carrying one of the party down into the crevasse with it. "Are you alive, Fred?" they shouted after him. "Yes!" "Are you hurt?" "No!" "Well, can you climb back up?" Came a faint echo: "I'm still f-a-a-l-lling!"

◆ INSANITY

Foreign Words and Phrases

won (Kor)
(wahn) inability to let go of something from the past or an illusion (e.g., a past love affair, position of authority, etc.)

il a le diable au corpse (Fra)
(eel ah le dee-AH-ble oh KOR) the
devil is in him; he is possessed

idée fixe (Fra)
(EE-day FEEX) *lit*: fixed idea; obses-
sion, preoccupation

meshuggener (Yid)
(meh-SHOOG-in-ah) wild, unpredictable, crazy person

loco poco (Spa)
(LOH-koh POH-koh) slightly crazy,
a little mad

Quotations

"A man that'd expict to thrain lobsters to fly in a year is called a loo-
nytic; but a man that thinks men
can be tu-rrned into angels be an
iliction is called a rayformer an' remains at large."

> Finley Peter Dunne (1867–1936),
> U.S. writer and humorist,
> Mr. Dooley's Opinions (1900),
> "Casual Observations"

"The world is becoming like a lunatic asylum run by lunatics."

> David Lloyd George, 1st Earl of Dwyfor
> (1863–1945), British prime minister

"If you talk to God, you are praying; if God talks to you, you have
schizophrenia."

> Thomas Szasz (1920–   ),
> U.S. psychiatrist, The Second Sin
> (1973), "Schizophrenia"

Classical Phrases and Myths

non compos mentis (Lat)
(nohn KOM-pos MEN-tis) *lit*: not in
control of one's mind; deranged, insane

"*Quos Deus vult perdere prius demen-
tat.*" (kwos DAY-us vult PER-
der-e PREE-us de-MEN-tat) (Those
whom God wishes to destroy, he
first makes mad.)

> Euripides (480 B.C.–406 B.C.),
> Greek playwright [Latin translation
> of Greek]

"*Auditis an me ludit amabilis In-
sania?*" (Do you hear it? Or is it a
delightful madness that makes
sport of me?)

> Horace (65 B.C.–8 B.C.), Roman poet,
> Odes, III, iv, l. 5

"*Semel insanivimus omnes.*" (We
have all been mad once.)

> Johannes Baptista Mantuanus
> (1448–1516), German clergyman

Jokes, Stories and Anecdotes

The explorer Friedrich Humboldt
once remarked to a Parisian doctor
who specialized in mental disor-
ders that he would like to meet a
lunatic. His friend delightedly arranged for Humboldt to dine with
two strangers. One was a model of
cool formality while the other gestured and talked wildly. Gazing at
the second stranger, Humboldt
whispered to the doctor, "Your lunatic amuses me." "But it's the
other one who's the lunatic," replied the physician, following
Humboldt's gaze. "The gentleman
you're looking at is [the famous
novelist] Honoré de Balzac."

> Friedrich Heinrich Humboldt, Baron von
> (1769–1859), German naturalist, traveler,
> and statesman

Committed in 1897 to an asylum,
the insane songwriter Hugo Wolf,
pointing to a large clock hanging in
the institution's dining room, once
asked, "Is that clock right?" "As far
as I can tell," answered an attendant. In a moment of lucidity, Wolf

asked, "Then what's it doing here?"

Hugo Wolf (1860–1903),
Austrian composer

◆ INSIGNIFICANCE

Foreign Words and Phrases

bagatelle (Fra)
(bag-ah-TELL) trifle, bauble, trinket

n'importe (Fra)
(nam-pohrt) it does not matter

Quotations

"Writing a book of poetry is like dropping a rose petal down the Grand Canyon and waiting for the echo."

Don[ald Robert Perry] Marquis
(1878–1937), U.S. writer and poet

Classical Phrases and Myths

res nihili (Lat)
(res NI-hil-ee) thing of no consequence, trifling matter

Jokes, Stories and Anecdotes

A young, inexperienced actor, anxious to give his very minor role the right interpretation, sought out Sir James Barrie, who was producing his own play, for advice. "I am glad you have asked me," Barrie said after reflecting. "Please convey while you act that the man you portray has a brother in Shropshire who drinks port."

Sir J[ames] M[atthew] Barrie (1860–1937),
British writer and playwright

◆ INSINCERITY

Quotations

"That's what show business is—sincere insincerity."

Benny Hill (1925–1991), British comedian

◆ INSOLENCE

Foreign Words and Phrases

chutzpah (Yid)
(KHUTZ-pah) unmitigated audacity or impudence, boldness

Quotations

"Bow, stubborn knees!"

William Shakespeare (1564–1616),
British playwright and poet, Hamlet
(1601), Act IV, sc. v

"Le tact dans l'audace c'est de savoir jusqu'ou on peut aller trop loin." (Being tactful in audacity is knowing how far one can go too far.)

Jean Cocteau (1889–1963), French writer,
artist and filmmaker, Le Coq et
l'Arlequin (1918)

Jokes, Stories and Anecdotes

Beau Brummell's quarrel with his former friend the Prince Regent, later George IV, shook fashionable society. According to Brummell, he was riding with his friend Beau Nash in London when they met the regent. The regent ignored Brummell, speaking only to the friend. When the regent continued on but was not yet quite out of earshot, Brummell asked loudly, "Who's your fat friend?"

George Bryan ["Beau"] Brummell
(1778–1840), British socialite

Hermann Goering, Hitler's lieutenant, collided with an Italian aristocrat at a crowded Roman railroad platform. The nobleman demanded an apology. Snapped Goering: "I am Hermann Goering." Replied the Italian: "Although insufficient as an excuse, as an explanation it is ample."

Hermann Wilhelm Goering (1893–1946),
German politician

◆ INSURANCE

Quotations

"What can't be cured must be insured."

Oliver Herford (1863–1935),
British-born U.S. humorist and illustrator

Jokes, Stories and Anecdotes

Two retired businessmen are on the golf links commiserating about their careers. "What happened to your business?" one asks the other. "Fire. Destroyed everything. What happened to yours?" "Flood," the first replied. "Really? How do you arrange a flood?"

Two rival aging starlets were forced to sit next to each other at a Hollywood function. "Honey," the first boasted, "Lloyd's once insured my breasts for $5 million." "Really," drawled the other, "What did you do with the money?"

Each summer, Henry Frick would transport his priceless collection of art treasures in a custom-built railroad car from New York to his estate at Pride's Crossing, Massachusetts. Journalist Oswald Garrison Villard once asked the one-time chairman of Carnegie Steel Company whether he was concerned about theft or damage to the artwork in transit. "Oh, no," responded Frick, matter-of-factly. "They're insured."

Henry Clay Frick (1849–1919),
U.S. industrialist

◆ INTELLIGENCE

Foreign Words and Phrases

Wunderkind (Ger)
(VOON-der-kint) lit: wonder child; child prodigy

Quotations

"The French are wiser than they seem, and the Spaniards seem wiser than they are."

Francis Bacon (1561–1626),
British lawyer and writer, Essays (1625),
"Of Seeming Wise"

"A smattering of everything and a knowledge of nothing."

Charles Dickens (1812–1870),
British writer, Sketches by Boz
(1836–1837), "Tales," ch. 3

"The test of a first-rate intelligence is the ability to hold two opposed ideas in the mind at the same time, and still retain the ability to function."

F[rancis] Scott [Key] Fitzgerald
(1896–1940), U.S. writer, Esquire
(February 1936), "The Crack-Up"

"Walt [Rostow] can write faster than I can read."

John Fitzgerald Kennedy (1917–1963),
U.S. president

"I think this is the most extraordinary collection of talent, of human knowledge, that has ever been gathered together at the White House, with the possible exception of when Thomas Jefferson dined alone."

John Fitzgerald Kennedy (1917–1963),
U.S. president, describing a state dinner
he gave for winners of the Nobel Prize,
April 1962

"Thou speakest wiser than thou art."

William Shakespeare (1564–1616),
British playwright and poet,
As You Like It (1600), Act II, sc. iv

"Some folks are wise, and some are otherwise."

Tobias Smollett (1721–1771),
British writer and surgeon

"His mind was like a soup dish, wide and shallow; it could hold a small amount of nearly anything, but the slightest jarring spilled the soup into somebody's lap."

I[sador] F[einstein] Stone (1903–1989), U.S. writer, describing politician and lawyer William Jennings Bryan

Jokes, Stories and Anecdotes

"I presume that there is much in the world of physics that puzzled you during your lifetime." said God to Albert Einstein upon his matriculation into heaven. "You will be glad to know that you now have the opportunity of understanding all, including the unified theory that you never completed." Barely suppressing his glee, Einstein gladly accepted the sheaf of papers from God. He looked through the sheets eagerly and rapidly, turned back to the first page, took a final look and handed them back to God with a sigh. "No, still wrong."

While visiting his old hometown of Far Rockaway, New York, the Nobel Prize–winning physicist and author Richard Feynman examined his high school records. Later, he remarked to his wife that his file revealed that his IQ was 124, "just above average." He was nonetheless delighted, because "to win a Nobel Prize was no big deal. But to win it with an IQ of 124—*that* was something."

Richard P. Feynman (1918–1987), U.S. physicist and writer

◆ INTEMPERANCE

Foreign Words and Phrases

gourmandise (Fra)
(goor-mon-DEE-suh)   self-indulgence, hedonism

Quotations

"Business was his aversion; pleasure was his business."

Maria Edgeworth (1767–1849), British writer, The Contrast, ch. 2

"My main problem is reconciling my gross habits with my net income."

Errol Flynn (1909–1959), U.S. film actor

"Puritanism. The haunting fear that someone, somewhere, may be happy."

H[enry] L[ouis] Mencken (1880–1956), U.S. critic and writer, Chrestomathy (1949), ch. 30

Classical Phrases and Myths

dum vivimus, vivamus (Lat)
(dum wi-wi-mus wi-WAH-mus) while we live, let us live (to the fullest)

Jokes, Stories and Anecdotes

While teammates on the Minneapolis Lakers, "Hot Rod" Hundley and Bob Leonard enjoyed notoriety for their nighttime shenanigans. When they missed a team plane, however, exasperated owner Bob Short summoned them to his office. Short first called Hundley in for a lecture and fined him the then-enormous sum of $1,000. Once outside Short's office, Hundley was anxiously asked by Leonard, "How much?" "Baby, a big bill," replied Hundley. "A hundred dollars?" "A hundred, damn. A thousand." Leonard's eyes filled with tears. Consolingly, Hundley said, "It's a record." Leonard's face brightened. "Let's go an' celebrate."

Rodney Hundley (1934–   ), U.S. basketball player

◆ INTERMENT

Classical Phrases and Myths

requiescat in pace (Lat)
(re-kwi-es-KAT in PAH-ke) may he
rest in peace (abbr: RIP)

sarcophagus (Grk)
(SAR-kof-ag-us) *lit:* flesh-eater, now
burial coffins

Jokes, Stories and Anecdotes

Humorist Robert Benchley, after
departing from a party on New
York City's Riverside Drive early in
the morning, stopped at Ulysses S.
Grant's tomb, scribbled something
on the back of a paper, and left it
at the door of the monument. The
note read: "Please leave one quart
of milk and cream.—U. S. G."

> *Robert Charles Benchley (1889–1945),*
> *U.S. humorist*

Someone who had not been notified
of the death of a renowned composer asked librettist W. S. Gilbert
what the composer was doing. "He
is doing nothing," replied Gilbert.
"But surely he is composing." "On
the contrary, he is decomposing."

> *Sir W[illiam] S[chwenck] Gilbert*
> *(1836–1911), British writer*

The British diplomat Baron Gore-
Booth once received the following
urgent telegram from the Middle
East: "Ruler has died suddenly.
Please advise." Gore-Booth's immediate reply: "Hesitate to dog-
matize, but suggest burial."

> *Paul Henry, Baron Gore-Booth*
> *(1909–   ), British diplomat*

Consenting (barely) to dramatist
Ben Jonson's request for a square
foot, after his death, in hallowed
Westminster Abbey, where many of
Britain's greatest literary lights are
interred, Charles I of England had
Jonson buried in an upright posi-
tion.

> *Ben Jonson (1572–1637),*
> *British playwright*

◆ INTERPRETATION & TRANSLATION

Quotations

"*Traduttori, traditori.*" (Translators,
traitors.)

> *Italian proverb*

"You continue to play Bach your
way, and I'll continue to play him
his way."

> *Wanda Landowska (1879–1959), Polish*
> *harpsichordist, to another musician*

"I'd like that translated, if I may."

> *[Maurice] Harold Macmillan, 1st Earl of*
> *Stockton (1894–1992), British prime*
> *minister, remarking unflappably at the*
> *United Nations in September 1960, after*
> *being interrupted by Soviet premier*
> *Khrushchev, who was banging*
> *his shoe on the table*

"*El original es infiel a la traducción.*"
(The original is unfaithful to the
translation.)

> *Jorge Luis Borges (1899–1986),*
> *Argentine writer and poet, reviewing*
> *Henley's translation of* Vathek *by*
> *William Beckford, Sobre el "Vathek" de*
> *William Beckford (1943), in Obras*
> *Completas (1974), p. 730*

Jokes, Stories and Anecdotes

Guido, a Mafia capo, asked the
godfather about a job for his deaf-
mute nephew, Roberto. The godfa-

ther determined that Guido's nephew would make a perfect bagman, as he would be unable to hear or speak of the underworld's activities. Months passed without incident until one day the godfather summoned Guido to his favorite restaurant. "Roberto's performed well, Guido," he said. "But his latest delivery is $300,000 short. Guido, I'm sending Bluto with you to find out how he made such a mistake." When they caught up with Roberto, Bluto put a gun to his head and told Guido to ask his nephew what had happened to the money. "The godfather is willing to forgive you if you tell the truth," Guido said in sign language. "So, where's the money?" His eyes popping in fear, Roberto signed back, "Forgive me. I'll never do it again. The money's behind a loose brick next to the toilet." "So what'd the kid say?" bellowed Bluto. "He said he doesn't think you have the guts to pull the trigger."

On a visit to China, a diplomat rambled for nearly 20 minutes in telling an anecdote. His audience was respectfully silent. When he had finished, his interpreter merely said four words. Everyone laughed uproariously. "How did you tell my story so quickly?" gasped the stunned diplomat. "Story too long," replied the interpreter. "So I said: 'He tell joke. Laugh.' "

Ferguson treated himself to his first luxury cruise and was assigned a dining table at which the only other diner was a Frenchman. Neither spoke the other's language. When they met, Ferguson began eating at once, but the Frenchman said in very courtly fashion, "Bon appetit." Ferguson, ashamed for not having introduced himself, replied, "Fergu-son!" This went on for several meals. Once, waiting for his dinner partner, Ferguson casually asked the steward where Mr. Bone-apatee might be. "Oh, you mean Monsieur D'Essaie," laughed the steward. "He'll be arriving shortly." "But if Bone-apatee is not his name," asked Ferguson, "why does he always announce himself that way to me at each meal?" "He is saying 'Good appetite— enjoy your meal,' " sneered the steward. Humiliated, Ferguson waited for dinner and, when he faced the Frenchman, enunciated clearly, "Bone-apatee." The Frenchman smiled and said, "Fairg-uzon!"

An American visitor in Berlin went to the Reichstag, accompanied by an interpreter, to hear the politicians speak. Prince von Bismarck soon began to engage in a debate, speaking with force and at length. Despite persistent nudges from the American, who was anxious to hear a translation, the interpreter sat listening with intense concentration. Finally, the American could no longer restrain herself and burst out, "What is he saying?" "Patience, madam," replied the interpreter. "I am waiting for the verb."

Otto Eduard Leopold, Prince von Bismarck (1815–1898), German statesman

In 1842, Sir Charles Napier won smashing victories in Sind, a region along the lower reaches of the Indus River in what is now Pakistan. With security in mind, and conscious that British public officials typically knew Latin, he dispatched news of his conquest in the one-word message, *"Peccavi"* ("I have sinned.")

Sir Charles James Napier (1782–1853), British soldier and administrator

◆ INVISIBILITY

Foreign Words and Phrases

pentimento (Ita)
(pen-tee-MEN-toh) *lit:* repentance; effaced detail that becomes apparent after time (e.g., mark left by a painter's erasure or alteration)

profil perdu (Fra)
(pro-FEEL per-DOO) *lit:* lost profile; profile of an object beyond one's blind spot

Classical Phrases and Myths

de non apparentibus et de non existentibus eadem est ratio (Lat)
(de non ap-PARE-en-ti-BOOS et de non ex-ist-EN-ti-BOOS) it is presumed that what does not appear does not exist, legal maxim

According to Greek mythology, Nephele (NEF-e-lee) was the cloud shaped to Hera's likeness by Zeus to protect Hera from the amorous advances of Ixion. Centaurus, the sire of the centaurs, was produced from the union of Nephele and Ixion.

Jokes, Stories and Anecdotes

As a fledgling comedian, Jackie Gleason stayed at a boardinghouse in a seaside town while performing at the local nightclub. Unable to pay his rent, however, he planned a ruse to avoid suspicion and his obligation. He lowered a suitcase containing his belongings from his bedroom window into the arms of a friend below, then strolled nonchalantly in his swim trunks out of the house toward the beach. Three years later he returned to the boardinghouse to pay off his debt and relieve the guilt. The landlady immediately recognized him but stepped back in horror as if he were a ghost. "Oh!" she exclaimed. "I thought you had drowned!"

> *Jackie Gleason (1916–1990),*
> *U.S. comedian*

◆ IRRESOLUTION

Quotations

"We know what happens to people who stay in the middle of the road. They get run down."

> *Aneurin ["Nye"] Bevan (1897–1960),*
> *British politician*

"I must have a prodigious quantity of mind; it takes me as much as a week, sometimes, to make it up."

> *Mark Twain [Samuel Langhorne Clemens]*
> *(1835–1910), U.S. humorist, writer and*
> *speaker,* The Innocents Abroad
> *(1869), ch. 7*

Classical Phrases and Myths

homo nullius coloris (Lat)
(HOH-mo NULL-ee-uskol-OR-ees) lit: man of no color; one who does not commit himself (to an argument, position, etc.)

agonistes (Grk)
(a-gon-IS-tees) one in (especially mental) conflict, contestant

Jokes, Stories and Anecdotes

A psychiatrist patiently listened to her confused patient before offering her insight. "It appears to me you have trouble making decisions, wouldn't you agree?" The confused soul pondered the question some time before answering, "Well, yes and no."

Although the partnership of Gilbert and Sullivan in writing light opera was eminently successful, it was a strained relationship. W. S. Gilbert, particularly angered by Sullivan's repeated declarations of intending to dissolve the partnership so that he could write "better music," observed, "He is like a man who sits on a stove and then complains that his backside is burning."

Sir W[illiam] S[chwenck] Gilbert (1836–1911), British writer

◆ IRREVOCABILITY

Foreign Words and Phrases

lo dicho, dicho (Spa)
(loh DEE-choh DEE-choh) that is said, is said; things once said cannot be retracted

Quotations

"Once the toothpaste is out of the tube, it is awfully hard to get it back in."

H. R[obert] Haldeman (1929–1993), U.S. statesman, commenting to John Wesley Dean on Watergate affair, April 8, 1973

Classical Phrases and Myths

"Et semel emissum volat irrevocabile verbum." (And once escaped a word may not be recalled.)

Horace (65 B.C.–8 B.C.), Roman poet, Epistles, I, xviii, l. 71

Concerned about his extraordinary military successes, the consul in Rome in 49 B.C. proposed that Julius Caesar should be recalled, his armies disbanded and a new commander appointed to take his place. Caesar could either return to Rome as a private citizen and face his hostile political enemies or march on Rome at the head of his loyal army and embroil it in civil war. Caesar advanced to the Rubicon River, the boundary between Gaul and Italy, where he could scarcely bring him-

self to issue the fatal order to cross. As he hesitated, a large apparition on the bank played a pipe, then snatched a trumpet from a soldier, blew a blast on it and crossed over the river. Caesar accepted this as a sign from the gods and led his troops over with the words: *"Jacta alea est."* (The die is cast.) Hence, *jacta alea est* is the phrase used to indicate irrevocably commiting oneself to a course of action.

Gaius Julius Caesar (100 B.C.–44 B.C.), Roman general and statesman

◆ JEALOUSY

Quotations

"It is not enough to succeed. Others must fail."

Gore Vidal (1925–   ), U.S. writer

Jokes, Stories and Anecdotes

Soon after Irish playwright Samuel Beckett married his lover Suzanne in 1961, her jealousy of his increasing fame and success began to sour their marriage. One day in 1969 Suzanne answered the telephone, listened briefly, said a few words and hung up. Turning to Beckett and looking stricken, she hissed, *"Quel catastrophe!"* (What a catastrophe!) She had just been informed that Beckett had been awarded the Nobel Prize for literature.

Samuel Beckett (1906–1989), Irish writer, playwright and poet

A friend of actress Beatrice Lillie, dining at another table, noticed a beautiful showgirl in Lillie's party. He had a waiter deliver a scribbled note to her. It read: "My God, Bea, who is that incredibly gorgeous creature at your table?" Beatrice Lillie scrawled an answer, which the waiter carried back. He opened it and read: "Me!!"

> *Beatrice Lillie (1898–   ),*
> *Canadian-born British actress*

◆ JOURNALISM

Quotations

"The printing press is either the greatest blessing or the greatest curse of modern times, one sometimes forgets which."

> *Sir J[ames] M[atthew] Barrie (1860–1937),*
> *British writer and playwright,*
> Sentimental Tommy *(1896), ch. 5*

"It was long ago in my life as a simple reporter that I decided that facts must never get in the way of truth."

> *James Cameron (1911–1985),*
> *British writer*

"Headlines twice the size of the events."

> *John Galsworthy (1867–1933),*
> *British writer and playwright*

"All the news that's fit to print."

> *Adolph Simon Ochs (1858–1935),*
> *U.S. publisher,* New York Times

"I write from the worm's-eye point of view."

> *Ernie Pyle (1900–1945), U.S. writer,*
> Here Is Your War *(1943)*

"Well, all I know is what I read in the papers."

> *Will[iam Penn Adair] Rogers*
> *(1879–1935), U.S. comedian*

"I'm sure if I have any plans, the Press will inform me."

> *Arthur Scargill (1938–   ),*
> *British labor leader*

"Freedom of the press in Britain means freedom to print such of the proprietor's prejudices as the advertisers don't object to."

> *Hannen Swaffer (1879–1962),*
> *British writer*

"Dead. That's what the man was when they found him with a knife in his back at 4 P.M. in front of Riley's saloon at the corner of 52nd and 12th Streets."

> *James Thurber (1894–1961),*
> *U.S. cartoonist and humorist, writing a*
> *lead after his editor instructed the novice*
> *journalist to write short dramatic leads*

"In the old days men had the rack; now they have the Press."

> *Oscar [Fingal O'Flahertie Wills] Wilde*
> *(1854–1900), British playwright,*
> *writer and wit*

"Most rock journalism is people who can't write interviewing people who can't talk for people who can't read."

> *Frank Zappa (1940–1993),*
> *U.S. musician and songwriter*

Jokes, Stories and Anecdotes

John Quincy Adams would often swim naked in the Potomac at dawn. Journalist Anne Newport Royall, who had been spurned repeatedly by President Adams for an interview about his pet project, the Bank of America, once tracked him to the river bank and sat by his clothes. She introduced herself and, resorting to screams whenever Adams tried to emerge, conducted surely the most unusual press conference known with the trapped politician.

> *John Quincy Adams (1767–1848),*
> *U.S. president*

A *New York Times* headline that read, "Elm Beetle Infestation Ravishing Thousands of Trees in Greenwich" was ridiculed by editor Theodore Bernstein in the *Winners and Sinners* bulletin distributed to staff. Under Bernstein's review entitled "Insex," he admonished, "Keep your mind on your work, buster. The word you want is 'ravaging.'"

Theodore Bernstein (1904–1979),
U.S. editor

The abolitionist and founder of the *New York Tribune,* Horace Greeley, riding the train to New York, sought to find out why a certain passenger was reading the rival newspaper, the *Sun.* Greeley began with small-talk and then inquired, "Why don't you read the *Tribune?* It's much more informative than the *Sun.*" "I also take the *Tribune,*" replied the other man. "I use it to wipe my arse." "Keep on with it," countered the perturbed Greeley. "Eventually you'll have more brains in your arse than you have in your head."

Horace Greeley (1811–1872),
U.S. publisher and politician

Newspaper proprietor William Randolph Hearst sent the artist Frederic Remington to cover events in Cuba following the explosion of the *Maine* in 1898. But the expected conflict between Spain and the United States did not immediately materialize, and Remington cabled Hearst, asking whether he should return. Hearst cabled back: "Please remain. You furnish the pictures and I'll furnish the war." Sure enough, due largely to inflammatory writing undertaken by the Hearst newspaper empire to expand circulation, the Spanish-American War began.

William Randolph Hearst (1863–1951),
U.S. publisher [authenticity controverted]

Joseph Pulitzer, after whom the Pulitzer Prize is named, believed that his newspaper, the *New York World,* should be so influential that even inhabitants of other planets would read it. When he once considered erecting an advertising sign in New Jersey that would be visible on Mars, he was dissuaded only after an aide inquired, "What language shall we print it in?"

Joseph Pulitzer (1847–1911),
Hungarian-born U.S. publisher

In compliance with his editor's instructions never to state as fact anything that could not be verified objectively, humorist Mark Twain, then a fledgling reporter, wrote the following account of a social affair: "A woman giving the name of Mrs. James Jones, who is reported to be one of the society leaders of the city, is said to have given what purported to be a party yesterday to a number of alleged ladies. The hostess claims to be the wife of a reputed attorney."

Mark Twain [Samuel Langhorne Clemens]
(1835–1910), U.S. humorist,
writer and speaker

◆ JUDGE & JURY

Foreign Words and Phrases

Kulikov (Yid)
(Kool-ih-kof) a politically expedient or pragmatic legal judgment

Quotations

"The public do not know enough to be experts, yet know enough to decide between them."

Samuel Butler (1835–1902), British writer

"A jury consists of twelve persons chosen to decide who has the better lawyer."

Robert Lee Frost (1874–1963), U.S. poet

Classical Phrases and Myths

"No one should be judge in his own case."

Publilius Syrus (c. 100 B.C.), Roman writer, Sententiae, 545

Cambyses II, a Persian ruler who was known for little more than being the father of Cyrus the Great, ordered that a judge who had been found guilty of corruption be flayed alive. Once the sentence had been carried out, the skin was used to cover the seat from which judgments were issued. Cambyses then appointed the dead judge's son to his father's position.

Cambyses II (d. 522 B.C.), Persian king

Jokes, Stories and Anecdotes

Desperate to avoid a murder-one conviction, a Texan bribed a juror to find him guilty instead of manslaughter. The jury was out for four days but finally returned a verdict of manslaughter. The grateful Texan cornered the juror afterward. "Thanks a heap, son," he said. "How in hell did you do it?" "It wasn't easy," the beaming juror replied. "The others were hell-bent on acquitting you."

◆ JUDGMENT

Quotations

"I don't care anything about reasons, but I know what I like."

Henry James (1843–1916), U.S. writer, Portait of a Lady (1881), vol. 2, ch. 5

Classical Phrases and Myths

res judicata (Lat)
(res YOO-dik-ah-ta) *lit:* thing which has been judged; closed case, matter that has been settled

ratio decidendi (Lat)
(RA-ti-oh day-kid-END-ee) method of decision-making; the essentials of a judgment, the reasons for a particular decision

sub judice (Lat)
(sub YOO-dee-kay) *lit:* under a judge; under judgment, still undecided

Jokes, Stories and Anecdotes

When asked whether he preferred Burgundy or claret, French gastronome Brillat-Savarin replied, "That, madame, is a question that I take so much pleasure in investigating that I postpone from week to week the pronouncement of a verdict."

Anthelme Brillat-Savarin (1755–1826), French writer and gastronome

Shown several canvases by a bodyguard who also enjoyed painting in his spare time, retired prime minister Winston Churchill observed, "They're much better than mine, but yours will have to be judged on merit."

Sir Winston Spencer Churchill (1874–1965), British prime minister and writer

◆ JUSTICE

Foreign Words and Phrases

à bon droit (Fra)
(ah bonn DRWA) *lit:* with good reason; with justice

Quotations

"The love of justice for most men is merely the fear of suffering injustice."

François, Duc de La Rochefoucauld (1613–1680), French writer, Maximes (1678), 78

"Lord, I wonder what fool it was that first invented kissing!"

> *Jonathan Swift (1667–1745),*
> *Anglo-Irish clergyman and writer,*
> Polite Conversation *(c. 1738),*
> *"Dialogue II"*

Classical Phrases and Myths

fiat justitia, ruat caelum (Lat)
(FEE-at yus-TEET-ee-a RU-al KEE-lum) let justice be done, though the heavens fall in ruin

According to Greek mythology, Rhadamanthus (rad-a-MAN-this) was the severe judge of three in Hades, the underworld, where one of his special duties was to bring to justice those whose crimes went undetected on earth. Earlier, he was known for his wise and just rule over Crete, having obtained the laws from his father, Zeus. Thus, to be *Rhadamanthine* is to be incorruptible and just.

Jokes, Stories and Anecdotes

The U.S. senator, traveling in his home state, asked his attorney to notify him as soon as a judgment was handed down in the District of Columbia case concerning his participation in an influence-peddling scheme. At 4 P.M. he received a cable that read, "JUSTICE HAS PREVAILED." The politician immediately wired back, "APPEAL AT ONCE."

◆ JUSTIFICATION

Foreign Words and Phrases

catalogue raisonne (Fra)
(kat-a-log RAYZ-ohn) catalogue of reasons, justifications

Quotations

"Every man, wherever he goes, is encompassed by a cloud of com-forting convictions, which move with him like flies on a summer day."

> *Bertrand Arthur William Russell,*
> *3rd Earl (1872–1970),*
> *British mathematician and philosopher,*
> Sceptical Essays *(1928),*
> *"Dreams and Facts"*

Classical Phrases and Myths

apologia (Grk/Lat)
(apo-LOH-gia) speech made in self-defense, esp. apology of Socrates at his trial in 399 B.C.

causa movens (Lat)
(KOW-sa MO-wens) reason for undertaking a particular action

The son of the Greek dramatist Sophocles, who gave posterity *Antigone* and *Oedipus Rex* among others, hauled his father to court to have Sophocles declared senile and therefore unable to cut the suspicious son out of his will. Sophocles, then 89, merely said, "If I am Sophocles, I am not out of my mind; if I am out of my mind, I am not Sophocles." He then read before the judges passages from his newest play, *Oedipus at Colonus*. The case was dismissed.

> *Sophocles (496 B.C.–406 B.C.),*
> *Greek playwright*

◆ KILLING

Foreign Words and Phrases

a la lanterne (Fra)
(ah lah LONG-tern) *lit:* to the lamp-post! lynch him!; slogan derived from the French Revolution

Quotations

"One murder made a villain
Millions a hero."

Beilby Porteus (1731–1808), British poet,
Death (1759), l. 155

"That depends on whom you kill."

George Bernard Shaw (1856–1950),
Irish playwright, answering if he hated
killing for pleasure

"*On tue un homme, on est un assassin.*
On tue des millions d'hommes, on est
un conqué rant. On tue les tous, on est
un dieu." (Kill one man and you are
a murderer. Kill millions and you
are a conqueror. Kill all and you are
a god.)

Jean Rostand (1894–1977),
French scientist and writer, Pensées d'un
biologiste (Thoughts of a Biologist)
(1939), p. 116

Classical Phrases and Myths

The Roman general Marcellus,
upon capturing Syracuse, gave special orders to spare the life of Archimedes (ark-i-MEED-eez). A
Roman soldier found Archimedes
drawing mathematical symbols in
the sand. Engrossed in his work,
Archimedes gestured impatiently
for the soldier to wait until he had
solved his problem, murmuring,
"Do not disturb my circles." The
soldier, enraged, slew the great scientist with his sword.

Archimedes (287 B.C.–212 B.C.),
Greek mathematician and scientist

Although Demosthenes is generally
considered the greatest orator of
classical Greece, the great Athenian
statesman and general Phocion was
a formidable rival. Demosthenes
once said to him, "The Athenians
will kill you, should they go into a
rage." "Or you," retorted Phocion,
"should they come to their senses."

Phocion (c. 402 B.C.–318 B.C.),
Greek statesman and general

Jokes, Stories and Anecdotes

William Brodie of Edinburgh, head
of the Incorporation of Edinburgh
Wrights and Masons, was respected
for, among other things, inventing
the drop. Previously, a person being
hanged was simply pushed off a
height; Brodie introduced the more
infallible system of trapdoor and
lever that became the legal standard
for hangings. It turned out that Brodie was also a successful burglar.
When an accomplice turned king's
evidence, Brodie was eventually ap-
prehended and condemned to die.
Brodie's invention was first tested at
his own execution; on the gallows
the hapless inventor inspected the
arrangements, pronounced them
satisfactory, and was efficiently *hoist*
by his own petard.

William Brodie (d. 1788),
British labor leader

"Lamb to the Slaughter" on *Alfred*
Hitchcock Presents was a 1958 epi-
sode in which a housewife killed
her husband with a frozen leg of
lamb, and then cooked it, having
invited the police who are investigating the murder to dinner. The
police eat the evidence.

Sir Alfred Hitchcock (1889–1980),
British film director

◆ KINDNESS

Foreign Words and Phrases

carita pelosa (Ita)
(kah-REE-tapeh-LOH-sa) generosity with return favor expected

rapprochement (Fra)
(rah-PROSH-mon) re-establishment
of friendly relations (especially between nations)

Quotations

"He was so benevolent, so merciful a man that, in his mistaken passion, he would have held an umbrella over a duck in a shower of rain."

Douglas William Jerrold (1803–1857), British playwright and humorist

"Be nice to people on your way up because you'll meet 'em on the way down."

Wilson Mizner (1876–1933), U.S. writer and wit [attributed also to Jimmy Durante]

Classical Phrases and Myths

"One good turn deserves another."

Petronius, Gaius [Petronius Arbiter] (d. c. 66), Roman writer, Satyricon, sec. 45

◆ KISS

Quotations

"The kiss originated when the first male reptile licked the first female reptile, implying in a subtle, complimentary way that she was as succulent as the small reptile he had for dinner the night before."

F[rancis] Scott [Key] Fitzgerald (1896–1940), U.S. writer

"I wasn't kissing her, I was just whispering in her mouth."

Chico [Leonard] Marx (1891–1961), U.S. film comedian defending himself after his wife had caught him kissing a chorus girl

"When women kiss it always reminds one of prize fighters shaking hands."

H[enry] L[ouis] Mencken (1880–1956), U.S. critic and writer, Chrestomathy (1949), ch. 30

"A kiss can be a comma, a question mark or an exclamation point. That's basic spelling that every woman ought to know."

Mistinguett (1873–1956), French dancer and singer

Classical Phrases and Myths

A kiss in ancient Rome was distinguished as a *basium* between acquaintances, an *osculum* between close friends, and a *suavium* between lovers.

◆ KNOWLEDGE & EXPERIENCE

Foreign Words and Phrases

dharma (Skt)
(DAHR-muhr) one's (comprehension of his or her) ideal and unique course in life

pundit (Hin)
(PUHN-dit) scholar who speaks with authority on issues, commentator

au courant (Fra)
(oh KOO-ron) up-to-date, familiar with

illuminati (Ita)
(il-loo-me-NAH-tee) *lit:* enlightened; (ones) enlightened and wise

Weltmann (Ger)
(VELT-mahn) lit: man of the world; cosmopolitan character

cognoscenti (Ita)
(koh-nyo-SHEN-tee) *lit:* connoisseurs; those knowledgeable in a field, about an event, etc.

connoisseur (Fra)
(konn-oh-SUHR) expert in a given field (arts, food, wine, etc.)

Quotations

"If he only knew a little of law, he would know a little of everything."

Anonymous remark about the lord chancellor, Lord Brougham

"It is costly wisdom that is bought by experience."

Roger Ascham (1515–1568), British writer and scholar

"The trouble with people is not that they don't know but that they know so much that ain't so."

Josh Billings [Henry Wheeler Shaw] (1818–1885), U.S. humorist, Josh Billings' Encyclopedia of Wit and Wisdom (1874)

"As scarce as the truth is, the supply has always been in excess of the demand."

Josh Billings [Henry Wheeler Shaw] (1818–1885), U.S. humorist, Affurisms (1865)

"The chapter of knowledge is a very short one, but the chapter of accidents is a very long one."

Philip Dormer Stanhope, 4th Earl of Chesterfield (1694–1773), British statesman and writer

"Experience is a comb which nature gives to men when they are bald."

Eastern proverb

"The years teach much which the days never know."

Ralph Waldo Emerson (1803–1892), U.S. writer and philosopher, Essays: Second Series (1844), "Experience"

"Experience is a good teacher, but her fees are very high."

William Ralph Inge (1860–1954), British clergyman

"Never say you know another entirely, until you have divided an inheritance with him."

Johann Kaspar Lavater (1741–1801), Swiss divine and poet, Aphorisms on Man (c. 1788), 157

"Children with Hyacinth's temperament don't know better as they grow older; they merely know more.

Saki [Hector Hugh Munro] (1870–1916), British writer, Toys of Peace and Other Papers (1919), "Hyacinth"

"Experience is the name every one gives to their mistakes."

Oscar [Fingal O'Flahertie Wills] Wilde (1854–1900), British playwright, writer and wit, Lady Windermere's Fan (1891), Act III

Classical Phrases and Myths

gnothi seauton (Grk)
(GNOH-thi se-OW-ton) know thyself; this maxim appeared at the Delphic Oracle and was taken up by the Sophists

gnosis (Grk)
(GNOH-sis) knowledge, understanding, especially of spiritual mysteries

"Nam et ipsa scientia potestas est." (Knowledge itself is power.)

Francis Bacon (1561–1626), British lawyer and writer, Meditationes Sacrae (1597), "De Haeresibus"

Jokes, Stories and Anecdotes

Examining a candidate for the medical degree, professor of medicine Joseph Hyrtl demanded, "Please describe to me the function of the spleen." The nervous student, sweat dripping from his brow, stammered, "Herr Professor, I-I knew it just a moment ago, but, but, I've forgotten!" "Damn you!" roared Hyrtl. "Now the only man in the world who understood the function of the spleen has forgotten it!"

Joseph Hyrtl (1810–1894), Austrian anatomist [variations also attributed to others]

◆ LAMENTATION

Foreign Words and Phrases

désole (Fra)
(day-ZOH-lay) disconsolate, heart-broken

Quotations

"Indeed the tears live in an onion that should water this sorrow."

*William Shakespeare (1564–1616),
British playwright and poet,* Antony and Cleopatra *(1607), Act I, sc. ii*

"It takes your enemy and your friend, working together, to hurt you to the heart: the one to slander you and the other to get the news to you."

*Mark Twain [Samuel Langhorne Clemens]
(1835–1910), U.S. humorist, writer and speaker,* Following the Equator
(1897), ch. 45

Classical Phrases and Myths

"Waste not fresh tears over old griefs."

*Euripides (480 B.C.–406 B.C.),
Greek playwright,* Alexander

"*Hinc illae lacrimae.*" (hinc il-LAY lak-RIM-ay) (Hence these tears.)

*Terence [Publius Terentius Afer]
(c. 190 B.C.–159 B.C.), Roman playwright,*
The Woman of Andros *(166 B.C.)*

In Greek mythology, Niobe (Nee-oh-bee), the daughter of Tantalus, was a very proud woman, particularly proud of her seven sons and seven daughters. The 14 beautiful children were slain by Apollo and Artemis because of Niobe's boasting, and were not buried for nine days. Grief-stricken, Niobe could not stop weeping for her children, and Zeus turned her into a marble statue with a face continually wet with tears. Thus, a *Niobe* is a weeping or an inconsolably grieving mother.

Jokes, Stories and Anecdotes

"My son, nothing is worth dying for," urged the priest. "Come from that ledge." "My neighbor took off with my wife," sobbed the disconsolate man. "But that was a year ago," responded the priest. "Well, he called me this morning," cried the man, "and he's bringing her back."

Two businessmen are depressed. The first heaves a sigh and says, "I thought September was bad, but then came October. Worse! But then November has been the worst in years and—" The other man breaks in. "Jeez, Stanley, you're complaining about trifling matters. I just learned that Doris had a stroke just before she rammed the Mercedes into a tree, and her boyfriend was in the car with her. What can be worse than *that?*" "I'll tell you," said Stanley. "December!"

◆ LANGUAGE

Foreign Words and Phrases

lingua franca (Ita)
(LEEN-gwa FRAN-ka) common tongue used to communicate between different nationals

patois (Fra)
(PAT-wa) local style of speech

Quotations

"Language is the dress of thought."

*Samuel Johnson (1709–1784),
British man of letters*

"Slang is a language that rolls up its sleeves, spits on its hands and goes to work."

Carl Sandburg (1878–1967),
U.S. poet and writer

"Yes, I always seem to lose something in the original."

James Thurber (1894–1961),
U.S. cartoonist and humorist, replying
when informed that his work was even
funnier in French than in English

Jokes, Stories and Anecdotes

A visiting American and an Englishman were going up in a London skyscraper when the Englishman said, "Drat, the lift's slow." "It's called an 'elevator,' " corrected the American. "In London it's called a 'lift.' " "Yes, but we Americans invented it," persisted the American, "and we call this an 'elevator.' " "That's all very well, old boy," sniffed the Englishman, "but who invented the language?"

The Austrian diplomat Prince von Metternich praised Lord John Dudley by telling him that Dudley was the only Englishman he knew who could speak French well. Metternich could not hide his contempt for Englishmen's inability to speak fluent French, adding, "The common people of Vienna speak French better than the educated men of London." Lord Dudley replied, "That may be so, but Your Highness will recall that Bonaparte has not been twice in London to teach them."

Klemens, Prince von Metternich
(1773–1859), Austrian statesman

Mike Romanoff falsely claimed to be an expatriated Russian prince. A young actor playing with Romanoff in the 1967 film *Tony Rome* sought to discountenance him by addressing him in fluent Russian. Roma-

noff only responded with a look of freezing disdain, later explaining, "The vulgarity of a stranger speaking to me in that tongue! We never spoke anything but French at court."

Mike Romanoff [Harry F. Gerguson]
(1890–1972), US restaurateur

When it was suggested to Bess Truman that she persuade her husband, President Harry Truman, to tone down his language after he had characterized a certain politician's speech as "a bunch of horse manure," she replied, "You don't know how many years it took me to tone it down to that!"

Harry S Truman (1884–1972),
U.S. president [attributed variations]

◆ LANGUAGE STYLE

Foreign Words and Phrases

bonton (Fra)
(bon ton) good style, polished manner

bel air (Fra)
(bel EHR) grace, poise, good deportment

Quotations

"A lot of people who don't say 'ain't' ain't eatin'."

Jay Hanna ["Dizzy"] Dean (1911–1974),
U.S. baseball player, retorting to
accusation that he was corrupting English
language students with his unruly diction
and grammar

"Cut out all those exclamation points. An exclamation point is like laughing at your own joke."

F[rancis] Scott [Key] Fitzgerald
(1896–1940), U.S. writer, correcting
a fledgling author's manuscript

"Backward ran sentences until reeled the mind."

Wolcott Gibbs (1902–1958), U.S. writer, satirizing the prose in Time Magazine

"Ducking for apples—change one letter and it's the story of my life."

Dorothy Parker (1893–1967), U.S. wit and writer

"Mr. Speaker, I smell a rat; I see him forming in the air and darkening the sky; but I'll nip him in the bud."

Sir Boyle Roche (1743–1807), British politician [authenticity unverified]

Classical Phrases and Myths

epea pteroenta (Grk)
(EP-ay-apter-o-EN-ta) *lit:* winged words, significant statement

Jokes, Stories and Anecdotes

In a student essay noting that "the girl tumbled down the stairs and lay prostitute at the bottom," the professor's correction in the margin read: "My dear sir, you must learn to distinguish between a fallen woman and one who has merely slipped."

After the night school English instructor had announced, "Tomorrow night we will take up syntax," the immigrant squirmed. "Oh no!" she exclaimed. "First they want tuition, and now they're collecting taxes!"

When Jean Harlow, the platinum blond 1930s movie star, met Lady Margot Asquith for the first time, she not only blundered in addressing Asquith by her first name but also in mispronouncing it as "Margot." Lady Asquith corrected her:

"No, no, Jean, the *t* is silent, as in 'Harlow.'"

Margot Asquith, Countess of Oxford and Asquith (1864–1945), British writer and socialite

A pedantic critic once challenged a Churchillian sentence on the grounds that he should not have ended the sentence with a preposition because this violated grammatical norms. Churchill countered with a note of his own: "This is the sort of nonsense up with which I will not put."

Sir Winston Spencer Churchill (1874–1965), British prime minister and writer

Attached to the mirror in her dressing room, the actress Minnie Fiske found a note from fellow actress Margaret Anglin: "Margaret Anglin says Mrs. Fiske is the best actress in America." Mrs. Fiske added two commas and returned it to Miss Anglin. Revised, the note read: "Margaret Anglin, says Mrs. Fiske, is the best actress in America."

Minnie Maddern Fiske (1865–1932), U.S. actress

Famous as world middleweight champion, Rocky Graziano set out to jump from the relatively safe world of boxing to the precarious one of show biz. It was politely suggested that he take lessons somewhere like the Actors Studio and polish up his syntax. "Why should I go to a place like that?" smirked Rocky. "All they do there is learn guys like Brando and Newman to talk like me."

Rocky Graziano [Thomas Rocco Barbella] (1922–), U.S. boxer

Josiah Henson, the ex-slave orator who was reputed to be the model for Uncle Tom in Harriet Beecher Stowe's novel, *Uncle Tom's Cabin*, was introduced to the archbishop of Canterbury while touring England.

Impressed by Henson's bearing and speech, the archbishop asked him at which university he had studied. Henson's solemn reply: "The university of adversity."

Josiah Henson (1789–1883), U.S. orator

Jerome Kern, composer for Broadway musicals, became increasingly annoyed with the affected articulation and theatrical gestures of a certain actress, particularly when she rolled her *r*'s. "Tell me, Mr. Kern," she finally said, "you want me to c-rr-ross the stage, but I'm behind a table. How shall I get acr-rr-oss?" "Why-y dear," Kern replied, "just r-r-roll over on your *r*'s."

Jerome [David] Kern (1885–1945),
U.S. composer

Noah Webster, who compiled the dictionary, was, predictably, a stickler for grammar. On one occasion, he was caught kissing the maid in the pantry. His wife was aghast. "Noah, I am surprised!" "No, my dear," Webster corrected her, "*I* am surprised; you are merely astonished."

Noah Webster (1758–1843),
U.S. lexicographer
[authenticity unverified]

◆ **LATENESS**

Quotations

"He was always late on principle, his principle being that punctuality is the thief of time."

Oscar [Fingal O'Flahertie Wills] Wilde
(1854–1900), British playwright,
writer and wit

"*Quant le cheval est emblé dounke ferme fols l'estable.*" (kwah leh sheh-VAL eh ehm-BLAY, dohnk fehrm ful les-TAB-leh) (When the horse has been stolen, the fool shuts the stable.)

Proverb, Les Proverbes del
Vilain (c. 1303)

Classical Phrases and Myths

terminus ad quem (Lat)
(TER-min-us ad kwem) final point in time; the latest possible date for an event or process

Jokes, Stories and Anecdotes

The civil servant, disfigured with bruises, a black eye, and an arm in a sling, and hobbling on crutches, showed up at the boss' office. The boss glowered at him and glanced meaningfully at the clock. "I fell off the balcony at home," explained the timid employee. Roared his boss, "And that took you an hour?"

To pay off some gambling Chico Marx wrote Heywood Broun a check and warned him not to cash it before 12 o'clock the next day. Broun complained later that the check had bounced. "What time did you try to cash it?" Marx inquired. "Twelve-o-five." "Too late."

Chico [Leonard] Marx (1891–1961),
U.S. film comedian

◆ **LAW & CONSTITUTION**

Quotations

"No matther whether th' constitution follows th' flag or not, th' supreme coort follows th' iliction returns."

Finley Peter Dunne (1867–1936),
U.S. writer and humorist, Mr. Dooley's
Opinions (1900), "The Supreme
Court's Decisions"

"The Common Law of England has been laboriously built about a mythical figure—the figure of 'The Reasonable Man.' "

Sir A[lan] P[atrick] Herbert (1890–1971), British writer and politician, Uncommon Law *(1935), p. 1*

"It is useless for the sheep to pass resolutions in favour of vegetarianism while the wolf remains of a different opinion."

William Ralph Inge (1860–1954), British clergyman

"Laws are like cobwebs, which may catch small flies, but let wasps and hornets break through."

Jonathan Swift (1667–1745), Anglo-Irish clergyman and writer, A Critical Essay upon the Faculties of the Mind *(1707)*

Classical Phrases and Myths

de jure (Lat)
(day YOO-re) recognized as right and lawful (*opp: de facto*)

lex non scripta (Lat)
(lex nohn-SKRIP-ta) *lit:* law which has not been written or recorded, customary law

obiter dictum (Lat)
(OH-bi-ter DIK-tum) incidental remark; in law, a remark by the judge that is outside the content of his or her judgment (*plu: obiter dicta*)

"Quid leges sine moribus Vanae proficiunt?" (What profit laws, which without lives are empty?)

Horace (65 B.C.–8 B.C.), Roman poet, Odes, *III, xxiv, l. 35*

Greek legislator and statesman Solon's new legal code for Athens included revising its constitution and introducing new laws, prohibiting loans based on the security of the borrower's person and measures to promote commerce. When Solon was challenged to declare whether he had given Athens the best laws, he replied, acknowledging their imperfections, "No, but the best that they could receive."

Solon (c. 639 B.C.–c. 559 B.C.), Greek legislator and statesman

◆ LAWLESSNESS & ANARCHY

Quotations

"Here, even the law of the jungle has broken down."

Walid Jumblatt (1949–   ), Lebanese militant

"Anarchism is a game at which the police can beat you."

George Bernard Shaw (1856–1950), Irish playwright, Misalliance *(1914), p. 14*

Classical Phrases and Myths

anomie (Grk)
(ah-NOM-ee) condition of despair brought on by a breakdown in the rules of conduct and loss of sense of purpose (from anomie: lawlessness)

Jokes, Stories and Anecdotes

A rabbi, a physicist, and a politician were arguing about whose profession was the oldest. "Surely mine is oldest," boasted the rabbi. "When Eve came from Adam's rib, that was a religious miracle." "But before that, order came from chaos," reasoned the physicist. "Only a physicist could have done that." "And first," interjected the politician, "someone had to create chaos. . . ."

◆ LAWYER

Quotations

"A solicitor is a man who calls in a person he doesn't know to sign a contract he hasn't seen to buy property he doesn't want with money he hasn't got."

Sir Dingwall Bateson (1898–1967),
British lawyer

"He has made a career of defending the scorned, the degraded, the oppressed—no matter how rich and powerful they are."

Art Buchwald (1925–   ),
U.S. humorist, commenting on attorney
Edward Bennett Williams

"If there were no bad people there would be no good lawyers."

Charles Dickens (1812–1870),
British writer

"The first thing we do, let's kill all the lawyers."

William Shakespeare (1564–1616),
British playwright and poet, King Henry
VI, Part II *(1591), Act IV, sc. ii*

"Bluster, sputter, question, cavil; but be sure your argument is intricate enough to confound the court."

William Wycherley (1640–1716),
British playwright

"*Nous savons tous ici que le droit est la plus puissante des écoles de l'imagination. Jamais poète n'a interprété la nature aussi librement qu'un juriste la réalité.*" (We all know here that the law is the most powerful of schools for the imagination. No poet ever interpreted nature as freely as a lawyer interprets the truth.)

Jean Giraudoux (1882–1944),
French writer and diplomat, La Guerre
de Troie n'aura pas lieu (The Trojan War
Will Not Take Place) *(1935), Act II, sc. 5*

Jokes, Stories and Anecdotes

An economist, a mathematician, and a lawyer were interviewed by the CEO of a large corporation for its presidency. The CEO asked each: "What is two plus two?" Economist: "The diminishing marginal returns of examining the problem force me to conclude the answer is four." Mathematician: "The answer is between three and five, plus or minus one." Lawyer: (shifting his eyes) "Anything you want it to be."

Following George Ade's after-dinner speech, a famed lawyer, with his hands buried in his pants pockets, began his speech: "Doesn't it strike the company as a little unusual that a professional humorist should be funny?" Ade waited for the laughter to die down before replying: "Doesn't it strike everyone as a little unusual that a lawyer should have his hands in his own pockets?"

George Ade (1866–1944),
U.S. humorist and playwright

Irish justice Lord Norbury was asked by fellow members of the bar to contribute for the payment of the funeral of a Dublin attorney who had died in poverty. Norbury asked what donation would be appropriate and was informed the no one had contributed more than a shilling. "A shilling!" Norbury exclaimed. "A shilling to bury an attorney? Why, here's a guinea! Bury one and 20 of the scoundrels."

John Toler, 1st Earl of Norbury
(1745–1831), Irish jurist

A young man claiming damages for an arm injury caused by a bus driver's negligence was being cross-examined by British barrister and later Conservative MP F. E. Smith. Smith directed, "Please show us how high you can lift your arm now." The plaintiff, his face distorted in pain, slowly raised his arm to shoulder level. "Thank you," said Smith. "And now, please show us how high you could lift it before the accident." The arm quickly shot straight up in the air. Case closed.

F[rederick] E[dwin] Smith, 1st Earl of
Birkenhead (1872–1930),
British lawyer and politician

◆ LAXNESS

Quotations

"In olden days a glimpse of stocking
Was looked on as something shocking
Now, heaven knows,
Anything goes."

Cole Porter (1891–1964), U.S. songwriter,
Anything Goes (1934 song)

Classical Phrases and Myths

ad arbitrium (Lat)
(ad ahr-BIT-rium) at will

durante bene placito (Lat)
(dur-ANT-ay BE-ne PLAK-ii-oh) *lit:* during good pleasure; as long as the authorities allow

◆ LAZINESS

Jokes, Stories and Anecdotes

A tramp was complaining to his companion about the hardships of hobo life. "Traveling on freight trains, dodging the police, sleeping on cold benches, wondering where your next meal is coming from, it's a hard life," he mused. "So why don't you get a job?" asked the second. The first tramp exclaimed, "What? And admit I'm a failure?"

"You're the laziest person I've ever met," roared the small business owner to his newest employee. "You have barely completed a month's worth of work since I hired you two months ago. Give me one reason why I should retain you." The employee shrugged and said, "Well, when I take a vacation, you won't need someone to fill in."

◆ LEADERLESSNESS

Quotations

"When I was a boy I was told that anybody could become President. I'm beginning to believe it."

Clarence Seward Darrow (1857–1938),
U.S. lawyer

"If a traveller were informed that such a man was the Leader of the House of Commons, he might begin to comprehend how the Egyptians worshipped an insect."

Benjamin Disraeli, 1st Earl of Beaconsfield
(1804–1881), British prime minister,
deriding Lord John Russell

"Power without responsibility: the prerogative of the harlot throughout the ages."

Rudyard Kipling (1865–1936),
British writer and poet replying to
Lord Beaverbrook [phrase repeated by
Stanley Baldwin, March 18, 1931]

"In Pierre Elliott Trudeau Canada has at last produced a political leader worthy of assassination."

Irving Layton (1912–   ),
Canadian writer

"*Eh, je suis leur chef, il fallait bien les suivre.*" (Hey, I am their leader, I have to follow them.)

Alexandre Auguste Ledru-Rollin
(1807–1874), French politician, shouting
from within a mob at the Paris barricades
during the Revolution of February 1848

Classical Phrases and Myths

"Vis consili expers mole ruit sua." (Force without mind falls by its own weight.)

> Horace (65 B.C.–8 B.C.), Roman poet,
> Odes, III, iii, l. 65

"An nescis, mi fili, quantilla prudentia regitur orbis?" (Dost thou not know, my son, with what little wisdom the world is governed?)

> Count Oxenstierna (1583–1654),
> Italian aristocrat, letter to his son, 1648

◆ LEADERSHIP

Foreign Words and Phrases

emir (Arab)
(eh-MEER) leader, ruler

rajah (Hin)
(RAH-jah) Indian prince; ruler

sheikh (Arab)
(shaykh) chief, tribal head

Quotations

"That the king can do no wrong, is a necessary and fundamental principle of the English constitution."

> Sir William Blackstone (1723–1780),
> British jurist, Commentaries on the
> Laws of England (1765–1769),
> bk. III, 17

"Charlatanism of some degree is indispensable to effective leadership."

> Eric Hoffer (1902–1983),
> U.S. labor leader and philosopher

"To lead the people, walk behind them."

> Lao-Tzu (c. 604 B.C.–531 B.C.),
> Chinese philosopher

"Only he can command who has the courage and initiative to disobey."

> William McDougall (1871–1938),
> British psychologist

"All the President is, is a glorified public relations man who spends his time flattering, kissing and kicking people to get them to do what they are supposed to do anyway."

> Harry S Truman (1884–1972),
> U.S. president, letter to his sister,
> November 14, 1947

"I never give them [the public] hell. I just tell the truth, and they think it is hell."

> Harry S Truman (1884–1972),
> U.S. president

"L'etat c'est moi." (lay-TAH seh mwah) (I am the state.)

> Louis XIV (1638–1715), French king,
> at the Perlement de Paris, 1651

Classical Phrases and Myths

paterfamilias (Lat)
(PA-ter-fam-EE-lias) head of family

charisma (Grk)
(kar-IS-ma) divinely conferred power; capacity to inspire enthusiasm and obedience in others; in Weber's terminology, the charismatic leader has innate qualities that give him or her the right to claim obedience

anax andron (Grk)
(AN-ax an-DROHN) leader of men; a term Homer applied to Agamemnon and others

"Multo tutius est stare in subiectione quam in praelatura." (It is much safer to obey, than to govern.)

> Thomas à Kempis [Thomas Hamerken von
> Kempen] (c. 1380–1471), German monk
> and writer, Imitatio Christi (c. 1420),
> bk. IX, ch. I

While Alexander the Great was leading his thirsty army across the desert, a soldier came up to him, knelt down, and offered him a helmet full of water. "Is there enough for 10,000 men?" asked Alexander. When the soldier shook his head, Alexander poured the water out on the ground.

Alexander III [Alexander the Great] 356 B.C.–323 B.C.), Macedonian king

While traveling in the Alps, Julius Caesar once came upon a poor and miserable village. A member of his entourage wondered idly whether the village's men struggled and schemed to be leader of their small community in a competition for civic honors. "For my part," Caesar replied earnestly, "I would rather be the chief man in this village than the second man in Rome."

Gaius Julius Caesar (100 B.C.–44 B.C.), Roman general and statesman

Jokes, Stories and Anecdotes

Benjamin Franklin, then America's minister in Europe, attended a dinner in Paris that included both the French foreign minister and the British ambassador, soon after George Washington's victory at Yorktown. The French minister proposed a toast: "Louis XVI, who like the moon fills the earth with a soft benevolent glow." The British ambassador replied with: "George III, who like the noonday sun spreads his light and illumines the world." Franklin answered with: "I give you George Washington, general of the armies of the United States, who, like Joshua of old, commanded both the sun and the moon to stand still, and both obeyed."

Benjamin Franklin (1706–1790), U.S. statesman and scientist

When the line from Henry Brooke's poem *Earl of Essex*, "Who rules o'er freemen should himself be free," was recited to literary lion Samuel Johnson, he observed, "It might as well be 'Who drives fat oxen should himself be fat.'"

Samuel Johnson (1709–1784), British man of letters

◆ LEADERSHIP TRANSFER

Foreign Words and Phrases

junta (Spa)
(HOON-toh) cabal seeking power

coup d'état (Fra)
(koo day-TAH) violent or unconstitutional change of government (English *abbr:* coup)

Quotations

"That's one small step for a man, one giant leap for mankind."

Neil Armstrong (1930–   ), U.S. astronaut making history on July 20, 1969, when he became the first human being to set foot on the moon. At the last moment, taking advantage of the delayed communications link with superiors on Earth, Armstrong reportedly pulled rank over fellow astronaut Buzz Aldrin to do it.

"Unused power slips imperceptibly into the hands of another."

Konrad Heiden (1901–1975), German writer

"You are pitiful isolated individuals; you are bankrupts; your role is played out. Go where you belong from now on—into the dustbin of history!"

Leon Trotsky [Lev Davidovich Bronstein] (1879–1940), Russian revolutionary, sneering at the Mensheviks, History of the Russian Revolution (1913), vol. 3, ch. 10

Jokes, Stories and Anecdotes

The lame duck was called upon to speak at his opponent's victory celebration. He dryly said: "I am reminded of an epitaph in the town cemetery that reads: 'I expected this, but not so soon.' "

Charles II, described by the Earl of Rochester as "a merry monarch, scandalous and poor," was popular with his subjects, unlike his brother James, Duke of York. James, riding one day in his carriage, attended by armed guards, once came upon Charles carelessly strolling through Hyde Park with only two attendants. The surprised duke stopped his coach and tactfully suggested to Charles that it was unwise to expose himself to grave danger. "Nonsense," said Charles good-humoredly. "No man in England would kill me to make *you* king."

Charles II (1630–1685), British king

Although he later admitted that the phrase attracted him more by sound than by sense, economist and ambassador John Kenneth Galbraith remarked to John Kennedy, regarding the Diem coup in South Vietnam and the prospect of a better regime, "Nothing succeeds like successors."

John Kenneth Galbraith (1908–1992),
Canadian-born U.S. economist
and diplomat

◆ LEARNING

Quotations

"Education makes a people easy to lead, but difficult to drive; easy to govern, but impossible to enslave."

Henry Peter Brougham, Baron Brougham
and Vaux (1778–1868), British lord
chancellor and statesman,
[authenticity unverified]

"Education is what remains when we have forgotten all that we have been taught."

George Savile, Marquis of Halifax
(1633–1695), British statesman and writer

"In my early years I read very hard. It is a sad reflection, but a true one, that I knew almost as much at 18 as I do now."

Samuel Johnson (1709–1784),
British man of letters

"When I was their age, I could draw like Raphael, but it took a lifetime for me to learn to draw like them."

Pablo [Ruiz y] Picasso (1881–1973),
Spanish-born French artist, visiting an
exhibition of children's drawings

"His knowledge of books had in some degree diminished his knowledge of the world."

William Shenstone (1714–1763),
British poet

"Education . . . has produced a vast population able to read but unable to distinguish what is worth reading."

George Macaulay Trevelyan (1876–1962),
British historian, English Social History
(1942), ch. 18

"I have never let my schooling interfere with my education."

Mark Twain [Samuel Langhorne Clemens]
(1835–1910), U.S. humorist,
writer and speaker

"The founding fathers in their wisdom decided that children were an unnatural strain on parents. So they provided jails called schools, equipped with tortures called education. School is where you go between when your parents can't take you and industry can't take you."

John Updike (1932–   ),
U.S. writer

"Education is an admirable thing, but it is well to remember from time to time that nothing that is worth knowing can be taught."

Oscar [Fingal O'Flahertie Wills] Wilde
(1854–1900), British playwright,
writer and wit

Classical Phrases and Myths

(empta dolore) experientia docet (Lat) (EMP-tah dol-OR-ay ex-peri-ENT-ee-a DOK-et) (painfully bought) experience teaches

"For the things we have to learn before we can do them, we learn by doing them."

Aristotle (384 B.C.–322 B.C.),
Greek philosopher, Nichomachean Ethics,
bk. II, ch. 1

"Sire, there is no royal road to geometry."

Euclid (c. 300 B.C.), Greek mathematician,
replying to Egyptian King Ptolemy I's
request for a faster way to learn
mathematical theorems

Jokes, Stories and Anecdotes

The best and the brightest military minds were studying modern U.S. military history at the War College. "So, Colonel," the instructor asked the top student for his oral final examination, "what were the most important lessons you learned here?" "First, sir, to stay far from Vietnam and, second, not to mess with those Vietnamese."

The exiled Rumanian King Carol once informed the British diplomat Sir Robert Bruce Lockhart that during his reign he had selected 14 of the brightest Rumanians for special training in the government service. He sent seven to England and seven to the United States to study their political and economic systems. "The seven who went to England were very smart—they all achieved great success in the government in Bucharest," said the king. "And the seven you sent to the States?" asked Lockhart. "They were even smarter," replied Carol. "They stayed there."

Carol II (1893–1953), Rumanian king

During a dinner a young girl asked Albert Einstein, "What is your profession?" Einstein replied: "I devote myself to the study of physics." The girl, astonished, said, "You mean to say you study physics at your age? I finished a year ago."

Albert Einstein (1879–1955),
German-born physicist

William Howard Taft, then chief justice of the Supreme Court, was in a discussion with Robert Hutchins, who, before becoming president of the University of Chicago, was dean of Yale Law School. "I suppose, Professor Hutchins," said Taft, "that you teach your students that the judges are all fools." "No, Mr. Chief Justice," answered Hutchins, "we let them discover that for themselves."

Robert Maynard Hutchins (1899–1977),
U.S. educator

Mark Twain used to say that it was possible to learn too much from experience. A cat, he said, that once sat down on a hot stove lid would never again sit down on a hot stove lid. The trouble was that it would never sit down on a cold one, either.

Mark Twain [Samuel Langhorne Clemens]
(1835–1910), U.S. humorist,
writer and speaker

241

◆ LEGALITY

Quotations

"Appeal. In law, to put the dice into the box for another throw."

> Ambrose [Gwinnet] Bierce
> (1842–c. 1914), U.S. writer and poet,
> The Devil's Dictionary (1911)

"For certain people, after 50, litigation takes the place of sex.

> Gore Vidal (1925–   ), U.S. writer

"The law is sort of hocus-pocus science, that smiles in yer face while it picks yer pocket."

> Charles Macklin (1697–1797), Irish actor
> and playwright, Love a la Mode (1759),
> Act II, sc. i

"A Constitution should be short and obscure."

> Napoleon I [Napoleon Bonaparte]
> (1769–1821), French general and
> emperor, Maxims (1804–1815)

Q: "Doctor, how many autopsies have you performed on dead people?" A: "All my autopsies have been performed on dead people."

> Actual court transcript

Classical Phrases and Myths

in re (Lat)
(in RAY) in the matter of (plu: *in rebus*)

lite pendente (Lat)
(LEE-tay pen-DEN-tay) while the case is pending

sub poena (Lat)
(sub PEEN-ah) *lit:* under a penalty; writ demanding, on penalty, that one attend court (English: subpoena)

amicus curiae (Lat)
(AM-ee-kus KUR-ee-ee) *lit:* friend of the court; in law, one who advises the court in a case not his own

◆ LEGS & FEET

Quotations

"Feets, do your stuff!"

> Bill ["Bojangles"] Robinson (1878–1949),
> U.S. dancer

"His legs, perhaps, were shorter than they should have been."

> Lytton Strachey (1880–1932),
> British writer, Eminent Victorians
> (1918), "Dr. Arnold"

Jokes, Stories and Anecdotes

"Now, son, why do you think a stork lifts one leg when it eats?" "Because, Daddy, if it lifted both, it'd fall over."

Asked to resolve many serious and frivolous disputes, Abraham Lincoln once was recruited to mediate an argument concerning the correct length of a man's legs in proportion to the size of his body. After listening intently to both sides, he announced that it was with great mental anguish he was deciding this significant issue about which so much bloodshed over the ages had been spilled. "It is my opinion," he concluded, "that a man's lower limbs, in order to preserve harmony of proportion, should be at least long enough to reach from his body to the ground."

> Abraham Lincoln (1809–1865),
> U.S. president

◆ LENIENCY

Jokes, Stories and Anecdotes

The labor leader and pacifist Eugene Debs was sentenced to ten years in prison for his speech in 1918 condemning World War I and criticizing persecution of persons under the 1917 Espionage Act. Undaunted, he ran his 1920 presidential campaign from the federal penitentiary in Atlanta, and received almost a million votes. When, on Christmas Day 1921, Debs was released on the orders of President Harding, he said, happily but unrepentantly, "It is the government that should ask me for a pardon."

Eugene Victor Debs (1855–1926), U.S. socialist and labor leader

◆ LIBERALISM

Quotations

"A rich man told me recently that a liberal is a man who tells other people what to do with their money."

Imamu Amiri Baraka [Everett LeRoi Jones] (1934–   ), U.S. writer

"The liberals can understand everything but people who don't understand them."

Lenny Bruce [Leonard Alfred Schneider] (1925–1966), U.S. comedian

◆ LIFE

Foreign Words and Phrases

rites de passage (Fra)
(REET duh pas-SAHJ) important landmarks in one's life

vie manquée (Fra)
(VEE mon-KAY) misdirected life

Quotations

"Life is a sexually transmitted disease."

Anonymous, London Underground graffito

"It seems that I have spent my entire time trying to make life more rational and that it was all wasted effort."

A. J. Ayer (1910–1989), British philosopher

"Life. A spiritual pickle preserving the body from decay."

Ambrose [Gwinnet] Bierce (1842–c. 1914), U.S. writer and poet, Devil's Dictionary (1911)

"Life is one long process of getting tired."

Samuel Butler (1835–1902), British writer, Notebooks (1912), ch. 1

"Life is the art of drawing sufficient conclusions from insufficient premises."

Samuel Butler (1835–1902), British writer, Notebooks (1912), ch. 1

"Life is a tragedy when seen in close up, but a comedy in long shot."

Charles Spencer ["Charlie"] Chaplin (1889–1977), British-born actor

"Life is an Incurable disease."

Abraham Cowley (1618–1667), British poet, To Dr. Scarborough, VI

"Life is a zoo in a jungle."

Peter de Vries (1910–1993), U.S. writer

"Life is a jest; and all things show it.
I thought so once; but now I know it."

John Gay (1685–1732), British poet and playwright, My Own Epitaph

"Life is made up of sobs, sniffles, and smiles, with sniffles predominating."

O. Henry [William Sydney Porter] (1862–1910), U.S. writer, Four Million (1906), "Gift of the Magi"

243

"Life can only be understood backwards; but it must be lived forwards."

> Soren Kierkegaard (1813–1855),
> Danish philosopher, Life

"Life is something to do when you can't get to sleep."

> Frances Anne Lebowitz (1950–   ),
> U.S. photographer, Metropolitan Life
> (1978), p. 101

"It's not true that life is one damn thing after another—it's one damn thing over and over."

> Edna St. Vincent Millay (1892–1950),
> U.S. poet, letter to Arthur Davison Ficke,
> October 24, 1930

"I postpone death by living, by suffering, by error, by risking, by giving, by losing."

> Anais Nin (1914–1977),
> French-born U.S. writer and dancer

"For when the One Great Scorer comes to mark against your name, He writes—not that you won or lost—but how you played the Game."

> Grantland Rice (1880–1954), U.S. writer
> and poet, Only the Brave (1941),
> "Alumnus Football"

"This world is a comedy to those that think, a tragedy to those that feel."

> Horace Walpole, 4th Earl of Oxford
> (1717–1797), British writer

"Vivre est une chute horizontale." (Life is a horizontal fall.)

> Jean Cocteau (1889–1963), French writer,
> artist and filmmaker,
> Opium (1930), p. 37

"La vie est un songe . . . nous veillons dormants et veillants dormons." (Life is a dream . . . we sleeping wake and waking sleep.)

> Michel Eyquem de Montaigne
> (1533–1592), French writer,
> Essays (1580), bk. II

Classical Phrases and Myths

"Vitae sunmma brevis spem nos vetat incohare longam." (Life's brief span prevents us from making far-reaching hopes.)

> Horace (65 B.C.–8 B.C.), Roman poet,
> Odes, I, iv, l. 15

Ancient Greek philosopher Thales often would declare that there was essentially no difference between being alive and being dead. When someone asked why, then, he chose life instead of death, he replied, "Because there is no difference."

> Thales (c. 640 B.C.–c. 546 B.C.),
> Greek philosopher

Jokes, Stories and Anecdotes

As an old man, French writer Bernard de Fontenelle was conversing with an elderly acquaintance. "Death has forgotten us," said the friend. Bringing his finger to his lips, Fontenelle replied, "Sh-sh!"

> Bernard de Fontenelle (1657–1757),
> French writer and philosopher

◆ LIFESTYLE

Foreign Words and Phrases

savoir vivre (Fra)
(sav-wahr VEEV-ruh) to know how to live; elegance, social grace, good breeding

nostalgie de la boue (Fra)
(nos-TAHL-gee de lah boo) lit: longing for the mud; yearning for the low life

Quotations

"All decent people live beyond their incomes nowadays, and those who aren't respectable live beyond other peoples'. A few gifted individuals manage to do both."

Saki [Hector Hugh Munro] (1870–1916),
British writer, Chronicles of Clovis
(1914), "The Match-Maker"

Jokes, Stories and Anecdotes

While visiting a West Virginia mine during the 1960 Democratic campaign, John F. Kennedy was asked by a miner, "Is it true you're the son of one of our wealthiest men?" Kennedy concurred. "Is it true you've never wanted for anything, and had everything you wanted?" Kennedy admitted so. "Is it true you've never done a day's work with your hands all your life?" Kennedy nodded. "Well, I'll tell you this," said the miner. "You haven't missed a thing."

John Fitzgerald Kennedy (1917–1963),
U.S. president

◆ LIMITS (ENCLOSURE)

Quotations

"The sky is the limit."

Miguel de Cervantes (1547–1616),
Spanish writer, Don Quixote de la
Mancha, *Part I (1605), bk. III, ch. 3*

"Good fences make good neighbors."

Robert Lee Frost (1874–1963), U.S. poet,
North of Boston *(1914),*
"Mending Wall"

Classical Phrases and Myths

"*Est modus in rebus, sunt certi denique fines,*
Quos ultra citraque nequit consistere rectum." (There is measure in everything. There are fixed limits beyond which and short of which right cannot find a resting place.)

Horace (65 B.C.–8 B.C.), Roman poet,
Satires, *I, i, l. 106*

◆ LITTLENESS

Foreign Words and Phrases

soupçon (Fra)
(soop-SOHN) *lit:* suspicion, conjecture; a tiny amount

bijou (Fra)
(bee-ZEW) *lit:* jewel; exquisite miniature

objet de vertu (Fra)
(OB-jay de VEHR-too) *lit:* object of quality; small work of art

Quotations

The two wits Robert Benchley and Dorothy Parker once shared a tiny office in the Metropolitan Opera House which was no more than a cramped triangle carved from a hallway. Commented Benchley: "One square foot less and it would be adulterous."

Robert Charles Benchley (1889–1945),
U.S. humorist

Classical Phrases and Myths

iota (Grk)
(ee-OH-ta) Greek letter *i;* a miniscule quantity

◆ LOUDNESS & FAINTNESS OF SOUND

Foreign Words and Phrases

fortissimo (Ita)
(for-TIS-see-moh) in music, very loud

a mezza voce (Ita)
(ah MEH-tsa VOH-chay) *lit:* at half voice; faintly

calando (Ita)
(kal-LAHN-doh) *lit:* going down; in music, softer and slower, fading away

à haute voix (Fra)
(ah oat VWAH) at the top of one's voice

Jokes, Stories and Anecdotes

The Oxford lectures of critic Walter Pater, whose writings were in the vanguard of the 1890s "art for art's sake" Aesthetic movement, were notoriously inaudible. Following a lecture, Pater said, "I hope you all heard me." Oscar Wilde replied, "We overheard you."

> *Oscar [Fingal O'Flahertie Wills] Wilde (1854–1900), British playwright, writer and wit*

◆ LOVE

Foreign Words and Phrases

chagrin d'amour (Fra)
(shag-ran dah-MOOR) *lit:* sadness of love, distress bred of unhappiness in love

inamorato/inamorata (Ita)
(in-a-mo-RA-toh/in-am-o-RA-tah) he/she who is in love

affaire de coeur (Fra)
(ah-FAIR de KUHR) matter of the heart; love affair

Quotations

"The desires of the heart are as crooked as corkscrews."

> *W[ystan] H[ugh] Auden (1907–1973), British-born poet, Letter from Iceland (1937), "Letter to William Coldstream, Esq."*

"How do I love thee? Let me count the ways.
I love thee to the depth and breadth and height
My soul can reach, when feeling out of sight
For the ends of Being and ideal Grace."

> *Elizabeth Barrett Browning (1806–1861), British poet, Sonnets from the Portuguese (1850), no. 43*

"In her first passion woman loves her lover,
In all the others all she loves is love."

> *George Gordon, Lord Byron (1788–1824), British poet, Don Juan (1821), Canto III, iii*

"Love, and a cough, cannot be hid."

> *George Herbert (1593–1633), British clergyman and poet, Jacula Prudentum (1651), no. 49*

"I die a queen. But I would rather die the wife of Thomas Culpeper."

> *Catherine Howard (1520–1542), British queen, uttering last words before being beheaded after King Henry VIII discovered that his fifth wife was still in love with her former fiancé [authenticity unverified]*

"Love is like the measles; we all have to go through it."

> *Jerome K[lapka] Jerome (1859–1927), British writer, Idle Thoughts of an Idle Fellow (1886), "On Being in Love"*

"Love is what happens to a man and a woman who don't know each other."

> *W[illiam] Somerset Maugham, (1874–1965), British writer and playwright*

"Birds do it, bees do it,
Even educated fleas do it.
Let's do it, let's fall in love."

> *Cole Porter (1891–1964), U.S. songwriter, Let's Do It (1954 song)*

"Absence diminishes mediocre passions and increases great ones, as

the wind snuffs candles and fans
fire."

François, Duc de La Rochefoucauld
(1613–1680), French writer,
Maximes (1678), 276

"Love looks not with the eyes, but
with the mind,
And therefore is wing'd Cupid
painted blind."

William Shakespeare (1564–1616), British
playwright and poet, A Midsummer
Night's Dream (1596), Act I, sc. i

"Of one that lov'd not wisely but
too well."

William Shakespeare (1564–1616),
British playwright and poet,
Othello (1605), Act V, sc. ii

"There are two tragedies in life.
One is not to get your heart's desire. The other is to get it."

George Bernard Shaw (1856–1950),
Irish playwright, Man and
Superman (1903), Act IV

"Love is the most ambiguous, de-
lirious, illogical emotion there is."

Sylvester Stallone (1948–   ),
U.S. actor

"'Tis better to have loved and lost
Than never to have loved at all."

Alfred Tennyson, 1st Baron Tennyson
(1809–1892), British poet,
In Memoriam (1850)

"Le coeur a ses raisons que la raison ne
connaît point." (The heart has its
reasons which reason knows nothing of.)

Blaise Pascal (1623–1662),
French mathematician and writer,
Pensées (1670), no. 4, 277

Classical Phrases and Myths

omnia vincit amor (Lat)
(OM-ne-ah WIN-kit AH-mor) love
conquers all (things)

"Per ćaputque pedesque." (Over head
and heels.)

Gaius Valerius Catullus (87–c. 54 B.C.),
Roman poet, Carmina, XX, l. 9

"Amantium irae amoris integratio
est." (a-MANT-ee-um ir-AY a-
MOR-is int-eh-GRAY-tee-oh) (The
quarrels of lovers are the renewal of
love.)

Terence [Publius Terentius Afer]
(c. 190 B.C.–159 B.C.), Roman playwright,
The Woman of Andros (166 B.C.)

Jokes, Stories and Anecdotes

While on an American tour, the
British actress Mrs. Patrick Campbell, typically in control of the situation, was once taken to dinner by
a shy, diminutive man. "Tell me
which would you sooner do," she
asked huskily, her magnetic eyes
focused on him, "love passionately,
or be loved passionately?" The shy
fellow took a deep breath, reflected,
then ventured, "I'd rather be a ca-
nary."

Mrs. Patrick [Beatrice] Campbell
(1865–1940), British actress

Queen Victoria and her Prince Albert
visited Florence several times as
young newlyweds, and were particularly fond of the Brunelleschi dome
surmounting the cathedral. Years after Albert had died, Victoria returned to Florence and found that
the dome had been restored. Outside
the cathedral, she ordered her carriage stopped, rolled down the window, and opened the locket that
hung about her neck. She turned the
miniature of her beloved husband to
face the dome and, after silently
sharing its magnificence with him,
closed the locket and hurried away.

Victoria (1819–1901), British queen

◆ LOVE, UNREQUITED

Quotations

"I never hated a man enough to give him diamonds back."

> Zsa Zsa [Sari] Gabor (1919–   ),
> Hungarian-born U.S. actress

"When a lovely flame dies,
Smoke gets in your eyes."

> Otto Harbach (1873–1963),
> U.S. songwriter, Smoke Gets in
> Your Eyes (1933 song)

"Scratch a lover and find a foe."

> Dorothy Parker (1893–1967), U.S. wit
> and writer, Not So Deep as a Well
> (1937), "Ballad of a Great Weariness"

Classical Phrases and Myths

According to Greek mythology, Anteros (AN-ter-os) was the brother of Eros and the son of Aphrodite and Ares. He was sometimes represented as the avenger of unrequited love, and sometime as the symbol of mutual love and tenderness.

Jokes, Stories and Anecdotes

George Gershwin was very fond of a woman who instead married someone else. Commented the great composer and songwriter, "If I wasn't so busy, I'd be upset."

> George Gershwin (1898–1937),
> U.S. composer and songwriter

The wife of playwright and wit George Bernard Shaw was asked during a joint interview how she had coped with her husband's many female admirers. By way of reply, Mrs. Shaw related an anecdote: "After we were married there was an actress who pursued my husband. She threatened suicide if she were not allowed to see him . . ." "And did she die of a bro-

ken heart?" "Yes, she did," interrupted Shaw. "Fifty years later."

> George Bernard Shaw (1856–1950),
> Irish playwright

◆ LOYALTY

Foreign Words and Phrases

(si) capo di tutti capi (Ita)
(see KAH-poh dee TOO-tee KAH-pee) (yes) godfather of godfathers

bushido (Jap)
(BOO-shee-doh) Samurai code of steadfast loyalty and honor

Quotations

"If you wish to win a man's heart, allow him to confute you."

> Benjamin Disraeli, 1st Earl of Beaconsfield
> (1804–1881), British prime minister

"I don't want loyalty. I want loyalty. I want him to kiss my ass in Macy's window at high noon and tell me it smells like roses. I want his pecker in my pocket."

> Lyndon Baines Johnson (1908–1973),
> U.S. president

Classical Phrases and Myths

semper fidelis (Lat)
(SEM-per fee-DAY-lis) always faithful

fidei defensor (Lat)
(fid-E-ee day-FEN-sor) defender of the faith; title ascribed to a sovereign and inscribed on coins

In Greek legend as described in Homer's Iliad, Patroclus (pa-TROH-klus) was Achilles' loyal friend who donned Achilles' armor to rally the Greeks and was killed. Grief-stricken, Achilles killed the great Trojan hero, Hector, and, contrary to traditional funereal treatment, dragged the corpse behind his char-iot as a trophy. Hence, *Patroclus* connotes a loyal friend.

In Greek legend, as described in Homer's *Odyssey*, Penelope (peh-NEL-oh-pee) was Odysseus' loyal wife who spurned wooers as she waited hopefully for the return of her husband for 20 years. Thus, *Penelope* connotes a loyal wife.

Jokes, Stories and Anecdotes

Jean Cocteau, the French writer, art-ist and filmmaker, confided his dis-appointment about one of his projects to his film students: "It's my worst work." One of his disci-ples said, "Among us, it's generally understood that you aren't its au-thor."

Jean Cocteau (1889–1963), French writer, artist and filmmaker

Theodoric the Great, king of the Os-trogoths and of Italy in the sixth century, was an Arian, but had a trusted Catholic minister. Seeking to ingratiate himself with Theodo-ric, the minister renounced his ten-ets to embrace Arianism. Theodoric had him beheaded, explaining, "If this man is not faithful to his God, how can he be faithful to me, a mere man?"

Theodoric the Great (c. 454–526), Ostrogoth king

◆ MACHINERY

Quotations

"Man is a tool-making animal."

Benjamin Franklin (1706–1790), U.S. statesman and scientist

"One machine can do the work of 50 ordinary men. No machine can do the work of one extraordinary man."

Elbert [Green] Hubbard (1856–1915), U.S. businessman and writer

"Men have become the tools of their tools."

Henry David Thoreau (1817–1862), U.S. writer, naturalist and poet

Classical Phrases and Myths

Having invented the lever and the pulley, Archimedes (ark-i-MEED-eez) proclaimed, "Give me a place on which to stand, and I will move the earth." Hiero of Syracuse chal-lenged him to put his words into action and help the sailors beach a large ship. By arranging a series of pulleys and cogs, Archimedes, unaided, was able to pull the great vessel out of the water and onto the beach.

Archimedes (287 B.C.–212 B.C.), Greek mathematician and scientist

◆ MAKEUP

Quotations

"In the factory we make cosmetics; in the store we sell hope."

Charles Revson (1906–1975), U.S. businessman

"A triumph of the embalmer's art."

Gore Vidal (1925–   ), U.S. writer describing Ronald Reagan

◆ MALE

Foreign Words and Phrases

bonhomme (Fra) (bon-OM) good, honest man

Ubermensch (Ger)
(OO-ber-mensh) Superman

machismo (Spa)
(mah-KEES-moh) (focus on) masculinity or virility

Quotations

"Long before the invention of lo-fat blueberry yogurt, pre-nuptial agreements and poodle psychologists, a man was a man."

> *Anonymous, advertisement for*
> *Arrow Shirts*

"Macho does not prove mucho."

> *Zsa Zsa [Sari] Gabor (1919–   ),*
> *Hungarian-born U.S. actress*

"The fucking you get isn't worth the fucking you get."

> *Dorothy Parker (1893–1967), U.S. wit*
> *and writer, appraising men*
> *[authenticity unverified]*

"It's not the men in my life that counts—it's the life in my men."

> *Mae West (1892–1980), U.S. film actress,*
> *I'm No Angel (1933 film)*

"Young men want to be faithful and are not; old men want to be faithless and cannot."

> *Oscar [Fingal O'Flahertie Wills] Wilde*
> *(1854–1900), British playwright, writer*
> *and wit, The Picture of Dorian Gray*
> *(1891), ch. 2*

Gerry (Jack Lemmon): "We can't get married at all ... I'm a man."
Osgood (Joe E. Brown): "Well, nobody's perfect."

> *Billy [Samuel] Wilder (1906–1993),*
> *U.S. film director and writer, and I. A. L.*
> *Diamond (c. 1900s), U.S screenwriter,*
> *Some Like It Hot (1959 film)*

Classical Phrases and Myths

In Greek mythology, the Amazons (AM-a-zonz) were a nation of single-breasted female warriors located in Asia or Scythia. Hence, an *amazon* refers to a large or robust woman, or a female soldier.

◆ MALE & FEMALE

Quotations

"There is more difference within the sexes than between them."

> *Dame Ivy Compton-Burnett (1884–1969),*
> *British writer, Mother and Son (1955),*
> *ch. 10*

"I'm not denyin' the women are foolish: God Almighty made 'em to match the male."

> *George Eliot [Mary Ann Evans Cross]*
> *(1819–1880), British writer, Adam Bede*
> *(1859), ch. 53*

"Man has his will—but woman has her way!"

> *Oliver Wendell Holmes, Sr. (1809–1894),*
> *U.S. writer and physician, The Autocrat*
> *of the Breakfast Table (1858), ch. 1*

"Men have as exaggerated an idea of their rights as women have of their wrongs."

> *Edgar Watson Howe (1853–1937), U.S.*
> *writer, Country Town Sayings (1911)*

"A man is as good as he has to be, and a woman as bad as she dares."

> *Elbert [Green] Hubbard (1856–1915),*
> *U.S. businessman and writer, The*
> *Notebook (1927)*

"You see an awful lot of smart guys with dumb women, but you hardly ever see a smart woman with a dumb guy."

> *Erica Jong (1942–   ), U.S. writer,*
> *Fear of Flying (1973)*

"Men have a much better time of it than women. For one thing, they marry later. For another thing, they die earlier."

H[enry] L[ouis] Mencken (1880–1956), U.S. critic and writer, Chrestomathy *(1949), ch. 30*

"In a world without women what would men become?" someone once asked humorist Mark Twain. He replied, "Scarce, sir, mighty scarce."

Mark Twain [Samuel Langhorne Clemens] (1835–1910), U.S. humorist, writer and speaker

"All women become like their mothers. That is their tragedy. No man does. That's his."

Oscar [Fingal O'Flahertie Wills] Wilde (1854–1900), British playwright, writer and wit, The Importance of Being Earnest *(1895), Act I*

Jokes, Stories and Anecdotes

French diva Sophie Arnould, after giving a supper for several distinguished guests, was visited by the lieutenant of police, who demanded their names. She said that she could not remember even one. The lieutenant persisted, "But a woman like you ought to remember things like that." "Of course, lieutenant," she replied demurely, "but with a man like you, I am not a woman like me."

[Madeleine] Sophie Arnould (1740–1802), French actress and singer

A pompous gentleman once asked the sharp-tongued actress Mrs. Patrick Campbell, "Why do you suppose it is that women so utterly lack a sense of humor?" "God did it on purpose," Mrs. Campbell answered, without batting an eyelash, "so that we may love you men instead of laughing at you."

Mrs. Patrick [Beatrice] Campbell (1865–1940), British actress

The author Edna Ferber enjoyed wearing tailored suits. When the dapper playwright Noel Coward ran into her once, and both were wearing similar suits, he remarked, "You look almost like a man." Replied Ferber, "So do you."

Edna Ferber (1887–1968), U.S. writer [attributed also to others]

"You are a man. I am a woman," began a woman seeking to embroil Professor John Mahaffy in a feminist argument. "What is the essential difference between us?" Mahaffy replied urbanely, "Madam, I cannot conceive."

Sir John Pentland Mahaffy (1839–1919), Irish scholar

◆ MANAGEMENT

Quotations

"There is something rarer than ability. It is the ability to recognize ability."

Elbert [Green] Hubbard (1856–1915), U.S. businessman and writer

"Executive ability is deciding quickly and getting somebody else to do the work."

J. G. Pollock (1871–1937), U.S. businessman

"Managing is getting paid for home runs someone else hits."

Casey Stengel (1890–1975), U.S. baseball manager

◆ MANIFESTATION

Quotations

"Some circumstantial evidence is very strong, as when you find a trout in the milk."

Henry David Thoreau (1817–1862), U.S. writer, naturalist and poet, Journal *(1906), entry for November 11, 1854*

Classical Phrases and Myths

res ipsa loquitur (Lat)
(res IP-sa LOK-wi-tur) *lit:* the thing in itself speaks; it is all rather obvious; the situation speaks for itself

Jokes, Stories and Anecdotes

While investigating the unusual but fatal one-car collision, the patrolman noticed a monkey playing on the wrecked car's trunk. "I wish you could tell me what happened," the cop mused. Surprisingly, the monkey raised its hands to its mouth in a drinking motion. "So they were drinking. Is that all?" The monkey shook its head and brought its hand to its mouth in a smoking motion. "So they were drinking and smoking. Is that all?" The monkey shook its head and brought its hands together in a lovemaking motion. "So they were drinking, smoking and screwing," the cop said. "So what the hell were you doing?" The monkey raised its hands in a driving motion and craned its neck over its right shoulder.

◆ MARRIAGE

Foreign Words and Phrases

suttee (Hin)
(SUHT-ee) Hindu custom of widows burning themselves on their husbands' funeral pyres

Quotations

"Wives are young men's mistresses, companions for middle age, and old men's nurses."

> Francis Bacon (1561–1626),
> British lawyer and writer, Essays (1625),
> "Of Marriage and Single Life"

"The most happy marriage I can picture or imagine to myself would be the union of a deaf man to a blind woman."

> Samuel Taylor Coleridge (1772–1834),
> British poet and writer

"The value of marriage is not that adults produce children, but that children produce adults."

> Peter de Vries (1910–   ),
> U.S. writer, Tunnel of Love (1954), ch. 8

"Marriage is too interesting an experiment to be tried once or twice."

> Eva Gabor (1923–   ),
> Hungarian-born U.S. actress

"Matrimonial devotion
Doesn't seem to suit her notion."

> Sir W[illiam] S[chwenck] Gilbert
> (1836–1911), British writer,
> The Mikado (1885), Act II

"The others were only my wives. But you, my dear, will be my widow."

> Sacha Guitry (1885–1957), French actor
> and playwright, consoling his fifth wife,
> who had sounded jealous of her four
> predecessors [variations also
> attributed to others]

"The wedding march always reminds me of the music played when soldiers go into battle."

> Henrich Heine (1797–1856),
> German poet and writer

"Marriage has many pains, but celibacy has no pleasures."

> Samuel Johnson (1709–1784), British man
> of letters, Rasselas (1759), ch. 26

"Marriages are made in heaven and consummated on earth."

> John Lyly (c. 1554–1606), British writer,
> Mother Bombie (1590), Act IV, sc. i

"There once was an old man of Lyme
Who married three wives at a time,
When asked 'Why a third?'

He replied, 'One's absurd!
And bigamy, Sir, is a crime!' "

*William Cosmo Monkhouse (1840–1901),
British humorist,* Nonsense
Rhymes *(1902)*

"After a few years of marriage a
man can look right at a woman
without seeing her and a woman
can see right through a man without
looking at him."

Helen Rowland (1875–1950), U.S. writer,
A Guide to Men *(1922)*

"A husband is what is left of a
lover, after the nerve has been extracted."

Helen Rowland (1875–1950), U.S. writer,
A Guide to Men *(1922), p. 19*

"It takes two to make a marriage a
success and only one a failure."

*Herbert Louis, 1st Viscount Samuel
(1870–1963), British statesman and
writer,* A Book of Quotations
(1947), p. 115

"Many a good hanging prevents a
bad marriage."

*William Shakespeare (1564–1616),
British playwright and poet,*
Twelfth Night *(1600), Act I, sc. iv*

"With all my heart; whose wife
shall it be?"

*John Horne Tooke (1736–1812),
British radical politician and philologist,
replying when advised to take a wife
[attributed also to Tom Sheridan,
son of Richard Brinsley Sheridan]*

"Marriage is like a dull meal with
the dessert at the beginning."

*Henri, Comte de Toulouse-Lautrec
(1864–1901), French painter*

"Marriage is a great institution, but
I'm not ready for an institution
yet."

Mae West (1892–1980), U.S. film actress

"A man likes his wife to be just
clever enough to comprehend his
cleverness, and just stupid enough
to admire it."

*Israel Zangwill (1864–1926),
British writer and playwright*

Classical Phrases and Myths

"Tecum vivere amem, tecum obeam libens." (With you I should love to
live, with you be ready to die.)

Horace (65 B.C.–8 B.C.), Roman poet,
Odes, III, xiii, l. 24

"By all means marry: if you get a
good wife you'll become happy; if
you get a bad one, you'll become a
philosopher."

*Socrates (469 B.C.–399 B.C.),
Greek philosopher*

Jokes, Stories and Anecdotes

"Heavens," sighed the wife, "I'm
convinced my mind is almost
gone!" Peering over his reading
glasses, the husband replied, "No
wonder—you've given me a piece
of it every day for 20 years."

The trouble with being best man at
a wedding is that there is no opportunity
to prove it.

After the newlywed couple made
love one night, he threw his pants at
her, saying, "Try them on." She answered:
"You know they're much
too big." "You got it," he snorted.
"Don't forget who wears the pants in
this house." Scowling, she plucked
her panties from the bed, and tossed
them at her husband. "Try them on,"
she ordered. Studying the garment,
he snickered, "Forget it! I'd never
get into these!" She headed for the
bathroom. "Until your attitude
changes," she said over her shoulder,
"that's absolutely right."

The husband explained his method
for making a marriage work. "We divide
up the decisions. The wife handles
the small ones, and I handle the

big ones." He then described his wife's small decisions. Asked a listener, "And what kind of big decisions do you make?" Answered the husband, "I don't know. There haven't been any big decisions yet."

British queen Alexandra was grief-stricken as King Edward VII lay on his deathbed. Her grief required her at first to turn a blind eye to his infidelities and sybaritic lifestyle, but later she remarked to Lord Esher, "At least now I know where he is."

> *Alexandra (1844–1925),*
> *Danish-born British queen*

A servant of Guillaume Bude, the French royal librarian, came running and breathlessly told his master that the house was on fire. "Inform your mistress," Bude instructed, waving him away. "You know that I leave all household matters with her."

> *Guillaume Bude (1467–1540),*
> *French scholar*

On a royal visit to the Cadbury co-coa plant, George Cadbury escorted Queen Mary while Mrs. Cadbury walked behind with King George V. Queen Mary, worried that the elderly Cadbury might get a chill due to the cold, said "Mr. Cadbury, please put on your hat." Cadbury hesitated. "Please, Mr. Cadbury—or I'll have the king command you to do so!" Her host still demurred. Then from behind came the resonant tone of Elizabeth Cadbury: "George, put your hat on." He did.

> *George Cadbury (1839–1922),*
> *British manufacturer and social reformer*

Asked what was the best advice he had ever been given, the WWII general Mark Clark answered, "To marry the girl I did." "And who gave you that advice?" "She did."

> *Mark Wayne Clark (1896–1984),*
> *U.S. general*

Upon moving into 10 Downing Street, the British prime minister's official residence in London, Denis Thatcher, husband of then-prime minister Margaret Thatcher, was asked by a reporter, "Who wears the pants in this house?" "I do, and I also wash and iron them."

> *Denis Thatcher (1915–   ),*
> *British businessman*

Soon after his marriage to Queen Victoria, Prince Albert stalked out of the room and locked himself in his private apartments. Victoria furiously pounded on the door. Albert called, "Who's there?" "The queen of England, and she demands to be admitted." Silence. Victoria again hammered at the door. "Who's there?" "The queen of England, and she demands to be admitted!!" Further silence, and the door remained shut. Again, fruitless and furious knocking. Then there was a pause, followed by gentle tapping. "Who's there?" The queen replied, "Your wife, Albert." The prince immediately opened the door.

> *Victoria (1819–1901), British queen*

◆ MASTURBATION

Quotations

"Don't knock masturbation. It's sex with someone I love."

> *Woody Allen [Allen Stewart Konigsberg]*
> *(1935–   ), U.S. comedian and*
> *filmmaker, and Marshall Brickman*
> *(1941–   ), U.S. humorist,*
> *Annie Hall (1977 film)*

"He's a fine writer, but I wouldn't want to shake hands with him."

> *Jacqueline Susann (1918–1974),*
> *U.S. writer, judging Philip Roth,*
> *author of* Portnoy's Complaint,
> *a novel partly about masturbation*

◆ MATHEMATICS

Quotations

"Mathematics may be defined as the subject in which we never know what we are talking about, nor whether what we are saying is true."

> *Bertrand Arthur William Russell,*
> *3rd Earl (1872–1970),*
> *British mathematician and philosopher,*
> *Mysticism and Logic (1917), ch. 4*

◆ MAXIM

Quotations

"A platitude is simply a truth repeated until people get tired of hearing it."

> *Stanley Baldwin, Earl Baldwin of Bewdley*
> *(1867–1947), British prime minister*

"All generalizations are dangerous, even this one."

> *Alexandre [fils] Dumas (1824–1895),*
> *French writer and playwright*

"Epigram: a wisecrack that played Carnegie Hall."

> *Oscar Levant (1906–1972),*
> *U.S. pianist and wit*

Classical Phrases and Myths

gnome (Grk)
(GNOH-may) maxim, aphorism

◆ MEANING

Quotations

" 'Then you should say what you mean,' the March Hare went on. 'I do,' Alice hastily replied; 'at least— at least I mean what I say—that's the same thing, you know.' 'Not the same thing a bit!' said the Hatter. 'Why, you might just as well say that "I see what I eat" is the same thing as "I eat what I see"!' "

> *Lewis Carroll [Charles Lutwidge*
> *Dodgson] (1832–1898), British writer and*
> *mathematician,* Alice's Adventures in
> Wonderland *(1865), ch. 7*

Classical Phrases and Myths

videlicet (Lat)
(WEE-de-LIK-et) *lit:* one may see; namely, that is to say (*abbr: viz*)

ad rem (Lat)
(ad rem) to the point, relevant to the matter under discussion, pertinent

Jokes, Stories and Anecdotes

"Maitre d'!" shouted the indignant restaurant customer. "There's a nail floating in my soup! What's the meaning of this?" "I couldn't say," replied the refined host, bowing deeply. "May I suggest a fortune-teller?"

◆ MEASUREMENT

Quotations

"I am the extent of a tenth of a gnat's eyebrow better."

> *Joel Chandler Harris (1848–1908),*
> *U.S. writer, replying how he felt on his*
> *deathbed [authenticity unverified]*

Classical Phrases and Myths

ex pede Herculem (Lat)
(ex PED-e HER-cu-lem) *lit:* (to measure) Hercules from his foot; to estimate the size or extent of the unknown whole from the known part, to extrapolate

Jokes, Stories and Anecdotes

Journalist Heywood Broun in a 1917 review of a play said that the performance of actor Geoffrey Steyne was "the worst to be seen in the contemporary theater." Steyne immediately sued. Later, while the case was pending, Broun had the opportunity to review the actor's performance in another play. This time he wrote: "Mr. Steyne's performance was not up to his usual standard."

> [Matthew] Heywood Campbell Broun
> (1888–1939), U.S. writer

◆ MEDIATION

Quotations

"Those who in quarrels interpose
Must often wipe a bloody nose."

> John Gay (1685–1732), British poet and
> playwright, Fables, Part I (1727),
> "The Mastiffs"

Classical Phrases and Myths

eirenicon (Grk)
(ay-RAY-NIK-on) proposal outlining terms of peace

◆ MEDIOCRITY

Foreign Words and Phrases

faute de mieux (Fra)
(foht de meeuw) for want of anything better; an inferior substitute

Quotations

"Genius and geniuses every way I turn! If only there were some talent!"

> Henri Bernstein (1876–1953),
> French playwright, visiting Hollywood

"Some men are born mediocre, some men achieve mediocrity, and some men have mediocrity thrust upon them. With Major Major it had been all three."

> Joseph Heller (1923–   ),
> U.S. writer, Catch-22 (1961), ch. 9

"The worst misfortune that can happen to an ordinary man is to have an extraordinary father."

> Austin O'Malley (1858–1932),
> U.S. physician and writer

"Never was ability so much below mediocrity so well rewarded; no, not even when Caligula's horse was made a consul."

> John Randolph (1773–1833),
> U.S. politician describing Richard Rush

◆ MEMORY

Foreign Words and Phrases

déjà vu (Fra)
(DAY-jah voo) the experience of seeing something that seems oddly familiar

tartle (Scot)
(TAR-tul) to fail (and hesitate) to recognize someone or something

Quotations

"I distinctly remember forgetting that."

> Clara Barton (1821–1912),
> U.S. social reformer, when reminded of
> a wrong done to her years earlier

"A memory is what is left when something happens and does not completely unhappen."

Edward de Bono (1933–),
British writer

"Many a man fails to become a thinker for the sole reason that his memory is too good."

Friedrich [Wilhelm] Nietzsche
(1844–1900), German philosopher

Jokes, Stories and Anecdotes

One day while in New York, the actor James Cagney saw a man across the street. "You see that fellow over there?" Cagney asked his wife. "He sat next to me in school. His name is Nathan Skidelsky." Though proud of her husband's incredible memory, Mrs. Cagney replied, "Prove it." Cagney went over and said hello. It really was Nathan Skidelsky. But he didn't remember Jimmy Cagney.

James Cagney (1899–1989)
U.S. film actor

As part of her nightclub act, Carol Channing would sometimes encourage members of the audience to ask her personal questions. Someone asked, "Do you remember the most embarrassing moment you ever had?" "Yes, I do," replied Channing. "Next question?"

Carol Channing (1921–),
U.S. actress and singer

American dancer Lydia Sokolova claimed to have assisted the Ballets Russes star Tamara Karsavina in interpreting a very successful role. When asked about Sokolova's contribution, the tempestuous Karsavina said flatly, "Lydia has very good memory, but she tends to rely upon it too much."

Tamara Karsavina (1885–1978),
Russian ballerina

◆ MIDDLE AGE

Foreign Words and Phrases

d'un certain âge (Fra)
(duhn SEHR-tan AHJ) middle-aged

Quotations

"The really frightening thing about middle age is the knowledge that you'll grow out of it."

Doris Day (1924–),
U.S. singer and film actress

"Middle age is the time when a man is always thinking that in a week or two he will feel as good as ever."

Don[ald Robert Perry] Marquis
(1878–1937), U.S. writer and poet

◆ MINISTRY

Quotations

"Archbishop: a Christian ecclesiastic of a rank superior to that attained by Christ."

H[enry] L[ouis] Mencken (1880–1956),
U.S. critic and writer

"How can a bishop marry? How can he flirt? The most he can say is, 'I will see you in the vestry after service.'"

Sydney Smith (1771–1845),
British clergyman and writer

"There is a certain class of clergyman whose mendicity is only equalled by their mendacity.

Archbishop Frederick Temple (1821–1902), British clergyman

Jokes, Stories and Anecdotes

Siiting next to Rabbi Adler at an official luncheon, Herbert Cardinal Vaughan asked him mischievously, "When may I have the pleasure of helping you to some ham?" Replied Adler, "At Your Eminence's wedding."

Hermann Adler (1839–1911), German-born British rabbi [attributed also to others]

A U.S. clergyman once condemned the great actress Sarah Bernhardt as "an imp of darkness, a female demon sent from the modern Babylon to corrupt the New World." Sarah responded with a note: "My dear confrere, why attack me so violently? Actors ought not to be hard on one another. Sarah Bernhardt."

Sarah Bernhardt (1844–1923), French actress

◆ MIRACLE

Foreign Words and Phrases

Wundersucht (Ger)
(VOON-duhr-soosht) fascination with miracles (public's appetite met by advertisers, evangelists, etc.)

Quotations

"For those who believe in God no explanation is needed; for those who do not believe in God no explanation is possible."

Father John Lafarge (1880–1963), British clergyman, commenting on the cures at Lourdes

---

◆ MISCONDUCT

Foreign Words and Phrases

Erlko nig (Ger)
(EHRL-kuh-nig) elf king, mischievous spirit

enfant terrible (Fra)
(on-FON tehr-REE-bluh) *lit:* terrible child; incorrigible (and embarrassing) child; *fig:* person whose unruliness creates difficulties

Quotations

"Oh dear me—it's too late to do anything but accept you and love you—but when you were quite a little boy somebody ought to have said 'hush' just once!"

Mrs. Patrick Campbell [Beatrice] (1865–1940), British actress, letter to George Bernard Shaw, November 1, 1912

"Time to me this truth has taught
('Tis a treasure worth revealing),
More offend from want of thought,
Than from any want of feeling."

Charles Swain (1801–1874), British poet, Want of Thought

Classical Phrases and Myths

The Greek mathematician Thales's mule was carrying a load of salt but accidentally fell in a river. The salt dissolved. Realizing that its burden was considerably lighter, the mule repeated the stunt. Thales's cure for the insolent mule was to burden the beast with sponges for the return journey.

Thales (c. 640 B.C.–c. 546 B.C.), Greek philosopher

Jokes, Stories and Anecdotes

While leading a group of tourists around the colleges of Oxford University, the British writer Charles

Calverley announced: "That is Balliol College. That is the Master's house. . . ." He then threw a stone at the study window. "And that," he continued, "is the Master."

Charles Stuart Calverley (1831–1884), British writer [attributed also to others]

"When I was a boy, my friends and I would wander the streets to find horses tied up to a post," began longtime mayor of New York, Fiorello La Guardia, trying to distinguish between mischief and delinquency for the police. "We'd unhitch one, ride him around town, then tie him up again." "Are you telling us that the mayor of New York was once a horse thief?" asked a policeman. "No," said La Guardia. "I'm telling you that he was once a boy."

Fiorello La Guardia (1882–1947), U.S. politician

French statesman Talleyrand overheard historian Claude Rulhirés complain that he was unjustifiably accused of being mischievous, "even though I have done only one mischievous thing in my life." Asked Talleyrand, "And when will that end?"

Charles Maurice de Talleyrand-Périgord (1754–1838), French diplomat

---

◆ MISFORTUNE

Foreign Words and Phrases

schlemiel (Yid)
(shleh-MEEL) one who is unlucky or clumsy, a fool, *e.g.*, one who falls on his back and breaks his nose

schlimazl (Yid)
(shleh-MAZL) Job-like person to whom everything bad happens, *e.g.*, the waiter who spills a bowl of soup is a schlemiel, the person he spills it on is a schlimazl

Quotations

"now and then
there is a person born
who is so unlucky
that he runs into accidents
which started to happen
to somebody else."

Don[ald Robert Perry] Marquis (1878–1937), U.S. writer and poet, archy and mehitabel (1933), "archy says"

"*Dans l'adversite de nos meilleurs amis, nous trouvons quelque chose qui ne nous deplait pas.*" (In the misfortune of our best friends, we find something that does not displease us.)

François, Duc de La Rochefoucauld (1613–1680), French writer, Maximes (1665), 583

Classical Phrases and Myths

"Misfortune reveals true friends."

Aristotle (384 B.C.–322 B.C.), Greek philosopher, Eudemian Ethics, bk. VII, ch. 2

"There's many a slip 'twixt the cup and lip."

Palladas (c.400), Greek writer [authenticity unverified]

Jokes, Stories and Anecdotes

The football player Bronko Nagurski, roughhousing with a teammate, fell out of a second-floor window. A policeman made his way through the crowd that had gathered and inquired, "What happened?" "I don't know," said Nagurski. "I just got here myself."

Bronko Nagurski (1908–1990), U.S. football player

◆ MISINTERPRETATION

Jokes, Stories and Anecdotes

"With which hand do you stir your coffee?" asked the child. "With my right hand," replied the social matron. "Oh," said the child, "don't you use a spoon?"

The peril of using irony as a rhetorical device was learned well by Lord Justice Charles Bowen. When acting as a Puisne judge, he was trying a burglar who, having entered a house by the top story, was captured downstairs taking silver. Ingenuously, or ingeniously, the accused claimed to be an eccentric addicted to perambulating on the roofs of adjacent houses, and occasionally dropping in "permiscuous" through an open skylight. Reportedly, the judge caustically summed up in his instructions to the jury: "If, gentlemen, you think it likely that the prisoner was merely indulging in an amiable fancy for midnight exercise on his neighbor's roof; if you think it was kindly consideration for that neighbor which led him to take off his boots and leave them behind him before descending into the house; and if you believe that it was the innocent curiosity of the connoisseur which brought him to the silver pantry and caused him to borrow the teapot, then, gentlemen, you will acquit the prisoner!" To the judge's great dismay, the jury did immediately acquit the accused.

Charles Synge Christopher Bowen,
1st Baron (1835–1894), British jurist

In 1958, the American writer Barnaby Conrad was badly gored in a bullfight in Spain. Later, at a New York restaurant Eva Gabor said to playwright Noel Coward, "Noel dahling, have you heard the news about poor Bahnaby? He vass terribly gored in Spain." Alarmed, Coward asked, "He was what?" "He vass gored!" "Thank heavens. I thought you said he was bored."

Sir Noel Coward (1899–1973),
British playwright and actor

As the daughter of an earl, Lady Katharine Sackville retained her title when she married journalist Frank Giles. While journeying abroad, they once received an invitation from the British embassy addressed to Mr. and Mrs. Giles. Giles called the embassy to correct the breach of protocol, and started to explain: "She isn't exactly Mrs. Giles—" "No problem," assured the voice at the other end. "Bring her along anyway. We're not at all stuffy here."

Frank Thomas Robertson Giles
(1919–   ), British writer

Conservative MP Neil Marten was guiding a group of his constituents on a tour of the Houses of Parliament. Lord Hailsham, then lord chancellor and wearing all the regalia of his office, came upon the group. Recognizing Marten among the visitors, Hailsham exclaimed, "Neil!" All of Marten's constituents promptly fell to their knees.

Neil Marten (1916–   ),
British politician

◆ MISJUDGMENT

Quotations

"Everyone complains about his memory yet no one complains about his judgment."

François, Duc de La Rochefoucauld
(1613–1680), French writer,
Maximes (1678), 89

"[Samuel] Johnson's aesthetic judgements are almost invariably subtle, or solid, or bold; they have always some good quality to recommend them—except one: they are never right."

Lytton Strachey (1880–1932),
British writer, Books and Characters
(1922), "Lives of the Poets"

Jokes, Stories and Anecdotes

Standing in front of a historic painting of a dirty but relaxed peasant at the museum, the society matron commented to her friends, "Isn't that like them. Too poor to buy decent clothes, but he can afford to have his portrait painted."

◆ MODESTY

Quotations

"He's a modest man who has a good deal to be modest about."

Sir Winston Spencer Churchill
(1874–1965), British prime minister
and writer, describing Sir Clement Attlee

"You've no idea what a poor opinion I have of myself—and how little I deserve it.

Sir W[illiam] S[chwenck] Gilbert
(1836–1911), British writer

"All men have their faults; too much modesty is his."

Oliver Goldsmith (1728–1774), Irish-born
British poet, playwright and writer,
The Good-Natured Man (1768), Act II

"Liking a writer and then meeting the writer is like liking goose liver and then meeting the goose."

Arthur Koestler (1905–1983),
British writer

Jokes, Stories and Anecdotes

The composers Johannes Brahms and Johann Strauss the Younger, who had each admired the other from afar, once met in Vienna.

Strauss handed his autograph book to Brahms, asking if Brahms would do him the honor of signing it. After Brahms had signed it Strauss later saw that Brahms had transcribed the first few bars of *The Blue Danube* and written underneath, "Unfortunately not by Johannes Brahms."

Johannes Brahms (1833–1897),
German composer

◆ MONEY

Foreign Words and Phrases

faux frais (Fra)
(foh fray) overlooked items excluded from a budget

il faut de d'argent (Fra)
(eel FOH de LAH-jon) it is necessary to have money

Quotations

"Money is like muck, not good except it be spread."

Francis Bacon (1561–1626),
British lawyer and writer, Essays (1625),
"Of Seditions and Troubles"

"Annual income twenty pounds, annual expenditure nineteen nineteen six, result happiness. Annual income twenty pounds, annual expenditure twenty pounds ought and six, result misery."

Charles Dickens (1812–1870),
British writer, David Copperfield
(1849–1850), ch. 12

"If you would like to know the value of money, go and try to borrow some."

Benjamin Franklin (1706–1790),
U.S. statesman and scientist,
Poor Richard's Almanac (1732–1757)

"They who are of the opinion that money will do everything, may very well be suspected to do everything for money."

George Savile, Marquis of Halifax (1633–1695), British statesman and writer

"Put not your trust in money, but put your money in trust."

Oliver Wendell Holmes, Sr. (1809–1894), U.S. writer and physician, The Autocrat of the Breakfast Table (1858), ch. I

"I don't like money, actually, but it quiets my nerves."

Joe Louis (1914–1981), U.S. boxer

"Money is like a sixth sense without which you cannot make a complete use of the other five."

W[illiam] Somerset Maugham (1874–1965), British writer and playwright, Of Human Bondage (1915), ch. 51

"One should look down on money but never lose sight of it."

André Prévot (c. 1911–   ), French citizen

"When I was young I used to think that money was the most important thing in life; now that I am old, I know it is."

Oscar [Fingal O'Flahertie Wills] Wilde (1854–1900), British playwright, writer and wit

Classical Phrases and Myths

radix nialorum est cupiditas (Lat) (RAH-dix ma-LOR-umest ku-PID-ee-tas) money is the root of all evil

The Roman emperor Vespasian, a military commander who came to power after the profligate Nero committed suicide, was anxious to restore the Roman state to solvency. Virtually everything was taxed, even Rome's public urinals. When his finicky son Titus protested that this tax was beneath the dignity of the state, Vespasian took a handful of coins obtained from its source

and held them up to his son's nose. "Non olet!" (It does not smell!)

Vespasian [Titus Flavius Sabinus Vespasianus] (9–79), Roman emperor

Jokes, Stories and Anecdotes

After obtaining the combination number of the safe from the bank cashier, one burglar tied and gagged him while the other burglars herded the other employees into a separate room. The burglars were about to leave after they had rifled the safe when the cashier made desperate pleading noises through the gag. Curious, one of the burglars loosened the gag. "Take the books, too!" whispered the cashier, "I'm $25,000 short."

The American tourist knew the dollar was low, but she didn't realize just how low until she was in Rome, threw three coins in the fountain, and was arrested—for littering.

In 1921, while with William Randolph Hearst's New York American, journalist, biographer and novelist Gene Fowler traveled on assignment to northern Canada, making much of the trip by private railroad car at a high fare. Upon his return, Fowler created one of his imaginative expense records to account for the bill. He concocted a list of items that might be thought necessary for an expedition to the far north— including a secondhand dogsled and a team of huskies to draw it. The auditor returned the account for failure to balance. The death of the lead dog, plus a commemorative headstone, added another $100, but the amount was still short. So Fowler added: "Flowers for the bereft bitch–$1.50."

Gene Fowler (1990–1960), U.S. writer

◆ MOTIVATION (INDUCEMENT)

Foreign Words and Phrases

élan vital (Fra)
(ay-LON VEE-tat) *lit:* vital impetus; life force, source of an individual's motivations

Quotations

"Never ascribe to an opponent motives meaner than your own."

Sir J[ames] M[atthew] Barrie (1860–1937), British writer and playwright, rectorial address, St. Andrews, May 3, 1922

"When I see a merchant overpolite to his customers . . . thinks I, that man has an axe to grind."

Charles Miner (1780–1865), U.S. writer, Essays from the Desk of Poor Robert the Scribe (1815), "Who'll Turn Grindstones"

"He never does a proper thing without giving an improper reason for it."

George Bernard Shaw (1856–1950), Irish playwright, Major Barbara (1907)

Jokes, Stories and Anecdotes

After the explorer Ernest Shackleton had approached David Lloyd-George seeking a sponsor for his next expedition, the Welsh statesman, always eager to improve upon his connections, introduced Shackleton to a wealthy acquaintance. Lloyd-George later asked Shackleton if the meeting were productive. "Very," replied the explorer. "He offered me 10,000 pounds for my expenses, provided that I would take you along with me to the Pole. And he promised me 1 million pounds if I were to leave you there by mistake."

David Lloyd George, 1st Earl (1863–1945), British prime minister

The playwright and diplomat Clare Boothe Luce once had the happy occasion to meet the inspiration for her dramatic work, George Bernard Shaw. "Except for you," she gushed, "I wouldn't be here." "And now, let me see, dear child," said Shaw, "what *was* your mother's name?"

George Bernard Shaw (1856–1950), Irish playwright [authenticity unverified]

◆ MOVEMENT

Foreign Words and Phrases

adagio (Ita)
(a-DAH-joh) slow(ly); in music, movement in slow time

accelerando (Ita)
(a-cheh-leh-RAHN-doh) in music, gradually gathering speed

allegro ma non troppo (Ita)
(a-LEH-groh mah non TRO-poh) in music, briskly but not too fast

con moto (Ita)
(kon MO-toh) *lit:* with movement; in music, with life

Classical Phrases and Myths

in transitu (Lat)
(in TRA N-sit-oo) in transit, in passage

perpetuum mobile (Lat)
(per-PET-u-um MOH-bil-e) perpetual motion

Jokes, Stories and Anecdotes

Q: "What is fast transportation?"
A: "When a farmer ships two rabbits 100 miles by truck and it arrives with two rabbits."

◆ MUSIC

Foreign Words and Phrases

cadenza (Ita)
(kah-DEN-zah) in music, elaborate
solo performance near finale

Quotations

"Good music is that which pene-
trates the ear with facility and quits
the memory with difficulty."

Sir Thomas Beecham (1879–1961),
British conductor, speech (c. 1950)

"A musicologist is a man who can
read music but can't hear it."

Sir Thomas Beecham (1879–1961),
British conductor

"I'll play it first and tell you what
it is later."

Miles Davis (1926–1991),
U.S. musician

"Playing 'bop' is like playing Scrab-
ble with all the vowels missing."

Edward ["Duke"] Ellington (1899–1974),
U.S. musician and composer

"I know only two tunes. One of
them is *Yankee Doodle* and the other
one isn't."

Ulysses Simpson Grant (1822–1885),
U.S. general and president, indicating his
dislike for music after an attending a
concert as president

"Fortissimo at last!"

Gustav Mahler (1860–1911),
German composer, seeing Niagara Falls

Classical Phrases and Myths

"*Sicelides Musae, paulo maiora cana-
mus!*" (Sicilian Muses, let us raise a
somewhat loftier strain!)

Virgil [Publius Vergilius Maro] (70 B.C.–
19 B.C.), Roman poet, Eclogues, IV, l. i

Jokes, Stories and Anecdotes

During the intermission of a concert
in which Sir Thomas Beecham's
conducting and the pianist's playing of a Mozart concerto were un-
derwhelming, a stagehand asked
Beecham, "Should we take the piano off or leave it on?" Beecham
thought about the second half of
the program, for which a piano was
not required. "You might as well
leave it on," he said. "It will probably slink off by itself."

Sir Thomas Beecham (1879–1961),
British conductor

For much of the year Prince Esterházy kept his musicians at Schloss
Esterházy in a remote corner of
northwestern Hungary, far from
their families. There, Haydn composed his Fifth "Farewell" Sym-
phony. At its first performance, for
the last movement, in which the in-
struments drop out of the score one
by one, each player, on completing
his part, blew out his candle and
tiptoed away from the orchestra.
Prince Esterházy accepted the hint,
and permitted the musicians a vacation.

Franz Joseph Haydn (1732–1809),
Austrian composer

With great effort, but unsuccessfully, the composer Franz Joseph
Haydn was trying to express a
storm at sea in a certain musical
passage. Exasperated, Haydn cried,
"The deuce take the tempest. I cannot do it!" and, setting his hands at
opposite ends of the keyboard, rapidly brought them together. Exclaimed the delighted librettist,
"That is it!"

Franz Joseph Haydn (1732–1809),
Austrian composer

Following the death of the great
composer and songwriter George
Gershwin, a well-intentioned ad-

mirer asked Oscar Levant to hear an elegy written by the admirer in honor of Gershwin. When he had finished playing the piece, the man turned to Levant for approval. "I believe," Levant said, "that it would have been better if you had died and Gershwin had written the elegy."

Oscar Levant (1906–1972), U.S. pianist and wit [attributed also to others]

Suspecting that the Philadelphia Orchestra's overfamiliarity with Richard Strauss's *Till Eulenspiegel* was to blame for its inauspicious rehearsal, Pierre Monteux stopped the piece and declared, "Gentlemen, I am sure that you know this piece backwards, but please, let us not play it that way."

Pierre Monteux (1875–1964), French conductor

Mozart, only two years old, was taken to a farm, where he heard a pig squeal. "G-sharp!" he chortled. A nearby piano confirmed his conclusion.

Wolfgang Amadeus Mozart (1756–1791), Austrian composer

At an evening party, Mozart bet the elder Haydn a case of champagne that he could not play on sight a piece Mozart had just composed. Haydn accepted the bet and sat at the piano in front of the sheet music, but only played a few bars. He protested that the piece could not be continued because the passage contained a note in the center while both hands were at opposite ends of the keyboard. Mozart replayed the composition. When he reached the impossible note, he bent forward and struck it with his nose. Applause.

Wolfgang Amadeus Mozart (1756–1791), Austrian composer [authenticity unverified]

Returning home inebriated one night, Savoy operetta composer Arthur Sullivan was unable to find his home among the identical row houses on his street. So as he walked along the row, he relied on his tone sense when he kicked each metal shoe scraper alongside the front entrances. Finally, one rang a familiar note. "B-flat," he muttered, and walked confidently into his home.

Sir Arthur Seymour Sullivan (1842–1900), British composer and conductor [attributed also to other composers]

◆ MUSICAL INSTRUMENT

Quotations

"[The harpsichord] sounds like two skeletons copulating on a corrugated tin roof."

Sir Thomas Beecham (1879–1961), British conductor

Jokes, Stories and Anecdotes

British conductor Sir Malcolm Sargent was once asked, "What do you have to know to play the cymbals?" "Nothing," he said, "just when."

Sir Malcolm Sargent (1895–1967), British conductor and organist

◆ MUSICIAN

Foreign Words and Phrases

maestro (Ita)
(mah-ESS-troh) master, teacher, orchestra conductor, title for eminent musician

Quotations

"I love Wagner, but the music I prefer is that of a cat hung up by its tail outside a window and trying to stick to the panes of glass with its claws."

Charles [Pierre] Baudelaire (1821–1867),
French poet

"There are two golden rules for an orchestra: start together and finish together. The public doesn't give a damn what goes on in between."

Sir Thomas Beecham (1879–1961),
British conductor

"You see, our fingers are circumcised, which gives it a very good dexterity, you know, particularly in the pinky."

Itzhak Perlman (1945–   ),
Israeli violinist, explaining why so
many great violinists were Jewish,
"60 Minutes," 1980 television program

Classical Phrases and Myths

According to Greek orator and satirist Lucian, Harmonides, a young flute player and scholar of Timotheus, began his solo at his public debut with so violent a blast that it was his last breath into his flute. He died on the spot.

Harmonides (c. 4th century B.C.),
Greek musician

Jokes, Stories and Anecdotes

With some of the musicians apparently unable to keep time during a bad rehearsal, Sir Thomas Beecham scolded one: "We cannot expect you to be with us the whole time, but maybe you would be kind enough to keep in touch now and again?"

Sir Thomas Beecham (1879–1961),
British conductor

A society hostess who had asked violinist Fritz Kreisler his fee to play at a private party was informed that the amount would be $5,000. The matron accepted but warned, "Please be aware that I do not expect you to mingle with the guests." "In that case, madam," replied Kreisler, "my fee will only be $2,000."

Fritz Kreisler (1875–1962), U.S. violinist
[attributed also to others]

Giocomo Meyerbeer and Gioachinno Rossini were rival opera composers who shared a cordial but intense rivalry. Conversing once with Meyerbeer, Rossini allowed how bored and melancholic he felt. "You listen," Meyerbeer replied consolingly, "to too much of your own music."

Giacomo Meyerbeer (1791–1864),
German composer and pianist

At a farewell piano concert, the pianist, composer and statesman Ignace Paderewski, by then well past his prime, performed poorly. Attending the concert, pianist Abram Chasins turned to fellow pianist Moriz Rosenthal and sighed, "The things that man has forgotten!" "What he forgets isn't so bad," Rosenthal observed. "It's what he remembers!"

Moriz Rosenthal (1862–1946),
Polish-born pianist

◆ NAKEDNESS

Quotations

"I have seen three emperors in their nakedness, and the sight was not inspiring."

Otto Eduard Leopold, Prince von
Bismarck (1815–1898), German statesman

"No. You see there are portions of the human anatomy which would keep swinging after the music had finished."

Sir Robert Helpmann (1909–1986), British choreographer, answering whether the fashion of nudity would extend to dance

When asked if she really had nothing on in her famous calendar photograph of the early 1950s, Marilyn Monroe, her eyes widening, purred, "I had the radio on."

Marilyn Monroe [Norma Jean Baker] (1926–1962), U.S. film actress

Classical Phrases and Myths

in puris naturalibus (Lat)
(in POOH-rees na-toor-AH-li-bus)
in the natural state, naked

Jokes, Stories and Anecdotes

George S. Kaufman made a business call on theatrical producer Jed Harris, renowned for his outrageous antics. Ushered into Harris's office, Kaufman found Harris seated stark naked at his desk. Kaufman smiled. "Jed, your fly is open."

George S[imon] Kaufman (1889–1961), U.S. playwright, writer and wit

---

◆ NARROW-MINDEDNESS

Foreign Words and Phrases

Einstellung (Ger)
(EYN-shtel-lung) in psychology, fixed reaction to a problem

Quotations

"He has the lucidity which is the by-product of a fundamentally sterile mind . . . Listening to a speech by Chamberlain is like paying a visit to Woolworth's: everything in its place and nothing above sixpence."

Aneurin ["Nye"] Bevan (1897–1960), British politician, describing Neville Chamberlain

"Conservative. A statesman who is enamored of existing evils, as distinguished from a Liberal, who wishes to replace them with others."

Ambrose [Gwinnet] Bierce (1842-c. 1914), U.S. writer and poet, Devil's Dictionary (1911)

"A fanatic is one who can't change his mind and won't change the subject."

Sir Winston Spencer Churchill (1874–1965), British prime minister and writer

"None so deaf as those who won't hear."

English proverb (c. 1500s)

"I will look at any additional evidence to confirm the opinion to which I have already come."

Lord Hugh Molson (1903–   ), British politician

"Aristotle maintained that women have fewer teeth than men; although he was twice married, it never occurred to him to verify this statement by examining his wives' mouths."

Bertrand Arthur William Russell, 3rd Earl (1872–1970), British mathematician and philosopher, Impact of Science on Society (1952), ch. 1

"He is one of the finest minds of the fifteenth century."

Franz Werfel (1890–1945), Czech playwright, Jacobowsky und der Oberst (Jacobowsky and the Colonel) (1944) [comment about a vain, narrow-minded aristocrat living in the 19th century]

Classical Phrases and Myths

homo unius libri (Lat)
(HOH-mo OON-ius LEE-bree) *lit:* man of one book; partisan; used disparagingly to indicate a person versed in only one text

Jokes, Stories and Anecdotes

The Scottish philosopher David Hume, renown as a skeptic, attended regular church services conducted by an ultra-orthodox minister. When a friend pointed out the discrepancy, Hume shrugged, saying, "I don't believe all he says, but he does. Once a week it is nice to hear a man who believes in what he says."

> *David Hume (1711–1776),*
> *British philosopher and historian*

◆ NATIVITY

Foreign Words and Phrases

habitué (Fra)
(ah-BEE-tew-ay) habitual patron of an establishment

Quotations

"If a man's from Texas, he'll tell you. If he's not, why embarrass him by asking?"

> *John Gunther (1901–1970), U.S. writer*

Jokes, Stories and Anecdotes

A New York debutante had met a charming man at a party, but as time wore on, he began to make his excuses. "I have to make my way out to Hoboken." "To Hoboken!" said the debutante. "Why would you want to do that?" "I live there," he explained. She countered, "But that's no excuse."

"All Rochester seems to be in New York this week," exclaimed George S. Kaufman's wife, after seeing a number of acquaintances from her hometown, Rochester, while they strolled down Fifth Avenue. Replied Kaufman, "What an excellent time to visit Rochester."

> *George S[imon] Kaufman (1889–1961),*
> *U.S. playwright, writer and wit*

◆ NATURE

Foreign Words and Phrases

Leitmotiv (Ger)
(LYT-mo-TEEF) *lit:* leading motive; theme associated with a person, event, institution or genre (especially music)

Classical Phrases and Myths

Natura abhorre vacuum
(nat-OOR-a AB-hor-re WAK-u-um) Nature abhors a vacuum

> *Benedict [Baruch] Spinoza (1632–1677),*
> *Spanish philosopher,* Ethics *(1677), pt. I,*
> *proposition 15: note*

"Nature does nothing uselessly."

> *Aristotle (384 B.C.–322 B.C.),*
> *Greek philosopher,* Politics, *bk. I, ch. 2*

"Nature, to be commanded, must be obeyed."

> *Francis Bacon (1561–1626),*
> *British lawyer and writer,* Novum
> Organum *(1620), "Aphorism 129"*

Jokes, Stories and Anecdotes

Frontiersman and fur-trapper Jim Bridger had received a serious wound during one of his numerous skirmishes with hostile Indians or wild animals. The man dressing it expressed concern that the wound would suppurate. "Don't worry," growled Bridger. "In the mountains, meat never spoils."

Jim Bridger (1804–1881),
U.S. frontiersman

A woman informed James Whistler that she had just traveled along the Thames from the country, and that there was an exquisite haze in the atmosphere that reminded her of Whistler's paintings. "Yes, madam," responded Whistler, "Nature is creeping up."

James Abbott McNeill Whistler
(1834–1903), U.S.-born British painter

◆ NECESSITY

Foreign Words and Phrases

force majeure (Fra)
(force mah-JUHR) irresistible force, overwhelming compulsion; in law, a contract clause to protect the signatories against acts of God and unavoidable accidents

Classical Phrases and Myths

necessitatem in virtutem commutare (Lat)
(nek-ESS-it-a-temin WIR-TOO-tem) to make virtue a necessity; Latin proverb

mater artium necessitas (Lat)
(MAT-er ART-ium ne-KESS-ee-TAH-tas) necessity is the mother of invention

"Yet do I hold that mortal foolish who strives against the stress of necessity."

Euripides (480 B.C.–406 B.C.),
Greek playwright, Mad Heracles, l. 281

"Necessitas non habet legem."
(nek-ES-si-tas nohn HAB-et LEG-

em) (Necessity has no law.)

Publilius Syrus (c. 100 B.C.),
Roman writer, Sententiae, 399
[recognition that moral codes break
down completely in certain situations]

"Necessitatem in virtutem commutare."
(NEK-es-sit-a-temin WIR-tu-tem KOM-mut-ar-ay) (We transmute necessity into a virtue.)

Quintilian [Marcus Fabius Quintilianus]
(c. 35–c. 100), Roman writer, Institutio
Oratoria, bk. I, 8, 14

Jokes, Stories and Anecdotes

Asked about the size of the police force in a little village, the sergeant replied, "Including me, four men." "But there can't be enough work in this little place to justify four men," remarked the inquirer. "There isn't," replied the sergeant, "but if weren't here, there would be."

◆ NEGOTIATIONS

Foreign Words and Phrases

pourparler (Fra)
(poor-par-lay) discussions, negotiations

nemawashi (Jap)
(NEE-mah-WASH-ee) behind-the-scenes maneuvering to forge consensus among differing factions

Quotations

"Awfully sorry, I didn't get that. Would you mind screaming it again?"

Sir Rudolf Bing (1902–   ), opera
administrator, to a trade union negotiator
for the Metropolitan Opera stagehands

"Let us never negotiate out of fear, but let us never fear to negotiate."

John Fitzgerald Kennedy (1917–1963), U.S. president, inaugural address, January 20, 1961

Jokes, Stories and Anecdotes

"I'm asking fifteen hundred a week," stated an actor while negotiating a contract with movie mogul Samuel Goldwyn. "You're not asking fifteen hundred a week," Goldwyn snapped. "You're asking twelve, and I'm giving you a thousand."

Samuel Goldwyn [Samuel Goldfish] (1882–1974), Russian-born U.S. film producer

---

◆ NEWNESS

Quotations

"Anything that calls itself new is doomed to a short life."

Tom Wolfe (1931–   ), U.S. writer

Classical Phrases and Myths

"Nihil est dictum, quod non est dictum prius." (Nothing is said which has not been said before.)

Anonymous comic poet

"Pereant, inquit, qui ante nos nostra dixerunt." (Confound those who have said our remarks before us.)

Aelius Donatus (c. 350), Roman educator

◆ NEWS

Foreign Words and Phrases

(les) actualités (Fra)
(lehz ak-too-al-ee-TAY) current events, news

cause célébre (Fra)
(kose sy-LEH-bre) lit: celebrated case; issue provoking great public interest; notorious scandal

Quotations

"When a dog bites a man, that is not news, because it happens so often. But if a man bites a dog, that is news."

John B. Bogart (1848–1921), U.S. editor [misattributed to Charles A. Dana]

Classical Phrases and Myths

"That proverbial saying 'Bad news travels fast and far.'"

Plutarch (46–120), Greek writer, Morals, Of Inquisitiveness

Jokes, Stories and Anecdotes

Whenever news was lacking during WWI, *New York Herald* owner James Bennett filled in the empty space with "Deleted by French censor."

James Gordon Bennett (1841–1918), U.S. newspaper owner and eccentric

King George IV of Britain detested his wife, Caroline of Brunswick, and they lived separately for all but their first year of marriage. In 1821, King George's groom of the bedchamber informed the king of the portentous news of Napoleon's death: "Sir, your bitterest enemy is dead." Exclaimed Caroline's husband, "Is she, by God!"

George IV (1762–1830), British king

Horace Greeley, founder of the *New York Tribune*, insisted that his journalists use the word "news" in the plural. Accordingly, he once sent a cable to a staffer: "ARE THERE ANY

NEWS?" Cabled back the staffer: "NOT A NEW."

Horace Greeley (1811–1872),
U.S. publisher and politician

◆ NOMENCLATURE

Foreign Words and Phrases

nom de guerre (Fra)
(NOM de GERR) pseudonym, stage name

nom de plume (Fra)
(NOM de PLOOM) pseudonym (of a writer)

sobriquet (Fra)
(soh-bree-KAY) nickname, false name

Quotations

"INXS."

Name of rock music band: In Excess

"Just note the crescendo."

Ezra [Loomis] Pound (1885–1972),
U.S. poet and writer explaining his
son's name, Omar Shakespeare Pound

"What's in a name? That which we call a rose
By any other name would smell as sweet."

William Shakespeare (1564–1616),
British playwright and poet, Romeo
and Juliet (1595), Act II, sc. ii

Jokes, Stories and Anecdotes

Q: "Do you know how the extinct Ono bird got its name?" A: "Because its scrotum hung below its feet, and when it approached a landing it would shriek, 'Oh, no! Oh, NO!' "

Thomas Beecham was once walking with his sister's friend, Utica Welles, and said to her, "I don't like your first name. I'd like to change it." "You can't," she replied, "but you can change my last name." And so they were married.

Sir Thomas Beecham (1879–1961),
British conductor

After sending his play to French playwright Tristan Bernard for review, a young playwright asked Bernard for suggestions for a title. Bernard, who had not yet read the manuscript, paused and then asked: "Are there any trumpets in your play?" Puzzled, the young dramatist replied, "No." "Any drums?" "No." "Well, why not call it 'Without Drums or Trumpets'?"

Tristan Bernard (1866–1947),
French dramatist and playwright
[attributed similarly to J. M. Barrie]

During the course of a conversation discussing his possible family relation with the Earl of Denbigh, whose family name was Fielding, novelist Henry Fielding was asked by the earl why the names were spelled differently. He could give no reason, replied Fielding, "except maybe that my branch of the family was the first to know how to spell."

Henry Fielding (1707–1754),
British novelist, playwright and lawyer

Someone complained to Dublin tax collector John Joyce, James Joyce's father, that his name had been spelled with two *ll*'s instead of one. Joyce inquired gravely, "Which *l* would you like to have removed?"

John Joyce (1849–1931), Irish bureaucrat

Richard Nixon, promoting his book *Six Crises* at a bookstore, asked all customers their names so that he could address each signed copy. One gentleman approached and grinned. "You've just met your seventh crisis," he said. "My name is Stanislaus Wojechzleschki."

Richard Milhous Nixon (1913–1994), U.S. president

The Nobel laureate and biochemist Albert Szent-Gyorgyi sent a paper to the scientific journal *Nature* that described a new sugar that he had isolated. Because this new sugar was of unknown structure but, like other sugars, required the suffix "ose," Szent-Gyorgyi suggested the name "ignose." *Nature*'s stern editors rejected his frivolity, requesting another name. He resubmitted "God-knows."

Albert von Nagyrapolt Szent-Gyorgyi (1893–1986), Hungarian-born U.S. scientist

◆ NONCONFORMITY (ABNORMALITY)

Foreign Words and Phrases

la différence français (Fra)
(la dif-FER-ons fron-SAIS) *lit:* the French difference, France's independence from other nations

appoggiatura (Ita)
(ahp-POH-djah-TOO-rah) in music, accented dissonant note

Quotations

"I feel like a fugitive from th' law of averages."

William ["Bill"] Mauldin (1921–   ), U.S. cartoonist, Up Front *(1945), cartoon caption*

"The exception proves the rule."

Proverb [As said by Robert Burton in The Anatomy of Melancholy *(1621–1651): "No rule is so general, which admits not some exception"]*

"Certainly nothing is unnatural that is not physically impossible."

Richard Brinsley Sheridan (1751–1816), Irish-born British playwright and politician, The Critic *(1779) Act II, sc. i*

Classical Phrases and Myths

lusus naturne (Lat)
(LOO-sus NAT-oor-ay) freak of nature, highly unusual natural occurrence

"*Natura il fece, e poi ruppe la stampa.*"
(NAT-ur-a il FE-kay ay POH-ee RUP-pay la STAM-pa) (Nature made him, and then broke mold.)

Ludovico Ariosto (1474–1533), Italian poet, Orlando Furioso *(1532), Canto X*

◆ NONEXISTENCE

Foreign Words and Phrases

néant (Fra)
(NAY-on) emptiness, nothingness

Quotations

" 'Contrariwise,' continued Tweedledee, 'if it was so, it might be; and if it were so, it would be: but as it isn't, it ain't. That's logic.' "

Lewis Carroll [Charles Lutwidge Dodgson] (1832–1898), British writer and mathematician, Through the Looking-Glass *(1872), ch. 4*

"The Dodo never had a chance. He seems to have been invented for the sole purpose of becoming extinct, and that was all he was good for."

Will Cuppy (1884–1949), U.S. writer, How to Become Extinct *(1941), p. 163*

Classical Phrases and Myths

nihil ex nihilo fit (Lat)
(ni-hil ex nil-EE-oh fit) *lit:* nothing comes from nothing; the argument from first cause, i.e., that matter

must have been created by a divine force

◆ NONSENSE

Foreign Words and Phrases

mumbo jumbo (W. Afr.)
(MUM-boh JUM-boh) routines of certain shamans who utter nonsense syllables to ward off evil spirits and impress tribal watchers

Quotations

"To appreciate nonsense requires a serious interest in life."

> Gilette Burgess (1866–1951),
> U.S. humorist and illustrator

"His nonsense suits their nonsense."

> Charles II (1630–1685), British king
> commenting on a certain preacher

"No one is exempt from talking nonsense: the misfortune is to do it solemnly."

> Michel Eyquem de Montaigne (1533–
> 1592), French writer, Essays (1580)

"Your damned nonsense can I stand twice or once, but sometimes always, by God, never."

> Hans Richter (1843–1916), Hungarian-
> born conductor, losing his temper—and
> command of the English language—with a
> second flutist at Covent Garden

"The King returns not to his sense, but to his nonsense."

> Horace Walpole, 4th Earl of Oxford
> (1717–1797), British writer, remarking
> acerbically after George III "recovered"
> from a bout of insanity

Classical Phrases and Myths

nihil ad rem (Lat)
(ni-hil ad rem) *lit:* nothing to the matter (in hand); irrelevant

◆ NUMEROUSNESS

Foreign Words and Phrases

troika (Rus)
(TROY-kuh) three-horse cart; also, three ideas or aspects of one idea

Quotations

"Even God Almighty only has ten."

> Georges Clemenceau (1841–1929),
> French prime minister, deriding President
> Woodrow Wilson's Fourteen Points for his
> 1918 peace proposal after WWI

Classical Phrases and Myths

variatim (Lat)
(WAH-ri-AH-tim) variously, in various ways

et cetera (Lat)
(et KET-te-ra) *lit:* and the rest; and so forth (abbr: etc.)

Jokes, Stories and Anecdotes

While in the presence of Edward VII, a young minister once pompously used the royal pronoun "we," although referring only to himself. The king at once remonstrated, "Only two people are permitted to refer to themselves as 'We'—a king, and a man with a tapeworm inside him."

> Edward VII (1841–1910), British king

At the conclusion of the debut of *Arms and the Man* the crowd was cheering wildly as the author took a curtain call. During a lull in the applause, someone called out in stentorian tones, "Shaw, your play stinks!" There was a horrified moment of silence, then Shaw exclaimed, "Sir, I quite agree with you, but what are we two against so many?"

George Bernard Shaw (1856–1950),
Irish playwright

◆ OBSTINACY

Foreign Words and Phrases

entêté (Fra)
(on-TEH-tay) obstinate

Quotations

"He has a first-rate mind until he makes it up."

Margot Asquith, Countess of Oxford and
Asquith (1887–1969), British writer and
socialite, describing Sir Stafford Cripps

"They defend their errors as if they were defending their inheritance."

Edmund Burke (1729–1797),
British statesman, philosopher and writer

"The difference between perseverance and obstinacy is that perseverance means a strong will and obstinacy means a strong won't."

Lord Dundee (1902–   ),
British statesman

"Like all weak men he laid an exaggerated stress on not changing one's mind."

W[illiam] Somerset Maugham (1874–
1965), British writer and playwright,
Of Human Bondage (1915), ch. 39

"I am firm. You are obstinate. He is a pigheaded fool."

Katharine Whitehorn (1926–   ),
British writer

◆ OCCULT

Foreign Words and Phrases

kabbalah (Heb)
(kha-BAH-la) (Jewish) mysticism

seance (Fra)
(say-ahnce) *lit:* a group meeting intended to contact spirits

voodoo (Hait)
(VOO-doo) a religion, involving the practice of magic rituals and spells, based on ancestor worship

Quotations

"Superstition is the religion of feeble minds."

Edmund Burke (1729–1797),
British statesman, philosopher and writer,
Reflections on the Revolution in
France (1790)

"No, it is better not. She will only ask me to take a message to [her deceased husband] Albert."

Benjamin Disraeli, 1st Earl of Beaconsfield
(1804–1881), British prime minister,
declining on his deathbed to receive a
royal visit from Queen Victoria

Jokes, Stories and Anecdotes

Sir Arthur Conan Doyle believed that communication with the dead was possible. He was once asked to visit a fellow author who was seriously ill. "I'll visit him tomorrow," promised Doyle. "But tomorrow could be too late—he may not last the night," he was advised. Replied Doyle, "Then, I'll speak to him next week."

Sir Arthur Conan Doyle (1859–1930),
British writer

Following the publication of an article by William Ralph Inge, the gloomy dean of London's St. Paul's church, a vengeful woman wrote him: "I am praying nightly for your death. It may interest you to know that in two other cases I have had great success."

William Ralph Inge (1860–1954), British clergyman

◆ OCCUPATION (BUSINESS)

Foreign Words and Phrases

métier (Fra)
(MAY-tee-yay) profession, calling, vocation

acharnement au travail (Fra)
(ah-SHAR-ne-mon oh trah-VYE) addiction to work

Quotations

"How can we be laid off if we own the company?

Lament of an anonymous Weirton Steel ex-worker, who was a shareholder of the company

"My career was as checkered as a tablecloth."

Sonny [Salvatore] Bono (1943–   ), U.S. entertainer and politician, And the Beat Goes On (1992)

"The chief business of the American people is business."

[John] Calvin Coolidge (1872–1933), U.S. president, speech in Washington, D.C., January 17, 1925

"Remember that time is money."

Benjamin Franklin (1706–1790), U.S. statesman and scientist

"Dr.—well remembered that he had a salary to receive, and only forgot that he had a duty to perform."

Edward Gibbon (1737–1794), British historian, Memoirs (Autobiography) (1796), p. 44

"The best career advice to give to the young is: 'Find out what you

like doing best and get someone to pay you for doing it.' "

Katharine Whitehorn (1926–   ), British writer

Jokes, Stories and Anecdotes

A priest, an attorney, a taxi driver and a politician are on a ship which suddenly hits an iceberg. "Save the women and children first," cries the priest. "Screw 'em!" exclaims the attorney. Taxi driver: "Do we have time?" Politician: "Do we have time?"

If sometimes clergy are defrocked and lawyers are disbarred, doesn't it follow that tree surgeons are debarked; cowboys are deranged; electricians are delighted; and dry cleaners are depressed?

Then there was the masseur who went out of business because he rubbed his customers the wrong way.

Why is it that when you need a lawyer, you can always find one?

An archaeologist is someone whose career lies in ruins.

British general Harold Alexander's assistant once asked Alexander the reason for his habit of tipping into his "out" tray any letters remaining in his "in" tray at the end of the working day. "It saves time," explained Alexander. "You'd be surprised how little of it comes back."

Harold Alexander, 1st Earl [Alexander of Tunis] (1891–1969), British general and statesman

Violinist Isaac Stern was introduced to Muhammad Ali at a New York party. "You might say we're in the same business," noted Stern. "We both earn a living with our hands."

"You must be pretty good," said Ali. "There isn't a mark on you."

Muhammad Ali [Cassius Clay] (1942–), U.S. boxer

Typically uncomfortable at formal dinners, the inventor Thomas Edison, a guest at one, was making his way back to his laboratory. Unfortunately, he was intercepted at the door by the host. "It certainly is a delight to see you, Mr. Edison," he said, and then he asked Edison, "What are you working on now?" "My exit."

Thomas Alva Edison (1847–1931), U.S. inventor

◆ OPINION

Quotations

"I never offered an opinion till I was sixty, and then it was one which had been in our family for a century."

Benjamin Disraeli, 1st Earl of Beaconsfield (1804–1881), British prime minister

"He thinks by infection, catching an opinion like a cold."

John Ruskin (1819–1900), British writer and social reformer

"He never chooses an opinion; he just wears whatever happens to be in style."

Leo Nikolaevich Tolstoy (1828–1910), Russian writer

Classical Phrases and Myths

ceterum censeo (Lat)
(KET-er-um KEN-see-oh) in my opinion

me judice (Lat)
(MAY YOO-di-kay) in my judgment

◆ OPPORTUNITY

Foreign Words and Phrases

en plein (Fra)
(on PLEN) completely, in full; bet placed on a single number on the roulette wheel, risk taken without insurance or security

Quotations

"Opportunity makes a thief."

Francis Bacon (1561–1626), British lawyer and writer, letter to Earl of Essex, 1598

Classical Phrases and Myths

"While we stop to think, we often miss our opportunity."

Publilius Syrus (c. 100 B.C.), Roman writer, Sententiae, 185

Jokes, Stories and Anecdotes

Amy Lowell so despised one of Boston's leading families, the Cabots, that she would even refuse invitations to any functions to which a Cabot had also been invited. About to board the *Devonian* for her annual European trip, she saw the passenger list and promptly disembarked. "There are 16 Cabots aboard the *Devonian* this trip," she explained to a journalist, "and God isn't going to miss such an opportunity."

Amy [Lawrence] Lowell (1874–1925), U.S. poet

◆ OPPOSITENESS

Foreign Words and Phrases

vis-à-vis (Fra)
(VEEZ-ah-VEE) concerning, regarding

276

Quotations

"Good taste and humor ... are a contradiction in terms, like a chaste whore."

> Malcolm Muggeridge (1903–1990),
> British writer and broadcaster

Classical Phrases and Myths

vice versa (Lat)
(WEE-ke WER-sah) inversely, the other way around

◆ ORIGINAL (AUTHENTICITY)

Foreign Words and Phrases

ébauche (Fra)
(ay-BOHSH) sketch, rough draft, model (in art, etc.)

Quotations

"Without an original there can be no imitation."

> George Grossmith (1847–1912) and
> Walter Weedon Grossmith (1854–1919),
> British writers, The Diary of
> a Nobody, *ch. 11*

"Of the author it has been observed:
Before they made him, they broke the mold."

> S[idney] J[oseph] Perelman (1904–1979),
> U.S. writer and screenwriter, Road to
> Miltown *jacket cover*

"*L'ecrivain original n'est pas celui qui n'imite personne, mais celui que personne ne peut imiter.*" (The original writer is not he who refrains from imitating others, but he whom no one can imitate.)

> Vicomte Françoise-René de Chateaubriand
> (1768–1848), French writer, Génie du
> Christianisme *(1802)*

Classical Phrases and Myths

ex nihilo (Lat)
(ex NI-hil-oh) from nothing

Jokes, Stories and Anecdotes

Two plays being performed on Broadway, one by Ruth Gordon, entitled *Over 21*, and the other by George Oppenheimer, entitled *Here Today*, contained thinly disguised characters based on Dorothy Parker. Parker grumbled that, although she had wanted to write her autobiography, she was now afraid to do so. "If I do, George Oppenheimer and Ruth Gordon would sue me for plagiarism."

> Dorothy Parker (1893–1967),
> U.S. wit and writer

◆ ORIGINALITY

Foreign Words and Phrases

echt (Ger)
(ekt) genuine

Quotations

"Originality is undetected plagiarism."

> William Ralph Inge (1860–1954),
> British clergyman

"What a good thing Adam had. When he said a good thing he knew nobody had said it before."

> Mark Twain [Samuel Langhorne Clemens]
> (1835–1910), U.S. humorist, writer and
> speaker, Notebooks (1935), p. 67

Jokes, Stories and Anecdotes

"Only you could have said that!" exclaimed an admiring friend after the French playwright Tristan Bernard uttered a most clever remark. Yet Bernard admitted that he had in fact read the quip in the newspaper that morning. "But you used it as your own!" cried the friend, aghast. Replied Bernard, "Yes, to make it authentic."

Tristan Bernard (1866–1947),
French playwright and writer

◆ ORNAMENTATION

Foreign Words and Phrases

bric-à-brac (Fra)
(brick-ah-brack) miscellaneous old trinkets, ornaments, etc.

okimono (Jap)
(OH-kee-moh-noh) decorative objects

Quotations

"[Be it resolved] that all women, of whatever age, rank, profession, or degree; whether virgin maids or widows; that shall after the passing of this Act, impose upon and betray into matrimony any of His Majesty's male subjects, by scents, paints, cosmetics, washes, artificial teeth, false hair, Spanish wool, iron stays, hoops, high-heeled shoes, or bolstered hips, shall incur the penalty of the laws now in force against witchcraft, sorcery, and such like misdemeanours, and that the marriage, upon conviction, shall stand null and void.

British Act of Parliament, 1670

"Diamonds Are a Girl's Best Friend." [Title of song (1949).]

Leo Robin (1900–   ),
U.S. songwriter

"She [Mrs. Stanhope] was rich in apparel but not bedizened with finery . . . she well knew the great architectural secret of decorating her constructions, and never descended to construct a decoration."

Anthony Trollope (1815–1882),
British writer, Barchester Towers, ch. 9

Jokes, Stories and Anecdotes

An actress who was a rival of French diva Sophie Arnould had received from her lover a magnificent diamond riviere. A bit long, the necklace, as worn by the actress, seemed to disappear down her cleavage. Sophie Arnould smirked, *"C'est qu'elle retourne vers sa source"* (It's just returning to its source).

[Madeleine] Sophie Arnould (1740–1802),
French actress and singer

The fabulously wealthy Mrs. Greville had the greatest disdain for ladies whose jewels were more spectacular than hers. An extremely wealthy American woman once discovered, to her horror, that the principal diamond had fallen from her necklace while she attended a gathering at Mrs. Greville's mansion. Everyone dropped to their hands and knees, searching for the diamond, and Mrs. Greville was overheard saying to a footman, "Perhaps this would be of assistance," as she handed him a magnifying glass.

Mrs. Ronald [Maggie] Greville
(1867–1942), British socialite

◆ OSTENTATION

Foreign Words and Phrases

bon viveur (Fra)
(bon vee-VUHR) one who lives luxuriously

grand luxe (Fra)
(grohn LOOKS) with much luxurious style

Quotations

"That's it baby, when you got it, flaunt it."

> Mel[vin] Brooks (1926–   ),
> U.S. actor and filmmaker, The Producers
> (1968 film)

"Conspicuous consumption of valuable goods is a means of reputability to the gentleman of leisure."

> Thorstein [Bunde] Veblen (1857–1929),
> U.S. scholar and philosopher, Theory of
> the Leisure Class (1899), ch. 4

Classical Phrases and Myths

Cornelia (kor-NEL-ee-a), the daughter of Scipio Africanus and wife of Tiberius Gracchus, was once called on at home by a wealthy Roman lady, who proudly showed off her jewelry to her hostess. The rich matron then challenged Cornelia to show off her own jewels. Just then, her two sons Tiberius and Gaius, who would grow up to become famed reformers of Rome's agrarian laws, entered the room. Gesturing toward her sons, Cornelia said proudly, "These are my jewels."

> Cornelia (c. 150 B.C.), Roman aristocrat

Jokes, Stories and Anecdotes

Alice Vanderbilt, the wife of financier Cornelius Vanderbilt II, was once having lunch with her son Reggie and his new second wife, Gloria, at the old Ambassador Hotel. Alice asked if Gloria had received her pearls. When Reggie interjected that he could not afford to buy any pearls worthy of his bride, Mrs. Vanderbilt calmly ordered that scissors be brought to the table. With the scissors she cut off about one-third of her own pearls, worth some $70,000. Handing them to her daughter-in-law,

she said, "There you are, Gloria, all Vanderbilt women have pearls."

> Alice Vanderbilt (c.1845–c.1930),
> U.S. socialite

The rose specialist and flamboyant dandy Harry Wheatcroft once came to a flower show sporting a carnation instead of the customary rosebud in his buttonhole. Said an astonished acquaintance, "What's this, Harry? No rose?" "Shh, I'm going incognito!"

> Harry Wheatcroft (1898–   ),
> British horticulturist

◆ OWNER

Classical Phrases and Myths

bona vacantia (Lat)
(BON-ah wak-ANT-ia) in law, goods whose legal ownership is unknown

Jokes, Stories and Anecdotes

Pointing to the presidential helicopter amid the other helicopters on the tarmac, the young Air Force corporal politely informed President Johnson, "This is your helicopter, sir." Replied Johnson, "They're all my helicopters, son."

> Lyndon Baines Johnson (1908–1973),
> U.S. president

◆ PAIN

Quotations

"Then the Elephant's Child put his head down close to the Crocodile's musky, tusky mouth, and the Crocodile caught him by his little nose

... At this, O Best Beloved, the Elephant's Child was much annoyed, and he said, speaking through his nose, like this, 'Led go! You are hurtig be!' "

> Rudyard Kipling (1865–1936),
> British writer and poet, Just So Stories
> (1902), "The Elephant's Child"

"For there was never yet philosopher
That could endure the toothache patiently."

> William Shakespeare (1564–1616),
> British playwright and poet, Much Ado
> About Nothing (1600), Act V, sc. i

"Nothing begins, and nothing ends,
That is not paid with moan;
For we are born in other's pain,
and perish in our own."

> Francis Thompson (1859–1907),
> British poet, Poems (1913), "Daisy"

Jokes, Stories and Anecdotes

When his mother told him his aunt soon would be visiting, the precocious wit George S. Kaufman, then only four years old, said, "That depends on your threshold of pain."

> George S[imon] Kaufman (1889–1961),
> U.S. playwright, writer and wit
> [authenticity unverified]

◆ PAINTING & ART

Foreign Words and Phrases

au premier coup (Fra)
(oh pre-MYER koo) *lit:* at the first blow; completion of an artwork in one session

beaux arts (Fra)
(boh ZAR) fine arts, also a grand neo-classical style of architecture

nature morte (Fra)
(nah-toor mort) stilllife, artistic representation of inanimate object

objet d'art (Fra)
(OB-jay-DAR) work of art

quadratura (Ita)
(KWAH-drah-TOO-rah) perspective paintings in a room, designed to deceive the eye

art brut (Fra)
(ar broo) *lit:* raw art; idea that all representations, whether graffiti or childish scribblings, are art

Quotations

"A product of the untalented, sold by the unprincipled to the utterly bewildered."

> Al Capp (1909–1979), U.S. cartoonist,
> describing abstract art

"Damn your nose, madam; there's no end to it!"

> Thomas Gainsborough (1727–1788),
> British painter, painting the portrait of
> actress Sarah Siddons

"Art is either plagiarism or revolution."

> Paul Gauguin (1838–1903),
> French painter

"Pity you had such bloody awful weather."

> George VI (1895–1952), British king,
> commenting to Modernist painter John
> Piper, who specialized in storm scenes

"We know that the tail must wag the dog,
For the horse is drawn by the cart;
But the Devil whoops, as he whooped of old;
'It's clever, but is it Art?' "

> Rudyard Kipling (1865–1936),
> British writer and poet, Barrack-Room
> Ballads (1892), "The Conundrum
> of the Workshops"

"There is nothing more difficult for a truly creative painter than to paint a rose, because before he can do so he has first to forget all the roses that were ever painted."

Henri Matisse (1869–1954), French painter, Notes d'un Peintre (1908)

"Art is a lie that makes us realize the truth."

Pablo [Ruiz y] Picasso (1881–1973), Spanish-born French artist

"What garlic is to salad, insanity is to art."

Augustus Saint-Gaudens (1848–1907), U.S. sculptor

"Every time I paint a portrait I lose a friend."

John Singer Sargent (1856–1925), U.S. painter

"My business is to paint not what I know, but what I see."

Joseph Mallord William Turner (1775–1851), British painter, replying to a naval officer pointing out that the ships in the landscape artist's view of Plymouth had no portholes

"Every portrait that is painted with feeling is a portrait of the artist, not of the sitter."

Oscar [Fingal O'Flahertie Wills] Wilde (1854–1900), British playwright, writer and wit

"L'Art pour l'art." (Art for art's sake.)

Victor Cousin (1792–1867), French philosopher and educator

Classical Phrases and Myths

Vita brevis est, ars longa. (WEET-a BRE-vis est, ars LONG-a) (Life is short, art is long.)

Seneca [Lucius Annaeus Seneca] (c. 4 B.C. -A.D. 65), Roman writer, philosopher and statesman, De Brevitate Vitae, I, i

ars est celare artem (Lat) (ars est kel-AHR-e AR T-em) the true purpose of art is to conceal art

In an ancient Greek contest of *trompe-l'oeil* effects, Zeuxis, pitted against Parrhasios, painted a boy holding a dish of grapes. Zeuxis painted the grapes so true to nature that birds tried to pick at them. Then Zeuxis asked his rival to draw back the curtain concealing the painting of Parrhasios. But this life-like curtain was itself painted. Zeuxis thus conceded defeat, since he had only fooled the birds, whereas Parrhasios had fooled Zeuxis, a painter.

Zeuxis (c. 424 B.C.-c. 380 B.C.), Greek painter

Jokes, Stories and Anecdotes

After studying an unremarkable modern watercolor in the window of a London art gallery, Shakespearean actress Dame Edith Evans commented to her companion, "I couldn't have that in my house. It would be like living with a gas leak."

Dame Edith Evans (1888–1976), British actress

Several sculptors contended that sculpture was superior to painting as an art form because it was not one-dimensional. A famed painter of the Venetian school, Giorgione, countered that a single painting could indeed show all sides of a figure without obliging the viewer to walk around the object. Giorgione convinced the skeptical sculptors by painting a nude with her back turned to the viewer, a pool of water at her feet to reflect the front, a mirror reflecting one side, and a burnished corselet the other.

Giorgione [Giorgione da Castelfranco] (c. 1477–1510), Italian painter

Regarded by some as the first Renaissance painter, Giotto, while a student of Giovanni Cimabue, painted a fly on the nose of a figure in one of the master's paintings.

The insect appeared so realistic that Cimabue tried repeatedly to brush the fly away when he returned to work on the picture. He then realized that he had fallen victim to a practical joke.

Giotto [Giotto di Bondone] (c. 1266–1337), Italian painter and architect [variations also attributed to others]

For 47 days Matisse's painting *Le Bateau* was displayed in the Museum of Modern Art in New York, during which time 116,000 people visited the gallery. Only after these days had passed did someone notice that the painting was hung upside down.

Henri Matisse (1869–1954), French painter

The shipping tycoon Stavros Niarchos once commissioned a portrait of himself to be painted by surrealist Salvador Dali for a fee of $15,000. As soon as his face had been sketched, he instructed Dali to finish the picture without him as a model. Dali did so, but completed the portrait with a naked body. He demanded $25,000, but Niarchos refused to pay for the unwanted work. Instead, Dali sold the painting to Aristotle Onassis, his client's chief rival, for $50,000. When Niarchos later saw the picture displayed on Onassis's dining room wall, he relented, asking his host, "How much do you want?" Onassis replied, "$75,000," which Niarchos promptly paid. He hid the portrait at home in a closet.

Stavros Niarchos (1909–), Greek industrialist

An American GI in Paris once declared to Picasso that he did not like modern paintings because they were unrealistic. Picasso said nothing. A few minutes later, the soldier proudly showed the abstract artist a snapshot of his girlfriend. "Heavens!," exclaimed Picasso. "Is she really as small as that?"

Pablo [Ruiz y] Picasso (1881–1973), Spanish-born French artist

---

◆ PARENTAGE

Foreign Words and Phrases

kyoikumama (Jap)
(key-OH-ee-koo-mah-mah) *lit:* education mama; mother who pushes a child for high academic achievement, *cf.* stage mother

Quotations

"There are times when parenthood seems nothing but feeding the mouth that bites you."

Peter de Vries (1910–1993), U.S. writer

Leontine: "An only son, sir, might expect more indulgence." Croaker: "An only father, sir, might expect more obedience."

Oliver Goldsmith (1728–1774), Irish-born British poet, playwright and writer, The Good-Natured Man (1768), Act I

"God could not be everywhere, and therefore he made mothers."

Jewish proverb

"Oh, what a tangled web do parents weave
When they think that their children are naive."

Ogden Nash (1902–1971), U.S. humorist, The Face Is Familiar (1940), "Baby, What Makes the Sky Blue"

"Parents—especially step-parents—are sometimes a bit of a disappointment to their children. They don't fulfill the promise of their early years."

Anthony Powell (1905–), British writer, A Buyer's Market (1952), ch. 2

"I can be president of the United States or I can control Alice. I cannot possibly do both."

Theodore Roosevelt (1858–1919),
U.S. president, sighing about his
daughter's interruptions

"If you must hold yourself up to your children as an object lesson (which is not necessary), hold yourself up as a warning and not as an example."

George Bernard Shaw (1856–1950),
Irish playwright

Classical Phrases and Myths

in loco parentis (Lat)
(in LOH-koh pah-REN-tis) in lieu of the parent

Agrippina was so consumed by her ambition to place Nero on the imperial throne that when the soothsayers whom she had consulted told her that "Nero will reign, but he will kill his mother," she replied, "Let him kill me, then."

Agrippina (15–59),
mother of Emperor Nero

Cambyses (kam-BIE-seez), the son of Cyrus the Great, a great conqueror of the ancient world, was reprimanded by his father for insolence. Cyrus noted that he would never have spoken to his own father in the same manner as had Cambyses. "But you were the son of a nobody," retorted Cambyses, "whereas I am the son of Cyrus the Great."

Cambyses II (d. 522 B.C.), Persian king

Cicero (SIS-e-roh), the Roman orator and statesman, was once mocked for his humble origins by Metellus Nepos, whose mother was known for her dissolute ways. Taunted Nepos, "I mean, who was your father?" Retorted Cicero, "It would be much harder for me to tell you who was yours."

Marcus Tullius Cicero (106 B.C.-43 B.C.),
Roman statesman and man of letters

Jokes, Stories and Anecdotes

The hushed courtroom waited with great anticipation for the judge's verdict in the widely publicized paternity suit. Emerging after long deliberation in his chambers, the brooding magistrate entered the courtroom and sat down behind the bench. Staring at the defendant, he suddenly produced a cigar from under his robes, and with a flourish handed it to the young man. "Congratulations," declared the judge, "you've just become a father."

The teacher of a writing class in which Isaac Asimov's mother was enrolled said to her, "Pardon me, Mrs. Asimov, but I am curious. Are you a relative of Isaac Asimov?" Barely restraining her pride, Mrs. Asimov said, "Yes, indeed. He is my son." "No wonder you're so good at writing," remarked the teacher. Drawing herself up to her full 58 inches, Mrs. Asimov said icily, "I beg your pardon. No wonder *he's* so good at writing."

Isaac Asimov (1920–1992), U.S. writer

◆ PARSIMONY

Foreign Words and Phrases

shnorrer (Yid)
(SHNOHR-er) beggar; cheapskate; bargain-hunter; sponger

Quotations

"It was said of old Sarah, Duchess of Marlborough, that she never puts dots over her *i*'s, to save ink."

Horace Walpole, 4th Earl of Oxford
(1717–1797), British writer

"There are many things that we would throw away, if we were not afraid that others might pick them up."

Oscar [Fingal O'Flahertie Wills] Wilde (1854–1900), British playwright, writer and wit

Jokes, Stories and Anecdotes

The youngster came home in great excitement, exclaiming, "Father, I ran all the way home from school behind the trolley, and saved a dollar carfare." His father angrily slapped him on the back and said, "Spendthrift! Why didn't you run home behind a taxicab and save three dollars?"

In one of his acts as the world's stingiest man, comedian Jack Benny was confronted by an armed robber who said, "Your money or your life." The demand was met with a long silence. Finally, the robber repeated: "Hey mister, what will it be, your money or your life?" Benny calmly replied: "I'm thinking! I'm thinking!"

Jack Benny (1894–1974), U.S. comedian

The humorist and writer Irvin Cobb was captured and questioned by the Germans with three other journalists during WW I as they traveled by taxi to the Belgian army headquarters. After about 36 hours of interrogation, Cobb finally asked one of his capturers, "Sir, whether or not you intend to shoot us, will you at least grant us one request?" The German, taken aback, asked, "What is that?" "Will you please tell the taxi driver to stop the meter?"

Irvin S[hrewsbury] Cobb (1876–1944), U.S. humorist and writer

The stingy proprietess of a boardinghouse presented to her boarders a plate of cold cuts sliced so thin they were transparent. Entertainer Joe Lewis, indicating the meats, asked her if she had cut them. "I did." "OK then, I'll deal."

Joe E. Lewis (1902–1971), U.S. entertainer

In 1925 Harold Ross founded *The New Yorker* magazine. Resources were stretched thin on the magazine's shoestring budget. When Ross reprimanded Dorothy Parker for not turning in a promised piece, she complained, "Someone else was using the pencil."

Dorothy Parker (1893–1967), U.S. wit and writer

A pay telephone from which John D. Rockefeller once made a collect call failed to refund his coin. So he rang the operator who, in order to mail the money to him, asked for his name and address. Rockefeller began: "My name is John D.... Oh, forget it! You wouldn't believe me anyway."

John D[avison] Rockefeller, Jr. (1874–1960), U.S. financier and philanthropist

◆ PARTY

Quotations

"The Party's Over." [Title of song (1956).]

Betty Comden (1919–   ) and Adolph Green (1915–   ), U.S. songwriters

Jokes, Stories and Anecdotes

Groucho Marx, never one to mince words, endured a stultifying party for a seemingly interminable evening. Finally, he rose to leave. "I've had a wonderful time," Groucho said to the host, shaking his hand, "but this isn't it."

Groucho [Julius] Marx (1895–1977), U.S. comedian [authenticity unverified]

The famed editor Maxwell Perkins decided to test the hypothesis that no one really listens to what others say at a boring cocktail party. While shaking his hostess's hand, he said, "I'm sorry I'm late, but it took me longer to strangle my aunt than I expected." "Yes, indeed," the social matron replied, "I'm so happy you came."

Maxwell Perkins (1884–1947), U.S. editor

◆ PAST

Foreign Words and Phrases

belle époque (Fra)
(BELL-a ay-POCK) *lit:* beautiful era; the period 1900–1914

Sehnsucht (Ger)
(ZAYN-zookt) longing, nostalgia

Quotations

"Nostalgia isn't what it used to be."

Anonymous graffito used as title of Simone Signoret book

"The only thing I regret about my past is the length of it. If I had to live my life again, I'd make the same mistakes, only sooner."

Tallulah Bankhead (1903–1968), U.S. actress

"It's deja-vu all over again."

Lawrence ["Yogi"] Berra (1925–), U.S. baseball player and manager

"Oh! the good times when we were so unhappy."

Alexandre [pere] Dumas (1803–1870), French writer and playwright

"They spend their time mostly looking forward to the past."

John Osborne (1929–), British playwright, Look Back in Anger (1956), Act II, sc. 1

"Those who cannot remember the past are condemned to repeat it."

George Santayana (1863–1952), Spanish-born U.S. philosopher, poet and writer, Life of Reason (1905), vol. 1, ch. 12

Classical Phrases and Myths

quondam (Lat)
(KWOHN-dam) former, once

laudator temporis acti (Lat)
(low-DAH-tor tem-POR-is AK-tee) *lit:* praiser of past times; one who prefers the past to the present

"Even God cannot change the past."

Agathon (447 B.C.–401 B.C.), Greek poet

◆ PATH (ROUTE)

Foreign Words and Phrases

camino real (Spa)
(kah-MEE-no ray-AL) *lit:* royal road; highway, best avenue to a given end

Quotations

"Sow an act, and you reap a habit. Sow a habit, and you reap a character. Sow a character, and you reap a destiny."

Charles Reade (1814–1884), British writer [authenticity unverified]

"There are two things to aim at in life: first, to get what you want; and, after that, to enjoy it. Only the wisest of mankind achieve the second."

Logan Pearsal Smith (1865–1946), U.S. writer, After-Thoughts (1931), "Life and Human Nature"

Classical Phrases and Myths

more suo (Lat)
(MOR-e SU-oh) in his own manner, fashion, habit, etc.

modus operandi (Lat)
(MO-dus OP-er-AND-ee) method of operation

cursus honorum (Lat)
(KUR-sus hon-OR-um) *lit:* course of honors; sequence of posts leading to leadership or authority

Jokes, Stories and Anecdotes

"We shall cross the river here," said an officer, placing his finger on the map before French statesman Duc de Richelieu and his aides as they planned a military campaign. "Excellent, sir," Richelieu replied, "but your finger is not a bridge."

> *Armand-Emmanuel du Plessis, Duc de Richelieu (1766–1822), French statesman*

◆ PATIENCE

Foreign Words and Phrases

tout vient à qui sait attendre (Fra)
(too vyen ah kee set ah-TEHN-dr) everything comes to him who waits

Quotations

"Patience, n. A minor form of despair, disguised as a virtue."

> *Ambrose [Gwinnet] Bierce (1842–c. 1914), U.S. writer and poet,* Devil's Dictionary *(1911)*

"I am extraordinarily patient, provided I get my own way in the end."

> *Margaret Thatcher (1925–   ), British prime minister*

Jokes, Stories and Anecdotes

An expectant father, who sported a week's growth of beard, was seated outside the maternity ward when he was spotted by another expectant father. "Good heavens!" cried the latter. "How long have you been waiting?"

A young musician once complained bitterly to composer Johannes Brahms about delays in getting his first opus published. Brahms counseled him to be patient: "You can afford not to be immortal for a few more weeks."

> *Johannes Brahms (1833–1897), German composer*

◆ PAYMENT (EXPENDITURE)

Foreign Words and Phrases

à compte (Fra)
(ah COM-te) part payment, installment

Quotations

"When some men discharge an obligation, you can hear the report for miles around."

> *Mark Twain [Samuel Langhorne Clemens] (1835–1910), U.S. humorist, writer and speaker*

Classical Phrases and Myths

"Although work ceases, expenses continue."

> *Marcus Porcius Cato [the Elder] (234 B.C.–149 B.C.), Roman statesman,* On Agriculture, *Bk. XXXIX, 2*

Jokes, Stories and Anecdotes

Reaching into his pocket after being presented with his restaurant bill, the customer somehow lost his balance and fell over. To onlookers he said, "The food was delicious—but wait till you get your bill!"

Later to become poet laureate and immortalized in Alexander Pope's *Dunciad* as the quintessential bore, the British actor and dramatist Colley Cibber in his first role on stage merely had to hand a message to a character played by the great Thomas Betterton. Paralyzed with stage fright, he botched the scene. Betterton later angrily demanded the name of the youth who had marred the performance. "Master Colley," was the reply. "Master Colley. Then fine him!" "But, sir, he has no salary." "No?" sulked Betterton. "Then put him down for ten shillings a week and fine him five shillings."

Colley Cibber (1671–1757),
British playwright

◆ PEACE & PACIFICATION

Quotations

"Peace, n. In international affairs, a period of cheating between two periods of fighting."

Ambrose [Gwinnet] Bierce
(1842–c. 1914), U.S. writer and poet,
Devil's Dictionary (1911)

"The quickest way of ending a war is to lose it."

George Orwell [Eric Blair] (1903–1950),
British writer, Polemic (May 1946),
"Second Thoughts on
James Burnham"

Classical Phrases and Myths

si vis pacem para bellum (Lat)
(see wees PAH-kem par-a BEL-lum) if you want peace, prepare for war

pax vobiscum (Lat)
(PAX woh-BIS-kum) peace (be) with you

halcyon (Grk)
(HAL-see-on) *lit:* kingfisher; calm, peaceful

"*Nunc patimur longae pacis mala, sae-vior armis*
Luxuria incubuit victumque ulciscitur orbem." (We are now suffering the evils of a long peace. Luxury, more deadly than war, broods over the city, and avenges a conquered world.)

Juvenal [Decimus Junius Juvenalis]
(c. 50–c. 130), Roman writer,
Satires, VI, l. 292

"*Ubi solitudinem faciunt, pacem appel-lant.*" (OO-bee SOL-ee-TOO-din-em FAK-ee-unt PAH-kem AP-pel-lant) (They create desolation and call it peace.)

Cornelius Tacitus (c. 55–117),
Roman historian, Agricola (c. 98), 30

Jokes, Stories and Anecdotes

On New Year's Eve at London's Garrick Club, Seymour Hicks implored the playwright Freddy Lonsdale to make up after a dispute with another club member: "Go over now and wish him a happy New Year." Freddy approached his antagonist. "I wish you a happy New Year," said Lonsdale, "but only one."

Frederick Lonsdale (1881–1954),
British playwright

◆ PENALTY

Quotations

"No! No! Sentence first, verdict afterwards!"

Lewis Carroll [Charles Lutwidge
Dodgson] (1832–1898), British writer and
mathematician, Alice's Adventures in
Wonderland (1865), ch. 12

"[O]ne is absolutely sickened, not by the crimes that the wicked have committed, but by the punishment that the good have inflicted."

Oscar [Fingal O'Flahertie Wills] Wilde (1854–1900), British playwright, writer and wit

---

◆ PERCEPTIVENESS

Foreign Words and Phrases

a prima vista (Ita)
(ah PREE-ma VEE-stah) at first sight, at first glance

Quotations

"Fleas know not whether they are upon the body of a giant or upon one of ordinary stature."

Walter Savage Landor (1775–1864), British poet and writer, Imaginary Conversations *(1824–1829),* "Southey and Porson"

"The question of common sense is always 'What is it good for?'—a question which would abolish the rose and be answered triumphantly by the cabbage."

James Russell Lowell (1819–1891), U.S. poet

Jokes, Stories and Anecdotes

A young woman was filling out a job application. To the question "Have you ever been arrested?" the applicant wrote "no" in the blank. To the next question, "Why?" intended for those who had been arrested, the unthinking lady wrote, "Never been caught."

The newcomer at the bar bet $200 that he could correctly identify the nature and ingredients of any drink placed before him. Bets were laid and the bartender concocted imaginative new drinks. Yet the man correctly identified the brand of the liquor ingredients, the age of the wines and their vineyards, and the countries of origin. He was accumulating a small fortune. A drunk at the end of the bar was observing closely. Sliding a glass with its amber contents down the bar, he shouted, "Identify that, wise guy." The liquor expert took his usual sip, then spat it out, choking. "That's piss!" "Of course," drawled the drunk, "but *whose?*"

A man rushed into a drugstore and worriedly asked the druggist if she knew how to stop hiccups. The pharmacist, without warning, punched him in the throat. The stunned man angrily demanded that the druggist explain her unusual behavior. "Well," said the druggist, confidently, "you don't have the hiccups now, do you?" "No," replied the coughing man, "but my wife outside in the car still does."

◆ PERFECTION

Foreign Words and Phrases

a merveille (Fra)
(ah mer-VAY) marvelously, wonderfully

pièce de résistance (Fra)
(pyes de ray-SEES-tonse) the highlight of a meal, collection, performance, etc.

Quotations

"Faultless to a fault."

Robert Browning (1812–1889), British poet, The Ring and the Book *(1868–1869), bk. IX, l. 1177*

"By different methods different men excel;

But where is he who can do all things well?"

Charles Churchill (1731–1764), British poet, Epistle to William Hogarth, l. 51

"He has not a single redeeming defect."

Benjamin Disraeli, 1st Earl of Beaconsfield (1804–1881), British prime minister, describing William Ewart Gladstone

"I am an idealist. I don't know where I'm going but I'm on the way."

Carl Sandburg (1878–1967), U.S. poet and writer, Incidentals (1907), p. 8

"There is this difference between the Church of Rome and the Church of England: the one professes to be infallible—the other to be never in the wrong."

Sir Richard Steele (1672–1729), Irish-born British playwright and writer

"Who am I to tamper with a masterpiece?"

Oscar [Fingal O'Flahertie Wills] Wilde (1854–1900), British playwright, writer and wit, protesting changes in one of his plays

"Le mieux est l'ennemi du bien." (leh myuh es lehn-eh-MEE doo byen) (The best is the enemy of the good.)

Voltaire [François Marie Arouet] (1694–1778), French philosopher, writer and wit, Dictionnaire Philosophique (1764), "Art Dramatique"

Classical Phrases and Myths

ad astra (Lat)
(ad AST-ra) to the stars, to the utmost

acme (Grk)
(AK-mee) culmination, point of perfection

Jokes, Stories and Anecdotes

An American singer debuting at La Scala was at first flattered when the discerning Italian audience clapped during the encore for her to sing an aria for the third time. Completely winded, she informed the crowd that she could not sing it again. Declared a member of the audience, "Keep singing it until you sing it right."

In painting a picture of a spirited horse, Nicolas Poussin had repeatedly failed to depict satisfactorily the foam around its mouth. Exasperated, he threw his sponge against the canvas, perfectly creating the effect for which he had labored.

Nicolas Poussin (1594–1665), French painter

In 1965 Nobel laureate and novelist John Steinbeck and his poodle Charlie, passing through San Francisco by car, stopped at a sidewalk cafe with advertising executive Howard Gossage. "Yesterday in Muir Woods, Charlie lifted his leg on a tree that was 50 feet across, a hundred feet high, and a thousand years old," Steinbeck said. "What's left in life for that dog after that supreme moment?"

John Steinbeck (1902–1968), U.S. writer

◆ PERIOD OF TIME

Quotations

"I spent a year in that town, one Sunday."

Warwick Deeping (1877–1950), British writer

"There was a pause—just long enough for an angel to pass, flying slowly."

Ronald Firbank (1886–1926), U.S. writer, Vainglory (1915), ch. 6

Classical Phrases and Myths

pro tempore (Lat)
(proh TEM-po-RAY) temporarily,
for the moment (abbr: pro tem)

Jokes, Stories and Anecdotes

"The Jewish people have observed
their 5749th year as a people," the
Hebrew teacher told his class. "By
comparison, the Chinese have only
observed their 4686th. What does
that mean to you?" There was silence until one boy raised his hand
and said, "That means that the Jews
had to do without Chinese food for
1063 years."

◆ PERMANENCE
(STABILITY)

Quotations

"When it is not necessary to change,
it is necessary not to change."

> *Lucius Cary, Viscount Falkland
> (1610–1643), British statesman,
> A Speech Concerning Episcopacy (1641)*

"*Plus ça change, plus c'est la même
chose.*" (ploo sa shahn-je ploo seh la
mehm shose) (The more things
change, the more they remain the
same.)

> *Alphonse Karr (1808–1890), French
> writer, Les Guêpes (January 1849), vi*

◆ PERPETUITY

Quotations

"Eternity's a terrible thought. I
mean, where's it all going to end?"

> *Tom Stoppard (1937–   ), British
> playwright and writer, Rosencrantz and
> Guildenstern Are Dead (1967), Act II*

Classical Phrases and Myths

in aeternum (Lat)
(in ai-TER-num) forever, eternally

◆ PERSEVERANCE

Foreign Words and Phrases

gaman (Jap)
(GAH-mahn) ability to endure
hardships patiently

Quotations

"Ah, well, there is just this world
and then the next, and then all our
troubles will be over."

> *Anonymous elderly lady quoted by
> L. O. Asquith*

"When I warned them [the French
Government] that Britain would
fight on alone whatever they did,
their generals told their Prime
Minister and his divided Cabinet,
'In three weeks England will have
her neck wrung like a chicken.'
Some chicken! Some neck!"

> *Sir Winston Spencer Churchill
> (1874–1965), British prime minister
> and writer, speech to Canadian
> Parliament, December 30, 1941*

Classical Phrases and Myths

illegitimi non carborundum (mock
Lat)
(il-LEG-ee-TEEM-ee non CARB-or-
UN-dum) don't let the bastards
grind you down (also, nil carborundum illegitimi)

"*Cras ingens iterabimus aequor.*" (Tomorrow we set out once more upon
the boundless sea.)

> *Horace (65 B.C.–8 B.C.), Roman poet,
> Odes, I, vii, l. 32*

Jokes, Stories and Anecdotes

"For the last time, I'm telling you that I won't let you kiss me!" exclaimed the coed. Her date responded, "I knew you'd give up!"

Numerous charities descended upon Harpo Marx while he was visiting New York to appear at benefits. Marx, after being plagued by one woman with 12 calls in two days, wearily agreed to her request. Still, the anxious woman cautiously called to escort him personally to the charity benefit. As they were departing from his hotel suite, the telephone began to ring. "Don't you want to answer it?" she asked Marx. "Why bother?" Marx sighed. "I'm sure it's you again."

Harpo [Arthur] Marx (1893–1964),
U.S. film comedian

◆ PERSONAL APPEARANCE

Quotations

"No man ever was as wise as [Edward] Thurlow looks."

Charles James Fox (1749–1806),
British statesman

"How can the Republican party nominate a man who looks like the bridegroom on a wedding cake?"

Alice Roosevelt Longworth (1884–1980),
U.S. socialite, ridiculing Republican
presidential aspirant Thomas E. Dewey
[authenticity unverified]

"He was very bald . . . with . . . the general look of an elderly fallen angel travelling incognito."

Peter Quennell (1905–),
British writer, describing André Gide,
The Sign of the Fish (1960), ch. 2

"It is not my appearance which now troubles me, it is my disappearance."

Thaddeus Stevens (1792–1868),
U.S. politician and lawyer, replying, near
death, to someone who had remarked on
his appearance

Jokes, Stories and Anecdotes

At a college reunion, one classmate exclaimed, "Jim, you've changed. You had thick, blond hair, but now you're bald. You used to be tan, now you're pale. You were trim, now you're obese. You've changed so much." "But I'm not Jim." "Good grief! You've changed your name, too?"

"Doctor, will the scar show?" asked the young lady. "That, madam," replied the doctor, "is entirely up to you."

The famed attorney Clarence Darrow was often ridiculed for his sloppy appearance. "I go to a better tailor than any of you, and pay more for my clothes," retorted Darrow. "The only difference is that you probably don't sleep in yours."

Clarence Seward Darrow (1857–1938),
U.S. lawyer

After a stage performance, a man came to John Gielgud's dressing room to offer congratulations. "I am so pleased to meet you," said Sir John, recognizing the man's face. "I used to know your son—we were at school together." "I don't have a son," was the chilly reply. "I was at school with you."

Sir John Gielgud (1904–),
British actor

A wild-eyed, Medusa-coiffed man passed the bar in the actor-frequented Lamb's Club at which the sardonic Ring Lardner was drinking. Lardner said nothing when he first spotted the man, but could contain himself no longer when he passed Lardner again: "How do you look when I'm sober?"

Ring [Ringgold Wilmer] Lardner (1885–1933), U.S. writer

"It is nice meeting old friends," said actor Llewellyn Rees, upon first seeing his friend and fellow actor Robert Morley after a long spell. "Many people think I'm dead." "Not if they look closely."

Robert Morley (1908–1992), British actor

◆ PETS

Quotations

"The great pleasure of a dog is that you may make a fool of yourself with him and not only will he not scold you, but he will make a fool of himself too."

Samuel Butler (1835–1902), British writer, Notebooks (1912), ch. 14

"To his dog, every man is Napoleon; hence the constant popularity of dogs."

Aldous Huxley (1894–1963), British writer

"The trouble with a kitten is THAT Eventually it becomes a CAT."

Ogden Nash (1902–1971), U.S. humorist, The Face is Familiar (1940), "The Kitten"

Jokes, Stories and Anecdotes

"I want a dog of which I can be proud," said the socialite. "Does this one have a pedigree?" "If he could talk," replied the kennel owner, "he wouldn't speak to either of us."

The man called the newspaper to place an ad offering $10 for the return of his wife's Pekingese. "That's a high price for a dog," offered the clerk. "Not for this one," said the man. "I strangled it."

"So how do you know your fish are happy? Fish can't talk," countered the dubious woman when her neighbor boasted that his fish liked their new aquarium. The neighbor replied, "Why, they're always wagging their tails."

Mrs. Patrick Campbell, the British actress, tucked her pet Pekingese inside the upper part of her cape in an attempt to smuggle it through customs. "Everything was going splendidly," she later remarked, "until my bosom barked."

Mrs. Patrick [Beatrice] Campbell (1865–1940), British actress

◆ PHILOSOPHY

Quotations

"[Philosophy is] unintelligible answers to insoluble problems."

Henry B[rooks] Adams (1838–1918), U.S. historian

"Truth is the object of philosophy, but not always of philosophers."

John Churton Collins (1848–1908), British writer and scholar

"The first step towards philosophy is incredulity."

Denis Diderot (1713–1784), French philosopher, encyclopediast and writer

"It is a great advantage for a system of philosophy to be substantially true."

George Santayana (1863–1952), Spanish-born U.S. philosopher, poet and writer, The Unknowable (1923), p. 4

"You could read Kant by yourself, if you wanted; but you must share a joke with someone else."

> *Robert Louis [Balfour] Stevenson*
> *(1850–1894), British writer and poet*

"The safest general characterization of the European philosophical tradition is that it consists of a series of footnotes to Plato."

> *Alfred North Whitehead (1861–1947),*
> *British philosopher and mathematician,*
> Process and Reality *(1929), pt. 2, ch. 1*

Classical Phrases and Myths

scepsis (Grk)
(SKEP-sis) *lit:* inquiry, philosophic doubt, sceptical philosophy

"*Amicus Plato, sed magis amica veritas.*" (Plato is dear to me, but dearer still is truth.)

> *Aristotle (384 B.C.–322 B.C.),*
> *Greek philosopher,* Nichomachean Ethics,
> *bk. I, ch. 6 [Latin translation of Greek]*

"*Nihil tam absurde dici potest, quod non dicatur ab aliquo philosophorum.*" (There is nothing so absurd but some philosopher has said it.)

> *Marcus Tullius Cicero (106 B.C.–43 B.C.),*
> *Roman statesman and man of letters,*
> De Divinatione, II, 58

Jokes, Stories and Anecdotes

The university president sighed as he went over the proposed budget. "Why is it that the physics department always requires so much expensive equipment? The mathematics department only asks for paper, pencils and erasers," he said, mournfully. "Even better, the philosophy department doesn't even ask for erasers."

At a party, a social matron overheard guests addressing a particular gentleman as "Doctor," and so she approached him and began reciting her long list of physical ills. "But, madam," the man countered, "I am a doctor of philosophy." "Oh," replied the lady, starting to walk away. "But what kind of disease is philosophy?"

The attendant at a greenhouse in Dresden noticed wild gesturing by a customer and demanded, "Who are you?" The customer, the pessimist Kantian philosopher Arthur Schopenhauer, looked blankly at the attendant and murmured, "If only you could answer that question for me, I would be forever grateful."

> *Arthur Schopenhauer (1788–1860),*
> *German philosopher*

◆ PHOTOGRAPHY & GRAPHIC ARTS

Foreign Words and Phrases

paparazzi (Ita)
(PAP-a-RAZ-zee) free-lance, leech-like celebrity photographers

Quotations

"The camera makes everyone a tourist in other people's reality, and eventually in one's own."

> *Susan Sontag (1933–   ),*
> *U.S. writer,* New York Review
> of Books *(April 18, 1974)*

"My dear Sir, I thank you very much for your letter and your photograph. In my opinion you are more like me than any other of my numerous doubles. I may even say that you resemble me more closely than I do myself. In fact, I intend to use your picture to shave by. Yours thankfully, S. Clemens."

> *Mark Twain [Samuel Langhorne Clemens]*
> *(1835–1910), U.S. humorist, writer and*
> *speaker, replying by form letter to*
> *correspondents claiming to be his double*
> *and sending photographs as proof*

Classical Phrases and Myths

camera obscure (Lat)
(KAM-er-a ob-SKOO-ra) *lit:* darkened room; box with an aperture and a sequence of mirrors by which an image is projected onto a screen (16th-century camera invention)

Jokes, Stories and Anecdotes

Closing the photography session with Winston Churchill on his 80th birthday, a photographer courteously remarked that he hoped he would photograph Churchill on his 100th. "I don't see why not, young man," growled Churchill. "You look reasonably fit to me."

Sir Winston Spencer Churchill (1874–1965), British prime minister and writer

Commissioned to take an official portrait of the pope, photographer Yousuf Karsh had been accompanied to the Vatican by Bishop Fulton Sheen, and was setting up his equipment in the presence of Pope John XXIII. "God knew 77 years ago that someday I would be pope," remarked the uneasy pope to Bishop Sheen. "Why didn't He make me a little more photogenic!"

John XXIII [Angelo Roncalli] (1881–1963), Roman Catholic pope

---

◆ PHYSICAL APPEARANCE

Foreign Words and Phrases

au premier coup d'oeil (Fra)
(oh pre-MYER koo doy) at first glance

Quotations

"Straight trees have crooked roots."

Proverb (c. 1500s)

"Oh, Vanity of vanities!
How wayward the decrees of Fate are;

How very weak the very wise,
How very small the very great are!"

William Makepeace Thackeray (1811–1863), British writer, Vanitas Vanitatum

Classical Phrases and Myths

fortuna nulla fides frontis (Lat)
(for-TOO-nu noo-la FEE-des FRUN-tis) do not trust in appearance; appearances are likely to deceive

prima facie (Lat)
(PREE-ma FAK-ee-e) at first glance, on first sight; prima facie case: one in which initial evidence is thought sufficient to justify further examination and prosecution

Non semper ea sunt quae videntur.
(non SEM-per ay-a sunt kwai WID-en-tur) (Things are not always what they seem.)

Phaedrus (c. 20), Roman fabulist, Fables, bk. IV, l. 5

Jokes, Stories and Anecdotes

A single man and a married couple were marooned on a tiny island whose main feature was a tall palm tree. The men took turns climbing it to search the sea for possible rescuers. Finally, the single man could contain his desires no longer but there was no chance for intimacy, even though the woman seemed willing to satisfy him. Atop the tree one day, the single man had an idea. "Hey, you two," he shouted below. "Stop screwing!" This bewildered the married man, for he was sitting far apart from his wife. The married man was scanning the horizon the next day from atop the tree, and then looked down at the figures below. "I'll be damned," he muttered. "It really does look like they're screwing!"

Horrified by the worn appearance of Sir Douglas-Home on a prerecorded television program she was watching, Lady Douglas-Home rushed upstairs and asked her husband as he was changing, "Are you feeling well? You look dreadful downstairs."

Alec Douglas-Home, Baron Home of the Hirsel (1903–   ), British prime minister

◆ PHYSICIAN

Quotations

"The whole imposing edifice of modern medicine is, like the celebrated tower of Pisa, slightly off balance."

Charles, Prince of Wales (1948–   ), British prince

"While the doctors consult, the patient dies."

English proverb

"God heals, and the doctor takes the fee."

Benjamin Franklin (1706–1790), U.S. statesman and scientist, Poor Richard's Almanac (1732–1757)

"He's a fool that makes his doctor his heir."

Benjamin Franklin (1706–1790), U.S. statesman and scientist, Poor Richard's Almanac (1732–1757)

"Some fell by laudanum, and some by steel,
And death in ambush lay in every pill."

Sir Samuel Garth (1661–1719), British physician and poet, The Dispensary (1699)

"Doctors think a lot of patients are cured who have simply quit in disgust."

Don Herold (1889–   ), U.S. humorist and artist

"What I call a good patient is one who, having found a good physician, sticks to him till he dies."

Oliver Wendell Holmes, Sr. (1809–1894), U.S. writer and physician

"My doctor gave me six months to live but when I couldn't pay the bill he gave me six months more."

Walter Matthau (1920–   ), U.S. film actor

"Either he's dead, or my watch has stopped."

Robert Pirosh (c. 1900s), George Seaton (c. 1900s) and George Oppenheimer (c. 1900s), U.S. writers, A Day at the Races (1937 film)

"Formerly, when religion was strong and science weak, men mistook magic for medicine; now, when science is strong and religion weak, men mistake medicine for magic."

Thomas Szasz (1920–   ), U.S. psychiatrist, The Second Sin (1973) "Science and Scientism"

Classical Phrases and Myths

Hippocrates (hip-POK-rah-teez) of ancient Greece was the first physician to reject customs and beliefs that body effects were the result of supernatural origins, instead believing that they were caused by climate, food and even government. *The Hippocratic oath*, named in honor of the founding father of medicine, expresses a commitment to ethical medical conduct and is signed by physicians beginning the practice of medicine.

Hippocrates (c. 440 B.C.–c. 377 B.C.), Greek physician

Jokes, Stories and Anecdotes

Randolph Churchill, the son of Winston Churchill, who never escaped the shadow of his father's fame, was hospitalized to have a lung removed. It was later announced that the trouble was not "malignant." Commented the English novelist Evelyn Waugh, "It was a typical triumph of modern science to find the only part of Randolph that was not malignant and remove it."

Evelyn Waugh [Arthur St. John] (1903–1966), British writer, Diaries of Evelyn Waugh (1976), "Irregular Notes 1960–69," March 1964 entry

Three men were considering what they would do if told they had but six months to live. Fred said: "If my doctor said I had six months to live I'd cash in everything and visit every prostitute in town." John said: "If my doctor told me I had six months to live, I'd travel around the world." Merv said: "If my doctor told me I had six months to live, I'd consult another doctor."

"He's a family doctor," said Fred to a friend. "He treats mine and I support his."

"I'm sorry," said the heart surgeon, "but you must have a bypass operation." The patient squirmed uneasily. "If you don't mind, I-I'd like a second opinion." "Not at all," replied the surgeon. "You're also ugly as sin."

Doctor with hypodermic needle: "Don't be alarmed. You'll feel a little prick." Patient: "But we just met."

Almost 90, Konrad Adenauer, still chancellor, succumbed to a heavy cold. His personal physician, aggravated by Adenauer's impatience, said, "I'm not a magician. I can't make you young again." "I haven't asked you to," snapped Adenauer.

"All I want is to go on getting older."

Konrad Adenauer (1876–1967), German chancellor

The secretary of wit Dorothy Parker visited her to take dictation on letters while Parker was recuperating in the hospital. "This should assure us," said Parker, pressing the "nurse" button, "of at least 45 minutes of undisturbed privacy."

Dorothy Parker (1893–1967), U.S. wit and writer

As a young man, the British poet laureate Tennyson was successfully treated for hemorrhoids by a young but well-known proctologist. Years later, as a famous poet and a peer of the realm, Tennyson again suffered a painful attack, so he revisited the proctologist. He expected to be recognized because of his fame, but the proctologist was silent until the nobleman bent over for examination and the physician remarked, "Ah, Tennyson."

Alfred Tennyson, 1st Baron Tennyson (1809–1892), British poet

---

◆ PHYSICS

Quotations

"There was a young lady named Bright,
Whose speed was far faster than light;
She set out one day
In a relative way
And returned on the previous night."

Arthur Buller (1874–1944), British writer, Punch (December 13, 1923), "Relativity"

Jokes, Stories and Anecdotes

A basic equation in theoretical physics is "e = h $\sqrt{\ }$," where $\sqrt{\ }$ is the

Greek letter nu (pronounced new). By simple algebraic manipulation, this is equivalent to $\sqrt{} = e/h$. So, "What's new?" could be answered by "e/h".

"So what was so great about Einstein that he should be so famous?" Irving asked his daughter, a physicist. "Well Papa, he developed the theory of relativity, which holds that some things, such as space and time, previously believed to be absolute, are actually relative." "What do you mean?" "Well, for a young man with his sweetheart, an hour might pass like a minute. But if he were sitting on a hot stove, a minute would seem like an hour." Irving stared at his daughter incredulously. "So tell me one more thing—is it from nonsense like this that Einstein made a living?"

One hundred Nazi professors published a book condemning Albert Einstein's theory of relativity after the great physicist had gone into exile. Einstein was untroubled. "If I were wrong," he said, "one professor would have been enough."

Albert Einstein (1879–1955), German-born physicist

◆ PITILESSNESS (CRUELTY)

Quotations

"When Hitler attacked the Jews I was not a Jew, therefore, I was not concerned. And when Hitler attacked the Catholics, I was not a Catholic, and therefore, I was not concerned. And when Hitler attacked the unions and the industrialists, I was not a member of the unions and I was not concerned. Then, Hitler attacked me and the Protestant church—and there was nobody left to be concerned."

Martin Neimoller (1892–1984), German theologian

"Yes, indeed, a good idea, but we will first have a little hanging."

Prince Felix Schwarzenberg (1800–1852), Austrian statesman and diplomat, agreeing to show mercy to captured rebels during the 1849 Hungarian uprising against Austrian domination

"He jests at scars, that never felt a wound."

William Shakespeare (1564–1616), British playwright and poet, Romeo and Juliet (1595), Act I, sc. i

"A single death is a tragedy, a million deaths is a statistic."

Joseph Stalin [Iosif Vissarionovich Dzhugashvili] (1879–1953), Russian statesman [authenticity unverified]

Jokes, Stories and Anecdotes

A Hollywood agent, in the throes of depression with lack of work, was contemplating suicide when suddenly, there was a puff of smoke, a flash of light—and the devil appeared. The devil said to the agent, "I've got a proposition for you. For the remainder of your career, I'll get you exclusive representation of all of the Hollywood *wunderkind*. But in return, your wife and children must die, and their souls shall burn in hell for eternity." The agent answers: "So what's the catch?"

An actor came home from work and was stunned to see that his house had burned to the ground. "What happened?" he asked the nearby fire captain. "Unfortunately," the captain said, "your agent came here several hours ago, raped your wife, murdered your children, and burned down your home." The actor was shocked. "My agent came to my house?!!"

While Louis was playing cards with several court members, a M. de Chauvelin was stricken apoplectic and promptly died. A courtier, seeing him fall, shrieked, "M. de Chauvelin is ill!" Louis turned and coldly surveyed the corpse. "Ill? He is dead," observed the king. "Take him away. Spades are trumps, gentlemen."

Louis XV (1710–1774), French king

◆ PITY

Quotations

"Pity costs nothing, and ain't worth nothing."

Josh Billings [Henry Wheeler Shaw] (1818–1885), U.S. humorist

"To these crocodile's tears, they will add sobs, fiery sighs, and sorrowful countenance."

Robert Burton (1577–1640), British clergyman and writer, The Anatomy of Melancholy (1621–1651), pt. III

"He best can pity who has felt the woe."

John Gay (1685–1732), British poet and playwright, Dione, Act II, sc. ii

"He reminds me of the man who murdered both his parents, and then, when sentence was about to be pronounced, pleaded for mercy on the grounds that he was an orphan."

Abraham Lincoln (1809–1865), U.S. president

"Alas! poor Yorick. I knew him, Horatio; a fellow of infinite jest, of most excellent fancy."

William Shakespeare (1564–1616), British playwright and poet, Hamlet (1601), Act V, sc. i

Jokes, Stories and Anecdotes

A woman was convicted of murdering her longtime husband by lacing his coffee with arsenic. At her sentencing hearing, the defense attorney knew that he had a difficult job in garnering the judge's sympathy for his client. "Was there any time during commission of this crime, Mrs. Jones," the attorney began hopefully, "that you felt pity for your husband?" "Oh, yes," she exclaimed, accepting his hint, "when he asked for a second cup."

When Ethan Allen's notoriously ill-tempered first wife died, a local man offered to help transport the coffin to the church. "You could call on any of the neighbors," he said to Allen. "There's not a man in town wouldn't be glad to help out."

Ethan Allen (1738–1789), U.S. patriot

The violinist Mischa Elman once gave a recital for friends of the family when he was seven, and elegantly played Beethoven's Kreutzer sonata. During one of the many long rests in the composition, one of the elderly ladies tapped him on the shoulder and whispered confidentially, "Play something you know, dear."

Mischa Elman (1891–1967), Russian-born U.S. violinist [attributed also to others]

◆ PLAIN SPEECH

Foreign Words and Phrases

c'est a dire (Fra)
(sehl ah DEER) that is to say; in other words

Jokes, Stories and Anecdotes

President Lincoln was being guided by the commanding general's aide,

298

Oliver Wendell Holmes, Jr., on an inspection of Union defenses at Fort Stevens while it was under siege. Lincoln, wearing his customary tall hat, rose for a better view when Holmes was showing the enemy trenches. At once there was a crackle of fire from Confederate lines. "Get down, you fool!" shouted Holmes, pulling the president under cover. He then realized what he had said, and worried that disciplinary action would be exacted. But when Lincoln left, he only commented, "Goodbye, Captain Holmes. I am pleased to see that you know how to talk to a civilian."

> *Abraham Lincoln (1809–1865),*
> *U.S. president*

◆ PLANNING & EXECUTION

Foreign Words and Phrases

cy prés (Fra)
(SEE-pray) in law, the attempt to execute a person's wishes as closely as possible even when the instructions (e.g., in a will) cannot be followed exactly

Quotations

"The best laid schemes o' mice an' men
Gang aft a-gley,
An' lea'e us nought but grief an' pain,
For promis'd joy!"

> *Robert Burns (1759–1796), British poet,*
> *To a Mouse (1782), l. 7*

"This very remarkable man
Commends a most practical plan:
You can do what you want
If you don't think you can't,

So don't think you can't think you can."

> *Charles Inge (1868–1957), British poet,*
> *Weekend Book (1928),*
> *"On Monsieur Coué"*

"Though this be madness, yet there is method in it."

> *William Shakespeare (1564–1616),*
> *British playwright and poet,*
> *Hamlet (1601), Act II, sc. ii*

"Procrastination is the thief of time."

> *Edward Young (1683–1765), British poet,*
> *Night Thoughts (1742–1745),*
> *"Night I," l. 393*

"For her own breakfast she'll project a scheme,
Nor take her tea without a stratagem."

> *Edward Young (1683–1765), British poet,*
> *Love of Fame (1725–1728),*
> *satire VI, l. 187*

◆ PLEASURE

Foreign Words and Phrases

mechaieh (Yid)
(ma-KEE-yah) a great pleasure

aware (Jap)
(ah-WAHR-ay) pleasure engendered by ephemeral beauty, e.g., by the blooming of cherry blossoms

nakhes (Yid)
(NAHK-hes) mixed pleasure and pride, especially of parent for a child

la dolce vita (Ita)
(lah DOL-che VEE-tah) the good life (in English, often pejorative)

Quotations

"A man hath no better thing under the sun, than to eat, and to drink, and to be merry."

> *Ecclesiastes 8:15*

"But pleasures are like poppies spread—
You seize the flow'r, its bloom is shed;
Or like the snow falls in the river—
A moment white—then melts forever."

> *Robert Burns (1759–1796), British poet,*
> *Tam o' Shanter (1793), l. 59*

"Pleasure is nothing else but the intermission of pain."

> *John Selden (1584–1654), British jurist*
> *and scholar, Table Talk (1892), "Law"*

"*Wer nicht liebt Wein, Weib und Gesang,*
Der bleibt ein Narr sein Leben lang."
(Who loves not woman, wine, and song
Remains a fool his whole life long.)

> *Martin Luther (1483–1546),*
> *German Protestant theologian*
> *[authenticity unverified]*

Classical Phrases and Myths

"No pleasure endures unseasoned by variety."

> *Publilius Syrus (c. 100 B.C.),*
> *Roman writer, Sententiae, 406*

Epicurus (ep-i-KYUR-us) was an Athenian philosopher from Samos who taught that fulfillment lay in pleasure—freedom from pain and peace of body and mind—and the absence of religious superstition and of the fear of death. He advocated moderation but his name later became associated with the unfettered meaning of pleasure. Hence, an epicurean is one living for pleasure, a hedonist.

> *Epicurus (c. 342 B.C.–270 B.C.),*
> *Greek philosopher*

Jokes, Stories and Anecdotes

After his film career, Groucho Marx was host of a popular television program in the 1950s, "You Bet Your Life." The routine for the show, of which much was typically cut prior to broadcast, consisted of Marx interviewing his guests before playing the game. Once, Marx was eliciting biographical information from one contestant, Mrs. Story, who proudly announced that she had 22 children. When Marx naturally expressed surprise, Mrs. Story defensively proclaimed, "I love my husband very much." "I love my cigar, too," Groucho drawled, "but I take it out once in a while."

> *Groucho [Julius] Marx (1895–1977),*
> *U.S. comedian*

◆ POETRY

Quotations

"I won't be able to stand here much longer, unless you put some fire into your verses or some of your verses into the fire."

> *Anonymous, established writer to an*
> *aspiring poet reading his pallid verses*

"It is a sad fact about our culture that a poet can earn much more money writing or talking about his art than he can by practising it."

> *W[ystan] H[ugh] Auden (1907–1973),*
> *British-born poet, Dyer's Hand*
> *(1963), foreword*

"The mind that finds its way to wild places is the poet's; but the mind that never finds its way back is the lunatic's."

> *G[ilbert] K[eith] Chesterton (1874–1936),*
> *British man of letters*

"Sir, I admit your general rule,
That every poet is a fool,

But you yourself may serve to show it,
That every fool is not a poet."

Samuel Taylor Coleridge (1772–1834),
British poet and writer

"Idleness, that is the curse of other men, is the nurse of poets."

Walter D'Arcy Cresswell
(1896–   ), British poet

"Immature poets imitate; mature poets steal."

T[homas] S[tearns] Eliot (1888–1965),
U.S. poet, Sacred Wood (1920),
"Philip Massinger"

"Twenty-five percent read me for the right reasons; 25 percent like me for the wrong reasons; 25 percent hate me for the right reasons. It's that last 25 percent that worries me."

Robert Lee Frost (1874–1963), U.S. poet

"[P]laying tennis with the net down."

Robert Lee Frost (1874–1963), U.S. poet,
defining free verse

"There's no money in poetry, but then there's no poetry in money either."

Robert [Ranke] Graves (1895–1985),
British poet and writer, speech at London
School of Economics, December 6, 1963

"To be a poet is a condition rather than a profession."

Robert [Ranke] Graves (1895–1985),
British poet and writer

"Your works will be read after Shakespeare and Milton are forgotten, and not till then."

Richard Porson (1759–1808),
British scholar, giving his opinion
to poet Robert Southey

"Very nice, though there are dull stretches."

Antoine Rivaroli, Comte de Rivarol
(1753–1801), French writer, reviewing a
two-line poem

"Poetry is to prose as dancing is to walking."

John Wain (1925–   ), British poet,
BBC radio broadcast, January 11, 1976

Jokes, Stories and Anecdotes

While Walter Lowenfels was bombasting at length on his views on the relationship of art and the decadence of society, playwright and friend Samuel Beckett listened without a word. Finally, Lowenfels burst out, "You just sit there saying nothing while the world is going to pieces. What do you want to do?" "Walter," sighed Beckett, "all I want to do is sit on my ass and fart and think of Dante."

Samuel Beckett (1906–1989), Irish writer,
playwright and poet

Robert Frost and other guests went outside to the veranda to watch the sunset following a dinner party. "Oh, Mr. Frost, isn't it a lovely sunset?" exclaimed one young woman. Frost replied, "I never discuss business after dinner."

Robert Lee Frost (1874–1963), U.S. poet

◆ POLITICAL & ECONOMIC THEORY

Foreign Words and Phrases

Realpolitik (Ger)
(ray-AL-po-li-TEEK) theory of politics shunning idealism and based on realism; politics of pragmatism

laissez faire (Fra)
(LESS-ay fehr) *lit:* allow to do; nonaction; the doctrine of governmental noninterference

Quotations

"When a nation's young men are conservative, its funeral bell is already rung."

Henry Ward Beecher (1813–1887), U.S. clergyman and writer

"The greatest happiness of the greatest number is the foundation of morals and legislation."

Jeremy Bentham (1748–1832), British philosopher

"Men are conservatives when they are least vigorous, or when they are most luxurious. They are conservatives after dinner."

Ralph Waldo Emerson (1803–1882), U.S. writer, poet and philosopher, Essays: Second Series (1844), "New England Reformers"

"Some fellows get credit for being conservative when they are only stupid."

Frank McKinney ["Kin"] Hubbard (1868–1930), U.S. humorist and writer

"What is conservatism? Is it not adherence to the old and tried, against the new and untried?"

Abraham Lincoln (1809–1865), U.S. president, speech at Cooper Union, February 27, 1860

"Communism is like prohibition, it's a good idea but it won't work."

Will[iam Penn Adair] Rogers (1879–1935), U.S. comedian, Weekly Articles (1981), vol. 3, p. 9

"I am reminded of four definitions: A Radical is a man with both feet firmly planted—in the air. A Conservative is a man with two perfectly good legs who, however, has never learned to walk forward. A Reactionary is a somnambulist walking backwards. A Liberal is a man who uses his legs and his hands at the behest—at the command—of his head."

Franklin Delano Roosevelt (1882–1945), U.S. president, radio address to New York Herald Tribune forum, October 26, 1939

Classical Phrases and Myths

salus populi suprema lex est (Lat) (SA-lus POP-oo-lee sup-RAY-ma lex est) the safety of the people is the supreme law; utilitarian belief that the only standard by which government can be measured is its impact on the material welfare of the governed

Jokes, Stories and Anecdotes

The widow of King Albert I of Belgium, Elisabeth, made a state visit in 1956 to Soviet-dominated Warsaw. She was assigned a chief of protocol to accompany her to Mass, and asked him, "Are you a Catholic?" "Believing, but not practicing." "Of course," said Elisabeth to the functionary, "so in that case you must be a Communist." "Practicing, Your Majesty, but not believing."

Elisabeth (1876–1965), Belgian queen

◆ POLITICIAN

Foreign Words and Phrases

politico (Ita) (po-LEE-tee-koh) politician, opportunist

revanchiste (Fra) (re-VANJH-sheest) political advocate of violent (vengeful) measures

Quotations

"I will undoubtedly have to seek what is happily known as gainful employment, which I am glad to say does not describe holding public office."

Dean Acheson [Gooderham] (1893–1971), U.S. diplomat, explaining his future plans after leaving his post as secretary of state

"The first requirement of a statesman is that he be dull. This is not always easy to achieve."

Dean Acheson [Gooderham] (1893–1971), U.S. diplomat

"Vote for the man who promises least; he'll be the least disappointing."

Bernard Mannes Baruch (1870–1965), U.S. financier and statesman

"The recumbents were re-elected. The rascals were not turned out by those who turned out. Same old House of Reprehensibles."

Herbert Eugene Caen (1917–   ), U.S. writer

"An honest politician is one who, when he is bought, will stay bought."

Simon Cameron (1799–1889), U.S. writer

"It is the ability to foretell what is going to happen tomorrow, next week, next month, and next year. And to have the ability afterwards to explain why it didn't happen."

Sir Winston Spencer Churchill (1874–1965), British prime minister and writer, explaining the desirable qualifications for a politician

"Mr. Chamberlain loves the working man; he loves to see him work."

Sir Winston Spencer Churchill (1874–1965), British prime minister and writer, describing Sir Joseph Chamberlain

"He's running for the office of ex-President, and he's won."

John Wesley Dean (1932–   ), U.S. lawyer, describing the elder statesman image of ex-President Richard Nixon

"People say he was like the banyan tree: nothing and nobody grew under his shadow. They are wrong. He was like the sun and let everything and everybody grow—even the weeds."

Indira Gandhi (1917–1984), Indian politician, reminiscing about her father, Jawaharlal Nehru.

"He was a power politically for years, but he has never got prominent enough to have his speeches garbled."

Frank McKinney ["Kin"] Hubbard (1868–1930), U.S. humorist and writer

"When a man assumes a public trust, he should consider himself as public property."

Thomas Jefferson (1743–1826), U.S. president, remark to Baron von Humboldt, 1807

"A statesman is a politician who is held upright by equal pressure from all directions."

Eric A[llen] Johnston (1896–1963), U.S. businessman

"Once there was a poor widow who had two sons. One ran away to sea, and the other became Vice President. Neither was ever heard from again."

Thomas Riley Marshall (1854–1925), U.S. vice president

"The most successful politician is he who says what everybody is thinking most often and in the loudest voice."

Theodore Roosevelt (1858–1919), U.S. president

"He knows nothing; and he thinks he knows everything. That points clearly to a political career."

George Bernard Shaw (1856–1950), Irish playwright, Major Barbara (1907), Act III

"My choice early in life was either to be a piano-player in a whorehouse or a politician. And to tell the truth, there's hardly any difference."

Harry S Truman (1884–1972),
U.S. president

"Reader, suppose you were an idiot. And suppose you were a member of Congress. But I repeat myself."

Mark Twain [Samuel Langhorne Clemens]
(1835–1910), U.S. humorist,
writer and speaker

"*Comme un homme politique ne croit jamais ce qu'il dit, il est tout etonne quand il est cru sur parole.*" (Since a politician never believes what he says, he is quite surprised to be taken at his word.)

Charles André Joseph Marie de Gaulle
(1890–1970), French president and general

Classical Phrases and Myths

Known for his unimpeachable honesty and for never pandering to the popular will, the great Athenian statesman Phocion once delivered an opinion that was unanimously approved. The shocked Phocion remarked to a friend, "Can it be that I am making a bad argument without knowing it?"

Phocion (c. 402 B.C.-318 B.C.),
Greek statesman and general

Jokes, Stories and Anecdotes

"What should we do about the abortion bill?" hollered the legislative aide from the other room. "Well," spluttered the congressman, "I suppose we ought to pay it."

Q: Why would a politician abandon an unpopular platform? A: Not due to seeing the light, but feeling the heat.

Winston Churchill entered the men's room in the House of Commons, and found Clement Attlee already standing at the urinal. Churchill positioned himself at the opposite end of the urinal. Taunted Atlee, "Feeling standoffish today, are we, Winston?" "Quite right," retorted Churchill. "Every time you see something big, you want to nationalize it."

Sir Winston Spencer Churchill (1874–
1965), British prime minister and writer

On Jack Paar's "Tonight Show" Malcolm Muggeridge allowed that despite his disdain for politics he had voted only once in his life. "I just had to," he explained. "There was this one candidate who had been committed to an asylum and upon discharge was issued a Certificate of Sanity. Well, now, how could I resist? What other politician anywhere has an actual medical report that he is sane?"

Malcolm Muggeridge (1903–1990),
British writer and broadcaster

President Coolidge, on the presidential yacht cruising the Potomac with guests, was standing alone at the railing overlooking the expanse of water, when someone exclaimed, "Bowed over the rail. What thoughts are in the mind of this man, burdened by the problems of the nation?" Coolidge finally rejoined the others, saying, "See that sea gull over there? Been watching it for 20 minutes: Hasn't moved. I think he's dead!"

[John] Calvin Coolidge (1872–1933),
U.S. president

◆ POLITICS

Foreign Words and Phrases

qualunquismo (Ita)
(kwal-un-KEES-moh) political and social indifference

raison d'état (Fra)
(ray-ZON day-TAH) lit: reason of state (security); used to justify actions

Weltpolitik (Ger)
(VELT-po-li-TEEK) theory that politics is global in scale

Quotations

"It doesn't matter who you vote for, the government always gets in."

John Bright (1811–1889), British politician, commenting on Benjamin Disraeli

"Th' dimmycratic party ain't on speakin' terms with itsilf."

Finley Peter Dunne (1867–1936), U.S. writer and humorist, Mr. Dooley's Opinions (1900), "Mr. Dooley Discusses Party Politics"

"Politics is not the art of the possible. It consists in choosing between the disastrous and the unpalatable."

John Kenneth Galbraith (1908–1992), Canadian-born U.S. economist and diplomat, letter to John F. Kennedy, March 2, 1962

"Don't buy a single vote more than necessary. I'll be damned if I'm going to pay for a landslide."

Joseph Patrick Kennedy (1888–1969), U.S. businessman and diplomat, telegramming instructions to his son, presidential candidate John F. Kennedy

"Any party which takes credit for the rain must not be surprised if its opponents blame it for the drought."

Dwight W. Morrow (1873–1931), U.S. lawyer and politician

"Politics has got so expensive that it takes lots of money to even get beat with."

Will[iam Penn Adair] Rogers (1879–1935), U.S. comedian, syndicated newspaper article, June 28, 1931

"Public life is the paradise of voluble windbags."

George Bernard Shaw (1856–1950), Irish playwright

"Politics is perhaps the only profession for which no preparation is thought necessary."

Robert Louis [Balfour] Stevenson (1850–1894), British writer and poet, Familiar Studies of Men and Books (1882)

"I just hold my nose and mark the ballot."

Frank Underhill (c. 1900s), Canadian citizen, answering how he could bear to vote Liberal (1967)

Classical Phrases and Myths

"*Homo si politikon zoon.*" (hoh-MOH si pol-IT-i-kon ZOH-on) (Man is by nature a political animal.)

Aristotle (384 B.C.-322 B.C.), Greek philosopher, Politics, bk. I, ch. 2

Ancient Greek philosopher Thales was taunted by lesser minds because, for all his wisdom, he had not accumulated any wealth. One year Thales, relying on his knowledge of meteorology, purchased all the olive presses in Miletus before predicting a bumper crop of olives. He charged high prices for his monopoly of presses, and in one season became extremely wealthy. Thales then sold all the presses again and returned to philosophy, having achieved his purpose.

Thales (c. 640 B.C.-c. 546 B.C.), Greek philosopher

Jokes, Stories and Anecdotes

When *National Review* editor and author William F. Buckley ran for mayor of New York City in 1965, his campaign was not taken very seriously, even by Buckley himself, because of his virtually nonexistent chances of election. When a reporter asked him what his first action would be if elected, Buckley answered, "I'd demand a recount."

William F[rank] Buckley (1925–), U.S. editor, writer and speaker

During the presidential race between Andrew Jackson and Martin Van Buren, a voter at a political rally cried out: "Three cheers for Jackson!" A Van Buren supporter shouted back: "Three cheers for a jackass!" "We won't quarrel," shouted the first. "You cheer for your man and I'll cheer for mine."

Andrew Jackson (1767–1845), U.S. president

Senator Claude Pepper of Florida was the victim of either political dirty tricks or the ignorance of his constituency. His opponent, George A. Smathers, in the 1950 senatorial election, cleverly "nonslandered" the politician by playing to the public's incomplete vocabulary and knee-jerk bigotry, thereby pulling votes away from Pepper in a landslide. He accused Pepper of indulging in celibacy, practicing nepotism, having a thespian sister and having a latent tendency toward overt extraversion. (Pepper went on to enjoy a long, illustrious career in the U.S. House of Representatives.)

Claude Denison Pepper (1900–1989), U.S. politician

A supporter said to Adlai Stevenson while he was the Democratic candidate for president, "Governor, every thinking person will be voting for you." "Madam," replied Stevenson, "that is not enough. I need a majority."

Adlai E[wing] Stevenson (1900–1965), U.S. politician

◆ POLLUTION

Jokes, Stories and Anecdotes

You know that pollution is bad when the leaves don't fall, they jump.

◆ POPULARITY & FAME (CELEBRITY)

Foreign Words and Phrases

enfant gité (Fra)
(on-FON GAH-tay) *lit:* spoilt child; one who receives undue flattery and attention

Quotations

"The celebrity is a person who is known for his well-knownness."

Daniel J. Boorstin (1914–), U.S. scholar and writer, The Image (1961), ch. 2

Joe Gillis (William Holden): "You used to be in pictures. You used to be big." Norma Desmond (Gloria Swanson): "I am big. It's the pictures that got small."

Charles Brackett (1892–1969), U.S. writer, Billy [Samuel] Wilder (1906–), U.S. director and writer, and D. M. Marshman Jr. (c. 1900s), U.S. writer, Sunset Boulevard (1950 film)

"I don't care what you say about me, as long as you say something about me, and as long as you spell my name right."

George M. Cohan (1878–1942), U.S. playwright, actor and songwriter, commenting to a reporter seeking information about Cohan's musical Broadway Jones, 1912

"Popularity? It's glory's small change."

> *Victor [Marie] Hugo (1802–1885),*
> *French poet, writer and playwright,*
> *Ruy Blas (1838), Act III, sc. v*

"Fourteen heart attacks and he had to die in my week. In MY week."

> *Janis Joplin (1943–1970), U.S. singer,*
> *commenting when the scheduling of her*
> *photograph for the front cover of*
> Newsweek *was displaced by*
> *Dwight D. Eisenhower's death*

"The nice thing about being a celebrity is that when you bore people, they think it's their fault."

> *Henry Kissinger (1923–),*
> *U.S. diplomat*

"In the future everyone will be famous for fifteen minutes."

> *Andy Warhol (1927–1987), U.S. artist,*
> Andy Warhol's Exposures *(1979),*
> *"Studio 54"*

"What rage for fame attends both great and small!
Better be damned than mentioned not at all!"

> *John Wolcot [Peter Pindar] (1738–1819),*
> *British poet,* To the Royal
> Academicians *(1782–1785)*

Jokes, Stories and Anecdotes

The film actress Ina Claire was briefly married to John Gilbert, the silent screen romantic hero. Asked during the marriage how it felt being married to a celebrity, Claire suggested, "Why don't you ask my husband?"

> *Ina Claire (1895–1985), U.S. film actress*

Film actress Joan Crawford, upon exiting New York's "21" one pleasant, sunny day, decided to walk home. "But, madam," her chauffeur warned her, "you'll be mobbed." Replied Crawford, "I should certainly hope so."

> *Joan Crawford (1904–1977),*
> *U.S. film actress*

The president of the University of Tennessee at Chattanooga did not at first recognize the English scholar John Erskine, who was visiting to give a lecture, when they were to meet at the train station. At dinner that evening, the president informed Erskine, "I asked one gentleman if he were John Erskine and he sternly said, 'I should say not.' Another I asked said, 'I wish I were.' Which demonstrates that at least one man had read your books." "It does indeed," mused Erskine, "but which one?"

> *John Erskine (1879–1951),*
> *U.S. educator and writer*

"Tell them who you are," suggested actor Gregory Peck's companion after they could not find a table at a crowded restaurant. "If you have to tell them who you are," Peck reasoned, "you aren't anybody."

> *Gregory Peck (1916–),*
> *U.S. film actor*

◆ POSTERITY

Quotations

" 'We are always doing', says he, 'something for Posterity, but I would fain see Posterity do something for us.' "

> *Joseph Addison (1672–1719),*
> *British writer and politician,*
> The Spectator *(August 27, 1714)*

"Posterity is as likely to be wrong as anybody else."

> *Heywood Broun (1888–1939),*
> *U.S. writer,* Sitting on the World *(1924),*
> *"The Last Review"*

"I do not think this poem will reach its destination."

> Voltaire [François-Marie Arouet] (1694–1778), French philosopher, writer, and wit, giving his opinion of Ode to Posterity to its author, Jean Jacques Rousseau

Classical Phrases and Myths

non omnis moriar (Lat)
(nohn OM-nis MOR-ee-ahr) *lit:* I shall not die entirely; I leave something for posterity

"*Serit abores quae alteri seculo prosint.*" (He plants trees for another generation.)

> Caecilius Statius (220 B.C.-168 B.C.), Roman writer, Synephebi

◆ POVERTY

Quotations

"I was so broke I couldn't afford lint for my empty pockets."

> Sonny [Salvatore] Bono (1943–   ), U.S. entertainer and politician, And the Beat Goes On (1992)

"When I was a kid, I was so poor ... that in my neighborhood, the rainbow was in black and white."

> Rodney Dangerfield [Jacob Cohen] (1921–   ), U.S. comedian

"I used to think I was poor. Then they told me I wasn't poor, I was needy. Then they told me it was self-defeating to think of myself as needy, I was deprived. Then they told me deprived was a bad image, I was underprivileged. Then they told me underprivileged was overused, I was disadvantaged. I still

don't have a dime. But I sure have a great vocabulary."

> Jules Feiffer (1929–   ), U.S. cartoonist

"I'm living so far beyond my income that we may almost be said to be living apart."

> Saki [Hector Hugh Munro] (1870–1916), British writer, Chronicles of Clovis (1914), "The Match-Maker"

"There were times my pants were so thin I could sit on a dime and tell if it was heads or tails."

> Spencer Tracy (1900–1967), U.S. film actor

Jokes, Stories and Anecdotes

What's the difference between a savings and loan executive and a pigeon? A pigeon can still make deposits on a Rolls-Royce.

◆ POWER

Foreign Words and Phrases

puissance (Fra)
(pwee-sahnce) power, influence, force; dressage event

juggernaut (Ger)
(JOOG-ehr-nowt) powerful thing

Quotations

"President Nixon says presidents can do almost anything, and President Nixon has done many things that nobody would have thought of doing."

Golda Meir (1898–1978), U.S.-born Israeli prime minister

"One, on God's side, is a majority."

Wendell Phillips (1811–1884), U.S. social reformer, speech November 1, 1859

◆ PRACTICAL JOKE

Foreign Words and Phrases

farçeur (Fra)
(fahr-SUHR) buffoon, joker

Jokes, Stories and Anecdotes

The Catholic mystic poet Paul Claudel once tried unsuccessfully to convert the novelist and leader of French liberal thought, André Gide. A few days after the free-thinking Gide's death in February 1951, a telegram bearing Gide's signature appeared on a bulletin board in a hall of the Sorbonne: "Hell does not exist. Notify Claudel."

André Gide (1869–1951), French writer

English Conservative the Earl of Halifax shared a train compartment with two priggish-looking strangers while traveling to Bath. The journey passed in silence. In the total darkness as the train passed through a tunnel, Halifax loudly kissed his hand. After the train had emerged from the tunnel, Halifax asked the matrons, "To which charming lady am I indebted for the lovely affair in the tunnel?"

Edward Frederick Lindley Wood, Earl of Halifax (1881–1959), British statesman and diplomat

Insulted by a Mrs. Tottenham, who lived on the fashionable Berners Street in London, the young Theodore Hook instigated his most fa-

mous practical joke. Hook mailed numerous invitations, on various pretexts, to people from all walks of life to visit her home at the same appointed time. Hook and his friends watched as everyone from the Lord Mayor of London and the Duke of Gloucester to chimney sweeps and tradesmen converged upon the hapless Mrs. Tottenham's house, reducing the usually prosaic Berners Street to a chaotic mess.

Theodore Edward Hook (1788–1841), British writer and wit

◆ PRECEDENT

Foreign Words and Phrases

apéritif (Fra)
(ah-peh-ree-TEEF) *lit:* appetizer; drink taken before a meal

hors d'oeuvre (Fra)
(or DUH-vre) *lit:* outside the work; extra dish usually served before a meal

Classical Phrases and Myths

vestigia (Lat)
(WEST-i-gee-ah) *lit:* footprints; traces, remains

ante bellum (Lat)
(AN-tay BEL-tum) the period (and climate of opinion) before a war (esp. the American Civil War)

Jokes, Stories and Anecdotes

"What were you before you were drafted?" demanded the drill instructor on the first day of boot camp. Replied the recruit, "Happy, sir."

Dorothy Parker once encountered Clare Boothe Brokaw, later Clare Boothe Luce, in the lobby of *Vanity Fair's* offices. "Age before beauty," said the sharp-tongued Brokaw, stepping aside. "Pearls before swine," replied Parker, gliding through.

Dorothy Parker (1893–1967), U.S. wit and writer [authenticity controverted]

◆ **PREDICTION (PREMONITION)**

Classical Phrases and Myths

absit omen (Lat)
(AB-sit OH-men) may it not be an omen; God forbid

Julius Caesar was warned by the augur Spurinna early in March of 44 B.C. that a great danger would befall him on the Ides of that month. On the Ides, Caesar was going as usual to the Senate house. As he passed Spurinna, Caesar said, smiling, "The Ides of March have come." "True, they have come," replied Spurinna, "but not yet gone." Caesar was assassinated later that day.

Gaius Julius Caesar (100 B.C.–44 B.C.), Roman general and statesman

The grandfather of Cyrus (SIE-rus), Astyages, king of the Medes, had a dream that caused him to fear that his grandson would usurp his throne, so he ordered Harpagus to kill the grandson at birth. Harpagus, unable to commit the murder, gave the infant to a herdsman, Mitradates, to leave for dead in the mountains. Mitradates took the infant to his home, where his wife, having just given birth to a stillborn son, pleaded for the life of the infant. They dressed the stillborn in the robes of little Cyrus and left him on the mountain, and Astyages received the hoped-for report of his grandson's death. Cyrus grew up to be a leader among men under the loving care of his foster parents. In 549 B.C., Cyrus, after conquering other lands, and encouraged by Harpagus, who had spared his life, led a revolt by the Persians against their Median masters and conquered his grandfather Astyages, thus realizing the old king's dream.

Cyrus II [Cyrus the Great] (d. 529 B.C.), Persian king

In ancient Greece, Delphi (DEL-fie) was the site in Phocis of the famous oracle of Pythian Apollo, whose pithy, cryptic answers from the priestess tended to be double-edged and figured greatly in Greek myth and legend. Hence, anything characterized as delphic is ambiguous or enigmatic.

Jokes, Stories and Anecdotes

When an astrologer correctly predicted that a lady at the court would die within eight days, Louis XI, a devout believer in astrology, was duly impressed. But he was convinced that the too accurate prophet was dangerous, so he plotted to have the man killed. "You claim to understand astrology and to know the fate of others," Louis said to the astrologer as he was being restrained. "Any last prediction about your own life?" "I shall die three days before Your Majesty," answered the astrologer. His life was spared.

Louis XI (1423–1483), French king

◆ **PREFERENCE**

Quotations

"Thomas's Guide to Practical Shipbuilding."

G[ilbert] K[eith] Chesterton (1874–1936), British man of letters, answering what books he would most like to have with him if he were stranded on a desert island.

Classical Phrases and Myths

"Quod enim mavult homo verum esse, id potius credit." (For what a man had rather were true he more readily believes.)

Francis Bacon (1561–1626),
British lawyer and writer,
Novum Organum (1620)

◆ PREJUDGMENT

Quotations

"Something I once critically wrote about him so prejudiced me against him that I have never read a word he's written."

Oliver Herford (1863–1935), British-born U.S. humorist and illustrator, answering what he thought of Arnold Bennett's work

Classical Phrases and Myths

"In the event of dispute, never dare to judge until you have heard the other side."

Euripides (480 B.C.-406 B.C.),
Greek playwright,
Heraclidae (c. 428 B.C.)

◆ PRESENCE

Quotations

"He regretted that he was not a bird, and could not be in two places at once."

Sir Boyle Roche (1743–1807),
British politician [authenticity unverified]

Classical Phrases and Myths

adsum (Lat)
(ad-SUM) lit: to be present; "I am present" (answer to roll call)

Jokes, Stories and Anecdotes

Lamenting the sparse attendance at PTA meetings, the PTA bulletin read: "This . . . is . . . the . . . way . . . the . . . meetings . . . sometimes look . . . to . . . the . . . principal . . . when . . . he . . . goes . . . to . . . the . . . meetings."
"Wouldlooklikethisifeverybodyattendedthemeetings."

◆ PRETEXT

Foreign Words and Phrases

arriè re-pensée (Fra)
(ahr-ree-EHR-pon-SAY) *lit:* behind thought; mental reservation; ulterior motive

Quotations

"When a fellow says it hain't the money but the principle o' the thing, it's th' money."

Frank McKinney ["Kin"] Hubbard (1868–1930), U.S. humorist and writer,
Hoss Sense and Nonsense (1926)

"Won't you come into the garden? I would like my roses to see you."

Richard Brinsley Sheridan (1751–1816),
Irish-born British playwright and politician, making an invitation to a young woman [authenticity unverified]

Jokes, Stories and Anecdotes

Pleaded the forgetful husband to his wife: "You can't expect me to remember your birthday when you never look any older."

A farmer asked a neighbor if he might borrow a rope. "Oh, I wish I could," replied the neighbor, "but the rope you requested cannot be given, for I use it to tie up milk."
"But milk cannot be tied up with rope!" "True, but when one does

not want to do something, any reason will do."

The boss asked the employee, "Do you believe in life after death?" "Sure do, ma'am." "Well, that makes sense, then," replied the boss, "because after you left for your father's funeral Friday, he came here to see you."

Lord Charles Beresford, a close friend of the Prince of Wales, later Edward VII, reportedly declined a late dinner invitation from the prince by cabling: "Very sorry can't come. Lie follows by post."

> *Lord Charles Beresford (1846–1919),*
> *British aristocrat [attributed*
> *also to others]*

◆ PRICE (FEE)

Foreign Words and Phrases

au prix cofitant (Fra)
(oh pree koo-TON) at cost price

prix d'ami (Fra)
(pree dah-MEE) special price for a friend

Classical Phrases and Myths

ad valorem (Lat)
(ad wal-OR-em) according to the value (of goods, etc.)

"Pro tali mumismate tales merces."
(pro TAL-ee MUM-is-mat-ay TAL-es MER-kes) (You get what you pay for.)

> *Gabriel Biel (c. 1425–1495),*
> *French clergyman, Expositio Canonis*
> *Missae, lectio LXXXVI*

Everything is worth what its purchaser will pay for it."

> *Publilius Syrus (c. 100 B.C.),*
> *Roman writer, Sententiae, 847*

Jokes, Stories and Anecdotes

A woman was trying on hats and asked the clerk, "How much is that big hat?" "$40," replied the clerk. "And that small hat there?" "$100." "And for that eansie one?" "$150." Asked the puzzled customer, "How much if I don't buy a hat at all?"

An airport official got into a heated exchange with Igor Stravinsky, the famed composer, insisting that Stravinsky pay an excess-weight charge. When the official began his rote explanation for the charge, Stravinsky exploded, "I quite understand the logic of it—what I am objecting to is the money."

> *Igor Feodorovitch Stravinsky (1882–1971),*
> *Russian-born composer*

The artist James Whistler had ordered some blank canvases that had been lost in the mail. Asked whether the canvases were of any great value, Whistler said, "Not yet, not yet."

> *James Abbott McNeill Whistler*
> *(1834–1903), U.S.-born British painter*

◆ PRIDE

Foreign Words and Phrases

maestoso (Ita)
(mah-ess-TOH-soh) in music, majestically, dignified

kinkaku (Jap)
(KEEN-ka-ku) aura of dignity, emblematic of the noble Japanese spirit

kvelling (Yid)
(KVEL-link) swelling with pride

Quotations

"Pride goeth before destruction, and an haughty spirit before a fall."

> *Proverbs 16:18*

"I left the room with silent dignity, but caught my foot in the mat."

> George Grossmith (1847–1912) and Walter Weedon Grossmith (1854–1919), British writers, The Diary of a Nobody, ch. 12

"If a man's from Texas, he'll tell you. If he's not, why embarrass him by asking?"

> John Gunther (1901–1970), U.S. writer

Classical Phrases and Myths

hubris (Grk)

(HUB-ris) overweening pride leading to disaster; in classical drama, a refusal to accept the authority of the gods, a character flaw leading to disaster

The captured Indian king Porus was brought before Alexander the Great, who asked how he wished to be treated. "Like a king." When Alexander asked Porus if he had anything else to request, Porus replied, "Nothing, for everything is understood in the word 'king.'" Alexander restored Porus's lands to him.

> Alexander III [Alexander the Great] (356 B.C.–323 B.C.), Macedonian king

The house of Greek philosopher Plato had rich and exquisite carpets covering the floor. When Diogenes the Cynic crossed the threshhold, he showed his contempt by stamping and wiping his feet on them, saying, "Thus do I trample on the pride of Plato." Observed Plato, "With greater pride."

> Plato [Aristocles] (c. 428 B.C.–c. 347 B.C.), Greek philosopher

Jokes, Stories and Anecdotes

"I feel as a horse must feel when the beautiful cup is given to the jockey."

> [Hilaire Germain] Edgar Degas (1834–1917), French painter and sculptor, answering how he felt seeing one of his paintings sell for a high price

Groucho Marx attended one of composer George Gershwin's parties, which were apparently given for the sole purpose of having the host show off and play his music. "Do you believe that George's music will be played a hundred years from now?" Groucho was asked. "Sure," he replied, "if George is here to play it."

> Groucho [Julius] Marx (1895–1977), U.S. comedian

Despite her age and ill health, the opera singer Ernestine Schumann-Heink came out of retirement during the financially difficult Depression. Having signed a contract to tour music halls, she was callously told by an interviewer, "Things must be really bad when a great Wagnerian contralto is forced to do ten-cent shows." "Young man, how can times be bad," countered the singer, "when children can hear Schumann-Heink for a dime?"

> Ernestine Schumann-Heink (1861–1936), German opera singer

◆ PRIVACY & SOLITUDE

Quotations

"The business of everybody is the business of nobody."

> Thomas Babington Macaulay, 1st Baron Macaulay (1800–1859), British statesman and writer, historical essays contributed to the Edinburgh Review (September 1828)

"If you're lonely while you're alone, you're in bad company."

Jean-Paul Sartre (1905–1980),
French philosopher, playwright and writer

◆ PROBABILITY

Jokes, Stories and Anecdotes

A prisoner, long ago judged guilty by his king, was condemned to death. Begging for a reprieve, the prisoner promised to teach the king's horse how to fly if his execution was delayed for a year. Skeptical, but nonetheless intrigued, the king obliged and set the man free. An acquaintance of the man later asked him, "But why delay the inevitable?" Explained the condemned man, "It is not an inevitability. The odds are four to one in my favor—(1) the king might die; (2) I might die; (3) the horse might die; (4) I might teach the horse how to fly."

◆ PROCREATION (REPRODUCTION)

Foreign Words and Phrases

enceinte (Fra)
(on-SEE-ent-e) pregnant

Jokes, Stories and Anecdotes

An actress who was a contemporary of French diva Sophie Arnould repeatedly became pregnant and, due to her sacrificed shapeliness, she regularly lost both theatrical engagements and lovers. "She reminds me of those nations that are always extending their boundaries," commented Sophie Arnould, "but cannot retain their conquests."

[Madeleine] Sophie Arnould (1740–1802),
French actress and singer

Sarah Bernhardt's roles always required such displays of passion, remarked fellow actress and admirer Madge Kendal, that Kendal felt she could not take her daughter to see Bernhardt's performances. "But, madame, you should remember that were it not for passion," Bernhardt replied, "you would have no daughter to bring."

Sarah Bernhardt (1844–1923),
French actress

Astonished to learn that the comedian Victor Borge had recently bought a chicken farm, a friend inquired, "Do you know anything about breeding chickens?" "No," replied Borge, "but the chickens do."

Victor Borge (1909–),
Danish-born U.S. comedian and pianist

Actress Joan Collins had enjoyed a relationship with director George Englund, but lost her temper when Englund's wife, Cloris Leachman, revealed symptoms of pregnancy: "That's my baby she's having!"

Joan Collins (1933–),
British-born actress

A woman from Zurich once wrote Irish playwright and wit George Bernard Shaw with an unusual proposal: "You have the greatest brain in the world, and I have the most beautiful body; so we ought to produce the most perfect child." Replied Shaw, "What if the child inherits my body and your brains?"

George Bernard Shaw (1856–1950),
Irish playwright

◆ PRODIGALITY

Foreign Words and Phrases

à tout prix (Fra)
(ah too PREE) at all costs, at any price

Quotations

"Riches are for spending."

> Francis Bacon (1561–1626),
> British lawyer and writer,
> Essays (1625), "Of Expense"

"Part of the loot went for gambling, part for horses, and part for women. The rest I spent foolishly."

> George Raft (1895–1980), U.S. film actor,
> explaining how he squandered about
> $10 million during his career

Classical Phrases and Myths

Nero's Golden House—Nero's palace—was possibly the world's most conspicuous example of conspicuous consumption and ostentation.

> Nero (37–68), Roman emperor

"Carpe diem, quam minimum credula postero." (KAR-pay DEE-em, qwam MIN-ee-mum KRED-oo-la POSTer-oh.) (Seize the day, put little trust in the morrow.)

> Horace (65 B.C.–8 B.C.), Roman poet,
> Odes, I, iii, l. 25

Jokes, Stories and Anecdotes

The renowned profligate James Bennett once gave a tip of $14,000 to the guard on a train—the guard promptly resigned from his job, and opened a restaurant. Another time Bennett, uncomfortable sitting on a thick wad of money, threw the batch into a roaring fireplace; when someone else sought to salvage the bills from burning, Bennett flung them back into the flames. And when Bennett's favorite table at a Monte Carlo restaurant was occupied, he bought the entire restaurant from the proprietor for $40,000, evicted the diners, enjoyed his meal—and tipped the ex-owner with the returned ownership of the restaurant.

> James Gordon Bennett (1841–1918),
> U.S. newspaper owner and eccentric

To impress his guests, the wealthy Roman banker Agostino Chigi held dinner parties *al fresco* at the Villa Farnese overlooking the Tiber and, at the end of each course, instructed all to throw their dishes and cutlery into the river. Unbeknownst to his guests, however, before each party his servants had rigged nets just below the surface of the water to enable the *poseur* to carry on his false extravagance.

> Agostino Chigi (c. 1465–1520),
> Italian financier

Barred from taking his Spanish royalties out of the country, Somerset Maugham opted to use the money to pay for a luxurious vacation in Spain. He stayed at an elegant hotel and dined extravagantly until he felt confident his bill would match the royalty figure. But when he went to the manager to pay his bill, the manager declared, "You have brought much good publicity to us. Therefore, there is no bill."

> W[illiam] Somerset Maugham (1874–
> 1965), British writer and playwright

◆ PRODUCTIVITY

Quotations

"Thou didst create the night, but I made the lamp.
Thou didst create clay, but I made the cup.

Thou didst create the deserts, mountains and forests,
I produced the orchards, gardens and groves.
It is I who made the glass out of stone,
And it is I who turn a poison into an antidote."

Anonymous Urdu poet

Jokes, Stories and Anecdotes

The customs official at a French airport looked suspiciously at suspense film director Alfred Hitchcock's passport, which simply described his occupation as "Producer." The agent demanded, "What do you produce?" "Gooseflesh."

Sir Alfred Hitchcock (1889–1980), British film director

◆ PROFUSENESS

Foreign Words and Phrases

revenons à nos moutons (Fra)
(re-VUH-noh ah no MOO-tohn) *lit:* let us come back to our sheep; let's get back to the main point

biqa viseki-(Kiri)
(BEE-kuh viz-EK-hee) to speak in veiled references, disguised speech using metaphors

Quotations

"He is one of those orators of whom it was well said, 'Before they get up, they do not know what they are going to say; when they are speaking, they do not know what they are saying; and when they have sat down, they do not know what they have said.'"

Sir Winston Spencer Churchill (1874–1965), British prime minister and writer, describing Lord Charles Beresford

"This particularly rapid, unintelligible patter isn't generally heard, and if it is it doesn't matter."

Sir W[illiam] S[chwenck] Gilbert (1836–1911), British writer, Ruddigore (1887), Act II

"The worst of Warburton is, that he has a rage for saying something, when there's nothing to be said."

Samuel Johnson (1709–1784), British man of letters

"Madam, don't you have any unexpressed thoughts?"

George S[imon] Kaufman (1889–1961), U.S. playwright, writer and wit, to a loquacious bore

"He can compress the most words into the smallest ideas better than any man I ever met."

Abraham Lincoln (1809–1865), U.S. president, describing a fellow attorney

"He [Thomas Macaulay] is like a book in breeches . . . He has occasional flashes of silence, that make his conversation perfectly delightful."

Sydney Smith (1771–1845), British clergyman and writer

Classical Phrases and Myths

An ambassador from Perinthus on a mission to Sparta spoke at great length, and then asked, "What answer shall I give to the Perinthians?" "You may say," replied the king, "that you talked a great deal—while I said nothing."

Jokes, Stories and Anecdotes

Asked to comment about a loquacious colleague, the senator said, "When he gets started, his tongue is like a racehorse; it runs fastest the less weight it carries."

Recounting an apparently interminable tale to wit Franklin Pierce Adams, a friend finally said: "Well, to cut a long story short—" "Too late," interrupted Adams.

Franklin Pierce Adams (1881–1960), U.S. writer

Lady Astor, the first woman elected to the House of Commons, frequently interrupted other speakers. Once, when castigated for this, she protested that she had been listening for hours before interrupting. Commented an exasperated colleague, "Yes, we've heard you listening."

Viscountess Nancy Witcher Langhorne Astor (1879–1964), U.S.-born British politician

The volubility of Tallulah Bankhead, who was once described as "more of an act than an actress," was legendary. After an interview with her, the magician Fred Keating remarked, "I've just spent an hour talking to Tallulah for a few minutes."

Tallulah Bankhead (1903–1968), U.S. actress

When asked if he found it disconcerting to see members of the audience looking at their watches during a long lecture, English scholar John Erskine said, "No, not until they start shaking them."

John Erskine (1879–1951), U.S. educator and writer

The music critic, Henry Taylor Parker, known by his initials HTP as "Hell to Pay," was so irritated by some persistent windbags seated near him that he finally turned on them and hissed, "Those people on-stage are making such a noise I cannot hear a word you're saying."

Henry Taylor Parker (1867–1934), U.S. writer

◆ PROGRESS & DEVELOPMENT

Foreign Words and Phrases

ça ira (Fra)
(sah eer-AH) it will be all right (French revolutionary song)

kaizen (Jap)
(KIE-zehn) small, gradual improvements over time (opp: unpredictable change)

Schlimmbesserung (Ger)
(shlihm-BES-air-oong) an "improvement" that makes things worse

Quotations

"The world is moving so fast these days that the man who says it can't be done is generally interrupted by someone doing it."

Elbert [Green] Hubbard (1856–1915), U.S. businessman and writer

"Progress was a good thing once but it went on too long."

Ogden Nash (1902–1971), U.S. humorist

"When you are getting kicked from the rear it means you're in front."

Fulton J[ohn] Sheen (1895–1979), U.S. clergyman, educator and writer

"In Italy for thirty years under the Borgias they had warfare, terror, murder, bloodshed—they produced Michelangelo, Leonardo da Vinci and the Renaissance. In Switzerland they had brotherly love, five hundred years of democracy and peace, and what did that produce. . . ? The cuckoo clock."

[George] Orson Welles (1915–1985),
U.S. actor and filmmaker,
The Third Man (1949 film)

◆ PROMOTION

Quotations

"By working faithfully eight hours a day, you may eventually get to be a boss and work twelve hours a day."

Robert Lee Frost (1874–1963), U.S. poet

"He wished all men as rich as he
(And he was rich as rich could be),
So to the top of every tree
Promoted everybody."

Sir W[illiam] S[chwenck] Gilbert
(1836–1911), British writer,
The Gondoliers (1889), Act II

Jokes, Stories and Anecdotes

One of the cleverest ways of asking a boss for a raise in pay was the approach used by John Kieran when he was the sports columnist of the New York Times. Feeling the need for an increase, but wanting to be tactful about it, Kieran went to his employer, Adolph Ochs, and said respectfully, "Mr. Ochs, working for the Times is a luxury I can no longer afford." He got the raise.

John Kieran (1892–1979), U.S. writer

◆ PROOF & FACT

Foreign Words and Phrases

prendre sur le fait (Fra)
(PROHN-dresoor leh FAY) to catch in the act

Quotations

"I loved Kirk so much, I would have skied down Mount Everest in the nude with a carnation up my nose."

Joyce McKinney (1950–   ),
British citizen, testifying at Epsom
Magistrates' Court (December 6, 1977)

Classical Phrases and Myths

quod vide (Lat)
(kwod WEE-de) lit: for which see; a reference or precedent (used in cross references) (abbr: qv)

ecce signum (Lat)
(EK-ke SIG-num) here is the proof

exceptio probat regulam (Lat)
(ex KEP-tee-oh prob-at REG-u-lam) the exception proves the rule

bona fides (Lat)
(BON-ah FI-des) documents proving identity or authority

Jokes, Stories and Anecdotes

"My mother-in-law just tried to run me over," said the shaken man, brushing off his clothes as he rose from the pavement, to the police officer. "The car hit you from behind," noted the cop, "so how do you know it was your mother-in-law?" "I recognized the laugh."

◆ PROPERTY (POSSESSION)

Quotations

You Can't Take It with You. [Title of play (1936).]

Moss Hart (1904–1961), U.S. playwright
and theater producer, and George S[imon]
Kaufman (1889–1961), U.S. playwright,
writer and wit

Classical Phrases and Myths

ktema es aei (Grk)
(KTAY-ma es ay) a possession forever; Thucydides describing his book on the Peloponnesian war

Jokes, Stories and Anecdotes

Following a train of limousines pulling up to a Hollywood theater for a premiere, the wit Wilson Mizner emerged from a dilapidated Ford and grandly threw his keys to the parking attendant. "What shall I do with it?" sneered the valet. Mizner called gaily, "Keep it," and swept into the theater.

Wilson Mizner (1876–1933),
U.S. writer and wit

◆ PROPRIETY

Classical Phrases and Myths

pro forma (Lat)
(proh FOR-ma) as a formality; pro forma invoice: one issued in advance of the dispatch of goods

Jokes, Stories and Anecdotes

The mayor was touring the new psychiatric ward and was amazed to see in one cell a distinguished man who was reading Homer in Greek and was naked except for a top hat. Noticing his visitor, the inmate rose, bowed, and said in cultured tones, "Sir, I perceive your incredulity in finding me here in the nude." "Yes," said the mayor cautiously, "I was curious to know why." "It's painfully obvious," replied the inmate. "The cell is maintained at a comfortable 70 degrees, and I have privacy. Since clothing is unnecessary for warmth, why bother?" "True," muttered the mayor, acknowledging the clear thinking. "But why the top hat?" The inmate shrugged. "Someone *might* come."

Lawyer and politician William Jennings Bryan was once called to propose a toast at a state dinner arranged shortly after the Russo-Japanese War for the touring Admiral Togo, whose brilliant tactics had destroyed the Russian fleet at the battle of the Sea of Japan. An embarrassing breakdown of protocol seemed inevitable, for Bryan was a strict Prohibitionist and refused to drink champagne. But Bryan made the toast as promised—though with a difference. "Admiral Togo has won a great victory on the water, and I will therefore toast him in water," said Bryan. "When Admiral Togo wins a victory on champagne, I will toast him in champagne."

William Jennings Bryan (1860–1925),
U.S. politician

◆ PROSTITUTION

Foreign Words and Phrases

maison de société (Fra)
(meh-ZON de SO-see-ay-tay) *lit:* society house; brothel (euphemism)

Quotations

"They don't know anything about ranching. They certainly don't know anything about keeping their calves together."

Debbie Reynolds (1932–   ),
U.S. film actress, describing the
prostitutes at Nevada's Mustang Ranch

Jokes, Stories and Anecdotes

Before taking a lunch break, the prostitute left a sign on the door: "Out to Lunch. Go Fuck Yourself."

Asked if he thought his contributions to five U.S. Senators had influenced them to assist him in obtaining favorable federal legislation, Charlie Keating, CEO of Lincoln Savings and Loan, which declared bankruptcy with over $2 billion in excess liabilities, baldly replied: "I want to say in the most forceful way I can: I certainly hope so."

Charles Keating (1924–),
U.S. businessman

The humorist S. J. Perelman was besieged by a bevy of importuning prostitutes while traveling in Taipei, but eventually shook them off, quipping, "A case of the tail dogging the wag."

S[idney] J[oseph] Perelman (1904–1979),
U.S. writer and screenwriter
[attributed also to others]

Four professors walked past a group of streetwalkers. "Ah," said one scholar, "a flourish of strumpets." "I'd say," said the second, "a jam of tarts." "Rather," said the third, "an essay of Trollopes." And the fourth said, "Or an anthology of pros."

◆ PROTECTION

Foreign Words and Phrases

Gestapo (Ger)
(ge-SHTA-po) German secret police under Hitler; also refers more generally to similarly brutal and severe organizations

Quotations

"I have never seen a situation so dismal that a policeman couldn't make it worse."

Brendan Behan (1923–1964),
Irish playwright and wit

"The terrorist and the policeman both come from the same basket."

Joseph Conrad [Teodor Jósef Konrad Korzeniowski] (1857–1924), Polish-born British writer, Secret Agent (1907), ch. 4

"Every society gets the kind of criminal it deserves. What is equally true is that every community gets the kind of law enforcement it insists on."

Robert Francis Kennedy (1925–1968),
U.S. statesman and politician

" 'Where they got you stationed now, Luke?' said Harry Tugman peering up stoutly from a mug of coffee. 'At the p-p-p-present time in Norfolk at the Navy base,' Luke answered, 'm-m-m-making the world safe for hypocrisy.' "

Thomas [Clayton] Wolfe (1900–1938),
U.S. writer, Look Homeward Angel
(1929), pt. 3, ch. 36

Classical Phrases and Myths

"*Sed quis cusiodiet ipsos Custodes*" (sed kwis kus-TOH-di-et IP-sos kus-TOH-days) (Who shall guard the guards themselves?)

Juvenal [Decimus Junius Juvenalis]
(c. 50–c. 130), Roman writer,
Satires, VI, l. 347

◆ PSYCHOLOGY

Foreign Words and Phrases

Lehranalyse (Ger)
(LAYR-an-al-y-ZE) teaching analysis; process in which Freudian psychologists are themselves analyzed as part of their training

Quotations

"The psychotic person knows that two and two make five and is perfectly happy about it; the neurotic person knows that two and two make four, but is terribly worried about it."

Anonymous physician on radio broadcast, 1954

"Any man who goes to a psychiatrist ought to have his head examined."

Samuel Goldwyn [Samuel Goldfish] (1882–1974), Russian-born U.S. film producer [authenticity unverified]

"Neurosis is always a substitute for legitimate suffering."

Carl Jung (1875–1961), Swiss psychiatrist

"The Man Who Mistook His Wife for a Hat." [Title of book (1985).]

Oliver Sacks (1933–   ), U.S. physician and writer

Classical Phrases and Myths

In Greek legend, Oedipus was left to die as a baby near Corinth. Unaware that he was the son of King Laius of Thebes and Jocasta, he tried as an adult to determine his origins, by consulting the oracle at Delphi. He was informed that he would kill his father and sire children by his mother. Terrified, he sought to avoid the fulfillment of the prophecy by leaving Corinth and, while traveling, killed a man in his chariot and members of his train. Oedipus later came upon the monstrous Sphinx, who slew all who could not answer the riddle "What goes on four legs in the morning, two in the afternoon and three in the evening?" Oedipus answered correctly, and the Sphinx then killed herself, thus freeing Thebes. Arriving in Thebes, which had just lost its king, Oedipus became king of Thebes, marrying Jocasta. Thebes prospered but was later beset by a plague; in trying to lift it, Oedipus learned that he had indeed killed his father and married his mother, thus fulfilling the Delphic oracle. Aggrieved, he blinded himself and passed the rest of his years as a miserable wanderer, led by his daughter Antigone and harassed by the Furies. Thus, an *Oedipus complex* is the psychoanalytical term for strong boyhood attachment to one's mother, based on youthful sexual feelings and often accompanied by hostility to the father, which sometimes lingers into adulthood.

Jokes, Stories and Anecdotes

Patient: "My wife thinks she's a set of drapes." Psychiatrist: "Tell her to pull herself together."

"Despite what you think, Mr. Smith," said the psychiatrist to the patient, "you don't have a complex. Actually, you *are* inferior."

When George Gershwin began undergoing psychoanalysis, his close friend, pianist and wit Oscar Levant, scornfully asked him, "Does it help your constipation, George?" Replied the composer, "No, but now I understand why I have it."

George Gershwin (1898–1937), U.S. composer and songwriter

In 1961 Tennessee Williams decided to quit having sessions with his psychoanalyst. When asked why the change of heart, the dramatist replied sincerely, "He was meddling too much in my private life."

Tennessee [Thomas Lanier] Williams (1911–1983), U.S. playwright

---

◆ PUBLIC SPEAKING

Quotations

"I do not object to people looking at their watches when I am speaking. But I strongly object when they start shaking them to make certain they are still going."

William Norman Birkett, Baron Birkett (1883–1962), British politician

"When I hear a man preach, I like to see him act as if he were fighting bees."

Abraham Lincoln (1809–1865), U.S. president

"Before I speak, I have something important to say."

Groucho [Julius] Marx (1895–1977), U.S. comedian

"Winston has devoted the best years of his life to preparing his impromptu speeches."

F[rederick] E[dwin] Smith, 1st Earl of Birkenhead (1872–1930), British lawyer and politician, mocking Winston Churchill

"When I am in the pulpit, I have the pleasure of seeing my audience nod approbation while they sleep."

Sydney Smith (1771–1845), British clergyman and writer

Classical Phrases and Myths

Demosthenes is generally considered the greatest orator of classical Greece, but he had to overcome a speech defect to give such powerful orations as his *On the Crown* or the three *Philippics*. Legend has it that Demosthenes cured his stammer by learning to speak slowly, putting pebbles in his mouth; learned to overcome the disturbance of audience noise by going to the seashore and speaking to the waves; strengthened his weakness of breath by reciting poetry as he ran uphill; and attained fine diction by confining himself in a cave and copying Thucydides' history eight times. To resist the temptation of going out into society, he shaved one side of his head, so that he would be too embarrassed to show himself in public. In this manner, he was able to hone the skills necessary to hold Athenian audiences spellbound by speaking simply, pithily and effectively.

Demosthenes (c. 384 B.C.–322 B.C.), Greek orator

Jokes, Stories and Anecdotes

"So, judge, what did you think of my first sermon?" asked the new minister. "There were only three things wrong with it," replied the frank jurist. "Just three? Not bad for my first attempt. What were they?" he asked. "First, you read it!" answered the judge. "Second, you didn't read it well! And third, it wasn't worth reading anyway!"

The topic of a literary debate held in Chicago in 1917 between poet and novelist Maxwell Bodenheim and playwright Ben Hecht was "Resolved—That People Who Attend Literary Debates Are Imbeciles." Hecht spoke first, closing his remarks with "The affirmative rests." Bodenheim, after looking over the audience, simply said, "You win."

Maxwell Bodenheim (1892–1954), U.S. poet and writer

Even though he held important political posts, Winston Churchill believed that his salary from the government service was inadequate, and so he supplemented his income by lecturing and journalism. Observed Churchill, "I live from mouth to hand."

Sir Winston Spencer Churchill (1874–1965), British prime minister and writer

Mark Twain and the lawyer and wit Chauncey Depew were both scheduled to speak at a banquet. Twain spoke first for about 20 minutes and met with great applause. Then Depew rose and said: "Before this dinner, Mark Twain and I agreed to trade speeches. He has just delivered mine, and I am grateful for the reception that you have given it. Unfortunately, I have lost his speech, and I cannot remember a word of what he had to say." He then sat down.

Chauncey Mitchell Depew (1834–1928),
U.S. lawyer and politician

A heckler shouted at Benjamin Disraeli while he was giving a speech: "Speak up, I can't hear you." Retorted Disraeli, "Truth travels slowly, but it will reach even you in time."

Benjamin Disraeli, 1st Earl of Beaconsfield
(1804–1881), British prime minister

William Evarts, a 19th-century secretary of state, enjoyed the reputation of being an entertaining after-dinner speaker. Asked to give a few comments at a holiday banquet, he rose to the podium and began, "You have been enjoying a turkey stuffed with sage, and now I trust you will enjoy this sage stuffed with turkey."

William Maxwell Evarts (1818–1901),
lawyer and statesman

"Gentlemen, the obvious duty of a toastmaster is to be so infernally dull that the succeeding speakers will appear brilliant by contrast," Clarence Kelland began his introduction of speakers at a banquet. From the speakers' table came an appreciative chuckle. "However, I've looked over the list," Kelland continued, "and I don't think I can do it."

Clarence Budington Kelland (1881–1964),
U.S. writer

Poetry anthologist Louis Untermeyer once returned his speaker's fee to a small, poorly funded group, suggesting that it put the money to good use. When he later inquired what purpose the group had found for the money, Untermeyer was informed that it had been placed in "a fund to get better speakers next year."

Louis Untermeyer (1885–1977), U.S. poet
and writer [attributed to others]

◆ PUBLIC SPIRIT & PATRIOTISM

Foreign Words and Phrases

monstre sacre (Fra)
(MON-struh SAC-reh) *lit:* holy monster; a scoundrel who marries his ambition or evil with good causes

Quotations

"Patriotism is the last refuge of a scoundrel."

Samuel Johnson (1709–1784),
British man of letters

"My fellow Americans, ask not what your country can do for you—ask what you can do for your country."

John Fitzgerald Kennedy (1917–1963),
U.S. president

"We do not love people so much for the good they have done us, as for the good we have done them."

Leo Nikolaevich Tolstoy (1828–1910),
Russian writer

"A reformer is a guy who rides through a sewer in a glass-bottomed boat."

James John ["Light-horse Harry"] Walker
(1881–1946), U.S. politician,
adapting Wilson Mizner's comment
about Hollywood

Classical Phrases and Myths

amor patriae (Lat)
(AM-or PAT-ree-ai) patriotism, love of country

In Greek legend, as recounted in Homer's *Odyssey*, Mentor was the Ithacan to whom Odysseus entrusted the education of his son Telemachus and the care of his house. Thus, a *mentor* is a wise and trusted adviser.

Jokes, Stories and Anecdotes

Although in deteriorating health, John Adams survived until the 50th anniversary of the signing of the Declaration of Independence—July 4, 1826. He briefly recovered consciousness from his coma and murmured his last words, "Thomas Jefferson lives." Unknown to him, Thomas Jefferson had died that same day.

> *John Adams (1735–1826), U.S. president*

While mayor of West Berlin, Willy Brandt was invited during a tour of Israel to view the great new Mann auditorium in Tel Aviv. Brandt congratulated Israel's naming the concert hall for the German writer Thomas Mann, but he was politely corrected by his host. The hall was actually named for a certain Frederic Mann of Philadelphia. Brandt asked, "So what did he ever write?" "A check."

> *Willy Brandt (1913–1992),*
> *German politician*

A generous supporter of the New York Philharmonic Society, industrialist and philanthropist Andrew Carnegie, was visited yet again at his mansion for a requested donation of $60,000. With his checkbook out, Carnegie suddenly demurred, saying, "No, I've changed my mind. Surely there are other people who like music enough to help." He asked the society secretary to raise half the amount, and then he would match it. The following day the society secretary returned, announcing that he had raised the necessary funds. Carnegie commended the man's enterprise and wrote out a check for $30,000. Curious, he asked, "Would you mind telling me who gave you the other half?" "Not at all. Mrs. Carnegie."

> *Andrew Carnegie (1835–1919), Scottish-*
> *born U.S. businessman and philanthropist*

The Earl of Chesterfield accepted Samuel Johnson's plea to become a sponsor of Johnson's classic *Dictionary of the English Language*—but only after the 11-year project already had been finished. Johnson's rebuke is legendary: he mocked Chesterfield, asking, "Is not a Patron, my Lord, one who looks with unconcern on a man struggling for life in the water, and, when he has reached ground, encumbers him with help?"

> *Samuel Johnson (1709–1784),*
> *British man of letters*

◆ PUBLIC, THE

Foreign Words and Phrases

canaille (Fra)
(KAHN-ayh) the common people, the rabble

homme moyen sensuel (Fra)
(om mwa-YEN SEN-swel) *lit:* man of average desires; ordinary man, typical man

Quotations

"The Lord prefers common-looking people. That is the reason He makes so many of them."

> *Abraham Lincoln (1809–1865),*
> *U.S. president*

"The public be damned. I am working for my stockholders."

> *William Henry Vanderbilt (1821–1885),*
> *U.S. industrialist, disputing with a*
> *reporter that the public should be*
> *consulted about luxury trains*

"Our supreme governors, the mob."

Horace Walpole, 4th Earl of Oxford
(1717–1797), British writer

"Really, if the lower orders don't set us a good example, what on earth is the use of them?"

Oscar [Fingal O'Flahertie Wills] Wilde
(1854–1900), British playwright, writer
and wit, The Importance of Being
Earnest (1895), Act I

Classical Phrases and Myths

vox populi (Lat)
(wox POP-u-lee) *lit:* the voice of the people; popular verdict, public opinion

hoi polloi (Grk)
(HOI pol-LOI) the many, the rabble

◆ PUBLICITY & ADVERTISING

Foreign Words and Phrases

claqueur (Fra)
(klah-CUHR) someone paid to applaud at a performance

Quotations

"A telescope will magnify a star a thousand times, but a good press agent can do even better."

Fred Allen [John Sullivan] (1894–1957),
U.S. comedian

"I want it so that you can't wipe your ass on a piece of paper that hasn't got my picture on it."

Lyndon Baines Johnson (1908–1973),
U.S. president, speaking to his press agent

"Clark helped us a great deal, and asked for only one small favor in return—that we advertise his law firm on the back of one-dollar bills."

John Fitzgerald Kennedy (1917–1963),
U.S. president, thanking Clark Clifford

Classical Phrases and Myths

ad captandum vulgus (Lat)
(ad kap-TAND-um WUL-gus) to capture (appeal to) the emotions of the crowd

Jokes, Stories and Anecdotes

P. T. Barnum so craved free publicity that he was overjoyed to read the four-page obituary about his own death in the *New York Evening Sun* newspaper—which had been arranged by his publicity agent. The master showman's business instincts did not desert him even as he was dying. His reported last words were: "What were the receipts today at Madison Square?"

P[hineas] T[aylor] Barnum (1810–1891),
U.S. showman

Despite—or because—clergymen across the U.S. denounced the actress Sarah Bernhardt as the "whore of Babylon," her performances were well attended. To the Episcopalian bishop of Chicago who had most ardently maligned her, Bernhardt sent a note and a bank draft. "I am accustomed, when I bring an attraction to your town, to spend $400 on advertising," the note read. "Since you have done half the advertising for me, I herewith enclose $200 for your parish."

Sarah Bernhardt (1844–1923),
French actress

A spurious announcement was distributed at the Republican Convention of 1912: "At 3 O'clock on Saturday afternoon Theodore ROO-

SEVELT WILL WALK on the WATERS of LAKE MICHIGAN.''

Theodore Roosevelt (1858–1919),
U.S. president

''As I was saying when I was interrupted. . .''

Eamon De Valera (1882–1975),
Irish prime minister and president
[attributed also to others]

◆ PUNISHMENT

Foreign Words and Phrases

mal juste (Fra)
(mal joost) just desserts, justified harm

Quotations

''I went out to Charing Cross to see Major General Harrison hanged, drawn and quartered; which was done there, he looking as cheerful as any man could do in that condition.''

Samuel Pepys (1633–1703),
British statesman and diarist, diary,
October 13, 1660

''Deserves to be preached to death by wild curates.''

Sydney Smith (1771–1845),
British clergyman and writer

Classical Phrases and Myths

''*Noxiae poena par esto.*'' (NOX-ee-ayPOH-e-na par ES-toh) (Let the punishment match the offense.)

Marcus Tullius Cicero (106 B.C.–43 B.C.),
Roman statesman and man of letters,
De Legibus, III, xx

Jokes, Stories and Anecdotes

During a fiery political speech at Ennis, Eamon De Valera, who would become Ireland's longtime prime minister and president, was arrested. Released after a year's imprisonment, he hastened back to Ennis, called a meeting, and began,

◆ QUALITY, SUPERIOR

Foreign Words and Phrases

comme le petit Jesus en culottes de velours (Fra)
(kom le puh-TEET HEZ-oo on KOO-lot de vel-OOR) like the Christ child in velvet pants

tashinamu (Jap)
(tah-sheh-NAM-oo) privately devoting oneself to a project or cause regardless of recognition or compensation

ding hao (Chi)
(ding how) excellent, very good

Quotations

''The last temptation is the greatest treason:
To do the right deed for the wrong reason.''

T[homas] S[tearns] Eliot (1888–1965),
U.S. poet, Murder in the
Cathedral (1935)

''The sun shineth upon the dunghill, and is not corrupted.''

John Lyly (c. 1554–1606), British writer,
Euphues: The Anatomy of Wit (1579)

''The road to hell is paved with good intentions.''

Old English proverb

''She has more goodness in her little finger, than he has in his whole body.''

Jonathan Swift (1667–1745),
Anglo-Irish clergyman and writer, Polite
Conversation (c. 1738), ''Dialogue II''

Classical Phrases and Myths

nulli secundus (Lat)
(NUL-lee se-KUN-dus) second to none

"Summum bonum." (Sum-mum BOH-num) (The highest good.)
Marcus Tullius Cicero (106 B.C.-43 B.C.), Roman statesman and man of letters, De Officiis, I, ii

---

◆ RAIN

Quotations

"The tanned appearance of many Londoners is not sunburn—it is rust."
Anonymous, during Britain's wettest winter on record, London Evening Standard (1961)

Jokes, Stories and Anecdotes

Harry came into the house, dripping wet. His sympathetic wife said, "It must be raining cats and dogs outside." "Yep," said Harry. "I just stepped in a poodle."

◆ RAPPORT

Foreign Words and Phrases

en rapport (Fra)
(on rah-POR) in sympathy, in agreement

Classical Phrases and Myths

nemini contradicente (Lat)
(NE-mi-nee kon-tra-dik-ENT-e) *lit:* nobody dissenting; without opposition, unanimous; generally describes the passage of a resolution in a debate (abbr: *nem con*)

Jokes, Stories and Anecdotes

Charles V, Spanish King and Holy Roman Emperor, was often involved in warfare and diplomacy in trying to assert title over vast but farflung lands that he had inherited. In 1521 Charles again became embroiled with François I of France over the empire's Italian lands. Said Charles, "My cousin François and I are in perfect accord—he wants Milan, and so do I."
Charles V (1500–1558), Holy Roman Emperor and Spanish king

When signing the first draft of the Declaration of Independence, John Hancock observed, "We must be unanimous, we must all hang together." To which Franklin muttered, "We must indeed all hang together, or, most assuredly, we shall all hang separately."
Benjamin Franklin (1706–1790), U.S. statesman and scientist [authenticity unverified]

◆ RASHNESS

Foreign Words and Phrases

bronco (Spa)
(BRAHN-koh) *lit:* rough, coarse; wild or untamed horse

risque (Fra)
(REES-kay) daring, hazardous (with an implication of indelicacy)

à corps perdu (Fra)
(ah COR per-DOO) *lit:* until the loss of the body; desperately, recklessly

Classical Phrases and Myths

ferae naturae (Lat)
(fer-EE nat-OOR-ee) uncivilized, undomesticated beasts

A group of mice finally called a council meeting to discuss how to deal with their dreaded enemy, the cat. A young mouse stood and said, "I propose that a bell be hung around the cat's neck. Thus, when she approaches, we can hear the bell beforehand and escape." The mouse sat down amid thunderous applause. When the clamor quieted down, an old mouse who had been silent said, "It takes a young mouse to think of such a bold plan. A bell would certainly warn us of the cat's approach. But I ask you, who is going *to bell the cat?*"

> *Aesop (c. 600 B.C.), Greek fabulist*

◆ REASONING

Foreign Words and Phrases

gedankenexperiment (Ger)
(gehd-AHN-ken-ex-PEHR-e ment)
lit: thought-experiment, to carry out an experiment mentally rather than physically

Quotations

"Deliberation. The act of examining one's bread to determine which side it is buttered on."

> *Ambrose [Gwinnet] Bierce (1842–c. 1914), U.S. writer and poet, Devil's Dictionary (1911)*

"You mentioned your name as if I should recognize it, but beyond the obvious facts that you are a bachelor, a solicitor, a freemason, and an asthmatic, I know nothing whatever about you."

> *Sir Arthur Conan Doyle (1859–1930), British writer, The Return of Sherlock Holmes (1905), "The Norwood Builder"*

Classical Phrases and Myths

a fortiori (Lat)
(ah fort-ee-OR-ee) conclusively, with even stronger reason

Jokes, Stories and Anecdotes

An American investment banker attended a Sherlock Holmes party in London. He was informed that another guest, a Dr. Osborn, was noted for his remarkable Holmesian deductions about people. When introduced, the banker wasted no time. He pointed to a man in the corner and asked Osborn for a deductive description. "Well, I should say he is a solicitor who lives near Dover with his wife and four children. He's had escargots, steak and asparagus for dinner." "Well done," the American said. "And that man there?" "I'd believe he is a dentist. He bets the horses, has two mistresses and just returned from a vacation in Amalfi." "Congratulations," said the impressed American. "And me?" "Hmmm," Osborn began. "You are from the Northeast—Boston, I should guess. You're 38, married and you graduated from Harvard." "Fantastic! How did you know that I graduated from Harvard?" "Because, sir, every time you pick your nose, I can see your ring."

◆ RECOMMENDATION

Quotations

"Oh! he is mad, is he? Then I wish he would bite some other of my generals."

> *George II (1683–1760), British king, replying to complaint that General James Wolfe was a madman*

Jokes, Stories and Anecdotes

Horace Greeley wrote an angry dismissal letter in his notoriously illegible handwriting to a journalist on his paper, the *New York Tribune*. Several years later, the two met. "Nobody could read the note," said the fired journalist, "so I represented it as a letter of recommendation and obtained several excellent opportunities by it. I am so very obliged to you."

Horace Greeley (1811–1872),
U.S. publisher and politician

Visiting the United States in 1797, French revolutionist and freethinker Constantin Volney sought a letter of recommendation from President Washington. Seeking simultaneously to avoid controversy over the man's opinions and offense to the Frenchman, Washington cagily wrote: "C. Volney needs no recommendation from Geo. Washington."

George Washington (1732–1799),
U.S. general and president

◆ REFUSAL (PROHIBITION)

Foreign Words and Phrases

taboo (Poly)
(tah-BOO) prohibited, sacred

verboten (Ger)
(fehr-BOH-ten) prohibited, forbidden, illegal

Quotations

"You know I cannot give you a baronetcy, but you can tell your friends that I offered you one and you refused it. That's much better."

Benjamin Disraeli, 1st Earl of Beaconsfield
(1804–1881), British prime minister

"Let's find out what everyone is doing,
And then stop everyone from doing it."

Sir A[lan] P[atrick] Herbert (1890–1971),
British writer and politician,
Let's Stop Somebody

"I will not accept if nominated and will not serve if elected."

William Tecumseh Sherman (1820–1891),
U.S. general, message to Republican
National Convention, June 5, 1884

Classical Phrases and Myths

nolo episcopari (Lat)
(NOH-loh e-pis-kop-AHR-ee) lit: I do not wish to serve; refusal of office

The Macedonian forces of Alexander the Great, accompanied by Anaximenes, captured Lampsacus while on expedition against the Persians. Anxious to save his native city from destruction, Anaximenes sought an audience with the king. Anticipating his plea, Alexander declared, "I swear by the Styx I will not grant your request." "My lord," Anaximenes stated, "I merely wanted to request that you destroy Lampsacus." Thus, he saved his native city.

Anaximenes (c. 400 B.C.), Greek philosopher

Jokes, Stories and Anecdotes

A pious-looking Mrs. Cohn carefully studied the display counter in the delicatessen. Finally, she pointed and said, "A half pound of the corned beef, please." The butcher said gently, "I'm sorry, but that's ham." Snapped Mrs. Cohn, "Who asked you?"

◆ REFUTATION

Classical Phrases and Myths

apagoge (Grk/Lat)
(ap-a-GOH-ge) reduction to absurdity, indirect proof by demonstrating

the falsity of the opposite point of view

reductio ad absurdum (Lat)
(re-DUK-ti-oh ad ab-SURD-um) method of disproving a proposition by assuming a conclusion to be incorrect and working back to find a contradiction

Jokes, Stories and Anecdotes

Harry came upon a seemingly crazy woman in the street who was dipping her hand into an apparently empty basket and then waving her hand about. Finally, he asked, "Pardon me, but what are you doing?" The woman said, "It contains antilion powder. By scattering it, I keep lions away." "But," Harry protested, "there are no lions within a thousand miles of here." And the woman said, "I told you it was effective."

"And yet you insist you're innocent," repeated the judge, "despite the proof that four witnesses saw you shoot the gun?" "If it's witnesses you want, your honor," replied the defendant, "I can produce 30 who didn't see me shoot it."

Former prime minister Sir Winston Churchill visited the House of Commons while in his 80s. His appearance distracted attention from the ongoing debate. Murmured one young MP to another, "Really, I don't believe he should come anymore. They say he's growing a bit soft upstairs." Churchill slowly turned in his seat and growled, "They say he can't hear, either."

Sir Winston Spencer Churchill (1874–1965), British prime minister and writer

A Pittsburgh running back ran on a breakaway play the length of the football field, closely followed by game referee Tiny Maxwell. Penn State's defensive captain insisted that the player had stepped out of bounds at his own ten-yard line, thereby nullifying his gain beyond. When he offered to show Maxwell the incriminating cleat mark, the official gasped, "If you want me to go back and look at that cleat mark, you'll have to hire a taxi."

Robert W. ["Tiny"] Maxwell (d. 1922), U.S. football player

◆ REGRETFULNESS

Quotations

"To Alphonse Allais, with regrets for not having known him. Voltaire."

Alphonse Allais (1854–1905), French writer and playwright [inscription in a volume of Voltaire found in the library of Allais]

"My one regret in life is that I am not someone else."

Woody Allen [Allen Stewart Konigsberg] (1935–), U.S. comedian and filmmaker

"Hindsight is always 20-20."

Billy [Samuel] Wilder (1906–), U.S. film director and writer

Classical Phrases and Myths

"Durum: sed levius fit patientia Quidquid corrigere est nefas." ('Tis hard: But what may not be altered is made lighter by patience.)

Horace (65 B.C.–8 B.C.), Roman poet, Odes, I, xxiv, l, 19

According to Roman mythology, the Furies (FYUR-eez) (Grk: Erinyes) were the snake-haired dogheaded goddesses Alecto, Tisiphone and Megaera sent from Tartarus of the underworld to punish and to obtain revenge from people who had not atoned for their crimes. Orestes was pursued by them for slaying his mother even though he had been required to do so; their punishment was not vindictive but just. Hence, to face *the furies* is to bear avenging spirits or remorseful pangs.

Jokes, Stories and Anecdotes

Asked to apologize for insulting a fellow member of Parliament, Anglo-Irish dramatist Richard Sheridan said, "Mr. Speaker, I said the honorable member was a liar it is true and I am sorry for it. The honorable member may place the punctuation where he pleases."

> *Richard Brinsley Sheridan (1751–1816),*
> *Irish-born British playwright*
> *and politician*

◆ REJECTION

Quotations

"A good many young writers make the mistake of enclosing a stamped, self-addressed envelope, big enough for the manuscript to come back in. This is too much of a temptation to the editor."

> *Ring [Ringgold Wilmer] Lardner*
> *(1885–1933), U.S. writer,* How to
> Write Short Stories *(1924)*

Classical Phrases and Myths

e contra (Lat)
(ay KON-tra) on the other hand, to take a contrary position

Jokes, Stories and Anecdotes

Queen Elizabeth lived in disgrace and obscurity during the reign of her half-sister Mary. When she ascended the throne, a knight who had previously behaved insolently toward her threw himself at her feet to beseech

her pardon. Gesturing to him to rise, Elizabeth dismissed him unceremoniously, saying, "Do you not know that we are descended of the lion, whose nature is not to prey upon the mouse or any other such small vermin?"

> *Elizabeth I (1533–1603), British queen*

◆ RELIGION (CULT)

Quotations

After all, what's a cult? It just means not enough people to make a minority.

> *Robert Altman (1922–   ),*
> *U.S. film director*

"There is only one religion, though there are a hundred versions of it."

> *George Bernard Shaw (1856–1950),*
> *Irish playwright,* Plays Pleasant and
> Unpleasant *(1898), vol. 2, preface*

"A church is a place in which gentlemen who have never been to heaven brag about it to persons who will never get there."

> *H[enry] L[ouis] Mencken (1880–1956),*
> *U.S. critic and writer*

"*L'homme est bien insensé. Il ne saurait forger un ciron, et forge des Dieux a douzaines.*" (Man is certainly mad. He could not create a mite, and makes gods by the dozens.)

> *Michel Eyquem de Montaigne*
> *(1533–1592), French writer,*
> Essays *(1580), bk. II*

◆ REMAINDER

Classical Phrases and Myths

caput mortuum (Lat)
(KA-put MOR-loo-um) residue left after distillation

et alia (Lat)
(et AL-ee-a) and other things or people (abbr: *et al.*)

Jokes, Stories and Anecdotes

After a friend had waxed in superlatives about his waterfront property, Groucho Marx gave his opinion. Groucho said, "Don't think much of it. Take away the ocean and what have you got?"

> *Groucho [Julius] Marx (1895–1977),*
> *U.S. comedian [authenticity unverified]*

◆ RENEWAL (RESTORATION & REVIVAL)

Foreign Words and Phrases

de nouveau (Fra)
(de noo-VO) anew, afresh

refacimento (Ita)
(ree-fach-ee-MEN-toh) recasting, remaking, rehash

Quotations

"If it ain't broke, don't fix it."

> *Anonymous*

Classical Phrases and Myths

de integro (Lat)
(day in-TEG-roh) afresh, from the beginning again

Jokes, Stories and Anecdotes

To the patient who awoke after the operation to have his gangrene-infected leg amputated, the doctor explained, "I've got good news and bad news. The bad news is that we took off the wrong leg." "My God," cried the patient, "what could be the good news?" "The other leg is getting better."

◆ REPRESENTATION

Quotations

"Because no tree has ever complained about its likeness."

> *Sir Winston Spencer Churchill*
> *(1874–1965), British prime minister and*
> *writer, answering why he preferred*
> *to paint landscapes rather than portraits*

"Mr. Lely, I desire you would use all your skill to paint my picture truly like me, and not flatter me at all; but remark all these roughnesses, pimples, warts, and everything as you see me, otherwise I will never pay a farthing for it."

> *Oliver Cromwell (1599–1658),*
> *British lord protector, to the*
> *portraitist of Charles I's court*

Classical Phrases and Myths

"I portray men as they ought to be portrayed, but Euripides portrays them as they are."

> *Sophocles (c. 495 B.C.–406 B.C.),*
> *Greek playwright*

Jokes, Stories and Anecdotes

The six-year old was guiding his crayon meticulously on the sheet of paper. "What are you drawing, Freddy?" "A picture of God, Mommy." "But Freddy, nobody knows what God looks like." "They will when I'm through."

◆ REPRESENTATIVE (AGENT)

Foreign Words and Phrases

mayordomo (Spa)
(mah-yor-DOH-moh) chief servant (restaurant, household, etc.) (English: *major-domo*)

aide de camp (Fra)
(ED de kom) trusted assistant, confidential adviser to a senior officer (abbr: *DC*)

Quotations

"My agent gets ten per cent of everything I get, except my blinding headaches."

> *Fred Allen [John Sullivan] (1894–1957),*
> *U.S. comedian*

"It is well known what a middleman is: he is a man who bamboozles one party and plunders the other."

> *Benjamin Disraeli, 1st Earl of Beaconsfield*
> *(1804–1881), British prime minister,*
> *speech, Magnooth, April 11, 1845*

Classical Phrases and Myths

legatus a latere (Lat)
(le-GAH-tusah LAT-e-re) *lit:* ambassador from the inner circle; the formal description of a papal legate

In Greek mythology, the Myrmidons (MER-mee-donz) were a warlike people of ancient Thessaly. According to Homer's *Iliad*, the Myrmidons were a tribe of warriors led by Achilles in the Trojan War who performed their warlike duties as faithfully and tirelessly as the ants from which they had sprung and for which they were named. Thus, a *myrmidon* is an obedient and unquestioning follower or a policeman, a henchman.

◆ REPUTE (ADMIRATION)

Quotations

"The greatest mistake I made was not to die in office."

> *Dean [Gooderham] Acheson (1893–1971),*
> *U.S. diplomat*

"To enjoy a good reputation, give publicly, and steal privately."

> *Josh Billings [Henry Wheeler Shaw]*
> *(1818–1885), U.S. humorist*

"If you would not be known to do anything, never do it."

> *Ralph Waldo Emerson (1803–1882),*
> *U.S. writer, poet and philosopher,*
> *Essays: First Series (1841),*
> *"Spiritual Laws"*

"He cast off his friends as a huntsman his pack,
For he knew when he pleas'd he could whistle them back."

> *Oliver Goldsmith (1728–1774),*
> *Irish-born British poet, playwright*
> *and writer, Retaliation (1774),*
> *l. 107 [describing David Garrick]*

"We always like those who admire us; we do not always like those whom we admire."

> *François, Duc de La Rochefoucauld*
> *(1613–1680), French writer,*
> *Maximes (1678), 294*

"It's better to be looked over than overlooked."

> *Mae West (1892–1980),*
> *U.S. film actress, Belle of the Nineties*
> *(1934 film)*

Classical Phrases and Myths

kudos (Grk)
(KEW-dos) glory, renown, fame

Jokes, Stories and Anecdotes

Charles Edison, son of Thomas Edison, was campaigning for the governorship of New Jersey in 1940. When introducing himself, he was anxious to dissociate himself from his father's repute: "I would not have anyone believe I am trading on the name Edison. I would rather have you know me merely as the result of one of my father's earlier experiments."

Charles Edison (1890–1969),
U.S. politician, son of Thomas Edison

To ensure continuing critical and thus popular acclaim for his operas, the German composer and pianist Giacomo Meyerbeer used his great wealth to buy off critics. When Heinrich Heine, one of the bribed critics, suddenly had his financial umbilical cord cut by Meyerbeer, he presciently, and scathingly, remarked, "Meyerbeer will be immortal while he lives and perhaps for a little time after, because he always pays in advance."

Heinrich Heine (1797–1856),
German poet and writer

A cynical but kindly man, comedian Fred Allen, once rescued a boy from being hit by an oncoming truck. After snatching the boy to safety, Allen snarled at him, "What's the matter, kid? Don't you want to grow up and have troubles?"

Fred Allen [John Sullivan] (1894–1956),
U.S. comedian

On his South Pole expedition, Sir Edgeworth David's assistant, Douglas Mawson, was in his tent when he heard from outside a muffled cry. He then heard Sir David ask from the same direction, "Are you very busy?" "Yes I am," replied Mawson. "What's the matter?" "Are you really very busy?" persisted David. "Yes," said Mawson, impatiently. "What do you want?" There was silence, and then, apologetically, David said, "Well, I'm down a crevasse, and I don't think I can hang on much longer."

Sir Edgeworth David (1858–1934),
Australian geologist and explorer

◆ RESIGNATION

Foreign Words and Phrases

que será será (Spa)
(KAY seh-rah seh-rah) what will be, will be

c'est la vie (Fra)
(seh lah vee) that's life!

Quotations

"I am in that temper that if I were under water I would scarcely kick to come to the top."

John Keats (1795–1821), British poet,
letter to Benjamin Bailey, May 21, 1818

"What cannot be cured must be endured."

François Rabelais (c. 1494–1553),
French scholar, physician and writer

◆ RESISTANCE

Foreign Words and Phrases

jacquerie (Fra)
(jack-ehr-REE) insurrection of the lower class (from a 15th-century peasant revolt led by Jacques James)

Putsch (Ger)
(pootsh) insurrection, attempted revolution

Quotations

"We mean to hold our own. I have not become the King's First Minister in order to preside over the liquidation of the British Empire."

Sir Winston Spencer Churchill (1874–
1965), British prime minister and writer,
speech in London, November 10, 1942

"A little rebellion now and then is a good thing."

Thomas Jefferson (1743–1826),
U.S. president, letter to James Madison,
January 30, 1787

Classical Phrases and Myths

gaudium certaminis (Lat) (GOW-diumker-TAH-min-is) the joy of the struggle

contra mundum (Lat) (KON-tra MUN-dum) against the world; generally, one who assumes an unpopular position against the majority

Jokes, Stories and Anecdotes

A large firm was once offered a remarkable pension plan with one hitch: every employee had to join. Within a week everyone had signed except for the mail clerk. No matter who talked with him—coworkers, boss, or the personnel director—he refused to budge. "I don't understand it. I won't sign!" he repeated adamantly. Finally he was brought to the firm's president. "I'll make this very simple for you," began the president. "We're on the 40th floor of this building. If you don't sign, I'll throw you off my balcony. Understand?" The mail clerk nodded, withdrew a pen and hastily signed up for the pension plan. "So why did you sign so easily now, yet make such a fuss about signing before?" asked the president. Replied the mail clerk, "You're the first person who explained it so I could understand."

◆ RESOLUTION

Classical Phrases and Myths

Persian envoys of Xerxes came to demand surrender of Leonidas, the Spartan king who led the death stand at Thermopylae. "You are foolish to resist," they said. "The Persian archers alone are so numerous that their arrows will darken the sun." "So much the better," replied Leonidas, unmoved, "we will then fight in the shade." He and his 300 Spartan troops were slain to the man after Ephialtes traitorously showed the Persians a path to their rear; their famous epitaph read: "Go, stranger, and to Lacedaemon tell, that here, obeying her commands, we fell." In the narrow pass, Xerxes had lost 20,000 men to the Greeks, whose number was reduced from 4,000 to 1,000 to 300, mostly by surrender.

Leonidas (d. 480 B.C.), Spartan king

Jokes, Stories and Anecdotes

Having finished writing a paper, Albert Einstein and an assistant searched the office for a paper clip and found one—badly mangled. They then looked for a tool to straighten it, and finally located a whole box of clips. Instead of using any of the many presentable clips, however, Einstein shaped one for straightening the bent clip. He explained to the assistant, "Once I am set on a goal, it becomes difficult to deflect me."

Albert Einstein (1879–1955),
German-born physicist

◆ RESPECT

Quotations

"Admiration, n. Our polite recognition of another's resemblance to ourselves."

Ambrose [Gwinnet] Bierce
(1842–c. 1914), U.S. writer and poet,
Cynic's Word Book *(1906)*

"Go into the street, and give one man a lecture on morality, and another a shilling, and see which will respect you most."

> *Samuel Johnson (1709–1784),*
> *British man of letters*

"I do honour the very flea of his dog."

> *Ben Jonson (1573–1637),*
> *British playwright, Every Man in*
> *His Humour (1598), Act IV, sc. ii*

"He was a great patriot, a humanitarian, a loyal friend—provided, of course, that he really is dead."

> *Voltaire [François-Marie Arouet]*
> *(1694–1778), French philosopher,*
> *writer and wit, at a nobleman's funeral*

"Save me from my disciples."

> *Oscar [Fingal O'Flahertie Wills] Wilde*
> *(1854–1900), British playwright,*
> *writer and wit*

Jokes, Stories and Anecdotes

The French minister for foreign affairs, upon first meeting Thomas Jefferson, who went to pay his respects after arriving in France in 1785 to represent the United States, inquired, "You replace Monsieur Franklin?" "I succeed him," Jefferson replied. "No one could replace him."

> *Thomas Jefferson (1743–1826),*
> *U.S. president*

◆ RESPONSIBILITY & ASSIGNMENT

Foreign Words and Phrases

ombudsman (Swe)
(OHM-budz-man) one who handles administrative matters for a government or other institution, and esp. one who fields complaints from outsiders or constituents

Quotations

"Damn it! Another bishop dead! I think they die just to vex me."

> *William Lamb, 2nd Viscount Melbourne*
> *(1779–1848), British prime minister,*
> *expecting difficulties again in appointing a*
> *replacement in the House of Lords*

Classical Phrases and Myths

per procurationem (Lat)
(per PROH-koor-AH-ti-oh-nem) by the action of an authorized agent (abbr: *pp*)

sui juris (Lat)
(SU-ee YOOR-is) (of age) capable of assuming full responsibility and exercising judgment

faber est quis que fortunae suae (Lat)
(FAB-er est kwis-kwe for-TOON-ai SU-ee) (every) man is the architect of his own fortune

Jokes, Stories and Anecdotes

"For this job we want someone who is responsible." The applicant responded, "That's for me. Everywhere I've worked, whenever something went wrong, I was responsible."

◆ REST & VACATION

Quotations

"A perpetual holiday is a good working definition of hell."

> *George Bernard Shaw (1856–1950),*
> *Irish playwright*

Jokes, Stories and Anecdotes

Q: How many socialites does it take to screw in a light bulb? A: Two—one to mix the martinis, one to phone the electrician.

Louis Brandeis was once criticized for timing a short vacation just before the start of an important trial. "I require the rest," explained Brandeis. "I find that while I can do a year's work in 11 months, I can't do it in 12."

Louis Dembitz Brandeis (1856–1941),
U.S. jurist

During a long rehearsal delay when the singers were becoming impatient, a stagehand offered to fetch a chair so that opera singer Feodor Chaliapin could sit down until the problem was resolved. "It is not my body that is tired, it is my soul," replied Chaliapin. "But my soul has no ass. So forget the chair."

Feodor Ivanovich Chaliapin (1873–1938),
Russian opera singer

One evening when Thomas Edison came home from work, his wife said to him, "You've worked long enough without a rest. You must go on a vacation." "But where on earth would I go?" asked Mr. Edison. "Just decide where you would rather be than anywhere else on earth," suggested the wife. Mr. Edison hesitated. "Very well," he said finally, "I'll go tomorrow." The next morning, he was back at work in his laboratory.

Thomas Alva Edison (1847–1931),
U.S. inventor

◆ RESTITUTION

Jokes, Stories and Anecdotes

Christoph Gluck accidentally broke a glass pane of a shop on the rue St. Honore in Paris, and offered to pay for the replacement. When quoted the price, Gluck withdrew the only bill he had, which was about twice the amount. The shopkeeper was about to run next door

to get change when Gluck stopped him. "Don't bother. I will make it fair." And he broke another pane.

Christoph Willibald Gluck (1714–1787),
German composer [variations also
attributed to others]

◆ RESTRAINT (MODERATION)

Classical Phrases and Myths

ariston metron (Grk)
(ar-EES-ton MET-ron) the middle course is the best; the golden mean should be pursued (Homer)

via media (Lat)
(WEE-A MED-i-a) middle course between two extremes

aurea mediocritas (Lat)
(OW-re-amed-i-OK-rit-as) the golden mean, the happy medium (axiom derived from Aristotle)

◆ REVENGE

Foreign Words and Phrases

vigilante (Spa)
(vee-gheel-AHN-tay) *lit:* vigilance, watchfulness; self-appointed person outside the law who seeks order and often revenge

Quotations

"I and the public know
What all schoolchildren learn,
Those to whom evil is done
Do evil in return."

W[ystan] H[ugh] Auden (1907–1973),
British-born poet, Another Time *(1940),*
"September 1, 1939"

"A man that studieth revenge keeps his own wounds green."

Francis Bacon (1561–1626), British lawyer and writer, Essays (1625), "Of Revenge"

"Whose house is of glass, must not throw stones at another."

George Herbert (1593–1633), British clergyman and poet, Jacula Prudentum (1651), no. 196 [hence the proverb "People in glass houses shouldn't throw stones"]

"Living well is the best revenge."

George Herbert (1593–1633), British clergyman and poet, Jacula Prudentum (1651), no. 520

"Don't get mad; get even."

Joseph Patrick Kennedy (1888–1969), U.S. businessman and statesman [authenticity unverified]

"Revenge is often like biting a dog because the dog bit you."

Austin O'Malley (1858–1932), U.S. physician and writer

"The verses, when they were written, resembled nothing so much as spoonfuls of boiling oil, ladled out by a fiendish monkey at an upstairs window upon such of the passersby whom the wretch had a grudge against."

Lytton Strachey (1880–1932), British writer, commenting on Alexander Pope, Books and Characters (1922), "Lives of the Poets"

Classical Phrases and Myths

nemo me impune lacessit (Lat)
(NEE-moh may im-PUN-ayLAK-es-sit) no one provokes me without impunity; crown of Scotland motto

lex talionis (Lat)
(lex tal-ee-OH-nis) the law of retribution (allowing a victim to retaliate)

While en route to Rhodes when it was politically expedient for Julius Caesar to leave Rome, his ship was attacked by pirates. Caesar was captured and held for nearly 40 days at a ransom of 12,000 gold pieces. During his confinement, he often joked with the pirates that he would capture and crucify them, a threat at which they sneered. When the ransom was paid and Caesar was freed, he immediately gathered a fleet, chased down the pirates and crucified each man.

Gaius Julius Caesar (100 B.C.–44 B.C.), Roman general and statesman

Jokes, Stories and Anecdotes

A truck driver parked his 16-wheeler outside the diner, walked in and ordered a burger. As he was served, three huge bikers swaggered in, grabbed the trucker's burger and divided it among themselves. The driver quietly paid his bill and left. "Either that wimp is chicken or he can't fight," one biker snickered to the waitress. "Can't drive, either," she said. "He just ran over three motorcycles."

The rude society matron screamed at the airline employee at check-in, criticizing everything, before she left in a huff. The next in line sympathetically commented about the airline employee's ordeal. "Oh, I got even," replied the checker. "She's flying to Los Angeles, but her baggage is on its way to Baton Rouge."

◆ REVERENCE

Foreign Words and Phrases

faux devot (Fra)
(foh DAY-voh) one of false piety

Quotations

"How holy people look when they are seasick!"

Samuel Butler (1835–1902), British writer

"Men never do evil so completely and cheerfully, as when they do it from religious conviction."

Blaise Pascal (1623–1662), French mathematician and writer

"I admire the serene assurance of those who have religious faith. It is wonderful to observe the calm confidence of a Christian with four aces."

Mark Twain [Samuel Langhorne Clemens] (1835–1910), U.S. humorist, writer and speaker [authenticity unverified]

Classical Phrases and Myths

Dei gratia (Lat)
(DE-ee GRAH-ti-ah) by the grace of God

Solon told a tale of a pious mother who prayed that her two sons be granted the greatest gift the gods could bestow. Both youths promptly died, quietly and peacefully.

Solon (c. 639 B.C.–c. 559 B.C.), Greek legislator and statesman

Jokes, Stories and Anecdotes

"Clare Boothe Luce, playwright and widow of the publisher of *Time*, became a Catholic in middle life and naturally had a convert's conviction. While ambassador to Italy, she was once engaged in an earnest conversation with the pope. Anxious to catch a newsworthy story, a reporter leaned over and heard His Holiness saying in accented English, "But you don't understand, Mrs. Luce. I already *am* a Catholic."

Pope John XXIII [Angelo Roncalli] (1881–1963), Roman Catholic pope [authenticity unverified]

◆ REVOLUTION

Quotations

"It is well known that the most radical revolutionary will become a conservative on the day after the revolution."

Hannah Arendt (1906–1975), U.S. political philosopher

"If there's no dancing, count me out."

Emma Goldman (1869–1940), U.S. anarchist, commenting on the Russian Revolution

Jokes, Stories and Anecdotes

When the tartest member of Franklin Roosevelt's new administration, Harold Ickes, was asked why FDR was so intent on shaking things up, he responded, "You can't fertilize a 40-acre field by farting through the fence."

Harold L. Ickes (1874–1952), U.S. statesman

◆ RIDICULE

Quotations

"It is not necessary that every time he rises he should give his famous imitation of a semi-house-trained polecat."

Michael Foot (1913–   ), British politician, describing politician Norman Tebbit

"With a pig's eyes that never look up, with a pig's snout that loves muck, with a pig's brain that knows only the sty, and a pig's squeal that cries only when he is hurt, he sometimes opens his pig's mouth, tusked and ugly, and lets out the voice of God, railing at the whitewash that covers the manure about his habitat."

William Allen White (1868–1944),
U.S. writer, describing H. L. Mencken

"Caricature is the tribute that mediocrity pays to genius."

Oscar [Fingal O'Flahertie Wills] Wilde
(1854–1900), British playwright,
writer and wit

Jokes, Stories and Anecdotes

The colonial Virginia representative John Randolph was embarked on a long speech, but was hectored by Philomen Beecher, a representative from Ohio, who kept shouting out, "Mr. Speaker, previous question." Finally, the irritated Randolph exclaimed, "Mr. Speaker, in the Netherlands a man of small capacity with a bit of wood and leather will, in a few moments, construct a toy that, with the pressure of the finger and thumb, will cry, 'Cuckoo! Cuckoo!' With less ingenuity and with inferior materials, the people of Ohio have made a toy that will, without much pressure, cry, 'Previous question, Mr. Speaker!' "

John Randolph (1773–1833),
U.S. politician

◆ ROMANCE

Quotations

"The resistance of a woman is not always proof of her virtue, but more often of her experience."

Ninon de Lenclos (1620–1705),
French socialite and wit

"Some of the greatest love affairs I've known have involved one actor—unassisted."

Wilson Mizner (1876–1933), U.S. writer
and wit, describing Hollywood romances

"Candy
Is dandy
But liquor
Is quicker."

Ogden Nash (1902–1971), U.S. humorist,
Hard Lines (1931), "Reflections
on Ice-breaking"

"Men seldom make passes
At girls who wear glasses."

Dorothy Parker (1893–1967), U.S. wit
and writer, Not So Deep as a Well
(1937), "News Item"

Jokes, Stories and Anecdotes

Man picks up woman in a bar. She: "Your place or mine?" He: "If it's going to be a hassle, forget it."

"Have you loved anyone else before?" he asked. "No, I've admired men for their intellect, looks, job and so on. But with you, dear, it's love—nothing else."

So chivalrous toward ladies was the British actor Robert Elliston that he would declare his love even to chance acquaintances. He did so in a stagecoach and, seeing the object of his favor becoming agitated, he told the lady that he hoped he had not exceeded the limits of decorum. "Perhaps not, sir," the lady retorted, "but your limits of decorum are so extremely liberal that you may possibly lose your way in the excursion."

Robert William Elliston (1774–1831),
British actor

Zsa Zsa Gabor once appeared on a television program in which guest celebrities were asked to opine on matters of romance. A woman asked the first question: "I'm breaking my engagement to a very wealthy man who has already given me a sable coat, diamonds, a stove and a Rolls-Royce. What should I do?" Zsa Zsa counseled, "Give back the coat."

Zsa Zsa [Sari] Gabor (1919–   ), Hungarian-born U.S. actress

◆ RUMOR

Foreign Words and Phrases

canard (Fra)
(kahn-AR) *lit:* duck; rumor, hoax

Quotations

"Rumour is a pipe
Blown by surmises, jealousies, conjectures,
And of so easy and so plain a stop
That the blunt monster with uncounted heads,
The still-discordant wavering multitude,
Can play upon it."

William Shakespeare (1564–1616), British playwright and poet, Henry IV, Part II (1598), introduction

"There are two things that will be believed of any man whatsoever, and one of them is that he has taken to drink."

Booth Tarkington (1869–1946), U.S. writer, Penrod (1914), ch. 10

Classical Phrases and Myths

oratio oblique (Lat)
(or-AH-tio ob-LEE-kwa) secondhand statements, hearsay

Jokes, Stories and Anecdotes

The movie actress Bette Davis was informed that a rumor that she had died was spreading throughout New York. She was unworried. "With the newspaper strike on I wouldn't consider it."

Bette [Ruth Elizabeth] Davis (1908–1992), U.S. actress

◆ SADNESS & DESPAIR

Foreign Words and Phrases

chagrin (Fra)
(shag-ran) sorrow, vexation

Quotations

"My spirits were so low I could have used my chin to shine my boots."

Sonny [Salvatore] Bono (1943–   ), U.S. entertainer and politician, And the Beat Goes On (1992)

Classical Phrases and Myths

de profundis (Lat)
(day pro-FUN-dees) *lit:* from the depths; (arising) from extreme despair or anguish, the first words of the Latin version of Psalm 180, one of the seven penitential psalms, and the title of a book by Oscar Wilde

In Roman mythology, Saturn (SAT-ern) was a god of agriculture, the harvest and gardening who was believed to have been deposed from his rule by his son Jupiter during the golden age of Janus. Hence, one who is *saturnine* is gloomy and grave.

◆ SAFETY & SECURITY

Quotations

"There is no safety in numbers, or in anything else."

James Thurber (1894–1961), U.S. cartoonist and humorist, The New Yorker (February 4, 1939), "The Fairly Intelligent Fly"

◆ SAGE

Quotations

"A wise man will make more opportunities than he finds."

Francis Bacon (1561–1626),
British lawyer and writer, Essays
(1625), "Of Ceremonies and Respects"

"A wise man sees as much as he ought, not as much as he can."

Michel Eyquem de Montaigne (1533–
1592), French writer, Essays (1580)

"Have more than thou showest,
Speak less than thou knowest,
Lend less than thou owest."

William Shakespeare (1564–1616),
British playwright and poet,
King Lear (1606), Act I, sc. iv

"He [Thomas Macaulay] not only overflowed with learning, but stood in the slop."

Sydney Smith (1771–1845),
British clergyman and writer

Classical Phrases and Myths

"It takes a wise man to recognize a wise man."

Xenophanes (c. 570 B.C.–475 B.C.),
Greek philosopher

The Delphic oracle was asked to name the wisest man in Greece, and Socrates received the accolade. On being told this, Socrates said, "Since the gods proclaim me the wisest, I must believe it; but if that is so, then it must be because I alone of all the Greeks know that I know nothing."

Socrates (469 B.C.–399 B.C.),
Greek philosopher

Jokes, Stories and Anecdotes

Nobel laureate physicist Robert Millikan's wife overheard the maid at their residence answering the telephone. "Yes, this is where Dr. Millikan lives," said the servant, "but he's not the kind of doctor that does anybody any good."

Robert Andrews Millikan (1868–1953),
U.S. physicist

◆ SAINTS & ANGELS

Quotations

"Every time a child says 'I don't believe in fairies' there is a little fairy somewhere that falls down dead."

Sir J[ames] M[atthew] Barrie
(1860–1937), British writer
and playwright, Peter Pan (1928), Act I

"There is no sinner like a young saint."

Aphra Behn (1640–1689),
British playwright and poet

"Saint, n. A dead sinner revised and edited."

Ambrose [Gwinnet] Bierce
(1842–c. 1914), U.S. writer and poet,
Devil's Dictionary (1911)

"The way of this world is to praise dead saints and persecute living ones."

Nathaniel Howe (1764–1837),
U.S. clergyman

"The tyrant dies and his rule is over; the martyr dies and his rule begins."

Soren Kierkegaard (1813–1855),
Danish philosopher

"I stopped believing in Santa Claus when I was six. Mother took me to see him in a department store and he asked for my autograph."

Shirley Temple [Shirley Temple Black]
(1928–   ), U.S. film actress
and diplomat

Jokes, Stories and Anecdotes

As Ethan Allen lay ill, the examining physician said, "General, I fear the angels are waiting for you." "Waiting, are they?" thundered the American Revolution hero. "Waiting, are they? Well, let 'em wait."

Ethan Allen (1738–1789), U.S. patriot

◆ SANCTIMONY

Quotations

"I am halfway through *Genesis*, and quite appalled by the disgraceful behavior of all the characters involved, including God."

J. R. Ackerley (1896–1967), British writer

"Moral indignation is in most cases two per cent moral, 48 per cent indignation and 50 per cent envy."

Vittorio de Sica (1901–1974),
Italian director

"Piety is the tinfoil of pretense."

Elbert [Green] Hubbard (1856–1915),
U.S. businessman and writer

"We have just enough religion to make us hate, but not enough to make us love one another."

Jonathan Swift (1667–1745),
Anglo-Irish clergyman and writer,
Thoughts on Various Subjects *(1711)*

Jokes, Stories and Anecdotes

A woman was late to the auditorium for the evangelical meeting. She spotted an empty aisle seat and asked the man next to it, "Is this chair saved?" "Perhaps," he replied, "but sit down and we'll pray for it together."

Senator, lawyer and diplomat Joseph H. Choate and Speaker of the House Thomas Reed were in a conversation when Choate proudly declared, "I have not drunk whiskey, played cards for money, or attended a horse race in 28 years." "I wish I could say that!" exclaimed the admiring senator. Commented Reed: "Well, why don't you? Choate said it."

Thomas Brackett Reed (1839–1902),
U.S. politician

◆ SCANDAL

Foreign Words and Phrases

shmeer (Yid)
(shmeer) smear; bribe; paint

Jokes, Stories and Anecdotes

A great scandal burst when the affair between a chorus girl and a young employee of J. P. Morgan made headlines. Morgan bluntly informed his protégé that he was disappointed in him. "I'm not a hypocrite," countered the young man. "I have not done anything that most young men in my situation haven't done behind closed doors." "You may be right," Morgan snorted, "but that's what doors are for, dammit!"

John Pierpont Morgan, Jr. (1867–1943),
U.S. banker

◆ SCHOOL

Quotations

"I was a modest, good-humoured boy. It is Oxford that has made me insufferable."

Sir Max Beerbohm (1872–1956),
British writer, caricaturist and wit,
More *(1899),* "Going Back to School"

"Public schools are the nurseries of all vice and immorality."

Henry Fielding (1707–1754),
British writer, playwright and lawyer,
Joseph Andrews *(1742), bk. III, ch. 5*

"Let schoolmasters puzzle their brain,
With grammar, and nonsense, and teaming,
Good liquor, I stoutly maintain,
Gives genius a better discerning."

Oliver Goldsmith (1728–1774), Irish-born British poet, playwright and writer, She Stoops to Conquer (1775), Act I, song

"You can still buy five years' education at one of the best schools for less than half the cost of a Bentley."

Lord James of Rusholme (1909–), British educator

Classical Phrases and Myths

alma mater (Lat)
(AL-ma MAH-ter) *lit:* bounteous mother; beneficent or protective institution (typically, school, college, etc.)

lyceum (Grk)
lecture hall, teaching place, literary institution; the Lyceum was the school and playing field in Athens where Aristotle taught

In ancient Greece, the philosopher Plato taught at the Academy, named from the grove of Academos outside Athens. Hence, an *academy* is a place of learning.

Jokes, Stories and Anecdotes

On the campus of the University of Chicago where he was longtime president, Robert Hutchins met the great Greek scholar Professor Paul Shorey, who commented, "My understanding is that you and Mr. Adler are having the freshmen read and discuss the great books at the rate of one per week." Hutchins nodded. "But, really, how you can do that?" protested Shorey. "When I was a Harvard senior, it took us a whole term to study the *Divine Comedy*." "That may be, Professor

Shorey," said Hutchins, "but our students are bright."

Robert Maynard Hutchins (1899–1977), U.S. educator

◆ SCIENCE

Quotations

"That is the essence of science: ask an impertinent question, and you are on the way to a pertinent answer."

Jacob Bronowski (1908–1974), British scientist and scholar, Ascent of Man (1973), ch. 4

"The most incomprehensible thing about the world is that it is comprehensible."

Albert Einstein (1879–1955), German-born physicist

Jokes, Stories and Anecdotes

While anchored off Jamaica in 1504, Christopher Columbus was perilously low on food supplies, but the Jamaican Indians refused to sell him any more. Several days later, informed by his almanac that a lunar eclipse was due that night, he threatened the Jamaicans that unless they brought him food he would blot out the moon. The Jamaicans dismissed his threat but when the lunar eclipse began, they returned terrified. Columbus offered to restore the moon if he received his needed supplies, an offer gladly accepted. The moon was duly restored, and Columbus received his food.

Christopher Columbus (1451–1506), Italian-born navigator [attributed also to others]

◆ SCRIPTURE

Quotations

"No public man in these islands ever believes that the Bible means what it says; he is always convinced that it says what he means."

> *George Bernard Shaw (1856–1950),*
> *Irish playwright*

Jokes, Stories and Anecdotes

"I have good news, and I have bad news," said Moses as he returned from the top of Mount Sinai. "The good news is that God has reduced the commandments to ten. The bad news is that adultery's still in."

In his hospital bed near the end of his life, film comedian W. C. Fields was discovered reading the Bible. Challenged on his motives in suddenly "finding" religion so near to his death, the lifelong agnostic Fields muttered, "Just looking for loopholes."

> *W. C. Fields [William Claude Dukenfield]*
> *(1879–1946), U.S. film actor*
> *and comedian*

◆ SCULPTURE & CERAMICS

Jokes, Stories and Anecdotes

On the mantel in his room, the five-foot-tall eccentric surrealist Alfred Jarry displayed a huge stone phallus. To a woman who had asked whether it was a cast, Jarry replied, "Madame, no, it is a reduction."

> *Alfred Jarry (1873–1907),*
> *French writer*

◆ SECRECY

Foreign Words and Phrases

capa y espada (Spa)
(KAH-pah ee es-PAH-dah) *lit:* cloak and dagger; clandestine, with intrigue

entre nous (Fra)
(ON-tray noo) *lit:* between us; between you and me, in confidence

Quotations

"Mum's the word."

> *Miguel de Cervantes (1547–1616),*
> *Spanish writer,* Don Quixote de la
> Mancha, *Part II (1615), bk. IV, ch. 44*

"Three may keep a secret, if two of them are dead."

> *Benjamin Franklin (1706–1790),*
> *U.S. statesman and scientist,*
> Poor Richard's Almanac *(1732–1757)*

"Whoever wishes to keep a secret must hide the fact that he possesses one."

> *Johann Wolfgang Von Goethe*
> *(1749–1832), German poet,*
> *playwright and writer*

"I have the most perfect confidence in your indiscretion."

> *Sydney Smith (1771–1845),*
> *British clergyman and writer*

Classical Phrases and Myths

in camera (Lat)
(in KAM-er-ah) *lit:* in a room; proceedings conducted secretly, esp. in law

sub rosa (Lat)
(sub ROH-sah) *lit:* under the rose (a mark of secrecy); (pledge to be) secret, in confidence

◆ SENSUALITY

Quotations

"Give us the luxuries of life, and we will dispense with its necessities."

> John Lothrop Motley (1814–1877),
> U.S. historian [misattributed often to
> Oscar Wilde]

Classical Phrases and Myths

According to Greek mythology, Eros (EE-ros) (Roman: Cupid or Amor) was the god of love. He fired arrows of desire, in later legend randomly. Thus, something *erotic* produces sexual excitement.

Sybaris (SIB-a-ris), an ancient city in southern Italy founded in 720 B.C., was renowned for the luxury in which its inhabitants lived and celebrated for its wealth. Hence, a luxuriant lifestyle is *sybaritic*.

Jokes, Stories and Anecdotes

"Goodness, what beautiful diamonds!" "Goodness had nothing to do with it, dearie."

> Mae West (1892–1980), U.S. film actress,
> Night After Night (1932 film)

◆ SEVERITY

Classical Phrases and Myths

The ancient Greek legislator Charondas had promulgated a law that prohibited citizens from carrying weapons into the public assembly. One forgetful day, he wore his sword into the public meeting. A citizen reproached him for violating his own law. Charondas said, "By Zeus, I will confirm it," drew his sword and killed himself.

> Charondas (c. 550 B.C.), Greek legislator

◆ SEX

Foreign Words and Phrases

sosi khui (Rus)
(SUH-si KHEW-ee) fellatio

mènage a trois (Fra)
(may-NAJE ah TRWA) three-sided relationship, a married couple together with a third lover

consumatto (Ita)
(kon-SOOM-ah-toh) sex, climax

Quotations

"That was the most fun I ever had without laughing."

> Woody Allen [Allen Stewart Konigsberg]
> (1935–   ), U.S. comedian and
> filmmaker, and Marshall Brickman
> (1941–   ), U.S. humorist,
> describing sex, Annie Hall (1977 film)

"If God had meant us to have group sex, I guess he'd have given us all more organs."

> Malcolm Bradbury (1932–   ),
> British writer

"It doesn't matter what you do in the bedroom as long as you don't do it in the street and frighten the horses."

> Mrs. Patrick Campbell [Beatrice]
> (1865–1940), British actress

"All I can say is that sex in Ireland is as yet in its infancy."

> Eamon De Valera (1882–1975),
> Irish prime minister and president,
> returning from France as a young man

"License my roving hands, and let them go

346

Before, behind, between, above, below."

John Donne (1571–1631), British poet

"Keep your eyes wide open before marriage, and half-shut afterwards."

Benjamin Franklin (1706–1790),
U.S. statesman and scientist,
Poor Richard's Almanac (1732–1757)

"It's like air . . . not important until you're not getting any."

Debbie Reynolds (1932–),
U.S. film actress, commenting on sex

"Sex is an emotion in motion."

Mae West (1892–1980), U.S. film actress

"Said a potentate grown and despotic
'My tastes are more rich than exotic.
I've always adored
Making love in a Ford
Because I am auto-erotic.' "

Anonymous

"I've slept with more women by accident than John Kennedy had slept with on purpose."

Lyndon Baines Johnson (1908–1973),
U.S. president

"It has to be admitted that we English have sex on the brain, which is a very unsatisfactory place to have it."

Malcolm Muggeridge (1903–),
British writer

Classical Phrases and Myths

In Greek mythology, Aphrodite (a-FROH-di-tee) (Roman: Venus) was the goddess of love and beauty. Hence, an aphrodisiac is a sexual stimulant.

Jokes, Stories and Anecdotes

Now that his son had turned 13, the father decided that he should discuss those matters that an adolescent ought to know about life. So he called the boy into the study, shut the door carefully, and said with impressive dignity, "Son, I would like to discuss the facts of life with you." "Sure thing, Dad," said the boy. "What do you want to know?"

Q: How can you tell when a socialite achieves orgasm? A: She drops her Gucci purse.

Three youngsters, six, seven, and eight years of age, walked past an open street-level window. The six-year-old looked in and waved excitedly to the others. "Look," he said. "A man and a woman are fighting in there." The seven-year-old looked in and said, "You fool, they are making love." Said the eight-year-old, "Yes, and badly."

Caroline of Brunswick returned after her foreign travels to claim her rightful place as Queen of England upon the accession of George IV. The king brought an action for divorce on the grounds of adultery and she was tried in 1820 before the House of Lords. A line of inquiry involved her conduct with the dey (governor) of Algiers. Chief Justice Lord Norbury noted: "She was happy as the dey was long."

Caroline of Brunswick (1768–1821),
British queen

President Calvin Coolidge and his wife were taken on separate tours of a government farm in the 1920s. Grace Anna Coolidge, standing by the chicken pens, inquired whether the rooster copulated more than once a day. "Oh, yes," replied the overseer. "Many times." "Tell that to the president," she said. When the president heard about the rooster, he asked, "Same hen every time?" "No, a different one each time." Coolidge replied, "Tell that to Mrs. Coolidge."

[John] Calvin Coolidge (1872–1933), U.S. president

Film comedian W. C. Fields was once asked by an interviewing reporter, off the record, for his opinions about sex. "On or off the record," replied Fields, "there may be some things better than sex, and there may be some things worse. But there's nothing exactly like it."

W. C. Fields [William Claude Dukenfield] (1879–1946), U.S. film actor and comedian

Gaston Palewski, Charles de Gaulle's chief of staff, was a renowned libertine. When he once offered to drive a woman home from a party, she politely answered, "Thank you, but I'm too tired. I think I'll walk."

Gaston Palewski (d. 1984), French statesman

Dorothy Parker once scathingly reported on the numerous pretty girls present at a Yale prom. "If all the girls attending it were laid end to end," she said, "I wouldn't be at all surprised."

Dorothy Parker (1893–1967), U.S. wit and writer

◆ SHOW BUSINESS

Foreign Words and Phrases

piéce rosée (Fra)
(pyes ro-ZAY) *lit:* radiant piece; amusing piece of writing, light play, etc.

scenes a faire (Fra)
(zen ah fair) lit: scenes which must be done; in copyright law, incidents or plots immune from copyright infringement liability because they

necessarily flow from common themes or ideas, i.e., stock scenes

Quotations

"Congratulations on your latest production. Sure it will look better after it has been cut."

Eddie Cantor (1892–1964), U.S. entertainer, telegram to film producer Irving Thalberg on birth of his son

Jokes, Stories and Anecdotes

The famous opera producer had no sooner passed through the pearly gates than St. Peter told him they had an opera for him to produce. The producer tried to beg off, but St. Peter explained that this was a special opera—the libretto was by Shakespeare. At first intrigued, the producer nonetheless declined. Then St. Peter said the music score was by Beethoven. The producer was strongly tempted but shook his head. "Set design by da Vinci," St. Peter persisted. "Libretto by Shakespeare! Original score by Beethoven! Set design by da Vinci!" the producer exclaimed. "I'll do it!" "There's just one catch," St. Peter said. "God has this girlfriend who sings. . . "

The human cannonball, after years of being blasted into a net, went to the circus owner and told him he was going to retire. "You can't!" roared the cigar-chomping boss. "Where will I find a man of your caliber?"

The librettist W. S. Gilbert, of Gilbert and Sullivan fame, was a perfectionist and martinet. An actor, refusing to allow Gilbert to browbeat him, drew up his shoulders and declared, "See here, I will not be bullied. I know my lines." "Possibly," sniffed Gilbert, "but you don't know mine."

Sir W[illiam] S[chwenck] Gilbert (1836–1911), British writer

Ringling Brothers, Barnum and Bailey Circus once commissioned choreographer George Balanchine to arrange the dance and retain a composer for a ballet for certain circus performers. Balanchine called Stravinsky, who 30 years earlier had written *The Firebird*, *Petrushka* and *Le Sacre du printemps*. "What kind of music?" asked Stravinsky. Balanchine replied, "A polka." "For whom?" "Elephants." "How old?" "Young!" "If they are very young, I will do it." Stravinsky's 1942 *Circus Polka* was performed at least 425 times.

Igor Feodorovitch Stravinsky (1882–1971), Russian-born composer

◆ SICKNESS

Foreign Words and Phrases

grand mal (Fra)
(grohn MAL) *lit:* great illness; epileptic seizure

Quotations

"I hope it's nothing trivial."

Irvin S[hrewsbury] Cobb (1876–1944), U.S. humorist and writer, learning that his disagreeable boss at the New York World, Charles E. Chapin, was ill

Classical Phrases and Myths

nocebo (Lat)
(NOHK-e-bo) *lit:* I shall displease; in medicine, a harmless substance that might make one sick because the person believes it will

Jokes, Stories and Anecdotes

It was a rough ocean crossing and Mr. Jones was suffering the tortures of the damned. While he was leaning over the rail, retching, a steward patted him, comforting, "It may seem unbearable, sir, but remember, no man ever died of seasickness." Mr. Jones turned his green countenance to the steward and cried, "For heaven's sake, man, don't tell me that. Only the hope of dying is keeping me alive."

◆ SIGHT

Foreign Words and Phrases

voilà (Fra)
(vwa-la) *lit:* look there; look at that

Quotations

"You see, but you do not observe."

Sir Arthur Conan Doyle (1859–1930), Adventures of Sherlock Holmes (1892), "Scandal in Bohemia"

"Vision is the art of seeing things invisible."

Jonathan Swift (1667–1745), Anglo-Irish clergyman and writer, Thoughts on Various Subjects (1711)

◆ SILENCE

Quotations

"Even a fool, when he holdeth his peace, is counted wise."

Proverbs 17:28

"Silence is become his mother tongue."

Oliver Goldsmith (1728–1774), Irish-born British poet, playwright and writer, The Good-Natured Man (1768), Act II

"That man's silence is wonderful to listen to."

> Thomas Hardy (1840–1928), British writer and poet, Under the Greenwood Tree (1874), ch. 14

"Silence: a conversation with an Englishman."

> Henrich Heine (1797–1856), German poet and writer

"Silence is the most perfect expression of scorn."

> George Bernard Shaw (1856–1950), Irish playwright, Back to Methuselah (1921), pt. 5

"Silence is the unbearable repartee."

> G[ilbert] K[eith] Chesterton (1874–1936), British man of letters

Classical Phrases and Myths

"I have often regretted my speech, never my silence."

> Publilius Syrus (c. 100 B.C.), Roman writer, Sententiae, 1070

A typically loquacious barber asked King Archelaus how he would like his hair cut. Answered the king, "In silence."

> Archelaus (c. 550 B.C.), Macedonian king

Jokes, Stories and Anecdotes

When Western Union offered to buy the ticker invented by Thomas Edison, the great inventor was unable to name a price. Edison asked for a couple of days to consider it. He talked the matter over with his wife, and she suggested he ask $20,000, but this seemed exorbitant to Edison. At the appointed time, Edison returned to the Western Union office. He was asked to name his price. "How much?" asked the Western Union official. Edison tried to say $20,000, but lacked the courage, and just stood there speechless. The official waited a moment, then broke the silence and said, "Well, how about $100,000?"

> Thomas A. Edison (1847–1931), U.S. inventor [authenticity unverified]

◆ SIMILARITY (CONSISTENCY)

Foreign Words and Phrases

tout ensemble (Fra)
(toot en-SEHM-ble) all together, in unison

Quotations

"Another, yet the same."

> Alexander Pope (1688–1744), British poet and writer, The Dunciad (1728–1743)

"I wouldn't say when you've seen one Western you've seen the lot; but when you've seen the lot you get the feeling you've seen one."

> Katharine Whitehorn (1926–   ), British writer, Sunday Best (1976), "Decoding the West"

Classical Phrases and Myths

alter idem (Lat)
(AL-ter EE-dem) another precisely similar

◆ SIN & WRONGDOING

Foreign Words and Phrases

pecadillo (Spa)
(peh-kah-DEE-lyoh) minor transgression, venial offence (from *pecado*: sin)

honi soit qui mal y pense (Fra)
(OH-nee swa kee mal ee ponse) shame on him who thinks evil (motto of the Order of the Garter)

Quotations

"All sin tends to be addictive, and the terminal point of addiction is what is called damnation."

W[ystan] H[ugh] Auden (1907–1973), British-born poet, A Certain World (1970), "Hell"

"Pleasure's a sin, and sometimes sin's a pleasure."

George Gordon, Lord Byron (1788–1824), British poet, Don Juan (1818), Canto I, st. cxxxiii

"Many are saved from sin by being so inept at it."

Mignon McLaughlin (c. 1930–   ), U.S. writer

"The only people who should really sin
Are the people who can sin with a grin."

Ogden Nash (1902–1971), U.S. humorist, I'm a Stranger Here Myself (1938), "Inter-Office Memorandum"

"Between two evils, I always pick the one I never tried before."

Mae West (1892–1980), U.S. film actress, Klondike Annie (1936 film)

Classical Phrases and Myths

peccavi (Lat)
(pek-KAH-wee) lit: I have sinned; to admit to being in the wrong

"The road to Hades is easily traveled."

Bion (c. 325 B.C.–c. 255 B.C.), Greek philosopher

◆ SINCERITY

Foreign Words and Phrases

po dusham (Rus)
(poh DEWSH-uhm) from the soul

Quotations

"It is dangerous to be sincere unless you are also stupid."

George Bernard Shaw (1856–1950), Irish playwright, Man and Superman (1903), "Maxims for Revolutionists: Stray Sayings"

"A little sincerity is a dangerous thing, and a great deal of it is absolutely fatal."

Oscar [Fingal O'Flahertie Wills] Wilde (1854–1900), British playwright, writer and wit, The Critic as Artist (1891)

◆ SINGING & OPERA

Foreign Words and Phrases

falsetto (Ita)
(fall-SET-toh) voice above the natural register of the singer

basso profundo (Ita)
(BAHS-so proh-FOON-doh) in music, very deep bass voice

coloratura (Ita)
(kol-orr-a-TOO-rah) colorful singing, with passages designed to display virtuosity

bel canto (Ita)
(bel KAN-toh) lit: beautiful singing; singing with full, rich tone

Quotations

"Swans sing before they die—
'twere no bad thing
Did certain persons die before they sing."

Samuel Taylor Coleridge (1772–1834), British poet and writer, Epigram on a Volunteer Singer

351

"Opera is when a guy gets stabbed in the back and, instead of bleeding, he sings."

Ed Gardner (1905–1963), U.S. comedian, "Duffy's Tavern," U.S. radio program, 1940s

"Anybody singing the blues is in a deep pit yelling for help."

Mahalia Jackson (1911–1972), U.S. singer

"Opera in English is, in the main, just about as sensible as baseball in Italian."

H[enry] L[ouis] Mencken (1880–1956), U.S. critic and writer

"She sang, of course, 'Mama!' and not 'he loves me,' since an unalterable and unquestioned law of the musical world required that the German text of French operas sung by Swedish artists should be translated into Italian for the clearer understanding of English speaking audiences."

Edith Wharton (1862–1937), U.S. writer, Age of Innocence (1920), bk. 1, ch. 1

Jokes, Stories and Anecdotes

During his long tenure as general manager of the New York Metropolitan Opera House, Giulio Gatti-Casazza once gently tried to comfort an auditioning tenor by telling him that he was not quite ready for the Met. "Not ready!" the singer exclaimed. "Why, I'll have you know that La Scala thought so much of my voice when I was with them that they insured it for 50,000 pounds." "Indeed," said Gatti-Casazza. "And what did La Scala do with the money?"

Giulio Gatti-Casazza (1869–1940), Italian-born operatic manager

The baritone was rehearsing for a production of *Pagliacci* in which the "daring" director called for Merrill to get on his knees and place his head in the lap of a typically huge diva during a passionate duet. Merrill protested that the diva did not have a lap, but to no avail. He protested again when he put his face in her crotch, the only place available, but the director was adamant about his staging. While singing the duet, Merrill's voice warbled. The director shouted, "What's the trouble?" "I think I'm getting an echo."

Robert Merrill [Robert Miller] (1917–1994), U.S. opera singer

At the conclusion of Wagner's opera *Lohengrin*, a magic swan appears onstage and carries back the hero in a boat it is pulling to rejoin the fellowship of the Knights of the Holy Grail. Once when the tenor Leo Slezak was singing the opera, the contraption malfunctioned and sailed off back into the wings. The stranded tenor gestured toward his wrist and blankly asked the audience, "When does the next swan leave?"

Leo Slezak (1873–1946), Czechoslovak opera singer [attributed also to Lauritz Melchior and Joseph Tichatschek]

◆ SINGULARITY

Foreign Words and Phrases

wabi (Jap)
(WAH-bee) a flawed detail that creates an elegant, beautiful whole

avoir cachet (Fra)
(ah-VWAR ka-SHAY) to have distinction (or authority)

Classical Phrases and Myths

de minimis non curat lex (Lat)
(day MIN-ee-mees non koo-rat lex) the law does not concern itself with trifles

Jokes, Stories and Anecdotes

The surgeon asked his newly wealthy patient, "So would you prefer a local anesthetic for your forthcoming operation?" "I can afford the best," replied the patient. "Get something imported."

Asked to sign a first-edition copy of his book, Alexander Woollcott coyly sighed, amid the approving murmurs, "Ah, what is so rare as a Woollcott first edition?" Replied Franklin Pierce Adams, "A Woollcott second edition."

> *Franklin Pierce Adams (1881–1960),*
> *U.S. writer [attributed also to others]*

◆ SKIN

Jokes, Stories and Anecdotes

While sitting at the famous Round Table in the Algonquin dining room, dramatist Marc Connelly had his virtually bald head rubbed by the hand of a passing man who sneered, "It feels just like my wife's behind." Connelly, not batting an eyelash, remarked, "So it does."

> *Marc Connelly (1890–1980),*
> *U.S. playwright [attributed also to*
> *Nicholas Longworth]*

◆ SLEEP

Classical Phrases and Myths

"All men whilst they are awake are in one common world: but each of them, when he is asleep, is in a world of his own."

> *Plutarch (46–120), Greek writer, Morals,*
> *Of Superstition*

Jokes, Stories and Anecdotes

Lying next to his wife, who was reading in bed, the movie director began to talk aloud in his sleep. "Darling, I know I can get away from my bitchy wife for a week. I love you so." Just then he awoke, with his wife glowering down upon him. Quickly, he mumbled as if still asleep, "OK, let's repeat that scene."

At a party where Alfred Hitchcock had been asleep for nearly four hours, his wife awakened him to go home. "But it's only one o'clock," Hitchcock, who habitually fell asleep at parties, protested. "The hosts may get the impression that we aren't enjoying ourselves!"

> *Sir Alfred Hitchcock (1889–1980),*
> *British film director*

◆ SLOWNESS

Foreign Words and Phrases

allargando (Ita)
(al-ar-GAN-doh) in music, slowing down gradually

andante (Ita)
(an-DAHN-teh) *lit:* walking; slow tempo (in flowing style)

Jokes, Stories and Anecdotes

Late for delivering a lecture, Thomas Huxley dashed into a cab and ordered the cabman to use top speed. The cabman cracked his whip and the horse jumped forward. As the cab was racing down the street, Huxley stuck his head out the window and asked the cabman, "Do you know where I want to go?" "No, sir!" exclaimed the cabman, "but I'm goin' as fast as I can!"

> *Thomas Henry Huxley (1825–1895),*
> *British biologist and philosopher*

As a country lawyer, Abraham Lincoln once had to hire a horse from the local stables for an out-of-town case. Returning the animal, he asked the liveryman whether he kept the horse for funerals. "Certainly not," was the reply. "I am glad to hear it," said Lincoln, "because if you did, the corpse would not get there in time for the resurrection."

Abraham Lincoln (1809–1865),
U.S. president

◆ SLYNESS

Foreign Words and Phrases

melin (Fra)
(meh-LON) clever

sechel (Yid)
(SEKH-el) street smarts

finesse (Fra)
(fi-NESS) delicacy; in bridge, an attempt to win a trick although a higher card is known to be held by an opponent

Quotations

"With foxes we must play the fox."

Thomas Fuller (1654–1734),
British physician

"A hoot owl bangs into the roost and knocks the hen clean off, and catches her while she's falling. But a scrootch owl slips into the roost and scrootches up to the hen and talks softly to her. And the hen just falls in love with him, and the first thing you know, there ain't no hen."

Huey [Pierce] Long (1893–1935),
U.S. politician, distinguishing Herbert
Hoover, the "hoot owl," from Franklin
Delano Roosevelt, the "scrootch owl"

"He skillfully avoided what was wrong
Without saying what was right,

And never let his on the one hand
Know what his on the other was doing."

Frank Scott (c. 1900s), Canadian writer,
deriding Canadian prime minister
W. L. MacKenzie King, 1957

Classical Phrases and Myths

"It is a profitable thing, if one is wise, to seem foolish."

Aeschylus (525 B.C.–456 B.C.),
Greek playwright, Prometheus Bound

According to Greek legend, Daedalus (DEE-da-lus) was the architect who designed the Labyrinth to hide the Minotaur at the behest of King Minos, who was ashamed of his wife's monstrous son. The Labyrinth was designed so that no one entering would ever find the way out and divulge what he had seen. To ensure that his secret was kept, Minos had Daedalus and his son Icarus imprisoned. Daedalus craftily made wings for his son and himself, but as they flew to freedom, Icarus ignored his father's pleas and flew too close to the sun, thus melting the wax that held the wings together. He fell to his death in what is now called the Icarian Sea. Minos sought to trap Daedalus and offered a rich reward to anyone who could run a thread through a spiraled triton shell. A friend of Daedalus brought him the shell; Daedalus attached a thread to an ant and, by putting honey at the other end of the shell, induced the ant to traverse the coiling chambers of the shell to the other end. When the friend presented the threaded shell for the reward, Minos knew he had located Daedalus, for nobody else could be so clever. Thus, the phrases *with the inventiveness of Daedalus* and *daedalean* denote artistic skill and complexity.

Jokes, Stories and Anecdotes

Aboard a trans-Atlantic liner a steward was walking along the promenade deck with a large bowl of soup. The ship took a sudden pitch, and he spilled the entire bowl onto the shirtfront of a passenger sleeping in a deck chair. Thinking quickly, the steward awakened the man and said consolingly, "Feeling better now, sir?"

The hardware-store owner became suspicious of his brightest shop clerk when he discovered that the man lived like a king on a meager salary of $100 a week. When confronted by his boss, the man explained that each week he would sell 300 raffle tickets at a dollar apiece. "But what are you raffling off?" the store owner asked. "My paycheck."

At breakfast, Mrs. Jones asked, "Didn't I hear the clock strike one when you came home last night?" "Yes, Mom," replied her daughter sweetly. "It would've struck 11 but I stopped it to avoid waking you."

King Louis XIV once showed some poems he had written to the influential literary critic Nicolas Boileau, asking for his opinion of them. "Sire, nothing is impossible for Your Majesty," replied the honey-tongued courtier. "Your Majesty has set out to write bad verses and has succeeded."

Nicolas Boileau [-Despreaux] (1636–1711), French writer

The rector of his church asked the notorious financier and railroad magnate Jay Gould for his investment advice for the preacher's life savings of about $30,000. Gould confidentially suggested stock in Missouri Pacific, which the rector purchased. Although the stock initially rose steadily, the stock nosedived several months later. When Gould presented the despairing minister with a $40,000 check to cover his losses, the minister acknowledged that he had in fact passed on Gould's stock tip to other members of the church congregation. "I know that," smiled Gould. "It was them whom I wanted."

Jay Gould (1836–1892), U.S. financier

◆ SMELL

Quotations

"Henry IV's feet and armpits enjoyed an international reputation."

Aldous Huxley (1894–1963), British writer

◆ SMOKING

Quotations

"A cigarette is the perfect type of a perfect pleasure. It is exquisite, and it leaves one unsatisfied. What more can one want?"

Oscar [Fingal O'Flahertie Wills] Wilde (1854–1900), British playwright, writer and wit, The Picture of Dorian Gray (1891), ch. 6

Jokes, Stories and Anecdotes

During a rehearsal of one of his plays, Oscar Wilde was angrily quarreling with Sarah Bernhardt over how her part should be interpreted. Having reached an impasse, Wilde drawled, "Do you mind if I smoke, madam?" Snapped Bernhardt, "I don't care if you burn."

Sarah Bernhardt (1844–1923), French actress

While sitting contentedly in a railway waiting room smoking a cigar,

Count Haeseler was told by a young lieutenant, the room's other occupant, "You ought not smoke that cabbage-leaf cigar in good company." With that, he offered Haeseler one of his own cigars. The count continued to smoke his own cigar, however, placing the gift into his pocket. "Sir, why are you not smoking my cigar?" queried the surprised lieutenant. Retorted Haeseler, "I shall wait, as you suggest, until I'm in good company."

Count Gottlieb von Haeseler (1836–1919),
German general

◆ SOBRIETY

Quotations

"I'd hate to be a teetotaller. Imagine getting up in the morning and knowing that's as good as you're going to feel all day."

Dean Martin (1917–   ),
U.S. singer and actor

Jokes, Stories and Anecdotes

After drinking several jugs of cheap wine in the chilly night, three winos passed out. Two later awoke to find that the third had died during the night. At the funeral home, the two surviving friends stood by the coffin of their departed buddy. "Boy, ol' Fred sure looks good, don't he?" the first remarked. "Well, he oughta. He ain't had a drink in three days."

Then there was the fellow who, having sworn off drink, passed five bars with nary a sideways glance, so, in sheer ecstasy, he went to another bar for a drink to celebrate his victory.

According to novelist Gertrude Atherton, William Randolph Hearst, referring to the heavy drinkers on the staff of his *San Francisco Examiner*, would say that no one suffered more from the drink habit than he, although he himself never drank.

William Randolph Hearst (1863–1951),
U.S. publisher

◆ SOCIABILITY

Foreign Words and Phrases

bonhomie (Fra)
(bon-OM-EE)   good-heartedness, good nature

Quotations

"The most exhausting thing in life is being insincere. That is why so much social life is exhausting."

Anne Morrow Lindbergh (1906–1994),
U.S. poet and writer

"The sight of you is good for sore eyes."

Jonathan Swift (1667–1745),
Anglo-Irish clergyman and writer, Polite Conversation *(c. 1738),* "Dialogue I"

"Familiarity breeds contempt—and children."

Mark Twain [Samuel Langhorne Clemens] (1835–1910), U.S. humorist, writer and speaker, Notebooks *(1935), p. 237*

Jokes, Stories and Anecdotes

Arguing a case in court, two lawyers began to hurl names at each other. "You amoebic moron!" cried one. "You ambulance-chasing shyster," countered the other. The judge rapped for order. "Let's proceed with the case," she said, "now that you two have introduced each other to the court."

◆ SOCIALISM & COMMUNISM

Quotations

"It is a socialist idea that making profits is a vice; I consider the real vice is making losses."

> Sir Winston Spencer Churchill (1874–1965), British prime minister and writer

"Send your son to Moscow and he will return an anti-Communist; send him to the Sorbonne and he will return a Communist."

> Felix Houphouet-Boigny (1905–   ), Ivory Coast president

"Der Sozialismiis ist nichts als der Kapitalismus der Unterklasse." (Socialism is nothing but the capitalism of the lower classes.)

> Oswald Spengler (1880–1936), German philosopher and scholar, Jahre der Etitscheidung (The Hour of Decision) (1933), pt. 1

Jokes, Stories and Anecdotes

Bon's Yeltsin, in an effort to bolster his popularity, visited an agricultural commune. "Well, comrade, how are the potatoes this year?" he asked a farmer. "Very well, Comrade President," the farmer answered. "If we stacked them, they would reach God." "But God does not exist, Comrade Farmer." "Neither do the potatoes, Comrade President."

An alarmed colleague nervously informed Georges Clemenceau, who was France's prime minister during WWI, "Your son has just joined the Communist party!" "Monsieur, my son is 22 years old," Clemenceau calmly replied. "If he had not become a Communist at 22, I would have disowned him. If he is still a Communist at 30, I will do it then."

> Georges Clemenceau (1841–1929), French prime minister

◆ SOLDIERS

Foreign Words and Phrases

Wehrmacht (Ger) (VEHR-mahkt) Hitler's armed forces

Quotations

"Soldiers in peace are like chimneys in summer."

> Lord Burghley (1520–1598), British writer

"Don't talk to me about naval tradition. It's nothing but rum, sodomy and the lash."

> Sir Winston Spencer Churchill (1874–1965), British prime minister and writer

"An army marches on its stomach."

> Napoleon I [Napoleon Bonaparte] (1769–1821), French general and emperor [authenticity unverified]

"I never expect a soldier to think."

> George Bernard Shaw (1856–1950), Irish playwright, The Devil's Disciple (1901), Act III

"Overpaid, overfed, oversexed, and over here."

> Tommy Trinder (1909–1989), British writer, describing American troops in Britain during WWII

"I didn't fire him because he was a dumb son of a bitch, although he was, but that's not against the law for generals. If it was, half to three quarters of them would be in jail."

> Harry S Truman (1884–1972), U.S. president, commenting on General Douglas MacArthur

Jokes, Stories and Anecdotes

During the Civil War, Reverend Henry Ward Beecher traveled to England to garner British support for the North. He was asked while addressing a disorderly crowd of Rebel sympathizers, "Why didn't you whip the Confederates in 60 days, as you said you would?" "Because," retorted Beecher, "we found we had Americans to fight instead of Englishmen."

Henry Ward Beecher (1813–1887),
U.S. clergyman and writer

◆ SOLUTION

Foreign Words and Phrases

il doit y avoir une solution (Fra)
(il dwah ee a-VWAH oon zo-LOOT-un) there must be a solution . . .

denouement (Fra)
(DAY-new-MON) *lit:* unravelling (of plot); resolution, outcome (usually of a play, novel, etc.), result

Quotations

"A desperate disease requires a dangerous remedy."

Guy Fawkes (1570–1606), British outlaw,
justifying the gunpowder conspiracy to
blow up the Houses of Parliament
(after Hippocrates)

Classical Phrases and Myths

deus ex machina (Lat)
(DE-us ex MAK-in-ah) lit: god from a machine; being or device invoked to solve an otherwise insoluble problem; in drama, the intervention of the gods (lowered onto the stage by a device) to settle a problem

An extremely thirsty crow had the apparent good fortune to happen upon a pitcher of water, but when it stuck its beak into the long-necked container, the water left was beyond its reach. About to give up in dispair, the crow hit upon an idea to quench its thirst. It found and dropped pebbles, one by one, into the pitcher, until the water level rose and, proving that *necessity is the mother of invention*, the crow was able to drink.

Aesop (c. 600 B.C.), Greek fabulist

At Gordium in Phrygia (Asia Minor) a chariot was fastened with cords made from the bark of a cornel tree. The knot was so intricately tied that no ends were visible, and the tradition was that the empire of the world should fall to the man who could untie it. When Alexander the Great conquered Gordium, he confronted the famous puzzle. Unable to untie the knot, he drew his sword and cut it. Thus, to *cut the Gordian knot* is to take forthright action and sidestep hindering complexities.

Alexander III [Alexander the Great]
(356 B.C.–323 B.C.), Macedonian king

Jokes, Stories and Anecdotes

"Given the present world situation," said the armchair philosopher, "the solution is not to be born at all. But I doubt that one person in a million is that lucky."

John Randolph and Henry Clay, two early American politicians, were fierce rivals. Once, the two politicians found themselves face to face on a plank—laid out in a muddy street—so narrow that they could not pass. "I never give way to scoundrels," said Randolph, standing his ground. "I always do," said Clay, stepping into the mud.

Henry Clay (1777–1852),
U.S. statesman and orator

◆ SOPHISTRY

Quotations

"Yes, it is a terrible disease. You either die of it, or go insane. I have had it myself."

Marie Edme Maurice, Comte de MacMahon (1808–1893), French general and president, while visiting a field hospital, encouraging a soldier ill with tropical fever

Classical Phrases and Myths

ignoratio elenchi (Lat)
(ig-nor-AH-tee-oh ay-LENG-hi) in logic, an irrelevant argument that ignores the point at issue

argumentum ex silentio (Lat)
(ar-gu-MEN-tum ex sil-ENT-ee-oh) *lit*: argument out of silence; argument based on the absence of firm evidence

petitio principii (Lat)
(peh-TEE-ti-oh PRIN-ki-pi-ee) in logic and law, to beg the question

argumentum ad individium (Lat)
(ar-gu-MEN-tum ad in-di-WID-ee-um) argument that appeals to prejudices

non sequitur (Lat)
(nohn SEK-wi-tur) *lit:* it does not follow; something that does not follow from that expressed immediately before

Jokes, Stories and Anecdotes

Baseball player Yogi Berra was once asked whether he would like the pizza he had ordered cut into four or eight pieces. "Better make it four," said Berra. "I'll never be able to eat eight."

Lawrence ["Yogi"] Berra
(1925–   ), U.S. baseball player
and manager

"His argument is as thin as the homeopathic soup that was made by boiling the shadow of a pigeon that had been starved to death."

Abraham Lincoln (1809–1865), U.S. president, describing Stephen A. Douglas

◆ SOUND

Foreign Words and Phrases

vibrato (Ita)
(vee-BRAH-toh) tremulous variation of notes in music or speech

Jokes, Stories and Anecdotes

At a college concert, Oscar Levant was playing a difficult piano passage when a telephone began to ring offstage. Levant continued, but as the ringing also continued the audience became restless. Without pausing, the pianist turned to the audience and said, "If that's for me, tell them I'm busy."

Oscar Levant (1906–1972),
U.S. pianist and wit

When a servant dropped a stack of plates and there was a great crash, Anglo-Irish playwright Richard Sheridan cracked, "I suppose you have broken all of them." "No, sir, not a one." "Then, man, you mean to say you have made all that noise for nothing?"

Richard Brinsley Sheridan (1751–1816),
Irish-born British playwright
and politician

◆ SPACE

Quotations

"Space isn't remote at all. It's only an hour's drive away if your car could go straight upwards."

*Sir Fred Hoyle (1915–),
British astronomer*

"In the United States there is more space where nobody is than where anybody is. That is what makes America what it is."

*Gertrude Stein (1874–1946), U.S. writer,
The Geographical History
of America (1936)*

◆ SPEECH

Foreign Words and Phrases

parlando (Ita)
(par-LAHN-do) *lit:* speaking; (singing) while clearly enunciating

Quotations

"The true use of speech is not so much to express our wants as to conceal them."

*Oliver Goldsmith (1728–1774),
Irish-born British poet, playwright and
writer, Essays: The Use of Language*

"To learn English you must begin by thrusting the jaw forward, almost clenching the teeth, and practically immobilizing the lips. In this way the English produce the series of unpleasant little mews of which their language consists."

*José Ortega y Gasset (1883–1955),
Spanish philosopher and statesman*

Classical Phrases and Myths

vox audita perit litera scripta manet (Lat)
(wox OWD - i - taPER - itLIT - er-a-SCRIP-ta MAN-et) the voice, once heard, perishes but the written word remains

◆ SPEECH DEFECT

Quotations

"Nobody was any more likely to drop an 'h' than to pick up a title."

*G[ilbert] K[eith] Chesterton (1874–1936),
British man of letters, commenting on the
upper-middle class world, so concerned
with respectability and propriety,
in which he was raised*

"[The actress Sandy Dennis has a habit of speaking onstage as though sentences] were poor crippled things that couldn't cross a street without making three false starts from the curb."

*Walter Kerr (1913–),
U.S. writer*

Classical Phrases and Myths

lapsus linguas (Lat)
(LAP-sus LING-wai) slip of the tongue

Jokes, Stories and Anecdotes

"I w-w-want to s-s-sell B-B-Bibles," the man said to the hesitant interviewer for a religious publisher seeking salesmen. Yet the man's past sales performance was excellent, so he was hired. When the company's yearly sales figures were compiled, to everyone's amazement, the man's sales were the highest. At the annual meeting, the president congratulated him and asked what was his secret for selling so many Bibles. "I just go to the d-d-door and say," the man answered, "'w-w-would you like to b-b-buy a B-B-Bible? Or I c-c-could c-c-come in and read it t-t-to you.'"

British conductor Sir Thomas Beecham was once traveling in the nonsmoking compartment on a train when a lady entered the compartment and lit a cigarette, saying, "I'm sure you won't object if I smoke." "No," replied Beecham, "provided that you don't object if I get sick." "I'm afraid you don't know who I am," the lady said haughtily, nonplussed. "I am one of the directors' wives of this train company." "Madam," said Beecham, "if you were the director's only wife, I should still be sick."

Sir Thomas Beecham (1879–1961),
British conductor

British cabinet member Ernest Bevin spoke with a thick brogue, using few aspirates. When Prime Minister Clement Atlee suggested that a two-member subcommittee be formed to investigate an issue, his foreign secretary Bevin proposed that it should consist of "You and I." The confused room did not know whether he had meant Atlee and himself or Ugh (Hugh Dalton) and Nye (Aneurin [Nye] Bevan).

Ernest Bevin (1881–1951), British labor
leader and statesman

As U.S. ambassador to Great Britain, Joseph Choate heard much of the cockney accent, in which "h's" are routinely dropped in speech. Passing a box marked "Drop Letter Box" on a London street one day, Choate observed, "That box must be full of 'h's.'"

Joseph Hodges Choate (1832–1917),
U.S. lawyer and diplomat

A young lawyer, awestruck in his first appearance before England's high court, could only stammer, "My lord, my unfortunate client— my lord, my unfortunate client— my lord—" "Go on, sir, go on," said the Lord Chief Justice Ellen-borough. "As far as you have proceeded hitherto, the court is entirely with you."

Edward Law Ellenborough, 1st Baron
(1750–1818), British lawyer and jurist

After returning from his first trip to Paris in 1894–1895, Knut Hamsun was asked, "Did you have difficulty in the beginning with your French?" "No," responded Hamsun, "but the French did."

Knut Hamsun (1859–1952),
Norwegian writer

Asked why he speaks unaccented English while his brother Henry speaks with a thick German growl more than 50 years after leaving Germany, Walter Kissinger replied, "I am the Kissinger who listens."

Walter Kissinger (1927–   ),
brother of Henry Kissinger

◆ SPEEDINESS

Foreign Words and Phrases

ventre à terre (Fra)
(VON-tre ah ter) *lit:* belly to the ground; very fast

paso doble (Spa)
(PA-so DOH-blay) *lit:* double step, quick march, quick-stepping dance

petite allegro (Ita)
(pe-TEET a-LEH-groh) in music, quick, fast movements

Jokes, Stories and Anecdotes

"What's it like to fly the Concorde?" a friend asked the suave actor after he disembarked from his first supersonic flight. "You know you're traveling faster than the speed of sound," he replied, "when the flight attendant slaps your face before you can get a line out."

It was said of James "Cool Papa" Bell in baseball's Negro Leagues that he was so fast he could switch the light off and be in bed before the room got dark.

> James ["Cool Papa"] Bell (1903–1989), U.S. baseball player

◆ SPIRITS, BAD

Quotations

"No, but I'm afraid of them."

> Marquise Marie Anne du Deffand (1697–1780), French aristocrat, answering whether she believed in ghosts [attributed also to others]

Classical Phrases and Myths

cacodaemon (Grk)
(kak-o-DEE-mohn) evil spirit, nightmare

Jokes, Stories and Anecdotes

When their favorite waiter died, a few of the dinner regulars tried to contact him through a medium. "To communicate with the dead," the medium advised those gathered at the round table, "we must all hold hands and say his name as one." The group locked hands, and in unison the men said quietly and reverently, "Moe Pagani." Nothing. They tried again. Once again, the waiter failed to show. Finally, after the third "Moe Pagani," the bald-headed man appeared as a spectral image floating above them. "Moe," said one, "it's good to see you, but did we have to call you three times?" The ectoplasmic waiter shrugged. "Jerk, this isn't my table!"

◆ SPORTS

Quotations

"Honey, I just forgot to duck."

> Jack Dempsey [William Harrison] (1895–1983), U.S. boxer, commenting to his wife, Estella, after losing his World Heavyweight title, September 23, 1926 [paraphrased by President Ronald Reagan after unsuccessful 1981 assassination attempt]

"All pro athletes are bilingual. They speak English and profanity."

> Gordie Howe (1928–   ), Canadian ice hockey player, 1975

"Next year, schedule the game on a Friday because they don't eat meat then."

> Robert W. ["Tiny"] Maxwell (d. 1922), U.S. football player, advising a Harvard football player whose finger had been bitten by a Notre Dame player

"Sure, winning isn't everything. It's the only thing."

> Henry ["Red"] Sanders (c. 1900s), U.S. football coach [misattributed often to Vince Lombardi]

"Some people think football is a matter of life and death. I don't like that attitude. I can assure them it is much more serious than that."

> Bill Shankly (1914–1981), U.S. football coach

Classical Phrases and Myths

It is a matter of historical record that the emperor of Rome won every event in which he entered during the Olympics held in A.D. 67. In fact, when Emperor Nero on one occasion fell from his chariot during a race, the other contestants politely (and prudently) waited until he had remounted and sped on before resuming the race.

Nero [Lucius Domitius Ahenobarbus]
(37–68), Roman emperor

Jokes, Stories and Anecdotes

A man was standing at the bar of his tennis club with a ball stuffed into one pocket of his shorts. "What's that?" asked an adjacent young blond, pointing to the bulge. "Tennis ball," he replied. "Ouch," she said. "I know how that must feel. I have tennis elbow."

Sighed the golfer, "I'd move heaven and earth if I could break 100 here." "Try heaven," observed his partner. "You already moved most of the earth."

Muhammad Ali was once asked by someone, irritated by Ali's constant boasts of "I am the greatest," how Ali performed at golf. "I'm the best," replied Ali. "I just haven't played it yet."

Muhammad Ali [Cassius Clay]
(1942–   ), U.S. boxer

A scout once excitedly called the oft-losing Chicago Cubs manager Charlie Grimm. "I've found the best young pitcher ever, Charlie! Every man who came to bat was struck out—27 in a row. No one even got a foul until there were two out in the ninth. The pitcher is standing here. What shall I do?" "Sign up the guy who got the foul," answered Grimm. "We're looking for hitters."

Charlie Grimm (1899–   ),
U.S. baseball manager

Joe Louis, knocked to the canvas by Tony Galento's surprise left, jumped to his feet before the referee began the count. "I keep telling ya to take the count when you're knocked down," Louis's trainer admonished him later. "Why didn't you stay down for nine like I've always taught you?" Growled Louis, "And let him get all that rest?"

Joe Louis (1914–1981), U.S. boxer

◆ STATISTICS

Quotations

"There are three kinds of lies: lies, damned lies, and statistics."

Benjamin Disraeli, 1st Earl of Beaconsfield
(1804–1881), British prime minister

Jokes, Stories and Anecdotes

Reading life statistics, she turned to him and asked, "Do you know that every time I breathe a man dies?" "Interesting," he returned. "Have you tried toothpaste?"

◆ STORYTELLING

Foreign Words and Phrases

raconteur (Fra)
(RAH-con-TUHR) skilled storyteller

roman fleuve (Fra)
(ro-MAHN FLUHV) *lit:* river novel; multi-generational novel charting a group or family

c'est tout dire (Fra)
(seh too-DEER) (one has said) all there is to say

animateur (Fra)
(an-ee-mah-TUHR) one who can simplify difficult concepts for the benefit of a general audience

roman à clef (Fra)
(ro-MAHN ah clay) *lit:* novel with a key; novel in which (intentionally) poorly disguised characters represent real people

Classical Phrases and Myths

horribile dictu (Lat)
(hoh-REE-bee-lay DIK-tu) horrible
to tell, terrible to relate

*"Mutato nomine de te
Fabula narratur."* (Change but the
name, and it is of yourself that the
tale is told.)

> *Horace (65 B.C.–8 B.C.), Roman poet,*
> *Satires, I.i., l.69*

Jokes, Stories and Anecdotes

With an implicating glance at the
handcuffed defendant, the prosecutor nasally asked the witness,
"And can you describe the man
who beat you?" "Sure can," answered the still-bruised man,
"That's what I was doing when he
slugged me."

The talented British stage actress
Mrs. Patrick Campbell went to Hollywood in the early 1930s to be considered for film roles. On the
customary mimeographed publicity
form, she filled in the requested de-
tails of her name, the color of her
hair and eyes, her height, her hob-
bies, and so on. Under the heading
"Experience," she entered, "Edward VII."

> *Mrs. Patrick [Beatrice] Campbell*
> *(1865–1940), British actress*

"Sir, what is poetry?" Samuel Johnson was asked. "Why, sir, it is
much easier to say what it is not,"
the great literary giant replied. "We
all know what light is; but it is not
easy to tell what it is."

> *Samuel Johnson (1709–1784),*
> *British man of letters*

On a visit one evening to Nathaniel
Hawthorne and his wife, novelist
Herman Melville told them a story of
a fight he had witnessed on a South
Sea island, in which one of the Polynesian warriors had wielded a
mighty club. Melville strode about
the room, demonstrating the heat of
battle. After he had left, Mrs. Hawthorne thought he had left empty-
handed and wondered, "Where is
that club with which Mr. Melville
was laying about him so?" A search
of the room revealed no club, so the
next time they saw Melville, they inquired about the club. It turned out
there was no club. It had simply been
a figment of their imagination, con-
jured up by the vividness of Melville's storytelling.

> *Herman Melville (1819–1891),*
> *U.S. writer*

"You haven't heard this, have
you?" Henry Irving asked Mark
Twain after beginning a tale. "No,"
replied Twain. Somewhat later, Irving paused and repeated his concern. Twain again assured him that
he had not heard the story. Just before the climax of the story, Irving
broke off again, pleading, "Are you
sure you haven't heard this?" "I
can lie once," groaned Twain, "and
I can lie twice for courtesy's sake,
but there I draw the line. I can't lie
a third time at any price. I not only
heard the story, I invented it."

> *Mark Twain [Samuel Langhorne Clemens]*
> *(1835–1910), U.S. humorist,*
> *writer and speaker*

Frank Harris, an unashamed plagiarist, once related as his own an anecdote recognized by a group of
friends as written earlier by Anatole
France. When he finished, Oscar
Wilde finally broke the embarassed
silence that fell upon the group.
"Frank," he said gravely, "Anatole
France would have spoiled that
story."

> *Oscar [Fingal O'Flahertie Wills] Wilde*
> *(1854–1900), British playwright,*
> *writer and wit*

◆ STRENGTH & RIGIDITY

Foreign Words and Phrases

sforzando (Ita)
(sfor-TSAND-oh) *lit:* forcing; sudden emphasis, usually followed immediately by a reversion to previous level

Quotations

"I hear the softest thing about him is his front teeth."

> Damon Runyon (1884–1946),
> U.S. writer, Colliers' (September 1926),
> "Snatching of Bookie Bob"

Classical Phrases and Myths

rigor mortis (Lat)
(RIG-or MOR-tis) the stiffness of a corpse, developing within hours of death

According to Greek mythology, Atlas (AT-las) was the Titan condemned to support the heavens on his shoulders for rebelling against Zeus. He was almost freed of the burden when Heracles assumed the weight, but Hercules tricked him into reassuming his place. A collection of maps is labeled an atlas because his figure was used to decorate the title page of Mercator's collection in 1595. An *atlas* is also a man with great physical strength.

In Roman mythology, Hercules (HER-kyoo-leez) (Grk: Herakles) was a hero who accomplished 12 great labors and also performed other extraordinary feats requiring prodigious strength. Hence, something *herculean* is of great strength or courage, or requiring such.

◆ STUDENT

Quotations

"When I was a student at the Sorbonne in Paris I used to go out and riot occasionally. I can't remember now what side it was on."

> John Foster Dulles (1888–1959),
> U.S. statesman

Classical Phrases and Myths

alumnus (Lat)
(al-UM-nus) student, learned person, graduate of an institution (plu: alumni)

Jokes, Stories and Anecdotes

"I'm going to the movies, Dad," said the teen. "Would you please do my homework for me?" "But it wouldn't be right," protested the father. "That's OK," replied the youth. "You can at least try.

◆ STUPIDITY

Foreign Words and Phrases

Dummkopf (Ger)
(DUHM-kopf) dimwit

Quotations

"His mind was a kind of extinct sulphur-pit."

> Thomas Carlyle (1795–1881),
> British historian, describing Napoleon III

"Dumb as a drum vith a hole in it, sir."

> Charles Dickens (1812–1870),
> British writer, Pickwick Papers
> (1836–1837), ch. 25

"Many a crown of wisdom is but the golden chamberpot of success, worn with pompous dignity."

Paul Eldridge (1888–   ),
U.S. writer

"The General is suffering from mental saddle sores."

Harold L. Ickes (1874–1952),
U.S. statesman, commenting on
General Hugh S. Johnson

"He doesn't have sense enough to pour piss out of a boot with the instructions written on the heel."

Lyndon Baines Johnson (1908–1973),
U.S. president

"That fellow seems to me to possess but one idea, and that is a wrong one."

Samuel Johnson (1709–1784),
British man of letters

"He was so dumb that he crawled under them for two years before he found out that they swung both ways."

Wilson Mizner (1876–1933), U.S. writer
and wit, commenting on American
heavyweight boxer Tom Sharkey, who
owned a saloon with swinging doors
at its entrance

"People think I've got the IQ of a hockey score. I'm supposed to be this primordial being who slurs his way through life."

Sylvester Stallone (1948–   ),
U.S. actor

"His wit invites you by his looks to come,
But when you knock it never is home."

William Cowper (1731–1800),
British poet, Conversation (1782), l. 303

"All he had on his mind when he cut my film was his hat."

Erich von Stroheim [Erich Oswald
Stroheim] (1885–1957),
Austrian-born U.S. film director

Jokes, Stories and Anecdotes

"Look at this!" exclaimed the professor to the basketball coach. "Your star player wrote '8 × 7 = 58.'" "Give him a break," replied the coach. "He only missed by one."

The boxer returned to his corner at the sixth-round bell seeing stars. "He's barely laid a glove on you!" his manager hollered. "Yeah? Well, check the ref 'cause somebody's clobbering me," the fighter replied. A minute into the next round, the outclassed boxer was felled. "Don't get up till nine!" his corner man yelled. The boxer strained to lift his head off the canvas. "So," he said. "What time is it now?"

◆ STYLE

Foreign Words and Phrases

haute couture (Fra)
(oat koo-TOUR) high fashion dress or designing

à la mode (Fra)
(ah lah mohd) in fashion

dé mode (Fra)
(DAY-mo-DAY) out of fashion, old-fashioned

glitterati (Ita)
(GLEET-er-ah-tee) the "beautiful" people, socialites

dernier cri (Fra)
(DAIR-nee-ay CREE) *lit:* the last word; the very latest, in fashion

Quotations

"One had as good be out of the world, as be out of the fashion."

Colley Cibber (1671–1757),
British playwright, Love's Last Shift
(1696), Act II

Classical Phrases and Myths

arbiter elegantiae (Lat)
(AR-bit-er el-e-GANT-ee-ai) arbiter in matters of taste, dictator of fashion

◆ SUCCESS

Foreign Words and Phrases

succès de scandale (Fra)
(suk-SEH de skan-DAHL) success resulting from scandal generated by a piece

succès d'estime (Fra)
(suk-SEH des-TEEM) critical but noncommercial success (e.g., entertainment)

eclat (Fra)
(AY-clah) brilliance, success

succès fou (Fra)
(suk-SEH foo) smashing success

rien ne réussit comme le succès
(REE-ah ne RAY u-see kom le SOOK-say) nothing succeeds like success; French proverb

Quotations

"How to become an old actor."

> *Henry Fonda (1905–1982), U.S. movie actor and director, answering what is the one most important thing that any young actor has to know*

"All you need in this life is ignorance and confidence; then success is sure."

> Mark Twain [Samuel Langhorne Clemens] *(1835–1910), U.S. humorist, writer and speaker, letter to Mrs. Foote, December 2, 1887*

Classical Phrases and Myths

bene merenti (Lat)
(BE-ne mer-ENT-i) (success) to those who deserve it

"Fire is the test of gold; adversity, of strong men."

> *Seneca [Lucius Annaeus Seneca] (c. 5 B.C.–A.D. 65), Roman writer, philosopher and statesman, Moral Essays, "On Providence"*

Jokes, Stories and Anecdotes

The mother of Picasso, a spectacularly successful artist, had great ambitions for him. When he was a child, his mother said to him, "If you become a soldier, you'll be a general. If you become a monk, you'll end up as Pope." "Instead," observed Picasso, "I became a painter and became a Picasso."

> *Pablo [Ruiz y] Picasso (1881–1973), Spanish-born French artist*

◆ SUCCINCTNESS

Foreign Words and Phrases

précis (Fra)
(PRAY-see) summary of argument, document, etc.

Quotations

"I take the view, and always have, that if you cannot say what you are going to say in twenty minutes you ought to go away and write a book about it."

> *Lord Brabazon, Baron Brabazon of Tara (1884–1964), British sportsman and politician*

"*S'il est un homme tourmenté par la maudite ambition de mettre tout un livre dans une page, toute une page dans une phrase, et cette phrase dans un mot, c'est moi.*" (If there be any man cursed with the itch to compress a whole book into a page, a whole page into a phrase, and that phrase into a word, it is I.)

Joseph Joubert (1754–1824),
French writer, Pensées *(1842)*

"Je n'ai fait celle-ci plus longue que parceque je n'ai pas eu le loisir de la faire plus courte." (I have made this letter longer than usual, because I lack the time to make it short.)

Blaise Pascal (1623–1662),
French mathematician and writer,
Lettres Provinciales *(1657), no. 16*

Classical Phrases and Myths

in nuce (Lat)
(in NUK-e) in a nutshell, put succinctly

Although Philip of Macedon, Alexander the Great's father, had conquered or formed alliances with all the major Greek city-states, militaristic Sparta remained stubbornly independent. Diplomacy having failed him, Philip sent a threat: "You are advised to submit without further delay, for if I bring my army into your land, I will ravage your farms, slay your people, and destroy your city." The Spartans sent back their answer, sufficient to deter Philip: "If." Thus, the word *laconic*, meaning brief, terse or concise, is appropriately derived from the area in Greece, Laconia (la-KOHN-e-a) whose capital was Sparta.

Philip II (382 B.C.–336 B.C.),
Macedonian king

Jokes, Stories and Anecdotes

Warned to keep her copy short and stick to the bare facts, the rookie reporter wrote for her first "accident" story: "L. Jones looked up the elevator shaft to see if the car was on its way down. It was. Age 52."

Excited about his first "big" story, the rookie reporter cabled his news-paper editor: "Column story on sinking ship. Shall I send?" "Send 600 words," was the reply. The eager reporter was dismayed, and wired back: "Can't be told in less than 1,400." Returned his editor: "Story of creation of world told in 600. Try it."

The new inmate was amazed to find a group of men shouting numbers at each other in the prison yard and laughing uproariously. "12!" said one, and everyone chuckled. "42!" said another and everyone guffawed. A guard explained to the perplexed new con, "They've swapped the same old jokes for so many years that everybody knows all the jokes by now. So they just call out their numbers." Just then someone called out, "207!" and everyone roared at length. The new con asked, "What was so special about that one?" "Oh, that was a story they had never heard before."

Attending the premiere of *The Squall* in 1926, humorist Robert Benchley grew increasingly edgy with the play's use of broken English. He whispered to his wife that if he heard one more word of it, he was going to leave. Just then a gypsy girl on stage delivered the lines, "Me Nubi. Nubi good girl. Me stay." Benchley rose to his feet. "Me Bobby," he said. "Bobby bad boy. Bobby go." And he left.

Robert Charles Benchley (1889–1945),
U.S. humorist

A clergyman once approached George Canning, a British foreign secretary, prime minister and accomplished practitioner of the put-down, following a church service, and asked his opinion of the sermon. Canning replied, "You were brief." "Yes," said the clergyman,

"you know I avoid being tedious."
"But you *were* tedious."

George Canning (1770–1827),
British prime minister and diplomat

On returning from church one Sunday morning, "Silent Cal" Coolidge was asked on what topic the minister had preached. After reflection, he answered, "Sin." "Well, what did he say about sin?" "He was against it."

[John] Calvin Coolidge (1872–1933),
U.S. president [authenticity controverted]

A magazine once requested a short piece from oil executive J. Paul Getty on the secret of his success, and enclosed with the request a check for 200 pounds. The fabulously wealthy entrepeneur obligingly wrote, "Some people find oil. Others don't."

J[ean] Paul Getty (1892–1976),
U.S. industrialist

Seeking to determine his publisher's opinion of the manuscript of *Les Miserables*, Victor Hugo sent them a note containing only: "?" He received the reply: "!"

Victor [Marie] Hugo (1802–1885),
French poet, writer and playwright

When director and playwright Russel Crouse asked playwright Eugene O'Neill to shorten the script of *Ah Wilderness*, O'Neill reluctantly agreed. "You'll be happy to learn I cut 15 minutes," O'Neill telephoned the next morning. Crouse enthusiastically exclaimed, "I'll be right over to get the changes!" "Oh, there aren't any changes in the text," O'Neill explained, "but you know we've been playing this thing in four acts. I've decided to cut out the third intermission."

Eugene [Gladstone] O'Neill (1888–1953),
U.S. playwright

◆ SUFFERING

Quotations

"Better to suffer than to die: that is mankind's motto."

Jean de La Fontaine (1621–1695),
French fabulist, Fables (1668), no. 16

"When I hear somebody sigh that 'Life is hard,' I am always tempted to ask, 'Compared to what?' "

Sydney J[ustin] Harris (1917–   ),
British-born U.S. writer

◆ SUFFICIENCY

Foreign Words and Phrases

molto (Ita)
(MOL-toh) much, very

Classical Phrases and Myths

quantum meruit (Lat)
(KWAN-tum ME-ru-it) *lit:* as much as was deserved; in law, fair recompense

quantum sufficit (Lat)
(KWAN-tum suf-FIK-io) *lit:* as much as is necessary; sufficient amount

quantum vis (Lat)
(KWAN-tum WEES) *lit:* as much as you will; as much as you wish

◆ SUICIDE

Foreign Words and Phrases

hara kiri (Jap)
(HAH-rah KEE-ree) *lit:* stomach-cutting; ceremonial suicide by disembowelment (in shame)

Classical Phrases and Myths

vae victis (Lat)
(vay VEEK-tus) don't commit suicide

Jokes, Stories and Anecdotes

A notably unintelligent impresario committed suicide by shooting himself in the head. Playwright Sir Noel Coward icily remarked, "He must have been a marvelously good shot."

Sir Noel Coward (1899–1973),
British playwright and actor

◆ SUPERIOR

Foreign Words and Phrases

Radfahrer (Ger)
(ROD-fahr-ur) a worker who is tyrannical to his subordinates yet fawns over his superiors

Quotations

"That detached and baronial air of superiority the Briton habitually affects when circumstances beyond his control bring him into the presence of creatures of a lesser breed."

Pierre Van Paassen (1895–1968),
U.S. writer and clergyman

Jokes, Stories and Anecdotes

Bellowed the indignant boss to his incompetent employee, "If I'd known I was hiring a horse's ass, I'd have done the job myself!"

◆ SURPRISE

Foreign Words and Phrases

tout coup (Fra)
(too koo) suddenly

coup de main (Fra)
(koo de MAHN) surprise attack, unexpected blow

Quotations

"What we anticipate seldom occurs; what we least expect generally happens."

Benjamin Disraeli, 1st Earl of Beaconsfield
(1804–1881), British prime minister,
Endymion, bk. ii, ch. 4

Classical Phrases and Myths

While Julius Caesar and some friends were dining together on March 14, 44 B.C., the question was raised: "What is the best kind of death?" Before the others could answer, Caesar exclaimed, "A sudden one." The next day he was assassinated.

Gaius Julius Caesar (100 B.C.-44 B.C.),
Roman general and statesman

Jokes, Stories and Anecdotes

A man walks into a bar with a dog and, after receiving his drink, informs the bartender that his dog is able to talk. When the bartender begins to protest, the dog says, "No, it's true. I can talk." The astonished bartender says, "Unbelievable. Here's ten bucks. Go to the pizza parlor down the street and surprise my friend Guido." "OK," says the dog, who takes the money and leaves. When he fails to return, the dog's owner goes out and sees the dog having his way with an attractive French poodle. "Rover, how can you do this?" says the man. "Well," replies the dog, "I've never had money before."

According to Bennet Cerf, playwright Eugene O'Neill's first marriage in 1909 occurred after his return from a gold prospecting adventure in Honduras. Following one of his drinking blackouts, he supposedly awakened one morning in a flophouse with a girl beside him. "Who the hell are you?" he sleepily asked. Replied his bedmate, "You married me last night."

Eugene [Gladstone] O'Neill (1888–1953), U.S. playwright

◆ TACITURNITY

Foreign Words and Phrases

incomunicado (Spa) (een-koh-mew-nee-KAH-doh) isolated, unable to be contacted

Quotations

"Never complain and never explain."

Benjamin Disraeli, 1st Earl of Beaconsfield (1804–1881), British prime minister

"Madam, if I did not know I would tell you."

William Henry Seward (1801–1872), U.S. statesman, replying to a question about the secret destination of troops

Jokes, Stories and Anecdotes

Issuing the usual pleasant flatteries to an attractive woman, Prince von Bismarck was rebuffed by her statement: "One can't believe a word you diplomats say." "What do you mean?" "When a diplomat says 'yes,' he means 'perhaps.' When he says 'perhaps,' he means 'no,' " she said. "And if he were to say 'no'—well, he's no diplomat." Bismarck responded, "Quite true, madam. We diplomats do speak in a language of subtexts. But I fear with you ladies the exact opposite is true." "Really?" she asked. "When she says 'no,' she means 'perhaps.' When she says 'perhaps,' she means 'yes.' And if she says 'yes'—well, she's no lady."

Otto Eduard Leopold, Prince von Bismarck (1815–1898), German statesman

As a cub reporter for the *New York World*, journalist and novelist Heywood Broun was assigned to interview Utah's Senator Reed Smoot. "I'm sorry," Smoot declined, "I have nothing to say." "I know," rejoined Broun, "now let's get down to the interview."

Heywood Broun (1888–1939), U.S. writer

"Silent Cal" Coolidge's successor as governor of Massachusetts, Channing H. Cox, visited Coolidge as vice president in Washington. Cox asked Coolidge why was it that both spent their days seeing a long list of callers and yet, while Coolidge left the office daily at five P.M., Cox was often detained up to nine o'clock. "You talk back."

[John] Calvin Coolidge (1872–1933), U.S. president

When asked what his plans were for the future, the extremely devious and secretive Mehmed the Conquerer responded, "If a hair of my beard knew, I would pluck it out."

Mehmed II (1432–81), Ottoman sultan

◆ TEACHER

Quotations

" 'That's the reason they're called lessons,' the Gryphon remarked, 'because they lessen every day.' "

Lewis Carroll [Charles Lutwidge Dodgson] (1832–1898), British writer and mathematician, Alice's Adventures in Wonderland (1865), ch. 9

"To teach is to learn twice."

Joseph Joubert (1754–1824),
French writer, Pensées *(1842)*

Classical Phrases and Myths

elenchus (Grk)
(ay-LENG-kus) logical refutation, esp. the Socratic method of question and answer

modus docendi (Lat)
(MO-dus dok-END-ee) method of teaching

Socrates (SOK-ra-TEEZ) was an Athenian philosopher whose ideas, though not written, survived in the works of Plato and Xenophon and profoundly shaped Western culture and philosophy. He challenged traditional philosophy and laid the foundation for the development of logic and ethics. Tried on the charge of corrupting Athenian youth, Socrates gave his nonconciliatory speech, the Apology, and drank the poisonous hemlock. The *Socratic method* denotes the teaching technique using questions and answers, by which basic premises or assumptions are challenged by logical extension, and *Socratic irony* is the pretense of ignorance to reveal the ignorance of others.

Socrates (469 B.C.-c. 399 B.C.),
Greek philosopher

Jokes, Stories and Anecdotes

A man and his young son were riding the ferry, and the youngster kept peppering his father with questions. "Who is that man, Daddy?" "Don't know, son," murmured the father, engrossed in his book. "How many people are on earth?" "Dunno." "How far away is the moon?" "Son, don't ask me so many questions! Overhearing the young boy's questions, another passenger remarked, "You sure do have a curious little kid." "Uh-uh," replied the father. "How else could he become as knowledgeable as his dad?"

After his retirement as longtime president of the University of Chicago, Robert Hutchins was disdainfully asked whether Communism was still being taught at the university. "Yes," answered Hutchins, "and cancer at the medical school."

Robert Maynard Hutchins (1899–1977),
U.S. educator

◆ TEACHING

Foreign Words and Phrases

guru (Hindu)
(GOO-roo) teacher, spiritual leader

Quotations

"I owe a lot to my teachers and mean to pay them back some day."

Stephen Leacock (1869–1944),
Canadian humorist and economist

"He who can, does. He who cannot, teaches."

George Bernard Shaw (1856–1950),
Irish playwright, Man and Superman
(1903), "Maxims for
Revolutionists: Education"

Classical Phrases and Myths

odium scholasticum (Lat)
(OD-ee-um sko-LAS-ti-kum) the acrimony of pedants and scholars; academic quibbling over minor issues

Jokes, Stories and Anecdotes

After being appointed professor of music at UCLA, the world-renowned Jascha Heifetz explained his career shift: "Violin-playing is a perishable art, and must be passed on as a personal skill. Otherwise, it is lost." He then added, "My old violin professor in Russia said that someday I would be good enough to teach."

Jascha Heifetz (1901–1987),
Russian-born U.S. violinist

◆ TELEPHONE

Quotations

"Well, if I called the wrong number, why did you answer the phone?"

James Thurber (1894–1961),
U.S. cartoonist and humorist,
New Yorker cartoon caption
(June 5, 1937)

◆ TELEVISION

Quotations

"It is a medium of entertainment which permits millions of people to listen to the same joke at the same time, and yet remain lonesome."

T[homas] S[tearns] Eliot (1888–1965),
U.S. poet

"Television is an invention that permits you to be entertained in your living room by people you wouldn't have in your home."

David Frost (1939–   ),
British television entertainer

"I find television very educational. Every time someone switches it on I go into another room and read a good book."

Groucho [Julius] Marx (1895–1977),
U.S. comedian

◆ TEMPERAMENT

Foreign Words and Phrases

méchant (Fra)
(MAY shon) naughty, spiteful

aigreur (Fra)
(ay-GRUHR) acrimony, acerbity, sourness, harshness

Quotations

"Some folks are so contrary that if they fell in a river, they'd insist on floating upstream."

Josh Billings [Henry Wheeler Shaw]
(1818–1885), U.S. humorist

"She looketh as butter would not melt in her mouth."

John Heywood (c. 1497–c. 1580),
British poet, Proverbs *(1546)*

"Some people are so sensitive that they feel snubbed if an epidemic overlooks them."

Frank McKinney ["Kin"] Hubbard
(1868–1930), U.S. humorist and writer

"A tart temper never mellows with age, and a sharp tongue is the only edged tool that grows keener with constant use."

Washington Irving (1783–1859),
U.S. writer, The Sketch Book of
Geoffrey Crayon, Gent. *(1819–1820),*
"Rip Van Winkle"

Classical Phrases and Myths

"Excitabat enim fluctus in simpulo."
(ex-KIT-a-bat EN-im FLUK-tus in SIM-pul-oh) (He would raise a storm in a teapot.)

Marcus Tullius Cicero (106 B.C.-43 B.C.),
Roman statesman and man of letters,
De Legibus, *III, xvi*

"You are seeking a knot in a bulrush."

Titus Maccius Plautus (254 B.C.-184
B.C.), Roman playwright, Menaechmi,
Act II, sc. i [hence, willing doubts and
difficulties where none actually exist]

◆ TEMPERANCE

Classical Phrases and Myths

The Stoics (STO-iks) were members of a sect, founded in Athens by Zeno in 308 B.C., who believed that men could only be fulfilled by simple living and submission to fate. In their philosophy, men should be free from passion, though not unfeeling, and the highest good is virtue, that is, a life conforming to nature. Thus, a *stoic* person is one who exercises self-control and lives austerely.

◆ TEMPTATION

Quotations

"Sex appeal is 50 percent what you've got and 50 percent what people think you've got."

Sophia Loren (1934–   ),
Italian film actress

◆ THEFT

Foreign Words and Phrases

la piñata (Spa)
(la pin-YATA) the papier-mache animals that children whack with a stick so they can plunder the candy inside; term also for rapacious pillaging

gonif (Yid)
(GOHN-if) a thief

Quotations

"After shaking hands with a Greek, count your fingers."

Albanian proverb

"Stolen sweets are best."

Colley Cibber (1671–1757),
British playwright, The Rival Fools
(1709), Act I

"He that first cries out stop thief, is often he that has stolen the treasure."

William Congreve (1670–1729),
British playwright, Love for Love
(1695), Act III, sc. xiv

"We will get everything out of her [Germany] that you can squeeze out of a lemon and a bit more ... I will squeeze her until you can hear the pips squeak."

Sir Eric Geddes (1875–1937),
British politician, regarding war reparations after WWI, speech at the Drill Hall, Cambridge, December 9, 1918

"The robb'd that smiles steals something from the thief."

William Shakespeare (1564–1616),
British playwright and poet,
Othello *(1605), Act I, sc. iii*

Classical Phrases and Myths

occasio facit furem (Lat)
(ok-KAH-si-oh FAK-it FOO-rem)
(the) occasion makes the thief

Jokes, Stories and Anecdotes

While presiding at a state dinner, Winston Churchill was discreetly informed that one of the distinguished guests had been seen to pocket a silver salt shaker. Churchill pocketed the matching pepper shaker and, at the end of the meal, sidled up to the purloiner, murmuring, "Oh, dear, we were seen. Perhaps we had both better put them back."

Sir Winston Spencer Churchill (1874–1965), British prime minister and writer

On January 31, 1874, Jesse James's gang robbed the St. Louis-Texas express train. While boarding the train, a gang member handed the conductor an envelope containing the following press release, which was published the next day in the newspapers: "THE MOST DARING TRAIN ROBBERY ON RECORD! The southbound train of the Iron Mountain Railroad was stopped here this evening by five heavily armed men and robbed of —— dollars. The robbers arrived at the station a few minutes before the arrival of the train . . . The robbers were all large men, all being slightly under six feet. After robbing the train, they started in a southerly direction . . . There is a hell of an excitement in this part of the country." The gang actually included ten men, and after the robbery they headed west, not south.

Jesse James (1847–1882), U.S. outlaw

While a rancher in the Badlands, Theodore Roosevelt and one of his cowboys lassoed an unbranded maverick steer on rangeland claimed by Gregor Lang, one of Roosevelt's neighbors. They lit a fire for the branding irons and, as the cowpuncher was applying the brand, Roosevelt said, "Wait, it should be Lang's brand, a thistle," in recognition of the rule that the steer was Lang's because it was found on his land. The cowboy persisted in applying the brand. "But you're putting on my brand!" "That's right, boss," replied the cowboy. "I always put on the boss's brand." "Drop that iron," ordered Roosevelt, "go back to the ranch and get out. I don't need you anymore." The cowboy protested, but Roosevelt adamantly declared, "A man who will steal for me will steal from me."

Theodore Roosevelt (1858–1919), U.S. president

The English criminal Jonathan Wild, who masterminded a huge robbery and fencing operation, was literally an outlaw until the instant he died. Climbing the gallows at Tyburn, Wild deftly picked the pocket of the priest administering last rites, and was triumphantly waving his trophy to the crowd below even as his unrepentant neck was snapped.

Jonathan Wild (c. 1682–1725) British outlaw

◆ THINKING

Quotations

"Doublethink means the power of holding two contradictory beliefs in one's mind simultaneously, and accepting both of them."

George Orwell [Eric Blair] (1903–1950), British writer, Nineteen Eighty-Four (1949), pt. 2, ch. 9

"Ils ne servent de la pensé e que pour autoriser leurs injustices, et n'emploient les paroles que pour déguiser leurs pensé es." ([Men] use thought only to justify their wrongdoings, and speech only to conceal their thoughts.)

Voltaire [François Marie Arouet] (1694–1778), French philosopher, writer and wit, Dialogue XIV (1766), "Le Chapon et la Poularde"

◆ THINNESS

Quotations

"There was a young lady of Lynn
Who was so uncommonly thin
That when she essayed
To drink lemonade,

She slipped through the straw and fell in."

Anonymous, The Limerick Book, *p. 150*

Classical Phrases and Myths

"A line is length without breadth."

Euclid (c. 300 B.C.),
Greek mathematician

Jokes, Stories and Anecdotes

Rail-thin playwright George Bernard Shaw reportedly once said to corpulent man of letters G. K. Chesterton, "If I were as fat as you, I'd hang myself." Replied Chesterton, "And if I were of a mind to hang myself, I'd use you as the rope."

G[ilbert] K[eith] Chesterton (1874–1936),
British man of letters
[authenticity unverified]

After the irascible dramatist and novelist Ferenc Molnár quipped that at the birth of the reed-thin journalist Felecki the midwife had thrown away the baby and kept the umbilical cord, the two became embroiled in a feud.

Ferenc Molnár (1878–1952),
Hungarian playwright and writer

◆ THREAT

Quotations

"You know what you were before I made you what you are now. If you do not immediately comply with my request, I will unfrock you, by God."

Elizabeth I (1533–1603), British queen,
threatening the proud Bishop of Ely

"My solution to the problem would be to tell them [the North Vietnamese] frankly that they've got to draw in their horns and stop their aggression. Or else we're going to bomb them back into the Stone Age."

Curtis E. LeMay (1906–1990),
U.S. general, Mission with LeMay
(1965), p. 565

"There is no terror, Cassius, in your threats;
For I am arm'd so strong in honesty
That they pass by me as the idle wind,
Which I respect not."

William Shakespeare (1564–1616),
British playwright and poet,
Julius Caesar *(1600), Act IV, sc. iii*

"We have ways of making men talk."

Waldemar Young (c. 1900s), U.S. writer,
Lives of a Bengal Lancer *(1935 film)*

Jokes, Stories and Anecdotes

"Just to inform you," said the football player to the owlish professor, "that Coach said that if I didn't get better grades on my next report card, someone was going to get beat up."

An airplane full of lawyers was hijacked. The terrorists declared that, until their demands were met, they would release one lawyer every hour.

A portly, scowling gentleman entered the separate compartment on the European train and, just before lighting up a thick cigar, noticed a pregnant young woman looking at him apprehensively. The man said gruffly, "I hope you don't mind my smoking this cigar." "Not at all," said the mother-to-be, "provided you don't mind my throwing up."

Learning that his eldest son was having an affair with a young French actress distressed British statesman and lawyer Lord Brougham. Brougham tersely wrote to his son: "If you do not quit her, I will stop your allowance." His son wrote back: "If you do not double it, I will marry her."

Henry Peter Brougham, Baron Brougham and Vaux (1778–1868), British lord chancellor and statesman

Handel played the harpsichord as an accompaniment to singers during a rehearsal of his opera, *Flavio*. "If you cannot follow me better," mocked the tenor, displeased with Handel's playing, "I'll jump on your harpsichord and destroy it." "Please do," answered Handel, "but advise me in advance so that I may advertise it. More people will come to see you jump than to hear you sing."

George Frideric Handel (1685–1759), German composer

◆ THRIFTINESS

Jokes, Stories and Anecdotes

Overhearing some fellow actors of a touring theater company complain about inadequate accommodations, actress Molly Picon interjected, "I never complain about such things— my grandmother brought up 11 children in four rooms." Asked an amazed actress, "How did she manage?" "Simple, she took in boarders."

Molly Picon (1898–1993), Yiddish-American actress

The Harvard and Oxford scholar George Santayana lived very simply, a trait inherited from his father. When he once asked his father why he always traveled third-class, the elder Santayana replied, "Because there's no fourth class."

George Santayana (1863–1952), Spanish-born U.S. philosopher, poet and writer [attributed also to Albert Schweitzer]

◆ TIME

Quotations

"Time wounds all heels."

Irving Brecher (1914–   ), U.S. writer, Marx Brothers Go West (1940 film)

"Time present and time past
Are both perhaps present in time future,
And time future contained in time past."

T[homas] S[tearns] Eliot (1888–1965), U.S. poet, Burnt Norton

"Time: That which man is always trying to kill, but which ends in killing him."

Herbert Spencer (1820–1903), British philosopher and economist, Definitions

Classical Phrases and Myths

"*Tempus edax rerum.*" (TEM-pus ED-ax RER-um) (Time is the devourer of all things.)

Ovid [Publius Ovidius Naso] (43 B.C.–c. A.D. 18), Roman poet, Metamorphoses, XV, 234

◆ TIME, MEASURE OF

Quotations

"It was a bright cold day in April, and the clocks were striking thirteen."

George Orwell [Eric Blair] (1903–1950), British writer, Nineteen Eighty-Four (1949), pt. 1, ch. 1

"My good man, why not carry a watch?"

Sir Herbert Beerbohm Tree (1853–1917), British actor and theater manager, encountering a man panting as he carried a heavy grandfather clock [variations also attributed to others]

Jokes, Stories and Anecdotes

Confirming her dates at the bar of the casino during the convention for attorneys, the prostitute recited, "John, seven-ish, Fred, eight-ish, Bill, nine-ish." She then surveyed all the men and yelled, "Ten-ish anyone?"

Humorists Robert Benchley and Dorothy Parker were visiting a speakeasy when a man showed them what he said was an indestructible watch. They tested this by banging it against the tabletop, then throwing it on the floor and stomping on it. The owner picked it up, put it to his ear, and said, in incredulous dismay, "It's stopped." Benchley and Parker chorused, "Maybe you wound it too tight."

> Robert Charles Benchley (1889–1945),
> U.S. humorist

A timid Paris theater callboy once notified the actress Sarah Bernhardt of the first act curtain with the words: "Madame, it will be eight o'clock when it suits you." She adopted the phrase thereafter as her cue.

> Sarah Bernhardt (1844–1923),
> French actress

Samuel Goldwyn, during the making of a film, had the rude habit of phoning his associates at any hour to inform them of his latest idea. For example, Goldwyn phoned N. Richard Nash in the wee morning hours while he was writing the screenplay for *Porgy and Bess*. Nash angrily asked, "Do you know what time it is?" Pause. Then Nash heard Goldwyn ask his wife, "Frances, he wants to know what time it is."

> Samuel Goldwyn [Samuel Goldfish]
> (1882–1974), Russian-born
> U.S. film producer

◆ TIMELINESS

Foreign Words and Phrases

salto mortale (Ita)
(SAL-to mor-TAH-lay) *lit:* somersault; critical moment, climactic

Quotations

"We must beat the iron while it is hot, but we may polish it at leisure."

> John Dryden (1631–1700), British poet,
> playwright and writer,
> Dedication of the Aeneis

Classical Phrases and Myths

annus mutatis (Lat)
(AN-nus mu-TAH-tees) year of change

in discrimine rerum (Lat)
(in-dis-KREEM-in-ay REHR-um) at the crisis point (of affairs), at the turning point

Jokes, Stories and Anecdotes

The new sales manager called the sales force together to lay down the law. "There's now a new regime around here—all work. That means from now on," she concluded, "I want you out of here and calling on your customers at the stroke of nine." Wisecracked one salesperson, "The first stroke or the last stroke of nine?"

◆ TITLE

Quotations

"If we all wore crowns the kings would go bare-headed."

> R. H. Benson (1871–1914), British writer

"I would rather be a beeress than a peeress."

*Mrs. Ronald [Maggie] Greville
(1867–1942), British socialite, commenting
on her great fortune inherited from her
father, John McEwen,
a Scottish beer baron*

"Kings are not born; they are made by universal hallucination."

*George Bernard Shaw (1856–1950),
Irish playwright*

◆ TOP

Quotations

"There is always room at the top."

*Daniel Webster (1782–1852), U.S. lawyer,
politician and orator, responding to advice
not to become a lawyer as the profession
was overcrowded*

◆ TOUCH

Foreign Words and Phrases

touché (Fra)
(too-SHAY) *lit:* touched (fencing);
well-done, good retort or response

Jokes, Stories and Anecdotes

Because he had remained on his deathbed for such a long time without any signs of life, John Holmes, the brother of Oliver Wendell Holmes, Sr., appeared to those gathered to have already died. Feeling no pulse, the nurse remarked that a surer test of whether he was alive was to feel his feet. "Nobody ever died with their feet warm," she said. At that, Holmes said his last words, "John Rogers did," referring to the Protestant martyr who was burned at the stake in 1555 during the reign of Mary Tudor.

John Holmes (1812–1899), U.S. lawyer

◆ TOURISM

Jokes, Stories and Anecdotes

An Apache Indian was staring with astonishment at the Manhattan skyscrapers when a New Yorker asked sardonically, "Do you like our city?" The Indian, shaking his head in wonder, replied, "Amazing. But tell me, sir, do you like our country?"

An American tourist stopped at an inn in a small Russian village and ordered a couple of sausage links for breakfast. Later, he received the bill and was shocked to see that he had been charged $20. He asked, "Is sausage scarce here?" Replied the innkeeper, "No, but Americans are."

◆ TRAVEL

Foreign Words and Phrases

bon voyage (Fra)
(bon voy-AHJ) have a good journey

Wanderlust (Ger)
(VAHN-der-loost) desire to wander
(suggests restlessness)

Quotations

"In America there are two classes of travel—first class, and with children."

*Robert Charles Benchley (1889–1945),
U.S. humorist, Pluck and Luck (1925)*

"Like all great travellers, I have seen more than I remember, and remember more than I have seen."

*Benjamin Disraeli, 1st Earl of Beaconsfield
(1804–1881), British prime minister*

"As the Spanish proverb says, 'He who would bring home the wealth of the Indies, must carry the wealth of the Indies with him.' So it is in travelling; a man must carry knowledge with him, if he would bring home knowledge."

Samuel Johnson (1709–1784),
British man of letters

"Travel is glamorous only in retrospect."

Paul Theroux (1941–   ),
U.S. writer

Classical Phrases and Myths

"A rolling stone gathers no moss."

Publilius Syrus (c. 100 B.C.),
Roman writer, Sententiae, 524

The *Odyssey* (OD-i-see) is an epic poem in 24 books attributed to Homer and generally treated as a companion to the *Iliad*. The poem celebrates the ten-year journey of wanderings and adventures endured by Odysseus and his men as he struggled to reach his home in Ithaca after the Trojan War. Thus, an *odyssey* is a long journey or a description of one.

Jokes, Stories and Anecdotes

"We're halfway there," remarked the man to his wife as they drove into New York from Washington, D.C. "Half!" said his wife. "We're only six blocks from our destination." "The other half is finding a parking place."

The 300-pound-plus William Howard Taft, once stranded at a small railroad station, was told that the express train would stop only if a number of people wanted to board it. Taft wired the conductor: "Stop at Hicksville. Large party waiting to catch train." To the confused conductor when the train stopped and he boarded, Taft said, "You can go ahead. I am the large party."

William Howard Taft (1857–1930),
U.S. president and jurist

◆ TRAVEL (BY AIR)

Quotations

"The airplane stays up because it doesn't have the time to fall."

Orville Wright (1871–1948) and
Wilbur Wright (1867–1912),
U.S. aviators, explaining the principles
of their Flyer's performance

Jokes, Stories and Anecdotes

Asked if he was afraid of flying, a train passenger replied, "No, crashing."

Before takeoff on an airplane flight, a stewardess reminded Muhammad Ali to fasten his seat belt. "Superman don't need no seat belt," replied Ali. Retorted the stewardess, "Superman don't need no airplane, either." Ali fastened his belt.

Muhammad Ali [Cassius Clay]
(1942–   ), U.S. boxer

When Sir J. M. Barrie's *Peter Pan* premiered in London in 1904, in it Peter told the Darling children that they would fly if they believed they could. Soon parents of injured children, who had taken Peter's advice literally, notified Barrie. He immediately included in the play a cautionary statement that children could fly, but only if they had first been sprinkled with "fairy-dust," which of course is difficult to come by.

Sir J[ames] M[atthew] Barrie (1860–
1937), British writer and playwright

◆ TRAVEL (BY WATER)

Quotations

"Go up to the bridge, give the admiral my compliments, and tell him he's not to let that happen again."

Victoria (1819–1901), British queen, to an attendant, after a giant wave in rough seas rocked the ship in which she was crossing to Ireland

Classical Phrases and Myths

The Phoenician ship transporting Xerxes and his troops, retreating from Greece back to Asia Minor, encountered a large storm, and the ship seemed likely to founder. When Xerxes asked the pilot whether they would survive, he answered that they were without hope unless the ship's load was substantially lightened. Addressing the Persian troops on deck, Xerxes said, "It is on you that my safety depends. Some of you may now show your regard for your king." A number dutifully threw themselves overboard. When the lightened ship came safely to harbor, Xerxes commanded that a golden crown be presented to the pilot for preserving the king's life. He then ordered that the man's head be cut off for causing the loss of so many Persian lives.

Xerxes (d. -465 B.C.), Persian king

◆ TREES & PLANTS

Quotations

"I think that I shall never see
A poem lovely as a tree. . .

Poems are made by fools like me
But only God can make a tree."

Joyce Kilmer (1888–1918), U.S. poet, Trees and Other Poems (1914), "Trees"

"Training is everything. The peach was once a bitter almond; cauliflower is nothing but cabbage with a college education."

Mark Twain [Samuel Langhorne Clemens] (1835–1910), U.S. humorist, writer and speaker, Pudd'nhead Wilson (1894), ch. 5

Jokes, Stories and Anecdotes

Nobel Prize–winning novelist William Faulkner invited a woman to accompany him one spring evening to see a bride in her wedding dress. After driving a distance, Faulkner entered a meadow, switched off the headlights and inched forward in the darkness. Finally, he stopped the car, announcing that the lovely bride was in front of them. When he turned the headlights back on, before them stood an apple tree in full blossom.

William Faulkner (1897–1962), U.S. writer

◆ TRUTH

Foreign Words and Phrases

vérité (Fra)
(vay-ree-TAY) realism in representative art

verismo (Ita)
(vehr-EEZ-moh) realism, objectivity

mokita (Kiri)
(moh-KEET-ah) the well-known but unspoken truth (due to social conventions)

Quotations

"A truth that's told with bad intent
Beats all lies you can invent."

*William Blake (1757–1827), British poet,
artist and mystic, Auguries of
Innocence (c. 1805)*

"Tis strange, but true; for truth is
always strange; Stranger than fiction."

*Lord Byron [George Gordon]
(1788–1824), British poet,
Don Juan (1818),
Canto XIV, st. ci*

"How often have I said to you that
when you have eliminated the impossible, whatever remains, however improbable, must be the
truth."

*Sir Arthur Conan Doyle (1859–1930),
British writer, The Sign of Four
(1890), ch. 6*

"I don't want to be right. I only
want to know whether I am right."

*Albert Einstein (1879–1955),
German-born physicist*

"The color of truth is gray."

Andre Gide (1869–1951), French writer

"It is always the best policy to
speak the truth—unless, of course,
you are an exceptionally good liar."

*Jerome K[lapka] Jerome (1859–1927),
British writer, The Idler
(February 1892), p. 118*

"It takes two to speak the truth, one
to speak, and another to hear."

*Henry David Thoreau (1817–1862),
U.S. writer, naturalist and poet,
A Week on the Concord and Merrimack
Rivers (1849), "Wednesday"*

"Truth is the most valuable thing
we have. Let's economize it."

*Mark Twain [Samuel Langhorne Clemens]
(1835–1910), U.S. humorist, writer and
speaker, Following the Equator
(1897), ch. 7*

"*La vérité existe; on n'invente que le
mensonge.*" (Truth exists; only lies
are invented.)

*Georges Braque (1882–1963),
French painter, Le Jour et la nuit:
Cahiers 1917–52 (Day and Night,
Notebooks, 1952), p. 20*

Classical Phrases and Myths

magna est veritas, et praevalebit (Lat)
(MAG-na est VER-ee-tas et PRIE-val-e-bit) mighty is truth, and shall
prevail

Jokes, Stories and Anecdotes

The Nobel laureate, mathematician
and logician Bertrand Russell related that only once was he able to
make the British philosopher and
his good friend George Moore tell
a lie. He used the subterfuge of asking, "'Moore, do you always speak
the truth?" "No." Remarked Russell, "I believe this to be the only lie
he ever told."

*Bertrand Arthur William Russell, 3rd Earl
(1872–1970), British mathematician
and philosopher*

◆ TYRANNY & SUBJECTION

Foreign Words and Phrases

czar/czarina (Rus)
(tsahr / tsahr-REE-na) name for
male/female prerevolution Russian
rulers (also *tsar/tsarina*)

Gauleiter (Ger)
(GOW-ly-ter) local Nazi party leader
(colloq: petty tyrant)

Fuhrer (Ger)
(FEW-rer) leader; Hitler's title

Fuhrerprinzip (Ger)
(FEW-rer-print-SEEP) *lit:* principle
of leadership; theory of unlimited

authority on which Hitler's regime was based

Quotations

"All men would be tyrants if they could."

Daniel Defoe [Daniel Foe] (1659–1731), British writer, The Kentish Petition (1712–1713)

"The secret of the demagogue is to make himself as stupid as his audience so that they believe they are as clever as he."

Karl Kraus (1874–1936), Austrian poet and writer, Spruche und Widerspruche (Dicta and Contradictions) (1909)

"Tyranny is always better organized than freedom."

Charles Peguy (1873–1914), French poet and writer, Basic Verities (1943), "War and Peace"

Classical Phrases and Myths

divide et impera (Lat)
(de-VEE-dayet im-PER-a) divide and rule; political maxim cited by Machiavelli

"Oderint dum metuant." (OH-der-int dum MET-u-ant.) (Let them hate me, as long as they fear me.)

Lucius Accius (c. 170 B.C.–c. 85 B.C.), Roman poet and writer

An innocent lamb, while drinking at a stream, was approached by a wolf shouting, "How dare you stir up the mud of the water I'm drinking?" "But I was downstream from you," bleated the lamb. "Don't argue," snarled the wolf. "You're the one who was saying those disparaging things about me last year." "Oh, no," protested the lamb. "I wasn't even born last year!" "Well," snapped the wolf, "I cer-

tainly won't let you talk me out of my supper." And, since any excuse will serve a tyrant, the wolf fell upon the helpless lamb and devoured her.

Aesop (c. 600 B.C.), Greek fabulist

Jokes, Stories and Anecdotes

"So, didja win that fight with your wife?" one bar patron asked another. "She came crawling to me on her hands and knees," boasted the other. "No kidding? What did she say?" "Come out from under that bed, you coward!"

◆ UGLINESS

Quotations

"She resembles the Venus de Milo: she is very old, has no teeth, and has white spots on her yellow skin."

Henrich Heine (1797–1856), German poet and writer

"The tartness of his face sours ripe grapes."

William Shakespeare (1564–1616), British playwright and poet, Coriolanus (1608), Act III, sc. ii

Classical Phrases and Myths

In Greek mythology, Medusa (MEE-doo-sa) was one of three Gorgons who dwelt in Libya. The only one who was mortal, Medusa was originally a beautiful maiden who had been transformed (by Athena for violating one of her temples) into a hideous monster with hair of writhing serpents and a face so fearful to view that whoever saw it was turned into stone. When Perseus confronted her, he cut off her head by averting his face and watching her reflection in the shield of Athena, who also guided his hand. Hence, a *medusa* is a hideous woman, one who it is impossible to look at without revulsion.

Jokes, Stories and Anecdotes

Night after night, comedian Fred Allen noticed an unsmiling, haggard-looking musician in the orchestra pit of a vaudeville house in Toledo, Ohio. Finally, Allen stopped his act and called out to him, "How much would you charge to haunt a house?"

Fred Allen [John Sullivan] (1894–1956), U.S. comedian

The journalist and wit Franklin Pierce Adams was mocked once when the humorist Irvin Cobb, upon spying a moosehead mounted over the mantel, cried, "My God, they've shot F.P.A.!"

Irvin S[hrewsbury] Cobb (1876–1944), U.S. humorist and writer

The notably immoral and ugly French Prince Conti, ready to embark on a trip, jokingly warned his wife, "Madame, I counsel you not to make me a cuckold during my absence." "Monsieur, you may leave without concern," she replied, "for it is only when I look at you that I desire to deceive you."

Prince Louis-Armand II de Conti (1695–1727), French aristocrat

Someone tactlessly insulted the scientist and satirist Georg Lichtenberg about his very large ears. "Ah," retorted Lichtenberg, "with my ears and your brains we'd be a perfectly splendid ass, would we not?"

Georg Christoph Lichtenberg (1742–1799), German physicist and writer

◆ UNACCOMPLISHED

Quotations

"The best of all our actions tend
To the preposterousest end."

Samuel Butler (1612–1680), British poet and writer, Genuine Remains: Satire upon the Weakness and Misery of Man, 1. 41

Classical Phrases and Myths

In Greek mythology, Sisyphus (SIS-ee-fus) was relegated to Tartarus, the lowest area of the Underworld, for his various crimes and deceptions. His punishment was to roll uphill a huge stone, which at the summit always rolls back downhill, thereby condemning him to eternal toil. Thus, a *labor of Sisyphus* is a task never completed.

Jokes, Stories and Anecdotes

The phrase "to do (or pull) a Brodie," meaning to attempt a risky stunt, originated in 1886 when Steve Brodie jumped off the Brooklyn Bridge 135 feet into the East River to win a $200 bet. The father of the heavyweight boxer Jim Corbett later met Brodie. "So you're the fellow who jumped over the Brooklyn Bridge," he said. "I jumped off it," corrected Brodie. "I thought you jumped over it," said the unimpressed old Mr. Corbett. "Any damn fool could jump off it."

Steve Brodie (1863–?), U.S. saloonkeeper

The inventor Thomas Edison had tried 50,000 experiments before he invented a new storage battery. When it was pointed out that he had endured an exorbitant number of failures to achieve results, he replied, "Results? Why, I have gotten

384

a lot of results. I know 50,000 things that won't work."

Thomas Alva Edison (1847–1931), U.S. inventor

◆ UNAFFECTEDNESS

Foreign Words and Phrases

wagoto (Jap)
(wah-GOH-toh) less stylized Kabuki acting style in which the hero is often a young lover or dandy

Classical Phrases and Myths

Sparta (SPAR-ta) was the ancient city in Laconia, Greece, renowned for the austerity and simple lifestyle of its citizenry. A child born in Sparta was examined by state representatives and, if found to be weak, was left to die on Mount Taygetus. A well-known story of Spartan hardiness and self-discipline involves the Spartan youth who stole a fox, hid it under his cloak, and stood silent and motionless as the fox gnawed at his vitals. The valor of Spartan warriors became proverbial, best illustrated in the battle of Thermopylae, where the Spartan contingent, under Leonidas's command, refused to surrender or be taken captive. Thus, a *spartan* object or life is austere, simple and enduring.

◆ UNCERTAINTY

Quotations

"Half the failures of this world arise from pulling in one's horse as he is leaping."

Julius Charles Hare (1795–1855) and Augustus William Hare (1792–1834),

British clergymen and writers, Guesses at Truths *(1827), Serial I*

"When in doubt, win the trick."

Edmond Hoyle (1672–1769), British writer [Hoyle's writings, particularly for the game of whist, were responsible for the saying "according to Hoyle"]

"When in doubt tell the truth."

Mark Twain [Samuel Langhorne Clemens] (1835–1910), U.S. humorist, writer and speaker, Following the Equator *(1897), ch. 2*

Jokes, Stories and Anecdotes

A man at a construction site was hit over the head by such a severe blow that he was knocked comatose. His family, convinced he was dead, arranged with a funeral parlor for his burial. But at the next dawn, the man suddenly regained consciousness and sat straight up in the casket. Confused by his physical surroundings, he rubbed his eyes and looked around. He thought: "If I'm alive, why in the world am I in this cushy, satin-lined box? But if I'm dead, why do I have to go to the bathroom?" This story was often told by President Harry Truman.

◆ UNCHASTITY

Quotations

"Only if you can calm her down."

Judy Garland [Frances Gumm] (1922–1969), U.S. entertainer and film actress, answering Jack Paar's question about another actress, "Isn't she a nymphomaniac?"

"If there were no husbands, who would look after our mistresses?"

George Moore (1852–1933), Irish writer, playwright and poet

"You were born with your legs apart. They'll send you to your grave in a Y-shaped coffin."

Joe Orton (1933–1967),
British playwright, What the
Butler Saw (1969), Act 1

"Young men want to be faithful and are not; old men want to be faithless and cannot."

Oscar [Fingal O'Flahertie Wills] Wilde
(1854–1900), British playwright, writer
and wit, The Picture of Dorian Gray
(1891), ch. 2

Classical Phrases and Myths

In Greek mythology, Actaeon (ak-TEE-on) was a hunter who one day discovered the chaste huntress goddess Artemis bathing. Offended, she turned him into a stag, and he was torn apart by his own hounds. An *actaeon* is a cuckold, one with horns implanted upon him.

According to Greek mythology, Priapus (*PRI-ay-pus*) was the god to promote fertility in women, crops and cattle. A son of Dionysus and Aphrodite, he was depicted as a faunlike deity with an erect penis. Thus, *priapism* refers to promiscuity and licentiousness.

In Greek mythology, satyrs (SAY-terz) were sylvan deities closely involved with the worship of Bacchus, the god of wine; they had somewhat bestial faces, horns on the foreheads and tails. In Roman mythology, they were depicted as goatlike men who followed Dionysus in his debaucheries. Hence, a *satyr* is one with a great sexual appetite.

Jokes, Stories and Anecdotes

Mary was getting married and was becoming more and more anxious about satisfying her forthcoming marital duties. She approached her friend Tanya, who knew everything about men. "I know this is very el-ementary," began Mary, "but is it all right to talk to your husband while you're making love?" Tanya pondered the question, then said, "I must admit that I've never done that, but I suppose you could—if there's a telephone nearby."

A man best known as a cuckold for his wife's infidelities was bragging about his young son to French comedy dramatist Georges Feydeau. "He's so devoted to his mother and so loving," boasted the proud father. "He's always 'under her skirts.'" Feydeau muttered, "Where he must meet a lot of others."

Georges Feydeau (1862–1921),
French playwright

Several acquaintances were gossiping about an older lady who had led a wild life as a single woman. Her confession of all her prior affairs to her husband before they married was offered to explain the success of the long and happy marriage. Praised all, "What candor! What courage!" Remarked the comedy dramatist Samuel Foote, "Yes, and what a memory!"

Samuel Foote (1720–1777),
British actor and playwright

When his Queen Caroline lay on her deathbed, George II, who was a notorious libertine, was nonetheless genuinely grieved. When she nobly begged him to marry again, he replied, "*Non, j'aurai des maîtresses.*" (No, I shall have mistresses.) Mourned the dying queen, "*Ah! Mon Dieu, cela n'empêche pas.*" (Ah! My God, [marriage] would not prevent that.)

George II (1673–1760), British king

An indefatigable lothario, the refined Joseph Giampetro bore a worried countenance and an opened letter when he was seen in a coffeehouse by a friend. The friend sympathetically inquired whether Giampetro had received bad news. "No, but whoever sent this letter says that he will strangle me if I continue to see his wife." "So keep away from the woman," advised the friend. "But which lady?" cried Giampetro. "The letter is anonymous!"

> *Joseph Giampetro (1866–1913),*
> *Austrian-born German actor*

◆ UNDERTAKING

Quotations

"Difficult do you call it, Sir? I wish it were impossible."

> *Samuel Johnson (1709–1784), British man*
> *of letters, showing his distaste for music*
> *after the performance of a violin virtuoso*

"So little done, so much to do."

> *Cecil John Rhodes (1853–1902),*
> *British-born South African statesman*
> *and financier, dying words*

Classical Phrases and Myths

actum ne agas (Lat)
(AK-tum nay AG-ahs) do not redo what has been done (colloq: get on with it)

◆ UNDESIRABLE

Foreign Words and Phrases

cavoli riscaldati (Ita)
(kav-OH-lee rees-KALD-ah-tee) *lit:* reheated cabbage; attempt to revive an old relationship (e.g., dead love affair) is messy, distasteful

Quotations

"Stop the World, I Want to Get Off." [Title of musical (1961).]

> *Anthony Newley (1931–   )*
> *and Leslie Bricusse (1931–   ),*
> *British songwriters and playwrights*

◆ UNFAIRNESS

Quotations

"He can't see a belt without hitting below it."

> *Margot Asquith, Countess of Oxford and*
> *Asquith (1864–1945), British writer and*
> *socialite, describing David Lloyd George*

"There is always inequality in life. Some men are killed in a war and some men are wounded and some men never leave the country . . . Life is unfair."

> *John Fitzgerald Kennedy (1917–1963),*
> *U.S. president, press conference,*
> *March 21, 1962*

"All's fair in love and war."

> *Francis Edward Smedley (1818–1864),*
> *British writer, Frank Fairlegh*
> *(1850), ch. 50*

"Quit fouling like a wimp. If you're gonna foul, knock the crap outta him."

> *Norm[an] Stewart (c. 1940–   ),*
> *basketball coach, to Missouri Tigers'*
> *six-foot-nine-inch Don Bingenheimer*

◆ UNFAMILIARITY

Classical Phrases and Myths

"*O tempora, O mores!*" (*oh TEM-por-a oh MOR-ays*) (Oh, the times! Oh, the manners!)

> *Marcus Tullius Cicero (106 B.C.–43 B.C.),*
> *Roman statesman and man of letters,*
> *In Catilinam, I, i, I [exclamation*
> *suggesting dissatisfaction with*
> *changing times, changing values, etc.]*

Jokes, Stories and Anecdotes

The artist Maxfield Parrish, who specialized in rendering beautiful nudes, once had a typically gorgeous model arrive at his studio. To delay confronting the blank canvas he invited her to share a cup of coffee. Suddenly, the studio buzzer rang. "Miss!" shrieked the panic-stricken artist, "For God's sake, take your clothes off! My wife is coming to check on me."

> *Maxfield Parrish (1870-1966),*
> *U.S. illustrator and painter*

◆ UNHAPPINESS & DISPLEASURE

Foreign Words and Phrases

kvetch (Yid)
(kvetch) to complain, whine or gripe (chronically)

ah, les bons vieux temps ou nous etions si malheureux! (Fra)
(ah les bon vyeu ton oo noo ay-TEE-on see mal-HEH-ruh) oh, the good old times when we were so unhappy!

con dolore (Ita)
(kon doh-LOHR-ay) in music, mournfully

Angst (Ger)
(ahngst) (feeling of) turmoil, frustration, anxiety, guilt

Quotations

"Unhappiness is best defined as the difference between our talents and our expectations."

> *Edward de Bono (1933–   ),*
> *British writer*

"[Ralph Waldo] Emerson is one who lives instinctively on ambro-sia—and leaves everything indigestible on his plate."

> *Friedrich [Wilhelm] Nietzsche*
> *(1844–1900), German philosopher*

Classical Phrases and Myths

"Forsan et haec olim meminisse iuvabit." (Someday perhaps even this plight shall be pleasant to remember.)

> *Virgil [Publius Vergilius Maro]*
> *(70 B.C.-19 B.C.), Roman poet, Aeneid,*
> *bk. II, l. cciii*

Jokes, Stories and Anecdotes

"The food here is simply awful," one woman exclaimed to her dinner partner on the cruise ship. "Yes," replied the other woman, "and the portions are so small."

The condemned traitor was being led out to be shot at sunrise. It was pouring rain, and the condemned turned to the lieutenant heading the execution squad, saying bitterly, "You are very cruel to march me in this downpour to be shot!" The lieutenant snapped, "You're lucky! You don't have to march back."

◆ UNIVERSE & COSMOLOGIES

Classical Phrases and Myths

cosmos (Grk)
(KOS-mos) the universe as an orderly whole

Jokes, Stories and Anecdotes

At a public meeting concerning Transcendentalism, Margaret Fuller, a pioneer of women's rights and social reform (as well as a Transcendentalist), rose in a moment of enthusiasm and cried, "I accept the universe!" To which Scottish-born historian Thomas Carlyle growled, "By God, she'd better!"

Thomas Carlyle (1795–1881),
British historian

◆ UNKINDNESS

Quotations

"Tallulah [Bankhead] is alway skating on thin ice. Everyone wants to be there when it breaks."

Mrs. Patrick Campbell [Beatrice]
(1865–1940), British actress

" 'Waldo is one of those people who would be enormously improved by death,' said Clovis."

Saki [Hector Hugh Munro] (1870–1916),
British writer, Beasts and Super-Beasts
(1914), "The Feast of Nemesis"

"Why be disagreeable, when with a little effort you can be impossible?"

Douglas Woodruff (1897–1978),
British writer

Classical Phrases and Myths

Draco (DRA-koh) was a seventh-century B.C. lawgiver who formulated the first written code of laws for Athens. On completion of the code, the citizens were so overjoyed that at a testimonial in his honor they showered Draco under a deluge of cloaks. Draco's code was said to have been written in blood because it mandated the death penalty for many offenses, and was mostly superseded by the code of

Solon in 594 B.C. Hence, anything *draconian* is harsh or severe.

Draco (c. 600 B.C.), Greek legislator

◆ UNKNOWN

Quotations

"'Tis very puzzling on the brink
Of what is Eternity to stare,
And know no more of what is *here*,
Than *there*."

Lord Byron [George Gordon] (1788–1824),
British poet, Don Juan Canto X
(1823), l. xx

"Nothing is so firmly believed as what is least known."

Michel Eyquem de Montaigne
(1533–1592), French writer,
Essays (1580), bk. I

Jokes, Stories and Anecdotes

When introduced to Nobel Prize–winning Ernest Hemingway in a restaurant, baseball great Yogi Berra, who read only the sports pages, was asked if he had ever heard of the famous writer. "I don't believe so," Berra admitted. "What paper does he write for?"

Lawrence ["Yogi"] Berra (1925–),
U.S. baseball player and manager

The poet Robert Browning's 1840 poem *Sordello* concerned pragmatism and its conflict with the human soul. The language was incomprehensible to many, including members of the London Poetry Society, who had asked Browning to interpret a particularly obscure passage. Browning read it through twice, frowned, and then, shrugging his shoulders, said, "When I wrote that, God and I knew what it meant, but now God alone knows."

Robert Browning (1812–1889),
British poet

◆ UNPREPAREDNESS

Quotations

"Magnificently unprepared
For the long littleness of life."

Frances Cornford (1886–1960), U.S. poet,
Rupert Brooke (1915)

Jokes, Stories and Anecdotes

Herford was a guest of honor at a banquet along with a famous general. Without prior warning, the hostess announced, "Mr. Oliver Herford will now improvise a poem in honor of this occasion." Herford, a modest and shy man, protested. "Oh no," he said, shrinking back in his chair, "have the general fire a cannon."

Oliver Herford (1863–1935), British-born
U.S. humorist and illustrator
[attributed also to Carl Sandburg]

◆ UNPRODUCTIVENESS

Quotations

"procrastination is the
art of keeping
up with yesterday."

Don[ald Robert Perry] Marquis
(1878–1937), U.S. writer and poet,
archy and mehitabel (1927),
"certain maxims of archy"

Classical Phrases and Myths

ex nihilo nihil fit (Lat)
(ex NEE-hil-oh NEE-hil fit) from nothing, nothing can be made

"The mountain labored greatly and produced a mouse."

Aesop (c. 600 B.C.), Greek fabulist

Jokes, Stories and Anecdotes

At the cafeteria, Fred could not help overhearing the conversation of four women at an adjoining table. Said the first, "Poor Mary. The doctor told her that she can't have any babies. Apparently, she's impregnable." The second tittered. "Dear, the correct word is 'impenetrable.'"Snorted the third, "Oh, what malaprops you are. The term is 'inconceivable.' " With her nose in the air, the fourth said, "No, the word is 'unbearable.' " Fred leaned over and said to them, "Ladies, the word you want is 'inscrutable'."

◆ UNSOPHISTICATION

Foreign Words and Phrases

klutz (Yid)
(klutz) chronically clumsy person

Quotations

"He is forever poised between a cliche and an indiscretion."

[Maurice] Harold Macmillan, 1st Earl of
Stockton (1894–1992), British prime
minister, describing a foreign secretary

"What makes us so bitter against people who outwit us is that they think themselves cleverer than we are."

François, Duc de La Rochefoucauld
(1613–1680), French writer,
Maximes (1678)

Jokes, Stories and Anecdotes

The Italian composer Cherubini was once given a score by an acquaintance, who said that it was by

Etienne Mehul. After studying the piece, Cherubini stated, "This isn't by Mehul, it's too bad!" "Then will you believe me if I tell you that it is mine?" asked the acquaintance. "No, it's too good."

Maria Luigi Cherubini (1760–1842), Italian composer

◆ UNTIMELINESS

Foreign Words and Phrases

rubato (Ita)
(roo-BAH-toh) *lit:* robbed; in music, deviation from strict time with notes lengthened or shortened

Quotations

"When written in Chinese the word 'crisis' is composed of two characters. One represents danger and the other represents opportunity."

John Fitzgerald Kennedy (1917–1963), U.S. president, Address, United Negro College Fund Convocation, April 12, 1959

"The time is out of joint;
O cursed spite,
That ever I was born to set it right!"

William Shakespeare (1564–1616), British playwright and poet, Hamlet (1601), Act I, sc. v

"*Trois heures, c'est toujours trop tard ou trop tôt pour ce qu'on veut faire.*" (Three o'clock is always too late or too early for anything you want to do.)

Jean-Paul Sartre (1905–1980), French philosopher, playwright and writer, La Nausie (Nausea), (1938)

◆ UNWILLINGNESS

Quotations

"If the people don't want to come out to the park, nobody's gonna stop them."

Lawrence ["Yogi"] Berra (1925–), U.S. baseball player and manager, commenting on poor attendance at New York Yankee games

Jokes, Stories and Anecdotes

When newspaper proprietor William Randolph Hearst offered columnist Arthur Brisbane a fully paid six-month vacation for his valuable work on behalf of the newspapers, Brisbane surprisingly refused. When Hearst asked for an explanation, the journalist provided two reasons. "The first is that if I stopped writing for six months it might hurt the circulation of your newspapers," said Brisbane. He paused, and then added, "The second reason is that it might not."

William Randolph Hearst (1863–1951), U.S. publisher

During a period when diplomatic relations with France were severely strained, King Henry VIII of England appointed a nobleman as his ambassador to French King François I. When the diplomat heard Henry's aggressive message, however, he pleaded to be excused, for if he delivered it, the diplomat pointed out, the enraged French king might well have him executed. If François killed him, Henry reassured him, Henry could retaliate by striking off the heads of a dozen Frenchmen in England. "But of all these heads, my lord," sighed the concerned diplomat, "there may not be one fitting my shoulders."

Henry VIII (1481–1547), British king

◆ UPPER CLASSES & ARISTOCRACY

Foreign Words and Phrases

grande dame (Fra)
(grohnde dahm) (haughty or snobby) aristocratic lady, great old ship, building, etc.

(le) gratin (Fra)
(le grah-TAHN) *lit:* topping of breadcrumbs or grated cheese; upper crust of society

haut monde (Fra)
(oat MOND) high society

elite (Fra)
(ay-LEET) the upper or privileged group(s)

créme de la créme (Fra)
(krem de la krem) *lit:* cream of the cream; the ultimate, the top level (generally, the upper classes)

Quotations

"It has been said, not truly, but with a possible approximation to truth, that 'in 1802 every hereditary monarch was insane.' "

Walter Bagehot (1826–1877), British economist and writer, The English Constitution, *ch. 4*

"For what were all these country patriots born?
To hunt, and vote, and raise the price of corn?"

Lord Byron [George Gordon] (1788–1824), British poet, The Age of Bronze *(1823), st. xiv*

"Everyone likes flattery; and when you come to Royalty you should lay it on with a trowel."

Benjamin Disraeli, 1st Earl of Beaconsfield (1804–1881), British prime minister

"The whole world is in revolt. Soon there will be only five Kings left— the King of England, the King of Spades, the King of Clubs, the King of Hearts and the King of Diamonds."

Farouk I (1920–1965), Egyptian king

"There are bad manners everywhere, but an aristocracy is bad manners organized."

Henry James (1843–1916), U.S. writer

"There are only about four hundred people in New York society."

Ward McAllister (1827–1895), U.S. socialite

"An aristocracy in a republic is like a chicken whose head has been cut off—it may run about in a lively way, but in fact it is dead."

Nancy Mitford (1904–1973), British writer, Noblesse Oblige *(1956), p. 39*

"When I want a peerage, I shall buy it like an honest man."

Alfred Charles William Harmsworth, Viscount Northcliffe (1865–1922), British aristocrat

"Ladies and gentlemen are permitted to have friends in the kennel but not in the kitchen."

George Bernard Shaw (1856–1950), Irish playwright

"All kings is mostly rapscallions."

Mark Twain [Samuel Langhorne Clemens] (1835–1910), U.S. humorist, writer and speaker, The Adventures of Huckleberry Finn *(1884), ch. 23*

Classical Phrases and Myths

optimates (Lat)
(op-ti-MAH-tays) the aristocracy,
the best people (often used sardonically or ironically)

Ancient Greece was divided into a
thousand independent city states,
of which Athens was the most
prominent. When Themistocles of
Athens was the most renowned
leader in all Greece, a politician
from a small provincial town called
Larissa said sneeringly to him: "A
great deal of your fame, Themistocles, arises from the fortunate accident of your birth in Athens. Had
you been born in Larissa, you
would not have become great."
Scornfully, Themistocles replied,
"Nor you, had you been born in
Athens."

> *Themistocles (c. 527 B.C.–c. 460 B.C.),*
> *Greek statesman*

Jokes, Stories and Anecdotes

The social matron advised her poor
cousin, "In Boston we consider only
our breeding." Responded her
cousin, "In San Francisco, we think
it's great fun, but we also do other
things."

Young Marie Thérèse was playing
with a maid one day and, taking
one of her hands, counted the fingers. "What?" she exclaimed. "You
have five fingers, too, just like me?"

> *Marie Thérèse Charlotte,*
> *Duchesse d' Angoulême (1778–1851),*
> *French aristocrat*

Princess Anne was a member of the
English equestrian team at the 1976
Olympics. In the only exception to
Olympic qualifying standards, she
was exempted from the required
physical examination, presumably
because her sex and purity had
been uncontrovertibly established
by virtue of her royal blood.

> *Princess Anne (1950–   ),*
> *British royal*

King George VI and Queen Elizabeth
went to see a Noel Coward–Gertrude Lawrence play at a London
theater. When they entered the royal
box, the audience rose to its feet in
deference. "What an entrance!" exclaimed Gertrude Lawrence. Retorted Coward, "What a part!"

> *Sir Noel Coward (1899–1973),*
> *British playwright and actor*

The British statesman Benjamin
Disraeli, who boasted a reputation
of being able to make a joke on any
subject, was once challenged by his
political rival William Gladstone.
"Make a joke about Queen Victoria." "Sir," replied Disraeli, "Her
Majesty is not a subject."

> *Benjamin Disraeli, 1st Earl of Beaconsfield*
> *(1804–1881), British prime minister*
> *[attributed also to others]*

On a state visit to Australia, the
Queen Mother found herself surrounded by a number of inquisitive
Australians at a garden party. Ever
gracious as the circle pressed closer,
the still smiling queen remarked
under her breath, "Please don't
touch the exhibits."

> *Elizabeth the Queen Mother*
> *(1900–   ), British queen*

Traveling by train to Compéigne,
the autocratic princess was politely
asked by the compartment's lone
other occupant if smoking would
bother her. "I have no idea, monsieur," Princess Metternich responded, a steely eye fixed on the

man. "No one has ever dared to smoke in my presence."

Princess Pauline Metternich (1859–1921), French aristocrat

◆ UPSTAGING

Jokes, Stories and Anecdotes

A fellow actress once said of Tallulah Bankhead: "She's not so great. I can upstage her any time." "Darling, I can upstage you," retorted Bankhead, "without even being on stage." In the play in which they were acting, one scene called for Bankhead to put down a champagne glass from which she had been drinking and make her exit while the other actress was engaged in a long telephone conversation. At the next performance that evening, Bankhead placed the half-full glass precariously on the edge of the table. The other actress was ignored as the audience, attention riveted on the glass, gasped. Bankhead had placed adhesive tape on the bottom of the glass, the other actress later learned, to ensure the success of her moment of triumph.

Tallulah Bankhead (1903–1968), U.S. actress

John Barrymore, displeased with his performance, was sitting dejectedly in his dressing room after his debut as Hamlet, later to become one of his most famous roles. A gentleman came in, threw himself at Barrymore's feet and kissed his hand, gushing, "O Great One! I enjoyed your performance so much!" Replied Barrymore, "Not half so much as I am enjoying yours."

John Barrymore (1882–1942), U.S. actor

Because children and animals invariably upstage others in a cast, actors are disinclined to perform with them. Sir Noel Coward, the British playwright, once attended a play in which a youthful "prodigy" occupied virtually every scene. "Two things should have been cut," he commented. "The second act and that youngster's throat."

Sir Noel Coward (1899–1973), British playwright and actor

◆ URBAN AREA

Quotations

"A big hard-boiled city with no more personality than a paper cup."

Raymond Chandler (1888–1959), U.S. writer, describing Los Angeles, The Little Sister (1949), ch. 26

"Crowds without company, and dissipation without pleasure."

Edward Gibbon (1737–1794), British historian, describing London, Memoirs (Autobiography) (1796), p. 90

"Washington is a city of Southern efficiency and Northern charm."

John Fitzgerald Kennedy (1917–1963), U.S. president

"City Life. Millions of people being lonesome together."

Henry David Thoreau (1817–1862), U.S. writer, naturalist and poet

"Only a city [San Francisco] as beautiful as this one could survive what you people are doing to it."

Frank Lloyd Wright (1869–1956), U.S. architect

Classical Phrases and Myths

"Divina natura dedit agros, ars humana aedificavit urbes." (DEE-vee-na NAT-ur-a DED-it agROS ars HUM-an-aay-DIF-i-kav-it URB-ays) (Di-

vine nature gave us the country, man's skill built the cities.)

*Marcus Terentius Varro
(116 B.C.-.27 B.C.), Roman writer,
De Re Rustica, bk. III, i, 4*

◆ USE

Jokes, Stories and Anecdotes

"Which is more important to us—the sun or the moon?" asked the teacher. "The moon," answered Bobby. "The moon gives us light at night when we need it, but the sun gives us light only in the daytime when we don't."

Winston Churchill was denounced in the 1930s as impetuous, contentious, unsound, inconsistent and an amusing parliamentary celebrity who was forever out of step. "We just don't know what to make of him," a concerned Tory MP said to Lady Astor, the first woman elected to the House of Commons. Lady Astor asked brightly: "How about a nice rug?"

*Viscountess Nancy Witcher Langhorne
Astor (1879–1964), U.S.-born
British politician*

◆ USELESSNESS

Quotations

"To many people dramatic criticism must seem like an attempt to tattoo soap bubbles."

*John Mason Brown (1900–1969),
U.S. writer*

"A blind man will not thank you for a looking glass."

English proverb c. 1700s

"There's no getting blood out of a turnip."

*Frederick Marryat (1792–1848),
U.S. writer, Japhet in Search of a
Father, ch. 4*

"God in His wisdom made the fly
And then forget to tell us why."

*Ogden Nash (1902–1971), U.S. humorist,
Good Intentions (1942), "The Fly"*

"When You're All Dressed Up and Have No Place To Go." [Title of song (1912).]

*George Whiting (c. 1900s),
U.S. songwriter [adapted by William
Allen White (1868–1944), U.S. writer,
describing the Progressive Party after
Theodore Roosevelt left the presidential
campaign, 1916]*

Jokes, Stories and Anecdotes

The actor Marcello Mastroianni once received a splendid gold watch from film producer Joseph Levine. Although the actor was already wearing a gold wristwatch, which could have created an awkward situation, Mastroianni simply took off his own watch and nonchalantly dropped it into a wastebasket.

*Marcello Mastroianni (1923–   ),
Italian actor*

After President Ford had lost five of the last six primaries in 1975, Ford's campaign manager, Rogers Morton, was asked if he planned any change in strategy. Morton replied, "I'm not going to rearrange the furniture on the deck of the *Titanic*."

*Rogers Morton (1914–1979),
U.S. businessman*

◆ VANITY

Foreign Words and Phrases

amour propre (Fra)
(ah-MOORPROH-pr) vanity, desire for admiration, self-esteem

folie de grandeur (Fra)
(fol-LEE de gran-DUHR) *lit*: folly of grandeur; the (ridiculous) desire to

seem great and surrounding oneself with trappings of power and influence

Quotations

"Lord Birkenhead is very clever but sometimes his brains go to his head."

Margot Asquith, Countess of Oxford and Asquith (1864–1945), British writer and socialite, praising faintly the English lord chancellor F. E. Smith, 1st Earl of Birkenhead

"To say that a man is vain means merely that he is pleased with the effect he produces on other people. A conceited man is satisfied with the effect he produces on himself."

Sir Max Beerbohm (1872–1956), British writer, caricaturist and wit, Quia Imperfectum, And Even Now (1921)

"Egotist, n. A person of low taste, more interested in himself than in me."

Ambrose [Gwinnet] Bierce (1842–c.1914), U.S. writer and poet, Cynic's Word Book (1906)

"H. L. Mencken suffers from the hallucination that he is H. L. Mencken—there is no cure for a disease of that magnitude."

Maxwell Bodenheim (1893–1954), U.S. poet and writer

"We are all worms. But I do believe that I am a glow-worm."

Sir Winston Spencer Churchill (1874–1965), British prime minister and writer

"[My wife is so self-involved that] when we make love, she calls out her own name."

Rodney Dangerfield [Jacob Cohen] (1921–   ), U.S. comedian, Back to School (1986 film)

"We are so vain that we even care for the opinion of those we don't care for."

Marie von Ebner Eschenbach (1830–1916), Austraian writer

"I could readily see in [Ralph Waldo] Emerson . . . a gaping flaw. It was the insinuation that had he lived in those days, when the world was made, he might have offered some valuable suggestions."

Herman Melville (1819–1891), U.S. writer

"The time he can spare from the adornment of his person he devotes to the neglect of his duties."

Samuel Johnson (1709–1784), British man of letters

"Tell me, George, if you had to do it all over, would you fall in love with yourself again?"

Oscar Levant (1906–1972), U.S. pianist and wit, to composer George Gershwin

"Hortense is the only woman I know who pronounces the word 'egg' with three syllables."

Dorothy Parker (1893–1967), U.S. wit and writer, describing her mother-in-law, whom she considered a poseur

"The bigger a man's head, the worse his headache."

Persian proverb

"Self-love seems so often unrequited."

Anthony Powell (1905–   ), British writer, Acceptance World (1955), ch. 1

"He fell in love with himself at first sight and it is a passion to which he has always remained faithful."

Anthony Powell (1905–   ), British writer, Acceptance World (1955), ch. 1

"It is our own vanity that makes the vanity of others intolerable to us."

François, Duc de la Rochefoucauld (1613–1680), French writer, Maxims (1678)

"I fall back, overcome with the glory of myself all rosy red,
And the knowledge that I, a mere cock, caused the sun to rise."

*Edmond Rostand (1868–1918),
French poet and playwright,
Chantecler (1907), Act II, sc. iii*

"When a man is wrapped up in himself he makes a pretty small package."

*John Ruskin (1819–1900),
British writer and social reformer*

"A buzz of recognition . . . heralded the arrival of Sherard Blaw, the dramatist who had discovered himself, and who had given so ungrudgingly of his discovery to the world."

*Saki [Hector Hugh Munro] (1870–1916),
British writer, The Unbearable
Bassington (1912), ch. 13 [a thinly veiled
reference to George Bernard Shaw]*

"I cannot tell you, madam. Heaven has granted me no offspring."

*James Abbott McNeill Whistler (1834–
1903), U.S.-born British artist, answering
whether he thought genius was hereditary*

"Mr. [James] Whistler always spelt art, and I believe still spells it, with a capital 'I.'"

*Oscar [Fingal O'Flahertie Wills] Wilde
(1854–1900), British playwright,
writer and wit*

"You can pick out actors by the glazed look that comes into their eyes when the conversation wanders away from themselves."

*Michael Wilding (1912–1979),
British actor*

"The way Bernard Shaw believes in himself is very refreshing in these atheistic days when so many people believe in no God at all."

*Israel Zangwill (1864–1926),
British writer and playwright*

Classical Phrases and Myths

"Fools take to themselves the respect that is given to their office."

Aesop (c. 600 B.C.), Greek fabulist

According to classical mythology, Narcissus was a beautiful youth who fell in love with his reflection in a pool of water, refused to leave the water's edge and died. He was turned into the flower that bears his name (also called the iris). Thus, one who is exceedingly vain, self-indulgent or self-loving is said to be *narcissistic*.

Jokes, Stories and Anecdotes

When asked why Harold Clurman, an influential theater director in the 1930s, continually studied his face in the mirror, his wife, Stella Adler, quipped, "He's trying to imagine how he's going to look on that horse when he's a statue in Central Park."

Stella Adler (1901–1992), U.S. actress

One of British politician Bejamin Disraeli's admirers, speaking about him to fellow politician John Bright, said: "You ought to give him credit for what he has accomplished, for he is a self-made man." "I know he is," retorted Bright, "and he adores his maker."

*John Bright (1811–1889),
British politician*

Firing Line host William F. Buckley once sent fellow author Norman Mailer a copy of his latest book. Chagrined not to find a personal message from Buckley on the flyleaf, Mailer turned promptly to the index to see if he had been mentioned. Next to Mailer's name in the index was the handwritten greeting "Hi!"

*William F[rank] Buckley (1925–   ),
U.S. editor, writer and speaker*

The famous actor Charles Macklin boasted in 1755 that he could repeat any speech after hearing it only once. Comedy dramatist Samuel Foote, who was present, challenged Macklin to repeat the following: "So she went into the garden to cut a cabbage leaf to make an apple pie, and at the same time a great she-bear, coming up the street, pops its head into the shop. What! No soap? So he died and she very imprudently married the barber. And there were present the picninnies, and the joblillies, and the Garyalies, and the grand panjandrum himself, with the little round button at top. . ." Macklin was unable to live up to his boast but the English language now has the phrase *"the grand panjandrum"* to describe an important, especially a self-important, person.

> *Samuel Foote (1720–1777),*
> *British actor and playwright*

Filling out a market research form, Nubar Gulbenkian, a British heir, came across a section labeled: "Position in life." He wrote: "Enviable."

> *Nubar Gulbenkian (1896–1972),*
> *British businessman*

The Canadian actor Raymond Massey obviously reveled in his tremendous success in his role as Abraham Lincoln. Sneered George S. Kaufman, "He won't be satisfied until he's assassinated."

> *George S[imon] Kaufman (1889–1961),*
> *U.S. writer, playwright and wit*

While walking in a fog, the English professor W.P. Ker and a friend saw a huge figure before them. When they caught up with the figure, it turned out to be Sir Edmund Gosse, an eminent biographer, translator and critic, whose appearance had been magnified by the atmospheric phenomenon called the Brocken specter. "I did not know whether you were the Brocken specter or an Oxford don returning to nature," remarked Ker to Gosse. When they continued on their ways, Ker asked his friend, "Could you notice how pleased Gosse was to be perceived, even in a fog, as an Oxford don?"

> *William Patton Ker (1855–1923),*
> *British scholar*

Theodore Roosevelt was described thus by one of his sons: "Father always had to be the center of attention. When he went to a wedding, he wanted to be the bridegroom; and when he went to a funeral, he wanted to be the corpse."

> *Theodore Roosevelt (1858–1919),*
> *U.S. president*

◆ VARIETY

Jokes, Stories and Anecdotes

The professor of sexual physiology at a medical school was lecturing his class: "And so, anatomically speaking, there are precisely 52 distinct positions possible in the sex act. If we classify these positions—" The knowledgeable girlfriend of one of the students raised her hand and said, "Sir, actually there are 53 distinct positions possible." The professor regarded her with a frown. "Miss, my statement reflects long and serious research in the field by highly respected authorities." "But I, too, speak with knowledge," she persisted. "In fact, from my own experience, I can vouch for the existence of 53." "Well, let's count them," sneered the professor. "First, there is the primary position of woman horizontal-dorsal, man horizontal-ventral—." "My God," cried the woman, "54!"

◆ VICTORY

Foreign Words and Phrases

conquistador (Spa)
(kohn-kees-tah-DOR) *lit:* conqueror;
Spanish conqueror of Mexico and
Peru; one who invades and exploits
on a massive scale

Quotations

"In defeat, unbeatable; in victory,
unbearable."

> Sir Winston Spencer Churchill
> (1874–1965), British prime minister
> and writer, describing the autocratic
> and arrogant Field Marshal
> Bernard Law "Monty" Montgomery

" 'You put so much stock in *winning* wars,' the grubby iniquitous
old man scoffed. 'The real trick lies
in *losing* wars, and in knowing
which wars can be *lost* . . . [N]ow
that we are losing again, everything
has taken a turn for the better, and
we will certainly come out on top
again if we succeed in being defeated.' "

> Joseph Heller (1923–   ),
> U.S. writer, Catch-22 (1961), ch. 23

"After a victory there are no enemies, only men."

> Napoleon I [Napoleon Bonaparte]
> (1769–1821), French general and
> emperor, ordering aid for a fallen Russian
> at the bloody Battle of Borodino (1812)

Classical Phrases and Myths

At Zela in Asia Minor in 47 B.C., Julius Caesar decisively defeated the
king of Pontus, Pharnaces II. His
victory was announced in Rome
with the simple but immortal
words: "Veni, vidi, vici" (WAY-nee,
Wee-dee, Wee-kee) (I came, I saw, I
conquered).

> Gaius Julius Caesar (100 B.C.–44 B.C.),
> Roman general and statesman

The invading Greek forces under
Pyrrhus (PIR-us), king of Epirus in
northwestern Greece, defeated the
Romans at Asculeum in Apulia in
279 B.C. When Pyrrhus was congratulated for his victory by a
Greek, he ruefully thought of all the
men, close aides and supplies he
lost, and sighed, "Another such victory and we are ruined." A *Pyrrhic
victory* is hence a victory at too high
a cost for the victor.

> Pyrrhus (319 B.C.–272 B.C.), Epirian king

Jokes, Stories and Anecdotes

At the Congress of Vienna in 1815,
following total defeat of the French
at the Battle of Waterloo, several
French officers proudly turned their
backs on the Duke of Wellington.
When someone offered the snubbed
victor sympathy, Wellington
bowed and said, "I have seen their
backs before, madam."

> Arthur Wellesley, 1st Duke of Wellington
> (1769–1852), British general
> and prime minister

◆ VIEWPOINT
(MENTAL ATTITUDE)

Foreign Words and Phrases

Gemfit (Ger)
(ge-MEWT) temperament; emotional impact

Weltanschauung (Ger)
(VELT-an-SHAU-ung) worldview,
philosophy of life

Weltgeist (Ger)
(VELT-gyst) prevailing spirit (of the
world, age, times, etc.)

Quotations

"I've made an odd discovery. Every time I talk to a savant I feel quite sure that happiness is no longer a possibility. Yet when I talk with my gardener, I'm convinced of the opposite."

Bertrand Arthur William Russell, 3d Earl (1872–1970), British mathematician and philosopher

"On n'est jamais si heureux ni si malheureux qu'on s'imagine." (One is never so happy or so unhappy as one thinks.)

François, Duc de la Rochefoucauld (1613–1680), French writer, Maximes, (1678), 49

Classical Phrases and Myths

conscia mens recti (Lat)
(KON-ski-amens REK-tee) conscious of being right

Jokes, Stories and Anecdotes

Three people of different occupations looked at the Grand Canyon. The priest said: "What a glory of God!" The geologist said: "What a wonder of science!" The cowboy said: "What an awful place to lose a horse!"

Two men were strolling down the street when the music of a nearby church's chimes danced through the air. One man commented, "Isn't that wonderful music?" "Can't hear you," replied the other. "Aren't those chimes beautiful?" "Whadja say?" "Isn't that lovely music?" "It's no use," said the other man. "Those pesky bells are so noisy I can't hear what you are saying."

◆ VIRTUE

Foreign Words and Phrases

kosher (Yid)
(KOH-shur) legitimate; pious; food ritually prepared in compliance with Jewish dietary laws

Quotations

"I'm as pure as the driven slush."

Tallulah Bankhead (1903–1968), U.S. actress

"I am willing to admit that I may not always be right, but I am never wrong."

Samuel Goldwyn [Samuel Goldfish] (1882–1974), Russian-born U.S. film producer, declining to change his mind about a particular script

"I prefer an accommodating vice to an obstinate virtue."

Molière [Jean Baptiste Poquelin] (1622–1673), French playwright, Amphitryon (1666), Act I, sc. iv

"Be virtuous: not too much; just what's correct.
Excess in anything is a defect."

Jacques Monvel (1745–1812), French actor and playwright

"Our virtues are most frequently only vices in disguise."

François, Duc de La Rochefoucauld (1613–1680), French writer, Maximes (1678), 179

"An Englishman thinks he is moral when he is only uncomfortable."

George Bernard Shaw (1856–1950), Irish playwright, Man and Superman (1903), Act III

"Always do right. This will gratify some people and astonish the rest."

Mark Twain [Samuel Langhorne Clemens] (1835–1910), U.S. humorist, writer and speaker, speech to the Young People's Society, Greenpoint Presbyterian Church, Brooklyn, February 16, 1901

"Few men have virtue to withstand the highest bidder."

> George Washington (1732–1799),
> U.S. general and president

Classical Phrases and Myths

bona fide (Lat)
(BON-ah FI-day) *lit:* good faith; genuine, correct, legitimate

"Video meliora, proboque; Deteriora sequor." (I see and approve better things, but follow worse.)

> Ovid [Publius Ovidius Naso]
> (43 B.C.–c. A.D. 18), Roman poet,
> Metamorphoses, VII, 20

The Feast of the Bona Dea were religious rites in ancient Rome to which only women were admitted. In 61 B.C. Julius Caesar's second wife, Pompeia, was accused of having commited adultery with the notorious profligate Publius Clodius, who had attended the feast in female dress. Caesar divorced Pompeia. Later, there was an inquiry into the desecration. Caesar declined to testify against Pompeia, so the court asked him why he had divorced her. He responded, *"Caesar's wife must be above suspicion."*

> Gaius Julius Caesar (100 B.C.–44 B.C.),
> Roman general and statesman

Jokes, Stories and Anecdotes

J. Edgar Hoover, longtime head of the FBI, was characterized by Washington insiders as "that Virgin Mary in pants" for so blatantly cultivating an image of pious rectitude, although the historical record indicates he was often corrupt.

> J[ohn] Edgar Hoover (1895–1972),
> U.S. statesman

◆ VULGARITY

Foreign Words and Phrases

mauvais gôut (Fra)
(MO-vay goo) bad taste

Kulturschande (Ger)
(KUL-toor-SHAN-duh) insult to good taste; crime against civilization

dégôut (Fra)
(day-GOO) distaste, disgust

Quotations

"His manners are 99 in a 100 singularly repulsive."

> Samuel Taylor Coleridge (1772–1834),
> British poet and writer

"That fellow would vulgarize the day of judgment."

> Douglas William Jerrold (1803–1857),
> British playwright and humorist, Wit and
> Opinions of Douglas Jerrold (1859)

"It's worse than wicked, my dear, it's vulgar."

> Punch Alamanac (1876)

"Vulgarity is simply the conduct of other people."

> Oscar [Fingal O'Flahertie Wills] Wilde
> (1854–1900), British playwright,
> writer and wit

◆ WAKEFULNESS

Quotations

"Without a wink of sleep."

> Miguel de Cervantes (1547–1616),
> Spanish writer, Don Quixote de la
> Mancha, Part I (1605), bk. II, ch. 4

"It was such a lovely day I thought it was a pity to get up."

> W[illiam] Somerset Maugham
> (1874–1965), British writer and
> playwright, Our Betters (1923), Act III

Jokes, Stories and Anecdotes

The Duke of Wellington once arranged for an appointment with young British statesman Palmerston at 7:30 A.M. When someone disclosed skepticism that Palmerston, who kept late hours, could keep the appointment, the unfazed Palmerston replied, "Of course I shall. It's perfectly easy—I shall keep it the last thing before I go to bed."

Henry John Temple, 3d Viscount Palmerston (1784–1865), British prime minister

◆ WAR

Foreign Words and Phrases

guerre à l'outrance (Fra)
(gerr ah LOO-trans) *lit:* war to excess; war to the bitter end; *colloq:* fight to the finish

guerrilla (Spa)
(geh-REE-lyah) *lit:* small war; unconventional warfare

Quotations

"The Falklands thing was a fight between two bald men over a comb."

Jorge Luis Borges (1899–1986), Argentine writer and poet, discussing the 1982 Falklands War

"*Der Krieg ist nichts anderes als die Fortsetzung der Politik mit anderen Mitteln.*" (War is nothing more than the continuation of politics by other means.)

Karl von Clausewitz (1780–1831), Prussian soldier and writer, Vom Kriege (On War) (1833)

"There was never a good war or a bad peace."

Benjamin Franklin (1706–1790), U.S. statesman and scientist, paraphrasing Cicero and Samuel Butler, letter to Josiah Quincy, September 11, 1773 [cf. "I cease

not to advocate peace; although unjust it is better than the most just war."

Cicero, Epistolae ad Atticum, bk. VII, epistle 14]

"Either war is obsolete or men are."

[Richard] Buckminster Fuller (1895–1983), U.S. writer, architect and engineer

"Little girl.... Sometime they'll give a war and nobody will come."

Carl Sandburg (1878–1967), U.S. poet and writer, The People, Yes (1936) [cf., Suppose They Gave a War and Nobody Came? (1970 film).]

"As long as war is regarded as wicked, it will always have its fascination. When it is looked upon as vulgar, it will cease to be popular."

Oscar [Fingal O'Flahertie Wills] Wilde (1854–1900), British playwright, writer and wit, The Critic as Artist (1891)

"*La guerre, c'est une chose trop grave pour la confier à des militaires.*" (War is something too serious to entrust to military men.)

Charles Maurice de Talleyrand-Périgord (1754–1838), French diplomat [attributed also to Georges Clemenceau]

Classical Phrases and Myths

jus contra bellum (Lat)
(yus KON-tra BEL-lum) *lit:* law against war; the "moral" law makes all warmongering unjust

jus in bello (Lat)
(yus in BEL-loh) *lit:* law in war; even in war moral constraints and conventions must be obeyed

"*Silent enim leges inter arma.*" (SILent EN-im LEG-es IN-ter AR-ma) (Laws stand silent in war.)

Marcus Tullius Cicero (106 B.C.–43 B.C.), Roman statesman and man of letters, Pro Milone, IV, xi

"In peace the sons bury their fathers, but in war the fathers bury their sons."

Croesus (c. 550 B.C.), Lydian king

Jokes, Stories and Anecdotes

During the Civil War the conspicuous gallantry of a Union cavalry officer rallying his troops on the field of battle so impressed Confederate General Richard S. Ewell that he ordered his soldiers not to shoot at the man. Stonewall Jackson later reprimanded Ewell, shrewdly noting, "Shoot the brave officers and the cowards will flee, taking their men with them."

Thomas Jonathan ["Stonewall"] Jackson (1824–1863), U.S. general

---

◆ WARNING

Quotations

"Fasten your seat belts, it's going to be a bumpy night."

Joseph L. Mankiewicz (1909–   ), U.S. writer, All About Eve (1950 film)

"There was so much handwriting on the wall that even the wall fell down."

Christopher Morley (1890–1957), U.S. writer

Classical Phrases and Myths

According to Greek legend, Cassandra was one of the 12 daughters of Priam, king of Troy. Her name has become synonymous with those prophets of doom whose warnings go unheeded until it is too late. She correctly predicted many events leading up to the fall of Troy to the Greeks in the Trojan War, the murder of Agamemnon by his wife Clytemnestra and the coming of Orestes to avenge him. Thus, *Cassandra warnings* indicate impotent wisdom.

Jokes, Stories and Anecdotes

The cop was writing out a speeding violation for the motorist when he happened to notice that the backseat of the man's car was packed with penguins. "If you don't want another ticket for operating an unsafe vehicle," instructed the policeman, "you'd better take them to the zoo." The next day the cop flagged down the same man speeding past—only this time he had the top down and the penguins were wearing sunglasses. "Didn't I tell you to take these penguins to the zoo?" demanded the policeman. "Oh, I did," replied the driver. "Today I'm taking them to the beach."

◆ WATER

Quotations

An American had spoken disparagingly of the Thames. "What have you in the Mississippi?" asked John Burns. Replied the American, "Water—miles and miles of it." "Ah, but you see," said Burns, "the Thames is liquid history."

John Burns (1858–1943), British writer

"Water, water, every where,
And all the boards did shrink.
Water, water, every where,
And not a drop to drink."

Samuel Taylor Coleridge (1772–1834), British poet and writer, The Ancient Mariner (1798)

◆ WEAKNESS (FRAGILITY)

Foreign Words and Phrases

pianissimo (Ita)
(pee-ahn-ISS-ee-moh) in music, very softly

morbidezza (Ita)
(mor-bee-day-tsah) *lit:* tenderness; extreme delicacy in painting style (generally used pejoratively)

Quotations

"The spirit indeed is willing, but the flesh is weak."

Matthew 26:41

"It's going to be fun to watch and see how long the meek can keep the earth after they inherit it."

Frank McKinney ["Kin"] Hubbard (1868–1930), U.S. humorist and writer

◆ WEALTH

Foreign Words and Phrases

rentier (Fra)
(RON-tee-eh) one living off rents and investments (usually used pejoratively)

nouveau riche (Fra)
(NOO-voh reesh) person of newly acquired wealth and status (usually pejorative)

Quotations

"All heiresses are beautiful."

John Dryden (1631–1700), British poet, playwright and writer, King Arthur (1691), Act I, sc. i

"I am rich beyond the dreams of avarice."

Edward Moore (1712–1757), British playwright, The Gamester (1753), Act II, sc. ii

"I am a Millionaire. That is my religion."

George Bernard Shaw (1856–1950), Irish playwright, Major Barbara (1907), Act II

"The wretchedness of being rich is that you live with rich people."

Logan Pearsal Smith (1865–1946), U.S. writer, After-Thoughts (1931), "In the World"

"Just what God would have done if he had the money."

Alexander Woollcott (1887–1943), U.S. writer, broadcaster and wit, viewing playwright Moss Hart's opulent country estate [attributed also to Wolcott Gibbs]

Classical Phrases and Myths

"He has not acquired a fortune; the fortune has acquired him."

Bion (c. 325 B.C.–c. 255 B.C.), Greek philosopher

According to Greek mythology, Midas (MIE-das) was a Phrygian king who, for taking care of Dionysus's friend, was granted any wish by the god. Midas wished that anything he touched would turn to gold. He was very happy but then realized that he could not eat or drink, so he was able to get Dionysus to retract the cursed wish of greed. Hence, to have the *Midas touch* is to have the ability to turn any activity into a financial success. But Midas fell victim to another mistake—he maintained that Pan the satyr, not the god of music, Apollo, had won a musical contest. For having ears unfit to judge a god's music, Apollo caused Midas to grow long ass-ears. Humiliated, Midas wore a cap, but could not conceal his deformity from his barber; the barber, who was tormented with his secret, whispered the secret into a hole by the river from which sprung reeds to reveal the disgrace.

Jokes, Stories and Anecdotes

Financier J. P. Morgan once announced in a burst of patriotism, "America is good enough for me!" Growled politician William Jennings Bryan, "Whenever he doesn't like it, he can give it back to us."

William Jennings Bryan (1860–1925),
U.S. politician

In "Rich Boy," part of his 1926 collection of stories *All the Sad Young Men* (1926), F. Scott Fitzgerald wrote "Let me tell you about the very rich. They are different from you and me." In 1936, Ernest Hemingway's *Snows of Kilimanjaro* contained the rejoinder, "Yes, they have more money."

F[rancis] Scott [Key] Fitzgerald
(1896–1940), U.S. writer

Oil executive J. Paul Getty was once asked by a journalist whether it was true that the value of his holdings then amounted to a billion dollars. After a pause, Getty answered, "I suppose so. But remember a billion dollars doesn't go as far as it used to."

J[ean] Paul Getty (1892–1976),
U.S. industrialist

Following a tour of the magnificent 39-room mansion of publicist and art-and-celebrity collector Benjamin Sonnenberg, the dramatist Tennessee Williams briefly excused himself to go the bathroom. Later, according

to Ben Sonnenberg, Jr., Williams said, "It looked so shabby when I took it out, I couldn't go."

Tennessee [Thomas Lanier] Williams
(1911–1983), U.S. playwright

◆ WEATHER

Foreign Words and Phrases

naya gryazi (Rus)
(NUH-yuh GREE-ahz-hee) black mud melted from snow, in which Nazis and Napoleon became stuck

mistral (Fra)
(mees-TRAHL) northwest wind

Quotations

"On a fine day the climate of England is like looking up a chimney; on a foul day, like looking down one."

Anonymous

"Some are weather-wise, some are otherwise."

Benjamin Franklin (1706–1790),
U.S. statesman and scientist,
Poor Richard's Almanac (1732–1757)

"There is really no such thing as bad weather, only different kinds of good weather."

John Ruskin (1819–1900),
British writer and social reformer

"Heat, madam! It was so dreadful that I found there was nothing for it but to take off my flesh and sit in my bones."

Sydney Smith (1771–1845),
British clergyman and writer, commenting
about the oppressive hot weather

"I did not attend his funeral; but I wrote a nice letter saying I approved of it."

Mark Twain [Samuel Langhorne Clemens] (1835–1910), U.S. humorist, writer and speaker

Classical Phrases and Myths

In Greek mythology, Typhon (TIE-fon), or Typhoeus, was a tremendous monster whose body consisted of serpents from the waist down and who had snake heads in lieu of hands. He fathered many other monsters: Cerebrus, the Hydra, the Chimaera, the Sphinx of Thebes, the dragon guarding the Golden Fleece and, according to some accounts, the eagle that gnawed at Prometheus's liver. Killed by a thunderbolt hurled by Zeus, Typhon was the personification of fierce windstorms. Thus, a *typhoon* is a wind of hurricane force.

In Greek mythology, Zephrus (ZEF-i-rus) was the personification of the gentle west wind. Hence, a *zephyr* is a gentle breeze.

Jokes, Stories and Anecdotes

The wife of the English viceroy in Ireland, Lady Carteret, once commented to clergyman and satirist Jonathan Swift how good the air was in Ireland. "For God's sake, madam," implored Swift, falling to his knees, "do not say that in England, for if you shall, they will surely tax it."

Jonathan Swift (1667–1745), Anglo-Irish clergyman and writer

One Sunday when Mark Twain and the writer William Dean Howells were leaving church, it began to rain heavily. Looking up at the clouds, Howells asked, "Do you think it will stop?" Replied Twain, "It always has."

Mark Twain [Samuel Langhorne Clemens] (1835–1910), U.S. humorist, writer and speaker

◆ WHOLE (COMPLETENESS)

Classical Phrases and Myths

corpus (Lat)
(KOR-pus) body, collection (of law, written works, etc.)

in extenso (Lat)
(in ex-TEN-soh) in its entirety, completely

ne plus ultra (Lat)
(nay ploos UL-tra) *lit:* nothing more beyond; no further beyond, furthest point attainable

in toto (Lat)
(in TOH-toh) as a whole, in its entirety, completely

◆ WILL

Foreign Words and Phrases

celui qui veut, peut (Fra)
(se-LWEE kee vuhr puhr) he who will, can; *colloq:* where there's a will, there's a way

Quotations

"If a man can't forge his own will, whose will can he forge?"

Sir W[illiam] S[chwenck] Gilbert (1836–1911), British writer, Ruddigore (1887), Act II

"I've conquered my goddam will-power."

Don[ald Robert Perry] Marquis (1878–1937), U.S. writer and poet, ordering a double martini after a month on the wagon

Classical Phrases and Myths

sponte sua (Lat)
(SPON-tay SU-ah) of one's own free will

"Hoc volo, sic iubeo, sit pro ratione voluntas." (I wish it, I insist on it! Let my will stand instead of reason.)

> *Juvenal [Decimus Junius Juvenalis]*
> *(c. 50–c. 130), Roman writer,*
> *Satires III, l. 223*

◆ WONDER

Foreign Words and Phrases

yugen (Jap)
(YOO-gehn) awareness of the universe's profundity that triggers wondrous feelings

Schauspiel (Ger)
(SHOW-speel) spectacle

Quotations

Bored Los Angeles housewife (Barbara Stanwyck): "I wonder what you mean." Insurance salesman (Fred McMurray): "I wonder if you wonder."

> *Billy [Samuel] Wilder (1906–1993),*
> *U.S. film director and writer,*
> *Double Indemnity (1944 film)*

Classical Phrases and Myths

mirabile dictu (Lat)
(mee-RAH-bee-lay DIK-tu) *lit:* marvelous to say; wonderful to relate (cf. horrible dictu)

stupor mundi (Lat)
(STU-por MUND-ee) wonder of the world

Jokes, Stories and Anecdotes

Fred watched in amazement as the man sitting next to him at the bar ordered a martini, poured out its contents, then nibbled away at the bowl of the glass until only the stem was left. He placed it in his shirt pocket and ordered another martini. This continued until he had six stems, and then left. The bartender, noting Fred's astonishment, remarked, "You look surprised." "I'll say," said Fred. "The idiot left the best part."

◆ WORDS & LETTERS

Quotations

"I'm not very good at it myself, but the first rule about spelling is that there is only one 'z' in 'is.'"

> *George S[imon] Kaufman (1889–1961),*
> *U.S. playwright, writer and wit, to a*
> *writer after reading a manuscript loaded*
> *with spelling errors*

"That woman speaks 18 languages, and she can't say 'no' in any of them."

> *Dorothy Parker (1893–1967), U.S. wit*
> *and writer, praising faintly*
> *a promiscuous acquaintance*

"Certain phrases stick in the throat, even if they offer nothing that is analytically improbable. 'A dashing Swiss officer' is one such. Another is 'the beautiful Law Courts.'"

> *John Russell (1919–   ),*
> *British writer, Paris (1960), ch. 11*

Jokes, Stories and Anecdotes

When a gang member's baby says "Mother!" he's learned his first half-word.

Q:"What do dyslexic theologians argue about?" A: "The existence of dog."

Reverend Henry Ward Beecher once received an insulting letter in the mail containing just one word: "Fool." During his next service, he exhibited the letter to his congregation, remarking: "I have known many an instance of a man writing a letter and forgetting to sign his name, but this is the only instance I have known of a man signing his name and forgetting to write the letter."

Henry Ward Beecher (1813–1887),
U.S. clergyman and writer

Film producer Samuel Goldwyn handed humorist James Thurber the completed screenplay "The Secret Life of Walter Witty" (Goldwyn's malapropism), warning him not to read the last 100 pages because they were too "bloody and thirsty." Thurber disobeyed the instruction, noting that he was "horror and struck."

James Thurber (1894–1961),
U.S. cartoonist and humorist

"What seven-letter word has three *u*'s in it?" humorist, short-story writer and cartoonist James Thurber once asked a nurse in a hospital in which he was staying. The nurse thoughtfully replied, "I don't know, but it must be unusual."

James Thurber (1894–1961),
U.S. cartoonist and humorist

"You don't suppose I've lost my incapacity for work, do you?"

Aristide Briand (1862–1932),
French prime minister, complaining about
a stack of documents to study

"Work expands so as to fill the time available for its completion."

C. Northcote Parkinson (1909–   ),
British writer, Parkinson's Law
(1958), p. 4

Classical Phrases and Myths

factotum (Lat)
(fak-TOH-tum) one who does everything; general manager

Jokes, Stories and Anecdotes

"He's the worst kind of worker—the shy, retiring type. His ledgers are a few million dollars shy, which is why he's retiring."

"Son, you're incredible," said the office manager to the new employee. "You've been here a month, and you're already two months behind!"

◆ WORKER

Foreign Words and Phrases

gajes (Spa)
(GAH-hays) perquisites and obligations of a job (outside job description)

Gastarbeiter (Ger)
(GAST-ahr-BYE-ter)   lit: guest worker; foreigner working (in Germany)

Quotations

"Often Daddy sat up very late working on a case of Scotch."

Robert Charles Benchley (1889–1945),
U.S. humorist, Pluck and Luck *(1925)*

◆ WORKPLACE

Quotations

"I go to them to save time. I've found that I can leave the other fellow's office a lot quicker than I can get him to leave mine."

Henry Ford (1863–1947),
U.S. industrialist, explaining why he
visited subordinates in their offices
rather than summoning them to his

"Yes, but keep the copies."

Samuel Goldwyn [Samuel Goldfish]
(1882–1974), Russian-born U.S. film
producer, granting his secretary's request
to destroy files that were more than ten
years old

Jokes, Stories and Anecdotes

Following his appointment as home secretary, Georges Clemenceau, later French prime minister, arrived punctually to inspect his new offices and staff. But when he toured the department with his aide, flinging open door after door, they found every office empty. They finally entered a room only to discover the lone staff member fast asleep, slumped on his desk. When the aide moved to awaken him, Clemenceau said, "Don't awaken him. He might leave."

Georges Clemenceau (1841–1929),
French prime minister

The writer and wit Dorothy Parker became lonely and depressed when she occupied a tiny office in New York's Metropolitan Opera House, so she had the signwriter who came to letter her name on the office door instead paint "Gentlemen."

Dorothy Parker (1893–1967),
U.S. wit and writer

◆ WORSHIP

Quotations

"He didn't actually accuse God of inefficiency, but when he prayed his tone was loud and angry, like that of a dissatisfied guest in a carelessly managed hotel."

Clarence [Shepard] Day, Jr. (1874–1935),
U.S. writer

"America has become so tense and nervous it has been years since I've seen anyone asleep in church—and that is a sad situation."

Norman Vincent Peale (1898–1994),
U.S. theologian

"Why is it when we talk to God, we're said to be praying—but when God talks to us, we're schizophrenic?"

Lily Tomlin (1939–   ),
U.S. comedian and actress

Jokes, Stories and Anecdotes

Benjamin Franklin as a youngster found the long graces his father said before and after meals extremely tedious. "I think, Father," said young Franklin, while helping his father salt down the winter's provisions one day, "if you say grace over the whole cask once for all, it would be a vast saving of time."

Benjamin Franklin (1706–1790),
U.S. statesman and scientist

When Edward Everett Hale, whose great-uncle was Nathan Hale, was chaplain of the U.S. Senate, he was asked, "Dr. Hale, do you pray for the Senate?" "No," he replied. "I look at the Senators and pray for the people."

Edward Everett Hale (1822–1909),
U.S. clergyman and writer

William Lawrence, the Episcopal bishop of Massachusetts, was out driving when he came upon another driver angrily swearing while he struggled to pry a flat tire from the rim. The bishop suggested, "Have you tried prayer, my good man?" The exasperated driver sank to his knees with his hands clasped and his eyes lifted heavenward. Again he inserted the tire iron, but this time the tire popped off.

Lawrence exclaimed, "Well, I'll be goddamned!"

William Lawrence (1850–1941), U.S. bishop [authenticity unverified]

◆ WRETCH

Foreign Words and Phrases

momser (Yid)
(MOHM-zer) evil bastard

(el) diablo (Spa)
(el DYAH-bloh) (the) devil, fiend

dybbuk (Heb)
(DIB-book) evil spirit; soul of a dead person which enters a living body

me de boue (Fra)
(AHM de BOO) *lit:* soul of mud; base soul, ungenerous spirit

il a les défauts de ses qualites (Fra)
(eel ah lay day-FOH de say KAL-ee-TAY) his faults spring from his very qualities

roué (Fra)
(ROO-eh) rake, profligate, cunning

Schweinhund (Ger)
(SCHWINE-hoont) *lit:* pig dog; villain, henchman

Quotations

"He was the mildest manner'd man That ever scuttled ship or cut a throat."

Lord Byron [George Gordon] (1788–1824), British poet, Don Juan Canto III (1816), l. xli

"I begin to smell a rat."

Miguel de Cervantes (1547–1616), Spanish writer, Don Quixote de la Mancha, Part I (1605), bk. IV, ch. 10

"As there is a use in medicine for poison so the world cannot move without rogues."

Ralph Waldo Emerson (1803–1882), U.S. writer, poet and philosopher, Essays: First Series (1841), "Compensation"

"Mad, bad, and dangerous to know."

Lady Caroline Lamb (1785–1828), British aristocrat, describing Lord Byron, Journal (March 1812)

"It is a sin to believe evil of others, but it is seldom a mistake."

H[enry] L[ouis] Mencken (1880–1956), U.S. critic and writer

"Better to reign in hell, than serve in heav'n."

John Milton (1608–1674), British poet and writer, Paradise Lost (1667), bk. I, l. 261

"He's the only man I know who has rubber pockets so he can steal soup."

Wilson Mizner (1876–1933), U.S. wit and writer, commenting on an unethical colleague [authenticity unverified]

"You're a mouse studying to be a rat."

Wilson Mizner (1876–1933), U.S. wit and writer

"He is a man of splendid abilities, but utterly corrupt. He shines and stinks like a rotten mackerel by moonlight."

John Randolph (1773–1833), U.S. politician, describing Edward Livingston

"Some wicked people would be less dangerous had they no redeeming qualities."

François, Duc de La Rochefoucauld (1613–1680), French writer, Maximes (1678)

"He has spent all his life in letting down empty buckets into empty wells; and he is frittering away his age in trying to draw them up again."

Sydney Smith (1771–1845),
British clergyman and writer

Classical Phrases and Myths

"Hic niger est, hunc tu, Romane, caveto." (That man is black at heart: mark and avoid him, if you are a Roman indeed.)

Horace (65 B.C.–8 B.C.), Roman poet,
Satires, I. iii, l. 85

Treachery and debauchery reached a feverish pitch preceding and during the reign of Nero (NEE-roh). Agrippina, his widowed mother, married her uncle Claudius, emperor of Rome, who had recently slain his first wife for her infidelities. Agrippina was not going to allow his design to have his son Britannicus named his successor to interfere with her determination to have her son Nero instead made emperor. So she encouraged Nero to marry his adoptive sister, who was Claudius's daughter. Then, before Claudius was able to clarify his plans for succession, the aged emperor died an agonizing death overnight, having been fed poisonous mushrooms in a stew by Agrippina, using a poison from Locusta. Nero became emperor, and gave Claudius a magnificent funeral. Nero later deified Claudius, wryly commenting that mushrooms were indeed the food of the gods, because by eating them, Claudius had become divine. Next, Nero had to eliminate Britannicus, who, of course, suspected foul play and had been cheated out of the throne. Locusta, knowing that Britannicus used a taster, first had Britannicus served an untainted drink which, he complained, was too hot. Cold water was quickly brought to him

and he unknowingly gulped down the poison. Nero watched, calmly amused, as Britannicus fell back and choked to death. Nero took his own mother as his mistress but, plagued with guilt, he had her put to death. He also falsely accused his wife Octavia of infidelity and—surprise!—had her poisoned so he could marry a wealthy patrician, Poppaea Sabina. Although Nero did not fiddle while Rome burned (the instrument had not been invented, and he was at his villa in Antium), his depravity had nonetheless eroded all popular support. He stabbed himself in the throat with the assistance of his scribe Epaphroditus in A.D. 68 on the anniversary of Octavia's murder.

Nero [Lucius Domitius Ahenobarbus]
(37–68), Roman emperor

Jokes, Stories and Anecdotes

The pope and an attorney arrived simultaneously at the Pearly Gates, and St. Peter showed them to their quarters. The pope was led to a small, spartan cubicle furnished with a cot, chair and Bible. The lawyer was shown to a huge chamber of marble with views and deluxe furnishings. "This is a mistake," the lawyer said to St. Peter. "Shouldn't the pope have this room?" St. Peter shook his head. "No. We've had many popes in heaven, but you're the first attorney."

At the 1913 premiere of Stravinsky's ballet score for *Le Sacre du printemps*, commissioned by Sergei Diaghilev, the audience in Paris nearly rioted. When the piece was next performed in Paris in 1952, it received enthusiastic applause. "There was just as much noise the last time," remarked Pierre Monteux, who conducted on both occasions, "but the tonality was different."

Igor Feodorovitch Stravinsky (1882–1971), Russian-born composer

◆ WRITING

Foreign Words and Phrases

homme de lettres (Fra)
(OM de LET-ruh) man of letters, writer, literary man

Kunstlerroman (Ger)
(KOON-stler-ro-MAN) *lit:* artist novel; novel about development of an artist's sensibility

Bildungsroman (Ger)
(BILL-doohngs-ro-MAN) *lit:* formation novel; novel tracing life and development of one character (e.g. *Madame Bovary*)

belles lettres (Fra)
(bell LET-re) serious literature

literati (Ita)
(lee-teh-RAH-tee) educated and well-read (people)

novela picaresca (Spa)
(noh-VEH-lahpee-kah-RES-kah) picaresque novel, adventure story about a single roguish hero

geflugelteWorte (Ger)
(ge-FLEW-gel-tuh VOR-tuh) *lit:* winged words; writings supporting differing sides of an issue

Festschrift (Ger)
(FEST-shrift) *lit:* festival writing; essays written to commemorate a distinguished scholar

Quotations

"The only people who like to write terribly are those that do."

Franklin Pierce Adams (1881–1960), U.S. writer

"After being Turned Down by numerous Publishers, he had decided to write for posterity."

George Ade (1866–1944), U.S. humorist and playwright, Fables in Slang (1900), p. 158

"A footnote is like running downstairs during the first night of marriage."

John Barrymore (1882–1942), U.S. actor [attributed also to Noel Coward]

"None of these people have anything interesting to say, and none of them can write . . . [What they do] isn't writing at all—it's typing."

Truman Capote (1924–1984), U.S. writer, appraising "Beat" novelists, televised interview, 1959

"Literature is the art of writing something that will be read twice; journalism what will be read once."

Cyril Connolly (1903–1974), British writer, Enemies of Promise (1938), ch. 3

"When I want to read a novel, I write one."

Benjamin Disraeli, 1st Earl of Beaconsfield (1804–1881), British prime minister

"The art of reading is to skip judiciously."

Philip Gilbert Hamerton (1834–1894), British writer, Intellectual Life, pt. iv, letter iv

"Gentlemen, you do me too much honor, but I have four reasons for not writing: I am too old, too lazy, too fat and too rich."

David Hume (1711–1776), British philosopher and historian, declining to update his best-selling History of Great Britain

"It takes a great deal of history to produce a little literature."

Henry James (1843–1916), U.S. writer,
Life of Nathaniel Hawthorne
(1879), ch. I

"To read between the lines was easier than to follow the text."

Henry James (1843–1916), U.S. writer

"A votary of the desk—a notched and cropt scrivener—one that sucks his substance, as certain sick people are said to do, through a quill."

Charles Lamb (1775–1834), British writer,
Essays of Elia (1823), "Oxford
in the Vacation"

"The art of newspaper paragraphing is to stroke a platitude until it purrs like an epigram."

Don[ald Robert Perry] Marquis
(1878–1937), U.S. writer and poet

"If you want to get rich from writing, write the sort of thing that's read by persons who move their lips when they're reading to themselves."

Don[ald Robert Perry] Marquis
(1878–1937), U.S. writer and poet

"A person who publishes a book willfully appears before the public with his pants down."

Edna St. Vincent Millay (1892–1950),
U.S. poet

"Henry James writes fiction as if it were a painful duty."

Oscar [Fingal O'Flahertie Wills] Wilde
(1854–1900), British playwright, writer
and wit, The Critic as Artist (1891)

"Literature is the orchestration of platitudes."

Thornton [Niven] Wilder (1897–1975),
U.S. writer and playwright

Jokes, Stories and Anecdotes

The poet T. S. Eliot was once asked by publisher Robert Giroux whether he agreed with the widely held belief that most editors are failed writers. "Perhaps," answered Eliot after some reflection, "but so are most writers."

T[homas] S[tearns] Eliot (1888–1965),
U.S. poet

Informed that writer Nancy Mitford was staying at a friend's villa to finish a book, Shakespearean actress Dame Edith Evans commented, "Oh, really? What exactly is she reading?"

Dame Edith Evans (1888–1976),
British actress

Thomas Jefferson was somewhat discomfited by the editorial revisions made by a committee reviewing his draft of the Declaration of Independence, so Ben Franklin told him a story: As a young man Franklin had had a friend who, having completed his apprenticeship as a hatter, was going to open his business with a signboard inscribed "John Thompson, hatter, makes and sells hats for ready money" over the depiction of a hat. When he asked for his friends' opinions, the first noted that "hatter" could be left off the sign, as "makes and sells hats" showed the nature of the business; the second remarked that "makes" was superfluous, as customers would be unconcerned with who had made the hats; the third pointed out that "for ready money" was unneeded because it was not local custom to sell on credit; the fourth, commenting on the remaining verbiage "John Thompson sells hats," suggesting deleting "sells" as no one would expect the hatter to give them away; and someone pointed out that "hats" was superfluous since there was the painted picture of a hat on the signboard. The board was hung reading "John Thompson" with a picture of a hat underneath the name. The story mollified Jefferson, and it was generally agreed that the committee's editorial work had improved the wording of the Declaration of Independence.

Benjamin Franklin (1706–1790),
U.S. statesman and scientist

Samuel Goldwyn hired a ghostwriter to write a series of articles to be published with Goldwyn's byline, but the writer had to be replaced when he became ill during the assignment. Goldwyn read the writing of the substitute and remarked with dismay, "It's not up to my usual standard."

Samuel Goldwyn [Samuel Goldfish]
(1882–1974), Russian-born
U.S. film producer

Aware that Ernest Hemingway's contract with Scribners barred the publisher from changing anything in his manuscripts, Maxwell Perkins, then an editor at Charles Scribner and Sons, thought that he ought to consult the patrician Charles Scribner on whether to delete the word "fuck" from Hemingway's manuscript for *Death in the Afternoon*. Then leaving the office to go to lunch, the elderly Scribner suggested discussing the issue upon his return, and so he jotted the single word "Fuck" on his notepad headed "What To Do Today."

Ernest [Miller] Hemingway (1899–1961),
U.S. writer

Nobel laureate Ernest Hemingway was asked by his young son Patrick to edit a story he had written. Hemingway reviewed the piece and then handed it back to the boy. "Papa," Patrick said, disappointed, "but you changed one word only."

"If it's the right word," replied his father, "that's a lot."

Ernest [Miller] Hemingway (1899–1961),
U.S. writer

The prolific Belgian novelist Georges Simenon, author of the *Inspector Maigret* series, was working on his 158th novel when film director Alfred Hitchcock called from America. "I'm sorry," answered Madame Simenon for the fast-writing author. "Georges is writing and I cannot disturb him." "Let him finish his book," Hitchcock said. "I'll hang on."

Sir Alfred Hitchcock (1889–1990),
British film director

After the publication of *Uncle Tom's Cabin*, a woman asked novelist Harriet Beecher Stowe if she could clasp the hand of the woman who had written the great antislavery novel. "I did not write it," Stowe modestly replied, "God wrote it. I merely did his dictation." Novelist and critic William D. Howells, however, noted that the text had to be largely rewritten in the margins of her proofs because God's diction, grammar and phrasing were so poor. Also, the book's practical inspiration was a pamphlet written by Josiah Henson, a runaway Maryland slave.

Harriet Beecher Stowe (1811–1896),
U.S. writer

The publisher of writer and transcendentalist philosopher Henry David Thoreau's *A Week on the Concord and Merrimack Rivers* wrote to Thoreau inquiring how he wished to dispose of 706 unsold copies of the 1,000-book edition. Thoreau asked to have them sent to him and, once stored, Thoreau noted in his journal, "I now have a library of nearly 900 volumes, over 700 of which I wrote myself."

Henry David Thoreau (1817–1862),
U.S. writer, naturalist and poet

◆ YOUNGSTER

Foreign Words and Phrases

bambino (Ita)
(bam-BEE-noh) baby, child

Quotations

"What music is more enchanting than the voices of young people, when you can't hear what they say?"

Logan Pearsal Smith (1865–1946),
U.S. writer, After-Thoughts (1931),
"Age and Death"

"What is childhood but a series of happy delusions."

Sydney Smith (1771–1845),
British clergyman and writer

"The child is the father of the man."

William Wordsworth (1770–1850),
British poet, My Heart Leaps Up (1807)

Jokes, Stories and Anecdotes

Concerned that six-year-old Becky still hadn't uttered one word, Mrs. Jones made an appointment with the pediatrician. Before leaving, she had Becky brush with adult toothpaste, since Becky had used up the children's brand. "Phew! This is awful!" snarled the little girl, spitting out the toothpaste. "You can talk!" exclaimed the joyful parent, tears running down her cheeks. "Why haven't you talked before?" "Everything's been fine until now."

The novelist and playwright Somerset Maugham, a homosexual, was convinced that retiring early at night would keep him young. Annoyed by this habit, the society hostess Emerald Cunard pressed him to remain one night as he was readying to depart soon after dinner. "I can't stay, Emerald," replied Maugham. "I have to keep my youth." "Then why didn't you bring him with you?" protested Lady Cunard. "I would be delighted to meet him."

Lady Emerald Cunard [née Maud Burke]
(1872–1948), U.S.-born British socialite

The pragmatist philosopher John Dewey's theories of education also influenced his own home life. One day as he was sitting in his study, which was directly below the bathroom, he felt a trickle of water run down his back. He raced upstairs to find his young son struggling to shut off the water to a bathtub overflowing with water and toy boats. Seeing his father, the youngster said sternly, "Don't argue, John. Get the mop."

John Dewey (1859–1952),
U.S. philosopher and educator

Elizabeth the Queen Mother and Princess Margaret, then a little girl, were on a walk when a woman came up to them, exclaiming, "So this is the lovely little lady we've heard so much about!" Margaret sternly replied, "I'm not a little lady. I'm a pri—" The queen firmly interrupted. "She's not quite a little lady yet. But she's learning."

Elizabeth the Queen Mother
(1900–   ), British queen
[authenticity unverified]

Actor Peter Ustinov, the proud father of a proper young daughter, took her to see her first opera, *Aida*, being performed at the Baths of Caracalla in Rome. During the scene in which a menagerie of animals parade on stage, virtually all of them suddenly relieved themselves. Staring aghast at the sight, Ustinov felt a light tapping on his shoulder. His daughter earnestly inquired, "Daddy, is it all right to laugh?"

> Sir Peter [Alexander] Ustinov
> (1921–   ), British actor and writer

◆ YOUTH (CHILDHOOD)

Foreign Words and Phrases

jeunesse dorée-(Fra)
(juh-NESS do-RAY) lit: gilded youth; wealthy, fashionable youth, yuppies

Quotations

"Youth would be an ideal state if it came a little later in life."

> Herbert Henry Asquith, Earl of Oxford
> and Asquith (1852–1928),
> British prime minister

"I thought he was a young man of promise, but it appears he is a young man of promises."

> Arthur James Balfour, 1st Earl of Balfour
> (1848–1930), British prime minister,
> describing Winston Churchill

"I'm not young enough to know everything."

> Sir J[ames] M[atthew] Barrie
> (1860–1937), British writer and
> playwright, The Admirable Crichton
> (performed 1902, pubd. 1914), Act I

"He is a man suffering from petrified adolescence."

> Aneurin ["Nye"] Bevan (1897–1960),
> British politician, describing
> Winston Churchill

"The great trouble with the young people today is their freedom; they can no longer disobey."

> Jean Cocteau (1889–1963), French writer,
> artist and filmmaker

"Vietnam was what we had instead of happy childhoods."

> Michael Herr (1940–   ),
> U.S. writer

"Boys will be boys, and so will a lot of middle-aged men."

> Frank McKinney ["Kin"] Hubbard
> (1868–1930), U.S. humorist and writer

"My salad days, when I was green in judgment."

> William Shakespeare (1564–1616),
> British playwright and poet, Antony and
> Cleopatra (1607), Act I, sc. v

"Youth is a wonderful thing; what a crime to waste it on children."

> George Bernard Shaw (1856–1950),
> Irish playwright

"Those whom the gods love grow young."

> Oscar [Fingal O'Flahertie Wills] Wilde
> (1854–1900), British playwright,
> writer and wit, The Picture of
> Dorian Gray (1891)

Jokes, Stories and Anecdotes

The judge reviewed with a jaundiced eye the defendant accused of peddling "Fountain of Youth" brew which, he advertised, would reverse the aging process. "Does the accused have a prior arrest record?" the judge asked the prosecutor. "Yes, Your Honor. He was arrested for the same offense in 1984, 1969, 1952, 1906 and 1835."

British zoologist Julian Huxley's tantrums as a youngster were not a problem for his illustrious grandfather, Thomas Huxley, also a zoologist, biologist and paleontologist. He said, "I like the way he looks you straight in the face and disobeys you."

Thomas Henry Huxley (1825–1895),
British philosopher

When the youthful Tom Dewey announced his candidacy for the presidency at the 1940 Republican convention, crusty old Harold Ickes, New Deal secretary of the interior, commented: "Dewey has thrown his diaper into the ring."

Harold L. Ickes (1874–1952),
U.S. statesman

♦ INDEX ♦

419

◆ Q ◆

◆ R ◆